The Woman Without a Hole

& Other Risky Themes from Old Japanese Poems,

or, 18-19c *senryû* compiled, translated & essayed

by

robin d. gill

---

*I*s the *Other Title* for *This Book* <u>simultaneousl*y* published</u>

as an

Ex*p*eriment

by paraverse press for reasons explained on the reverse

The tentative title (*Octopussy, Dry Kidney & Blue Spots*) had so many detractors, the author created a second title, *The Woman Without a Hole*, that he was *also* happy with, and sent out both to acquaintances, for *their* votes and opinions.

Pro *Octopussy*

Keep to the *Octopussy* title, Robin. I'd put in front *'(Per)Verse Snatches* . . . but then, I'm an Aussie, where 'snatches' are 'cunts'. PD, iconoclastic author and transl. of italian verse

Hmmm, what a dilemma... I guess I'd go with the *Octopussy* title, though.
LD, always tasteful author, anthropologist & ex-geisha-no-tamago

Pro *Hole*

I don't think you want to use "Octopussy" in your title, just because (for anyone aged more or less 50 or so, at least) it is a word effectively patented by Ian Fleming, no less precisely than "incarnadine" and countless other such words are "owned" by Shakespeare, . . . Then again, it just might work as a (mild) provocation. _The Woman Without a Hole_ would /probably/ work better as your title. It raises a question in need of answering. Forget about *Dry Kidney*, etc. This is just weird in a not intriguing way. LC, brilliant and always critical scholar of japanese literature at CUNY

It's a less complicated, dynamite title, and you have good complications in the table of contents (#26 is a favorite). JS, author & publisher of the avant-garde in english, japanese and thai

I have long been interested in senryu and it is high time we had a new anthology of them out in English. For what it's worth, I like best *'The Woman Without a Hole'*.
TS, scholar and prolific author on japanese visual culture at SOAS

Other

This needs thinking about. *The Woman Without a Hole* would have trouble with constipation. Your thoughts focus on an aspect of the woman that your age dictates. (Still it would be an unpleasant surprise.) My age focuses on regularity as the primary goal of a good life. JS, my godfather, a novelist of grace still wearing shit-kickers in his 80's

Or, *Rise Ye Dildos* (a pun on my 2003 book, *Rise, Ye Sea Slugs!*) D, *aka* chibi, haikuist

I have no specific suggestions for your title (but I'll buy the book either way, the table of contents is great). LN, promising young scholar of japanese r at FIU

Summary & Decision

At first, the two titles were tied 4-4 (the above is a sampling of responses), but all the slower responders went for the *Hole* that wasn't. Votes dictated that I should throw back the *Octopussy*, but two respondents who favored it were, of all correspondents, the most comfortable with lugubrious topics and represented just the type of reader I hoped to attract. Recalling my frustration when, years ago, I tried and failed to convince a Japanese publisher to go along with my idea for an experiment with two very different sorts of titles for the same book, I thought, *Hah! Now is the time!* As an author-publisher, *I can do this*. Once and for all, we shall see just how much a book is judged by its *title*. We shall see whether the oddly perverse, and seemingly plagiarist pop trilogy or the elegant riddle wins out. &, *Thank you, everyone!* - rdg

Edo townsmen amused themselves by reading and writing senryu, not caring whether it qualified as poetry.

Makoto Ueda, introducing his anthology of the same [1]

セックスは頭でするものでございます.

Sex is something you do with your mind.

黒木香 Kuroki Kaoru [2]

Si enim quod verbo significatur id turpe non est,
verbum, quod significat, turpe non potest.

If what a word designates is not filthy,
the word, itself, can neither be.

Cicero *Fam.9.22* [3]

With all its humor there is a sense of real delight in what may be called obscenity for its own sake.

C. E. S. Wood re. Mark Twain's *1601* [4]

1. *Light Verse From the Floating World* (1999). Japanese had no generic term for "poetry," and *still* do not, but *if* they did, that would have been true.

2. *Furutsu Hakusho* (1987), by Kuroki Kaori, an adult video actress famous for scary long, black and prolific underarm hair, as well as outrageous statements about sex, made in a uniquely affected language, mixing polite grammar and a post-modern lexicon.

3. *Cicero Fam.9.22.* Thanks to Peter Dale for finding the quote, and apologies for altering the translation to re-create the rhyme-sense at the expense of the logical symmetry.

4. *1601* by Mark Twain, produced by David Widger @ Project Gutenberg. C.E.S.Wood was responsible for printing Twain's bawdy "conversation," which he described as *"brutally British rather than lasciviously latinate,"* a perfect description of senryû!

All translations, unless otherwise indicated,

笑・句

are from the original Japanese by the author.

笑・具

本書中、他者に翻訳クレジットを明記したもの

笑・婦

以外の英訳は、すべて筆者による珍文、駄文也.

ショック

A *shôku* 笑句 is literally a laugh-*ku*, or a smile-*ku*, for japanese use the same chinese character 笑 for both ・It is not in japan's largest dictionary, as are *shôgu* 笑具, *laugh-tool* or, 1) something to make people laugh, 2) an adult tool, such as penile armor, and *shôfu* 笑婦, *laugh-lady*, or street-walker (properly 娼婦)・One could call *shôku* 笑句 a positive name for the negative *bareku* 破礼句, literally, break-etiquette-*ku*・In 1835, the editor of the famously dirty collection of senryû, 柳の葉末, used it to describe the *ku* he and his bawdy buddies found or made ・ Granting them to be 'humorous poems,' (J. ソルト), we might qualify: *these* humors are the type that *fill, drip* or *spurt* from the page. ・ To some, they may prove to be a real *shokku* ショック, i hope a salutary one. 〆

Dirty Themes from 18-19c Japanese Poems,

Octo*p*uss*y*, D*r*y *K*idney & B*lue* *S*pots

or, senryû compiled, translated & essayed

by

robin d. gill

穴可穴
非常穴
paraverse press

This is the 8 th book published by paraverse press, home of truly creative nonfiction, which is to say, nonfiction that is neither journalism, nor history, nor how-I-overcame-this-or-that. We are afraid our books will not help you get rich, healthy or up-to-date. Whatever their subject, they offer one thing, always the same yet different; and *that* is ideas,

"food for thought,
all you can eat!"

but, please quote freely, so long as you cite this book and take care to check the ***Errata*** at **http://www.paraverse.org**

We invite the Library of Congress to help us catalog for, as you can see below, this book has many faces! Meanwhile please enjoy our Publisher's Cataloging-in-Publication:

Octopussy, Dry Kidney & Blue Spots
– Dirty Themes from 18-19c Japanese Poetry –
or, senryû compiled, ~~introduced~~, translated, ~~interpreted~~ and essayed by robin d. gill.
Includes the Japanese originals, romanization, a bibliography, poet and poem indexes.

ISBN # 0-9742618-5-8 (pbk)
13-digit: 978-0-9742618-5-0

1. Senryû – Translations into English
2. Poetry – Obscene – Japanese
3. Japan – Edo Era (17-19c)
4. Sex – Ethnology – Japan
5. Humor & Curiosities
6. Nonfiction – essay

I. gill, robin d.

1st edition, 2007, Fall.
(call it a reading copy, too)

Printed by Lightning Source in the United States and United Kingdom; distributed by Ingram, Baker & Taylor, etc.; available from Amazon , B&N, etc..

◎

For more information, please visit our web site, www.paraverse.org.
If you have further questions, write us at info@paraverse.org, or uncoolwabin@hotmail.com, or whatever e-mail address is given at the site (or works). *Forget snail-mail!* Your poor author-publisher *is* a snail.

about that "dirty" subtitle

Usually, creating a subtitle is fun, but this one was hell. Why? Because any subtitle my correspondents and I came up with disappointed more people than it pleased.

Since I mentioned the possibility of going the University Press route, P.D. put me on the high road with *Scurrilous Poetics of ~*. While I do engage in literary criticism, the book is for the most part a good read because it is 90% eye-opening theme with far more example than analysis. Such a subtitle would belie that, and frighten off more lay readers than it would attract scholars.

Then, there is the B-word. Many called for it. I understand. *Everybody* likes *Bawdy*. That word has charm. Like a good-looking man or woman, *Bawdy* can get away with murder. The main title of the only inexpensive anthology of x-rated verse in English worth mentioning, *"a pleasant collection,"* edited by E.J. Burford and published by Penguin, is *Bawdy Verse*. No one minds if it includes maids doing it with dogs, buggered colts & *etcetera*. Unfortunately, the B-word evokes an Elizabethan world far too loud and lusty for the more urban/e world of senryû. If applied to things Japanese, *bawdy* would have to be reserved for the far freer, dirty folk-songs (pp 173, 314, 410).

Because senryû *is*, in part, *truly offensive*, I also thought to emphasize its *badness,* while playing with the Supreme Court's silly idea of "socially redeeming value" (Why not just say titillation for titillation's sake is fine?): *Poetry Beyond Redemption*. It was not at all popular. *Christianity* kept popping up in the comments, and, Lord knows, I already had enough trouble trying to keep my books divorced from those of Oxford Theologian Robin Gill (*Hah!* He will love *this* one!).

My first idea for the *main* title was to stress the novelty of the translation. *The Un-publishable Poetry of Japan,* or *The Poetry None Dared Translate!* But, wouldn't you know it, someone *had*. And it was even someone I once met, though I had not known he did it. He only translated 66 of them – here I have *thousands* – but I was no longer Columbus. I would have to settle for being the pickle-dealer, as someone (Emerson, right?) called Amerigo V..

So, instead, I made a title that would indirectly say the book is a miscellany full of intriguing subjects of a possibly risqué nature to be revealed in due course (After reading this book, you will know why an *octopussy* could give a man *dry kidney* and their baby a *blue spot*).

And, for that subtitle, over the objections of all and horror of one (my mom), I finally settled on *"dirty,"* because, while *some* but not most of the senryu are *erotic*, *some* but not most are *lewd, obscene, pornographic, ribald, scurrilous*, and so forth, almost all fit into the promiscuous snatch of *"dirty."* Moreover, this word is the only one I could find that seems utterly *unaffected* and boasts a pedigree (etymology) with no inherent class pretensions. Of course, it does have some bad connotations, but so does *bad*, itself – that never stopped *it* from becoming good, did it? And self-denigration is *taihen* Japanese! – r.d.g.

凸

dedicated
to the editors of
nihonkokugodaijiten
japan's largest dictionary
because it must have taken
great courage to use so many
senryû, some clearly obscene,
as examples, when others
had yet to appreciate
their importance
for philology
& history.

凹

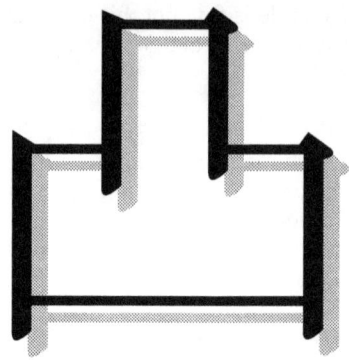

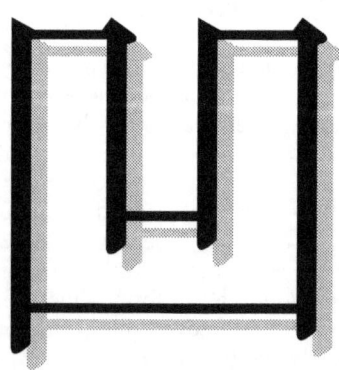

目 次　Contents

出典の表示、或は勝手な一語略字斗り

Abbreviations I created to save space and avoid acronyms.

~~~~~~

- *Leaf* 葉 1835/6. *Yanaginohazue*. Willow Leaftips. 『柳の葉末』
- *Million* 万 1757-1789. *Mankuawase*. Myriad-*ku*-gathered. 『川柳評万句合』
- *Mu* む 1750 - 1761. *Mutamagawa*. Warrior-gem-river. 『俳諧武多摩川』
- *Pluck* 摘 1776-1801. *Suetsumuhana*. Safflower (end-pinch-blossom). 『誹風末摘花』
- *Willow* *# only*. 1765 - 1841. *Yanagidaru*. Willow Barrel. 『誹風柳多留』 (a number alone is *Willow*, unless elsewise indicated, as is the Japanese practice).
- Nothing at all. 失出典か何もない。スペース次第の省略もあるが。Source is lost, not yet found, or there was no room for it (your author is also the book designer).
- *Ku* c̲ source name+date (in Japanese). Mostly *zappai* found in Suzuki, or *Cuntologia*.
- OJD: dictionary:see *biblio* 日本国語大辞典 ◎上記の略字以外の日本語出典+年付のある句の多くは鈴木『艶句の世界』か玩宮隠士『女陰万考』等掲載の雑俳か。

<u>Sources will usually *not* be Englished</u>. If you cannot read Japanese, it should not matter. Cite *me!*（詳細は、付録にて。失典句の出典先ご存知の場合、教えてください！）

~~~~~~

About my compilation and translation

~~~~~~

Selecting poems to translate is like casting. The easy thing to do, and the most common, is to select what one expects the audience to immediately appreciate. That is why Hollywood turns Chinese fashion-model beauties into geisha. It is why so many translated poems make sense to you with no explanation to speak of. But, it is the odd-looking movie star or poem that takes some time to get used to that often ends up affecting you deeply. Of course, I occasionally drop a poem I love in the original that translates poorly, but I try to select poems to draw out themes rather than to make my job, or the reader's, easy. True, a helluva lot is lost in translation when poems are not selected for translatability, but I do my damndest to reincarnate the poetry in new bodies equally appealing though little like the original, and try to make up for the inevitable losses by finding something similar in type though different in particulars, and using multiple translations to preserve ambiguity or more information than could be Englished into one *ku*. When pushing my "poetic license," as space (design) permits, I try to include a word-for-word translation so you may revoke it as you please. Other times, I may provide the same simply to fill an extra line on the page. Finally, in this book, as others, I try to aim so that if I miss, it will be on the side of wit.

About the *Information* crammed into the back of the book.

~~~~~~

All my books of translated poetry contain *Humpty Dumpty* (idiosyncratic usages), *Japanglish* (not standard, but the equivalent of *Clockwork Orange's* Nadsat) Portmanteau (couplings of meaningful roots) and otherwise invented words. As haiku is too short for descriptive phrases to replace words English lacks, such license, cannot be helped. I try to explain each at least once, but if you jump around, or, heaven forbid, have a memory as bad as mine, now and then, you may need to take advantage of the *Glossary*. The *Bibliography* and *Index* may also surprise you.

X X X

F o r e w o r d

Warning!

The censor forbids the translation, and it is not worth learning Japanese just to read them. – R.H. Blyth *Japanese Life and Character in Senryû* [1]

Only a few verses are given here, not the best, but the best printable ones. – R.H. Blyth: *Edo Satirical Verse Anthologies*

Contemporary sensibilities may be offended by implications of sexism, classism, agism, or child abuse, but I present them anyway. Not to do so would be to indulge in self-censorship (which is one of the few indulgences that I do not allow myself). – John Solt: *Willow Leaftips*

~~~~~~

A *senryû,* like a haiku, is a 17-syllabet verse, or, to use the Japanese term, *ku,* equivalent in length to 7 or 8 English beats, tending to have two or three possible breaks, though, also like haiku, they are almost always printed in a single line, the better to squeeze dozens, or scores of them into a page. [2] Indeed, the first major collection/s of *senryû* by the *ku* judge, or "point-man" (*tenja*) whose name became one with the form, Karai Senryû (柄井川柳 1718-1790), had no less than 60 *ku* per page! [3] If haiku is a personal poetry of shared seasonal themes, *senryû* tends toward third-person caricature and urban themes. As with limericks, the blunt, black humor of many old *senryû* makes it hard to concede them the status of poetry, which, we in the English language tradition, whether we admit it or not, expect to be *somewhat* fancy, if not lyrical. Some *ku,* lacking rhyme and meter, may not even seem like "ditties;" but, even so, they are usually *witty,* if for no other reason than that they are not only brief but cryptic enough to be *riddles.* Even *senryû* specialists, who may be amateurs, often, for whatever reasons, medical doctors, [4] extol the importance of brain-storming (輪講 ring-discussions /sessions), *i.e.,* collective interpretation, and though he (almost *always* a *he*) may well be one of the top authorities in the field, always ends his foreword or afterword with a request for other researchers or readers to help correct anything found lacking or wrong.[5] In other words, senryû is not for passive readers; it is a poetry to be *solved.*
~~~~~~

Historically speaking, *senryû* is not only the *low-ku* sibling to the *high-ku*, but a monozygotic twin. In early-phase *haikai* – 14 and 17-syllabet chains of light, lively, and often zany, linked-verse that started as an off-shoot of the more formal *renga* – risqué, or even *raunchy* poems, bearing little or no relation to seasonal phenomena and poems as patently pure as any haiku written today were mixed indiscriminately, much as we find with the *Epigrams* of Martial, Aristophanes' drama or even Lucretius' philosophical prose-poem *De Rerum Natura.*[6] My inclination is to follow the promiscuous practice of the ancients, East and West, before the modern idea of "obscenity" was born by segregating the *dirty=bad* from the *clean=good.* [7] But, for fear of offending, or, worse, losing readers, I only introduced enough *senryû* into my books of translated haiku [8] to show the mutual influence, or, rather common stream of both, and few of those senryû were as dangerous (?) as many you will see here. The reverse is not true. No one stops reading a "dirty" book because it has something *clean* in it. So, I will include in this book, with a total of about 1300 senryû, enough haiku to clearly demonstrate where the sibling forms unite and where they part, as well as add an element of beauty missing in *senryû*, which will hitherto be written simply "senryu," for enough English speakers are familiar with the word to justify its complete naturalization.

Continued after the last chapter

The foreword continues for twenty pages, not including eight pages of notes. To resume reading please go to page 435, but first, do note that while there are advantages to knowing more about the history of senryu and what makes it special before reading this book, readers without a scholarly interest in senryu (most of you, I presume) might appreciate the rest of the foreword more *after* reading enough of the book to *want* to know more. I will mention only one point made later here: when encountering occasional sick humor, please remember that the place where senryu took off, Edo (now Tokyo), was not only the world's largest city but so lopsidedly male that horniness was endemic. Also, if, you do not hail from the part of the English world where *cunt* is a term of endearment, and may be offended by the language I must use to be fair to the original, please go straight to the two-page *apologia "Being Blunt about Cunt"* (pp 463-4).

Notes to the *Foreword*

1. *Citations.* Please note that chapter-notes will not be used for giving information that may be found in the Appendix. Moreover, they will be called *Eddies*, to reflect their purpose being primarily aesthetic and natural, rather than pedantic. The eddies in most chapters will not be numbered and are best read after the chapter is. They will, on the whole, be less like notes than these for the foreword. Page numbers (proper citations) will not be given unless I deem it necessary or they are provided by someone (where it would be rude to erase them). See Hilaire Belloc *On Footnotes*, for my opinion of them.

2. *Syllabet, etc.* "Syllabet" was coined by the author because the Greek term used by linguistics for a short and uniform syllable, *mora,* is indeed Greek to all but specialists. Please see the *Glossary* ㊤ if you would further pursue this or other terms.

3. *Sixty Ku (poems) Per Page?* My source is senryu scholar Okada Hajime's message to the readers in his selection from Senryû's *Million* (mankuawase). Okada's book has only 10 *ku* per page, for most have short explanations. I photocopied his facsimile of the 60-*ku*/pg original (pg 434), and a page from a 20c senryu anthology with exactly the same number of *ku*/pg (pg 490). Iwanami's tiny pocket-books have 18 *ku*/pg. Compare this to the one or two, rarely four *ku* per page common in English, despite the lack of explanation. To my mind, "we" are getting gypped and the lives of our trees are being taken too lightly; but, to be honest, few have thanked me for offering thousands of *ku* at a price one usually pays for hundreds (but my statistics could be better c̲ *this* book), while many have told me they wished for less poems and larger margins. If you appreciate what Japanese once took for granted, please let me know in person and in reviews. This has gone on for *years* now, and I am almost ready to give in to the oh-so-tasteful, wasteful majority.

4. *Medical Doctors and Senryû.* The first round-robin treatment of all four volumes of *Pluck* (suetsumuhana), published in 1982, was undertaken by a group of physicians in Tokyo's Minato Ward. In Japanese, to examine something thoroughly is *to stick a scalpel into it* (*mesu o ireru*), and, so, one of the participants of a second round-robin try at the same (Saibara et al. 1995) writes, they did so *with literal incision*. I have not seen the book, but can imagine that figuring out old poems often dealing with the body would intrigue doctors used to round-robin brainstorming sessions for difficult medical cases.

5. *どうか叱正をもって御指導をいただきたい。* "By all means, give us your guidance, both scolding and corrections." These words were found near the end of the introduction to the 1995 *Pluck* round-robin, delightful because the participants do not wait for the readers but disagree or correct one another. The willingness not only to admit to mistakes but to show them to all is what I most admire in an author. Even, Okada Hajime, the man who knew the most about senryû, wrote in the introduction to his *Million ku* selection that *"the interpretation of old senryû is really difficult; one must consider the collective input* (crowd-wisdom 衆智) *for and against* [an interpretation] *and call the most reasonable* (妥当な) *interpretation the right one* (正解)."

6. *De Rerum Natura.* Lucretius graphically describes a theory that vigorous movement by women reduces the chance of pregnancy. But, note, his poem-essay is not X-rated as the others mentioned. It is PG (parental guidance) level. Lucretius develops not only atomic theory, but myth interpretation, dream theory, psychosomatics and much more. You need not read Martial (we will quote him later only because he was the dirtiest) or Aristophanes, but *if you have not read Lucretius, your basic education is incomplete.*

7. *Segregating the Obscene.* I oversimplify when I say the ancients did *not* and we *do*. I hope you do not mind my poetic license extending to the essay at times!

8. *My Haiku translations.* I have published four books with 7,000 haiku in the original Japanese and over 10,000 translations (See pp 501-3). I try to save the wit found between hitherto neglected layers of meaning while developing the seasonal themes from which individual haiku come and to which they return. Though careful not to give *senryû* more than a minor part in these books, the hundreds I *have* introduced are nonetheless a substantial addition to the body of translated *senryû* because that body is very, very thin.

Pronunciation & Transcription

Like Spanish, Japanese has 5 vowel sounds: *Buenos Aires*. You must pronounce, not blend, them. A diacritical mark indicates long-vowels, written double in Japanese. A double consonant means you pause slightly before belting it out. Like German, Japanese has many words which are compound. Determination of a "word" is arbitrary; likewise my use of hyphens. Most beginners love them; most specialists hate them. Old senryu had some interesting peculiarities *in the Japanese*, which I have, as far as possible given MS-Word's limitations, left as is to help those who would learn to read in the original.

<u>*The Story of a Priest and His Queen*</u>

川柳で読む道鏡と女帝の物語

1

一

馬の如き
Two Like Horses

~~~~~~

As Japanese cultural pride, riding a wave of economic growth and forecasts of "Japan-as-Number One" in the 1970's and 80's, reached levels of boastfulness unknown since the late-16c, the early-7c Regent and Crown Prince Shôtoku 聖徳 Taishi's words on cultural relativism – *what seemed right to others might seem wrong to us, and vice versa* – were constantly bandied about to illustrate the contrast between the flexible, tolerant Japanese and the ossified, absolutist "desert-spirit" of the Judeo-Christo-Islamic West. His mid-8c great ^{x11} grand-daughter Kôken Tennô 孝謙天皇, later Shôtoku Tennô 称徳天皇, whom we will, after senryu, call *Empress* (Jotei "woman-emperor), may not have found everything so relative. According to a story probably better known in the 18c than Shôtoku Taishi's statement, she urinated upon a certain Buddhist Sutra she claimed was false. Evidently, it was *not*, because supernatural punishment was visited upon her. Her *quim and desire* (source of all suffering) grew to enormous proportions. Senryu lost the *desire* and, with it, the point of the story, but found great joy in the Empress's physical *size* – it is easy to hyperbolize or metaphor. This example is from the relatively late (1835) and notably c/rude *Leaf* collection.

新鉢の頃が女帝は乳母の味 葉三
arabachi no koro ga jotei wa uba no aji
(new pot's time, jotei-as-for wetnurse-flavor)

the empress

even virgin
her purse was wide
as a wet nurse

her first time
it was already wide
as a wet nurse

The "taste" suggests the perspective of one who knew her from inside, so to speak. An *arabachi*, or new pot, is the sex of a pubescent girl, a virgin, or the first coitus of the same. A wet-nurse was stereotypically the anti-virgin, *very hairy*, *huge* and *horny*. She will have her own chapter. Back to the Empress:
~~~~~~

女帝ハ九十六ひだでおわします 摘 3-9
jotei wa kyûjû-roku hida de owashimasu pluck
(empress-as-for ninety-six folds-with is[honorific])

empress kôken
pray be told, had six
& ninety folds

A standard vagina had 48-folds. Another *Pluck ku* wonders: *"Who could be / so patient or bold to count / fold by fold?"* (四十八ひだとハよくもかぞへたり摘 1-7 *shijû-hachi hida to wa yoku mo kazoetari*). This figure coincides with the birth-date of the Buddha, Month 4, Day 8 (Months as well as days are numbers in the Sinosphere). On that day, a *Leaf ku* jokes, the good *"Wife Maya's / forty-eight folds were kept / waiting in vain"* (摩耶婦人四十八ひだ待ちぼうけ 葉三 *maya-bujin shijû-hachi hida machiboke*). The birth was Caesarian. Back to the Empress and her size:

医者親子ともに女帝は御寵愛 葉 19
isha oyako tomo ni jotei wa gochôai

doctor, parent &
child, together in place,
enjoy Her Grace

doctor, parent &
even the page enjoy her
royal patronage

Standard 'feeling-up' was two-fingered – there are many clear diagrams of the proper way to do it, some depicted, believe it or not, from within! The outside pictures clearly show the *parent-finger* (our thumb), *doctor* (also medicine-, our ring-) finger and *child*-(pinky)finger curled back and not entering the *Mons veneris* with the people-pointing-(index-) and middle-fingers. Or, poetically (in prose), *"By the gate, doctor, parent and child must wait"* (門口で医者と親子が待っている「甲子夜話」文政四: 1821). So this is no mere finger puppet (*yubi-ningyo*), but what amounts to a whole hand within the *cave of love* suggested by the characters for Imperial Grace. That is a pretty picture compared to the next:

吸筒のやうに女帝のねれる音 葉十三
suizutsu no yô ni jotei no nereru oto leaf
(suck-tube-like empress's warming-up sound)

her majesty
primed the sound of water
in a bucket

The *suizutsu* is not really a bucket but a *canteen* made from a large tube of bamboo. Japanese pay much attention to wetness as a sign of readiness. Sexy passages/scenes in books/movies are called "wet-spots" (*nureba* 濡場). When the large-sexed Empress walked about, you could hear the prime of her desire slushing about like bilge-water in a small sail boat in a rough sea. At first, I thought *nereru* a mistake for *nureru,* or "get wet," but it is almost surely a different verb meaning "to warm up" (pp.144-8).

道鏡が出るまて牛蒡洗ふやう 摘 1-8
dôkyô ga deru made gobo arau yô pluck
(dôkyô arrives-until burdock washing-like)

Queen Slackeesha

until dôkyô came
her sex was like washing
burdock in the sea

Several times longer than a carrot, the burdock root is not short, but *thin*, rarely thicker than a finger. The simile in the senryû is still in common use today. Dôkyô was a well-endowed bonze, who became her lover and rose to be Prelate. The following couplet style translation might be titled: *a fitting mate.*

Until Dôkyô sex was pure futility –
Try washing a burdock in the sea!

The real burdock is washed because it is eaten. Unlike carrots, with that childish flavor better left to the likes of Bugs Bunny, the slightly woody earth-taste of the burdock satisfies the discriminating adult palate (That carrot and not burdock is part of French cuisine proves that gourmet or not, the taste buds of the French and their following have yet to grow up). A slightly less conventional simile:

蛇が蚊をのんでるところへ弓削が出る
ja ga ka o nonderu tokoro e yuge ga deru 摘 3-4
(snake/s mosquito[acc] drinking place-to yuge arrives)

yuge appeared
when a snake was swallowing
a mosquito

yuge shows up
for a snake ravenous from
eating mosquitoes

Yuge is another name for Dôkyô. Mosquitoes stabbed/thrust (*sasu*), which made them male analogs, while snakes, despite their outside form, were functionally female: they *swallowed,* or *sheathed* things. Most Japanese have read a *Tale of Uji* where a traveler awakens from a scrumptious wet-dream to find by his side a snake lying dead with foam coming from its mouth. Asphyxiated. (Tyler:1987)

道鏡ハ人ン間にてハよもあらじ 万 明三
dôkyô wa ningen nite wa yomo-araji million

as a human
in this world dôkyô
is peerless

This *ku* (& its draw, "how interesting"おもしろい事) is boring but not completely dead, for it makes the reader continue: "but *of course* / there is the *horse!"* That makes it better than the following odd-sounding (a 4-9-4 syllabet-break) *ku* from *Willow:*

からだハ人間てへのこは馬なり 柳21
karada wa ningen de henoko wa uma nari ス-3

His body was human, his cock was horse.

The *ku* is saved only by the ellipsis of his name. But, even a horse was *thin* compared to this exemplar of massive manhood later re-incarnated in *ukiyoe:*

道鏡ハ居ルとひざか三ッ出来 万宝
dôkyô wa suwaru to hiza ga mitsu deki 十三
(dôkyô-as-for sits and knees-the three can)

When Dôkyô sat down, all eyes would freeze:
To see he had not two, but — three knees!

"All eyes would freeze" is entirely my invention. Is it acceptable? I suppose it depends whether you appreciate rhyme.

おやかすと道鏡 イ八にかくれんぼ
oyakasu to dôkyô mara ni kakurenbo 葉16
(erects when dôkyô's dong-by hiding-would-boy)

Parlor Games
(in jotei's court)

when *It* stood
and dôkyô sat, they could
play *peek-a-boo*
o'er his lap!

dôkyô erect
a child finds it perfect for
hide-n-go-seek

dôkyô's yard
kids find room to play
hide-n-go seek

comin' to get you
ready or not! one hides behind
dôkyô's pride

Did children find Dôkyô's colossus a good place to hide behind or did he and the Empress play such games? But because the game and the person who hides are both *kakurenbo* a direct yet good translation is hard. Sorry to overdo it trying to compensate. Until the 20c, "yard" was a common word for penis.

眼病の蝉道鏡のイ八で啼 葉十六
ganbyô no semi dôkyô no mara de naki
(eye-diseased cicada dôkyô's dong-at crying)

a myopic cicada
comes to cry on
dôkyô's cock

To fully appreciate this *Leaf ku* you must know something about song-bug behavior (shared by some birds). The deafening high-decibel noise coming from little cicada is amplified by their taking care to select not only large trees but *solid* ones to cry on. That way, there is less sound leak. The cicada may have been blind (their eyes can film over) but he knew good wood when he felt it.

此 イ八忽チ大木と弓削おやし 葉二六
kono mara tachimachi taiboku to yuge oyashi
(this dong instantly great tree and/says yuge erects)

◎ yuge demonstrates his power to the empress ◎

let this cock become
your mighty tree, instantly
says he, growing hard

Yuge = Dôkyô, again. *"To Yu"* suggests *to iu*, or, "so saying." I was tempted to translate just: *"This cock / makes a giant tree / instantly."* It *sounds* better than the above. I couldn't do it. The original deserves more. It depicts a Dôkyô who is not the proverbial *fool with a tool*, but a man endowed with wit enough to play upon the Confucian dictum for leaders to become giant trees to shelter their subjects, and does so with phrasing that alludes to a song called *Old Pine* written hundreds of years later! Moreover, pine (*matsu*) suggests "pine-mushroom" (*matsutake*), the symbol of an ideal, large-glans, upcurved manhood, while "*tachimachi* = instantly" includes "stand/erect" (*tachi*). All this wit lost in translation speaks well to the quality of the better *ku* of the famously coarse *Leaf.*

大キさわ天迄とゞく のこなり 万安五
ôkisa wa ten made todoku henoko nari million
(largeness-as-for heaven-until reach/ing pecker is)

his ticket up

as for its size
his cock was said to rise
clear to heaven

that was a cock
large enough to dock
on heaven's shore

the size we relate:
his peter reached clear to
the heavenly gate

A similar *ku: "What good fortune – / Up the Cloud-well the huge head / of a cock!"* (運のよさ雲井へまらの大天窓 葉別八 *un no yosa kumoi e mara no ô-atama*), or

megacephallus

up the cloudgate
a cock's mighty head!
heaven smiled

These are pictures of Jack climbing up his own bean-stalk. Or, should we say lifting himself up by something other than his bootstrap? There was a corollary reason Dôkyô was worthy of Imperial matronage: *"Yuge's tribute: / A cock in the rough unsullied / underground"* (地下で穢さぬ荒閉を弓削献じ 葉 三十 *jige de kegasanu ara-mara o yuge kenji*). He was virgin because none could possibly have taken him in. "Underground" is a literal translation of what the Imperial Court called mortals below (*chika*). Another *ku* touches upon Dôkyô's humble origin, by paradoxically referring to a "cloud-spirit," which could rise when strange things were happening or soon to happen. Usually it had Imperial ramifications:

.

みんかんにへ　このうん気ふとく立チ 万
minkan ni he<u>no</u>ko no unki futoku tachi million 天五
(commoner's house/s-from cock's cloud-spirit/s thickly rise/s)

from a hovel
vapor ominous and thick
rise above a prick

Do you see the missing letter in the above Japanese senryû and a previous one? That is because the book I found it in was published when Japan was occupied by the Allies or still pretending to share in Usanian Puritanism. *Henoko* is not a polite name for the penis. Okada's explanation was: *"Dôkyô. Like the cloud raised by an atomic bomb."* He had to write "Dôkyô" because most modern readers might not recognize what the old *ku* referred to. Without such help, one must read many senryû to understand the themes to understand the senryû. It becomes a sort of double acrostics. Of course, the same may be said for all Japanese poetry, but it is especially true for the short forms and perhaps more for senryu, with its riddle-like quality, than for haiku. The *ku* also may play on a line from a Japanese mythology of beginnings. *"There is a sword, and if there is a cloud-spirit rising above it, it is called the Sword of the Myriad Clouds of Heaven."* (「一つの剣あり、その上に雲気ありければ、天の藂 (むら) 雲の剣と名づく」大日霎尊?). At any rate, Dôkyô, following his cock, rises to the occasion, goes to heaven – which in ancient Japan meant the Imperial Court on Cloud Nine (the term is 九重の雲 *nine-fold-cloud/s*) – where he remains to serve his Empress. If only "Heaven" figured in Japanese coital trope, we might find a tit for tat: they could take each other to heaven. But *senryû* did find ways to make it clear that the Empress got off. My favorite reproduces the sound she is supposed to have uttered when coming. As is usually the case, word-wit does not travel:

ホ～
ホウッ
ホウギョ～
*ホウ*道鏡に*ギョ～*
*ホウギョ!*崩御崩御と詔*ホウギョ!*
dôkyô-ni hôgyo-hôgyo to mikotonori 摘 3-18
(dôkyô-to "-demise-exalted demise-exalted" [says/goes] imperial edict)
◎ *an imperial bull to dôkyô: her exalted demise, exalted demise!* ◎

The Chinese character used for a member of the Imperial family dying (the 崩 *hô* above) also means "collapse." It is one of two characters commonly used to write "destruction," and, by itself, the "slide" of an "earth-slide," commonly caused by monsoon rains or typhoons. Such connotations are more suggestive of orgasmic cataclysm than "demise" or "pass away." Moreover, repeated, *"hôgyo hôgyo!"* sounds like the Empress is further gone than "one of the Mayds of Honour" whom Sir Walter [Raleigh] was "getting .... up against a tree in a wood" within his garden who "cryed in extasey, *Swisser Swatter Swisser Swatter!*" (*Aubrey's Lives*) Since the Empress is no Pope, "Bull" is wrong but "edict" sounds like a decree, "notice" would be a minor matter and "announcement" too long and vague, etc. In other words, the combination of high language and the low echo of the original senryû defeat this translator. But, of course, I must *try*, using the tricks of our own language, even if it means turning the Empress into a Queen and dressing the story, to use a Japanese idiom, with some fins and tails:

.

Royal Lovemaking

Dô-dôkyô, dear, We die! We die!
Long live the Queen!
The chamber-maids cry.

~~~~~~

The Witty *Petit Morte*

Dôkyô, your Queen is dead! she cries.
Then, long live the Queen!
He, dying, replies.

~~~~~~

The Coming of the Queen

Dôkyô, Her Highness p-pa-passes away!
A Royal Edict ends the night's love-play.

After ten years of such play, at age 53, she died for good. The accursed Empress found even Dôkyô could not sate her desire — some *ku* gleefully point out he could only come once (道鏡ハ一ッかいたもつ斗リ也　摘 3-18 *dôkyô wa ikkai tamotsu bakari nari* pluck) [1] — and took to using a *Yamato yam* 大和芋 (but, today, usually called *tororo imo*) as a dildo. Long as a horse and often thicker, slightly bumpy and productive of abundant white slime when grated or strongly rubbed, this watery yet crisp tuber, grated and mixed with a sprinkling of laver, soy sauce, a quail's egg and *wasabi*, is generally used to dip buckwheat noodles in – yes, Japanese usually *dip* their buckwheat noodles in a sauce, or wash, rather than *soak* them in it; but, according to Sasama's *Eropedia*, this "yam" has medical as well as culinary applications. Containing several stimulating chemicals (*arantoin, aruginin, jiasutahze?* chemists may recognize and re-spell), it is used to treat burns and abrasions, as well as serving for a topical aphrodisiac and dildo. Unfortunately, it has one serious drawback. The *yamato-imo* (*Dioscorea Japonica*) is fragile in the way of all starchy things. It *snaps* if quickly bent. Well, a monster-sized yam broke off in the Empress and would not come out. A nun physician from Kudara

(Southwest Korea) turned up in the nick of time and oiled up her hands to work it out; but, before her work was done, one of her body-guards whipped out his sword and beheaded her, supposedly because he took the nun for a bewitched fox (doubtless the salacious nine-tailed one particularly feared at the time). So the Empress dies and our hero loses his position on top of Cloud Nine and passes the few remaining years of his life at a temple dedicated to the Physician of Souls 薬師寺 – doubtless celibate unless he found another mare – and, as so often happens with the famous, no longer rests in one piece, for, if Nishizawa is correct, his incorruptible penis-bone was eventually dug up, ground into powder and – as the reader can already guess – drunken by men eager to get what the spam in our e-mail promises all of us still today. *"You say they are made of cavernous tissue?"* writes Nishizawa, *"That is the difference between the thoughts of a layman and an obscenitologist like me. But, surely you have heard this old song:*

したきゃ　させます　千百晩も・マラの背骨が　折れるまで
shitakya sasemasu senbyaku ban-mo / mara-no senaka-ga oreru made
(if you want, i give: a thousand-hundred nights-even / prick's backbone breaks until)

If you want it, you got it babe,
For your sake, I'll stay hard as a rock!
Yea, I'll fuck you forever, or until
— I break the backbone of my Cock!

Perhaps the best part of the story of Dôkyô and the Empress is *the story of the story.* According to an official history, written in 772, Dôkyô, a physician as well as teacher of Zen, cured the Empress of a serious illness earning her trust and before long served as Hô Ô (the same word, 法王, usually reserved for the Christian Pope) and what amounted to co-Emperor. *That is all.* But, within fifty years, rumors had it that they had slept together "as husband and wife". The rumors fermented into song. Dôkyô's rapid advancement was attributed to having a *virile* member. Since he didn't tire of her either, in this age where men tended to be polygamous, it came to be thought she, too, must have been blessed with an exceptionally good part. As the centuries passed, the story took a turn for the better – if *interesting* is better – when the pair's outstanding *qualities* turned into *quantities*. By this time, it would seem that Buddhist priests had gained the same reputation their Christian brothers enjoyed in Chaucer's England: they were synonymous with a bountiful natural endowment. Granted, in Dôkyô's case, *super*natural would be the more fitting word. By 1444, he was said to have had "more than a horse" (馬陰過レ量可レ笑); and, finally, two years later, a book written by a Buddhist priest explains how the Empress happened to become large enough to appreciate a horse. *Heaven forbid, she pissed upon a sutra!*

one saving grace

While senryu black humor can be cruel, and there are so many *ku* about various types of male and female members that they will fill 3½ more chapters, big women and small men are very rare. Could that be because so many of us are (or have) worried about our size that the subject was unconsciously avoided?

~ *eddies* ~

★ **Article 10 of The Seventeen-article Constitution** (十七条憲法) **dated 604 and attributed to Prince Shôtoku** as translated by William George Aston a century ago:

> *X. Let us cease from wrath and refrain from angry looks. Nor let us be resentful when others differ from us. For all men have hearts, and each heart has its own leanings. Their right is our wrong, and our right is their wrong. We are not unquestionably sages, nor are they unquestionably fools. Both of us are simply ordinary men. How can any one lay down a rule by which to distinguish right from wrong? For we are all, one with another, wise and foolish, like a ring which has no end. Therefore, although others give way to anger, let us on the contrary dread our own faults, and though we alone may be in the right, let us follow the multitude and act like them.* (Thanks to Wikipedia, easily found)

.

1. *Pissing on Things.* The *reason* I had so many senryu about the priest and empress on paper ready to scan in and reform into the above essay to kick off this book was because Issa wrote a haiku demanding a captain not piss on the floating moon (for translations + explanation see *A Dolphin in the Woods*) that I chaptered with a dozen more of his *ku* treating sacrilegious, or possibly sacrilegious excretion [A] (eg. *Facing West / I do not even piss: what / a moon tonight!* 西むいて。。– a play on an old story of a monk who would not fart pointing in the direction of the Pureland), his friend's 7-7 (*Urination forbidden! / Violets and Dandelion!* 小便無用菫蒲公英) and dozens of senryu about improper or outrageous pissing, including some with the phrase Issa used in this and other *ku,* the most memorable of which has mosquito larvae dancing a sutra: *"Urination Forbidden"* 小便無用. [B] Blyth caught *some* of the *senryu* (a man impudently pissing *willow style* (*yanagidare*), *i.e.,* in a large arch into a ditch where a sign forbids the same; another aiming at a *torii* mark (because the gateway of a Shinto shrine physically demarcates the point of entry into sacred space, it came to mean *"Do not pollute here."*). Blyth's selection of senryu are as innocent as Issa's haiku. To put Issa in context, mine were not.

A. *The Innocent Sacrilege.* The hyper-sexed Buddhist Pope and Empress are a splendid counter to the fine-tooth saw of the subtle Far East, a cloyingly sweet world of porcelain, humble honorifics and pretty haiku. But they sharpen the teeth of the opposite saw of bizarre Eastern spectacle. To pull the teeth of both saws together, nothing beats the following stories from the *P'aegwan Chapki* of O Sukkwon, a 16c Korean, who treated history with the warm and witty touch of John Aubrey, whom his otherwise fine translator-editor should have mentioned rather than Montaigne:

> In the beginning, Cheju Island was inhabited not by men, but by spirits who emerged from the ground. This was at Mohung Cave, north of Mount Halla. The eldest spirit was named Yang Ulla; the second, Ko Ulla, and the third Pu Ulla. Ko Hu, a descendent of Ko Ulla, bore the title songju and was an able statesman of Silla. In Koryo and in the present dynasty, descendents of the Ko clan have passed the civil examinations and become ministers.
>
> During the Cheng-te era (1506-1521), one Ko filled a post in the Palace Guard ..... When a certain military official named Yi returned from a trip to Cheju, Ko asked him if he had seen Mohung Cave. Yi replied, "I saw it and urinated into it." Ko was speechless. (Peter H. Lee: *A Korean Story-teller's Miscellany* Princeton 1989)

I was tempted to rewrite the punch-line: *"Saw* it? I *pissed* in it!" but, on second thought, realized Lee's translation made more sense. Anyone dumb enough not to have known the sacred nature of that cave would not have replied in a witty manner. Yahoo Yi was just reporting what he did. Issa's "captain", likewise, had no designs on the moon. If it were a small pond without a ripple, and the water was black enough to actually show a moon about the size of a bullfrog, I can well imagine a drunk trying "to piss out the moon" (*Hudibras*), and succeeding, too. But Issa's captain, assuming the culprit was the captain, was merely responding to the call of nature – If a real cowboy is someone who *can pee from the saddle without getting his chaps wet* (country music producer Billy Sherrill), then shall we say that a seasoned skipper ("old conch" where I come from) can piss from a small boat on a choppy day and put every drop in the sea? Speaking of which, there is a senryu about something similar though not explicit: *The horse-boy / whips out one every inch / as splendid* (馬かたハおさ／＼まけぬものを出し *umakata wa osa-osa makenu mono o dashi.*) He is, presumably, pissing (staling!?) while he walks. The original uses psychological mimesis (*osa-osa*) to make *it* sway like the mighty limb of a tree in the breeze though the comparison is with the horse.

Note: a horse-boy (*umakata*) is not so much a groom, though he does groom the horses, as a man who ran in front of horses to clear the street, keeping people from getting run over and the rider from risking execution for homicide in crowded Japan. For more on horse-boys, especially one with "well-turned calves" that so excited Elizabeth Scidmore, see the *Horse* chapter in *Topsy Turvy 1585*. You may also learn why *there were no signs forbidding pissing in public in Kyôto* (As noted by a senryû – everything interesting was noted by senryû – within five solid pages re. waste recycling in the *Architecture* chapter).

B. *Pissing as a Sign of Disrespect.* Humans do not piss to mark territory and show little natural tendency to do it when angry. We are more likely to do it out of fear, excitement or physiological sympathy, such as those who bepissed themselves in close proximity to bagpipe music, as noted by the bard. *Rhetoric* is another matter. Being "pissed off" is old hat, and William Hogart's *Frontisspiss* to a 1763 polemical pamphlet (Found in *Let Newton Be*) illustrates *pissing-as-dissing* with an old witch sitting on a crescent moon literally pissing down upon books on earth.

★ We will not have many more notes about notes in this book, so please do not get pissed off.

~~~~~~

2. *The Wages of Supernatural Sin*. If a woman may be given a slack cunt, what happens to her male equivalent, the jerk who pisses on the moon or worse? While no pissing is involved, a folk-tale in Issa's *My Spring* gives the basic idea:

> In the country of Shinano [Issa's province], in a place called Black Slope, there lived a doctor Nakamura somebody-or-other, who brought a disaster upon himself by beating to death a pair of mating snakes. That very night, a terrible pain broke out in his private parts, which subsequently rotted and fell plunk off, killing him et cetera. His son, Santetsu, inherited his profession. This young man was hung far better than average, boasting a particularly thick and sturdy *matsutake*-like erection [see pp. 107, 109 re. this mushroom, the ideal penis]. When he married and was set to celebrate the nuptials for the first time, the massive pole that stood before him instantly turned into a sobbing little thing as limp as a lamp-wick. The shame, the embarrassment, the chagrin! He tried another woman to no avail. He tried a hundred different mistresses, but not restored to his former self and so disturbed he is nearly mad, now lives as a recluse. So don't [you, reader] ignore such news as something out of the *Tales of Uji* [Tale 15] or other old fables; this type of thing can be seen *now*, with your own eyes. Gossip has it that a snake's vindictiveness won't settle for anything less than the extinction of the line. Thus, we can see that everything alive, even fleas and lice, like humans, really want to live. To kill them, especially while they are mating, is a very sinful thing.

A Japanese friend, an editor and antiquarian of high repute, to whom I mentioned this
~~~~~~

story said: "Most farmers *hate* snakes. As soon as they see them they kill them. There is something Freudian here." So, *is Issa adding fear of castration to Buddhist karma to try to convince people to let snakes live in peace?* ◎ As an aside, I would like to remind my readers *where* this story was found. Issa's *My Spring* is mostly a collection of *ku* but not all Issa's, with sporadic prose passages of which the most famous is the description of his darling little girl, with the onomatopoeic names she gave to animals before she could properly speak, her endearing way of making a Buddhist prayer (repeating a phrase she had heard Issa use) to a Shinto New Year's decoration and so forth. When we find out she dies, we are touched to tears. The above fable, with its graphic description of an erect penis is found only pages before. *My Spring* made Issa's name. And, here is my question: *Were Japanese odd to find nothing prurient in that cock in such a context? Or, are we for segregating sex from other matters so strictly?*

見事也・下疳を蚯蚓と云ふ丁稚 大花笠 享保中
migoto nari / gekan o mimizu to iu chôji 鈴

◎ *beautifully put* ◎
her fav'rite child calls her
canker a worm

Another ♀eg. of *the wages of peeing on things*. This is a capped-verse and not a senryu *per se*, though it could be. Sayings claim that peeing on worms can make your member sore and swollen (which may be remedied by washing a worm) or simply bring bad karma (*bachi ga ataru*). The child who has seen the chancre his or her father brought home to mother either heard the father make the claim she brought it upon herself or put together the warning not to pee on worms with what he has seen. Call it a precocious mondegreen.

~~~~~~

3. ***Those Forty-eight Folds* – Not to be Mistaken for *Wrinkles!*** Henry Miller's cock-sure protagonist in *The Tropic Of Cancer* (1934) had a rude proposition: *"I will ream out every wrinkle in your cunt."* If you think of beds as an ironing boards, cocks as irons and women as clothing, why not? Otherwise, the Japanese fold (*hida*) is far kinder than Miller's "wrinkle." (Since writing this, I found two *ku* mentioning cunt "*shiwa*= wrinkles," but both mention their *faces*, so I guess it means the flaccid labia. Do only the Hindis, with their love for deep folds in the neck and back, *never* conflate the two, as one comes from welcome superfluity and one from regrettably insufficient humours?

~~~~~~

4. *Another Three Knees?* Nishizawa (1985) writes that an anonymously authored 「天保風説見聞秘録」 (Tenpôstylexplanationseenheardsecretrecord) book, records that when, in the seven-month of 1835, a freak-show promoter (見世物師) went to Ushigomi 牛込 to try to buy (the right to display) a thirty-three year-old commoner (we'll skip his name and many more details of the precise address) with a member huge enough to be rare across the ages, he was found seated with it "extending several 2.8 sun (over 3 inches) *beyond his knees*." As this was the same year the *Leaf* introduction was penned, I went back to check on the third knee *ku,* but, *no!* That *ku* appeared in *Million,* generations earlier.

~~~~~~

5. *Arm Puppet.* We will come across more finger-puppets elsewhere, but only one arm puppet, for the Empress, manipulated by Dôkyô:

between bouts
yuge plays puppet master:
an arm puppet
~~~~~~

あいだには腕人形を弓削つかい
aida ni wa ude-ningyô o yuge tsukai 46-5

In Amer-english this practice, rare and humorously named in Japanese is, yuck, called "fisting." As long as we are looking at manual matters, here is a *ku* found in Nishizawa:

両の手で孝謙帝は御にぎり 46-33
ryô no te de kôken tei wa on-nigiri

with both hands
the august imperial grip
of the empress

the empress gasps
at what she deigns to grasp
with both hands

The Empress's name, Kôken, would not fit in translation because I needed "august imperial" and "deigned to" for *on,* as the stock translation, "honorable" would not work.

~~~~~~

5. *Ominous Vapor.* Do you recall the *ku* about vapor rising from Dôkyô's mighty manhood (up through the humble hovel/s)? So, apparently, did a later senryu:

どうきやうでなくてもぬけばゆげが立 摘
dôkyô de naku to mo nukeba yuge ga tachi 2-18

dôkyô or not,
it will steam when just
whipped out

whipped out
it will steam, = yuge rises
dôkyô or not

Japanese dislike central heating, so for half of the year, that is still true today. There is no small humor in the gloss, for the juvenile silly-serious tone of contradiction pretends to miss the literary/religious significance of the vapor in the previous *ku* and takes it literally while it puns on Dôkyô's other name, Yuge, a homophone for "steam."

~~~~~~

6. *When Size* Really *Does Not Matter*. The switch from sexual potency to size could also be seen as the vulgarization of a legend. Size, more than anything else, has always captured the attention of the masses. The first man of modern letters, Montaigne, who was painfully aware of a paltry endowment, once wrote

> What mischief is not done by those enormous pictures that boys spread about the passages and staircases of palaces [I guess graffiti was no more confined to restrooms then, than now!]! From these, women acquire a cruel contempt for our natural capacity. (trans. __________)

Imagine what he would have thought about Japanese spring(erotic)-prints! What makes Dôkyô harmless, even to the most delicately membered male, is that he is clearly an anomaly fit for an anomaly, rather than someone to be measured up against. Moreover, as mentioned, size was suspect, extremely large ones were thought to tend toward being soft and not up for repeated bouts (contrary to the little ones on sumo wrestlers that could come back to come time and time again). Here is an indirect implication of the same –

道きやうハ長命丸をはけてぬり 万
dôkyô wa chômei-gan o hakete nuri 明三

pope dôkyô, he
laid his long-life salve on
with a trowel

long-life cream:
dôkyô wiped on the whole
damn shell-full

Then again, with the Empress's desire matching her size, maybe it could not be helped.[A] One amusing thing. This medicine is a millennia ahead of time. Since most such was sold in clam-shells, I brought that into the second reading. *Hakete* means either to buy in bulk or pour something all on, but *nuri* means paint/wipe on, so it was tricky to translate.

A. As one reader found this chapter so offensive to women suffering from largeness that she thought I should find another to start the book with, let add that, *first*, the Empress is an *anomaly*, not just *large* but, like Dôkyô, enough so to be used for hide-and-go-seek (I suspect such a grotto *ku* is out there among the hundreds of thousands of senryu I have *not* read) and, as such, should rather be of some *consolation*, in the same way that the existence of decocked and hooded men (pp. 184, 201 and ch. 19, respectively) offer some consolation for small men. And, *second*, as we shall see later (pg.117), there was a counter-argument in favor of *loose* ones, so they were not *entirely* shafted so to speak by senryu. And, finally, let me point out that demeaning references to a man's size – not a woman's – can be found almost any day on primetime television sitcoms in Usania. In this area, *it is clearly men, not women who are constantly reminded of their shortcomings.* ◎ So, picky readers – which does not mean all readers, for I know some of you may think *me* a prude – please note that the book has an overall balance, & try not to rush to judgment. For the sake of the other readers, I will not be making many (or, possibly, *any*) more boring qualifications of this sort.

---

7. *Behind the Legend.* The first draft explanation for the odd story of the accursed Empress was simply this: *While Shinto and Buddhism eventually came to terms with each other, the clash of indigenous and imported sensitivities and interests, like that of Celts and other Northern peoples with Christianity in North Europe, evidently created some very interesting – make that weird – tales*. On second reading, it seemed hopelessly naive. Thanks to Blyth's history of Zen I knew that Buddhists, or at least Zen Buddhists were at home with excrement, but they were more likely to laugh about it. And, even if the pissing-on-a-sutra idea was slanderous rhetoric used to battle Shinto on its own terms – it was concerned with purity and pollution – and suitable for the tail-end of a long era of wars, when even once mild religions fought with no holds barred, [A] why should Buddhists have anything against an Empress who was said to have shared power with *their* Dôkyô? Wiki has a paragraph with what seems the most reasonable explanation. When the Empress died of small-pox, she was the end of her Heaven Warrior Line 天武天皇系. The newly reigning Heaven Wisdom Line 天智天皇系 of Emperors might have found it in their interest to promote or allow folk legends to sully the name of their ancestral rival. Extrapolating from Wiki, we can imagine this legend eventually took root and grew branches, [B] perhaps in the literature of rival sects of Buddhism favoring rival lines of Emperors, to finally blossom in outlandish, yet innocent senryu.

A. *Religious Wars in Japan.* Compared to Europe, where quitting a religious sect (apostasy) was a capital crime and Jews who converted to Christianity to save their lives were later exhumed and burned, Japanese authorities were tolerant, even when Buddhist zealots engaged in armed confrontation with other sects. When Buddhist secular power threatened the hegemony of the rulers, however, they did not hesitate to burn their temples, militant monks included, to the ground. For a picture of Buddhist and Christian missionaries going at it in the gleeful way we might now associate with adolescent boys (eg., the head of a literally "blasted idol" landing in a commode!) though the stakes were higher, see ch. 3 & 4 of *Topsy-turvy 1585* (2004), a book translating and explicating 611 contrasts between Europeans and Japanese according to Luis Frois, S.J..

B. *Branching Legends.* One of the first branches grew a second one. Believe it or not, another colossal cock arose to battle with Dôkyô for the Empress's favors. After losing out, Blessing-beauty (how his name 恵美 translates) fomented a rebellion and, if I read correctly, went down fighting. We will skip him and all complex matters that do not pertain to senryu in this book.

Dôkyô Drollery. ~~*A Ku That Touches Upon a Still Current Usanian Fashion Problem*~~ . . .

袴着のころが道鏡へのこ也 摘 4-33
hakamagi no koro ga dôkyô henoko nari
(*hakama* wearing ~~era/times~~/right-size dôkyô cock becomes)

~~*when hakama*~~
~~*came to be worn, dôkyô*~~
~~*was in best form*~~

~~*wearing a hakama*~~
~~*everyone is hung*~~
~~*like dôkyô*~~

~~*hakama boasting*~~
~~*legs so long only dôkyô*~~
~~*could fill them*~~

~~*the perfect size*~~
~~*for wearing a hakama*~~
~~*dôkyô's pecker*~~

~~*to wear hakama,*~~
~~*& fit them, you'd need*~~
~~*what dôkyô had*~~

~~The legs on the culotte-like trousers worn for formal events by the nobility were so long they covered the feet and dragged behind like a train on a dress. I am glad to see the Japanese themselves thought these trousers, which turn feet into knees and require one to kick the train out in front for each step, ridiculous (For a full page of astonished reactions to this dysfunctional clothing by Europeans: see item 1-6+ in *Topsy-turvy* 1585). I was stymied by the *koro* until finding in my OJD (日本国語大辞典) that the 6th usage of *koro* was an abbrev. of *koroai* (頃合). Nowadays, Usanian youth wear their crotches around their knees. In my time, certain shirts with long tails were popular; stuffed in (and we had to tuck them in by regulation), they made a boy look like he had a lot down there – much the way horse and cow tails were used to fill codpieces in Elizabethan England. Of course, no one explained it like that. Such shirts were just "high quality." Could the knee-crotch (the butt-crack hanging out is merely a side-effect) be a clever way to avoid comparisons of male equipment or pretend every boy is a Dôkyô? I have read numerous explanations for the fashion but, oddly, not one mentioned what role, if any, penis insecurity or the desire to look or seem big, played in starting it. This may be more proof yet that, even if men are rich and powerful, male problems have been neglected more than female ones~~.

first hakama
when all little boys boast
dôkyô's cock

first hakama
when every little boy
is a dôkyô

Believe it or not, there are words in both French and Japanese for showing ones erasures: *"sous rature,"* and *"misekechi"* (I only learned of them when Professor Lewis Cook of CUNY described what I did on p. 375 of *Cherry Blossom Epiphany* to someone else on GG's *kigo* blog). First, I only crossed-out the first translation above. But when I tried out my reading on a respondent, he replied that *hakamagi* was not just the literal meaning but a coming-of-age ceremony for little boys (age 3-7, depending on the local circumstances and custom), when they first wore them. If so, *my* new reading is what you see above. But my respondent's was that the *ku* was a gag to the effect that the rest of the man's body kept growing, so *it* became comparatively small. (「子どもの頃は道鏡なみの巨根だったのに（からだの他の部分が成長して今では普通だ）」というギャグ). To wit,

first hakama
back when he had a cock
like dôkyô's

first hakama
'back then i was hung
like dôkyô'

Though I recall telling a friend in Scotland that lambs are interesting, indeed, for judging from those I could see across the river, the little ones are born with full-size tails which shorten proportionately as the rest of the body grows, I do not get the impression that most little boys start with three legs. But, if you think of an old man with what Japanese call a lantern (with all the folds) between his legs, who likes to talk of his magnificent past, I suppose this might do for hyperbole. Perhaps, a specialist on senryu will weigh in on this most interesting ku before the next edition (Remember to check the errata and glosses at paraverse.org from time to time).

宗因批判=点取の『大阪独吟』より。559 道鏡や音に聞えし音羽山　560 かたりもつくさじ其果報者　561 身体も次第にはり上げ／＼て　562　天竺振旦からかさの下（ありがたくも此寺の一本からかさか）563　大きにもやはらげ来る飴は／＼　564 あつかひ口もねぢた月影。さて、研究者にはこの連句の完全解釈を頼みます。わが手持ちの解釈に出てくるのが先ず、古今歌の「音に聞えし音羽山の。。。年をふるかな」。そこまではいいが、道鏡を「勢力絶倫で音に聞えた」という引き続きの説明が、どうも変。勢力でなく、大きさがである、問題は。あの音もどうかな？かの「万句合」の天七の句には「どふ／＼／＼といふほとのへのこなり」とあり、「馬」を連想するのも一つポイントでは？と訊きたい。558 は、たしかに腎水に触れるが、連想は古い発想の絶*倫*から絶大への過程を通るからこそ、563 は、後に川柳に出てくる巨根の弱点、つまり象の鼻へと転じるよう。解説者が、色々と難しいところを拾ってくださったが、道鏡のどこかがミソか、きちんと捕まえなければ、元句の機知も、漏れてしまうでは？

Dôkyô Equivalent. Where is the Occidental Dôkyô? Like Dôkyô, hired partly to help make the Empress well (侍二看病「続日本記」32), Rasputin is the obvious choice — but wrong because he was not paired with the right Catherine, namely, the Great one who, we are told could accommodate, and eventually died under, a horse. Taking literary figures, Rabelais played with the gargantuan baubles of his characters, but they were giants; *proportionately speaking*, for all we know, they could have been Greek (The statues commonly seen today. Or did the big ones suffer proportionately more from the ravages of time and censors?). The closest I can come to Dôkyô in "our" traditional (?) literature is this description of a monster cock in John Cleland's *Memoirs of a Woman of Pleasure*: *"its enormous head seem'd in hue and size, not unlike a common sheep's heart; then you might have troll'd dice securely along the broad back of it."* That *is* big and the attention given to the head almost Japanese (see pg. 107, 118-9). When Fanny's friend Louisa gamely takes it all in, she is said to be "gorg'd with 'the dearest morsel of the earth'" – shades of poor Romeo's dead corpse! Unfortunately, its owner was no clever bonze. The only patrimony of a fool, a common enough conceit in "our" bawdy to have a name, it was *a fool's bauble*.

◎　道鏡もうき世ハ廣ィ物ト言イ　摘　四・六　◎

その壱つ　better late than never　#1

Broader Significance of Dôkyô and the Empress's Affair. Treating historic themes in Japanese erotic images, Timon Screech mentions our Empress under yet another name:

> Unlike the Continent, Japan had a (truncated) history of female rulership, and the role that sex had played in this was not forgotten. Most famous was the *shujô* Abe (posthumously Kôken) who almost ruined the state . . . through her infatuation with a handsome monk called Dôkyô; this resulted in her deposition, after which no women ruled for 900 years . . . Whatever the historical facts, it was believed that what Abe had liked about Dôkyô was his penis, said to be mammoth. This scurrilous insinuation, already current in the thirteenth century, was popularized in the eighteenth. (*Sex and the Floating World.* University of Hawaii Press: 1999)

Whether her "infatuation" was really the root cause of the civil unrest is an open question; but it is interesting to see so much has been made of the relationship. I was only disappointed not to find the pair among the 149 prints in Screech's book. Is it possible that the graphic artists neglected this theme so popular in senryu because they had no way to depict the couple with surety because the genitals of *all* the men and women in the *shunga* (spring-prints) are humongous?

その弐つ better late than never #2

~~~~~~

Dôkyô and the Flower Flask. For the third time, I am two days from paginating and then indexing the 30+ files comprising this book. But, speaking of the devil, when I searched for the term *takara-awase* (treasure-matching/assembly) because it was the name for a print by Kunisada (or a book with them) found in Screech (1999) and discussed in ch.4., this morning (Sept.6, 2007), I found it at a site defining terms and concepts associated with *rakugo*, the art of the story-telling comic or the comic story teller. For you to get it, please pretend that in English, too, a *flask* and *vase* are the same word. No, to make it easier, I will use the Japanese word *bin* that means both.

"The Flower *Bin*" Tools of the Edo Era 「花瓶」江戸時代の道具

> Speaking of *shi-bin* [urinal/s], the *shi-bin* belonging to Yugen Dôkyô, famed for his gigantic penis, was brought to a convention called "treasure-matching" in the Edo era. These "treasure-matching conventions" were the origin of our *rakugo* (comic story-telling). After all, the procedure was to bring any treasure – or whatever you felt was a treasure – there, set it up on a stand covered with fine cotton cloth and try to convince the audience why it was a treasure like none other in the whole wide world.
>
> These conventions were held by crazy-verse masters 狂歌師達 and none other than Utei Enba, the man who was to found the genre called *rakugo* was one of those who made his debut in such a meet. So you see, from the get-go, there was this affinity between *shi-bin* [urinal/s] and *rakugo*. But this goes deeper yet, it speaks to what Edo was all about. It was a time when tools were not thrown out. They were just used for other things, restored as saleable goods at used-tool shops and not rarely morphed to reappear in a new guise. You might say they were not only alive but very lively creatures, indeed. Back then, it was nothing at all for a *shi-bin* [urinal 溲瓶] to become a *ka-bin* [flower vase 花瓶]. (カッパライ先は TBS 落語研究会 新・落語掌事典 落語演目「か」)

Long ago, I read Issa's *ku* where he calls his urinal his number-one treasure (perhaps,一の宝) in the winter. I simply thought it a decent *ku,* for it brings out the cold almost as well as a sentence in his journal where he admits to peeing out a hole in the door or wall when he drank too much (I guess the urinal was full), but now I think he was also alluding to knowledge of the above "treasure-matching" story. I realize the mere mention of Dôkyô's urinal, which I imagine must have been so large it was carried to the treasure-matching meet dangling from a pole carried by two professional movers, does not justify such a large discussion. *My* intention is to help any reader who may have failed to find any humor in the hyperbole in this chapter to loosen-up and try another. You are in a foreign country. It may take some time to catch on, but I am sure you will. (I apologize, if any readers feel they do not need any such babying and I am talking down to them. Remember, you are not my only reader. Please imagine some of the others who may be reading with you.)
~~~~~~

馬の捌きを学べば、月も無事

— 2 —

アンネの比喩尽し
No Taboo on Metaphor!

~~~~~~

許々多久の罪も消へ(ゆ)べし秋の月 一茶
kokodaku no tsumi mo kiyubeshi akinotsuki issa 文政一
(every-bit-of sin/crime-even vanish-should, autumn-moon)

all of our sins
should vanish tonight:
the fall moon

Where our full moon brought out the witches and werewolves, the Japanese moon, a reflection of Buddhist Law, sent them packing! It was even credited with making wild beasts behave themselves. In Japanese art, we see picture after picture of the farmer's most feared adversary, the wild boar, sleeping peacefully. Perhaps, this difference in attitude was why the Portuguese Jesuit Luis Frois recorded in 1585 that, "man, woman or child, we fear the night," while "in Japan, to the contrary, neither grown-ups or little ones have any fear." Issa's *ku* is, first of all, praise for a moon so bright and clear no dust/sin/stain clouds its mirror/ face and by implication all it reflects; but, he seems to take this Shintô concept of purity a step further having the moon vanquish sin/s with moonshine cleansing us of our mind-dirt, much as the Sun dries up and disinfects crud, 2) or sucks up the same like a sin-eater (poor people who ate up people's sins at funerals in Europe). The only thing a moon like this shares with our accursed orb is a verbal association with the menses. I don't think Issa, as a religious Buddhist, cared for that association. When he mentions a period – whether a memory of his wife's, his host's wife's or that of the Goddess of Spring, Sao-hime – he uses a different euphemism:

めぐり日と俳諧日也春の雨 一茶
megurihi to haikaibi nari haru no ame issa 文政八
(cycling-round-day &/so haikai day becomes, spring-rain)

her day comes   *her day comes*   *her period comes*
round: perfect for haikai *so, too, friends in haikai* *so it's my haikai day*
with spring rain   *and spring rain*   *with spring rain*

And, he wrote one *ku* that suggests a Buddhist reading of menses using senryu vocabulary while remaining unassailably innocent: *"Clams spit out their waste (crud/garbage) on a (full) moon night* (*hamaguri no gomi o hakasuru tsukiyo kana*)." With *clam* so common a metaphor for cunt, and moon for *menses*, the *ku* cannot help equating menstruation with purification. The clams do not pollute a pure moon so much as join in the collective purification. The second *ku* clearly mentions a period, but Issa was between wives that Spring, so is it a memory or, does it refer to the circumstances at another's house? He was on the road hosting *haikai* jamfests here and there. Did Issa or others set the dates for their all-night linkverse jamfests to take advantage of the wife's moon duty or is it purely fortuitous? *Haikai day* is a neologism. A poetry meeting (*kukai*) is most likely, but studious Issa could have been reading up on old *haikai*, which included much that would later be left to senryu. Take, for example, link-verses #1738-39 & #1741-43 in what is considered the representative collection of early-phase *haikai,* the *Enoko-shû* (重頼 Shigeyori ed.犬子集 1633), or "puppy collection."

1. Longing to go all the way as high as Mt Fuji 恋をするがの富士の山ほど
2. Giddy from the sight of their fat white rumps; 若衆のしほ尻に心まどはして
3. Nip those boys' cheeks so you won't stay blue 尻にくひつき思ひはらさん
4. I'd be happy just to be a louse born in her undies! せめて君のゆぐの虱と生ればや

1) The original is "making love as *much* as Suruga's Fuji." The famous lover of *The Tales of Ise* had to go & go (ejacul. punning) to Suruga (行き行てするがのくににいたる) .
2) The orig. mentions "young-crowd"(catamites), and white-sand-butt/s. Fuji was compared to such a rump in *Tales of Ise* and there were dazzling white sand Fujis in gardens.
3) More like *bite & latch on to* in the orig. I trust you can tell what cheeks are referred to?
4) A switch of sex to a "you," meaning a female sweetheart. English wanted a "her." The "you" (君) also meant "ruler;" so the abject wish fits. Undies = a loin-wrap.

5. I'd throw myself in just to be remembered 身をなげしんで思出にせん
6. If I only had a deep pool of the water you pissed 君さまの小便水の渊もがな
7. We cannot suck mouths waving a red flag さはりありつゝ口もすはれず・我君↓
8. And that long nose on my dear must be counted a flaw の鼻のながきやきずならん
9. A lie so apparent in the color of his face うそは面の色に見えけり・泪にと硯↓
10. Made with bottled teardrops that turned out to be ink ～のすみを目にぬりて

5) Like a warrior who commits a heroic suicide.
6) *Piss Me a Pond* rather than *Cry Me a River?* In a *waka*, Saigyô (1118-90) wanted to do the same in a pool of his own tears shed for his sweetheart.
7) The actual word is *sawari*, a hindrance, which means menstruation. *We/I/he.*
8) A long nose would get in the way (But ↓ is Pinocchio foreshadowed?)
9) A bald-faced lie is called a red-lie in Japanese, and that was the color of the tip of the famously long nose of a woman in *The Tale of Genji.*
10) Referring to a ladies' man who carried a bottle of water for teardrops on command, who accidentally brought ink and blackened his reputation instead.

Enough early-*haikai*. That should do to show the senryu we will see were no newly invented dirtiness. Other *ku* in the above sequence equate *love* with *pus* released from a inflammation in a manner reminiscent of Samuel Johnson on *love* as the holding/release of *farts*. Haiku, like senryû, was born in a septic, natural environment. And, both gained from the practice of linked-verse, which cultured highly imaginative associations in the same manner rhyme did for us –

> ....[rhyme] hath beene so farre from hindering their [sonnet writers] inuentions, as it hath begot conceit beyond expectation, and comparable to the best inuentions of the world: for sure in an eminent spirit whome Nature hath fitted for that mysterie, Ryme is no impediment to his conceit, but rather giues him wings to mount and carries him, not out of his course, but as it were beyond his power to a farre happier flight.

I give you Samuel Daniel's words harking from a time when "v" was written "u" because I feel rhyme is unappreciated and am not sure that Frost's comments about playing tennis without a net, which describe why form *in general* is an asset, suffice to rebut those who turn their fear of letting rhyme take the tiller into rhetoric against it! What rhyme or linked-verse (including capped *ku*) does is pull the individual poet out of the ruts our minds naturally make. While most senryu is not actually born of *haikai* linked-verse, the wit required to write and read them was. Sorry to keep you waiting. Here is this chapter's first senryu:

信女の月をよどませる和尚様　摘
shinjô no tsuki o yodomaseru oshô-sama pluck 4-32
(believing-woman's moon=religion / dirtied/blocked/stagnated monk[subj+suffix])

the shining moon
of a lay sister clouded
by brother monk

This *ku* manages to capture both the Buddhist and the woman's moon, but fails to properly English because we must use two words, "menses" and "month," instead of one. Moreover, we have no single word for blocking a flow, causing stag-nation and loss of pristine clarity. When we think of a still section of river, we are more likely to imagine it as clear – from settling down – than cloudy! Like the opposing interpretations of "a rolling stone gathers no moss," we have a metaphorical mismatch; but, here, the difference is phenomenological rather than psychological. What irony! The priest (an *oshô* is a well-off bonze who may head a small temple) has stained the moon of her spiritual purity, while stopping the flow of her period, i.e. impregnated her!

西鶴も漏る月役の女小屋　表若葉 享保 17
saikaku mo moru tsukiyaku no onna-goya (寄合にけり／へ)
(saikaku even leaks moon-duty's woman/women-small-bldg)

◎ *they do gather* ◎

even saikaku
missed that little hut
for moon duty

even saikaku
left this scene in wraps
moon-duty hut

Moonshine and moonwater (月の水) *leak=moru* through grass roofs and menstrual pads in English as in Japanese, but the figurative usage was lost in translation for English takes it to mean sharing secret information rather than failing to pick up on something. According to the poet who responded to the draw I made the title,

Ihara Saikaku (1641-93), master of the erotic novel, who depicted women in more places and ways than any other writer, missed them gathering *there*. I would guess Saikaku did not so much *miss* them as *avoid* them because he, like most men, was not turned on by blood; as one late *Willow ku* put it, *"Snapping turtle shrinks before his wife's full moon"* (すっぽんも縮む女房のお月様 105 *suppon mo chijimu nyôbô no otsukisama.* Note that *moon* and *marsh turtle* are standard trope for the *exalted* and the *lowly*, respectively, as well as the *period* and the *penis*.)

もれ出る月明らかに小豆飯
more-izuru tsuki akiraka ni azukihan 33-10
(leaking-appears moon clearly-by adzuki-rice)

in the leaking
rays of moonshine, red beans
and white rice

Another *ku* has a fire kindled to cook the dish as the light leaks in, but all such *ku* do not English well for we have never paid much attention to "leaking" moonlight and that light cannot also be the moon. Words or not, in parts of Usania, feminists know that the first-tide (*hatsushio* 初潮) was celebrated in Japan by eating a bowl of white rice with little red *azuki* beans and have adopted the practice or created their own for their daughters. I like to think some may have got the idea from reading Blyth's translation of a *senryû* with little brother puzzled about why the family was eating special food (once, not just beans but white rice was a rare treat) and his sister was on the high-horse.

豆に花咲くと小豆の飯をたき 61-6
mame ni hana saku to azuki no han o taki
(bean-on flower blooms so bean rice cooking)

when the flower
is on the bean, its time
to cook bean-rice

もう娘花見に小豆飯をたき 28-3
mô musume hanami ni azuki han o taki
(already daughter blossom-viewing-for bean...)

a missy already
her blossom-viewing food
red-bean rice

初めてのお客に赤の飯をたき 45
hajimete no okyakyusan ni aka no han o taki
(first-time guest-for red rice[acc] cooking)

a guest's first visit
the white rice just exquisite
with those red beans

初花の祝儀たがいにおほゝ也
hatsuhana no iwagi tagai ni obobo nari 130
(first-bloom's celeb. mutual [hon+]bobo become)

the celebration
of her first bloom: now it's
obobo for both

娘の初役顔までが赤の飯 28
musume no hatsuyaku kao made ga akanohan
(daughter/girl's first-period face-until is redrice)

her first period
is that red on her face
rice or a blush

A cunt is a *bean*. A *bobo* is an adult cunt. The "o" is an honorific. We can imagine the mother speaking sweetly to her daughter. *Flower* and *guest* are some of many other names for the menses. But leaking moonshine, blooming vines and bowls of special food for honorable guests create a picture a bit too pretty. *"Her mother / all smiles for the first / seven days"* (初めての七日を母はにこにこし万明二宮 2 *hajimete no nanuka o haha wa nikoniko shi*) goes one senryu, implying that subsequent periods might not be so cheerfully marked. And that is to be expected, for they were bothersome. When, to use Papua New Guinean idiom, *"Mun i kilim meri"* (the moon, he kills Mary – T. sione: Tok Nogut in *Maledicta II* [*meri* = *wife* and *kilim* also means *injure/abort*]), Japanese women staying in separate rooms or, in some localities, separate houses, ate food cooked on different fires from different pots. As the pseudonymous author 玩宮隠士 of *Cuntologia* put it, *"Even the gods hated menstruating women. Until the end of the Edo era, it was taken for granted that menstruating women were forbidden to enter shrine precincts"* (女陰万考 1996). This meant seven days per month! Since most festivals were held in Shinto shrines, this means women lost out on a lot of fun.

初詣娘鳥居を断られ 失典
hatsumôde musume torii o kotowarare
(first-visit daughter shrinegate denied)

first shrine visit
a girl is denied entry
at the red gate

おく家老鳥居の前でぎんみをし万
okugarô torii no mae de ginmi o shi 明 3
(palace elder shrinegate-before screens)

a palace elder
stands by the shrine gate
screening them

A girl, off to the Shrine to get a good start for the new year, is hijacked by the moon. Did she *just* get her first period and was made to wait outside the gate– *torii* is usually red, so I made it so – by her parents, or was there a guard looking for guilty faces? The second *ku* imagines an old chamberlain by the *torii,* a doorless gate close to the inside of the character 開, scrutinizing girls. It was a response to the fine draw *"Why not just ask them?"* (たつね社すれ *tazune koso sure*)! Another, perhaps playing against that, even more mischievously suggests,

國家老開を見せたらどんな顔 葉
kunigarô bobo o misetara donna kao 三三
(country-hose-elder cunt[acc] shown-if what face)

why not show a cunt
to that old chamberlain
just to see his face!

show 'im your cunt
just to see his expression:
the country elder

The chamberlain here, a *kunigarô,* is one left in charge of the "country = *kuni*," or provincial fiefdom, when the lord is serving time in Edo, but we must skip further such details in favor of better ones to come. The *ku* is juvenile and amusing mostly because of its relationship to the character built by previous *ku.*

Moon Against Moon

またぐらのぎんみをとげる月見前
matagura no ginmi o togeru tsukimi-mae 末 1-23
(crotch-storage/godown's inspection[acc] carry-out moon-viewing-pre)

faithfully carried out
her godown's inspection
pre-moon-viewing

before the moon
an inquisitor pays a call
on her godown

crotch godowns
receive the inspectors
for the tsukimi

One *Pluck* round-robin participant thought the high-falootin expression *"ginmi o togeru* = execute an inspection" was samurai-speak; but another showed examples of its adoption by townsmen when they wanted a hyperbole for something being checked out. This careful scrutiny concerns the preparation of moon-viewing dumplings for either the 15th night of the mid-Fall Harvest moon-viewing, or the 13th night of the following month, both of which were important Buddhist celebrations because the moon and its light reified Buddhist Law and Mercy, the grace of which bathed the earth and all on it, as described at the start of the chapter. If the wife were impure, the husband would have to make the dumplings, which were food for the viewing, decoration and an offering, instead. On the one hand, this would be a welcome break for the wife who normally would mortar, knead and *round* (they are shaped into balls) the moon-viewing dumplings; on the other hand, she would feel bad not to be able to fete the moon, to whom she might feel related in a less Buddhist but more intimate way than her husband.

お月見をていしゆに十五丸メさせ
o-tsukimi o teishu ni jûgo marume sase 4-6

for moon-viewing
the master is made to make
the fifteenth round

十三夜又かとてい主おん丸め 露丸評明
jûsanya mata ka to teishu on-marume 三大 2

the thirteenth night
"not again!" says her husband
rounding them off

Though a purity-centered religion from the start, Shintô was not really *that* down on menses, and to the degree it may have been, the idea of shrine-gate inspection may have been new, arriving only centuries before the arrival of senryu, as Shinto re-enshrined itself in competition with Buddhism. The dumpling taboo might be older, for many Buddhist sects were terribly clear about the impurity and inferiority of women, whom they held must be reincarnated as a man before they had any chance of enlightenment. Menstruation was only the easiest pretext for denying women access. Some temples, or entire mountains of temples, were off-limits to all women *all of the time*, some for all but on special occasions. The respectful "o" before the moon and "on" before rounding, could not be Englished, as "honorable" would sound ridiculous and, worse, make the translation too long.

what bad timing!
the sun chosen turned out
to be the moon!

what bad timing!
we chose a day that was
her monthly

間の悪さ日は選んだが月になり 84-37, &
ma no warusa hi wa eranda ga tsuki ni nari 85-2, 136-18
(interval's badness sun/day/date-as-for choose but moon/menses becomes)

Bad circumstance is universal, but in a culture where lucky dates were carefully selected by taking the permutations of calendars of various cycles – such a mishap would be particularly galling. The original *ku* is stunningly simple; but lacking the *sun=day* and *moon=month* equivalence, English does poorly with it.

七日さへ休ミやせぬと女房出る 摘 3-20
nanuka sae yasumi ya senu to nyôbô deru

who can take off
seven days! says the wife
as she goes out

One cannot tell whether the wife leaves the special moon-duty hut or a small house in town where there is no such place, but the comment makes great sense. Not that anyone really vacationed those seven days. The moon-duty hut would have been a workshop for indoor work like sewing mosquito or fishing nets and a million other indoor chores. And, if the "seven days" was official, it is possible many women did their moon duties just that long, no more or less, regardless of their actual course: *"His wife always catches colds that last just seven days"* (お内儀ハ七日とかきる風をひき 摘 4-18 *onaigi wa nanuka to kagiru kaze o hiki*). There is also a *kyôka* (31-syllabet crazy-verse) in *Cuntologia* suggesting that periods could be faked to avoid sex. The author suggests husbands keep tabs on their wives to be sure they are not getting gypped.

Ignoring the Red Flag

猿猴の月に手をだす新世帯 柳
enkô no tsuki ni te o dasu arasetai willow 82
(monkey's/ee's moon-to hand[acc] stick out[= engage in] new-household)

like monkeys
can't keep their hands off the moon
the newlyweds

like a monkey
can't keep his hands off the moon
the bride groom

newlyweds
like that monkey reaching
for the moon

The menses are sometimes called the *"moon's water."* Water is where the proverbial Chinese monkey tries to scoop up the reflection of the moon. Sex-crazed newly-weds, renowned for *"doing what is done at night in the day"* (新世帯夜する事も昼間する 摘一五 *arasetai/arajôtai yoru suru koto mo hiruma suru*) are a popular stereotype in senryu. *"To newly-weds / an abstinence night / is monkey business"* (庚申をうるさく思う新所帯 失典 *kôshin o urusaku omou arasetai* – more on abstinence night & the monkey connection in a few pages). Though *"Confucius says / Thou shall not take / a sleeping chick"* (senryu is lost, but note that unlike Usanian Confucianisms, it plays on something actually in the *Analects*), *"The new wife can't even take a nap / without her husband getting into her twat"* (also lost). I have seen half a dozen on the newly-wed ignoring periods, but that reaching monkey is the wittiest.

猿猴と知らず炬燵で手を伸ばし
enkô to shirazu kotatsu de te o nobashi 83-70
(monkey [it's?] know-not kotatsu-at hand [acc] reach out)

not knowing he
was that monkey, reaching
under the kotatsu

~~he reaches out~~
~~under the table, unaware~~
~~a monkey's there~~

In a first draft, twelve years ago, I wrote "water is not obligatory, for the monkey is also known to have red-colored privates;" but the 猿猴 is a *Chinese* monkey with a long tail and not a macaque with an ugly red-rump, like those in Japan. I completely missed the real wit in the *semantic ellipsis*. Namely, the protagonist does not know he is *acting like* the proverbial monkey reaching for the moon.

お月見の豆に手を出しはじかれる 165
o-tsukimi no mame ni te o dashi hajikareru

reaching out for
a moon-viewing bean his hand
is flicked away

Sweet potatoes and dumplings were common moon-viewing food, but *beans*? Long before its "re-discovery" in the modern West (it was known of old – "we" forgot a lot), the clitoris was recognized and called a "bean" in Japan. Moon-viewing was a serious religious rite, not a good time to horse around, even if the moon did not imply the wife was having her period. The final verb is witty for reversing the usual relationship between hand and bean. While the "moon= menses" metaphor continues strong today, in the heyday of senryu it was nosed out by a metaphor now obsolete: *the horse,* or, rather, *riding one*. Evidently, menstrual gear resembled riding, and failure to take care could result in a spill.

Learning to Ride

月やどるらんそろ／＼ぼろをため 121 乙
tsuki yadoru ran sorosoro boro o tame

she'll soon be
putting up the moon: we
better save rags

Boro was not necessarily rags, so if we forgive the use of a modern word, *"Here comes the moon / We'd best stock up soon / on cardboard!"* might be another possibility. I am unsure if the wit is in the saving of a lowly item or in the poverty of a family that would have to prepare for menstruation in the way the Usanian middle class saves to retire. Since senryu did not seem to pay much attention to poverty, the former is more likely. Putting up the moon (*tsuki yadoru*) was not so original in Japanese as in English, for it is a stock phrase used for anything from dew drops to soup to the tear-wet sleeves of lonely lovers, *i.e.,* wherever moonlight or the moons reflection might be found. This usage might be seen as a parody of the lyrical one. But that late Willow ku, stands alone. Senryu were interested in a newer metaphor, the horse. I do not know when it started, but here are examples:

1. *First time to ride. / Her mother hands-over / the pony's reins.*
2. *Her first horse! / How quickly girls become / good riders!*
3. *Galloping / out to the outhouse / for urgent matters.*
4. *A woman doing / some mighty fancy riding / in the restroom.*
5. *She kept loose reins / and now her slip / is stained.*
6. *Play in the horse's belly cinch / now a red stain makes her wince.*
7. *A maid embarrassed – scolded for falling / off her horse.*
8. *The housewives / have horses that eat as much / as nanny goats.*
9. *Every time / a horse stales it devours / bales of paper.*

1. 乗り初めに駒の手綱を母伝授 62 *norisome ni koma no tazuna o hahadenju*
Or, *passes down, i.e.* a tradition. And "*~some=starts*" puns on "stain."
2. はつむまに乗ルと娘もうまく成リ *hatsu-muma ni noru to musume mo umaku-nari*
Or, *horsey,* for *muma* is a childish pronunciation. 万　宝十一
3. 雪隠へ馬でかけ出す急な事 87 *setchin e uma de kakedasu kyû na koto*
Japanese has no "gallop," but going out quickly for a horse must be that.
4. せつちんで手綱さばきをする女 摘 1-7 *setchin de tazuna-sabaki o suru onna*
With squat holes rather than stools, they must have ridden like jockeys.
5. 手綱がゆるいと帷子へしみが出来 摘 4-19 *tazuna ga yurui to katabira e shimi ga deki*
The *katabira* is both an undergarment and a dangerously thin sole summer garment.
6. 馬の腹帯が延び候赤くしみ 39 *uma no hara-obi ga nobi soro akaku shimi.*
She must have puffed up her belly when she pulled the girth cinch.
7. 下女はづかしい落馬してしかられる 万 天元 *gejo hazukashii rakuba-shite shikarareru*
How pitiful! There is a Japanese expression: like wasps stinging a teary face.
8. 奥様のお馬も羊ほど喰らい 32 *okusama no o-uma mo hitsuji hodo kurai*
Japanese lacks number. It could be *"a housewife's horse"* if you prefer. Since Japanese used more paper than cloth, introducing goats was a stroke of genius.
9. 馬の小便其度に紙を喰 121 内 *uma no shôben sono tabi ni kami o kuu*
Actually, palace stables in Japan had wooden floors and the horses' stale was caught in long-handled scoops by their attendants! (see *Topsy-turvy 1585*, item # 8-24)

If Blyth did not translate any of the above senryû, it is not because the censors would have stopped him. 4, 7, 8 and 9 should have been good enough for his anthologies, so I can only suspect that he felt the subject was, unlike the farts, shit and piss with which he was at home with, was, aside from the red beans, taboo. But enough talk, we have many more horses to go.

浅草を食っているのは下女が馬 失典
asakusa o kutte-iru no wa gejo ga uma

and the ones
eating short grass are
maids' horses

the horse eating
asakusa short grass
is the maid's

Paper was not only paper but much of the cloth in Japan. From warm paper kimono to fancy handkerchiefs to sex and moon-duty, it ruled supreme. Japanese dresses had to be unsewn and resewn to be washed, so it was especially important to avoid stains and, to this end, both cardboard-like scraps to absorb blood and fine water-resistant paper were combined. Not all could, however afford the best riding gear. Asakusa, a place name that translates as "short-grass," was also a cheap brand of paper. Finally, someone put the horses and paper together without the goat.

10. *A female warrior / upon a horse: call her / unapproachable.*

11. *The wife's horse / makes her husband lie / down his spear.*

12. *The honorable horse / so you'd better stop! /* Brushed off by the maid.

10. 女武者馬に乗ってよせ付けず 86 *onna busha uma ni notte yose-tsukezu*
The only women riding (not just carried on) real horses were bushi class (samurai).
11. 女房の馬で亭主の槍を寝せ 113 *nyôbô no uma de teishu no yari o nese*
I am lost. Is it possible the allusion is to the size of a horse's genitals?
12. お馬だよよしなと下女ははねつける 35 *o-uma dayo yoshina to gejo wa hanetsukeru*
If this translated as well as it reads in the original, it would deserve a full page.

The maid's "*honorable* horse" is an atrocity, the revenge of a language that has no subtle yet unmistakable way to express respect against one that does. In Japanese, a one-phoneme prefix does the trick. The horse in the earlier *ku* mentioning a goat's appetite also gets an honorific "o," either to bring out the contrast with the lowly goat, or because that was how women talked. Be that as it may, that honorific only works fully in the last *ku*, where the maid uses it to elevate the status of a part/function of her body, and, speaking in its exalted behalf rather than for her humble self – imperiously brushes her master off his customary high-horse. It is as good as anything in Shakespeare.

お馬には牛は使わぬ長局
o-uma ni wa ushi wa tsukawanu nagatsubone
([hon.]horse-as-4 ox-as-4 uses-not cham.maid)

the honorable horse:
the chamber-maid puts her ox
out to pasture.

長局牛をやすめて馬に乗り
nagatsubone ushi o yasumete uma ni nori
(cham.maid ox[acc] rest-lets horse-on mounts)

the chamber-maid
puts her ox out to pasture
& mounts a horse

The *nagatsubome* is a lady-in-waiting or chamber-maid of the palace of the Shôgun or a Daimyô. Since most of the women rarely if ever slept with their lord, I avoid the term harem, but males over seven were not allowed and the women were bored. As we will see later (ch.4), these women were synonymous with *masturbation*, and generally used dildos made from water buffalo horn called in short simply *ushi,* "cow/ox." The "o" before *her* horse in the first *ku* seems less an honorific than a reflection on the elegant language of women of the court.

水馬とも出られず海士は針仕事
suiba to mo derarezu ama wa hari-shigoto 失典
(water/sea-horse though go-out-not diveress-as-for needle-work)

a seahorse mount
but the diver stays home
does her sewing

even a seahorse
must stay on land, divers
have sewing days

Unlike English, where the sea-*horse* and not the sea-*dragon* is the generic term, in Japanese, the *dragon-child* (*umi-no-tatsugo*) is the common term. But, in this case, the horse had to be brought into the picture. Female divers called *ama* spend hours in water too cold for men with their thinner layer of protective fat. But, with sharks around, they had to take time off for the "seahorse." (Ah, just in case you wondered, our hippo is *river*-horse in Japanese.)

a diver sewing
she cannot go out even using
the water-horse

One of my dictionaries, that concentrating on words made from Chinese characters, gave me the *seahorse*; but my 12-volume OJD did not. Instead, it had only *"water-horse,"* defined as a technique used by samurai to get horses to cross rivers or other stretches of water, where the rider slid off and swam by the horse when the water got too deep for it to touch bottom and climbed back on as soon as the horse started to get its footing. Because facetious military analogies were more common than fantasy creatures, I regret to say that *this* water-horse seems the more likely to be correct here. Sewing was a typical activity for someone killing time usefully.

馬だからよしなと女房尻を向け
uma dakara yoshina to nyôbô shiri o muke 112
(horse because stop-it! as/says rear faces/turns-to [him]))

the horse is here
so whoa! says his wife
turning her back

i'm a horse, so
whoa! says wife turning
her back on him

"Horse because" allows the original to simultaneously refer to being *on* the horse and being *one*. When asked whether or not an order is ours or not, we may reply *"I'm* the hamburger!" or *"I'm* the hotdog!" but English cannot do that here. Point-ing her butt at him is idiomatic for spurning his advances, yet, we also get a wee hint of another possibility, for even some men who were not newlywed were willing to ride sorrel mares. As one *ku* put it *"Polluted? Who cares! / Now the wife is really / in a quandary"* (けがれてもよいとはきついはずみ様 摘1 *kegarete mo yoi to wa kitsui hazumi yô*). The only thing worse than that would be this: *"If you're a horsey, / how about your fart-hole?" / says fool-husband* (お馬なら屁の穴でもと馬鹿亭主 105 *o-uma nara he no ana demo to baka teishu*). This is my first encounter with an anus so named, but horses know which hole to use (The spellbinding logic used by Boccacio's priest on another man's wife is far better). I hope there is a *ku* somewhere out there that properly tails a horse! If the Japanese could only pun on *ass* like English – for once, *we* are the homophonically blessed – there would surely be a *ku* like *"If her horse / is stuffed, why, then, / feed her ass!"* or, *"Horsey* ***won't*** *– / So the newly wed sees / if the ass* ***will,"*** or, *"When her horse / is bridled, her ass may / be tailed!"* etc.

~~~~~~

Pietro replied, *"Mother of God, I did not want that tail there. You were putting it too low down. Why did you not say to me, 'Make it yourself'?" "Because,"* answered Dom Gianni, *"you would not know the first time how to stick it in so well as I can."* (from *Dioneo's Story*, Day Nine of Boccaccio's *Decameron!*)

~~~~~~

こらえ兼ね亭主が好きで赤えぼし
koraekane teishu ga suki de aka-eboshi

red goose barnacle
on the husband who loves it
too much to wait

he couldn't wait
so her husband wears his
high red hat

he couldn't wait
so she loves her husband
and his red dog

The red hat is a cross between the tall phallic hats worn by Japanese nobles in classic times and a Chinese equivalent of *"Love me love my dog,"* where the dog is an unstylish bright red hat. It is the only senryu I recall with a husband who is neither a newly-wed nor suffering from the clap (we will see soon) who wants to have anything to do with his wife at that time. Note that the "red hat" metaphor (his cock? her sheath?) implies the wife reluctantly indulges his kinky desire.

女房が落馬をするとすぐに乗り 65
nyôbô ga rakuba suru to sugu ni nori

soon as his wife
falls off her horse, up he
jumps for a ride

七日迄まつて女房をらくはさせ万宝九
nanoka made matte nyôbô o rakuba sase

he waits a week
then knocks his old lady
right off her horse

At first, I only appreciated the first *ku*, for it adds a whole new twist by turning the horse under the woman into her and is clever for playing with the universal idea of jumping right back on (better with no "he," as in the original). Wives in both *ku* are *nyôbô,* but I made the second "old lady" to match the rude behavior of her spouse, who is nonetheless amusing for sticking so strictly to the calendar, or rather the conventional period regardless of what the real one might be. Unfortunately, there were days where *jumping back on* was not allowed.

馬はもういいが今夜は庚申 86
uma wa mo ii ga konya wa kanoezaru

Blue Warrior

the horse finally
in the stable, but tonight
he is not able

The night written 庚申 and pronounced Kôshin or Kanoezaru, originally a night of waiting-up for a major Buddhist guardian demon/deity, called "Blue Warrior" – perfect here, for the English meaning of blue – was hijacked by the popular Taoist monkey, found in the tail of the colloquial Kanoe*zaru*. In the Sinosphere, the horse stood for desire (*id*) and (believe it or not) the monkey for control (*super-ego*). Monkeys were painted leading heart-horses by the reins, and actually brought around to bless stables once a year. That night, abstinence was observed. Originally, it was because giving in to one's desires when you might be surprised in the act by a deity of a religion preaching for people to hold their horses was verboten; but, later, the reason changed to fear any child conceived that night *would grow up to be a thief.* As always, rationalization came to the rescue:

けつをするぶんはかまわぬかのへ 申 摘
ketsu o suru bun wa kamawanu kanoezaru 2-17

blue warrior day
doing it from behind is
no cause to mind

a piece of ass
no trouble with that
blue warrior day

I cannot tell if the "ass" is his wife's or a boy's. It is probably the wife. Since there are a few lines to fill at the bottom of the page, let me add that in the *Pluck* anthology it came from there are nine *ku* starting with *ketsu*=ass/anus and only one of the buggered is female beyond doubt (at a nunnery).

りちぎ者・かゝもふけふは何日めじや 笠付類題句
richigimono · kaka mô kyô wa nan-nichime ja 天保五

< he is upright >
"old lady, just how many
days are we at?"

This wonderful find of Suzuki's is almost mid-19c, yet is a capped verse, called a *kasazuke,* so it is probably from the Kinki (not kinky) parts Southwest of Tokyo (Osaka, Kyoto, Nagoya, etc.). The expression *kaka* is used for an older wife who is no cuteypie, and tends to be the household dictator. Usually, she has many children. And, as the saying goes, *"The upright guy is buried in children"* (律義者の子沢山 *richigimono no kodakusan*). A man who is a steady worker creates the stability needed to make and nurture children. It may also be, the *ku* suggests, because he goes by the biological clock. The next *ku*, I like even better:

七日斗カなんのこつたと女房いひ 摘
nanuka baka nan-no kotta to nyobo ii 1-35
('seven-days only what things[!#?]'wife says)

get a life!
seven days are nothing
says his wife

what's seven days
out of your life! stop bitching
says his wife

just seven days
what's the big fuckin' deal!
says the wife

seven whole days
a big ado about nothing
laughs his wife

Many more *ku* observe husbands with flagging interest in frustrated wives. Perhaps, the complainer should consider herself lucky. But this 1776 *Pluck ku* hasn't even gotten us to the *real* monkey business involving sorrel horses.

When Men Ride Horses, *Clap!*

~~~~~~

馬もなんともおもわない女郎げび 万
uma mo nantomo omowanai jorô gebi 天四

the two-bit whore
doesn't give a damn
about *her* horse

馬上のたたかい淋病の薬なり 75
bajo no tatakai rinbyô no kusuri nari

A joust on horseback
in other words, medicine
for a dose of clap!

Gonorrhea was rampant in Edo, with its large population of single men who bought sex from whores such as this one who did it *every* day. I do not know if the sorrel horse cure was taken seriously or not, but senryu poets enjoyed it.

1. *To cure your clap ・ why, of course! This time try ・ to ride a horse!*

2. *Clap the diagnosis ・ Suddenly he's interested ・ in horses!*

3. *For clap you can ・ mount bareback to fight it ・ barehanded.*

or, *For clap, you go ・ mount a horse to do battle ・ without arms.*

淋病の薬馬にも乗ってみろ 96 *rinbyô no kusuri uma ni mo notte-miro*
淋病と号して馬に乗りたがり 59 *rinbyô to gô shite uma ni noritagari*
りん病に馬上ながらも無手と組み 万宝九 *rinbyô ni bajô nagara mo mute to kumi*

The last, and oldest *ku* (1759), plays with two meanings of *handless.* It was the term for period used in the Imperial Palace *and* alludes to the sufferer's being forbidden to post on his medicine horse. He was to insert his stricken member, stay put and not *go* ("come"). Moreover, if the man availing himself of this "clinic that comes round once a month," were to really ride, that is, *"use his hips,*
~~~~~~

the medicine turns to poison" (もし腰を使えば薬毒となる 万?安五 *moshi koshi o tsukaeba kusuri doku to naru*). Luckily for women, such rules of combat probably kept most men from trying it. None of the *ku* explain the logic behind the cure. Could it be trans-sensual correspondence where burning pain is quelled by flame-red menses? Purification by blood where the disease is supposed to flow off with the woman's courses? Perhaps it is human nature to do painfully difficult things in the expectation that effort, however misguided, will be rewarded by some benevolent power that keeps tabs on the balance of our happiness/misery. Needless to say, the healthcare provider was unhappy. Here, I *had* the perfect example: *"Back in the saddle / to banish the curse? His wife / would vanish first!"* (うちかへす病気女房きへたがり *uchikaesu byôki nyôbô kietagari* 6-32). Unfortunately, a re-reading revealed the disease made a *come-back* rather than *being beaten back;* and that meant *Dry Kidney* disease (pg 121), not the clap.

Consider *The Gross*

月役ハいるかのあじとつび虱 葉別4ウ
tsukiyaku wa iruka no aji to tsubijirami

moon-duty time
it tastes just like dolphin
says the cunt-crab

Syunroan notes that, *unlike whale*, dolphin is very bloody. Since whale, excluding blubber, is far from bloodless, it *must* be, though I doubt it matches the red of *sakuraniku*, cherry-meat, *i.e., horse!* This *ku* borrowed from my book-to-be of salacious marine poetry (*The Mullet in the Maid*) is a rare example of *found* in translation: in Japanese, *lice* are not called "crabs." I saved it for late in the chapter to make a point about the diversity of grossness. This *ku* seems grosser than the cure-for-clap *ku* for being so specific: it rubs our noses in the menarche, yet it is far less *obscene* if we consider the possibility women really were used to treat clap like that. Now, how about the next senryu (Ueda's trans.) from the introduction to *Light Verse from the Floating World*? How gross is *it?*

the moon makes her grieve	*tsuki mireba*
over thousands of things –	*chiji ni kanashiki*
His Lordship's widow	*gokôshitsu* (K 3)

After admitting to avoiding senryu that "violate our sense of decency," Ueda made an exception for the above example *"only because it uses a euphemism for a word that is normally shunned in respectable poetic language."* After noting it "alludes to a *waka* by Oe Chisato (fl. 897-903) . . renowned for its expression of the vague melancholy felt by a sensitive person looking at the autumn moon," he explains the senryu only shows its true color with the "widow," in the last line, for, then, readers would know the "moon" (*tsuki*) alludes to the menstrual period of a young widow, remembering among the *"thousands of things"* the *"time she spent with her husband in the bedroom."* Not all readers find that allusion, but even granting it was intended, a widow *in senryu*, is either paired with the priest more interested in her hole than the departed husband's soul or another paramour, or recalls her husband while masturbating. *Thinking about sex when she has a period* seems too arbitrary a reading. The grief, or pathos here probably comes less from erotic memories than from *childlessness*, because 1) a period is not so much the time to think of sex, as *of failure to become pregnant* (Issa's notebook records his wife's periods when he was hoping for children: just imagine how aware the women were!) 2) she is not just a widow, but one in a family *line* where bearing a *male* child mattered and 3), there is a homophonic suggestion of "blood[line]" in "thousand" (both are *chi*). Not that such details matter. What *bothers me* and should bother all of us is that we must tiptoe so gingerly around supposedly delicate matters in books intended for literate adults. In the Victorian Age, the masses were denied access to obscenity the more highly educated elite enjoyed in Latin. That is to say, the ruling class treated the ruled as children. Today, *all of us* who live in Usania are patronized, or, to give credit to women for the role they have played in creating the new censorship (pc hysteria?), *matronized.*

世は花よ身には月水の七日後家 へらずロ
yo wa hana yo mi ni wa sawari no nanuka-goke 元禄七 1694
(world-as-for blossoms/festive! body/self-as-for hindrance's 7-day widow)

the world in bloom
while she's in moon-water
a seven-day widow

the world parties
while the seven-day widow
serves the moon

the whole world
parties! i'm in the doghouse
a seven-day widow

This antedates all the senryu in this chapter, not to mention Karai Senryû's birth. The draw, if it is a draw and not just the 7-7 that came before in a *haikai* link-verse, is actually poetic: *"Just cannot stay still / the shadow of a dog"* (只も居られずかげぼしの犬 *tada mo irarezu kageboshi no inu*). I put it into the last reading, sort of. At any rate, here we do have a widow, as part of a phrase describing what a young woman who enjoys sex must feel for those seven-days each month. According to Suzuki, the "moon-water" in Chinese characters here is pronounced *sawari* (hindrance = menstruation).

風呂へ下女入らぬで手代安堵する 太平楽
furo e gejo hairanu de tedai ando suru 享保九

seeing the maid
stop at the tub, the clerk
sighs with relief

the maid doesn't
take a bath so the clerk
gains a reprieve

Even a period can be a breath of fresh air. This is probably the perspective of a man afraid that knocking up the maid-servant might ruin his chance to marry the boss's daughter and take over the company, is it not? After that scare, he should realize it is safer to masturbate (pp 66-7). One wonders, however, how he manages to spy on her and whether that was what got him in trouble to start with.

あま寺ハ七日ハ俗クの心あり 万 宝十
amadera wa nanuka wa zoku no kokoro ari man
(nunnery-as-for sevendays-as-for secular-heart/mind is)

at the nunnery
for seven days women feel
their secularity

for seven days
the nuns feel closer to their
holes than holy

This refers to having periods and not the Festival of the Star Lovers on Day Seven of the Seventh Moon because the *draw-ku* was *mama naranu koto,* which might be Englished as "Some things can't be helped (because there are limits to one's freedom)." It is ironic because when these women lived in the secular world, they were secluded from it for those seven days. Yet, when they leave that world for the religious one, that experience becomes their link to it.

月に七日は髪もそこねず 折句庫
tsuki ni nanuka wa kami mo sokonezu 寛政二

every month, seven days,
when hair is not harmed

This is a 7-7 *oriku,* or "folded-ku," where the first part came off another *ku,* and not your usual senryu, but thematically it could be. It was not easy for a Japanese woman to guard her fancy hairdo (or a man to guard his, in many cases). That is one reason for the pillows almost narrow enough to be string instrument bridges! So, it was easy for women to look good when they were untouchables.

A Refresher

(こりゃまさしく閉口の句)

開の中カ才の字にする月七日 葉25
bobo no naka sai no ji ni suru tsuki nanuka

開 ⇒ 閉
BΘBΘ

the *kai* in the gate
becomes *sai,* closed
seven days a month

The character meaning "open," as in "open for business," in Chinese or Japanese was 開, while the one meaning to close-up or close-out is 閉. I would have liked to put an X over the O's in *bobo*, that was not among the choices of font. The 開

in the *ku* could be pronounced *kai* rather than *bobo,* and it would sound better that way because of the *kai/sai* rhyme, but the meaning would be too hard to pick up aurally as *kai* is not only "cunt" while *bobo* is. You will find the two characters 開 *open* and 閉 *closed* in all Sinosphere-friendly elevators.

~ eddies ~

Skipped Ku. I missed many good *ku* I would have liked to have had in this chapter, because it was one of the first written. Your author, addressing you now as his editor, designer and publicist, finds it just too much trouble to rearrange almost 20 pages, losing time better spent on other work that no one will do for him. The first comes from Senryû's *Million* series and was published in 1775:

初花にたばこをつけて大さわぎ 万 安四
hatsuhana ni tabako o tsukete ôsawagi

putting tobacco
upon her first flower: talk
about commotion!

what an uproar
she treats her first blossom
with tobacco!

Tobacco – only introduced to Japan two centuries earlier – explains Okada Hajime, was used as a coagulant to stop bleeding. If the carefully orchestrated red bean rice celebrations seem too good to be true, remember slip-ups are also part of Japan and senryu.

初花と云う新馬に娘乗り 36
hatsuhana to iu arama ni musume nori
(first blossom as say new-horse-on daughter rides)

first-bloom:
the name of the baby green
the girl rides

their daughter rides
a newly-broken horse
called first-bloom

おてんばも地道に歩行初の馬 101
otenba mo jimichi ni shokô hatsu no uma
(tomboy/giglet too earthroady walk first-horse)

first horsey
even a wayward girl
is grounded

first horsey
even flying giglets come
down to earth

Newly-broken seems a bit crude compared to the Japanese "new-horse," meaning a horse ridden for the first time, so I asked my equestrian sister whether any word was out there and she said that sometimes such a horse is called a "baby green." Now that you know what the horse is about, no more explanation is needed for the first *ku.* The second is another matter. Otenba is usually translated as a tomboy, but it is really a kooky girl in sui generis (pardon my Latin if it's wrong). Old words like *hoyden* (literally a *heathen*) and *giglot* or *giglet* or even the plainer but still playful *filly* would be better. While *(o)tenba* is most commonly written 御転婆 (hon. tumble-aunt), the fun here is in the homophone, 天馬 *flying horse.* Pegasus has become a pony on a lead.

御役中出入りを止める表門 109
o-yaku-chû deiri o tomeru omote-mon

when on duty
none go in or out
the front gate

This is too simple, but it would have been effective right before the husband who couldn't wait suggested the other gate. Another senryû is even simpler:

一年に八十四日湯に行けず 162
ichinen ni hachi-jû-shi hi yu ni ikezu

every year
84 days she cannot go
to the baths

When I asked my equestrian sister if we had any standard number of days such as Japan's seven, she indignantly replied (as I imagine my other sister would reply) that *everyone is different*. True. But, do we lose or gain by keeping menstruation so hush-hush; and, don't stereotypes, which are wrong for everyone by definition, help keep it visible?

血の池も構わず売るは安地獄 115
chi-no-ike mokamawazu uru wa yasujigoku

what's cheap hell?
where they sell without scruple
ponds of blood

A "cheap hell" (*yasu-jigoku*) is a cheap brothel with women far less fortunate than the unfortunate courtesans. The women are working through their periods. There is a macabre wit at work here, for women who aborted children were bilked out of money (centuries earlier, mind you) by traveling nuns who told them that they would go to hell and end up in such a pond of menstrual blood unless they interceded with the prayers (and incense sticks and whatever – just like the Catholics of the time) they could buy.

~~~~~~

2. ***Issa, the Moon and Menstruation, Revisited.*** It may be improper to "revisit" and correct things that have not been properly published. But, when I like the order of things in an essay, I am not about to change it even if it is my own and I have every right to do so. Issa, practicing Buddhist or not, *did* actually call menstruation with a moon name in other haiku. I knew that, too, a dozen years ago, but put the *ku* into a different chapter, and with 3000 pages for them to get lost in, never caught the contradiction until now:

月の役に犬も並んで月見かな　一茶 文政四
tsukinoyaku ni inu mo narande tsukimi kana

for moon-duty
the dog also joins us
moon-viewing

her moon comes in
so out we go moon-viewing
with the dog in tow

Because Issa often writes of duties – in his old age he called his summer naps his *sleep-duty* – I first thought it meant *his duty to view the moon*, but the term was in common use, the dog is "also" with him and Issa enjoyed moon-viewing with his wife – my favorite is a summer moon, where he rests his head on her cool rump – she may be with him (Find it
~~~~~~

at the online magazine Simply Haiku or in *HIC! haiku in context* if/when it is published). It is hard to find moon-viewing menses in senryu, for the metaphor takes over the complete *ku*. *"The moon-viewing / comes before the pampas / – what a loss!"* (薄より月見の早いおちゃっぴい 97 *susuki yori tsukimi no hayai ochappii*) is a good example. Pampas grass (*susuki*=sawgrass, properly eulalia or *Miscanthus sinensis*) was cut and sold for moon-viewing party props in urban areas, so one might wonder if the *obana* bloom (tail-flower) was late that Fall; but my OJD told me that this pampas (*susuki*) was synonymous to a courtesan or lower-ranking woman of pleasure's *miagari*=body-raised, which is to say when she is in dry-dock and not carrying customers. Ideally, her period would coincide, but it came early, so she lost income. You might say it put her *in the red*. But, I think two senryu in *Cuntologia* may be about coinciding periods and moon-viewing:

月見には女房の嫌う女郎花 77
tsukimi ni wa nyôbô no kirau ominaeshi

moon-viewing
how his wife detests
wench flowers

かかあの月見宿六はさえぬ面 72
kakaa no tsukimi yadoroku wa saenu tsura

the old lady's
moon-viewing clouds her
old man's face

For the first, imagine the man moon-viewing with his buddies while his wife worries he will take advantage of her being out of commission to play around. The flower in question (*Patrinia scabiosaefolia*) blooms in Fall, season for moon-viewing. For the second, the word used for the husband might be called affectionate denigration or a denigrating term of endearment: *yado* is lodging and *roku* short for *rokudenashi*, a *good-for-nothing*. The matron who would be the central organizing force for a family (with many generations and maybe relatives, too) moon-viewing is unable to do so that year. Again, for the umpteenth time, for I have never seen anyone else point it out, *the haiku is personal*, while the traditional senryu gives us a situation, a situation comedy, if you will.

~~~~~~

3. *Temples Off-limits to Women:* Buddhist or Shinto, temples and shrines sought the same high ground, graced with the authority of time in the presence of huge trees and boulders, the mountains. A *ku,* the source of which I have regrettably lost, jokes about the practice of gender taboos:

ありがたさへのこを嫌ふやまハなし天八幸2
arigatasa henoko o kirau yama wa nashi 万?

land of our fathers

thank your lucky stars
tain't a mountain near or far
that hates pricks

let's be grateful
and what i mean is, no mountain
hates the penis

The "your" reflects my understanding of senryu as a literature (?) by and for men. Here is a case of women kept down, literally. There were some exceptions to the rule:

金玉を門ン外トに置くまつか丘 万明二
kintama o mon-soto ni oku matsugaoka

all bollocks will
be left outside the gate
at pine-wait hill

The nunnery on Matsuoka hill in Kamakura was a refuge from maltreatment and for
~~~~~~

seeking divorce (pg 84). The "pine" (*matsu*) in the name is homophonic with "wait." There were also mountains where women could practice their faith halfway up the top.

きんたまの光リの見へる女人堂 万
kintama no hikari no mieru nyojindô man 宝十
(gold-balls/gems' shine's see-can woman's hall/pavilion)

basking in *what!?*

the woman's hall
from whence they catch sight
of the ball-shine

the light from
golden jewels can be seen:
woman's hall

Japanese men tended to be very close to their mothers, so even mountains where women were not allowed into the holy of holies, could have facilities for retired mothers to live and work for their salvation nearby, especially if the temples catered to nobility (see *Topsy-turvy 1585* (2003)). Also, women were allowed on some sacred mountains *one day per year*, on day 15, the full moon of month 7. Here are two of three Issa *ku* about it:

三井寺や先湖を見るおばゞ達 一茶
mitsui-dera ya mazu umi o miru obaba-tachi

a rare sight

three-well temple
first, they gaze on the sea
grand aunties

能なしや女見に行三井寺へ 一茶
nônashi ya onna mi ni yuku mitsuidera e

the open mountain

a good-for-nothing
goes out for some girl-watching
to three-well temple

Many women never got far enough from their fields to visit the ocean. Issa made a touching observation. His second *ku* makes it clear which sex has the biggest problem with pure thoughts and needs regulation! It is also a confession. Issa often called himself a good-for-nothing. His most common self-description, repeated in a dozen or so *ku,* was *one who neither lit incense nor farted*, i.e., neither contributed to society, nor to his religious duty, but neither did much harm. Proto-senryu haikai, i.e. the *Mutamagawa*, caught this temple in Issa's part of the country at least a half-century before Issa did:

三井寺も一日は咲く女郎花　武玉川　十五
mitsuidera mo ichinichi wa saku ominaeshi mu 15

at mitsui temple
blooming for one day
maiden flowers

Issa has scores of maiden flowers. Since they include *ku* that are risqué, I tended to translate the plant as a *wench flower* or even a *whore flower!* This flower became a staple of male poets after an abbot confessed to falling off his horse onto one in a *waka*. I could not find anything the least voluptuous in the scrawny plant, but Issa found they moved well – for that I think the swing of the wild Chrysanthemum, with its slow *S* stems the best – and described them wriggling (*kuneru*) in the moon-light in a way I had to translate as grinding to catch the sexy nuance. Eventually, I will compile the haiku and you may attach them to this book, for, in many ways, they seem very senryu.

~~~~~~

Monkeys and the Moon. While most animals rely upon oil spreading out from their snouts to prevent dust from flowing into their mouths when they drink, monkeys clear away the floating dust with their hands, could that have something to do with the fiction
~~~~~~

of their reaching for the moon? Also, it is possible that monkeys were seen washing sweet potatoes a couple hundred years before a certain female monkey, subsequently named for the potato (*imo*) was said to have done so. Yayû (1701-83), a haiku poet I am fond of, writes: *"It still grows / though rubbed by simian hands / the three-day moon"* (猿の手に摩つとも尽きし三日の月 也有 *saru no te ni mazu to mo tsukiji mika no tsuki*)

~~~~~~

A Horse that May Be for Real. At first, I thought the following *ku* 失典 was about menses-as-riding; but considering the bride was from the country, I changed my mind:

婚礼の日に馬に乗る田舎娵 再現
konrei no hi ni uma ni noru inaka yome

sure enough
she saddles up to take her vows
the rural bride

her wedding day
and her very first ride
a rural bride

Even though she is from the country, the bride, unlike samurai women, only rode a horse once in her lifetime, when she went to the groom's house for her betrothal.

~~~~~~

A Kernel of Validity in the Awful Clap Cure? In his detailed investigation and analysis of the nitty-gritty of esoteric tantric yoga, which is to say alchemy via the body, David Gordon White describes how the menstrual blood of certain women (they had different names depending upon the moonphase of their period!) were used to activate mercury with the sulfur in their blood (mercury+ sulfur=cinnabar?). Some sources advised men to place the mercury wrapped in cloth inside their wife's vagina, others advised them to bind or stabilize mercury by placing it in their own urethra together with menstrual blood from the right woman (through urethral suction, the "fountain pen technique," first practiced with water, light, milk, cooling, clarified butter, lubricating, huney, sticky and a challenge and finally mercury, extremely heavy), or specify sexual intercourse toward such ends (I simplify whole chapters). Since doses of mercury were used for the clap, one wonders if the combination of the medicine and intercourse with women having their periods might have had a wee bit of positive effect on the healing of the man.

~~~~~~

Catching Clap & Curing It. Another parallel. If a *Leaf ku* is correct, there were odder magical remedies for clap than incomplete sex during a period: *"Three cunt hairs / – a remedy found nowhere / in medicine"* (開の毛三本医学にもない薬 葉 別五 *bobo no ke sanbon igaku ni mo nai kusuri*). One is advised to burn these hairs and drink down the ashes with *sake!* Syunroan marvels at this folk remedy, then continues to note that it was believed that *clap was caught by discontinuing coitus so "small-water" sat in the pipes,* so to speak. I could not figure out how that dovetailed with those three hairs, but I would not be so quick to laugh about the belief. Flushing out the urethra by coming might better one's odds of not picking up disease. Such a reasonable hypothesis might also help explain the unreasonable remedy, where the patient having coitus with a menstruating woman does *not* come, *i.e.,* a magical reversal after one has the disease.

淋病は首を拾ったかわりなり 失典
rinbyô wa kubi o hirotta kawari nari

call the clap
a bargain in exchange
for his head

The husband had a right to kill the paramour, who escapes with his head by committing *coitus interuptus*, which gives him a dose. A less clever *ku* simply says *"A paramour*
~~~~~~

with the clap was sloppy about love" りんびやうに成ル間夫は不首尾なり 万明二 *rinbyô ni naru maotoko wa fushubi nari*).

~~~~~~

A Modern Womenstruation ku (*anzu saki jiai kiwamaru waga mensu* – Tokizane Shinko)

Apricots bloom
self-love in extremis
my menstruation trans. Higginson

I found this *ku,* considered a senryu today – though *I think* we should call it something else★ because, 17-syllabet or not, the *content and style* is more similar, if not identical to *tanka* (31 syllabets) – in William J. Higginson's classic international *saijiki, Haiku World.* Note the Japanese word for period, from *menstruation*, but unlike our long ugly Latinism – or "period," which is almost as bad, *mensu,* is a fine, poetic word. The *jiai* in the original is usually used with respect to other people, *go-jiai o,* when telling them to *please take care of themselves*. The verb *kiwamaru* means taking something to the extreme, going all out with. English's lack of such a verb probably sparked Higginson's exceptionally creative *in extremis* translation (I only made one change: capitalizing the "apricots" because, to my eyes, a left-margin arrangement demands capitalization.)

★ Please note that I am not taking issue with W.H. calling Shinko's *ku* a senryu. I am taking issue *with a convention accepted in Japan.* I *have* Tokizane Shinko's best known work, 『有夫恋』 *Yûfuren* ("Have Husband Loves/Romance/Affairs"). It is full of excellent 17 syllabet *ku* about the feelings, many sexual, of a married woman. Most of them are far too personal, too emotionally deep to be called senryu in the traditional sense. Yet, in the afterword, I see novelist Tanabe Seiko, to whom I was once introduced as my perfect bride, since I had declared I wanted someone literally well-rounded (that's a story you may ask me about if we ever meet), calls Shinko *the Yosano Akiko of the world of senryu.* Yosano Akiko may have brought her personal passion into *tanka* (so did her husband whose *tanka* is included in *Rise, Ye Sea Slugs!* (2003)), but *tanka* already had passion, senryu had none. So, I repeat, Tanabe and others who call Tokizane's work senryu (including the poet and her publisher, I guess) are *wrong*. What Tokizane has done is create 17-syllabet *tanka* which, to differentiate from the standard 31-syllabet form should be called *tanku* 短句 or *haika* 俳歌 (or, bearing in mind Tokizane's love for the word "willow," the *ryû* in senryû, in her honor, we might call it 柳句、俳柳、短柳、柳歌、*ryûka, hairyû, tanryû,* or *ryûka,* respectively).

~~~~~~

Cuntologia included one stanza from an undated (probably 20c) song published in 1979 :

Once a month, even the cunt,
must bite the paper and cry tears of blood.

月に一度はおまんこでさえも 紙をくわえて血の涙 魔山人『赤湯文字』
tsuki ni ichido wa omanko de sae mo kami o kuwaete chi no namida 1979

Unlike the lonely Navel (pp 191-2), Cunt – the *manko* in the song is closer to cunt (blunt and none too pretty) than the *bobo* common in old senryu – is generally treated with respect as a shrine and enjoys an active social life. The bloody tears, as old Sinosphere trope are more often than not crimson. Regardless, they English well enough. The idea of holding something in one's mouth, however, cannot be expressed poetically in English where such a verb is missing. The cunt may *hold* paper *in its mouth*, but the soul of wit, brevity is lost, I tried to play on "bite the bullet," but it didn't work, did it?

~~~~~~

One Blue Monkey I don't want to allow to escape. The Kanôezaru or Blue Monkey Day
~~~~~~

most often called Kôshin, if you recall, is not about menstruation; it shares its characteristic of being a time when sex was taboo, the subjects came together in senryu. This particular *ku,* a *maekuzuke* predating senryu by sixty some years, however, has nothing to do with the menses. It says: *"Blue Monkey Day / they're still rubbing-off crud / at the bath-house."* (庚申に垢掻いて居る風呂や者　寄太鼓　元禄十四 *kôshin ni aka kaite iru furoyamono*). Suzuki writes the draw すかたん／＼／＼ (*sukatan-sukatan-sukatan* or, *sukatan-tan-tan*) to mean something violating common sense (常識はずれ) and interprets the whole to mean that women who help customers wash their backs but sometimes reach in front and entice men up to the second floor for paid sex are still selling it despite the date. I think the draw may rather mean that the customer, a single man who may not even know what day it is, to his disappointment finds the bath girls doing the real work rather than skipping up to the second floor. Since the original has no "still," modern logic would favor Suzuki, but my reading is favored by the OJD definition of *sukatan* as *"not getting what one is counting on."* Be that as it may, the verb I made "rub" is actually "scratch," though I could not use it with the "crud" because it just would not work in English. It is what Japanese use for the primate behavior we call "grooming." Suzuki did not mention that because it is common knowledge among his readers, but he should have mentioned something else I first learned from reading Issa's word-book (and checked with the OJD): the people who did this work at baths, especially the women (湯女 *yuna*) were popularly called "monkeys" (*saru*). So, whatever reading turns out to be right, there is wit in bringing the monkeys together.

~~~~~~

Note to Suffering Readers. The Eddies will become shorter and more fun to follow with each chapter except for some dealing with male color, perhaps because I felt uneasy with the subject as I do with this one, which I was sucked into by the lively metaphors. The best *eddies* tend to run about a tenth the length of the chapter, not a quarter like this one.

~~~~~~

Offer to Potential Collaborators. My original aim was to pursue a few metaphors of menses and let someone else combine them with anthropological and ethnographic research. So, I never did try to find out things such as how mistresses and maids worked out their respective periods or how Japan transitioned from special moon duty huts to in-home taboos, etc.. I welcome either glosses (with the researcher's name) to add to an enlarged future edition or, better yet, reprinting this chapter or parts of it in a book on the subject. The same thing goes for every chapter.

~~~~~~

又も光献辞
second dedication

~~~~~~

Equestrian Arts and Menstrual Gear. This chapter is dedicated to a Prince who loved and eventually married an equestrian (whose first name in Japanese would be *tsubaki*), and once expressed his love as desire to be something stuck in her person. *There* is someone who would understand *haikai!* I'll bet he has also read in Harris's *My Life and Loves* how delighted his grandfather, or great grandfather was with limericks and other dirty ditties. God bless the English and may they never lose their bloody awful sense of humor and one word!

Toodle-oooooooooooo

Where the Turtle and Baby Legs Play
亀たちと赤ん坊ヶ素足の遊びどころ

三 3

乳母ヶ池の恋
The Wet Nurse's Pond

~~~~~~

日本中鵜呑顔なる巨燵哉 一茶
nihon-jû unomigao naru kotatsu kana 文化十
(japan-within cormorant-drinking face/s become kotatsu!/is)

throughout japan
kotatsu stuffed full
as cormorants!

a country full of
stuffed cormorants
our kotatsu!

The modern *kotatsu* is a small electric heater attached to the bottom of a table covered with a quilt to retain the heat. Families without central heating winter there. Old style *kotatsu*, still seen in farm houses and mansions of the wealthy, include a pit below the table, so one can sit at ease, as on Western chairs, but level with the floor and the eyes of little children. Cormorants are known for voraciously stuffing their gullets (the bottom, which is tied by the cormorant-masters). Fish tails and heads dangle from their open beaks. During a cold-front, many *kotatsu* would have had more people crammed into them than fully fit, and seeing them emerge from it to greet a guest would have resembled a cormorant disgorging its gullet. I also imagine a New Year holiday (the day in it dedicated to people doing service jobs, *yabuiri*), when farmers and workers usually too busy to sit joined Issa and other good-for-nothings (writers, like me). After all, to swallow *anything, i.e., be lacking in discrimination, fall for a line or theory,* in Japanese is "to cormorant swallow." Haiku and senryu both love *kotatsu*, but if the former pays attention to what goes on *above* the table, the latter dwells on what goes on *below* its closed skirt, the stuffing within the stuffing so to speak:

こたつにて毛雪駄をはく面白さ
kotatsu nite ke-setta o haku omoshirosa 2-4
(kotatsu-at, hair-slipper/s [acc]-put-on-interestingness)

sitting tight above
but below the kotatsu, hoh!
a hair-slipper

interesting, this
wearing fur slippers within
the kotatsu
~~~~~~

Did the first page fail to produce the wet-nurse? No. She was the *slipper* worn in the early *Willow ku*, for wet-nurses exampled hairy twats. Footsie was not the only play in town under the *kotatsu*~~: *"From the hem, a hand enters to work – the puppet master"* (裾から手を入れ人形を遣ってる[袂からの誤記か]失典 *suso* [*tamoto?*] *kara te o ire ningyô o yatteru*). We will return to "finger-puppets" later, but this *ku* is probably a misprint: a woman reaching in "from her *bossom*" would be much wittier. Moreover, the wet-nurse is not a likely candidate finger-puppet; *she* required more than a few fingers~~. One more *kotatsu* before returning to our *uba:*

人形を見るはこたつの猫ばかり 61
ningyô o miru wa kotatsu no neko bakari
(puppet[acc] sees-as-for kotatsu's cat only)

the puppet
is only seen by one
kotatsu cat

the only one
who gets to see puppets
is the pussy

Fingering by another or oneself was called "finger-puppet/try." Cats love to squeeze under the hem of the *kotatsu's* skirt and stay until their hair gets singed.

乳母ここはなんだと足で毛をなでる 摘
uba koko wa nanda to ashi de ke o naderu 1-4

nursey, what's this?
while stroking her hair
with his feet

England's painter of domesticity, Hogarth (or *maybe* Hogarth), shows a contented couple, husband reading in a chair, wife knitting on the floor, *with his daddy-toe clearly buried in her pubic hair.* Newlyweds do this in senryu, but wet-nurse +child+foot are more common. Why? *First*, they were proverbially hairy down there, as befits a changeling who would gobble down anything; *second*, as women who had given birth many times, they tended to be large; and, third, they were supposedly as desirous of sex as the infants were for their milk (perhaps because they were poor and afraid to lose their job?), and seductive, because they wore loose clothing "open down to their navels" and sat in informal, revealing ways, rather than the proper Japanese woman's knees-together posture (closed-crotch underwear only spread after the 1932 Shirokiya department-store fire, when women jumping to their deaths revealed too much). Let us look at the three characteristics, *hair*, *size* and *desire*, one at a time, before returning to the most disgusting "poems" about playing footsie ever composed. *Hair:*

乳母ここはももんじいかと足をやり
uba koko wa momojii ka to ashi o yari 50-11

"nursey, is this
the momonjii monster?"
his foot extends

giving it a poke
with his foot: *nurse, is this*
the boogieman?

A *momonjii*, or *momonjaa*, was said to be so hairy it had only one feature: it could pop open a frightfully large mouth or eye. Like our "boogieman," it scared kids into doing the will of their caretakers, *i.e.,* behave themselves and fall asleep.

乳母の開見えお坊っちゃんわっと泣き
uba no bobo mie obocchan watto naki 葉 12

seeing nursey's
bobo, the young master
burst out crying

seeing the bobo
of his wet-nurse, the boy
began to wail

The word used for the boy, "little monk+diminuitive (*obocchan*)" suggests a pampered child likely to misbehave. Did nursey flash on purpose to keep him in line? Other senryu suggest kids were not the only ones who dreaded this *bobo.*

乳母野糞穴恐ろしやと蛇は逃げ
uba noguso ana osoroshiya to hebi wa nige

an outdoor crap
how terrifying! snake flees
the wet-nurse

taking her shit
al fresco, the wet-nurse
terrifies snakes

While Japanese were not terrified of snakes as Europeans who, because of their religious superstition, tended to think of them as evil, there was one circumstance where Japanese may have feared snakes. Women, in senryu, were warned to be careful when they urinated lest a snake take that opportunity to crawl up their vagina (after which they had to be lured out with frogs). No, *come to think of it,* most of those cases had to do with the snake-lady who let them crawl up there!

乳母寝相穴恐ろしや恐ろしや
uba nesô ana osoroshiya osoroshiya 63-7

wet-nurse sleeps
behold this holy terror
this awful hole

sleeping wet-nurse
how hairy, how scary
how hairy keri

Nesô, meaning *the appearance or posture of someone asleep,* is a great Japanese word. If you sleep prim, you have a good *nesô,* if you sprawl, you have a bad *nesô,* but the wet-nurse's *nesô* is literally frightful: the intensifying adverb *ana* is a homophone for "hole" (the same has been used in haiku to describe bug intelligence as *ana-kashikoi,* or *hole/very-smart* when the cold comes).

乳母が開程に達磨の大欠び 葉 13
uba ga bobo hodo daruma no ôakubi

a wet nurse's twat?
like a tremendous yawn
by bodhi-dharma

wet nurse's twat
the bodhi-dharma's yawn
encompasses all

While the Bodhi-dharma's inertia, reflected in his silence and ability to bounce right back up, which makes him the name for a roly-poly doll, is such that, one can imagine his yawn is awe-inspiringly huge, size is not what really makes this work. It is his full beard.

熊の巾着さん出して乳母昼寝 39-9
kuma no kinchaku-san dashite uba-hirune

her bear purse
on display, wet-nurse takes
a beauty nap

乳母がまへもくぞうがにのごとくなり
ubagamae mokuzôgani no gotoku nari 摘 *1-6*

the wet-nurse
in front the spitting image
of a hairweed crab

the wet nurse
is that a hairweed crab claw
or her snatch?

The "bear" is our "beaver;" the "beauty" is mine. The large claw of said crab (*mogusa-gani,* the above's dialect) is hairy. Crabs usually meant a strong pinch and some watertrade women were said to tatoo them, c̲ the labia minora fleshing the claw.

乳母玉の門昼見ても真っ黒し 151
uba tama no kado hiru mite mo makkuroshi
(wet-nurse-gem-gate daytime seeing even pure-black)

the jewel gate
of the wet-nurse pitch black
at high noon

the open gate
of the wet-nurse attracts
fireflies at noon

Hair is not always dark, but darkness is hairy, not bald, and both can terrify. The fireflies are borrowed from an early-20c North Florida 'lying' match between Afro-Americans putting down each other's blackness before it was beautiful (See Zora Neale Hurston's masterpiece, *Mules and Men*). Now, the second characteristic, *size:*

乳母ひるね山ぶし法螺の貝を出し 61
uba hirune yamabushi hora no kai o dashi

wet-nurse napping,
out comes the king conch of
a mountain wizard

If the *Mons veneris* is a mountain, the bearded and bushy-haired esoteric Buddhist mountain wizard (*yama-bushi*) is the woman's sex. These wizards are always pictured carrying conch horns. No wee cowry shell for the wet-nurse! If you have looked at typical conchs – the ones I found growing up in Florida – you know that the King Conch has much bigger lips than queen conchs and that is why I – not the original – made it a *king*. They also have beautiful, smooth pink openings which help us see why *concha* can mean vagina in Spanish. Japanese mountain wizard trumpets tend to be more like a whelk. The lips are less spectacular and the hole is big and dark. But some may have been colorful.

乳母昼寝既に開から破傷風 葉4
uba hirune sude ni kai kara hashôfû

wet-nurse naps
her cunt at noon already
a running sore

閻魔のあくび斯あらん乳母あぐら
enma no akubi kore aran uba agura 126

yama's yawn would
not be wrong: a wet-nurse
sits cross-legged

Hashôfû, or "burst-wound-wind," now means *tetanus*. It was a blister, boil or infected wound as pretty as a monkey's rump. My first translation, before being disappointed with what I found in the dictionary, was like Solt's: "*while the wet nurse naps / from her open crack / a miasmatic breeze.*" I mean not to embarrass him; *miasma*, the bad airs preceding germ theory was just too attractive an idea to let pass *twice*, and not wholly wrong, for the *ku* itself plays with the *nominal* wind coming "cunt-*from*," and it could be a precursor to feverish loving. "Already"(*sude ni*) is, however, important. A nap in Japanese is "day/noon-sleep" and a start-up time gives some natural life to the breeze that isn't. Regarding the second *ku,* Yama (Enma), the terrifying but good King of Hades, was bearded and the inside of his mouth blood red from punishing himself for punishing sinners by swallowing molten metal several times a day. The senryu may play with Buson's famous haiku equating a red peony withYama's tongue.

それでもと乳母だいだいを入て見る
sore de mo to uba daidai o irete miru 葉7

hmm, maybe this
will fit, too! a wet-nurse
with a bigerade

Senryu about hollow metal balls called *rin no tama,* a pair of which were inserted in the vagina for a woman to enjoy by herself, with a dildo, or with a man, abound:

りんの玉芋を洗うが如くなり 摘
rin no tama imo o arau ga gotoku 1-7

the jingling balls
it is just like washing
round potatoes

Not all of these sex toys jingled, but size-wise, they were always small potatoes compared to the *bigerade,* a citrus the size of a large grapefruit, or even the head of a baby. Usually found on top of New Year's Decorations, its name, *daidai* is homophonic with "large-large." Ping-pong ball-sized Japanese potatoes are rough-skinned and jostled together like gems being polished to get the dirt off.

大風のうわさ女護の乳母は待ち
ôkaze no uwasa nyôgô no uba wa machi

the wet nurses
on woman's island can't wait
for typhoon season

woman's island
rumors of a typhoon excite
the wet nurses

The Isle of Women is one of my favorite Edo Era fictions. We will have a chapter about this place where women, like Pliny's sea mares, have congress and issue with the Wind. Another *ku* has the wet-nurse *spreading wide*, vulgarly demanding that a storm *"come on!"* (嵐でも来いと女護の乳母拡げ *arashi de mo koi to nyôgô no uba hiroge*).

うばが池指で瀬ぶみをして這入
uba-ga-ike yubi de sebumi o shite hairu 葉 31
(wetnurse pond fingers-c shallows tread doing creep-enters)

wet-nurse pond
you finger-wade in until
you're swimming

wet-nurse pond
fingers test the water
then you're in

睾も引込みそうな乳母が池 76-33
kintama mo hiki-komisô na uba-ga-ike &121
(balls even/too pull-in-seems-wetnurse-pond)

wet-nurse pond
where even your balls
risk drowning

The pond is by far the most common trope for a wet-nurse's sex, though "wet" is not in *uba*. A "pond" is a sizeable body of water, the plants evoke hair and the water, desire. Topographical *ku* are hard to translate without changing details. For, example, without the fingers two *ku* back, we could have *Wet-nurse pond / you tread the mud and then you're / treading water.* So let me present more in a perfunctory fashion:

1. *The grass here / grows wild and wolly / Wet-nurse pond.*
2. *Trying to flee, / flea's caught in duckweed: / Wet-nurse pond.*
3. *Wet nurse pond: / You enter zubuzubu, / not kerplunk!*
   Wet-nurse pond: / You zubuzubu in & out / to take a dip
4. *At night, Leviathan slips heavily into wet-nurse pond.*

1.草ぼう／＼と生い茂るうばが池 *kusa bôbô to oi-shigeru ubagaike*
The bôbô (thickly overgrown) is an expansive play on *bobo*, the female sex. 57-3
2.逃げる蚤うばが池藻にからんでる *nigeru nomi ubagaike mo ni karanderu*
Poor flea, too, is afraid. *Mô* is a type of *algoid*. All I could find was "duckweed." 101-3
3.ズブズブズブと入水する乳母が池 *zubuzubuzubu to jusui suru ubagaike*
Zubuzubu is a typical sound of wet rubbery friction, *i.e.* sex. 120-26 ↑ 103-12 ↓
4.夜は大蛇がのたり込む乳母が池 *yoru wa orochi ga notari-komu ubagaike*
What *lope* is to a wolf, *notari*+movement is to a large snake. "Heavily" did the trick.

The Leviathan, the wet-nurse's awesome husband, is an *orochi*, not Orochi, the mythical serpent who demanded maidens for food until killed by a hero who was smart enough to get him drunk, but 'just' a python. While I am trying to stick with metaphor unique to the wet-nurse, some are shared with the large-sexed Empress (ch.1). For example, one *ku* has the wet-nurse brought to a climax by the "brigade of five" whom she "swallows whole" (五人組丸呑みにして乳母よがり 神の田艸 *goningumi maru nomi ni shite uba yogari*). This was expressed more cleverly with the Empress by naming the *other* three fingers. Another *ku* has a hairy (tiny auxiliary roots) burdock beset by the wet-nurse's grating bowl (毛牛蒡へ乳母擂鉢をおっかぶせ *kegôbo e uba suribachi o okkabuse*). Again, I prefer the proverbial burdock washed by the *sea* of the Empress. But here is one wet-nurse size *ku* as good as any of the Empress's. It plays upon a misunderstanding – urban folklore – involving a species of animal unknown in the Americas.

乳母狸十畳敷の開を出し 葉
uba tanuki jûjo-jiki no kai o dashi 10
(wetnurse *tanuki* ten-mat-sized cunt[acc] displays)

wet nurse tanuki
displays a twat that covers
ten tatami mats

A *tanuki* is a raccoon-faced fox about the size of fat miniature collie with shy charm and wonderfully cunning character that give them deservedly ample space in folklore and legend. The females are rarely mentioned in senryu. The males *are* because their scrotums are said to be large enough to cover *eight* tatami mats (about 200 square feet). The reason male tanuki had stupendous family jewels will be explained in the *Balls* chapter. Here, suffice it to note that nothing is ever said about their pricks, which, dwarfed by those gargantuan balls, are never even noticed. Considering that, it doesn't make much sense to grant female tanuki enormous cunts; unless, that is, we are talking about the proverbial wet nurse. And, now, we will bring *size* to a close with this:

ひろい事しりつゝ乳母をくどくなり 万
hiroi koto shiri tsutsu uba o kudoku nari 安元
(widething knowing while, wetnurse[acc] persuade is)

knowing her size
he would still seduce
a wet-nurse: why?

knowing she's slack
he would still have a crack
at the wet-nurse

The original has no question but I saw no reason not to pose it and gain some compensation for losing the wonderful "wide thing," which doesn't work in English. There *may* be an allusion to a well-hung monk, for the "wide way" was congress with women, whose vaginal grip was generally not so tight as that of a boy's anus, the narrow, and, for a monk, proper way. Or, it might just mean that the wet-nurse, being a loose woman, was the only one he would dare to mess with – which takes us to the hairy, large-sexed wet-nurse's *behavior*.

wet nurses on fire

よかる顔みて乳母こわい／＼ 摘
yogaru kao mite uba kowai kowai 2-25

seeing the face
of the wet-nurse crying
i'm scared!

nursey crying
as she comes, baby cries
at the sight

A *yogaru-kao* is the face of one making cries peculiar to women nearing orgasm; the fear of the child expressed in Japanese is *kowai-kowai, "scary, scary."*

とぼされる乳母ねんねこが消えるやう
tobosareru uba nenneko ga kieru yô 葉 *1*
(excited/lit wet-nurse: lullaby vanishes-seems)

5
loudly
the nanny
begins to die
before she ends
the lullaby
4
rockaby baby
in the treetop
his wet nurse
falls first!
3
before coming
to the end of the lullaby
wet nurse comes
2
when nanny gets turned on
we hear the lullaby turn-off
1
a wet nurse on fire, the lullaby goes up in smoke

<u>*Tobo*</u>*sareru*, which may play on <u>*bobo*</u>*-sareru*, to be "cunt-done," *i.e.,* "fucked," means to be lit as a candle or lamp is lit, while the vanishing *kieru* is what happens when a flame is put out. The only way I could match that sound and sexual excitement as effectively as the original is to use modern slang such as *turn-on/off.* I substituted English pun on *coming*. Still, lullabies dying in mid-song are clean enough. Mix wet-nursing and sex, and it gets really messy.

crying she comes
'mid milk, milk, milk!
the wet-nurse

よがってる乳母そこら中乳だらけ
yogatteru uba sokora-jû chichi-darake 葉 21
(love-crying wet-nurse, all-over milk/dugs lots-of)

crying loudly
as she comes the wet nurse
soaked in milk

wet nurse cries
& as she comes, behold
the milky way!

the wet nurse

crying loudly
as she comes bouncing boobs
spewing milk

This is the third usage of *yogaru/yogari* in the chapter. I passed over it earlier, but the word will come up again and again in this book, so let us try to get it clear. It is a verb/adjective for the outer manifestations of ecstasy, especially the sounds made by women in or approaching orgasm. English has its *moan* that becomes a *groan* when giving birth, but moaning is just one sound. What about the *cries* and *yelps*? Do Japanese women make more noise? Or, is it simply a an unexplained gap in our vocabulary? A similar gap in Japanese is also demonstrated in the *ku*. The same word *chichi* is used to finger a mother's "milk" and her "tits" (*chichi* also means "papa" – to think that we, too, used to call breasts "paps" but context rules it out here). But the ambiguity caused by that gap is helpful. We may imagine *both* full breasts and milk flying about. This next *ku*, a sibling from the same *Leaf* collection suggests the latter reading (liquidity) was probably the main one:

乳母ちぎる内座敷中屎だらけ y 40-10
uba chigiru uchi-zashiki-jû kuso-darake &葉 7
(wet-nurse fucks, inner-parlour-throughout, shit-messy)

wet nurse fucks
what bliss! the room's now full
of shit and piss

while wet nurse
gets laid the inner parlour's
paved with shit

Some say *if it isn't dirty, it isn't good sex*. I am not of that school. But, in support of the wet-nurse, I would like to explain that we are talking here of the baby whose needs are neglected while the wet-nurse plays, not lack of personal hygiene or sodomy. Truly stinky *bobo* stereotypically belong to the overworked maid and not the wet-nurse.

こん／＼をかぶって乳母をやつゝける 摘
konkon o kabutte uba o yattsukeru 3-9

with a kon-kon
on his face, he gives it
to the wet-nurse

鬼に成天狗に成て乳母をする 摘
oni ni nari tengu ni natte uba o suru 2-7

becoming demons
or tengu, men make love
to wet-nurses

Kon-kon are the soft yelps made by a fox, and the name for said animal in baby-talk. The nurse's lover wears a fox mask to amuse the kids so they do not cry and catch the attention of a neighbor, or, if he is the father tired of waiting the mandatory 75 days of post-partum abstinence, his wife. Since cheating husbands typically claimed to be possessed by foxes, the mask is symbolically apt. Demon or tengu (proboscis goblin/wizard) masks *also* suggest the supernatural powers one might want to do battle with the nanny's gargantuan snatch. Many readers may have seen *shunga* = spring-picture of this, though there is a good chance it was explained as husband and wife.

Easily Grossed Out? Skip the Next Two Wet-nurses!

The next two senryu take us back to the start, to the hair-slipper. One is innocent enough, but the other is a fantastically disgusting senryu – a good match for the grossest limerick. If you have read such limericks, you know what I mean. If you have not you will.

ませたがきうばの毛せったつつかける 雪の花
maseta gaki uba no ke-setta tsutsukakeru round-robin にて
(precocious kid wet-nurse's hair-slipper poke into)

precocious boy
nursey's hair slipper suddenly
is on his foot

just like that
the precocious boy wears
a hair slipper

how precocious!
suddenly popping into
nursey's hair shoe

This is the rare *ku* where a child takes the initiative with his nurse. The adjective, "precocious" is masterful. It makes what would be normal behavior by a rambunctious boy – and, better behavior than kicking or kneeing someone in the balls as obnoxious little Occidentals are apt to do – something amusing.

田舎乳母赤子の足を毛切れさせ 万
inaka-uba akago no ashi o kegire sase 明六
(country wet-nurse baby's leg/s [acc] hair-cuts make)

the men away,
a country wet nurse
gave baby's legs
3rd degree hair-burn!

pity the wet-nurse
in the country, alone!
baby's feet are hair-burnt
down to the bone!

imagine that!

a country wet-nurse
gives hair-burn
to baby's
leg

"Hair-cuts" are serious abrasions usually born of vigorous pumping sex with a woman whose stiff pubes closely encircle the vulva. But why *"country?"* First because country wet-nurse were thought to be shameless. One senryu even has them urinating while facing you (田舎乳母小便するにこちら向キ 万 明元 *inaka uba shôben suru ni kochira muki*). And second, with all the men in Edo, lonely without women, writing and reading senryu, the outlying country experienced what Issa and others called a "drought of men" (*otoko-hideri*). The unfortunate baby, having been burnt once, will presumably never try to stick his foot into a "hair-slipper" under a *kotatsu!* Some readers may be *horrified* by such a *ku*, not to mention behavior. An Edoite might have chuckled to his buddy, *"A baby's foot! Come to think of it, you couldn't make a better dildo! The way it can grip things like a hand and wriggle all about, our cocks could not compete!"* What do you think? Are such words *dangerous?* Or, just *silly?* To me, the latter. But silly or not, the *ku* is interesting for reversing the usual nurse-child relationship, which has the woman awakening the child's sexuality rather than satisfying her own desires. English diary literature is *full of* boys fondly remembering their nurses fondling them (women wrote few diaries of their sexual development and/or conquests) and sketches by the extraordinarily tender artist of sexual development and the erotic, Mihaly Zichy (1827 - 1906) depict a raw-boned nanny fellating a bashful boy and a younger baby-sitter fingering a tiny curly-haired girl, whose eyes are glazed over in ecstasy (See Poul Gerhard: *Pornography or Art?* which includes a small sampling of Japanese erotica, too. 1968/71). Today, Usanians live in a simple world, where all sexual contact between adults and children is considered equally evil and criminal, whether the adult 1) enjoys pleasuring the child while not excited him/herself, 2) enjoys pleasuring the child while excited h/self or 3) sexually excites h/self with no regard for the child. In most ages & places, 1) would be accepted behavior, 2) laughable and, perhaps ill-advised but hardly criminal, and 3) either ignored (as happening to others) or considered a capital crime.

.

This I would like to see in a movie!

小侍御乳母とのゝを見たといふ 万
ko-samurai o-ubadono no o mita to iu 明四

little samurai
says he saw honorable
wet nurse's

小侍御乳母がまたにはさまれる 万
ko-samurai o-uba-ga-mata ni hasamareru 明四

little samurai
caught scissored between
nanny's thighs

小さむらひ乳母居風呂へ入レてやり
ko-samurai uba iburo e irete yari 万安五

the little samurai
is put into the bath tub
c̲ the wet nurse

The first reverses a story about a wet nurse claiming to have seen a little samurai's privates – part of a story about a girl who pretended to be a boy because an heir was needed – but accurately portrays the manner in which samurai were given missions to test their courage from a tender age. The draw is *"How he is praised!* (*homerarenikeri*). In the second, *the wet-nurse* (*nanny* for the meter) caught such a tyke engaged in close reconnaissance and holds him tightly against her crotch (*mata*), for which the draw is *"Isn't that sweet!"* (いとしかりけり). The third is more like the proverbial lioness pushing her cubs into the ravine.

~~~~~~

~~~~~~

~ *eddies* ~

~~~~~~

Hanky-panky in the Kotatsu. A Japanese feminist of the cunt-positive school once wrote a book with a title that translates as "the playhouse under her skirt" (上野 千鶴子著『スカートの下の劇場』(裙子底下的劇場＝台灣中文版). One might compile an illustrated book of things that happen under the skirt of the table-heater. Perhaps, this senryu could start it:

瓜田より炬燵の足が疑わし 摘 3-4
kaden yori kôtatsu no ashi ga utagawashi

more suspicious
than walking with melons,
legs in a kotatsu

guiltier than
a melon patch: legs
in a kotatsu

A common saying in the Sinosphere: "If you are *seen* in a melon patch, you'll be considered a thief," *i.e.,* avoid even the suspicion of wrong-doing. Another version: *"A melon patch / goes c-out saying but / kotatsu, too* **. . .** くわでんハ元よりこたつもいましめる 22-4 *kaden wa moto yori kotatsu mo imashimeru*). Watch your step, . . . *and your footsie!*

下で人形遣うの猫知らず 神の田艸
shita de ningyô tsukau no neko shiruzu

(not kipling's cat)

the puppet show
below while even pussy
does not know

No, we have not just read this. The pussy in the *ku* in the main text came in from the cold. It was within the skirts of the table and saw the show. This one is probably paying attention to the snacks on top of the table (which are not mentioned).

~~~~~~

Fear of Snakes. In one of the oldest chronicles of Japan, a shuttle jumps up from a toilet to pierce and kill a woman. Perhaps that helps to explain why a general lack of snake-phobia (see *Topsy-turvy 1585*, item 14-14, for a page and a half of historical comparison with Europe) is seemingly contradicted by fear of violation while doing one's business.

~~~~~~

Orochi Just-so Story. Orochi, is both a particular serpent-god and anaconda/boa. I recall a *just-so* story, from somewhere in the Amazon. First Man had a huge snake of a penis that could creep across the ground and into huts to violate women while he napped in his hammock. One day, it went up a woman's skirt and, entering her, got hungry for the stew cooking and popped right up through her mouth and into the pot where it gulped down the entire content before leaving as it had come. Of course, this killed her. The other women picked up their knives and ran after the killer. The onslaught was so fast the first man had only time enough to protect what he could grasp. So, that is all men have.
~~~~~~

<u>*Masturbation as a Public Good*</u>

千擦りも美徳という常識

四 4

当て擦り等
Different Strokes

~~~~~~

千ずりをかきおふせたが支配人 葉四
senzuri o kaki-ofuseta no ga shihainin
(1000-rubs stroking-bore-the control-man)

delayed gratification

the clerk who beat
his rivals by beating off
alone? – the boss.

the masturbator
is the one who became
the master later

he who made do
with jacking off is now
the company boss

Senzuri, a "thousand-rubs." The quantity often means "many" in Japanese. Idiom is idiom, but that doesn't stop the stereotypical hick-samurai, the asagiura from taking it literally: *"'bout fifty jerks is plenty to get us'uns off"* (五十摺りぐらいで身供罷りすむ 葉 18 *gojû-zuri gurai de midomo makari-sumu*). That *ku* is a witty re-do of *"About fifty / and a thousand-strokes / is done"*(五十ほどかくと千ずりしまいなり」万 安四 *gojû hodo kaku to senzuri shimai nari*). Samurai, even hicks, were supposed to do their business with dispatch (eating & pooping in a minute so as to be ready for an attack), but the secret for success at anything big is not *that.* It is *delayed gratification.* The boss, above, had the discipline to take care of himself for years – or decades – in order to work up the ranks until he was made manager, passing over others who let things get out of hand by wasting their, and the company's time and money on prostitutes or marriages they could not afford.

当テがきもちがわず主の聟に成り 葉別三
ategaki mo chigawazu nushi no muko ni nari
(aimed-stroking errs-not: boss's groom becomes)

All that jacking off did not fly wide
the boss's daughter is now his bride!
~~~~~~

Here, the harmless behavior once called, and still considered "the solitary *sin*," by some, is proof of good character in *two* ways. *The first* is present in another version of this masturbatory success story, *"Years of beating off – the reward: a share in the family name"* (せんづりのほうび家名を分ヶて出シ万 安元 *senzuri no hôbi kamei o wakete dashi*). *I.e.,*, the *deferred gratification*, already mentioned. *The second* is that the clerk jerked while thinking of the girl – *ate-gaki* means "*aimed*, or directed-stroking" [1] – who would become his wife. *Think about it.* Surveys show that the minds of *most* people engaged in coitus tend to wander to the greener ass on the other side of the fence, town, TV, etc.. Excluding a tiny minority lucky to be fucking each other from the inside out, who can deny porn-star and self-styled "advocating vagina" Kuroki Kaoru's assertion that "*even sex* [coitus] *could be called 'two-person masturbation,' couldn't it?*" The long-term masturbator and boss's daughter match because the 10% or so of men who married into their wife's family (*irimuko*) had to accept an inferior role, as did women who married into a man's. Stereotypically, he is "spread under the ass" (*shiri-ni shikareta*) of his wife. The self-control of the master masturbator will come in handy for life, or at least until the old master and his wife retire.

おえ脈が二分たらぬ婿のイ八 葉 29
oe-myaku ga nibu hodo taranu muko no mara
(hard-on's throb/arteries 20% amount lacks groom[son-in-law]'s cock)

eighty degrees
of hardness: the cock of
a son-in-law

the son-in-law
has a cock that erects
eighty percent

twenty percent
lacking: the hardness of
a muko's cock

A *muko* was not his own man. In divorce, the wife took all; he could even *"have his hole taken by her paramour"*(入りむこと間男迄にあなとられ 摘 1-30 *irimuko to ma-otoko made ni ana d/torare*), if we take the pun-reading of *anadorare* (despised), *ana torare* (hole-taken). *"Even when hard, the muko seldom gets to put it in"* (おへたとて入むこめつたにハならず 摘 1-35 *oeta tote irimuko metta ni wa narazu*). He needs *her* permission for what was usually a man's right. Without it, all can do is sneak off to the w.c. for another thousand-strokes! In such circumstances, how could his testosterone count *not* drop & weaken the timber of his manhood?

我指で在スが如く後家よがり 葉末六
waga yubi de imasu ga gotoku goke yogari

the widow cries,
coming with her own finger
as if it were him

like his being
within the widow's finger
makes her cry

Seeing how Solt (1996) sidestepped the lack of a good verb (*yogari*) for *love cries* – "*with her finger / as if he were inside / the widow's orgasm*" – I added "coming." The verb *imasu* gracefully indicates *his* presence through her finger while alluding to a phrase in the *Analects* (祭ること在ますが如く 岡田) about how festivals (祭 *matsuri/u:* see pg. 163) allow the presence of those no longer with us. The accompanying refrain for the first *ku,* below, is *"The wind-chime goes tinkle, tinkle!"* Skipping the finer points of the juxtaposition, let me point out that the *tinkling* mimesis, *chinchin,* is a "penis" homophone. The second *ku's* refrain is untranslatable, but suggestive of doing things briskly, one after another.

ちいさい箱から爺を出す後家
chiisai hako kara toto o dasu goke
ちん／＼と風鈴ちん／＼と 延享四
(*chin-chin to fûrin chin-chin to*)

she takes papa
out of a little box
the widow

箱へことりと後家のきぬ／＼
hako e kotori to goke no kinuginu
是はさて是はさて／＼／＼ 延享四
(*kore wa sate kore wa sate sate sate*)

click goes the lid
of her box, a widow's
morning after

Whoever first called the practice of self-consolation *"the solitary sin"* did not know Japanese. If a man avoids disease and saves money=time by taking care of his own business before he has the means to marry, is it not his self-discipline laudworthy? *And, how about this widow?* Who dares say it would be more moral for her to betray her love, repress her memories, and, if you will pardon my vernacular, go out and get laid? Likewise for the maid-servants, who, as we shall see in *their* chapter, did not have shiny horn dildos kept in pretty paulownia boxes – the closing of the box with the mimesis *kotori to* shows the widow, ever the diligent housewife, does all things with alacrity in contrast to the classical love term *kinuginu,* suggestive of the slow and sad send-off of a lover in the morning – but, as I was saying, even these maids with their odd and, yes, *gross* dildo substitutes (radishes, potatoes, mullets) satisfying their natural urges by themselves rather than betraying the youths who wait for them back in the country are acting heroically. And so, too the most common example of moral masturbation, the ladies in the palaces of the Lords of Japan – concubines/ladies-in-waiting/chamber-maids. *Don't all who fucking themselves refrain from the greater pleasure of being inside of or wrapped around another person in order to live up to their responsibilities deserve our praise?* A *Million ku* replies: *"Those who make do with dildos are good people"* (張形ですんでいるには人がよし 万明六 *harikata de sunde-iru ni wa hito ga yoshi*). But, what about she who *overdoes it with the dildo fastened to her heel?* Or the lady-in-waiting *envied for having four or five of them* (長局四五本もってそねまれる 摘 2-3 *nagatsubone shi, gohon motte sonemareru*)? Or a bachelor who buys and fits out a block of congealed root starch (later!)? Would *that* be perverted? The answer is still *No!* It would only show they are highly sexed, and make their forbearance all the more heroic. (左下 135-11)

お局の悋気かゝとへ角が生え
otsubone no rinki kakato e tsuno ga hae

green with envy
the chambermaid's heel
grows a horn

長局足を早めてよがるなり 摘 2-31
nagatsubome ashi o hayamete yogaru nari

stepping faster
the lady in waiting has
started to cry

Because the movement of a dildo attached to a heel is not so closely tied to oneself as the same done by hand, it would feel more *other,* like the real thing.

湯加減がよくてのぼせる長局
yû kagen ga yokute nobaseru nagatsubone

our lady in waiting
flushes when the water
feels just right

164-19

あつ燗で楽しんでいる長局
atsukan de tanoshindeiru nagatsubone

our lady in waiting
enjoys sitting back with
a warm one

156-2

きうなときやひやで用ル長つほね 万 明五
kyû no toki ya hiya de mochiiru nagatsubone million

in a hurry
the lady in waiting can
use it cold

Judging history from senryu alone, masturbation was the chief duty of the lady in waiting or chamber-maid. Peckers by the peck: *"Ladies in waiting / every woman has / one prick"* (長局一チ女にへのこ壱本ッゝ 摘 1-35 *nagatsubone ichi-jo ni henoko ippon zutsu*). It's good they didn't have to share; Japanese, unlike the "individualistic" West, usually have their own chopsticks, bowls and cups. Senryu assure us they find their substitute *"good enough"* (はりかたハずいぶんよしと局いひ 摘 1-21 *harikata wa zuibun yoshi to tsubone ii*), – for *"not one irretractable foreskin"* (越前ハ壱本もない長つほね 摘 1-13 *echizen wa ippon mo nai nagatsubone.*) hides among them, and gives instructions on filling the thin ox horn with warm water. The first *ku* above has the warmth "just right," *i.e., like the real thing*; the "warm one" in the second seemingly refers to warm *sake* but alludes to the dildo. The "cold" (*hiya*) in the third usually refers to chilled drinks or soup and thus hints at the liquid within the horn and vagina as mouth.

馬程の牛を局は持っている 28-11
uma hodo no ushi o tsubone wa motteiru

our lady in waiting
has an ox that is built
like a horse

長つほねちいさいを取りわらハれる万
nagatsubone chiisai o tori warawareru 天五.

a lady in waiting
picks out a small one and
gets laughed at

These women may have little experience c̲ *men*, but nonetheless grow jaded and gradually increase the size of their dildos. When a novice visiting the "sundry goods man" (小間物屋 *komamonoya*), shyly goes for one of small caliber. . .

かたい奥扨はりかたハよくうれる 摘 1-33
katai oku sate harikata wa yoku ureru

chastity saved
by spending on dildos
a tight palace

a tight palace
don't the dildos sell
like hotcakes

a palace run
on rectitude, how those
dildos sell

おく中のすれ／＼へ　こ壱本なり 万 明八
oku naka no sure sure henoko ippon nari million

within the chambers
lots of friction: it is hard
with just one cock

Rectitude sells dildos. *Katai-oku* in the first *ku* means a "morally upright inner-chambers." Who knows what percent of the beauties were monopolized by the Shôgun and daimyos, but the friction between women vying for the ruler evoke Solomon, or, rather Mark Twain's sympathy for his "copulation cabinet of seven hundred wives and three hundred concubines" kept starving for sex by "this creature with the decrepit candle," as he described the sex that is weaker in bed.

二千九百九十九人ハ水牛 36-3 &
nisen kyûhyaku jûkyû nin wa suigyû 121 内 25

for two thousand
nine hundred and ninety nine
– water buffalo –

water buffalo
for two thousand nine hundred
& ninety nine

鈴の音でかゝとのうごく長つほね 万 安元
suzu no oto de kakato no ugoku nagatsubone million

moving their heels
to the tinkling of a bell
ladies in waiting

Of 3,000 women in the Inner Palace that night only one is solaced by the real thing; a bell is jingled when he comes so the time can be recording in case there is issue. A less creative *ku* mentioned the *"Three thousand / taking turns owning / one male-root* (男根壱本三千人の廻り持ち *dankon ippon sanzen-nin no mawari-mochi*). The allusion is to a legendary Emperor of China. No ruler of Japan had anywhere *close* to that many women. Still, the sex ratio these women had to endure was even worse than that endured by the poor single men of Edo. While senryu writers may joke about the dildos, *did they not also identify with these women?*

相イ方の無イはかゝとでほねを折 末摘 1-10
aikata no nai wa kakato de hone o oru ねかひ社すれ／＼
(partner-not-as-for heel-with bone[acc] break [i.e.bust one's balls])

being alone
she breaks the bone
of her heel

~~*without a man*~~
~~*to bust his balls, she blisters*~~
~~*her own heels*~~

partnerless ones
must bust the balls
of their heels

長つほねくじに勝たか下に成り 万明七
nagatsubone kuji ni katta ga shita ni nari million

the chambermaid
who won the draw
is on the bottom

お局は若い女中にさせるなり 摘 3-9
otsubone wa wakai jochû ni saseru nari pluck

the lady-in-waiting
has a young woman to
help her make do

They could strap on dildos or use a common one with a *tsubo,* or sword-guard/ stopper between to pleasure one another. My second version of the first *ku* is a teaser reading someone unfamiliar with these women might come up with. The last two have little poetry, but are instructive as to the poet's attitude toward women doing women. These women prefer to play the female role, showing they are not lesbians but making do without men. Other more clever mutual-masturbation *ku* translate no better: *"Bored mistresses / horn-felt intercourse / between oxen"* (牛どうし角つきあひの妾部や（押しつおされつ／＼／＼）新雪みどり 享保 14 *ushi dôshi tsuno tsuki-ai no mekakebeya.*). No poetic license can make up for the loss of the stab-match = *tsuki-ai* = relationship pun and the fact that Japanese bull-fights were head-to-head pushing matches (the draw is *push and be pushed*).

牛の果テ又世に出て色おとこ 万 宝十三
ushi no hate mata yo ni idete iro otoko million
(cow's/ox's end, again world-in/to appearing)

the ox dies &
is reborn from his horn
as a playboy

the end of an ox
and its rebirth on earth
as a lady's man

moving on to
greener pastures, an ox
serves a lady

dead, an ox rises
to heaven in the right hand
of a chambermaid

水牛ハおかしい角のはへたやつ 万
suigyû wa okashii tsuno no haeta yatsu 安二

water buffalo
are the ones that grow
strange horns

はりかたといつたか車引キおちど
harikata to itta ga kurumahiki ochido 同

that's a slip up!
she meant a dildo but got
one for a cart

牛の角もぐと女がふたり出来 摘
ushi no tsuno mogu to onna ga futari deki 2-24

an ox's horns
torn off they can make
two women

an ox's horns
can satisfy two girls
when torn off

The first imagines an Edo city dweller who has seen dildos but not the source.

The women went on field trips (blossom-viewing, herb-hunting etc.) by ox-cart (some very fancy). Poets sure got many laughs out of the lonely dildo. I would like to see more *ku* for the one's made of tortoise shell. Imagine the drooling old face of the tortoise whose shell ended up *there!* Or, if made of sea-turtle, it could have circled the world before buying the farm on Mons veneris, etc..

おれがのは昔細工と局いい 摘 4-5
ore ga no wa mukashi saiku to tsubone ii

"mine is good
old-fashioned craftsmanship"
says the tsubone

長つぼねそこを／＼と一人いゝ 万
nagatsubone soko o soko o to hitori ii 明七

that's the spot!
that's the spot! –the soliloquy
of a chambermaid

A really good dildo – thin-walled enough to feel fleshy, yet thick enough to last, bumpy enough to stimulate yet not enough to injure – like a good man, was probably hard to find; but, if the humor in the first *ku* is in the act of boasting about a dildo rather than a lover, that would be significant, because a century later boasting was in bad taste and complaining was acceptable. Or, is she just a lady in waiting too long? The second *ku* is sad if you think too much about it.

どこのうしのほねか御つほねひぞうがり
doko no ushi no hone ka o-tsubone hizôgari 万安四
(where's cow's/ox's bone? [hon.]chambermaid treasures)

the pillow talk of
a chambermaid: from what ox
did you sprout?

Hizôgari (秘蔵がり) means *being very fond of someone*, treasuring them as one's favorite. It is usually used for a minion or a mistress, not a dear dildo. The original wit turns the "horse = *uma*" in a common expression for a no-one coming from god knows where: a "wherever from horse's bone" (*doko no uma no hone*) – from horse-bone collectors in China? – into a cow/ox = *ushi*." The term is derogatory, but *if said in the right tone of voice by a lover*, oddly enough seems endearing. I think this is my favorite *ku* of this chapter, but only in the original.

Pre-senryû Dildos for Perspective

~~~~~~

Eastward bound / Who goes to swive / someone's daughter?
Over Love's Mountain / goes Sir Dildo.

~~~~~~

Over Love's Mountain / Goes Sir Dildo
Carrying a love-letter / in his fake heel, / Off he goes!

東路や　誰が娘とか契るらむ　　逢坂山を越ゆるはりかた　大筑波集
逢坂山を越ゆるはりかた　　恋の文入れて旅立つ具足櫃　　油糟 寛永

The first of the link-verse pairs is from the classic early *haikai* anthology *Inu-tsukuba-shû* (1536), considered by some the starting point for haiku and senryu, and the second from a slightly later one. Both have a foot in old romance and a foot in folk tradition, with an element of *haikai* surprise. (Found in Sasama)

dildo, whose enemy?

はりかたへいつそすいつくおしい事
harikata e isso suitsuku oshii koto 摘 2-9

it hurts to see
how tightly it sucks up
to that dildo

はり形ハきつい毒さと女医者 摘
harikata wa kitsui doku sa to onna isha 4-23

dildos are a hard
medicine to take, says
the lady doctor

はりかたが無イと仲条まだはやり 摘
harikata ga nai to chûjô mada hayari 1-10

without dildos
the abortionist is still
in big demand

until dildos
can be had, abortion
will be a fad

The dildo had two loyal enemies. Understandably envious men (see the eddies for a sample of the long comical English complaint in poetry), and the doctress, who made her living aborting fetuses with drugs. The original of the second *ku* says *kitsui doku,* or, "a harsh poison." A softer reading to the effect that it is emotionally trying for the women who use dildos to avoid pregnancy is less likely, for senryu favor blacker wit, i.e., and the inverse relationship of dildo and abortion.

finger teams and finger puppets

男は五人女は二人組　紅の花
otoko wa gonin onna wa futarigumi

digital dosage

for a man
a team of five, two will
do a woman

こんな時誰でもと下女二人組　神田連組連句集
konna toki dare demo to gejo futarigumi (from a renku!)

"this is when i can
do it with anyone" – the maid
plays team o' two

when she'll do it
with anyone, the maid's
own team o' two

"now i can do it
with anyone i want to"
a maid at team-o-two

Dildos attract poets. They are dramatic: *"The chambermaid / has one that was cut-off / right at the hairline!"* (毛のさかひ目から切たおつほね持チ 万 安七 *ke no sakai-me kara kitta o tsubone mochi*); *"An everlasting / pecker: that's what the lady / in waiting bought!* (万年ももちいるへ_こつほねかい 万 安五 *mannen mo mochiiru henoko tsubone kai* [*mannen* is the same word later used for a *fountain*-pen]). And they make for interesting metaphor: *"Every night / the chamber-maid puts a skirt / on her ox"* (うしにすそ毎ばん_せる長局 万 安四 *ushi ni suso maiban saseru nagatsubone*), *"The chamber-maid / has a bit of ox broth / for her nightcap* (長つほね牛の湯つけを喰てねる 万 安四 *nagatsubone ushi no yu-zuke o kuchiteneru*), as two *ku* I overlooked earlier put it. *But stop.* Two *fingers* suffice for the lowly servant-maid to have her prince. Most Japanese women (there were far more gejo=maidservants than *nagatsubone= chambermaids*), like men, got off *digitally*. *Cuntologia* includes a term for rubbing the clitoris, *sane-senzuri,* "clit-thousand-strokes," the same *senzuri* found in the male term, but I find no senryu with it. Instead, we have the *"two-team"* introduced above, and *"Sniggling c / that middle-finger while / squeezing cunt"* (中指でさねを釣ってる握りぼぼ 葉 9 *nakayubi de sane o tsutteru nigiri-bobo*), *"Writing the Tale, / now and then, Shikibu / clutched her cunt"* (物語り式部おり／＼握りつび *monogatari shikibu oriori nigiri-tsubi.*), with, respectively, *nigiri-bobo* and *nigiri-tsubi,* or *squeeze/clench/ clutch/ed/ing-cunt*. The Tale is the early-11c *Tale of Genji* (Read it yourself to see if you can guess where the author might have been carried away). As you can see, I just cannot decide how to best English these terms. *Thank goodness* there is another, more colorful expression:

歌舞伎見ながら人形のおもしろさ
kabuki minagara ningyô no omoshirosa 27

watching kabuki
how interesting to work
your puppet, too

the fun of it!
watching kabuki with
your puppet

見物のするだんまりは指二本 61-39
mimono no suru danmari wa yubi nihon

mummery
in the audience, ah,
two-fingers

人形に情をうつして泣く娘 新編 39
ningyô ni jô o utsushite naku musume

putting her heart
into her puppetry
a maiden cries

empathizing
with her own puppet
a maiden cries

putting her heart
into a puppet, the girl
starts to moan

下で人形遣うの猫知らず 神の田艸
shita de ningyô tsukau no neko shirazu

what pussy
doesn't know: a puppet
show below!

Respecting the last *ku – do you recall the puppetry below the skirt of the heated table (kotatsu) viewed only by the cat?* I do not know the date of the complementary *ku* above it which turns "cat-needs-not = *neko irazu*" (rat poison) into "cat-*knows*-not = *neko shirazu;*" but, one confession is in order. Until taking a slow second look at this puppetry in senryu, I wrongly assumed the fingering had to be done by another person. But, *no*, to make a puppet it is enough for the fingers to be under a woman's open-ended clothing, even though it be her own. Back to clearly moral masturbation:

千摺で斗り萬歳年をとり 葉 22
senzuri de bakari manzai toshi o tori

beating his meat
the manzai man picks up
another year

the manzai men
always masturbate from
year to year

Manzai combine stand-up comedian, clown and door-to-door begging. Every year they hit the road for the New Year holidays. Senryu, written from the point of view of hard-up men, recognize that the manzai, at least when on the road away from home, share their agony. Again, I ask, *Is the manzai man avoiding the temptation to stray by taking care of himself, not acting in an admirable way?*

極ずいたわけ挊でごほり／＼ 葉 11
gokuzui tawake senzuri de gôri-gôri leaf

the simpleton
does a thousand strokes
and has one!

ready to drop
after a thousand strokes
the fool stops

falling apart
from a thousand strokes
one slow bloke

After moral masturbation, we have the descriptive variety. One sub-variety might be called moronic description, a hick samurai, slooooowly counting each stroke – he probably can't count to a thousand anyway – *"hii, fuu, mii . . . "* (千摺りを一イ二ウ三イとかぞへて見 葉 別六 *senzuri o hii fuu mii to ka kazoete mi*). *Ooone, twooo* does not work. English cannot express stretched-out pronunciation as successfully as Japanese. Even if we wrote *"one," "won,"* the pronunciation of the *"ooo's"* would turn into a hard "u." By comparison, the above *ku* was easy to translate. How does its response to a literal reading of the Japanese (not found in Chinese) word for *masturbation*, "thousand strokes," compare to the response of the asagiura (hick samurai, who did it in 50 strokes) a few pages ago? I once read a small tome titled *Ten (or, was it twelve or thirteen?)Types of Ambiguity*. What I see in senryu makes me wish for another such analysis titled *Ten (or, was it twelve or thirteen?) Types of Moronity* using examples from senryu.

仰向いてせんずり臍がにわたづみ
ao-muite senzuri heso ga niwatazuni

lying face up
self-pleasure turns a navel
into a puddle

masturbating
face up makes a puddle
of a navel

masturbating
face up, the navel as
a holding-pond

This description (出典求む!) seems more concrete than even the asagiura's fifty strokes, but probably should not be taken for a recording of a one-time happening. I doubt any male has *not* created such a pond on at least one occasion. (*How sad to think not one of those tadpoles in the puddle will ever lose its tail!*)

倅大悦ひよめきで反吐をつき 葉七
segare tai-etsu hiyomeki de hedo o tsuki

my joyful son
his fontanel throbbing
regurgitates[*]

Segare, or "son" is a classy, yet humble way to refer to one's own penis. Here, this common idiom is turned into a complex metaphor. Syunroan points out that a *heavenly* ecstasy or joy, 天悦, once referred to the consummation of the loves of a man and woman – overlay the characters for "two" (二) and people (人) and you get "heaven" (天) – while *great* ecstasy or joy, 大悦, such as you see in this *ku* referred to sexual pleasure for *one*, whether in one-sided homosexual love or onanism – for just "one" (一) is overlaid upon person (人). The fontanel (little-fountain), or soft spot on the crown/back of a baby's head, is called *hiyomeki*, a word with the sound-sense of pulsing/breathing movement, or *odori, i.e.,* "dancing [spot]" in Japanese, and Syunroan opines that the details (slight changes in the head of the penis as it nears ejaculation) suggest a masturbatory observation.

Devil's Tongue for a Merkin?

こんにゃくをめゝっこにする花のよひ
konnyaku o memekko ni suru hana no yoi 32-8

~~*making a cunt*~~
~~*from the devil's tongue*~~
~~*blossom drunk*~~

choosing konjak
that looks like nookie
on blossom eve

~~*a blossom drunk*~~
~~*turns his konjak into*~~
~~*a piece of tail*~~

Konnyaku, or *konjak* as it is sometimes written in English is also *devil's tongue* according to my Japanese-English dictionary, though the definition found in my English-English dictionary "a foul smelling fleshy herb, *Hydrosme rivieri,* of the Old World tropics" suggests otherwise (for it is found in temperate Japan). The starch is cooked and formed into springy – close to whale blubber – rectangular or round blocks which have a somewhat off-color, sexy smell (whether foul or not depends on your taste). ~~I suppose it would be *possible* to take a round block and fashion it to look like a vulva just for the hell of it, but, this is, after all a senryu, and it is more likely a lonely drunk is preparing to jack off with a piece of konjak while sitting in the bloomshade under the falling petals. ◎ *So, I thought;* but~~ Okada notes *there is a bona-fide way konjak is prepared where it looks that way (probably to hold the sauce=flavor)!* ◎ But why, specifically, *hananoyoi,* a "blossom drunk," i.e., getting drunk while blossom-viewing (not only acceptable, but *de rigor:* see *Cherry Blossom Epiphany*)? ◎ *While such a word exists, more likely the eve=yoi before the blossom-viewing and they are making box lunch.* ◎ The *konjak ku* of Haiku Saint Bashô, who probably loved it for embodying the Tao in its tastelessness, include one with a few plum petals garnishing a serving of konjak *sashimi,* and another vaguely connecting it to cherry blossoms. This Issa *ku* lies midway between Bashô's culinary aesthetics and the above senryu:

花咲て妹がこんにやくはやる也 一茶
hana saite imo-ga-konnyaku hayaru nari 文化四
(flowers bloom, sister=potato konjaku popular becomes)

cherries bloom
and sweet gal konnyaku's
the going thing

cherries abloom
your sweety-pie's konnyaku
may start a fad

cherries bloom
and young men dive into
konjak pies

Imo, or (little) sister, is a term of endearment, something like "baby" or "sweety" in English. Eg., *"Spring-thaw / one sock [drying] on / sister kotatsu"* (Buson), a *kotatsu* being the skirted table-(t)heater we have seen used for trying on hair-slippers. So, we need not make too much of the *imo*. But, when you consider that poor Issa had to bachelor it for decades, despite being highly sexed, he surely tried *konjak* himself and couldn't help thinking of the second reading. Issa also plays with a reversal, for the *konnyaku* comes not from a "devil's tongue" in Japanese, but from what is called a *konnyaku imo* – or *konnyaku* "potato" *and* is a homophone with the term of endearment. The middle-reading makes most sense as a friend's wife prepared such a blossom-viewing lunch for him and his friends about the time the *ku* was composed. Now back to senryu. I have encountered the following *ku* many times but oddly failed to catch its source.

蒟蒻がすぎて倅は役に立たず
konnyaku ga sugite segare wa yaku ni tatazu
(konjak did too much, son-as-for use/role-as-stand-not)

too much
konjak has ruined
his son

He overdid his konjak-off-ing . . .
Now his poker's good-for-nothing.

The devil's tongue he overdid
– now his son won't do as bid

He doesn't find women much fun;
– too damn much devil's tongue!

The devil's tongue charmed
his once filial pole:
It will not stand for
a husband's proper role.

He used the devil's tongue
rather than his hand:
Now it won't stand
up and work.

the devil's tongue
cooked his goose: women
are all too loose

In Japanese, a "good-for-nothing" is one who "cannot *stand* [his/her] role." That is, konjak feels so good that regular use ruins a man for sex with a woman. One supremely boring senryu says *"He wields a tube-spear of konjak, the bachelor"* (蒟蒻の管鑓遣ふ独り者 *konnyaku no kudayari tsukau hitorimono*). The tube-spear (*kudayari*) had a thick tubular handle in which the thinner shaft with its tip was set. But, whether a slit is cut into a slab of konjak or it is cored/bored into a tube, it is more than just a hole. It has *spring* and *quivers*. Some *ku* develop the metaphor of *konjak* as cowardly because of that – remember Shakespeare's great word, *"quake-buttocks?"* – but we will stick to self-consolation.

馬鹿案じ茹で蒟蒻で火傷をし 六七
baka anji yude-konnyaku de yakedo o shi

a foolish idea:
boiling konjak and
getting burnt

Konnyaku, like the ox horn dildo, or rarer ox horn *merkin* – we used to have names for concave masturbation devices before ridiculous Christian superstitions made self-responsibility a sin – called *azumagata* 吾妻形, literally, "my-wife-shape" (also, sometimes written 東形, or East-shape as shorthand & for other reasons) could be warmed. For whatever reasons, konnyaku *prose* beats its *poetry* (the *ku* tend to be *exceptionally* poor) so let me summarize some examples:

.

1) An undated story (found in *Cuntologia*) called *"The Konjak Wife"* suggests personification, such as Issa's "sister/baby konjak," was not unheard of (a servant boy who overhears a bonze greeting the slab of konjak he shared his bed with every night, slips a prickly chestnut husk into "her" twat and . . .).

2) Another story, from a book printed when Issa was fourteen: "Having been given a gem-stalk that is hardly run-of-the-mill karma, no mistresses or widows will consort with poor Hiko-saburo. In fact, none of the world's women will give me the time of day. Not finding an Empress with a wide pussy like Yuge (Dôkyô) of old, I

> must live until I die, as I do now, a life bereft of joy. Although I do have money for pussy crafted from wax and konjak, that does not suffice to make me happy." (枕童児抜差万遍玉茎安永五 cited in IBID)
>
> 3) Passages from a book of bedroom advice dated 1822 (Issa would have been sixty), suggest cutting a slit with a blade-like skewer, rolling the slab of konjak in thick paper, placing it on hot ashes or in warm water, then taking it out and enveloping it in a cloth sheath. The sheath sounds practical as it would require less konjak as it could maintain the pressure without breaking and blot up excessive moisture, and, we are told, it should feel "no different from the gem-gate of a middle-aged woman." Best of all, it concludes with a proper admonition to take care to "bury it in the earth" and not just "leave it lying wantonly about." (閨中紀聞枕文庫 cited in IBID)

The second story is clever. By starting with a mention of widows (reputed to like big ones), we are lead to think the man shares Montaigne's plight (*"even the matrons . . look dimly on a man whose member's small,"...*) and, only later, does the *tragi-* gets its *-comedy*, when mention of Dôkyô and his Empress reveal the protagonist is *over-* rather than *under-*endowed!

こんにゃくでなめるハ男不心中 摘
konnyaku-de nameru-wa otoko-fushinjû 1-12
(konjak-with lick-as-for man not-heart-centered)

a twit for a twat, or
cunning cunnilingus

using konjak
for his tongue, the man's
just having fun

using konjak
to tickle her fancy, he's
not all there

The original says "licking with konjak." Since *licking* can mean *fucking*, as well as *to make a sucker of someone*, my first image was a half-hard penis flopping around where it should be poking. As konjak is said to have spermicidal properties, my second guess, was that it was a pessary. Men buying sex made a big thing of whether or not they were allowed to come in an unloaded vagina or not – a local regular (expected to help out with abortion or birth-related expenses) might, while a traveler would have to make do with a "pop-gun" (*kamideppô*) as paper-packed vaginas were called. I imagined a courtesan pretending to be in love with a man, while keeping her options open by slyly assassinating his sperm. The only problem with this interpretation, besides the fact the last five syllabets rightly read mean the *man* is not really madly in love, is that this use of konjak was not yet popular. Then, I read one more of those stories:

> A man convinced a girl to have sex with him saying, "If I lick you, will you let me do it?" After she agreed, he secretly fashioned a tongue out of konjak, held it in his mouth and commenced "licking." The girl said "For some reason, it feels cold down there!" The man catching she was on to him quickly swallowed it, saying "What do you mean? There's no konjak here!" (さしまくら　安永二 1773 in *Cuntologia*)

This made it almost certainly about cunnilingus. The clincher was another senryu with licking down there meant to show the sincerity of a man's love for a man (see *shinjû* . . . in *The Dirty Bonze* chapter). Be that as it may, what most attracts me to konjak is, first, that it, like the ox horn, may serve in both a concave and convex capacity (though the preponderance of usage for each is contrary) and second, male use of it for masturbation is rationalized by a sort of folk benediction, the origin, and consequently meaning of which, is still under debate. The three readings of "konjak's sand-exorcism/brush-off/rid' (*konnyaku-no suna-barai*) and the related "[a] man's sand-ridding/brush-off/exorcism" (*otoko no suna-barai*) I have encountered are: 1) Because konjak was made by a lot of treading and sand fell off a man's balls; 2) Because eating konjak once a month cleans up, or detoxifies the guts; and, 3) Because it was thought bad for a man not to ejaculate at least once a month and konjak was the favored receptacle. 1) is ridiculous, for few people actually made konjak. 2) is possible for konjak "is nearly impossible to digest and passes directly into and through the intestines, scrubbing the intestine walls and absorbing toxic substances as it goes along." One late-period *Willow ku* riddles the idea:

宝永四年こんにゃくの値が上り
hôei shinen konnyaku ne ga agari 柳 149
(hôei four-year konjak price-the rises/ed/ing)

hôei year four
the price of konjak
goes sky high

The fourth year of Hôei is 1707. That year, Fuji erupted. A fissure opened on the Southeast side from which a lateral volcano, to be called Mt Hôei (2702 m) sprouted up. A broad area not far from Edo ate a lot of the fall-out that year directly from the sky or in the clean-up. This was assumed to cause renal calculosis – for everyone knew a grain of sand in the urinary tract was hell – so a lot of konjak was eaten and the price rose. Note that the senryu was written about 130 years after the fact. That makes it a little late to be regarded as history.

こんにやくを小便桶でうりに来る *konnyaku o shôben oke de uri ni kuru* 22-16
Coming to sell konjak c̲ a piss pail – Still unsolved. To trade for fertilizer...?

The *Wages* of Masturbating

二才のつらにせんずりのかきだまり
nisai no tsura ni senzuri no kaki-damari 万安 六
(greenhorn's face-on 1000-rubs' stroke/scratch-puddle/rubbish)

teenage faces
what a mess is made
beating off

greenhorn faces
spotted with the puddles of
a thousand strokes

on the face
of a greenhorn, scum
from beating off

Okada Hajime explains: *nikibi,* "pimples." Don't we have the same superstition in the Occident? The Japanese – or, at least, senryu writers – were so highly aware of the verticality of a young man's erection that they might also have found it appropriate that he shot himself in the face! Be that as it may, there is a link between pimples and beating off: both peak at the same time in the life cycle. A 7-7 *ku* introduced by Suzuki puts it like this: *"Transfixed by spring pictures / a face full of pimples* 春画に見入る面皰出た皃 紀の玉川一 文政二 鈴 *shunga ni miiru nikibi deta kao*).

The Wages of *Not* Masturbating

布袋のせんずりどふも手が届き兼 葉十三
hotei no senzuri dômo te ga todoki-kane

putai's arms
can't reach & can't beat
his own meat

putai cannot
console himself: his arms
are too short

Even Gods were roasted by senryu. The fattest of the Seven (Chinese) Gods of Good Fortune, the pot-bellied Putai (Japanese: Hotei) is kidded here for being constitutionally incapable of masturbating. Poor Putai was no Zeus capable of changing form and seducing mortal women either. About three hundred senryu later, we discover the horrid result of *not* masturbating:

仕舞いにハ布袋唐子を痔持にし 葉末三二
shimai ni wa hotei karako o ji-mochi ni shi

too much happiness

in the end
putai gave his chinaboy
a case of piles

The *pole-makes-piles* idea was common in senryu, as it was a common idea in the culture.*** Sex and senryu scholar Syunroan Syuzin thought the idea was that Putai sodomized his boy servant because he was too ugly to attract women. As he was a 唐 =T'ang Dynasty (618-907) Zen monk, his seldom attractively drawn face may be based on historical fact, but I think it more likely this was composed as a follow-up for the *ku* that observed he could not masturbate. At the same time, Putai does sometimes have the features I imagine on a chubby, wine-quaffing old man, gay in both meanings of the word. And, reading Leupp's *Male Colors*, I found out *why* I was left with that vague impression. Putai was "often shown dallying with fair youths in Tokugawa paintings." Of course! I missed it, for I had assumed those boys were young *women,* understandable, for Leupp's example shows a "young female-role actor." But, the "chinaboy" in the *ku* refers to a younger boy yet – the equivalent of the Japanese *chigo* – Putai's road companion and servant (originally, he was pictured handing out sweets to poor children – did they morph into a servant or servants?). Note that the same character for Chinese 唐 is used for the "T'ang" Dynasty from which Putai, and for that matter, widespread pederasty, came from, and is even today the most common adjective for "Chinese" things. Today, Putai is generally written Butai for the same reason Peking starts with a B, but I prefer the P for Hotei because he is often conflated with the Buddha in the Occident. Also, Putai, either because of the felicitous resemblance to putti, the jolly infant boys (*puttine*) found in baroque sculpture, or for the "plump" association, simply sounds more fitting.

水牛かなけれハ水もくさるとこ 万 明五
suigyû ga nakereba mizu mo kusaru toko million
(hydro-cow/buffalo/s not-if water too putrefy about)

without bubalus
bubalis, her sweet water
would go bad

water buffalos
without them their paddies
would grow foul

You can recognize the dildo here. The water buffalo (I used the scientific name once to avoid repeating "water") was important for the condition of the paddies in parts of Japan. The "water" here refers to the spirit of life, the sexual humors. Overspending it was bad, but so was letting it go stagnant. Referring to the black cat typically kept by a girl with consumption, another *Million ku* snorts *"For her medicine / a black pecker would work / better than a cat"* (ねこよりもくろいへのこがくすりなり 万 安六 *neko yori mo kuroi henoko ga kusuri nari*). Dark cocks were held to be more vigorous (cause and effect confused?). Be that as it may, the concept is consistent. One must *keep the juices flowing*, whether with the help of 1-horn ox-power or the devil's tongue (I helped with the Japanese translation of a book on supramolecular biology by Hans Selye, discoverer of medically defined stress, and I was amazed to find he had observed how the disruption of blood-flow by objects planted in lab animals – physically induced stress – could cause cancer. The importance of good circulation is not an odd pre-scientific idea better left to Chinese medicine or Indian yoga, but a fact of life medical science has yet to pay sufficient attention to). And, now, what I'd call a particularly senryu senryu:

せんずりをかけと内儀は 湯屋で鳴り 摘 2-15
senzuri o kake to naigi wa yuya de(do?)nari

'masturbate!'
his better half hollars
at the bath

'go beat off!'
a wife thunders out
at the bath

One mixed bath. Two readings. Mine has her husband embarrassing her by getting an erection (perhaps they are abstaining for she recently gave birth). Not that she means he should masturbate then and there in public, as a certain Greek philosopher did at a theater to show his appreciation for the play. She just thinks he should learn to take care of himself. Nishizawa (1985) explains that Edo baths could be very crowded, especially in the tiny door between the dressing room and the baths, as much so as trains at rush-hour today – so frottage could hardly be avoided. Instead of a horny husband, some stranger got too familiar, or she thought one did.

はり形ハくるしからずとまつかをか 万安元
harikata wa kurushikarazu to matsugaoka million

easy divorce

with a dildo
it is not painful at all
matsugaoka

If a woman in an abusive relationship could flee to and remain at Matsugaoka temple for three years (celibate, of course, for no men were allowed), she could get a divorce whether or not her husband wanted it. This *ku* depicts the dildo as a plus for a woman and a possible minus for a possessive husband who would prefer to think his member indispensable.

The Oddest Onanism Poem Ever

I hesitate to introduce this next *ku*, as my faithful readers will find it again when I finally publish a potpourri of salacious marine senryu, *Mullets In Maids*. But this crab *ku* is so ridiculous, I cannot help wanting to share it, repeatedly!

蟹の十ン摺りうろたへてツイ羅切 葉
kani no senzuri urotaete tsui rasetsu 別八

crab consoles
himself & in his dither
cuts it off

crab beats off
and in his excitement
loses his meat

a crab's masturbation
can end in castration!

★ A great illustration by a top cartoonist of just such a crab, who, taught to masturbate, injures himself, will be found in the aforementioned *Mullets*, when and if it is published.

~ eddies ~

Aimed Masturbation. As explained in the text, the idea of *ate-gaki* – "targeted masturbation" or "aimed stroking" – done by a man while imagining a specific woman one loves or desires rather than a vague ideal women, multiple women or parts of women (or men, if one is homosexual) was old hat in the world of senryu But, while *ategaki* might also be apt for clitoral masturbation, it definitely did not cover dildos because *k/gaki* is a superficial stroking or *scratching*. A clever *Leaf* senryu invented a new term (until I find an earlier instance), *ate-ire,* or "targeted insertion," just to squeeze in that dildo!

似顔絵であて入れをする長局
nigaoe de ateire o suru nagatsubone 葉6
(resemble-face-with aim-insert-do chambermaid)

staring at an actor print
the harem chambermaid
inserts her dildo trans. solt

an actor's likeness
for the chamber-maid's
targeted insertion

Solt's translation captures the action perfectly, and Screech's *"Using a 'likeness picture' / She sticks it in / The serving woman"* serves to bring out the fact that pictures were *used* – a well-made point in his book, *Sex and the Floating World*, is that hard *or soft* (clothed) pictures could be *used* for masturbation – but neither of these previous translations caught the wit, which in senryu, is to say the poet's intent. It is, of course, the invention of that *new term*. As there is no TM to indicate it is new, one must waste a lot of time on senryu to catch it (Syunroan explains, but because of my familiarity with ategaki, I had cracked it on my own!) Screech also opines that a dildo *or* fingers could be stuck in. *The words by themselves could allow it*, but I have yet to find a single *nagatsubone* who used her fingers. For *that* you need an ordinary maidservant, a *gejo,* not one who wears fine clothing in a palace! There is no intrinsic reason why a *nagatsubone* could not use her fingers. It is just that *senryu is stereotype*. There is a semiology of senryu as of painting. Mere guessing won't do. In senryu, the dirty-minded wet-nurse or maidservant are usually the only women who got excited from looking at spring-prints, *i.e.* hard porn.

The likeness pictures in question generally show actors beautifully clothed and focus on their facial expression. I see this as the pictorial equivalent of the romantic novel, which most women prefer to, say, *The Pearl* or, for that matter the erotica of their own Anäis Nin. Having written this, I found two fascinating exceptions in Timon Screech's book. *First*, Illustration 105, an 1826 print (宝合わせ) by Utagawa Kunisada shows likenesses of two famous actors, together with supposed likenesses of their erect penises!. In the 1980's and 90's, Japanese male writers filled tabloids with details of the pudenda (from pubes to inner reaches of the vagina) of actresses and singers, so in one sense, it would seem little has changed – faces and genitals are still being matched – but, a *man's* privates! This I had not seen before. Could the chambermaids have had the romantic face *cum* cock to gaze upon?(!) *Second*, and particularly apropos of the subject of this eddy, the third illustration in his book shows a man ejaculating *upon a picture* of a courtesan hung on the wall besides which he is seated. That in itself is only interesting because the courtesan seems to be completely clothed, and the man seems too old to get turned on so easily – but when taken together with that word, aimed-stroking (*ategaki*), which appears well before the date of the painting (c.1830), we have a target that is supposed to be in the mind (purely from memory or with the aid of a picture), taken literally. Near the end of his book (between illus 141 and 142), Screech comes back to this print, or rather, illustration for a book of dirty pictures by Teikin, because of its title, Production (作業) and what was written with it:

> every drop of semen is the seed of a child, and you must sow it in the good furrow of women to reap a bountiful reward of offspring." (Screech:1999)

Screech notes that by 1800, "ten percent of the entire shogunal expenditure went on assistance to increase childbirth," and that "with fears of depopulation came changes to the acceptability of masturbation, which newly became an instance of waste." If I ever have the opportunity to read the post volume-24 Willow in order, this move from a masturbation-friendly to masturbation-unfriendly society is something I must look for!

.

男湯を女ののぞくきうな用 3-26
otoko yu e onna no nozoku kyû na yô

a woman peeks
into the male bath
an emergency

Men peek because they are turned on, but women . . . Biological and cultural influences are so closely entwined and researchers carry so many chips on their shoulders that, unless I am mistaken, we have yet to comprehend the extent of sexual similarity/difference in visual turn-ons (or turn-offs). This means scientific experiments first of all but hints for those experiments may be found throughout our cultures. Senryu suggests possible experiments by exploring countless by-roads of "looking." Here is one more –

一弐まひ見りや直キおえるしよじやく也 万 天元
ichi ni mai miri ya jiki oeru jojaku (女若) *nari*

the ones erect
after just a page or two
love boys & girls

Is it possible that bi-sexuals are quicker to react to pictures? I would guess this is bunk, but the Kinsey Institute or someone could test it out.

> Most art historians are unwilling to make statements about the history of sexuality, and in any case they seldom concern themselves with *use* at all, and when that use is masturbation, they wish to proffer nothing. Shunga have become 'art' and their context has contracted to that which academe allows for artistic genres . . .

A friend told me of Screech's book which arrived only a day or two before I was ready to call it quits and paginate. His attention to the *uses* of dirty pictures as a clean subject for research – not to mention his attention to senryu ("they are hugely useful for evidence of sexual mores and will be cited repeatedly") – was long overdue. So, I had to read and comment. This book got delayed by a week and lengthened by, maybe a dozen pages, for which you are paying a dollar more for this book (Thanks a lot, Laura!)

~~~~~~

2. *Sex as Masturbation & Kuroki Kaoru*. By turning her long underarm hair into trademark obscenity, this unabashed porn-star helped ridicule the government censors' into liberating pubic hair. I do not know how much of her thought is hers and how much her beloved producer, 村西監督 but her talk and books are refreshing. Another translation of the statement quoted in this chapter:

"You know, we could just call coitus 'masturbation for two'."

(「セックスも『二人オナニー』という表現ができるわけですよね」とは、「常に『主張するヴァギナ』でありたい」と云う＝黒木香『フルーツ白書』ワニブックス 1987)。　英訳不可能のおまけに、もう壱つ：「作品を生むということ。これは一種のマスターベーションではないでしょうか。小説家の方ですと、マスを埋めながらマスをかく——　と。」（同）

~~~~~~

Alternate to "A Thousand Strokes." One senryu suggests that a reason the Asagiura hick samurai thought of the literal meaning of a thousand strokes might be that it was not the common term in the outskirts of greater Edo where he came from: *"Gotôchi's thousand strokes in my country is called hand-cunt* (*te-bobo*)" 御富地のせんずり國の手ぼぼじゃて　葉 二八 *gotôchi no senzuri kuni no tebobo jate*).

~~~~~~

Dildo Details. Do you recall *"Our lady in waiting / flushes when the water / fools her"* (湯加減がよくてのぼせる長局 pg 70)? Here is the best machine translation can do c it:

> Having become shape of the tube, pouring the hot water, you call Hari[swollen/phallic] shape that it used. Therefore, *'hot water allowance* [temperature/adjustment] *being good, the long bureau* ["lady in waiting"] *which is dizzy* [giddy/excited]*'*, long bureau doing, the long hot water in the sense that you were dizzy. If only you were dizzy at the long hot water, it does not become Senryu. It is allowance of the hot water which was inserted in the Hari shape to which hot water allowance is plugged and 'the cow'[ox] is possible in angle of the water buffalo.

Even with the explanation fore and aft and my assistance in brackets, it is hopeless, isn't it! A very loose translation was the only way to make sense of it. The horns are said to be shaven thin enough that they give like flesh when properly moistened and warmed. The cavity was filled with absorbent cotton, to create the proper pressure and "skin" temperature. With some fine horn dildos, the warm liquid absorbed by the cotton, could, if I understand correctly, ejaculate through a hole when squeezed. Evidently, it was not easy to learn just how long and at what temperature to soak the horn inside and out to prepare a heavenly dildo. While ox, i.e. water-buffalo horn was better than *wood*, there was another material that had the fleshy give of the horn *and* even smoother skin, yet was easier to prepare: *"A chamber maid / with the ways and means / rides a turtle"* (長局くめんのいいのは亀に乗り *nagatsubone kumen no ii no wa kame ni nori*). Yep, tortoise-shell.

~~~~~~

Two Styles. The senryu I translated "*my joyful son, / his fontanel throbbing, / regurgitates*" (pg 77) and the long paragraph following it, were presented by Solt *sans* explanation as follows: '"*his thrilled cock in spasms / like a baby / upchucks a bit*" (1996). Because the words of the original are less difficult than "fontanel," my translation is stylistically wrong, while Solt's, which reads better, is right. From what hat in his brain did he pull that marvelous *upchuck* out of? But, by explaining about "son" meaning *penis*, I convey *information* some readers may enjoy knowing, and by using *fontanel*, though a difficult word in English, I share with readers the fine perception of the poet, thus showing what extraordinary sensitivity (?) may be found in crude subject matter. *Translation is a matter of aim.* Most translators choose to maximize information or optimize style. My aim changes depending on the poem and context in which I give it.

~~~~~~

Devil's Tongue (Konnyaku/Konjak/Elephant-Foot Taro) in 20c Cartoons I Saved. Most readers have probably see a bit of Japanese *manga*, but it is only one variety of what is out there. On the train returning from work, I preferred short 4-frame black humor often oddly and even poorly drawn – for they were printed or not printed on the basis of their wit – to those pretty (if you like huge eyes, etc) novelettes. This is the first time I have put that research to work. I hope you will not find something contemporary too vulgar! I will spare you the images, but if I do not report on *konjaking off,* who will?

1) Illustrations of the best way to prepare a bar of *konjak* for action, followed by a picture plus mimetic sound-track of an ugly chubby boy using it (*zuko-zuko korya, ehwai! zuko-zuko*), who gives it a name and kisses his "Rumi" (a Japanese girl's name) good night!

2) A couple takes an afternoon bath on a hot, smuggy day. Getting a beer from the fridge, he sees a piece of konjak and goes to it. She comes out of the bathroom and he gets bonked over the head by what looks like a proverbial rolling pin.
~~~~~~

3) An old man enters a "love hotel" with a young woman, and dies in the saddle so to speak. The next frame shows a pimply young man in a cheap apartment dead on a slab of *konjak*, discovered by his older sister who coldly declares *"that type of younger brother is the pits."*

4) A man with a 20-year *konjak history* (コンニャク愛好歴２０年) meets a woman who has enjoyed *baibu*, vibrators, for 15. So they try "swapping." As they go to it in the foreground, a vibrator and slab of konjaku pleasure each other in the background

5) Two young men discuss *pasokon*. One says they are great for playing with and the other agrees, assuming *pasokon* means the usual thing, "personal computer." Soon the other man finds out (graphically), to his horror, the other meant "personal *konjaku*."

6) Less a cartoon per se than illustration for an advertisement thinly disguised as an article. A *sopurando* (called *toruko* until the Turks complained), *i.e.*, *soapland* (massage parlor) girl shows how she uses *konjaku* for *sumata-purei* 素股プレイ "bare-crotch-play," letting her client penetrate a slit in the bar which she squeezes between her thighs (you see her – not just cartoons – a tel.#, hours and prices. Unbelievably, the ad claims the *sopurando* employs "a konnyaku craftsman who has created work as fine as *herring-row ceilings* and a *thousand-worms* (names for vagina to die for), with names like *"The Narrow Road to the Interior"* (Bashô's most famous work) or 奥飛馬＋蝉五条.

7) A pretty girl *ninja* rides up to an ugly male *ninja* on a giant slug. He tries salt on it to no avail, then, *Eureka!* He cuts a slit in the slug and goes to it. As he pumps away in the final scene he cries *"It's konjak! Konjak! konnyaku da!* (x2) The girl *ninja* in the background looks dejected, *"Oh, no! I was planning to eat it later!"* (It is very tempting to translate the *konnyaku* as "devil's tongue" in such cases!)

~~~~~~

Konjak and Poets. Issa offered a block or lump of *konjak* to Bashô on his deathday (anniversary). He recognized Bashô's Taoist orientation, his love for this representative *non-food.* Some today take pride in the fact that only the Japanese *choose* to eat this relatively flavorless starch that is hard to prepare. I like to imagine Bashô ridding himself of excess sand, exorcising the dirt of existence before departing for the ultimate New World. Sincerely enacted, even a folk superstition born of mistranslation from the past can be as significant, as sacred, as high liturgy. Whereas others used the devil's tongue to exorcise their bowels and balls, Bashô let it clean his soul.

~~~~~~

From a Machine Translation of an article on senryu + dildo, so poor the font is reduced.

> Long bureau [lady-in-waiting] drinking the liquor with the hot sake, in the sense that it has become drunk. You call to the advanced part of these Hari [dildo] shapes the woman rapture circle . . . long bureau of the shogunate harem, in order to be sung to this much in Senryu, you probably use Hari shape actively? Therefore "as for the upper curvature when value does Harima, the extent which is the phrase, notion store", [←a senryu about an upward curving phallus costing more] as for long bureau bought Hari shape secretly, it is thought. And, the hot water was poured, with "the turtle" and "the cow" etc nighttime stealthily it probably consoles the self? "The cow" and "the turtle" probably use inserting there, but in that case, stimulus to the bean clogging clitoris it probably is the finger? "The bean" says that it was the code word which points to the woman shade [her sex], but from the point of view of form, it is thought as the thing which pointed to the clitoris. There is also a phrase that "the son [penis, it should be the subject=eater!] you eat even with the bean of the current horse [the menses] which comes". It is the phrase which the form of the help flat young husband who carries out bloody kunniringusu[cunnilingus] vis-à-vis the new wife makes closely resembling. [the newly-weds introduced in the menses chapter].

I have been told not to waste space for things like this, but feel compelled to show non-translators how much more intelligent translators are than software.

~~~~~~

Dildo Vocabulary. In Burton's notes to *The Nights,* he mentions Chinese practices. " . . . the French *godemiché*(?) and the Italians *passatempo* and *diletto* (whence our "dildo"), every kind abounds, varying from a stuffed "French letter" to a cone of ribbed horn
~~~~~~

which looks like an instrument of torture." His *words* interest me. *Diletto* sounds like a dull stiletto, but the best by far is the understated *passatempo, i.e., time-passer* of the Italians! And Burton adds "*For the use of men they have the "merkin,"[FN#410] a heart-shaped article of thin skin stuffed with cotton and slit with an artificial vagina: two tapes at the top and one below lash it to the back of a chair.*" Japan is part of the Sinosphere, but chairs were not in use, so that was one *merkin* no Japanese ever used for jerkin'.

Dildo Poems in English. The idea of dildo-in-the-service-of-morality is found in The *Dildoides* of Samuel Butler in Hudibras (1672). First, he notes the potential for equality for those born small (suggesting an artificial enlargement rather than dildo proper), then notes a parallel: "*For Souldiers maim'd in chance of War / We artificial Limbs prepare;/ Why then should we bear such a Spight /To Lechers hurt in am'rous Fight*" (infected with the pox). And, he notes how they may protect the honor of widows:

Did not a Lady of Great Honour
Marry a Footman waiting on her?
Were one on these, timely apply'd
It had eased her Lust and saved her Pride

Though the defender of the dildo concluded, *"I therefore hold it very foolish / Things so convenient to abolish,"* the prosecutor won, as he spoke last and, in reality, a load of imported dildos were "burnt without Mercy" in Feb. 1671. Burford's *Bawdy Verse* is full of dildo poems, starting with Nashe's which includes these memorable lines:

Poor Priapus, thy kingdom needs must fall
Except thou thrust this weakling to the wall.

The Dildo That Was Not. I hate to embarrass a translator and friend, but if you, reading about erotic things Japanese, came across the *dildo* on the left below, take care –

.

肥後ずいきすばこの虫のやうに出シ 葉七又摘 3-15
higo-zuiki subako no mushi no yô ni dashi pluck / leaf
(higo-tarostem tapeworm-like-as removing)

the dildo from Higo *is pulled out* *like a tapeworm*	*Higo zuiki –* *You pull it out* *like a tapeworm*	*Higo armor –* *After the battle, behold,* *a tapeworm!*

– *for there is no such dildo.* A *higo-zuiki* is a long ribbon of vegetable fiber – Taro stems from Higo, down in Kyushu – wrapped neatly down a man's penis and back up where it is tied with a bow-tie. One *Pluck* senryu specifies 7 wraps around beyond which the head (glans) sticks out (肥後芋茎七巻まいてつらを出し 摘 1-8 *higo zuiki nana-maki maite tsura o dashi*). The idea is to thicken the penis and give it some ribs the better to tickle a big woman). It often came off during intercourse and had to be fished out (for a fun illus., see Poul Gerhard: *Pornography or Art* 1968/71). Maybe we could call it "Higo *armor"* though it is not so solid as the *tasuke-bune,* life-saving boats, which is to say dildo-like devices men could wear over their penises. Except for the wrong "dildo," the translation on the left is closer to the original than mine. Also, I would guess the inspiration for the *ku* was yet another earlier one in *Pluck*, from where the tapeworm *ku* was pinched by *Leaf:*

名玉はしりをたゝくところげ出る
mei-tama wa shiri o tataku to koroge deru pluck 1-30

the famous balls
you smack her behind
and out they roll

These smooth hollow metal balls called *rin no tama* had bits of quicksilver and other metal fragments within that clinked or I imagine sometimes jingled when the ball warmed up within the woman. Because of that one might think the *rin* the *rin* for bell 鈴 but it is not. The name 琳の玉 came from China with it. The *ku* above has plagiarized actual instructions. Needless to say, the Higo armor would not come with instructions comparing the product to a tapeworm. While we are on *rin no tama,* however, let me give you one more exceptionally astute *ku:*

りんの玉どっちの為か知れぬ也 35
rin-no-tama do'chi no tame ka shirenu nari

the jingle balls
who can tell which one
gets the benefit?

rin no tama
the unknown is this:
whose bliss?

Besides sound, these balls delight by erratic movement due to having irregularly shaped smaller balls solid, or with mercury, within the hollow balls you see, so I assumed they were a masturbatory device for women, pure and simple. Even reading the most common *ku* cited on the subject is: *"Rin no Tama: / Wives will not quickly / give their consent"* (りんの玉女房急には承知せず摘二 *rin-no-tama nyôbô kyû ni wa shôchi sezu*) only made me assume the men liked to see their wives auto-excite. What the above *ku* reveals is that these balls were also meant to stimulate the men who poked broad vagina. Or, writes Sasama, "a man might just want to experience the new sensation though I must admit to not feeling so drawn, perhaps due to a deficient curiosity."

> "Those *rin no tama* I've heard about – were they for a woman's pleasure or for a man's?"

Only days after writing the above, I found the above in Liza Dalby's *Geisha* (University of California Press: 1998) which I have been reading on and off for almost a year. Her description beats mine. First, the size is "a little larger than a quail's egg." Then, this, on the *effect:*

> Nestled deep within the vagina, the *rin no tama* moves when a woman does, not exciting great waves of pleasure exactly, but making her aware of that part of her body. "You know, I tried it once, " said Futami, "and it was no big deal. It made me giggle every time I felt the 'clink.' My guess is that it is really for the man's pleasure. A man would probably get a kick out of that little clink every time he entered."

This is followed by a story about *kumquats* which you will have to buy the book to read, but what fascinates me is how this question about *rin no tama* was still floating around almost two hundred years after the senryu wondered.

~~~~~~

Bath Erections. Today, the water is scalding hot: erections are unlikely. At the time the senryu were composed, that was generally not true. Another *ku* from about the same time:

おやかしてなへる迄居ル風呂の内 万 明八
oyakashite naeru made iru furo no uchi million
(erecting/ed wither/droop until be/stay bath inside)

growing hard
he's stuck until it falls
in the bath

his erection
must go before he can
leave the bath
~~~~~~

五 5

鼻の落度
Losing Nose

~~~~~~

たかの名におはなおちよハきつい事 摘
taka no na ni ohana ochiyo wa kitsui koto 1-24
(hawks[street-walkers' names-as hon.-flower[=nose]
hon.1000-eras[=drop-will]-as-for tough thing)

a bad joke

street-walker names
like sherri or rose: try to enjoy them
without your nose!

flowery names
for old whores say your nose
is next to blow!

It's easy enough to translate the "[night-]hawks," as street-walkers, but name puns are indeed *kitsui*, tough! I could not re-create the Japanese, which takes two common street-walker names meaning "flower" and "thousand-ages" and puts them together to get a homophonic phrase meaning *your honorable nose falls off*, which is to say, you contract the disease the Portuguese brought from Africa or the Americas, or Africa, probably via Europe to Japan, syphilis.

川岸へ出る河童は鼻を抜きたがり
kawagishi e deru kappa wa hana o nukitagari
(river-bank-to appearing kappa-as-for noses remove-wanting)

among kappa
who cruise the land
noses are an item
in big demand

~~~~~~

river-bank kappa

are those
who itch for
your nose

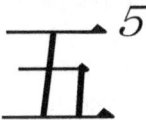

Kappa rank right next to the thunder demons as Japan's most interesting supernatural creature. They are generally depicted as bird-beaked, web-footed, turtle-carapaced yet sometimes finned humanoids with (since the 19c) a depression on the head where they balance water when they emerge from ponds or rivers. They were said to drown or cause people to waste away by stealing their butt-gem (尻子玉), perhaps the sphincter, as macaroni-shaped gems once were strung up, and because it seems appropriate for something said to live under vortexes to pull the plug on their victim, and because of the parallel with thunder demons who went for navels which, when you think of it, also mark the end of tubes!

鼻塚も築べき程に鷹はやり 22 &
hanazuka mo tsuku beki hodo ni taka hayari 94-11
(nose-mound even make-ought/could amount hawk popular[v.])

that night-hawk
so popular, she could make
a nose-mound!

When Hideyoshi attempted to conquer China through Korea (late-16c) and destroy potential domestic competition by forcing the powerful Christian states in the South to take the lead in the invasion, he created a bloodbath. Most Japanese do not know as much about that history as they should – as Usanians do not know about what Mexicans call *La Guerra de la Injustia* – but everyone knows about the mounds made from ears and noses brought back for the body count. The night-hawk referred to might be "One-year Oshun" ("Hitotose-oshun") so named for reputedly putting down 360 men one New Year's night over a century after Hideyoshi's death, in the reign of the dog-loving 8th Shôgun Yoshitsune. Impossible, according to Sasama, who gives statistics about war-time sex-slaves (sometimes so busy they ate and peed in bed!) showing 50 men/day was about the limit. He guesses One-*year* Oshin serviced 12 men that night, one for each *month* of the year. Be that as it may, there were certainly "rush-hours" in the trade, where whores would rush from customer/cubicle to customer/cubicle, splashing their *bobos* with water enroute. Such partitioned shops and the whores who worked in them, were called (*kirimise*), literally "cut-shops." An older, less interesting *ku* fails to take it all the way to the noses: *"That girl turns / so many tricks she could make / a mound of pricks!* (まら塚を築べき程な流行ッ子　葉十 *marazuka o tsuku-beki hodo na hayari'ko*) It may play on the *cut* in the name of her place of work. I will change that name, also was used for the girls, to improve the next translation:

切見世ハたんぶ迄うたがハれ 1-36
kirimise wa tankobu made utagaware

c a cut-rate
even bumps are thought
to be cankers

Most men found such conditions revolting. As always, we have an exception. Hick samurai called Asagiura were undaunted by filth. They reveled in it:

~~ひつしよなくされてもかゝる浅黄うら 摘 2 28~~
~~*hissho na [hissô na?] kusarete mo kakaru asagiura*~~
~~[correction: hisshonaku sarete mo kakaru asagiura]~~

~~*asagiura*~~
~~*don't blink at whores*~~
~~*who stink*~~

~~*asagiura*~~
~~*even the rotten ones*~~
~~*turn 'em on*~~

~~[correction: treated roughly / those asagiura still / keep coming]~~

~~A more accurate reading would have them "go for the *wretchedly rotten* [ones]:" My use of the unexpected meaning of "blink" saved the above senryu, but neither it nor most Asagiura senryu I have seen are worth saving. Only teenage boys would appreciate these yahoos who like going down — in Japanese, *making tongue puppets* (*shita-ningyô* 舌人形) — on night-hawks, cum in bordello waiting rooms, step on dog shit while engrossed in watching them mating, etc. (pg.417).~~

鉄砲の疵年を経て鼻に抜け
teppô no kizu toshi o hete hana ni nuke

the musket bruise
years later made its way
out of his nose

the musket bruise
spread so in time he paid
through the nose

Another name for disease-ridden cheap whores was *muskets*. It is hard to say if it was because if you were not careful they could blow up in your face or just that they were deadly and could kill at a distance, if not in feet, in years. As odd as it sounds, Japanese shot with the butt of the gun straight in front of them rather than on the shoulder, so it is no wonder that there was injury from the recoil. What I find amazing here is that the expression "paying through the nose" should work so well in translation. Most musket-whore *ku* translate poorly because they play on the *tama=bullet=ball=gem=beauty* homophones (eg. いい玉で鉄砲見世はどんと当て *ii tama de teppô mise wa don to ate*). Still, I am no fan of these *ku* even in the original language; so long as you want a metaphor, *go all the way*, like the English poets, with their street-walkers-as-*man-o-war*, *i.e.* battleship hyperbole! The idea of women wanting to spread disease = take male noses = is itself ludicrous. But, it is understandable. We laugh at what we fear, and Japanese, of all people, valued their noses. Nose size and class were closely correlated. The nose was thought indicative of a man's *fortune* (See *Topsy-turvy 1585,* item #1-4) as well as *natural endowment!* I learned of the former from a friend whose mother told fortunes (she sent me a book, too) and the latter, a commonplace, from hearing it in conversation and seeing it in cartoons. Senryu did not miss it:

見合い互いに気をつける鼻と口 138-11
miai tagai ni ki o tsukeru hana to kuchi

the marriage-match
couples sizing up each other's
nose and mouth

marriage matches
the noses and mouths sizing
each other up

A Japanese match-marriage was usually not forced. At the first meeting, the couple looked each other over, talked, then, separately, gave their opinions about continuing to the match-maker. An earlier *ku*, *"The bridegroom's nose is not to the taste=mouth of the bride"* (花嫁の口に似合わぬ聟の鼻 万安八 *hanayome no kuchi ni niawanu muko no hana*), though better than the above *ku* in Japanese, will not English for lack of a way to express *taste* with the word "mouth." Needless to say, that mouth represented the female part, as the nose did the male's (因みに A Japanese gynecologist 滋賀医大の笠井先生 measured 3,200 women and reported *no* correlation).

馬のはなもちっと大キそうなもの 万安八
uma no hana mo chitto ôkisô na mono 1779
(horse's nose also somewhat large-seeming thing)

a horse's nose
when you think about it is
pretty big, too!

a horse's nose
is also a pretty damn
large thing

a horse's nose
is itself pretty
damn big

This *ku* draws our attention to the horse's large nose *and* provides confirmation of the nose-penis linkage. Even today Japanese express sexual excitement in cartoons by showing youths *spouting blood* out their nostrils like harpooned whales. The phenomenon is even found on T.V.. No actual blood, mind you. A male comic might accent the effect of a low-angle shot of a beauty in a bikini, or whatever, by turning to the camera with big wads of tissue stuck in his nostrils!

日本人喧嘩腰でも己指す 敬愚

a pushy japanese
pointing at himself
instead of you

Japanese rarely point at others, but they belong to a minority of people who indicate themselves, not by touching or thumping gorilla-like on the chest, but by pointing an index finger near or on the tip of their nose. The *ku* is mine, *ad hoc*.

~~~~~~

四ツ目やの本家ははなをおやしてる
yotsumeya no honka wa hana o oyashiteru

at the home office
of the four-eyes, they
erect their noses

先づ鼻をはなせと天狗喧嘩分け 105-15
mazu hana o hanase to tengu kenka-wake

"first let go of
my nose!" breaking up
a tengu fight

The Four-eye/s is a knot that serves as an emblem and eyeglasses have nothing to do with the shop. It sold aphrodisiacs and potency creams of which "long-life-*maru*" was most famous. A conflation of the desire for a long-lasting erection and the longevity sought by esoteric discipline may explain why the red-faced mountain wizards with long noses that jut straight out from the face – so much so
~~~~~~

that masks of *tengu* are sometimes depicted in use as dildos – became the company emblem. Such a large mask was found on the front of the headquarters.

鼻ハともあれへのこをばたすける気　摘
hana wa to mo are henoko o ba tasukeru-ki 3-17
(nose-as-for however pecker[acc+emph.] help-feeling)

come whatever
happens to his nose, he will
treat his pecker

his nose is the one
who runs a risk to help
pleasure his prick

Most poor men, which meant most men in the world, have always – for centuries, at any rate – been forced to chose between no sex other than masturbation, or dangerous sex. And, in Edo, where men outnumbered women 2 or 3 to 1 and the lion's share of these women went to those wealthy enough to keep more than one (and that includes maids), the odds of getting free, safe sex were exceptionally low. Bright men, terrified of venereal disease, generally choose the former (there is even a book on onanism in Japan 木本屋『オナニーと日本人』インタナル出版昭和五一) until they made enough money to marry. My first translation has two readings, an ambiguity found in the original. The man is either treating himself to a whore, taking a chance with his nose – as my second translation poeticizes – or will take a painful course of treatment to help his pecker though he knows his nose will still end up in the nose mound. I also wonder if "helping" – which could be "saving" – the pecker at the expense of the nose could also refer to side-effects from treatment with heavy metals that could save the genitals but speed the destruction of the features. When Swift, in *The Progress Of Beauty*, writes *"When Mercury her Tresses mows / To think of Oyl and Soot, is vain, / No Painting can restore a Nose, / Nor will her Teeth return again,"* he refers not only to venereal disease, but to the mercury in the white powder used for makeup.

すっぱりと治りましたと鼻が落ち 16
suppari to naorimashita to hana ga ochi -16

cured and clean
as a whistle, then, off
drops 'is nose!

cured and clean
as a pipe, then, cough! and
'is nose blows off

せめて鼻ならバまだしもへのこ落 玉川初代
semete hana naraba madashimo henoko ochi

if only it were
just the noss . . . cough again
& his cock falls off

his nose sorely
missed, yet now he's pissed
his cock is gone

his nose lost
but a man's still a man!
*then **it** fell off!*

I added the "cough" in a few of the readings to see if I could not lighten things up a bit. This is the stuff of nightmare (I only understood the true horror, and early onset of third-stage syphilis when I saw photos of Civil War soldiers suffering from it).

鼻が落ても萬物の霊 む十八
hana ga ochite mo banbutsu no rei

nose or no nose
the king of creation

Man as primate, the superior animal was found in the Sinosphere, too. At first, I imagined an epidemic of noselessness taken facetiously as a *lése majesty* to the entire human race, but on closer reading, the 7-7 *ku* either depicts a poor soul consoling himself for at least being human – gratitude for being born a man, just one step from Buddhahood, was something taught to all in the Sinosphere – or a noseless man mistreating a horse. Only finding the 5-7-5 *ku* before it would tell.

はなくたにからしがきいて大わらい
hanakuta ni karashi ga kiite ôwarai 41-5-9?

the wages of stupidity

people laugh aloud
to see how pepper gives his
rotten nose the smarts

This is cruel, but after coming up with "smarts," I could not resist adding the title.

よし田町皆ぞう兵の手にかゝり摘
yoshidachô mina zohei no te ni kakari 1-5

yoshidachô
everyone falls into the hands
of the irregulars

yoshida town
those irregulars will take
anybody down

If Yoshiwara, literally "lucky-*meadow*," was known for its luxurious, carefully orchestrated prostitution – no sex first visit – Yoshida, literally "lucky-*field/ paddy*" was a popular red zone. The military term is a nod toward the large number of men of the samurai class – none too wealthy at the time – living nearby, but the point is well-taken. A source I have misplaced explains: *"This Pure Land [a nickname for Yoshidachô] is no different from a harbor town. If they catch you when you are passing by, they won't let go even if thunder should ring out. It is a terrifying place."* I know most of my readers will find it hard to believe that men may be *forced*. But, anyone who has experienced such pressure, knows the writers do not exaggerate. In my early twenties, I was once dragged off a street on the edge of Texas Town (Seoul, Korea) by an extremely attractive woman and her friends. Having boxed, wrestled and practiced judo, I was not terrified, but because of my loneliness (no sex with anyone but myself in a year and three wet dreams in a single night – someone gave me ginseng wine – but days before!), I was tempted and barely came up with a non-violent defense, which was to pretend I had v.d.! *It worked.*

よし田丁女房かせぐをはなにかけ
yoshidachô nyôbô kasegu o hana ni kake 摘 2-28
(yoshidachô[place] wife/wives' earning[acc] nose-on-place/bet)

◎すいな事かな◎
It's the cool thing!

in yoshidachô
men bet their noses
on their wives' income!

in yoshidachô
men are damn proud
of their wives' income!

Yoshiwara's "courtesans," had few customers and were unmarried, while the free and busy prostitutes of Yoshida were often married. The above *ku* plays upon homophonic readings of the phrase involving the nose. A parody has the wife nose-proud of her earnings (吉田町かせぐをかかあ鼻にかけ 35-37 *yoshidachô kasegu*).

吉田町おおかた鼻は夏座敷 65
yoshidachô ôkata hana wa natsuzashiki -17
(yoshidachô most [people] nose-as-for summer-parlor)

lucky-field town
most folk boast noses like
summer parlors

In the summer, most houses in Japan open up between rooms and without to a degree only found on a carousel in the Occident. Symptoms of syphilis noted in Europe include eating away the *bridge* of the nose, but many Japanese had no obvious bridge to start with. The perforation of the membrane between the nostrils is what comes up most often: *"Even noses have empty shops in Yoshida-chô"*(鼻にまで明店のある吉田町 *hana ni made akidana no aru yoshidachô*). "Even" may imply the husbands are pimps and the shops just fronts for the real business. And, it is not just Lucky Town. *"The guardhouse at the crossroads where even noses lack shôji* (辻番は鼻の障子もないところ 56-32 *sujiban wa hana no shôji ga nai tokoro*). Crossroads guards were low-level police and stereotypically received favors from nighthawks. The guard and place are one word in the original, the *shôji* is a paper partition and the "even" indirectly describes the tiny guardhouse.

はなくたな下女おひやくろが出ぬといふ
hanakuta na gejo oiyakuro ga idenu to iu 摘 1-3
(nose-rot-maid [tooth]blacking-the appear-not says)

the noseless maid
says her tooth black just
won't come out!

the maid cries
her black won't come out
a rotten nose

If husbands could be infected by their wives, maids could be infected by their husbands who consorted with a prostitute during their long period away from home working in the city, or by their playboy masters. "Ohakuro" is the polite, woman's way to pronounce the *tooth blacking* married women once wore. Because of the maid's syphilitic nose, her pronunciation (*oiyakuro*) is a bit off. What does that have to do with the black on her teeth? We shall now see:

こふかへとおはうろ壺へぶらり出し 46-4
~~kô kae~~ kôka e to ohaguro tsubo e burari dashi

~~like this? how far?~~
~~he asks, dangling it into~~
~~the blacking jar~~

off to the w.c.
he into the blacking jar
dangling, pees

~~like this, my love?~~
~~he asks, dangling it into~~
~~the blacking tub~~

There were secret recipes and magical spells to make the black glossy; I read that one was to get a man to squat over the jar. I think that piece (lost) was wrong to cite this *ku* (hence the cross-out), but I know urine was one ingredient used to bring out the black in the largely iron wash and that male urine had special properties not found in female. The "solution" for the previous senryu is that the poor maid with a syphilitic nose cannot attract a man to help beautify her teeth!

世界一鼻毛天国日本万歳

Long Live Japan, Nostril Hair Superpower of the World!

Having read all the volumes of Frazer's *Golden Bough* – a hundred times more fun than Claude-Levi-Strauss – I thought nothing in Japan could possibly amaze me. I was wrong. Nothing prepared me for the literature of 鼻毛 *nose hair.*

もろもろの鼻毛あつまる神子の皃 52-4
moromoro no hanage atsumaru miko no kao

the eyes of miko
gathering hair from nostrils
of a multitude

watching miko
as they collect hair from
countless nostrils

A *miko* is a shrine maiden. Dressed in a pure white robe, she is in charge of handing out charms and exorcisms, reading fortunes and other such things which are best done – or, spiritually, most effective – if one can read the mind of the other party. In Japanese, trying to figure out what is on another's mind is called *reading* [their] *nose-hair*. Senryu using the expression are almost all about *mistresses*. Reading their master's nose-hair was said to be their job. I like this early-19c *ku* for being the exception and for making me recall another metaphorical connotation of hair (pronounced *ke*, not *kami*) as impure thought. Not finding more interesting nose-hair senryu, I will switch for a while to haiku.

月影や鼻毛のばして待ちぬらん 宗因 連歌
tsukikage ya hanage nobashite machinuran sôin (1604-82)

what moonshine!
i'll let my nose hair grow
while i'm waiting

Without locating this *ku* from a link-verse (perhaps easy had I access to the data bank the university-affiliated enjoy), I cannot explain it, but I like it all the same. The next, by Onitsura (1660-1738), a contemporary of Bashô's some prefer to the Master, himself, is both odder and easier to read: *"When moving / it plucked not a nose hair / the blooming plum"* (宿替に鼻毛もぬきぬ梅の花 鬼貫 *yadogae ni hanage mo nukinu ume no hana*). The *ku* probably celebrates a successful transplanting, for there was a legendary plum that flew to join its master. (in *The Fifth Season* &/or *Cherry Blossom Epiphany,* we have it grooming itself like a bird). Plum (Japanese flowering apricot) blossoms have long stamens which cast beautiful shadows in the early morning or evening sunlight. Before I read Onitsura's *ku* I wrote a number of *ku* on them myself. Unfortunately, *flower* and *nose* are not homophones in English, so stamens and nostril hair are perfect strangers.

老の春初鼻毛抜今からも 素堂 (1641-1716)
rô no haru hatsu-hanage nuku ima kara mo

an elder's spring
pulling my first nostril hair
on the first day

In Japan, the spring means the New Year, a fifth season beyond time for the re-creation of the world. Every year all is done for the first time. Haiku is full of *first this* and *thats*. Nostril hair, far from romantic, is loved by haiku poets, not as a figure of speech but as a reflection upon age and loneliness. My first awareness of its literary possibilities came from a nonfiction novel by Inoue Hisashi called *Katei-kôron* (Family Debate). The author, forced to surrender his place at the *kotatsu* (quilt-skirted table) to his wife and three daughters, sat alone at his desk, pulling out nostril hairs and arranging them in a row upon a piece of paper, his manuscript. Inoue has long since remarried, but I am stuck with that image.

いへばえに鼻毛植けり花の蘂 調和 1637
iebae ni hanage uekeri hana no shin chôwa -1715
(housefly/ies-to/by/for nose-hair plant/ing blossoms' stamen/s!)

nostril hairs
growing on houseflies?
dark stamens

do house-flies
transplant our nose hair
into flowers?

the house flies
plant hair in my nose
pollination

The post-position *ni* has too many possible readings so I cannot tie the poem together. But, knowing from experience that dust/pollen speeds growth of nostril hair I favor the poet blaming the flies for his itchy nose. それとも家栄えか?

秋の雲泪なそへそ鼻毛ぬき 不角 (1651-1743)
aki no kumo namida na soe so hanage nuki fukaku

autumn clouds
let's have no tears over
pulling nose hair

Haiku can be so damn difficult that a translator feels like pulling out his hair. I do not find nose hairs particularly painful to pull and fail to find any natural relationship between that and rain clouds in the Fall. I would guess that the allusion is to Bashô feeling his age while watching clouds in this season of shortening days and dying leaves. Nose hair growth is as much a mark of aging as white hair. Note the poets' longevity! (未解：雪の立山不二見西行 鼻毛ぬけ 杉良)

& Snot!

鼻屎を喰て禿は叱られる 103-10
hanaguso o kutte kaburo wa shikarareru

a *kaburo*
is scolded for eating
her snot

Pretty round-faced pre-teen girls dressed like dolls to play their bit-parts in the adult drama of the pleasure quarters helped courtesans with little chores. But dolls did not pick their noses. An earlier version (拾遺八編) has her *tied up* (*shibarareru*), instead.

鼻屎を何の気も無く丸めて見 122?
hanaguso o nan no ki mo naku marumete mi 32? 別

rolling snot
into a ball just to see
if you can

just for fun
trying to make a ball
out of snot

Snowball in slow motion? One wonders how far this has been pursued. Up to golfball size? Baseball size? Softball size? Beachball size? Is it in Guinness?

~ eddies ~

Another version of the first senryu of the chapter is *"With that face* / [+ the same puns] . . ." (あの顔でお花（鼻）お千代（落ちよ）はきついこと *ano kao de ohana ochiyo wa kitsui koto*). I have no source for it. An unrelated *ku* makes a fascinating aside on naming:

かわゆくもにくゝも無イといい名つけ 万 安四
kawayuku mo nikuku mo nai to ii na tsuke million

those neither
beauties nor dogs are given
good names

for the girls
neither good nor bad get
pretty names

Nose Value and Face Value in Japan. To merely say that in Japanese the features of a face are called its *"me-hana-dachi,"* or "eyes-nose-standing," does not communicate what this *means*. I learned on a boat to Japan over twenty years ago. I was twenty one. A young Japanese woman, 19 or 20, who had spent a year or so in the USA and Canada working as a maid, was on the same liner (President Wilson). She was not a beauty, but she was not bad-looking either. Or so *I* thought. *She* was convinced another Japanese woman who – if you ask me was not half as cute as she was – was *much* better looking. "Why?' I asked, genuinely surprised. Her answer was, "She has a high nose!" My friend, like most Japanese from farm or low-class roots at the time was bridgeless. Despite the fact that the overall configuration of her face was pleasant enough that she had little to complain about, as far as she was concerned, a beak was the thing. She told me about pulling on her nose and singing a song in order to make it grow. It never did.

~~~~~~

Partition-Store Whores At Work. Full disclosure: My first sexual experience was in such a cubicle on my sixteenth birthday in Mexico.

切見世の押売り開をなすり附け 葉4
kirimise no oshiuri kai o nasuri-tsuke

pussy pushing
cubicle cuties just
rub it into you

穴端でおいで／＼は下湯の手
anabata de oide oide wa shimoyu no te 165
(hole-bank-at come, come!-as-for under-warm-water-hand)

by the hole-side
come over! come over! c
her low yu hand

her hand dripping
warm water, come here
dear, come here!

切店ハ洗ひさらしの開を売 葉26
kirimise wa araisarashi no bobo o uri

cubicle district
here they sell you freshly
washed pussy

cubicle shops
where they sell you pussy
freshly washed

The *anabata,* or hole-bank/edge, means the place where *"below-yu"* – *yu* being something English lacks a word for, warm-water, was used to douche after sex. It was thought to have some prophylactic value. *Hole-side/edge* also alludes to the danger involved, because the term is usually associated with being one foot in the grave. The lively language (which I cannot match) proves that not all late-period *Willow ku* (165 is the pen-penultimate volume) were so moribund as is often claimed. In the last *ku*, playful when you think of how 'freshly washed' usually makes you feel about something, no "district" is mentioned, but such establishments are generally not alone and I don't care for "store/shop/s." A c.1980 memory, too, of posters for various clubs/bars/joints in the blue-collar districts of Tokyo: *fureshu giyaru* (Fresh girls)! Forgive my "cubicle cuties," for the first *ku,* but I thought *kirimise* girls were young and pretty (unlike the night-hawks) until reading that the famously horrid *gojû-sô*, whom I thought were prostitutes in their fifties were named for their market value which was *fifty* (let's say *cents*) a shot and that they were the lowest type of prostitute within the ranks of the *kirimise.*
~~~~~~

なまおへなのをつつばめる五十ぞう 摘
nama-oe na no o tsutsubameru gojûzô 1-34

a fifty-rate
cramming them in
half-erect

五十そう引キつり込んでかぎをかけ 万
gojûzô hiki-tsuri-konde kagi o kake 明七

a fifty-rate
drags them in and
locks the door

One can imagine that not a few noses were lost for very little pleasure. But, I had a very good experience and the young doctor! who took me (he had just finished his year of social service – which doctors in Usania might benefit by), later that day gave me my next birthday present, a prescription for a shot of Penicillin, which he injected in my *gluteus maximus* just to be safe. And that is why I still have *my* nose to this day.

~~~~~~

Tooth Blacking. In *Topsy-turvy 1585* item 2-16 (2004), after giving the reactions to blacking by centuries of astounded European visitors, I hypothesized that black teeth might enhance the erotic appeal of women by making them less threatening or increasing the mimicry of the nether and upper mouths. Today, April 1, 2007, I encountered a new theory in a new book just received from its author, Liza Dalby: *East Wind Melts the Ice*.

> Geisha today may be the only women left in Japan today who still paint their faces white. When my geisha sister did my makeup for the first time, she warned me to cover my mouth when I smiled. I thought she was giving me a lesson in female etiquette. I forgot her advice, and when I saw a photograph of myself, teeth bared in a smile, I was horrified. Suddenly I understood – with skin painted matte white, one's teeth cannot help but look dingy yellow in contrast. (University of California Press: 2007)

I would not have come up with that in a thousand years. From this experience, Dalby deduced that Heian era women would have blackened their teeth to save their red, white and black aesthetics from "distracting yellow." I hope some reviewer noted this simple yet stunningly significant – for all interested in color psychology – discovery!

~~~~~~

Blacking Magic. Thunberg, in the 18c, recorded that not only iron filings and vinegar but "urine and sake" were used for ingredients. Perhaps urine of men had ingredients not found in that of women which could help explain the need for a man's contribution for ideal tooth black. But, we must take the senryu with a grain of salt. One can no more say what percentage of women in Edo actually enlisted men to help with their blacking than we can say what percent of women in San Paolo give men coffee filtered through their panties to make them fall in love.

~~~~~~

Lost and Found Nose. This is not a Japanese story. It is related by a 16c Italian "vendor of secrets," a type of writer that played an important role in the evolution of open modern science from its secretive past. "A Spanish gentleman named Signer Andres Gutiero, twenty-nine years of age, was strolling through the camp one day and came to words with a soldier. They drew weapons and with a backhand stroke the soldier cut off Signor Andre's nose, which fell in the sand, and i saw it because we were together. The quarrel ended, and the poor gentleman remained without a nose. So holding it in my hand, all full of sand, I pissed on it, and having washed it with urine I attached it to him and sewed it on very firmly, medicated it with balsam, and bandaged it. And I had him remain with it thus for eight days, believing the nose was gong to rot. However when I untied it I found it was very well attached again. I medicated it only once more and it was healthy and free, and all Naples marveled at it." (from William Eamon: *Science and the Secrets of Nature* Princeton 1994) Here, piss, which is generally treated as *pollution*, has served the purpose of a crass but important form of *purification*: sterilization.
~~~~~~

Pine Mushrooms & High-Bobos
上反りの松茸と臍隣の上開

六[6]

凸と凹の鑑
㊤ – Ideal Members – *I*

~~~~~~

The vulgar taxonomists of Edo identified (or invented) countless types, and composed various rankings, of the genitals. One ideal characteristic was shared by both sexes: *height.* a "goose[glans]-high" (*karidaka*) "up-curve"(*uwazori*) was usually the top penis; an "up-opener/cunt," *jôkai,* or "high-attached/fix" (*uwa-tsuki*) the ideal vulva. Women first:

お妾は臍を去ること一二寸 摘
o-mekake wa heso o saru koto ichi ni sun 4-14
([hon]mistress-as-for navel[acc] depart thing one two inches)

the mistress's
is only an inch or two
from her navel

the paramour's
leaves her navel less
than two inches

his sweet mistress?
her qualification is an inch or
two from her navel

The impossibly close figure of one or two inches suggests 1), a man hopelessly in love with his mistress – if a crush can turn pockmarks into dimples (a Japanese proverb), could the perceived distance to the navel vary inversely to the intensity of the love? 2), a fool boasting to a buddy; 3), a husband rationalizing his "needs" to his wife by cruelly exaggerating the difference between her and the mistress; 4) a wife sarcastically quoting her husband, 5) or exaggerating something he said. The honorable/polite "o" prefixing "mistress" (mekake) suggests 1) with an ironic tone, or 4), 5), but it is hard to say.

広いこと臍のきわまで裂けている 摘 2-14
hiroi koto heso no giwa made sakete iru pluck
(wide thing: navel's shore/edge-until splitting is)

that *is* wide!
split clear to the edge
of the navel
~~~~~~

Was this poet tired of hearing "close to the navel" so often? Or, was it a picture that inspired him? While the world has focused on men with their fire-hydrant-sized cocks in *shunga-e,* or spring-pictures, some of the women are equally awesome sheelalagigs, cloven to the navel (as was the anus of a catamite in Martial). But that *ku* is the exception to the navel rhetoric of desirable closeness:

別段に臍に近いで売りつめぬ 再現
betsudan ni heso ni chikai de uritsumeru

so close to the navel
her customers too are a cut
above the rest

臍迄が遠い女郎は売り遠し 梅柳
heso made ga tôi jorô wa uridoshi 天保 2

her navel being
none too near, the whore
is far from busy

The first *ku* actually says she packs them in. Was *up* favored over *down* purely for psychological reasons? I think *not*. Few Japanese women have buttocks large enough to raise the vagina's angle above horizontal when lying flat with their legs straight. A high vulva would matter more than with a people where most women had built-in cushions to accomplish that (one could check for correlations here). Needless to say, an upper would not facilitate *rear* entry. As one epigram (not a poem in the original 臍の下お開低いのは尻から有) puts it,

Far from the button? Never mind!
Low cunts are good – from behind!

But, with courtesans or mistresses usually chosen for their faces, women better equipped for frontal sex had an advantage. Of course, if a woman raises her legs high enough she can always be up front. In an undated *laugh-tale* (笑話: humorous folk-tale), a newlywed on her first post-marital visit home tearfully confesses to her rustic mother about discovering she was a low-fix: "*Low, my arse!*" replies her feisty mother, *"The next time 'e tells ye so, just plug up ye ears with ye heels and that will be the end o' that!"* (『寄噺の尻馬』二, in *Cuntologia*). Still, a woman cannot be doing that all of the time and pillows are ponderous.

じれてへ事下タ反りに下がりぼぼ 葉四
jiretee koto shita-zori ni sagaribobo

a frustrating thing:
down-curve and low-cunt trying
to make ends meet!

"Down-curve" is not quite right. *Sori/zori* is taut no matter the direction of the arch. So the down-curve is not flaccid. Many cultures recognize *size,* which, to be sure, *does* matter. The *Kamasutra* wisely divided men and women into *hare, horse* and *elephant* and considered the implications for proper match-making. But, the state-of-the-art erotics of Edo Japan go beyond mere dimension: *Who would have thought to consider cunt angles and cock curves?* Since a down-bend would hit the G-spot better that an upbend if the coitus were from behind, the above *ku* would seem to have an unstated premise: *intercourse, unless otherwise stated, is frontal.* But does biology agree with culture on that norm?

色事の太刀は皇子も下へそり 失題折句
irogoto no tachi wa kôshi mo shita e sori 享保中 鈴
(color-thing[sex]/s' great-sword-as-for imperial-child even/also downwarp)

when it comes to
swords in bed, even a prince
warps down

imperial or not
the great sword welded in bed
bows its head

Unlike "our" Excalibur, the ceremonial "great sword" (*tachi*) was slightly curved. Hung horizontally from a sash, the concave side was up, *i.e.,* the ends were high, the middle low (see item # 1-25+ in *Topsy-turvy 1585*). Neither "warp" or "curve" is as tense as *sori,* which has no hint of flaccidity even when curving down. I thought of "arches," for no arch is weak unless broken, but "arches down" seemed *awkward.* This is brave *lèse-majesté* even for the tolerant Tokugawa – allowed, perhaps, out of kindness to the majority of men who either curve not, or curve slightly *down,* and might think, from all those pictures of upward soaring cocks, they alone had a problem. I suspect the inspiration for the *ku* was Emperor Shitakawa's down-curve in a Moronobu print (*Wakaku Bijin Asobi* in P. Rawson: 1968).

けつを拭きゃ糞を撫込む下り開 葉 15
ketsu o fukya kuso o nadekomu sagaribobo

wiping her ass
crap gets rubbed into
a down-cunt

Unlike the *down-curve* cock, the *down-cunt*, has at least two obvious disadvantages. This is one. Always wiping toward the anus can help prevent urinary tract infection of the down-cunt and her partner but, other things being equal, an up-cunt is naturally more hygienic. Cunnilingus is the other.

愛想に上開という女医者 摘
aisô ni jôkai to iu onna isha 4-4

the lady doctor
socializing, tells her
she's an upper

to be friendly
the doctress tells her
she's an upper

Perhaps the biggest question raised by themes such as the *uppers* and *downers* is: *How widespread are these concepts?* From senryu, one gets the feeling that everyone was aware of such things. If not, would a female gynecologist – to be blunt, abortionist – really *say* such a thing?

色キ道のかゞみにもなるへの子なり
iroki-michi no kagami ni mo naru henoko nari

the way of sex
and the cock that was both
mirror and rex

a mirror, it stood
cock-sure for the way of sex
its very paragon

Dôkyô of the huge cock's name (ch.1) literally means "way-mirror." In Japanese, "mirror" and "exemplar" are homophones (*kagami*). Despite all those Japanese prints with male members large enough to be divided among a dozen normal men, huge cocks were not highly ranked. They were thought so hard on a woman she might even divorce the source of her pain. There are many *ku* and even a word, *blue=pale wife,* for the ailing mate of a man who was too well endowed, eg. *"The pale wife of a man who looks like a tile-dragger [it touches the tiles in the baths]"* (板ねぶとおぼしき人の青女房 摘 2-21 *itanebu to oboshiki hito no ao-nyôbô*)

大きいと言い兼ねている松ヶ丘 摘
ôkii to ii-kaneteiru matsugaoka 2-23

matsugaoka:
she could not say it
was too big

unable to say
because it's too big:
matsugaoka

Women could not divorce men as easily as men women – *"he is so large I hurt"* would not be a sufficient reason – but there was a no-questions asked way to escape, usually used for rare cases of domestic violence: fleeing to a temple that served as a sanctuary for women. Matsugaoka is the most famous of such run-into (*kakekomi*) temples where a woman could take refuge and divorce after three years. Male size also has a drawback regardless of the wife's size. There is the "elephant-nose" who suffers from the same softness Twain's "mammoth cod" did. I guess that's reassuring for the rest of us. Had women written senryu, they might have consoled themselves by claiming a tight vagina would suffer in child-birth: all advantages of life are also handicaps, or, poetically speaking, *should be.*

長いまら下女の部屋迄五つん這い 葉
nagai mara gejo no heya made itsutsunbai 21
(long cock maid/servant's/s' room/s-until five-crawls/ing)

crawling toward
the maid's room on all fives
mr. long pecker

mr. long pecker
heads for the maids' room
on all fives

No one is jealous of the maid, here. A wee bit more than average was considered good, but "long" cocks were thought poorly of. See these two Edo era listings:

一黒、二雁高、三反、四鉄砲、五麩、六白、七錐、八長、九大、十小
1. Black, 2. Goose-high, 3. [Up]warp, 4.Iron-muzzle (musket), 5. Wheat-gluten, 6.White, 7.Awl (small glans? phimosis?), 8. <u>Long</u>, 9. Big (wide), 10. Small (thin).

一麩、二雁、三反、四傘、五赤銅、六白、七木、八太、九長、十すぼえ
1. Wheat-gluten, 2. Goose, 3. [Up]warp, 4. Umbrella (wide-glans edge), 5.Copper, 6. White, 7. Wood (hard, like 4., above), 8. Thick, 9. <u>Long</u>, 10. Tapered(phimosis)

You can see the "goose-high" and "up-warp" glans in the top three in both ten-type lists (『子種蒔』&『女大楽宝開』respectively), while the "long Johns are near the bottom. That was because they tended to hit the cervix. Dark (1=black,

5 = copper in these two lists, but often "purple") marked a vigorous member – cause and effect is tricky, for usage does tend to darken the skin – and was generally ranked in the top five, in contrast to the female ideal of whiteness for the same. Hardness (5 = iron, 5 = copper) got a mixed judgment, because, like thickness and length, they could be rough on a woman. The *kasa,* or umbrella, in the second listing is usually assumed to go along with the goose, but it can be found on a less high-flying member. English calls the glans' *overhang* Japanese sex gourmets consider of prime importance for stimulating a woman a *corona* – an imperfect make-do term, for though it may ring something (the sun, at least), we tend to think of crowns which go up rather than out – but it is only salient to students of anatomy. The Japanese listings, however odd, make far more sense than the English-speaking world's simplistic fixation on the long and short of it alone. An upward arc has a beautiful plantlike purity (?), while a raised penis pointing ahead seems more like a cobra glaring out, or a predator on the prowl. Even imperfectly erect, the up-curve is a more perfect antithesis of, or freedom from, the mammal world, where life is generally condemned to droop. It laughs off gravity, floating lightly upward like a mushroom reaching for the light.

道鏡の塚から出たかさ松茸 摘 3-24
dôkyô no tsuka kara deta kasa-matsudake

and it rose again
from the grave of dôkyô:
the pine mushroom

up from the ground
of dôkyô's burial mound
the pine mushroom

Dôkyô, the Buddhist monk of humble birth whose phenomenal cock raised him above all but his expansive Empress (ch.1). The original has a "kasa" inserted just before the "matsudake" or pine-mushroom. The thick-shafted mushroom in question always has a glans-like head, but the *kasa* type is particularly broad, with a hefty overhang. Anyone who has looked carefully at "spring-prints" has probably noticed *three things* about the penises: 1) the huge size, 2) large veins &/or other convolutions on the shaft and 3) disproportionately large glans. The first is easily explained: the artists exaggerate sexual members to give them special attention as the point of the picture is *sex* (not beautiful bodies, as common in Occidental depictions of the same). The second, less often noted, makes sense if a tradition of landscape art with angular trees and craggy peaks is married to a concept of throbbing, abundant, overflowing fertility (Japan's myths of the beginning) and Japanese-style attention to decorative detail. The third, which ought to attract great attention, but oddly has not, intrigues me most of all, but I will leave that discussion for the *Eddies*, so as not to lose the larger flow.

かさのないものは女のおえたなり 摘
kasa no nai mono wa onna no oeta nari 2 - 32
(corona/margin-lacking thing-as-for woman/en's erected is)

if it's lacking
a corona, that hard-on
is a woman's

the uncrowned
erection: it belongs
to a woman

sans corona
whatever erects is some
thing female

The reference is to a *clitoris*. While it may have a foreskin-like hood, its head has no overhang. As we will see in the chapter on *Sex*, Japanese, perhaps because they were attentive to the clitoris, had a concept of female arousal-as-erection. The *ku* may *also* be read as a dig at a penis with no head to speak of. That is why I put the *ku* here rather than with other clit covens scattered throughout the book.

ちんぽこをかうしてなさゐとろうそくや
chinpoko o kôshite nasai to rôsokuya 摘 4-16
(pecker[acc] this do [polite imperative] says candleshop)

'this is the way
you want your cock' says
the candle man

The candle-maker in Japan makes candles that, contrary to Occidental candles, come to a head rather than to a tail. That is, they taper *down:* they are broader at the *top*. While they do not have a head separate from the shaft, they are much thicker at the head, i.e., the end that burns.

.

上ハ反りのまら尺八のやうにおへ 葉七
uwazori no mara shakuhachi no yô ni oe

an up-curve
cock erects just like
a shakuhachi

I have seen this Englished as *"Erecting like / the upwards curve of a / Threatening shakuhachi"* (though from *Leaf*, not by Solt) and know exactly what happened. The translator was not familiar with the odd but simple shorthand character for *mara* (cock) 亻八, which is seen on almost every page of most books of dirty senryu but in no dictionary I have yet seen, and confused it for the closest *bona fide* character, *ada* 仇. I do not have the original *Leaf*, but the Syunroan-annotated version. I thought he or his publisher did not want to mess with a character that would give trouble to the printers and some readers, but some other *ku* in it do have 亻八, so it would seem that slightly different spellings (if it can be called that) go back much further. Be that as it may, the Romanization (*age-sori no ada shakuhachi no yô ni soe*) showed the translator was also unfamiliar with the pronunciation of the basic term for an up-curve cock, *uwazori*, not *age-sori*, and the common slang for "erect," *oe,* not *soe!* Sorry to get off-track, but three words wrong in a poem as short as a senryu bothered me, especially when a term as specialized as a *shakuhachi sori,* or *shakuhachi curve* was explicated at length while the more basic concept of the up-curve was barely addressed . . . Syunroan put it well when he wrote that in a world where the metaphors/ synonyms for phallic things 陽物 span the gamut from elegant to vulgar, *this is a classy* (上品) *metaphor for a first-class penis*. Aside from the obvious length and, for a flute, exceptional thickness, a *shakuhachi* curves upward (with a slight ridge along the convex bottom sometimes) and the end that juts out (*i.e.,* is farthest from the mouth) is of bigger diameter than the blown end. Since it was typically played by someone whose face was under a hat and the end was blown over so the instrument was at a right angle rather than protruding out from the mouth like a recorder and, consequently, tends to point *down* on the whole, but by curving-up near the end, it sounds *out* rather than just earthward. It is also claimed that, aside from this functionality, a curved bamboo has a richer sound. So even though it is not played fully erect, so to speak, the fact it is convex below and has a larger head is what makes its shape not only phallic but ideally so.

松茸をさかさに植て子が出来る
matsudake o sakasa ni uete ko ga dekiru 37-36

a pine mushroom
planted upside down will
give you a child

for offspring
plant a pine mushroom
upside-down

If this just contrasts the manner of planting most plants and planting humans, the wit is as small as the head of said mushroom/penis is large. But, *if* it is the case that a mushroom so planted can grow baby mushrooms (the spore being attached to the underside of the head/top), it is a pretty clever parallel. Compare it to the following late-17c haiku:

松たけやゐろりの中に植て見る　涼兎
matsudake ya irori no naka ni uete miru ryôtô

pine mushrooms!
what if i try planting them
around the hearth

pine mushrooms
i'll try planting them
within the irori

The Japanese hearth is only slightly raised from the floor and looks like a sandbox around a fire. Skewers were planted in the sand. There were no plants unless planted for fun. Maybe the poet means only that the mushrooms would transform the *irori* into a magical garden – chances are he received a gift of the mushrooms and is repaying the donor with food for the mind – but I cannot help recalling the joke about men on the beach with only their mushrooms poking up through the sand when an old maid complaining of the dearth of men where she comes from happens upon them and gurgles with delight to find a place where "they grow in the wild." Well, *here*, they have been domesticated.

松茸は酒蛤は湯で風味
matsudake wa sake hamaguri wa yû de fûmi

to bring out the best
soak pine mushroom in sake
clams in hot water

松茸や笠着ておどる鍋の内
matsudake ya kasa kite odoru nabenouchi

pine mushrooms
dancing with their hats on
in the stew-pot

A *senryu* on the left; an early haiku by S.S. Longhead, now known as Teitoku (1570-1653) on the right. Some sweet *sake* may bring out the flavor of pine mushroom and clams are good scalded, but the wit is in the allegory. As explained in chapter 9, men benefit from a drink and women from exercise or a hot bath before sex. The haiku is not so *knowing* about sexual matters, but still plays with erotic trope. Stewpot-as-woman is well developed in Japan (ch. 24). S.S. Longhead's mushrooms are dying where every mushroom wants to die.

椎茸のりん気松茸踏みつぶし
shiitake no rinki matsudake fumitsubushi 60-25
(Cortinellus s.'s envy Armillaria m. tread-squash)

a wee mushroom
jealousy stomps flat
a pine mushroom

the jealousy
of a shiitake stomps
a matsudake

Someone from a country where infant circumcision is universal might be pardoned for thinking the little *shiitake* mushroom belonged to a boy who took out his penis envy on the wrong species, but, *no*, the *shiitake* turns out to be a chignon mimicking their cluster-form. And the chignon is really the palace maid (御殿女中 chamber-maid?) who wore that style. On a mushroom hunt, she takes vicarious revenge on a *matsudake* reminding her of a paramour who is doubtless away using his gift to pleasure another woman. But the hairstyle may not be all of the metaphor. According to *Cuntologia,* the sliminess of the mushrooms, or the soup in their immediate vicinity, makes them additionally stand for the wet-for-sex horniness of the cunts of these lonely women. As a really poor *ku* puts it *"The matsudake / and the shiitake do / a delicious thing"* (椎茸と松茸うまいことをやり *shiitake to matsudake umai koto o yari* 37).

松だけを握ツてさがみねばるなり 摘
matsudake o nigitte sagami neburu nari 3-14

just grasping
pine-mushroom, a sagami
becomes slimy

まつ茸を見てもさがみハはづむ也 摘 3-14
matsudake o mite mo sagami wa hazumu nari

a sagami will
orgasm at the sight of
a pine-mushroom

The Sagami is a maid-servant from Sagami, all of whom were reputably insatiable. We will encounter them again in the chapter on maid-servants.

松茸の元草をわけ虱狩り
matsudake no moto kusa o wake shirami-gari

parting the grass
around the pine mushroom
hunting for crabs

For once, I can say *gained* in translation! Thanks to the "crabs," English beats Japanese (Not knowing *this* crab, a Japanese musicologist had sea crabs commuting to the anus in translation of a dirty-blues song!). Not caught outside, "lice" are hardly ideal; but the *ku* does not entirely betray mushroom kind, as the stereotypical verb associated with them is "hunting." That gives us a hunt within a hunt.

茸取って大声あぐる女かな 子規
take totte ôgoe aguru onna kana 明治28
(mushroom/s taking great-voice raise/ing woman/en!/?/'tis)

the huntress
taking a mushroom, raises
a hue and a cry

ah, women!
singing out each time they
bag a mushroom

shouting out
with each mushroom bagged
the huntresses

Shiki (1867- 1902), one of the two fathers of modern haiku (the other being Kyoshi), had a strong imagination. His *ku* could be from life, or a new twist on Orpheus. In another, he elaborates: *"One party / was solid women / mushroom hunting* (一むれは女ばかりの茸狩 *hito mure wa onna bakari no kinoko-gari*). Were it a mixed group, the women might have covered their mouths and stifled their responses.

松茸はにくし茶茸は可愛らし Shiki 同
matsudake wa nikushi chadake wa kawairashi

pine mushrooms
spiteful; tea mushrooms
adorable!

Both manly and pee-wee mushrooms excite us in different ways. The "spiteful/ hateful"(*nikushi*) expresses male envy or female attraction toward someone who attracts you despite yourself. The feelings are honest, hence the *ku* is haiku, but fits the stereotypes so perfectly it *could be* a senryu. Two years later –

つれの者の松茸取りし妬み哉
tsurenomono no matsudake torishi netami kana

hoh, jealousy!
her companion bagged
a pine mushroom

松茸を得ずして帰る女哉
matsudake o ezu shite kaeru onna kana

just a woman
returning without bagging
a pine mushroom

returning without
one pine mushroom! – you call
yourself women?

The first *ku* has no pronoun, but "one's companion" will not do, so I guessed from the second, specifying sex but not number. It could be a party of women returning without their prize. I made it singular to gain the "a" after adding the "just," which was my creative take on the ambiguous *kana.* We could take the *ku* in a male vs. female romantic insult exchange as per the third reading, a paraverse. Either *ku* might work as a senryu, the first, as is, and the second, had promiscuous sleeping festivals (雑交寝) also called "mixed-fish-sleep" (雑魚寝) been developed as a theme in senryu (I only came across one. See sundry *ku* chapter 29).

茸狩の帰らんとする女かな 子規
takegari no kaeran to suru onna kana shiki
(mushroom-hunt/ing's return-would do woman/en!/?/'tis)

at the point
of return, women hunting
mushrooms

women about
to go home from hunting
mushrooms

my, my, women
trying to pull out from
a mushroom hunt

This is the least senryu of Shiki's mushroom hunts and the best. He captures the nature of a scavenging or collecting-style hunt, whether it is for mushrooms or sea shells. But let's go back to the early hunts of haikai:

茸狩のあるが中にも是見さい 大独
takegari no aru ga naka ni mo kore misai

mushroom hunting
many well-endowed but
'take a look at this!'

茸狩や夢にも似たる辷り道 柳居
takegari ya yume ni mo nitaru suberimichi

mushroom hunting
a slippery trail like
we were in a dream

The first *ku* comes from linked verse (*ls* but probably 17-18c), follows a *ku* with an umbrella-like hat, and proceeds one with the erotic word "color." The verb ending tell us that a woman speaks to a woman. The second 18-19c *ku* echoes a Bashô *ku* mentioning the danger an evening shower brings to the hunt. Issa goes further, falling on his ass only to come up with a mushroom. The idea of mushroom hunting as frantic competition goes back at least to Bashô's time:

松茸や人にとらるる鼻の先 去来
matsudake ya hito ni toraruru hananosaki

a pine mushroom
snatched by another right
under my nose

松茸や鼻の先たる哥がるた 其角
matsudake ya hananosakitaru utagaruta

a pine mushroom
the song-match card right
under your nose

Nose and mushroom are a good match, but Kikaku's metaphor beats Kyorai's straight *ku*. Card competition was fast and furious. Women excelled in it, and Kikaku has a preface about maids out mushroom hunting. Old Issa, who laments being beaten out by women hunters, had mixed feelings about this sort of hunting and notes how mushrooms can be trampled when people get too competitive:

初茸や見付けた者をつき倒し 一茶
hatsudake ya mitsuketa mono o tsukidaoshi

first mushroom
i push over the one
who finds it

初茸や踏つぶしたをつぎて見る 同
hatsudake ya fumitsubushita o tsugite miru

first mushroom
trampled and crushed, i
try mending it

五六人只一ッ也きの子がり 一茶
go roku nin tada hitotsu nari kinoko-gari

a mushroom hunt
five or six men with but one
between them

茸がりのから手でもどる騒かな
takegari no karate de modoru sawagi kana

what a ruckus!
home from a mushroom hunt
bare-handed

Issa wrote mushroom *ku* enough for every year he lived, sixty five in all. Many are interesting, but I particularly like the second *ku* above, written when he was 60, which seems a prototype for penis reattachment surgery. Some more readings:

having stepped on
the year's first mushroom, i
try to rejoin it

trying to repair
the year's first mushroom:
i stepped on it

Issa's *ku* often show a playfulness wrongly considered senryu. The *ku* with one mushroom between half a dozen men, however, could well be a senryu. Imagine, if you will, a gigantic phallus paraded about town, as groups of men do every year in many parts of Japan and contrast that to the mighty hunters with one mushroom.

松茸や引まくり行山の裾 素丸
matsudake ya hikimakuriyuku yamanosuso
(pine-mshrm/s!/? pull-tucking-go mt's hem)

pine mushrooms
we go around lifting up
the hill's hems

羽織を松に着せて茸狩 千代
haori o matsu ni kisete kinoko-gari
(cloak[acc] pine-on hanging mshrm-hunt)

mushroom hunt
hanging my wing-weave
on a pine tree

The first *ku* by one of young Issa's employers, Somaru (1712-95), postdates the second by Chiyo (1701-75), but the vocabulary has an early haikai feeling. There is irony in exposing a mountain, generally, female, to bag cocks. If that irony were not so allusive, we might have a senryu. Chiyo's *ku* has a modern touch recalling Loretta Lynn's song of first-sex where she hangs her angel wings upon a devil's horns. "Wing (or Feather)-weave or not, a short outer robe is not angel wings and a pine is no devil, but having heard Loretta sing and knowing what a pine mushroom stood for, not to mention the contrast of black *haori,* green pine-needles, white skin, red thonged sandals (they had to be) and the game, the *ku* is erotic to *me*.

雁高はくはえて引くと思うなり 摘
karidaka wa kuwaete hiku to omou nari 3-23

with a goosehigh
you think of mouthing
then pulling on it

with that big head
you bet they get pulled
from the audience

After the fine mushroom *ku,* this may seem a let down, but I want to end the chapter with some classic style dirty senryu. The *goose-high*, you might recall is pretty much the same as a pine mushroom – a soaring head-trip. The first reading, that of a neophyte, imagines a big lollipop or a new way of mushroom hunting (actually, I took notes on an "F-cup girl" competition on Japanese late-night TV (mid-nineties), where a bevy of beauties hunted for pine mushrooms while wired for their pulse. Finding one, we see a girl's heartbeat rise from 90 to 140 and that was *before* she bounced up and down and all but inserted it into her bikini.) The Japanese verb *kuwaeru* means to *hold by an orifice* and is most commonly used for pipes. It could work for the mouth above or its nether counterpart. But the experienced reader would know that in the argot of Edo's nightlife, *kuwaeru* meant that *a man was singled out from an audience by a geigi,* which is to say a female performer, a singer, dancer maybe a stripper or even a woman who had sex with members of her audience. So, the correct picture (or, solution) is not a *giga-glans* sucked within an orifice, but a performer literally pulling the masterpiece out from a number of men because of and, perhaps, *by* his member.

雁高は抜くとき藪の音がする　末摘
karidaka wa nuku toki yabu no oto ga suru 3-27
(goosehigh-as-for pull-out time thicket's sound makes)

the goosehigh
pulling out, the thicket
makes a sound

the fancy cock
pulling out it makes
a cheesy sound

the goosehigh
pulling out you hear it
in the thicket

At first, "thicket" had me stumped. I misread it as "bog," for it was easy to imagine the large glans-as-plunger sounding like a foot pulled from mud. A thicket may indeed pop now and then, when abrupt temperature change affects bamboo cells, but that is only known by we who have lived by such places and the sound is too dry for sex. The thicket was also a place for men and women to meet for secret sex. Though quiet because of the abundant foliage, it would echo *that,* but this *thicket* is more likely 1) argot – In the sexual underworld (花柳界), it referred to *pubic hair*, so one can hear the suction sound right through the pubic mound with its bushy cover; or, 2) an allusion to the metaphor "Releasing a fart within a thicket," *i.e., doing something dirty where none can notice*. Here, it would be literal: the goosehigh creates a vaginal fart. I tried to capture some of the riddling quality with the last reading, where I hinted at *cutting the cheese.* Or is the above all wrong and *nuku* here means "draw," as a sword, *i.e.,* expose the penis. If so, the sound would come from an awestruck person or people because of the expression 藪に目, or *a thicket never lacks for eyes.*

麻羅でもひけをとらぬが江戸の色
mara de mo hike o toranu ga edo no iro 葉 1
(cock-with-even loss[acc] take-not is/the edo-color/eros)

never second
even with cocks, the color
belongs to edo

even with cocks
edo's eros means never
admitting defeat

This alludes to the cocky purple-goose-high mentioned earlier. Edo was identified with the purple fields of Musashi-no and *edo-murasaki,* or, "Edo purple" dyeing technique and the purple silk was renowned throughout Japan. While the Edo-as-number-one mentality was collective – my first reading follows Syunroan in that – Edoites were also famously competitive as individuals, never backing down (see ch 31 "Fighting, or the Edoite *hanami* in *Cherry Blossom Epiphany*), so there may also be room for Solt's reading *"An Edo man's lust / is never to let his cock / be defeated."* My second reading tries to retain both possibilities.

too well- hung
he cannot kiss for fear
of losing his tongue

poor goose-high
is out of luck – he cannot
*kiss **and** fuck!*

I *just* made up this senryu (口すえば舌が危なき大かり高), but would bet my bottom-dollar there is such a *ku* out there, because cock-type lists sometimes warn that the owner of one of these masterpieces *must not kiss while fucking lest a woman in the throes of ecstasy bite it off* (鈴木 p.134 頁)! In Japanese tradition, we find no chimpanzee smacks. If prints are correct, Japanese frenched even before lips touched! Kissing was a *tongue* rather than *lip* thing. But what really matters here is how, once again – I recall writing the same in other chapters – we encounter *the kindness of folk wisdom*. Most of us are not lucky enough to have the perfect cock (or cunt), but, heh, *we*, at least, can kiss while we fuck. Sour grapes? *Of course*. But, what's wrong with that? There is *veritas* in vinegar, too.

more wheat gluten

Lacking a metaphor (the *sine qua non* for decent translation) for an expandable substance and not wishing to be sidelined from more central matters of form and size, I first relegated the *other* top cock – that was *first* in one ranking but way back in *fifth*-place in another – the very odd *fû mara*, to the footnotes. But true to its character, this monster grew, so I have decided to maintext it nonetheless.

大敵と見て恐るべからず麩イ八 葉
taiteki to mite osorubekarazu fu-mara 12

the enemy's huge
it quakes but not in fear
a sponge cock

she's a giant?
worry not! the foohmara
is compliant

According to my J-E dictionary, this *fu* is "wheat-gluten bread." I can recall buying cardboard-like *pads* of it, and how it expanded into a fat sponge when simmering (it was never eaten *as bread* but as a sop that starts off in the soup). The texture seems dry even when wet, and it tastes like the proverbial cardboard, but who cares! Something like Jesus' loaf it can expand to fit any pot. As such, it is perfect for any woman. The "big enemy" above need not be taken literally. One's nemesis is also one's love in *Japanspeak* and it may well have been the spirit of most premodern sexual relations throughout the world, including Europe. Even today, do not situation dramas tend to depict the sexes as *at war*, but in a fun way, even in the Occident? In other words, one more reading is possible:

whatever she
turns out to be, no worry
for foohmara!

big and lethal
to her eyes, but fear not!
it's a fooh-cock

Inserted within a tight woman, it will not expand and hurt her, but, if she balloons inside, as not a few women do, it can match her. That this cock was well known is indirectly proven by another senryu describing an elderly couple as "dried octopus and wrapped-up *fû"* (開干蛸まらハ苞麩の老夫婦　葉末　別十 *bobo hitako mara wa tsutofû no rôfufû*). The octopussy (ch. 8), once top of the line, is no longer succulent and the *fû* is a thin dry strip that, like one which has well-passed its use-by date no longer swells up when placed in water. *What splendid relations this couple must have enjoyed!* But, to return to the functional *fû*. With cocks like this, is it any wonder Japanese pop is the capital of morphing? Excluding the pinky-sized dried trepang that reconstitutes as a large cucumber, the closest thing to the *fûmara* with international coinage would probably be a dog's cock, alleged to inflate after insertion to better lock-in until orgasm. I would not be surprised if the authors of the Japanese penis typologies read the Chinese essayist/playwright/novelist Li Yu's masterpiece *The Carnal Prayer Mat.* The protagonist has a successful operation to graft such a dog's prick to his own, in order to gain an organ giving women enough pleasure to make adultery worth risking one's life for. But, when it comes to dog sex, a *Leaf* senryu takes the prize. Forget Archimedes. "*From the cunt [fucking] of dogs / [we/someone] thought up / screw work*" (犬の開から思ひつくねじ細工　葉 別七 *inu no bobo kara omoi-tsuku neji-saiku*). To think this 17-syllabet *Just So Story* was thought up despite the fact Japanese neither *screw* nor *get screwed*, metaphorically speaking!

妻は夫を麩じやとも知らず産ならべ　折句駒むかへ
me wa tsuma o fu ja to mo shirazu umi-narabe 大明七

the cock-lucky wife

without knowing
her husband was a fooh
child after child

in the dark about
a fooh's changing girth
birth after birth

It is not just that the wife had no other man to compare it with to know how blessed she was, as Suzuki points out, but that she would not have any reason to think about size when, after her second, third, fourth or fifth child, she grew slack down there. The *ku* is excellent.

~~~~~~
~~~~~~

~ eddies ~

~~~~~~

Close to the Navel. I recall as a teenager dancing a slow dance to *"Come on Baby Light My Fire"* at a youth center in Coral Gables, thinking how nice it would be if the place I wanted to enter (but never had) were only in the vicinity of the belly-button – or the very same – so I could easily slip it in *while dancing!*
~~~~~~

~~~~~~

Had women written senryu. The following sentence from pg 106, was too good to cut and in a general sort of way correct, but wrong in its particulars.

> *Had women written senryu, they might have consoled themselves by claiming a tight vagina would suffer in child-birth: all advantages of life are also handicaps, or, poetically speaking, should be.*

Since writing this, I have found *ku* – near-senryu *zappai* – likewise, almost surely by men, which *do* mention a disadvantage of a tight twat, indirectly at least:

つがもない・難産このもしがる若気　田植笠
tsugamonai · nansan konomoshigaru wakage 享保中

outrageous!
youthful desire favors
difficult births

outrageous!
the young favor birth
with danger

The last 7-5 in this *kasazuke ku* caps the first 5. Can you guess what, then, is so outrageous? Young men think gaining a mate with a tight twat is what life is all about. If they get that, they think they should count their lucky stars; unfortunately, however, women so blessed (from the man's point of view), were reputed to be likely to experience difficult births and run a high risk of dying from the complications. I doubt, however that this would apply to the exceptionally elastic octopussy of ch.8.

~~~~~~

Un-ideal Members. Because this chapter concerns ideal members, the contrary must get its due elsewhere. The hooded male member has its own chapter, but not the egg-plant nor the slack cunt. Here is one of the latter, particularly clever for its vocabulary:

弓削の道嚊・これもと睾丸しんきがる 伊勢冠付 文化中
yuge no dô kaka // koremo to kôgan shinkigaru 鈴

yuge's old lady
this, too! she frantically
stuffs in his balls

Yuge is Dôkyô of the huge cock and his "old lady" is the Empress of the huge twat. We have slang for a large women either co-coined by the poet who supplied the crown (*kamuri*) for the *ku* and defined by the one who finished it, or borrowed from literature. The balls would be on her husband, with a normal-sized member. Another *ku* from the same collection claimed a "Yuge's old lady" had to stuff her "cheeks" with *rin-no-tama* (弓削の道嚊・ほばらにやならぬりんの玉 文化十 *yuge no dô-kaka hobara nya naranu rinno-tama*) the jingling or clinking balls we have seen and will see for satisfying sex.

だがひろくしたと女房ハいゝこめる 摘
da ga hiroku shita to nyôbô wa ii-komeru 1-9
('who wide made?' wife-as-for says- enter[silencing other])

'so who's the louse
who made me so wide?' she says
to silence her spouse

'so who's to blame
for making me slack?' says she
taking him aback

A tiny women may stay exceptionally tiny because of lack of experience with anything substantial, but a large cock (monsters excluded) would not make a reasonably tight woman grow slack. The woman here is blaming the man for fathering her many children.

開くらべ・さゝいがら投げ込れたり 伊勢冠付 鈴
kai kurabe // sazai-gara nage-komeretari 文化三

she shell <vs> she shell

a cunt/shell match
they toss in a bout with
turbo cornutus

a cunt/shell match
a turban shell added
to ratchet up

There is one way cunt size is more interesting than cock size. One never hears of men contesting to see who has the *smallest*, but one *can* find women taking pride in what they can take in. The shell in question, *sazae* in Japanese, is a fist-metaphor. So we have Japanese women – at least as imagined by Japanese men – doing what post-1970's Usanians and their copycats do to the air, pushing fists into *it*. The words play on shell-matching games, an appropriate woman's pastime, as one senryû (I am saving for another book) pointed out. Notice how the cunt 開, usually pronounced "bobo" in senryu, is *kai* here. That is because shell 貝 is pronounced like that. My forced *"she shell"* cleverness can not make up for the absence of that natural pun.

~~~~~~

Head vs Shaft Cultures. If you have ever tried to mimic genres of music, you know that some tend to start solid and stretch out their warbles at the end of the phrases while others do so at the start of the phrases and up solid. I believe the former is more likely with a language like Japanese or Korean which puts its tonal energy in the tail of the verb at the tail of the sentence, but I have not examined the world of music enough to say for sure. Likewise for cocks. Some cultures depict them as shafts and may even have them end narrower than they begin, while others depict them as mushroom-like, with the shaft serving more to hold up the head than as the thing itself. Only a close examination of the conceptual penis, culture by culture by one party and art culture by culture by another party not knowing of each other's work followed by a correlation of their respective analyses could tell for certain if there are physiological reasons for the difference or if it is arbitrary. Or, there may be more subtle psychological motives involved. I considered neoteny, for babies have proportionately larger heads than adults. Could more neoteny-ous peoples tend to favor large glans? Yet, most Chinese art does not depict large glans on cocks and Japanese did *not* favor large heads *on people*. All that is certain is that Western Europe, like most of Africa, is, on the whole, shaft-centric. Art generally depicts the glans as only the tip of the penis and not a true *head* going *out* as well as *up* from the neck. The ancient chalk-delineated erection on the 170-220 foot (everyone's figures differ!) "Cerne Giant" in Dorsetshire England within which women slept to conceive, is representative. The glans is nothing much. This worldview even extends to real mushrooms, for a cap that curves up from the edge showing its "gills" is called "convex," while a head-centered culture, looking down at the crown would call it upside-down. I first came to feel the enormity of the difference when I saw mushroom-like penises on Shinto/Buddhist votive tablets. The heads were so large that I doubt most Occidentals would know what they represented! Even Screech (1999), an expert on reading Japanese erotic images, who *would* know(and translates three fine *zappai* or senryu on Mt. Inari called "male" for its fungi), describes the mushroom shape in a typically Occidental fashion as only "vaguely penile," finds the parasol penile only in its "erectility" and, like the mushroom, fragility, and grossly overvalues the "phallic shape" of the telescope. When he grants that he does "not necessarily think it legitimate to go
~~~~~~

through the sum of pictures of the Floating World and propose every *long, thin* object as a phallic symbol,"(my italics), I cannot help wondering if he fully appreciated the coequal or greater importance of the cap (*kasa*) with the shaft in the Japanese *idea* of a penis, which, as hard as it may be for Occidentals to grasp, is *not* something "long and thin." If the reader will pardon a vulgar example, even today, the 1990's Usanian porn star a *New Yorker* article called "a life-support system for his penis," would have had a hard time getting hired in Japan, for despite the length and proven durability of his member, porn producers there would not be impressed with a cock whose glans was half the diameter of the shaft. Peter North would need glans enlargement surgery (popular in Japan) before he made a yen.

大根が太れば嬶が漬けたがる 折句道しるべ
daikon ga futokereba kaka ga tsuketagaru 明四

thick daikon
make the old lady hot
to pickle them

a thick daikon
is what the old lady
would pickle

The *daikon*, as most readers may know, is the enormous white radish. They are used as metaphors for shapeless legs, and even a small one would be thicker than a penis, but we get the idea. This *ku* shows that the ideal cock partly depends on the woman's needs. The *ku* is acrostic. Suzuki does not tell us (or does not know) what they word is. Could this be *dabutsu* [*fu* can be read *bu*] 陀仏 i.e. the old wife prays to Buddha as the God/ess of mercy (short for *amidabutsu*) for such a thick one to come her way? Or *tabutsu* [and *da* as *ta*] 他物 i.e., another's (not her husband's)thing? Or *daibutsu,* 大仏 the colossal Buddha, if thick is what she wants!

~~~~~~

Further Fooh Thoughts. Screech writes that 18-19c Japanese pornography differs from Europe's in 1) "though the penis is depicted as large and hard, this is mitigated by its association with soft symbols," 2) "the vagina is shown as equal in power and size to the penis" and 3) the visual symbols show "the female organs are not merely inert enclosures." On the w/hole I agree, but most of those huge cocks, do *not* look particularly *hard*. The balls are craggy, but how "hard" can veins, suggestive of lightning, and the huge glans, more suggestive of rubber than bone or wood, be? Even the shafts are not spear handle-smooth like "ours." but have folds suggestive of spongy abundance to spare. The mushroom does not *mitigate* the hard image, it is part of the basic penis concept.

~~~~~~

Size Matters in Japan!? 上 ***Don't Believe the Artists***. Unlike some Europeans, whom rumors have it, wondered if Japanese really were so big, the Japanese knew the truth. So I didn't really expect anyone to point it out. The following capped verses were among the dozen or so senryu about spring pictures Suzuki included with his erotic zappai:

春の雨・手よりは太い画空事 五色墨
haru no ame / te yori wa futoi esoragoto

◎ *spring rain* ◎
more than a hand across
woodcut lies

絵空事・膝頭よりすさまじく 小柴垣
esoragoto / hizagashira yori susamajiku

◎ *woodcut lies* ◎
even her kneecap pales
by comparison

The first *ku,* dated 寛政五 1793, reminds me of something I saw most recently on the last frame of a three-part illustration in a *Pillow Pocket Book* 枕文庫 by Keisai Eisen 渓斎英

泉 published between 1822-36. The first shows a hand under the belly of a just starting-to-erect penis, the second tickling its semi-erect-throat and the one in question has it resting, fingers spread on top of the *glans*. The finger tips do not quite reach to the edge. My guess is that is the type of thing that referred to as picture-empty-things. For the second *ku,* dated 文化一 1804, I added the pronoun "her" rather than, say, "a" or "your" because the woman's kneecap is commonly portrayed in the spring-pictures. The word *esoragoto*, which is the final word in one *ku* and the cap in the other means both a picture that does not agree with the reality and hyperbole to the point of lie. *Fantasy* would be a less critical way to put it, and a kinder translation yet would be what Timon Screech used for the tongue-in-cheek title of an extraordinary book by that name written in 1797, *Artistic License.*

~~~~~~

Size Matters in Japan!? 下 *The* ***Relativity of It***. One of two usage examples of "small-front" (小前) in *Cuntologia* (女陰万考) was from a Tenpo Era (1830-44) book and combines the ideal of matching sizes, like the *Kamasutra*, with a *method* for doing so!

> *The Market of Fronts* – Long ago it was the custom for the youths and maidens of the appropriate age to come to this spot and, tucking up their front hems, show their cocks and cunts to one another so the large cocks could seek out the wide cunts and the small-fronts (little cunts), the tiny peckers, and the skin-covered (*phimosis*) weenies the hairless (immature) cunnies, and in that way all find the parts that agreed with their own. (『旅枕五十三次』)

~~~~~~

The Premise that Frontal Intercourse is the Default Position. That frontal intercourse was not the first choice in *all* cultures is obvious from the etymology of "missionary position." The bias for said position in some cultures may come from the association of superiority and being on top where men rule, a tendency to distinguish "us" from the stereotypical animal, and likewise to emphasize one's difference from other cultures where sodomy is common. It is not just a Christian concept. Edo era Japan also had frontal sex as the default position (though enjoying many others) – it was called the fundamental or true position (*hontc* 本手, *honma-dori* 本間どり、等」). In ancient Japan, that was by no ways the case. As more than one blogger points out, the first gods learned how to put his extra part into her missing one by watching *sekirei* (wagtail/s) (*Motacillidae*) do it, and that means . . . And, in case you don't know how birds do it, quips one, the "back" radical is in one of the bird's characters 鶺鴒 (back:背)! Yet, for all of this, there is a bias in favor of the *front,* which dove-tails with that for the *up*. Aside from physical considerations and nominal considerations – female parts in Japanese could be called "the front" (*mae*) or "front-hole" (*mae-ana*) as opposed to the rear one – the *front* is desirable for being metaphysically contrary to the *back*. Even with the heavy use of night soil for fertilizer and more scatological elements in the mythological beginnings than commonly encountered (see Leupp), Japanese still thought of shit as dirty and the psychological connotations of *front/before* tend to be better than *behind/after*.

~~~~~~

Down-curve Cock also Shitty? If the *down-cunt* was judged more difficult to *keep* clean, the *down-curve* was called a *kusokaki* cock (糞掻き麻羅), or "shit-scrapper." An internet know-it-all explains that in the "proper 正常位 (missionary) position, a down-bender would stimulate the vagina wall on the anal side so that, rather than feeling good, the woman would feel like taking a shit (!). This is patently ridiculous, for riding high in this position to better rub the clitoris would do the same regardless of the bent of the cock and we do not find women running to the toilet for *that!* The more likely explanation for the name is purely physical similitude. The shape of the instrument employed for scraping shit off the inside of commodes, *like any scraper*, bends down.
~~~~~~

<u>*Pretty Wives as Husband-killers*</u>
美人妻こそ夫の命になる

七 [7]

色男乃果テは
Dry Kidney Disease

気のとくさへのこ斗にみやくが有 摘 2-25
kinodokusa henoko bakari ni myaku ga ari

ah, the pity of it!
his only pulse, his life
is in his prick

a damn shame
only his pecker has life
worthy of the name

Here lies a man beat by his own meat. Like the maid who is a slow poke except for when it comes to getting poked, he is literally a good for nothing.

よそでへりますと内儀はいしゃへいひ
yoso de herimasu to naigi wa isha e ii 6-40

it gets used up
outside, says the wife
to the doctor

He is having sex with someone else. So *she* is not to blame. For *what?* The answer will come soon enough. Only decades ago, it sufficed for Blyth to explain a senryu that he translated *"It's all right now, — / What do doctors / Know about anything!"* (*mô shite mo ii no sa isha ga nani shitte* 51) as follows: "In this case, it is the man speaking, but in the following the woman is to blame: *'A relapse; / His wife wishes / to disappear.'* (*uchikaesu byôki nyôbô wa kietagari* 6-32)." Then, just four more words: "With shame and confusion." (Blyth:1961) Today, more explanation is required. When Ueda (1999) translates a *Willow* senryu *"the beautiful wife / boiling his herb medicine / that doesn't work,"* and notes only that "very likely the medicine is an aphrodisiac," I feel a disconnect. A wealthy old man *could* have a beautiful young *wife*, but stereotypically – and *senryu was mostly stereotype* – such a man would have a *mistress* (*mekake*), not a wife, whose sole duty is helping her old sugar daddy get it up, boiling that medicine. As it stands, the problem is almost surely one that anyone up to the mid-20c would have immediately guessed: *the husband is not husbanding his vital juices.* If there is any medicine he does *not* need, it is an aphrodisiac!

生キて居ルものハへ　ことめかけなり 万
ikiteiru mono wa henoko to mekake bakari 天四
(living thing-as-for pecker and mistress only)

what still lives?
only his pecker and
his paramour

あいそのつきた男女房で腎虚 万
aisô no tsukita otoko nyôbô de jinkyo 寛元
(charm's exhausted man wife-with kidney empty)

unloved men
getting dry-kidney from
their wives

left by a lover
the man still gets wasted
by his wife

Finally, the name of the subject, or disease, itself: *jinkyo*, literally, "kidney-empty." *Kenkyusha's New Japanese-English Dictionary* has a fine definition: *"men's emaciation due to sexual intemperance."* It is a wasting disease, what was called *a case of nerves* back in the day when we, too, believed sex could deplete energy, leading to debilitation. With liquids involved, my translations generally exchange *dry* for *empty* to gain a syllable. The *ku* above is a blend of *two* stereotypes. If dry-kidney is one, the other is that of a man who fucks his wife a lot because he has the hots for someone else who refuses his advances – *You say he goes on and on? / Madam, your husband is . .* (もぎ放しあれおかみさんだなさんが 摘 3-34 *mogippanashi are okamisan dana-san ga*) ~~– or is too closely monitored – a wife may keep close guard on a pretty servant for whom he has the "maid-bug" (*gejo-mushi* あまりさせたかるのも下女虫のせい 摘 4-31 *amari sasetagaru no mo gejo mushi no sei* – Nope "maid-bug's more likely her~~ own libido.). Psychologically speaking, this, and not a one-night stand, or visits to the Pleasure Quarter is the *real* "fucking around." The poor wife in such circumstances would be hard put to stop her husband, as she wasn't the *source* of his desire but only the *outlet*.

がになつて女じんきよじや無イといひ
ga ni natte nyobo jinkyo ja-nai to ii 9-31

adamantly
the wife denies: dry-kidney
it is not!

A wife's first duty in Japan, as in the West, was to help keep her husband alive and in good health. That, and not just the embarrassment of thinking the doctor and others will imagine all that fucking is why, as another senryu puts it, without naming the disease (for guessing it is the point), dry-kidney is *"a disease that brings shame to the wife"* (女房に恥をかかせるやまひなり 24-4 *nyôbô ni haji o kakaseru yamai nari*). The adamant denial reminds me of when I interviewed children about bugs on a train in Japan. I asked a boy about the last bug that caught his eye and he said "a cockroach," his mother, whom I thought was sleeping, jumped up and declared he'd *never* seen one in his life.

嫄の身になッてうれしいじんきよ也
yome no mi ni natte ureshii jinkyo nari 万1-30

'tis a disease
that makes the bride happy
dry kidney

お妾ハめうりのために腎虚させ 摘
o mekake wa me uri notameni jinkyo sase 4-9

the mistress
empties his kidney to gain
a reputation

Thanks to the doctor's diagnosis, does a young husband allow his wife – *bride* in Japanese includes the first few years when the couple live with his parents and she is hazed – to finally get some sleep at night, or, does the disease prove she is literally loved, as we see in the second *ku* that might describe a fin de siecle Western vamp? Well-loved seems more likely, for the "bride" would be proud of winning the battle for her husband's love with his mother. Psychological victory or not, the disease will end in defeat for both women: *"The cause of death / dry-kidney – his wife / now suffers"* (ちんきよにて死ンだを嫁ハくろうがり 摘 1-12 *jinkyo nite shinda o yome wa kurogari*): She is blamed by his family, and the sudden loss of his erection – not him, for he was no help for anything else – is hard on her.

とかくまだおへますかなとさじをとり 摘
tokaku mada oemasuka na to saji o tori 1-34

a cock-sure diagnosis

so, let me see,
he still has erections, right?
taking the spoon

reaching for
the spoon, i take it he still
has erections

An editor of a round-robin annotated *Pluck* explains "the focus seems to be on the *mottomo-rashi, i.e.,* specious, facial expression of the doctor" who is confident enough of his diagnosis to pick up the spoon, which means to start compounding the medicine, before he is finished questioning. In Japan, most physicians were medicine-doctors, in the sense that they took care of their own pharmacy. Unfortunately, modern English has no concept of medicines that are good fortifiers, enhancing virility in the sense of making a man and his sperm funda-mentally healthier, as opposed to one that simply makes a man horny or last longer. These two different categories of medicine tend to be conflated when all medicine related to sex is wrongly called an *aphrodisiac*.

床についてもおやしてる病也 摘 4-24 *toko ni tsuite mo oyashiteru yamai nari*

it's a disease
where you stand erect while
lying at ease

lying in bed
it still raises its head with
this disease

Even if "empty-kidney" was diagnosed, the man wouldn't necessarily go along with the prescription. He was, after all, a *sexaholic.* A patient in an illustrated sketch-book quoted by the *Pluck* round-robin editors, put it like this: "I'm going down fighting with cunt; I don't need medicine; don't need a thing; no matter what, cunt is *good!"* (*bobo to uchijini da, kusuri mo nani mo iranu, tokaku bobo ga ee*).

ここはまだいきてござると女房なき
koko wa mada ikite-gozaru to nyôbô naki 2-16
(here-as-for still alive [+hon.], says wife crying)

he's still alive
at least right here!
cries the wife

The stiff with a hard-on is an old saw, but do all stiffs stand? Those hung by the neck are said to. Those shot, do not, unless you put a cork in them (I am guessing, here). I don't really care to investigate further, but will be happy to add a note if any reader who is well-versed on this matter sends me a gloss. Here, it suffices to point out that Japanese, or senryu, at least, make it a mark of the dry-kidney man.

執念の深サへのこハ死にきらず 葉七
shûnen no fukasa e henoko wa shini-kirazu

incredible
tenacity: his cock just
refuses to die

desire runs
this deep: a cock that
will not die

The disease was psychosomatic; imagination and erection go hand in hand. The dry-kidney man wanted to fuck forever, and his *semper paratus* got the message. This *ku* seems strangely fitting in Japanese because *shûnen*, or "tenacity" also means "vindictiveness" and is most strongly identified with snakes.

魂魄爰に止まっておへてゐる 天元桜三
konpaku koko ni tomatte oeteiru

his spirit
has perched here
he's erect

this is where
his soul has stopped
the erection

his spirit
made it this far and
stands still

Soul Pole

his spirit
settled on his cock
a dry-kidney death

魂魄男根に止まって腎虚死に 葉
konpaku mara ni todomatte jinkyo-jini 25

Japanese had more than one soul. The *konpaku* is the one that leaves the body in dreams and tends to hang-around in this world (49 days was standard) after death. How stiff were these undying spirits? one *Million ku* describes *"A prick that could / pass through an iron wall / put in a coffin"* (てつへきもとをるへ こをくわんへ入レ 万天元 *tetsuheki o tôru henoko o kan e ire*).

泣きながら女房へのこへ土砂をかけ 安六梅四
nakinagara nyôbô henoko e suna o kake

while crying
the wife at his cock
throws sand

crying, the wife
throws sand upon the
part with life

According to Okada Hajime, sand blessed by the proper party of the esoteric Buddhist Pure Word sect for throwing upon dead bodies to make them bendable for burial purposes (Japanese coffins were usually more like tubs) was borrowed to treat hard cases of priapism. Or, cold cases of the same, as above.

ゆかん場のわらいじんきよで死ンだやつ
yukanba no warai jinkyo de shinda yatsu 摘 1-12

おしわけにけり／＼
pushing their way in!
pushing their way in!

laughs from the bathing room,
a guy who died of dry kidney

The *yukanba* (湯灌場) was a room for bathing corpses to clean them of this world's impurities before sending them on to the next. The draw-*ku* suggests those working at this solemn job wanted to see the double-stiff!

病上りどくだ／＼と持上げてる 葉 24
yami-agari doku da doku da to mochi-ageteru

convalescence

"it's poison!
po-poison!" she cries
heaving up

No one is puking. We are back to the wife, or mistress, and her still living stiff. She is as horny from the long fast as her convalescing husband (I put the first part of the *ku* into the title) and her desperate warning has just broken into a love-cry as she starts heaving up her buttocks to meet his thrusts half-way.

そち次第・嬶よ長生きさせてくれ 田みの笠
sochi shidai kaka yo naga-iki sasete kure 元禄 13

it's up to you,
mama, let this old man live
a long life!

よわい事・かかは仏か手を合せ 神酒の口
yowai koto kaka wa hotoke ka te o awase 安永 4

he's a weak one
is mama god? papa's hands
clasped together

Suzuki Katsutada comments on the first *ku*: "the wife is not always the one in a weak position. A man may be tortured by his wife's promiscuity and cuss her out, or he may unashamedly pray for her to help him out." As it is the lover and wife who may be legally killed if caught in the act, I think it more likely the husband is begging off his wife's demand for sex, as each act was, to use a country music expression for smoking cigarettes, antedating the government's label warnings, *driving nails in my coffin* (sung by Ernest Tubbs). The *hotoke* in the second, can mean "buddha/god" or "saint." As irony it might mean she is really not a saint but promiscuous, or it could be a homophonic pun on "let me alone!" Suzuki's reading has the advantage, for it is found in other cheating-related *ku, eg.,* from *Pluck,* " *'My husband's a saint' / she uses the line / to get laid all the time"* (わたしらが内は仏とやたらさせ 1-22 *watashira ga uchi wa hotoke to yatara sase*). It is sometimes said that behind every saint one finds a martyr. This would be an exception to the rule. Seriously, it is an excellent line: any man with the least libido, is likely to take pity on such a woman. Still, Suzuki may be wrong, for "weak" may mean weak-willed in the face of his own desire.

乳母か来て聞ク毒断ハ二人リまへ 万
uba ga kite kiku dokudan wa futari-mae million 宝13
(nurse-maid-the coming hears poison-block-as-for two-servings)

気を付にけり
being careful

wet-nurse comes
to hear the patient cannot
have her, either

nanny comes &
listens – hers, too, is
contraindicated

English lacks a word for things or behaviors that are contraindicated. The "two-servings" in this subtle early senryu mean that she as well as the wife have been taken into consideration by the doctor, who guesses the husband may be spending more in his own home than his wife realizes. And wives, say senryu, often didn't get it. One *ku,* with *"a horrendous thing"* (すさましい事) for the draw, gives an example: *"The drinking alone / did him in, or so / his widow thinks"* (酒でのみ死んだと後家ハ思って居 万 明五 *sake de nomi shinda to goke wa omotteiru*). Who could imagine making love could be deadly?

とぼす度だんだんにへる身の油 葉31
tobosu tabi dandan ni heru mi-no-abura

Body as Lamp

Each time you light that wick –
It drops a bit: your oil reserves

While the idea of a fixed amount of sexual energy is ridiculous, there is far more validity to the idea of sex as debilitating than is usually admitted by those who would smirk at the Victorians or psychoanalyze the roots of fascism. People – even scientists – who experience life as a natural building up of excess calories that must be dieted or partied off, lack the ability to empathize with the psychology of those who must fight to maintain flesh over their skeletons, spend life in fear of wasting away, and are more often then not tired. If my multi-volume haiku *saijiki* ever makes it to the *Summer*, one of the themes included in the first book will be *natsu-yase,* a seasonal malady most Japanese desperately fought. As a *ku* of Issa's put it *"At my hut / even the weeds suffer from / summer wasting"* (我庵は草も夏痩したりけり *waga io wa kusa mo natsuyase shitarikeri*). *Natsu-yase* is literally, "summer-thinning," as in growing thin, and we should note that "thin" is written with radicals indicating it is a disease. I translated it as "wasting" to bring out the connotations *thin* no longer has in a topsy-turvy world where obesity, the natural fruit of health and wealth is treated as a disease.

ぼぼの生酔日の色が黄に見へる 葉末八
bobo no nama-ei hi no iro ga ki ni mieru leaf
(pussy's drunkenness sun-color-the yellow-as see)

To a cunt-drunk fellow
– the sun looks yellow!

To the pussy-plastered –
the sun no longer alabaster

(a published mistranslation: "*on a day when / her pussy is drunk / the world appears yellow*")

A womanizer is called a color-man (*iro-otoko*). Would too much of that color change the color of the sun? Here is the explanation by a specialist in the literature of sex born in 1934: "Anyone who has had the experience probably understands, but when a man comes two or three times at a time and does this for two or three days in a row, he becomes somewhat hung-over or dazed and it is popularly said that 'the sun looks yellow.'" I do not know how many English-language readers will nod in agreement, but I would not be surprised to find sexually active but chronically thin men who agree, not with the detail of the yellow sun – as we always draw the sun yellow, we would have a hard time noticing the same! – but in the more general sense that many ejaculations in a short time affects or may be felt in the eyes or that general area. Disproving vague claims of energy depletion, or precise ones of protein loss or material exchange (such as ancient Indian ones equating drops of blood with drops of cum) is easy, but completely misses the point here. Emission may well deplete certain trace elements, zinc and copper, for example, that are vital for ocular health. And we are just starting to recognize the role of many trace elements . . . .

りんじうをきたなくさせる美しさ　こころごころに 万
rinjû o kitanaku saseru utsukushisa *kokoro-gokoro ni* 安二

beauty enough
to make it very hard
to pass away

beauty enough
to destroy all hope for
a good death

his last days
are sullied by her
her beauty!

This is not necessarily a dry-kidney *ku*. It may only concern the effect of beauty. *Rinjû* is the period before a death when everyone knows death approaches. Like birth, it can last minutes or days. A good *rinjû* does not so much depend upon the age of death or the cause but the attitude of the dying party. If there are no regrets, it is good; if there are regrets or rage at the world, it is bad. Here, we imagine someone old enough that dying should have been accepted if not welcomed, sad to go because he must leave behind beauty which he would have liked to continue to enjoy. When we say *"You can't take it with you,"* we mean *"money."* To this man, it is his honey, the embodiment of *beauty*. I think the draw means such thoughts were on everyone's mind.()

行過ぎて気の毒そうな年女房 住吉躍
yukisugite ・kinodokusôna toshi-nyôbô 元禄 13

coming too often
how wretched a sight!
the older wife

二人目の女房の顔も悪くなり 折句駒むかへ
futarime no nyôbô no kao mo waruku nari 宝暦三

the appearance
of his second wife also
goes downhill

These are the female equivalents of dry-kidney. An older wife getting lots of service from her young husband would only age faster. Or, more commonly, a young wife who enjoyed being "stabbed to death" (「大物で突き殺した」鈴木) too many times by her well-endowed husband is replaced by another willing sacrifice to priapus. Note that the second *ku* does not even mention the cause. The stereotype was that well established. Still, women in senryu are as likely to waste away from consumption born of failure to consummate a one-sided love-affair or just remaining virgin, as from excessive orgasms. In that sense, they differ from men. A cat companion is *de rigeur* for such women, or senryu about them anyway: *"A black cat / his mistress has a short / leash on life"* (くろねこをみじかい玉の緒でつなぎ 柳 22-10 *kuro-neko o mijikai tama no o de tsunagi*). Always black, it was thought good for tuberculosis or pining away from other causes.

命がもの種・かねの生る樹を退く美男水加減
inochi ga monotane kane no umaru ki o noku binan 文政一
(life's things-seed money bares tree[acc] leave/escape pretty-man)

◎ life's the seed of all ◎
pretty boy kisses goodbye
to his money tree

The "beautiful man" I changed to "pretty boy" is the same character found in *"Just too much! / A gigolo takes leave of / the widow"* (あんまりで・後家の暇とる男妾小柴垣文化 1 *anmari de// goke no hima to no otokoshô*). One wonders if these Japanese gigolos weren't being a bit selfish, wanting to keep their jelly-roll and sell it too, but the point is that the widows threatened to milk their kidneys dry.

実にへのこ遣へどへらぬ身の宝 葉 18
jitsu ni henoko tsukaedo heranu mi no takara

reality: cock's
a treasure you can use
and not use up

This does not *really* contradict dry-kidney. The penis, like the moon, recovers, but the juice of life is another thing. It, according to most pre-modern traditions, is an unrenewable resource. The "reality" of the *ku* recalls the title of a collection of sayings from various sutra used as temple school (*terago*) primers, *"Real Word Teachings"* 実語教, and one of the sayings in it: *"True wealth is the treasure that lasts a lifetime"* (「富はこれ一生の材(たから)にある」).

めおとながらや夜を待らん・夕めしに腎の薬の汁をして 貞徳
meoto-nagara ya yoru o matsuran ・yûmeshi ni jin no kusuri no shiru o shite
(female-husband[mates] while! night[acc] wait! // evening-meal-for kidney-medicine-soup does)

man and wife, yet, still,
they can't wait for night

for his supper
he takes soup, herbal
for the kidney

This 7-7+5-7-5 link-verse sequence by Teitoku (1570-1673) predates senryu dry-kidney. It does not mention *jinkyo*, but "kidney," together with passion, made that clear. In the *Young-crowd* chapter, we have another *haikai* sequence with the word. But the disease was not *that* popular a topic, so I doubt it came to be synonymous with the person in *haikai*. *Mr.* Dry-kidney was probably a senryu invention. But *why* were there so many senryu about *jinkyo?* Did the lean poor men who wrote senryu and saw too many dirty prints masturbate too much, thus gaining first-hand knowledge, and interest in the subject? *Perhaps*. But, there is a better explanation for what is happening here. The thought of a serious down-side to being married to a beautiful woman, having an octopussy mistress, or enjoying not only lots of sex but variety as a gigolo, must have been of no small consolation to these lonely men.

ぢんきよのくやみうらやましそうにいゝ 万
jinkyo no kuyami urayamashisô ni ii million 安八

the condolences
for her dry-kidney – is that
an envious tone?

words of sympathy
for the late dry-kidney, some
seem envious

Just who is envious of whom! A woman with a husband who can't get it up jealous of the wife with a husband who couldn't get it to stay down? A man with an unattractive wife who would have preferred his friend's fate? One last chuckle:

大名ハ見た斗リても水かへり 万 宝十
daimyô wa mita bakari de mo mizu ga heri million

まんかちなこと
"that's just too much!"

just by looking
a great lord can run
his well dry

lord daimyô
runs down his water
just by looking

I am unsure if the *draw* I loosely Englished as the title refers to the monopolization of so many beauties by one man or the idea that the body humour of a man surrounded by dozens if not hundreds of beauties is so heated up it can evaporate out through the eyes, even if his ejaculations are held in check. Today, in much of the world, it is hard not to live like that daimyô, for beautiful men and women are continually broadcast for our viewing pleasure.

はからしい病気女を見るもどく 摘 2-10
bakarashii byôki onna o miru mo doku

what a ludicrous
disease! just looking at
women kills you

an absurd disease
where women kill you by
looking at them

a crazy disease
just looking at a woman
will do you in

By now, the reader should no longer need an explanation. So I won't give one.

~~~~~~

~~~~~~

~ *eddies* ~

~~~~~~

Lead Quote that Was Not. I thought of putting the following passage from Frank Harris's *My Life and Loves* vol.2 at the head of the chapter, but forbore because I did not want to give away the nature of dry-kidney too soon.

> I never dreamed . . that one day in my old age I should sing the praises of chastity; but clearly I see now that chastity is the mother of many virtues. There's a story of Balzac that illustrates my meaning, I think it's told by Gautier. The great novelist came in one day with a gloomy face. "What's the matter?" asked Gautier.
>
> "I had a wet dream last night," Balzac replied, "and consequently shall not be able to conceive any good story for at least a fortnight; yet I could certainly write a masterpiece in that time."
>
> I found out that the chastity must not be continued too long or one would become too susceptible to mere sensuous pleasure; the semen, so to say, would get into one's blood and affect the healthy current of one's life. But to feel drained for a fortnight after one orgasm . . . proves to demonstrate that Balzac, like Shakespeare, must have been of poor virility. Didn't Shakespeare . . .

.
While Harris's seduction for seduction's sake is disgusting, his diary is a must for both the sex and the literature (I loved the debate about the advantages of various languages. It is a mistake to read Anäis Nin and not Harris (and Casanova.))

~~~~~~

Blyth, Ueda and "the beautiful/good wife." When Ueda translated the same *ku* Blyth (1960) translated *"The good wife / Is decocting a medicine / That won't do any good,"* he was right to make her "beautiful," for coming before a woman "good" meant that; but, Blyth was using his poetic license to set up the poem for his explanation which was: *"She is too beautiful; he can't keep away from her."* In other words, if you saw just the translation you might think Blyth didn't get it; yet, seeing the explanation, it is clear Blyth did, Ueda didn't. That is because (I repeat myself) Blyth was old world, Ueda new.

~~~~~~

Throwing Sand. The idea of throwing sand to soften things is not limited to dry kidney in senryu. We find it used to soften up an uptight woman a bad bonze wants to make (pp. 202-3) and we find it in metaphor: *"The third meeting: you would think the prostitute had sand thrown on her"* (三會目女郎に土砂をかけたやう 摘 4-32 *sankaime jorô ni suna o kaketa yô*). On the first two visits to the Pleasure Quarters of Yoshiwara, a man's patience and pocketbook are tested. He does not get to sleep with the courtesan until his third visit.
~~~~~~

Loventropy. A limited resource may be measured in many ways. If Indians tended to calculate the cost of semen in terms of the cost of making it compared to the cost of making blood, the Japanese thought in terms of quotas. Not only were a man's *days* numbered, but his orgasms as well. Judging from the quota I saw (2,000), I have already used up several of my lives! But, as I have said, I do not mean to contradict the usefulness of medical ideas based on limits. Modern medicine, which only discovered some salt made sugar-water more easily absorbed after the invention of the first artificial heart, is still only beginning to understand what the body needs and how best to supply it. There is much still to be learned from health beliefs and practices around the world.

Healthy Sperm. There is much more to "empty-kidney" than my brief sketch indicates. One of the symptoms, worn-out (thin) sperm explains Issa's *alopecia* (white hair from a young age) – *his father overdid it* – the early death of Issa's and Kiku's five children: *He overdid it* – there are several days in a row where Issa, playing catch-up in his fifties, has coitus three times per night (note in his journal) and why Issa's last child Yata, lived: "because with [his last wife] Yao, he was over sixty and only managed to do it once a day." These are not *my* theories. They are commonplace, except, perhaps, the part I quoted, which Nishizawa Kitaru may have been the first to come up with. Issa's *journal* (spare notes + haiku) also show he drank egg-*sake* and suddenly got interested in snakes, both good fortifying food). Issa died shortly after impregnating Yata.

Recovering from Dry Kidney? I found two senryû that, at first glance, *seemed* to contradict the idea of dry-kidney as a disease where one can get it up though too tired to get up. At first, I worried that my understanding was wrong, but . . . you will see.

じんきょの容体昨今はおへませぬ
jinkyo no yôtai sakkon wa oemasenu 柳 37 & 葉 24
(kidney-empty's condition evening-now-as-for [he is]erect-not)

the dry-kidney's condition –
since last night, no erection.

In the original, the last 5's *oemasenu,* a polite negative of the verb "to erect," tells us the wife is reporting to the doctor. I cannot tell if the sexpert explicator of *Leaf*, Syunroan Syuzin, fails to pick up on the meaning/wit or assumes it will be grasped by readers, for he only mentions a dry-kidney as someone who used up his supply of vital juice. I asked myself, *Where is the wit?* The answer is that it lies entirely in the interpretation of what would usually be *bad* news as *good* news. The wife is reporting *progress* to the doctor, as not erecting for a couple days would do a man with dry-kidney good and show he may have a chance to recover – something very rare – after all. I only used two lines because the original *ku* clearly splits mid-way.

じんきょしたはりかた局二本持チ 万安 6
jinkyo shita harikata tsubone nihon mochi million

dry-kidney'ed
dildos – the lady-in-waiting
has two of them

One might think the dildos were simply worn out, and were no longer hard enough to do their work, but when you recall that a man with dry-kidney not only can get hard but *is* hard practically all the time because he just cannot stop thinking about sex, this is puzzling, until you recall that the good dildos used by these women in the palace held water. Well, the "kidney-empty" ones would have sprung leaks and, not holding water be put to pasture if it were, dry.

Dry Kidney and the Nature of the War Between the Sexes. In a culture where importance is placed on husbanding one's vital juices and pride is taken at being self-disciplined and dexterous, one finds coitus tends toward becoming a *contest* rather than *congress*, a battle of body and will power won by making the other party come first and more often than you do. This might sound horrid to a culture where people just naturally (?) make love. But, since men and women can, to some degree, learn to come faster or slower, this adversarial attitude toward sex probably results in more satisfaction for all. Whether they have participated in it or not, all literate Japanese are aware of the idea of make-the-other-come-first warfare, and that is why Kuroki Kaoru, the controversial porn-star I quoted on page 3, once pointed out that she was a revolutionary because her attitude was that whoever comes first *wins*, and she was happy to gain victory after victory, which is to say, lots of orgasms for her fans to enjoy. I have never seen her in action (as she was so thin I would not have bought a video even if I had a video player, which I did not), but whenever I came across her interviews I always listened, for it is rare to find anyone who *talks in ideas* in public (Some say, her producer was the brains, but if so, she must have had a photographic memory, for whatever she said always made good sense). I thought I mentioned this *coitus-as-contest* mentality elsewhere in the book, and searched for it after reading Screech's hypothesis that the division of heads from tails by clothing or mosquito nets in spring-prints was "intended to diminish the power of the picture to present sex as adversarial" and that this and other gimmicks "attempt to counteract a danger inherent in pornography, of a battle emerging between the partners." (1999) My position would be that *battle is fine*, so long as it is willingly engaged in, which is to say, *a game*. What is tricky for the modern/foreign viewer is to judge the winner in the contests from the picture. Is the woman or man who has just enjoyed an orgasm, and lies there basking in the afterglow, the winner or the loser? It depends. (This is not to say all the sex depicted is fine. Even in the 18c and early 19c when most sex depicted was, as Screech points out, egalitarian and seemingly consensual (with one partner a bought woman, it was a "Shungatopia") there were some rape scenes just as in senryu. But their existence should not detract from the fun of healthy adversarial sex.

さきんずる時は女房ふそく顔 万
sakinzuru toki wa nyôbô fusoku-kao 安元
(precede[another] time-as-for wife dissatisfied face)

~~*when he beats*~~
~~*her out, his wife looks like*~~
~~*a sore loser*~~

~~*when her pappy*~~
~~*comes first, mama sure*~~
~~*looks unhappy*~~

coming before
his wife, she looks far
from satisfied

Is she not satisfied only because of not coming herself? Or, could she be disappointed that her husband did not "win" by the traditional standard? I crossed out the first reading because it reverses the traditional win and lose concept and that would be going too far, though real women may well have preferred to "lose" the dry-kidney battle and win in the same manner as Kuroki Kaoru would. The second reading bored me. With the last, the "far" brings our attention to her eyes and life to the *ku.* I first had the reverse translation, too (*when the wife / comes before pappy, she / looks unhappy*), but respondent Y felt the grammar made that highly unlikely. I cannot recall any other *ku* about someone coming first.

Worms and Octopussy
蛸壷にミミズ千匹

八[8]

凸と凹の鑑
㊦ – Ideal Members – *II*

~~~~~~

爰が開だという所が蛸は口チ 葉 10
koko ga bobo da to iu toko ga tako wa kuchi
(here cunt is say place-the octopus-as-for mouth)

this here place
called the bobo is the mouth
octopus-wise

Yes, a cephalopod has its mouth between its legs. But, *so what?* It is far more interesting to note, after the best made-in-Japan insult I know, that your opponent resembles an octopus, i.e., *has a head full of shit!* This first senryu is one of a minority of *tako*=octopus *ku* that do not directly touch upon the main subject of the chapter, the *Octopussy*. I will include some more, though they may not even hint at it, because I suddenly realized that Blyth and Ueda did not only skip obscene senryu but short-changed *nonsensical* senryu. *Why?* Probably because nonsense – fantastic ideas, the imagination – has no place if senryu is defined as a humorous poetry based on real observation of how humans live, alone.

蛸の雪隠どの足でまたぐやら 105-43
tako no setchin dono ashi de matagu yara

an octopus
on the pot, which legs does
it squat with?

How would one number the legs? Clockwise from center-front looking up? down? The original uses the polite term, originally a euphemism, for toilet, "snow-hidden" (ordure fell into soft material, such as sand or feathers, within which it disappeared). I use pot, loosely, for the toilets were not stools. Rather than sitting, Japanese *squatted* over an oblong hole (past-tense, for a majority of Japanese toilets are now Occidentalized), rear rather than front facing the door.
~~~~~~

蛸曰く人の疝気は我が頭痛 103-25
tako iwaku hito no senki wa waga zutsû

says the octopus
what men call lumbago
i call a migraine

says octopus
the lumbago of man is
our headache

Lumbago was a pelvic complaint that peaked in winter months and, in Japan at least, was a highly visible disease, for it was also associated with the enormous balls (where the lumbago bug (*senki mushi*) was said to hide out) of some famous beggars, one-man walking freak-shows, who, artists would have us believe, used carrying poles to lug, or wheel-barrows to cart their excess baggage around.

蛸の切腹天窓をば一もんじ 160-2
tako no seppuku atama o ba ichi monji

an octopus
cuts its belly with a cross
on its head

octopus commits
seppuku: cutting across
its forehead

Perhaps I should have pronounced the self-evisceration "harakiri" (belly-cutting) here despite the more formal "seppuku" (cut-abdomen) suggested by the order of the Chinese characters. Japanese allows the freedom of pronouncing something as if the characters were reversed with some (not all) words and, here, the subject is a reversal, speaking of which,

女房が蛸で亭主がうなり出し
nyôbô ga tako de teishu ga unaridasu 50

his wife a tako
the husband is the one
who groans aloud

an octopus wife:
he does the groaning
every night

What is an *octopussy?* The simple explanation is *a woman with exceptionally good suction.* When you think about it, *suction* is a great thing, not only does it feel good but proves a hole has no leak – it is whole, ... Isn't it ridiculous that *"sucks"* in English describes a substandard item or a deplorable situation?

蛸の味万民これを賞翫す 123
tako no aji manmin kore o shôgan su 別
(octopus's flavor myriad folk this[acc] prize do)

the whole world
appreciates the flavor
of an octopus

If we are talking about the food, it is true. Unlike squid, octopus is not at all fishy and it has a much better *hagotae,* or "tooth-reply" (the English term *mouthfeel* is too general). I love both and would eat more if they were not so damned bright. Other things even, I try to eat as low on the brain-chain as possible. But this is senryu. It means all *men* love octopussy.

蛸壷といへば漁師の嫁笑ひ 70-8
takotsubo to ieba gyoshi no yome warai

called an octopus pot
she cracks up: the bride
of a fisherman!

called octopus pot
a fisherman's young wife
laughs aloud

There is a senryu that claims an *octopus* and a *draw-purse* do not taste all that different (大同小異巾着と蛸の味 108-7 *daidô koi kinchaku to tako no aji*), but that is mistaken. A draw-purse (*kinchaku*) is a vagina that pulls tightly shut at the mouth. The "octopus," is an abbreviation for an octopus *pot* (*takotsubo* 蛸壷), which is to say, a trap for an octopus. It has a relatively restricted entrance, which makes it superficially like a draw-purse, but the high regard for the octopussy suggests there must be something more. Grappling arms, or *legs* if you prefer, with suction cups alone seem to offer an alternative etymology. But that would leave the pot's role in the metaphor unexplained. If Sasama is correct, it is not the shape of the pot or the snug fit of the octopus within. It is what *happens* when you reach down it to pull out the octopus. Yes, the octopus grabs hold of the arm. Having felt that herself, the fisherman's wife knows the metaphor inside-out.

御寵愛足が八本ないばかり 安四礼 1
gochôai ashi ga happon nai bakari (又秘蔵は)
(favorite/adored legs-the eight not only 女陰万考に)

his favorite
you can almost see
her eight legs

his mistress
begs but one thing
eight legs

Concubine #1

from the way
he begs, we know
what she hides:
eight legs

"Lacks only ~" means *as good as has*. *ergo* she is an octopus. That works in English, as per the second reading ("begs" could be "lacks" or "wants," but I wanted the rhyme), but the rhetoric is, or was, more common in Japan.

いっちょく上がった蛸が御意に入り
icchoku agatta tako ga goi ni iri 88-5, 10

the very highest
octopus is the octopus
our lord favors

the elevated
octopus wins the heart
of his lordship

A literal translation would be that "the first-best-raised-octopus-honorable-heart-enters" (いっちょく＝「一番よく」). While, a so-called *high-fix*, or *up-cunt* was said to often be an octopussy, this was not always so; but, among a 100% cephalopod harem – nonsense, for women were chosen for facial beauty and political reasons – the senryu imagines an important personage enjoys, the one with it closest to the navel would be most beloved. (There's a wee possibility *agatta* also means *bashful*.)

けい中へ入ッて妾はたことなる 摘 2-37
keichû e haitte mekake wa tako to naru

as she enters
the boudoir, his mistress
turns octopus

in the boudoir
his mistress turns into
a cephalopod

One of the top 100 country hits of all time has a wife (not mistress, of course) who is a prim and proper *lady* until she closes the door of the bedroom and *lets her hair fall down* transforming instantly into a man-eating *woman*.

たこつぼの水上げ奇也床の花
takotsubo no mizuage ki nari tokonohana 80-7
(octopus-pot's unloading strange becomes bed-flower)

~~*octopus pots*~~
~~*out of water make strange*~~
~~*bed flowers*~~

the unloading
of an octopus pot makes
a rare bed-flower

~~*strange catch*~~
~~*found in the octopus pot*~~
~~*a bed-flower*~~

This is one of those *ku* I only keep because of the chance I will do a Japanese version of the book someday. A "bed-blossom" is a star of the boudoir. Some people have beautiful faces, some have more hidden graces. *Mizuage,* literally, "water-raising" is much more difficult here. At least four of its meanings are played upon. 1) A ceremony where a geisha or courtesan is deflowered (pardon my English, in Japanese she turns into a flower), ideally by a wealthy man who will be her patron and treat her well so as to not harm her long-term earning ability; 2) Unloading something caught from a boat, and by extension the catch itself; 3) By further extension, earnings from any business deal; 4) Cutting and otherwise preparing the stem of a flower for arrangement in water so it can keep a long time and also how that flower sucks up water. In addition to this, I should add that the courtesan as an extension of her private part was considered a boat. One might think she should be "launched," but to her proprietor, this was her first catch, as the man paid a huge sum to have first honors.

たこつぼでけつの毛迄も吸ィ取られ 摘
tako-tsubo de ketsu no ke made mo sui-torare 3-12
(octopus-pot-by/because ass's hair-until-even sucking-taken)

an octopussy
even his asshole is
stripped of hair

かの蛸魚に越前肥後を吸い取られ
ka no tako ni echizen higo o sui-torare

by those octopi
skin-trapped & stem-wrapped
alike sucked in!

また蛸に引ったくられた鎧形 47-
mata tako ni hittakurareta yoroigata -29

snatched again
by the hungry octopus
her man's armor

The echizen is a man with *phimosis* (ch.19). He could use help pulling his *glans* from hiding. *Higo* is short for *higo-zuiki,* the stem of taros grown in Higo, next to Echizen. These long stems were wrapped around (neatly crisscrossing in all the pictures) thin penises to beef them up and give the vagina a bit of a ribbing. Some old men probably tied them extra tight at the base to shore up their erections, but they got slimy and tended to slip off. Other thin or flaccid men wore "armor" made of tortoise shell around the penis shaft. Those did not come off so easily, but an octopus evidentally made short work of them. The use of such devices seems out of place here since an octopussy fits any penis perfectly. 81-8 ↓

イボがあるほうが蛸だと女房言い
ibo ga aru hô ga tako da to nyôbô ii

"the octopus?
it's the warty one"
says his wife

奥様の蛸で妾はあがったり
okusama no tako de mekake wa agattari

the wife's tako
puts his old mistress
out of business

The fun with the first *ku* is imagining the situation. It must be this: the husband mentions a *tako* as in *octopussy* and his wife says something in reply, though she really had no idea what he was talking about, and he snorts, "Oh yeah, what do *you* think an octopus is?" Her answer, which means she can tell it apart from a *squid*, reveals she has not an inkling of what he was talking about. The "old" is added to the second *ku* to fill space and because I imagine that the man was happy to poke around with someone of fast wit with a pretty face *when he was younger,* but now needs a really good twat to keep *it* up. One *ku* has a mistress *"become good by copying an octopus"* (たこの真似するがお妾上手なり 摘 2-7 *tako no mane suru ga omekake jôzu nari*), but that is only true to a degree, a small degree. A woman can become a "draw-purse" (*kinchaku*) by doing exercise to strengthen her gate-control, but an octopussy's undulating grip from the lips to the cervix is only come by naturally.

同し弐朱出して天蓋かいあたり 万
onaji ni shu dashite tengai kai atari 宝九

paying out
the same two bits and striking
a ciborium!

The *tengai,* or "heaven's lid" is the bowl-like hat of a bonze, for which he was called a tako, or "octopus," which alludes, then, to our *octopussy*. The draw was *"A rare thing it is! A rare thing it is!"* (*mare na koto kana* (x2)).

惜しい事壷は蛸だが面は芋 45 肌が鮫 106
oshii koto tsubo wa tako da ga tsura wa imo /hada ga tako

what a pity
the pot of an octopus
mug of a spud

what a pity
the pot of an octopus
skin of a shark

To escape the ugly "pot," I was tempted to translate: *"What a pity / an octopussy wasted / on shark-skin [spud face];"* but the original syntax was wittier.

芋面も蛸の果報に生れつき 摘 3-9
imozura mo tako no kahô ni umaretsuki

the potato face
with god's good grace
got an octopussy

縁付くは芋面に蛸させるなり 摘 3-22
enzuku wa imozura ni tako saseru nari

fortune smiles
when a potato face weds
an octopussy

With respect to the "mug of a spud" on the previous page or the potato faces here, we are talking about people scared by severe acne or small pox. The first *ku* means a woman cursed above but blessed below. The second either means the same as the first *ku,* or that a man with a small-pox-ruined face lucks out by gaining a wife who can make his nights heavenly. I favor the second reading because the prehensile member doesn't necessarily bring happiness to its owner. Regardless, there is wit here: octopus = bonzes were said to ravish potato fields.

蛸が牛咥えて引くや長局 新編 10
tako ga ushi kuwaete hiku ya nagatsubone

an octopus
pulls about an ox?
(lady-in-waiting)

edo harems
where octopussies
swallow oxen

We encountered the "lady-in-waiting" or "chamber maids" in the onanism chapter. If you recall, ox horn dildos were *de rigor* for the preservation of chastity in the palace womens quarter. I doubt they were all octopussies because beauties were generally chosen for their faces, not their fannies, though I could not resist using the word harem, strictly speaking incorrect, for the women in Japane were not restricted from going out and most did not engage in sex with their lord.

蛸壷にまぎれ込たる大海鼠
tako-tsubo ni magire-komitaru ônamako
(octopus-pot-into luck-into-enter big-sea-cucumber)

wandering into
an octopus pot,
a large seaslug

105-12,14

There are numerous octopussy senryu combining with other sea-life, particularly a large number of shells, each pertaining to a certain type of cunt. I will leave most to *The Mullet and the Maid*, if, for nothing else, because the descriptions and names of the various species, or families require too much introduction for readers unfamiliar to them to make single *ku* translations worthwhile. A quick sampling of some common marine metaphor (the normal, not ideal), mentioning only familiar items, may be found in the eddies. Now, let us get to those worms.

~~~~~~

A Thousand Worms & Herring Roe

開の雑物数の子の肌ざわり 葉 14
bobo no zômotsu kazunoko no hadazawari
(cunt's variety-thing number-child[=herring-roe]'s skin-feeling)

a personal effect
of the bride's bobo, the feel
of herring roe

a sundry good:
the herring roe feeling
in her bobo

dressed inside
as well as out, her trousseau
is herring roe

Zômotsu, "sundry-things," itself means many things and one is the clothing and other personal effects in a bride's trousseau. *Herring roe* is short for a "herring roe-ceiling" (*kazunoko tenjô* 天井) and is the most common description of a stimulating texture on the dorsal wall of the vagina. I recall reading that childbirth can develop blood vessels and nerves in the vagina in ways favorable to both parties in coitus and that this herring roe is only found in women who have had childbirth. But I have not yet read enough (and probably never will) to know if that explanation was standard at the time the senryu was composed (which I also do not know). If it was, than we are talking about a bride that has already given birth. Herring roe is not, however, as highly ranked as the so-called "thousand-worms," *mimizu senbiki* (蚯蚓千匹), which is to say a vagina, that seems to quiver and tingle and squirm on all sides of the penis.

章魚でいい蚯蚓千匹だけは嫌
tako de ii mimizu senbiki dake wa iya
(octopus-c̱ ok worms-a-thousand only-as-for yuck)

keep it octopus
call me anything but
a thousand worms!

octopus, okay,
just don't call me that!
a thousand worms

I came across the term "a thousand worms" (*mimizu senbiki*) more often than "octopussy" (*tako[tsubo]*) in the evening sports newspapers commonly read by commuters on Japanese trains in the 1970's, 80's and 90's (There was always a
~~~~~~

column or two speculating on genital details and responsiveness of women based on the characteristics of an actress's face or a "soap-girl's" body, etc.), but if there are senryu about those worms – I thought I would find *many* when I began writing this chapter – I must have lost them. So, I made up the above *ku*, which includes an opinion I read somewhere and share, namely, that *a "thousand worms" is the same thing as an octopussy.*

海恋し腎の水まで吸い取られ
umi koishi jin no mizu made sui-torare

pining for the sea
even his liver water
is all sucked up

This one, too, is made-to-order. I am summing up a sentence about the octopussy from what would seem to be a late-18c or early-19c typology of male and female parts (失題艶道物) which claims that *"only this octopussy* (*tako-bobo*) . . . *by tightly holding and stimulating the cock within like this, will empty a man's liver"* (. . . 男の腎虚するはこの蛸ぼぼに限れり). You may note some contradiction between this and what was said in the chapter on dry-liver. The *ku* introduced there made the wife's beauty, i.e. *face,* the culprit. Here, it is something deeper within, yet further from the heart, that speaks directly to his part. If visual beauty can backfire, so can *tactile beauty*, if something that *feels* delectable can be so defined.

~ *eddies* ~

Fantasy, not only a problem for senryu. In my essays of themes in haiku, I have given favored treatment to fantasy, because it has been largely ignored by editors who believe that haiku only has room for objective realism, perhaps with some feeling, but only if it is "sincere." Oddly enough, a few such haiku escape the usual censure and make it big, Shôha's sea cucumber talking to the moon jellyfish (see *Rise, Ye Sea Slugs!*) and Bashô's wish to see the face of the famously Ugly God while blossom-viewing are such.

Some Marine Metaphor. The most common marine metaphor, and perhaps the most common metaphor for a cunt in senryû is the vulvic clam, a metaphor also found in folk-song. I do not know how old this folk song (next page) from Tsugaru (Northeast Japan) presented by Takenaka Rô as an example of a song still sung as it was before the drive to become a modern "civilized" state cleaned the country of its dirtiness, leaving the folk "castrated," (かくて、ニッポン人は去勢される。。。『にっぽん情哥行』), but since the genre of folksong (and probably this one) is far older than senryû, it is a good a place to begin as anywhere.

磯のはまぐり 掘るよりも　わたしのはまぐり　ほらせたい　十三潮「坊様おどり」
iso no hamaguri horu yori mo hitori-banareta yama oku de watashi no hamaguri horasetai
(shore's clam/s dig rather than, isolated mountain-outback-in my clam/s dig-want[you to])

invitation

forget the clams,
on the sea-shore, dear!
come to the mountains
and dig mine!

The big difference between folk-song and senryû is that, in the latter, clams do not generally speak for themselves. The metaphor may be more than one reading makes apparent. The clams on the shore may not be clams. This may well have originated as a woman-of-the-hills versus a woman-of-the-shore song. They are described by their consumers, men:

蛤は芝居でむだなしおをふき 万
hamaguri wa shibai de muda na shio o fuki 宝 11
(clam/s-as-for drama-at/for wasteful brine[acc] blow?/wipe?)

~~*the clam*~~
~~*squirts brine in vain*~~
~~*on stage*~~

the clams
squirt brine in vain
at plays

those clams
at the plays, wiping off
wasted juice

Buried in the sand with the slightly opened edges of the shell all that is visible the clam is said to be a perfect simulation of the real thing. And it was known for squirting brine. ~~The stripper should not. She is actually turned on when she should only be faking it~~. At first, I was not attentive enough to the fine points of the grammar, the significance of the *wa* (as-for), which makes the *ku* express something about clams/women [and their cunts] *in general.* Women were known for losing themselves in drama and having crushes on the actors (see pg. 85). The squirting/wiping (both *fuki*) pun could not be Englished.

まんちう舟やき蛤て入リをとり 万明四
manjû-bune yaki-hamaguri de iri o toru

high-tide

a boat-dumpling
rakes in the cash with
her baked clam

In *haikai*, people usually traveled to the beaches of Kuwana for clams, broiled on pine cones/balls (*fuguri*) but they could be had elsewhere, too. As editor Okada Hajime explains, it's hard to say whether the floating whore called a boat-dumpling (or boat-nuns!) is actually selling this item on the side – a metaphorical front – or keeping her own clam warm with a "crotch-fire" heater, that her cold-weather customers pay to baste.

へのこを握ってうなぎを釣った夢 葉 7
henoko o nigitte unagi o tsutta yume

gripping his cock
he dreamed that he
caught an eel

cock in hand
he sniggled an eel and
then woke up

Kikaku's dream of a mighty battle, waking up to flea-bites, or, rather, his haiku about it is well known. This later senryû is not. Why so? That is something to think about.

濡イハは女房うなぎの手あんばい 葉 24
nuremara wa nyobo unagi no te anbai

a wet pecker
luckily his wife is
a good sniggler

his wet penis
his old wife knows how
to handle eels

Whether the cock is not fully erect from the start, comes quickly so his wife wants to try to coax a bit more life from it or revive it for another round we do not know. But, we may imagine that she has become a skillful sniggler, or better yet eel-handler.

~~~~~~

Metaphor's Victims. According to a book (十九「金草鞋」初) dated 文化十 1813, female seafood venders had trouble plying their trade for fear their loud advertisements might be taken the wrong way. For example, to walk the streets shouting *"Octopus! Octopus!"* might lead people to think she was boasting of something else she was selling. As a result, the cries had to be altered to "Fish-octopus!" so the cephalopod would not be confused for the two-legged variety. The complaint is written in a journalistic manner and the editor of *Cuntologia* notes that it shows how these slang terms had become the common idiom. I would guess the complaint was pure spoof and am not bold enough to guess how well known the slang was. But, pseudo or not, it is an interesting phenomenon to contemplate. I will translate the passage in full for *The Mullet In the Maid.*

~~~~~~

Women Who have had Children. As there is apprehension over what the pas-sage of a child can do to the width of the woman's vagina, it is good to have pre-modern testimony to the effect that birth is not necessarily bad for a woman's sexuality.

開がわりしたと産後に亭主する 葉 5
kai-gawari shita to sango ni teishu suru

post-partum sex
it's like you got a new cunt
her old man says

sex after birth
so you traded in your cunt
her hubby says

The herring roe ceiling said to follow childbirth was part of the increase of "miscellany" (雑物 *zômotsu*) or "furniture" (道具 *dôgu*) within the vagina, said to feel good to both parties. Syunroan Syuzin has a long 1835 quote detailing the way the vagina of a woman who has given birth once is the best-outfitted (!) one of all. Note: we are not talking about sex just after birth, but after the 75 day post-partum period was over and the new and "improved" (Solt) pussy was again open for business.

~~~~~~

Herring Roe and Lice. Remember "anything but worms" (pg139)? It is possible my unconscious mind played tricks with the following senryu (c.1800) translated by Blyth:
~~~~~~

虱にたとへ数の子で叱られる 23-23
shirami ni tatoe kazunoko de shikarareru

scolded for
comparing herring roe
to lice

Besides re-parsing, centering and changing "and" to "to" (because a *tatoe* is making one thing stand for another), the translation is as Blyth did it. I have never cracked lice, but I have cracked hundreds if not thousands of fleas, and the ones full of blood (or, babies, if Issa is to be believed) make a sound that at least felt through the back of the nails seems similar to the roe between the teeth. Which is to say, this would not be about a woman's part, and if it was my memory, my memory was wrong.

~~~~~~

▲ ***One more Octopus!*** Reading *"The octopus doctor / – no place for women / to frequent"* (たこ薬師女の参ルとこでなし　万宝十三 *takoyakishi onna no mairu toko de nashi*), I was fascinated to encounter one more odd octopus in Japan. But what did he do? Diving into my OJD, I learned that this is a pharmacist/doctor who specializes in treating *baldness* and – get ready for the best part! – *all the patients must swear off eating octopus for life!*

◎ オマケ ◎

ロチュウチュウ蛸かいな味のよさ 119

~~~~~~

< next page >

My ***Octopussy*** Embarrassment, or *apologia*, in the classic sense of rationalizing something the nincompoops may well object to.

< next page >

~~~~~~
~~~~~~

Beware of *Fraud!* there is *octopussy* and there is *O C T O P U S S Y*

*Googling "octopussy," horror of horrors – it was the name of an old James Bond movie!
How can that be?! Were such a woman's private parts central to the movie? Or,
did James meet a cephalopod that purred? Avant-garde composer Sadie
met a holothurian (sea cucumber) that did. One never knows.
But, how did such a salacious movie title
ever pass the censors? And,
tell, me: will i now
be sued?*

*Thank
God for
Wikipedia
and all (including
me, I guess,) who contribute!*
I was getting nowhere in my Octopussy investigation,
which followed the discovery of being scooped by decades by
Ian Fleming. *"The title, 'Octopussy' is said to have come from a coracle
owned by Blance Blackwell that was given to Fleming at his home in Jamaica.
In the short story, 'Octopussy' is the name of Major Dexter Smythe's pet octopus.
For the film, the Bond girl is actually named 'Octopussy', saying it was the nickname
for her used by her father (Smythe). Magda, a henchwoman of the title character, also
refers to her cult-member tattoo of an octopus as, 'My little octopussy'."* We know the
contributor was not Usanian because the quotations were placed outside of the commas.
A *'coracle'* is a small circular boat from Wales or Ireland made of bark or oiled cloth
or something – perhaps I have seen one depicted by Lear – but the point to be made
is that agent James Bond did not invent the name for a woman with a particularly
clinging member, and hence Fleming's *octopussy* and mine are two completely
unrelated words that happen to be spelled the same. Any native speaker
of English living in a country where *cunts* are called *pussies,*
who translated poems about women called *octopuses*
because of their literally succulent members
could not call them anything but
"octopussy/ octopussies!"

of a different ilk: fleming's *vs.* mine

It Starts with Warming Up

ねるハ、ねれるカラ

九 9

凸+凹の過程を
Sex, *the* Process *of* ~

~~~~~~

練れた開 *Warming Up*

~~~~~~

女房ハかごでかゑつてしかられる
nyôbô wa kago de kaette shikarareru 17-4
(wife-as-for basket-by returning scolded-is)

using a sedan
to go home his good wife
is chewed out

the wife returns
in a basket and gets
a tongue lashing

ちか道をかへつて娵ハしかられる
chikamichi o kaette yome wa shikarareru 16-3
(shortcut[acc] returning bride-as-for scolded)

the young wife
is scolded for taking
a short cut home

くたびれて来たか女房のみやけなり 安二
kutabirete kita ga nyôbô no miyage nari 礼四
(exhausted came-that wife's present becomes)

arriving home
dead-tired is a gift
from the wife

bringing a gift
home: the good wife
is exhausted

Can you *guess* what is happening? Another version of the first *ku* has the more polite *okusama* for wife, but it is not needed as only well-off people could afford two or four-human-power taxi service, which some might call a palanquin but was often nothing more than what it was called, literally in Japanese, a *basket*.

折リ／＼は遠道させてあじをつけ 万
oriori wa endô sasete aji o tsuke 明三

from time to time
he has her walk the long way
to add some spice

he has her labor
the long way home, to add
flavor sometimes

now and then
for seasoning, he has her
take the long-cut

If the first three *ku* did not tell you what is going on, this one in three readings surely does. I invented the "long-cut" in the last reading because, in the original, it is a perfect antithesis of the "short-cut" (遠道 *vs.* 近道). Still, none of the four senryu above actually include *nereru/nereta,* a verb usually meaning *knead/ed*, but, in senryu context, always meaning one thing, *physical exercise undertaken to make a woman more responsive a sex partner.* A few more *ku*, with the word, which I will usually translate as "warming/ed up," explicit:

能く練れる事神の如し御百度 158
yoku nereru jishin no gotoshi o-hyakudo -11
(well kneads thing-god-like [hon.+]100-times)

heavenly indeed
a hundred prayers leave her
all warmed up

神楽堂ねれつくねれつくと亭主打ち
kaguradô neretsuku neretsuku to teishu uchi 46-37
(kagura-shrine warm/knead-get [x2] husband whips)

spurring her on
her pilgrimage, hubby is
hot on her tail

kagura shrine
warm up! warm up! hubby
spurs her on

神楽堂ちょっと一ねれ十二文 56-39,
kaguradô chotto hito-nere jûni mon 68-19

kagura temple
each warm up stint
twelve pence

The walk from shrine to shrine (Shintô) or temple to temple (Buddhist) or from one temple to another and back within a temple complex to offer a prayer or petition at each for a hundred times in a single stretch is called what my dictionary translates as "a hundred times worship." I think we might call it a frantic pilgrimage or prayer walk or many other things. Twelve *mon* was the cost of a small bottle of *sake* or a candle. I imagine one or the other was offered at each stop. The misuse of sacred activities and holy places to improve one's sex life evidently delighted those who wrote senryu, for there are scores of them. *"God-play-slope / Even the cave door softens / c hundred-times"*(御百度で岩戸もねれる神楽坂 *ohyakudo se iwato mo nereru kugarazaka),* if I may mention but one, representative of how these *ku* do not translate. Kagurazaka is only a place name, but taken literally hints at Mons veneris which is a good place for that grotto . . .

神楽堂 美しいほど よくねれる 34-35
kagura-dô utsukushii hodo yoku nereru

kagura shrine
the prettier they are the more
they warm up

Do beauties need to prove they love as good as they look? Or, is it because mistresses, whose livelihood depends upon being good in bed, also look pretty?

足る事を知らず蛸だに六阿弥陀 106-19,27
taru koto o shirazu tako da ni rokuamida

not content to leave
good alone, an octopussy
does six-buddhas

ねれて来て七番に成る六あみだ 末摘
nerete kite nanaban ni naru rokuamida 1-29

his wife returns
in need of a seventh round
six-buddhas

coming home
warmed up for a 7th round
six-buddhas

つふの無ィやうにねれるハ六あみた 同
tsubu no nai yô ni nereru wa rokuamida 2-30

kneaded enough
to lose all of her lumps
six-buddhas

Similar to the "hundred-times," this course (30 kilometers (七里半) in Edo) , usually reserved for the equinoxes, went from one Buddha statue to another. The "octopussy" (ch.8) needs no warm up. Re. the second *ku,* I first thought the walk home made it seven, but *ban* (番) also means *bout*, a round of sex. While *nereru* can mean "knead," that connotation is rarely developed. With the last *ku*, grains of *mochi* are pounded into a glutinous rice "cake" or "dumpling" (nothing like either, but English has no word for springy food (except the negative *rubbery*) – a gap in our culinary vocabulary which leaves us bereft of a needed metaphor). A cognate senryu has the *"present for hubby kneaded as much as millet-mochi,"* (ていしゆへのみやげあわ餅ほどにねれ 同 1-12 *teishû e no miyage awamochi hodo ni nere*) lascivious in the original because *millet* (*awa*) and *froth* are homophones.

とろふりと　れたを女房みやけなり
tôrori to nereta o nyôbô miyage nari 万安六

that's his gift
from the wife: kneaded
onto slime

We have seen the "gift from the wife" expression already, but this is a big improvement, at least in Japanese. The translation per se is no problem, but *slime* is not favored in English. Most native-speakers of English think of amphibian's mating, drool, mucous and other yucky things. In Japanese, the first thing one thinks of is half-a-dozen delicious, slimy foods. Again, we are at a loss for metaphor because of our culinary poverty. One robin does not make the spring, and okra by itself doesn't change a thing. Unless you have eaten slimy foods enough to have gotten over your prejudice, no amount of explaining will do.

機織りは遠道よりもよく練れる
hataori wa endô yorimo yoku nereru 40-29

using a loom
kneads one better than
a long road

其晩は片練れになる機の足
sono ban wa katanere ni naru hata no ashi

that evening
it was half-warmed up
her loom leg

40-29 ↑ Senryu like looms. On page 340, we'll find how working a loom makes the labia speak. Evidently, not all looms required both legs to work.

泥くさくぼぼのねれるは田植なり葉
doro-kusaku bobo no nereru wa taue nari 20

when bobos
stinking of mud warm up
rice-planting

rice planting
that's when muddy bobo
get warmed up

And it is when every man wishes for webbed hands and feet and eyes on his head. If we stand tall to be close to heaven, frogs can see it sitting down, thank you.

盆踊り踊り過ぎたる練れ加減
bon-odori odori-sugitaru nere-kagen

bon-dancing
too much is just right
for a warm-up

ねれるのを楽しみにして笛を吹き
nereru no o tanoshimi ni shite fue o fuki

looking forward
to a warm kneaded one
blowing his fife

The second senryu (摘 3-7) is a gem and would make a fine erotic haiku. The fife/ flute (*fue*) is, with the drum (and sometimes *shamisen*) the main instrument for the *bon* (all soul?) dances. Its notes are not delicate, though they may trail off in a fine flourish of complexity and the initial note usually blasts forth like an elemental force of nature or, if you have heard him, Tito Fuentes.

日帰りに練馬の里へ亭主やり 47-4
higaeri ni nerima no sato e teishu yari

her husband has her
go home to nerima
same day return

The wife's hometown, which includes the word "kneaded/ing" (*neri*) in it, is a long walk away, yet he wants her to come back the same day rather than spending the night there, so he can enjoy her tired but sexually responsive body.

練れぬはずくすねた銭で駕籠に乗り
nerenu hazu kusuneta zeni de kago ni nori 39-13

not kneaded? in fact
with coins tucked away she paid
for a sedan back

It would seem not all wives appreciated having to labor for better sex.

ねり供養見て来た女房湯へやらず
neri-kuyô mite kita nyôbô yu e yarazu 61-11

his wife back from
the saints' procession won't let
him take a bath

The early summer processions at temples around Japan called *neri-kuyô,* included Buddhist priests wearing the masks of saints and young children. The same *neri* for kneading is in the name of the procession because it is what the various parade-style walks (one could do an entire dictionary of such walks, one of which, described by Kaempfer in 1692, beats Monty Python's best) are called, and the association is that she, too, is well warmed-up for sex and wants her husband to fuck her well. Like walking, a hot bath helped a woman warm up for good sex, but for a man, it was thought to soften him and dissipate energy. For men, *sake* was recommended, for it slowed him down a bit while increasing the blood flow (I doubt the latter is true, but the way it reddens faces on half of all Japanese, it sure would seem to be the case). So, too, was another beverage:

茶によったのハ女房もうれしかり
cha ni yotta no wa nyôbô mo ureshikari 天三追善

high on tea
his old wife, too
is delighted

Supposing this means that caffeine keeps him awake – a man cannot snore and pleasure his wife at the same time – I added "old." Her husband is older yet.

女房のきらいはねれたへのこなり 葉20
nyôbô no kirai wa nereta henoko nari 天四類句有

what all wives
deplore is a pecker
already kneaded

what wives hate
is a pecker already
all warmed up

男のはねれてさっぱりいかぬ也
otoko no wa nerete sappari ikanu nari
(man's as-for kneaded completely do-won't becomes)

a man's part
warmed up is not
hot to trot

warmed up
a man's turns into
a cold fish

warmed up
a man's part is
useless as a fart

Not just a warm bath, but all warming up was thought bad for a man. This is a fact. With men, it tends to stand up when we sit or lie down. I would not be surprised if this were the main reason why women are forced to do, or if you think it a good thing, get to do, most of the hard labor in many parts of the world, especially where it is hot and men would sweat off too much energy. Men have good reason to be lazy.

ねれたへのこを提灯と申すなり 万
nereta henoko o chôchin to môsu nari 天六

kneaded cocks
you might call them
paper lanterns

I.e., flaccid, encircled with folds, like that of an old man, which were called lanterns. This is not to say kneading *always* worked for women either:

六阿弥陀練れは練れたが死んだよぅ
roku-amida nereba nereta ga shinda yô
(six bud. knead-if kneaded but dead-like/seem)

six-buddha walk
she kneaded and kneaded but
dead is still dead

六阿弥陀婆ァ無駄に練れて来る
roku-amida babaa muda ni nerete kuru
(six budds old-lady uselessly kneading comes)

six buddha walk
gramma returns, her kneading
went for naught

The "still" in the first *ku* (89-27↑) might be uncalled for. We cannot tell if the old lady's wasted effort, assuming it was an effort and not just incidental to the outing, failed to warm up a dried-up twat, or succeeded in *that* but failed to arouse grandpa's interest. Regardless, getting warmed up is no guarantee (31-30↑) of continuation to the next step, but first, the male equivalent to being warmed up.

勃・生したり *Erecting*

Because "erection" is too long for something common, we prefer "hard-on" or "boner." Japanese lacks a *noun* for the same but has what we lack, a good folksy-sounding verb specific to erection, *oeru/oyasu/oyakasu* (勃 or 生). This verb had the colloquial feeling proper to improper poetry and was much used. Yet today, Japanese use a verb closer to "erect," which we will not mention again: *bôki-suru.*

勃えたのを帯にはさんでしめ殺し
oeta no o obi ni hasande shimegoroshi
(erected one [acc] obi/sash-in/by scissored, squeeze-murder)

standing cocks
strangled between the wraps
of their sashes

catching a ferret
between the folds of his sash
and choking it

Obi sashes are thick and hard and wrapped several times around the torso. Such a method of killing by concealment may work when one is occupied with work but, like setting backfires, probably backfired (wet sashes). The above is no great *ku*, but beats generalizations such as *"Even hard-ons / are a waste says / the single man"* (勃してもつまりませんと独り者 *oyashite mo tsumarimasen to hitori-mono*), which, oddly is better when the hard-ons are exchanged for *farts* (pg. 369). Another *ku* c̲ cock-in-sash ends happily with the name of a stream forded by the *Tale of Ise* loverboy (おへたのを帯へはさんで河内越 *oeta no o obi e hasande kawachigoe*).

おやかして洗濯をする側へ落ち 万
oyakashite sentaku o suru soba e ochi 安六
(erected/ing, laundry doing[person]side-to falling)

becoming erect
he lands next to a maiden
washing laundry

landing next to
the laundress who gave him
the erection

his cock cap-
-sizes him into the river
from his cloud

A Chinese sage (久米仙人) fell from his cloud into the river when he saw the white thighs of a woman washing laundry. Allusions to this legendary happening abound in Japanese literature. I do not know if he ever got back up. The *erect* in the original is transitive 他動的, hence the second reading, but such a usage may only be respectful. My first third reading was *"his cock stands / while he falls ~."*

神棚にまでおやしている遊女町 43-17,
kamidana ni made oyashite-iru yûjo machi 23
(god-shelf-until erected playwoman (courtesan) town)

they're even erect
up on their god shelves
the playgirl town

The god-shelf is a household shrine or altar and the play-girl is a literal translation for what is usually Englished as courtesan. They did indeed place phalluses there. The senryu captures the titillating atmosphere from the male viewpoint by pretending that anything in the presence of these women can't help but erect.

耳をほる娵を見ていておやすなり
mimi o horu yome o mite-ite oyasu-nari
(ear[acc] dig bride[acc] seeing erect-become)

the newlywed
gets hard watching her
clean his ear

耳を掘る嫁を見て居てツイおやし
mimi o horu yome o mite-ite tsui oyashi
(ear[acc] dig bride[acc] seeing ends-up erecting)

seeing his bride
clean his ear he ends up
with a hard-on

↑2-22. People in love like to watch their lover concentrating. ↑葉別 2. Japanese clean ears with thin wooden spoons. Mothers do it for children and wives for husbands. It takes concentration and is only possible when the tool is in the hands of a dexterous and calm person in a quiet environment. A "bride" means a wife of short-standing, though she may be called a bride *for years* to differentiate her from her mother-in-law, the "wife" of the greater household.

生えたかと豆のもやしをなぶる也 52-2,
oeta ka to mame no moyashi o naburu nari 65-13
(erected?[asks] & bean's sprout/flame[acc] strokes)

are you erect?
he asks while stroking
the bean sprout

sprouting yet?
he asks while he strokes
the hot bean

The Japanese verb for erection seems to share something with *growing*, for like growing hair, the character chosen (生) is one that primarily means *life*. One feels the suitability of the verb for a culture that was fertility rather than creation-centered. Here, the English hard-on was impossible for it concerns "a" hard-on, while it is a woman whose readiness for sex is being questioned by the man who is diligently tickling her clitoris. The *moyashi* has two possible readings. Most probably it is the slight enlargement of the clitoris like a bean starting to sprout. Change "erect" to "ready" or "aroused" if you wish. I left it above to bring out the difference in the Japanese verb, which can be used for women, too, and ours which cannot. One unisex verb arrived in the egalitarian 1960's: *turned on*, but it is based on modern technology, and would be ludicrous in a translation of pre-modern poetry.

おやしたも知れぬで女罪深し 摘
oyashita mo shirenu de onna tsumi-bukashi 1-10
(erected even know-cannot-from woman/en sin-deep)

how heavy the sins
of women, for who can tell
when they're erect

though aroused
we cannot tell, so women
are close to hell

Same arousal or not, the hidden sin is deeper. Japanese also had different terms for female arousal. The way they are introduced suggests that the verbs used for both sexes may have been proper to the clitoris alone and barely acceptable as a description of the woman's entire sex –

うじゃじゃけたように女はおやす也
ujajaketa yô ni onna oyasu nari 4-8
(ripe-like woman/en-as-for erect is/are)

like ripe fruit
swollen and oozing, women
get aroused

over- ripe fruit
tingling with bugs: women
when aroused

おへるかわりに女房も朝うじゃけ
oeru kawari ni nyôbô mo asa ujake 葉 四
(erect replacing-c wife's/wives' too morning-ripe)

waking up hard:
wives have their morning
ripeness instead

instead of morning
erections, wives have their
rutty swarming

With men, the verb in the first *ku, oyasu,* means *erection* but, here, it means arousal in a more general, but still specifically sexual sense. Unfortunately, even two readings fall short of the sensual *uja-ujaketa.* The hot, swollen, throbbing, ripeness seems to ooze from the word itself. The verb *oeru* in the second *ku* means a penile erection, period, for it is given *ujake* as a counterpart. Another wet-as-aroused *ku* from *Leaf* brings us back to the moment we have reached: *"When her face burns / The water brigade / leaves her pussy"* (顔が火になると開から水を出し 葉別 2 *kao ga hi ni naru to bobo kara mizu o dashi*). Meanwhile –

すずロにたらり男根の三番叟　葉
*suzuguchi ni tarari dankon no sanba-*sô leaf 8
(bell-mouth-in/from dripping male-root's third performance)

tô~tô~ tarari, indeed!

drooling from
his bell mouth, peter's
last prelude

Japanese have bells of metal and wood with slit-like openings slightly enlarged at both ends. The meatus of the glans penis is like that, hence "bell-mouth." The *sanba-sô* is the third of the prelude acts to a Noh Play and is immediately followed by the main act. The crazy codger typically heads-off his remarks with *tôtô tarari* which, in one composition (大観本謡曲) was expanded to *tôtô-tarari-tararira, tarari-agarirarari.* In the original *ku* we have *tarari* alone. It means to dangle or drip down profusely. The *tôtô,* not actually in the *ku* has more meanings than one can shake a stick at. Among them, "at long last," "a massive flow of water," "a drum sounding out," "the sound of wind-bells or (hollow?)

gems," "sassy refrains from old songfests (mostly settling who sleeps with whom)" or "the shout (掛け声) used in *kendô*" while on the attack with the wooden or bamboo sword. The OJD has the etymology down as not yet known (語義未詳). I wonder if there might not be an Indian connection . . .

穴際 *Littoral*

指先で名所をさがす開行脚 葉末
yubisaki de meisho o sagasu bobo-angya 8ウ
(fingertip/s-with famous-places[acc] search cunt-pilgrimage/tour))

hunting for all
the famous spots: a digital
bobo pilgrimage

the scenic tour
of the bobo: let your fingers
do the walking

Where does it begin to be called sex? Do fingers count? Solt (1996) translates directly *"fingertips search / for famous sights /on pussy pilgrimage."* Some Japanese pilgrims might better be called tourists. As temples were sights, the attitude of the walker was what counted. For hundreds of years, Japanese have compiled lists of sight-seeing locations in given locales. Syunroan (1995) lists nine places to see in or in the area of the *bobo*. How many can you think of? He also gives a *ku* that I passed up on once, but on second thought, must translate:

谷の清水を指で汲む面白さ 126-65
tani no kiyomizu o yubi de kumu omoshirosa

how much fun
to draw pure valley water
with your fingers

To Japanese, such water was virtually sacred and typically drunk from cupped hands. Does equating the *bobo* with a shrine and pre-coital lubrication to pure (and purifying) spring water, etc. make up for the offensiveness of other senryu?

交合 *Coitus*

床コ闇に成るとへのこの手力雄
tokoyami ni naru to henoko no tajikara-o 葉 8
(bed-dark-to become and/when cock's hand-strength-male)

when utter darkness
comes to bed the crotch-child
becomes armstrong

床闇の岩戸に指の手力雄 新
tokoyami no iwato ni yubi no tajikara-o 39-7
(bed-darkness's cave-door-in fingers'handstrength-male)

when utter darkness
comes to bed, the cave-door's
held by fingerstrong

When Amaterasu-omikami shut herself up in the cave leaving the world in "perpetual dark" (*tokoyami* 常闇), a God whose name literally translates as Hand-strength-male held open the rock/door used to seal the cave after the Goddess peeked out to see what the commotion was (a raucous dance or striptease – by starlight, I guess – by another goddess caused the uproar). The bed (床 *toko*) is a homophone of "perpetual," hence "bed-dark." The second, later *ku,* bests the previous one in the original because maintaining a logical link – *arm* and *finger* – beats radical change. In *translation*, however, the cock in the first worked better because I made it a *crotch-child*, so it could grow into an adult Armstrong. I am not being *utterly* irresponsible in this, for the word for cock in the original, *henoko*, sounds like *a child* (子 *ko*) of the *he*, which can mean "fart," something identified with crotches. At any rate, the cave door is now ajar and –

ぬっと入れる所が天の美碌なり 葉六
nutto ireru tokoro ga ten no miroku nari leaf

that moment
you slip it in is a gift
from heaven

heaven's grace
the moment when you
first slip it in

This *ku* borrows from an old saying that *sake* is a gift from heaven. Thinking of the soft warm feeling of single-malt down the throat, I guess a woman might feel the same. The *ku* is smoother than another *Pluck ku* cited by Syunroan: *"A cock you'd think would hiss when stuck in"* (ぬっと入れたらぢうといいそなへのこ 万八・摘 2-33 *nutto iretara jû to ii so na henoko*). The sound *jû* is that made by something red-hot thrust into water. There are few insertion *ku.* The exception is this type: *"Poking it in / then trying to pull it out / in Ise's absence"* (ぬっと入れまず抜いてみる伊勢の留守 摘 1-11 *nutto ire mazu nuite miru ise no rusu*). There are *dozens* such. When Ise set off on his pilgrimage he had a spell put on his wife so if her chastity were violated she and her lover would stick together. That supposedly came to pass. When Kaempfer visited Japan in the 18c, he reported it as recent news, not knowing it was a 9c tale!

イ八の背にさね琴高の心持チ 葉
mara no se ni sane kinkô no kokoromochi
(cock-back-on, cunt/clitoris kinko's feeling)

a cunt riding
cock-back knows what
kinkô felt

who's carping?
clit on cock feels good
as quin gao did

like a clitoris
stuck to a big prick:
how kinkô felt

The cock is finally *in* for good. Kinkô was the Chinese sage musician, Quin Gao (Wade-Giles: Ch'in Kao). After a couple hundred years of austerities in the mountains, Zither Kao deliberately sank underwater one day in front of a crowd of witnesses. When he came up days later, he was on a huge carp that either changed into a dragon and flew him to heaven or took him back down to the Dragon's magical palace under the sea. Pick your legend. We find a *ku* describing scale-marks on this sage's crotch. Funny, but not so much as another *ku* putting *hexagons* on the buttocks of Japan's Rip van Winkle, Urashima Tarô, who rode a sea-turtle to the same palace (in Blyth). Sexpert senryu researcher Syunroan Syuzin noted there were many pictures of Kinkô cradling his zither seated on his carp that the senryu writer may have seen but that it took "monstrous powers of association" to leap from sage to clitoris (or upper-half of the vulva, for *sane* could also mean the labia minora) and carp to penis (「その連想たるや凄まじい」). Or, was the leap in the opposite direction? Syunroan *also* wrote:

> This idea was arrived at from something actually seen during intercourse. It describes the form of the little red head of the clitoris in contact with the dorsal side of the penis. In seated-position one can see something like this. (Syunroan: 1995)

With Japanese pornographic paintings showing grossly out-of-proportion male and female parts, the poet would hardly need to make the observations at first hand but, be that as it may, as part of my work translating a calendar edited by Japanese designer Sugiura Kohei, I happened upon a print by Harunobu (1724-70) that predates the senryu by decades and vitiates the need to make the poet a creative genius. This "missing link" depicts a *woman* seated on a carp. She reads a scroll we know is a love letter because this fish often served as shorthand for "love/ romance" because its name *koi* is homophonic for it. The curved ends of the scroll and the eddies about the fins and tail of the mighty fish bespeak her turbulent state of mind. Her free hand reveals three fingers, perhaps a love-triangle. *How can the carp=love take her to heaven – albeit not the same as that of the saint – just like that, which is to say suggest the senryu?* Harunobu thoughtfully emphasized the physical nature of the love-affair with red-layered *labial kimono hems* (all opening directly in front, in the style of a prostitute, rather than staggered for modesty) and her knees drawn up together in front of her forming the clitoral hood. Surely, the author of the senryu saw or heard about such a painting (or a copy of it); which I, neither Japanese, nor denizen of old Edo, knew to be sexy (*before* knowing of the *Leaf* senryu), the moment I saw *it!* Finally, something I have yet to see mentioned. If the senryû was composed by one with exceptional interest in the vocabulary of sex – which was probably the case – he would have known one of the many synonyms for clitoris and the sensitive area immediately around it was *kingen* 琴絃 or, "zither string," a term coming from the same Ch'ang Era China as the zither-playing saint!

カカッポウの豆を突っつくトトッポウ
kakappô no mame o tsuttsuku totoppô

pappa coo-coo
peck, peck, pecking mamma
coo-coo's bean

pappa pooh
peck, peck, pecking mamma
pooh's bean

Bean *ku* have such a cheerful ring to them. While bean *can* mean the clitoris, a pecking movement suggests it means cunt here. The "poh" I made "coo-coo" and "pooh" is the sound made by dove/pigeon/s *and* a ludicrous derogatory suffix.

尻の穴時々なでるマラの咽 葉別七
shiri no ana tokidoki naderu mara no nodo

from time to time
it strokes the bum-hole:
a cock's throat

Woman's legs raised high, man on top, long-draw poking bent to touch ventral wall of vagina, perhaps? Details aside, the *ku* has a nice, natural feel to it. We are not going to see more penile-vaginal/anal action in this chapter. Other examples are scattered about the book, for sex in senryu as in real life is rarely just sex. It tends to come with a role. Instead, we will see one last *finger* – in retrospect, *fingers* deserve *an entire chapter*, but they, too, as part of senryu sex are here and there, relating to stereotypes – at the bottom of the page. First, a pause in the act:

足音のたんびにこしをつかいやめ 摘
ashioto no tanbi ni koshi o tsukai-yame 1-25

at the sound
of each footstep their hips
come to a stop

their hips halt
now and then the sound
of footsteps

I have tried to select general descriptions of sex for this chapter. At first, I thought this must be a young married couple with nosey parents – too specific – but, on second thought, it could be adulterers, parents with children or premarital sex. Haven't we all had to pause for footsteps at some time or another?

嵐の夜娵存分に大よがり 葉 28
arashi no yo yome zonbun ni ô-yogari

a stormy night
the young wife can cry
as she pleases

the young wife
cries loud as she likes
stormy nights

This is implicitly limited, but we applies to more women than the stereotype. In thin-walled Japanese apartments, people still await stormy nights to let loose. *Yogari* is not synonymous with orgasm for most love-cries/yelping precede it.

指ほどに子壺は解さぬイ八の先 葉 32
yubi hodo-ni kotsubo wa gesanu mara no saki
(finger amount-as child-jar(womb)-as-for crack/open-not cock-tip)

for tickling locks
on baby jars, fingers beat
the cock by far

cock tips beaten
by fingers when it comes to
opening wombs

not as good as
fingers for cracking baby safes
the tip of a cock

"What pleasure / when the bell [penis tip] touches / the baby jar" (あなうまし子壺へ鈴のあたる時 葉13 *ana-umashi kotsubo e suzu no ataru toki* leaf) enthuses a boring *Leaf ku.* This, also in *Leaf,* is *much* better. According to a 1772 book 色道無限算開記, *"when a woman reaches the acme of pleasure* (至極気のゆく時) *her baby-jar=womb opens and sucks in the head of the cock* (魔羅の頭を吸い込むなり)" (『女陰万考』にて). So the above *ku* is probably a confirmation of the sexual pleasuring ability of the fingers rather than a comparison of, say, men to abortion doctors. The first reading borrowed an Australian jargon for jimmying a lock. The door to the womb was given great attention by senryu, but it is hard to know if that was because sharing such esoteric knowledge was fun, or, to the contrary, it was that common. The latter seems likely, for, I have seen illustrations of it and, while the English-speaking world had no popular word or even well-known slang for the cervix that I know of, Japanese had "flower-heart," "half-quail egg," "soroban bead," all probably from Chinese, and, the favorite for senryu, "mullet's belly button," (鯔の臍 *ina no heso*), which I am willing to bet my *shirikodama* is of Japanese origin. Still, this deep-fingering *savior faire* is less extraordinary to me than the high percentage of prints showing not only foreplay but clitoral fingering simultaneous to vagipenile coitus.

死ぬ、死ぬ *Le Petit Mort*

死ますの声にまつこの水をのみ　摘 初十
shinimasu no koe ni matsu kono mizu nomi pluck
([i/he/she]die/dying voice-for wait this water drink)

after hearing
"i'm dying," it's time:
"drink this water"

Japanese typically would wet their whistle before walking to the other side. But, *this* death-wait is facetious. The phrase "*Drink this water*" was part of the instructions for SS Long Life, which, painted on the penis was supposedly so potent a man would last *forever*, unless he took special measures. Believe it or not, the man was to *drink a cup of water* as soon as his partner started to orgasm. It would instantly break the spell and allow him to come: a perfect, mutual finale. I cannot help being suspicious of whether the senryu was not the work of a copywriter for the manufacturer of the potency cream, for it reminds one of the warnings (*"if erection persists for more than four hours, see your physician"*) for such medicines on Usanian television. The *Pluck* senryu may have been inspired by a less clever earlier *ku*: *"Come on, it's time / to drink your water!" – his wife / is satiated"* (もふ水をのみなと女房たんのうし 万明3 *mô mizu o nomina to nyôbô tannô shi*).

いのち也・死ぬる／＼とかすか也　安永四
inochi nari shinuru shinuru to kasuka nari 神酒の口

(life/fate/one's-love-become [i] die x2 and faint becomes)

"my life! my life!
i die! i die! i die!"
and it grows faint

waking up alive
i die! i die! resounds
ever so faintly

"i die! i die!"
is the easy part: *to death*
do us part

Life and death, side-by-side. "Life" means a sweet-heart. A person's name with "life = 命" tattooed under it means a vow of being lover's until death. Lovers thinking of committing a double-suicide usually did that. But, *inochi nari* can also mean something so good it is one's *raison d'être* or waking to find one is, against all odds, still alive. The last reading above is less a translation than a paraverse, inspired by the overload of possibilities, or concocted of frustration. Obviously the idiom of Christian marriage ceremony is out of place, but . . .

おっかさん死んじゃいやだと目を覚し 梅柳
okkasan shinjya iya-da to me-o sameshi 天保二
(mother die-as-for dislike-do and eyes open)

mommy, don't die!
cries the little boy
waking at night

wee eyes open:
mother, don't die!
mother don't!

What's a child to think? As another *zappai ku* puts it: *"Patching things up: / their child thinks that they / are fighting again"* (仲直り子は又喧嘩かと思ふ *nakanaori ko wa mata kenka ka to omou* 折句袋 安永八).

生きたり死んだり麩也蛸也 若の浦
ikitari shindari fu nari tako nari 文化二
(living etc dying etc gluten-bread is octopus is)

they come alive
then, coming, die: he, sponge
she, octopussy

living and dying
time and again, the sponge
and the octopus

Sex need not end in one round or even two. Here the dying becomes part of a cycle including coming to life. Ostensibly, this is about two people blessed with exceptionally reactive organs refreshing each other so much they cannot help wanting more. But, with both organs marked by the ability to expand and contract, we almost feel their sex as a slow breathing process or a union of primordial blobs. As explained before (pp 106-7, 115-6), the penis type named after a food with enormous expansive power, the wheat-gluten *fooh-mara*, that I turned into sponge here has the ability to fit any vagina. One thinks of a sea cucumber slipping between the crevices of rocks and anchoring itself. The *Octopussy*, just an *octopus* or *octopus pot* in Japanese, likewise has the ability to *grip* any penis.

男の悦声・しかし死ぬは言わざりし 冠付伊勢
otoko no yogari, shikashi shinu wa iwazarishi 文化十

◎ *a man's love-cry* ◎
but you'll never catch him
saying: *"i die!"*

I *guess* "ecstatic voice" here is pronounced *yogari.* But is it true for love-cries *everywhere?* If so, could it prove Byron's take on love being everything to a woman but only something to a man? Or, is it because being stabbed to death is more archetypical than being strangled? Or, because women lose it in coitus in a way men, who had to guard against attack by other men do not? Or, are women just more liable to emotional hyperbole? Or, are men afraid of *the real thing?*

長床坊・女の腹で卒中風　あふ夜
nagatokobô onna no hara de socchûbu 宝暦 1

◎ *mr long poke* ◎
on a woman's belly
has a stroke

◎ *stroke-all-night* ◎
has a stroke alright
on her belly

No, they're not afraid of this. At least not according to every Japanese senryu-sex-ologist I have read. All claim the same thing. *This is how every man wants to go.* In Japanese, one comes by *going*, so it sounds much better, too.

Aftermath その後

よわりふすへのこのたらす水ッ鼻 葉末
yowari-fusu henoko no tarasu mizuppana 15 オ
(weakened-hiding/lying-low cock drips water-nose)

the cock turns
shrinking violet with
a runny nose

lying low
a sniveling coward
once a cock

the spent cock
dribbling watery snot
bides his time

I must send this *ku* to Swedish friend, JF, a self-proclaimed literary snotologist. True, it is not pea-green as Joyce's choice example, but he may find it curious.

イ八の樋開の鋳型で子を拵エ 葉別
mara no toi bobo no igata de ko o kosae 2

with a pecker for
a sprue and a pussy for
a mold: babies!

the child they hold
made c̲ a pecker sprue
and pussy mold

to cast a child
use a cock for the sprue &
cunt for the mold

Recalling the counting song I first heard sung on a mostly black (and more girls than boys) bus going to a Coral Gables Senior High School football game in 1966 or 7, the *six with the dick* and the *seven in heaven* is followed by the *doctor-is-late* eight and *the-baby-is-mine* (or was it *fine?*) nine.

~~~~~~

~~~~~~

~ *eddies* ~

~~~~~~

★ ***Following the Sex Act*** from *warm-up* to *cool-down* was just one possible way to do it.

色けつきちやるめらといふ声を出シ <わらひ社すれ>
iroke tsuki charumera to iu koe o dashi 万明七

c̲ sex appeal
comes a voice like
a charamela

老の楽しみ人形をよく遣ひ 149-9
rô no tanoshimi ningyô o yoku tsukai

how old men
get off – doing a lot
of puppetry

黒あぶらへのこの毛をば染のこし 摘3-15
kuro-abura henoko no ke o ba somenokoshi

her black oil
enough remains to dye
his cock hair

Another approach toward sex might have been a chapter on sex life from childhood play with the wet-nurse, as we have seen, the grainy double-reed flute voice of a girl coming of age, as above (the draw says, "something to laugh at") to old men with livelier fingers than cocks and prostitutes who dyed their pubes – black-oil means a dye – I added the "her" and "him." (オマケ： チンてうで ちもだとしんそう ぬかしたり（うらみ社すれ） 万 安四. つまり、提灯で餅（をつく）如きの老人半勃起を、新造がうまく捗る)

~~~~~~

Sedans, Palanquin, Baskets. In Japan, horse or cow-drawn vehicles were far less common than man-borne. For crowded cities and mountains (both common in Japan), such transport was safer and smoother. While Europe had manned sedans in crowded urban entertainment zones (for riding one's horse drunk was a bad idea and stages not allowed), they could not go far because they were too heavy and the poles held by hand rather than resting on the shoulder. (See the endnote for ch 8, *Horses,* in *Topsy Turvy 1585*.)

~~~~~~

Slimy Foods. Others besides *okra* include 1) long tubers called *yama-imo* which grated make white, grainy slime, 2) fermented soy-beans called *nattô*, which whipped up ooze a slime with tiny hairs like gossamer, 3) the *himiji* mushroom which in a hot soup surrounds itself with a jelly like found with some fish spawn, 4) *mitsuba*, a three-leaved parsely with an elegant aroma, 5) raw squid cut in thin strips and eaten as noodles, 6) sea cucumber and 7) , 8) the entrails of both of these creatures, and 9) raw egg, particularly
~~~~~~

the white. Of these, 4) is the most important, for its elegance forces one to rethink slime.

~~~~~~

Japanese Warm-up Walks. There is no little irony here. To think that Japanese, who, like others in the Sinosphere, were *shocked* at the European practice of taking a constitutional, which is to say walking around in circles not trying to get anywhere (see *Topsy-turvy 1585*, item #1-27+), should be the ones to discover a practical benefit of walking!

~~~~~~

4. *Exercise, Bath, Drink before Sex: Male vs. Women.* A modern scientific study I read and lost confirms the benefit of exercise before sex for women but not for men. We might also study the bath and drinking. Re. drinking, the Japanese meant *some* was good for men, not a lot: 酔たイ八 尻餅をつく開の土手 *yotta mara shirimochi o tsuku bobo no dote –*

A drunk pecker / falls on his ass and lies / on mons veneris
A drunken cock / slipping on the cunt's dyke / lies belly down .

~~~~~~

Erection and The Inconvenience of Being a Man. Not only is a woman's secret "erection" more sinful, we have a "woman's feeling" that "*a man's must really get in the way,*" in the same *Pluck* (男のハじやまになろふと女の気 1-15 *otoko no wa jama ni narô ...*)

~~~~~~

5. *Phalluses on God-shelves.* More on the fate of these phalluses kept by courtesans after they were outlawed by the Tenpo Reforms of 1831 (Yes, before Japan was "opened") in I-forget-which-of-my-books, or Sasama, p.58-9, if you read Japanese.

~~~~~~

6. ***Stuck to a Big Prick and How Kinkô Felt.*** The original does not say "stuck to," but the word, which I borrowed from Solt (*a clitoris stuck to a prick / is how Kindaka / must have felt*) has the right sense. Checking Solt's rendition of the saint's name, which did not pan out, and re-checking my own, I was delighted to find Kinkô had homophones, perhaps purely fortuitous, meaning pleasure (欣幸) and [a body being] fixed in place (禁拘). But, more important, I feel I may have missed something here. I glossed over the feeling part of the metaphor: "how Kinkô felt" on that huge carp. In *Male Colors* (1995/7) Leupp observes that there may have been a greater proclivity for the men of Tokugawa Japan to want to experience not only male color, as was probably true for the majority of human cultures, but *both sides* of it, i.e., *inserter* and *insertee*. If so one may also wonder whether Kinko, too, may have been thought to have felt pleasure at having something massive between his legs as he rode the big fish bareback. But all of this is only allusion, caricature, the juvenile play of men. For a really erotic encounter with a carp, indeed the most erotic trans-species love scene I know of, you would do better to read the hot "Cold Fish" chapter of a novel called *Lady Onogoro's Lover* by Allison Fell. The cold fish is Hanako's human lover. The huge carp uses his "tickling barbels" and powerful sucking mouth to satisfy her in a lubricious two-page love scene as extraordinary in its way as Virginia Wolff's dying moth was in its.

~~~~~~

Labial Kimono Hems. The sleeve as the vale of tears where lover's wear their hearts has received ample attention by many interested in Japanese literature. There are also many pictures (Chinese and Japanese) where the woman's arm seems like a penis entering her own sleeve which is red-colored (or has a red slip sleeve) inside. The hem, perhaps, has been overlooked. To comprehend the sexiness of the hem-as-labia in the picture of the courtesan on the carp, some more explanation may be necessary (though I may find the picture and put it on the cover or back-cover as you will see or not see). First, one old folk song from Tsugaru, in Aomori prefecture, as transcribed by Takenaka:

沖の大船　白波わける　あなたわたしの　すそ分ける　十三潮「坊様おどり」
oki no ôbune / shiranami wakeru / anata watashi no suso wakeru

Big boats offshore split the breakers
You split my hem wide open

The reason the Occident – or, at least English – does not share this conceit with Japanese is because our lapels and hems are completely divorced with our pull-on or pull-over dresses, and, separated with wrapping or buttoned clothing, for the horizontal hem meets the frontal lapels at a right angle rather than merging as it did with the long, tatami-dragging kimono of the noblewoman or courtesan. If we have a labial look-alike it is the collar+lapels, but that is on the upper-part of the body and hence less suitable a metaphor.

むかふから・めいしよこのもし壱つまへ　三また竹
mukô kara // meisho konomoshi hitotsumae　享保中

◎ *from the front* ◎
the famous site looks fine:
hems in a line

The "famous-place," a sightseeing mecca, mentioned in this capped verse is the cunt, of course. The courtesan wears up to a dozen layers of clothing, but all opening in the front, not only do they mimic labia, they may flash the real thing when they go by in high-stilt-shoes in their advertising parades (my name for the annual processions).

~~~~~~

8. *Beans, Beans, Beans.* There are even some rock-scissors-paper *ku.* Nonsensical, they are hard to get: *"Sometimes, the scissors, paper, rock is a bean"* (じゃん拳の石は折々豆になり 164-2 *janken no ishi wa oriori mame ni nari*). *"The janken scissors sometimes scissors-out the bean"* (じゃん挙ンの鋏で実子をはさみ出し 葉 別七 *janken no hasami de sane o hasami-dashi*). I know the vulva is sometimes likened to a scissors, squeezing the legs together would make the bean=clit stand out, and paper could clean up after play, but I will leave a real translation to whoever can.

~~~~~~

★ *My Favorite Senryu Testimony of How a Traditional Fertility Culture Views Sex.*

お祭りをわたしわたして氏子出来
omatsuri o watashite watashite ujiko deki 48-33

from festival to
festival we go, ergo
we have ujiko

passing down
coitus to coitus
to all of us

Ujiko says my Japanese-English dictionary is/are "parishioners" or "people under the protection of a community deity." This is to so-called a tutelary deity or a *genius loci. Matsuri* is a festival or celebration with elements of worship *and* intercourse, close relations over space and time. The *watashite,* or crossing-over may pun on *watashi de,* "by me," by individual acts over time a *clan* is made. A clearer statement was made in a *Leaf* senryu *"We celebrate to keep our blood-lines intact* (御祭りハ先祖の血筋切らぬ為メ 葉 12 *omatsuri wa senzo no chisuji kiranu tame).* These cultural memes English poorly.

~~~~~~

A *Ku* I Gave Up on, Or the Limits of Translation, demonstrated c̲ bells & Croc. Mouths.

鈴をふるたび鰐口は練れるなり
suzu o furu tabi waniguchi wa nereru nari
(bell[acc] shakes/wags each-time crocodile-mouth-as-for knead/warm-up is)
~~~~~~

when the bell swings
one crocodile mouth sings
and one limbers up

Even if English had a word for warming up for sex by physical exercise, what can be done with a "crocodile mouth" that means both the split between a woman's legs and the slit on the lower edge of a bell shaped like a hollow dong (or a large metal tambourine with both two sides covered) that is struck with a large rope shaken – ideally you make a wave run up it on the last shake after you've shaken it to and fro creating a swing that grows with each shake the worshipper/ supplicant gives it. Even then it sounds in a dull tone hardly compensation enough for the work of getting it (the good thing is that means little children can't make enough noise with it to become obnoxious). the woman walks the next leg of the pilgrimage her husband will benefit from in bed when he applies his bell-mouth (the meatus resembles the hole on small Japanese bells) to her larger croc.

~~~~~~

Two Parts of Sex Neglected in this Chapter. One is the Kiss. It was neglected on purpose, for its role in Japan was smaller than in the Occident. Prints depict plenty of tongue-twining between lovers in mid-coitus, but with respect to husband and wife, I think the following *Pluck ku* tells it all:

口迄ハすつたがしやまの多イ内
kuchi made wa sutta ga jama no ôi uchi 摘 2-9
(mouth until-as-for sucked obstacles many within)

he kissed as far
as her lips when love was still
full of obstacles

He may still kiss = suck on her arm, breast or neck when their sex heats up, but he no longer seeks out her tongue (not lip, for Japanese).

~~~~~~

The Other is Fingering. Senryu and sex-instruction books both give *much* more space to fingering (*kujiru*) than the few example *ku* might indicate. I touched upon its importance of "finger puppetry" here and there in other chapters, so I hope the reader will forgive the brief presentation.

娘も十四牛の角文字　折句だはら　寛政五
musume mo jû-shi ushi no tsuno moji

a girl of fourteen
ox-horn letters

This *zappai* would have gone right by me without Suzuki's explanation. The representative ox horn letter is い "i," and it is first associated with the word いとし*"itoshi,"* meaning dear, and thus with romance (恋心), thoughts of which well up at this age *and,* at the same time, evokes her first use of an ox-horn masturbatory device called a *kujiri.* It is *not* the ox-horn dildos, i.e. penis substitutes, used by the chamber-maids, but more of a finger extension, a little tube that is slipped over the index finger (at least in a picture). To me, the existence of what might be considered a "finger-substitute" rather than a "penis substitute" tells as much as a picture (and there are many) about the extraordinary attention given to fingering by the Japanese.

The Love Poet Without One

今一つの恋歌人

ナ[10]

穴なし小町
The Missing Hole

~~~~~~

古今の序小町斗りは穴がなし
kokin no jo komachi bakari wa ana ga nashi 49

the kOkin fOrewOrd
kOmachi the sOle One
withOut a hOle

穴もないくせに恋歌は何事ぞ
ana mo nai kuse ni koi-uta wa nanigoto yo
(hole even not despite, love-songs-as-for what thing! 127-82)

what's the idea!
making love songs when you
have no hole!

what the hell?
a holeless wonder gives us
songs of love?

歌で見りゃ穴はなしとも思われず
uta de mirya ana wa nashi to mo omowarezu 105-31
(songs/poems-from considering-if hole-as-for not [+emph] think-not))

from her songs
who would think she was
missing a hole!

Ono Komachi was the most famous poetess of love in ancient Japan. The *Kokinshû* (905) was the second major anthology of poetry and famous partly for Ki no Tsurayuki's long foreword, which naturalizes the birth of poetry by not only mentioning gods and ancient poets but the *birds*, the *frogs* and the *bugs*, who are given the patent – anything not to give it to the Chinese! (if you will pardon my cynicism) – for bringing song, in Japanese identical with poetry, into the world. So, Komachi, reputeably known to no man, and still believed to have never broken her hymen *if she had one*, was not only an oddity among humans but the entire natural creation. The first senryu plays upon a sub-genre of senryu making
~~~~~~

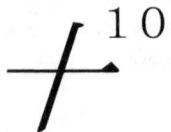

riddles about the composition of the poets in the famous *Hundred Poet One Poem* [each] Collection. The other two are but two of dozens expressing doubt that a virgen for life could write love poetry.

穴もない小町を玉に疵と言
ana mo nai komachi o tama ni kizu to ii
(hole even not komachi[acc] gem-on-blemish as say 91-8)

holeless komachi
they call her a perfect gem
with a flaw

komachi they call
perfection flawed only for
lack of a hole

玉にきずないのが小町たまにきず
tama ni kizu nai no ga komachi tama ni kizu
(gem-on flaw not is komachi gem-on flaw)

lack of a flaw
is the flaw on the lovely
gem komachi

These *ku* play on a common expression of regret for something extra-ordinarily beautiful yet lacking in one area. While Japanese did not call the female part *nothing* as some of the English did, the paradoxical metaphor works well enough. One *ku* that communicates nothing in translation: *"Too bad! / And her father's name was / Yoshizane!"* とつさまはよしざねだのにおしい事 摘 2-10 *tossama wa yoshizane na no ni oshii koto*). His name is a homophone for a *"good cunt."*

ことわりゃ毛斗りながら穴はなし
kotowari ya ke bakari nagara ana wa nashi
(objection!/: hair only while hole-as-for not 73-34)

out of human
control: having the hair yet
lacking a hole!

you be judge:
can there be no hole where
there is hair?

まれ人で出来そこなひハ小町なり 万 安四
marebito de deki-sokonai wa komachi nari

a divine beauty
left undone? komachi
is the only one

The word starting the first *ku, kotowari* means 1) a judgement as to the reasonableness of something; 2) something beyond the power of humans to change. I favor 1), for Japanese, on the whole, were kinder to oddity than, Europeans, who would rather tie a rooster that laid an egg to the stake and burn him/her than celebrate nature's sense of humor. Japanese cheerfully acknowledged Komachi's unique nature, calling varieties of holess bamboo *komachi-dake,* eyeless needles *komachi-bari,* and a solid koto bridge (usually, they look like towers) a *komachi-kotoji. Marebito*, in the second *ku,* is a god-like visitor or beauty.

コハ珍事小町に臍が二つあり 99
kowachinji komachi ni heso ga futatsu ari
(scary-rarething komachi-on navels two are)

scary rarity:
komachi has two not
one navel

spooky rare
komachi boasts two
belly buttons

The second navel is her unperforated tenth hole. I have no source/date for this *ku,* but a sentence about a vagina fashioned like a navel appears in 1785 (see *eddies*).

極内で小町も一度外科に見せ 52-33
gokunai de komachi mo ichido geka ni mise

show komachi
to a surgeon just once,
hush, hush

Secluded or not, Japanese had their eyes wide open. Knowledge of the natural variety of bodies was relatively wide-spread in Edo era Japan. A book of treasure/gem/ball-like things published in 1807 includes an illustration of a pretty Kintama-musume, Gold-gem[testicled]-Girl, who made her livelyhood displaying herself (Reprinted in the *Ball Book*). She is lying on her side, pulling up her enormous balls enough that we can see the doctor's huge penis well up her vagina. Notes claim he was the one who treated her balls, making a medical error (not specified) that cost her life. Other oddities such as women without proper holes were never burnt at the stake but simply marveled at in this curious culture. Gadgets with invisible workings – mechanical toys or automata – were popular, and it was inevitable that some thought of a practical solution.

七小町気楽な時もなかりけり む
nana-komachi kiraku na toki mo nakarikeri

seven komachi
not a time in her life was
free from care

The noh ballads 謡曲 "Seven Komachi," each treating different aspects of her life, were popular. From early-period *hakkai* she typified a beauty whose beauty was a jinx, but the emphasis in senryu came to be her sex life or absence there-of. The last *ku,* from Kei Kiitsu's pioneering *Mutamagawa* collection, is boring, the next two, both originally from Senryû's *Million,* as a set, really make us chuckle.

九十九夜車に斗リ疵を付ケ 万宝 11
kujûku yo kuruma ni bakari kizu o tsuke

ninety-nine nights
and the only scars he left
were in the cart

ninety nine nights
and he only made his nicks
on the ox-cart

下女ならば九十九番はさせるとこ 葉4
gejo naraba kujûku ban wa saseru toko millions/leaves
(maid-if 99th time/round/s[eve]-as-for do-made-to situation[bed])

with a maid
he would have been made
all 99 times

now, a maid
would let you make her
all 99 times

下女ならは九十九ばんはきれるとこ
gejo naraba kujûku ban wa kireru toko 摘 2-16
(maid-if 99th time/round/s/eve-as-for effected situation)

if maid, instead
he would've died in bed
for the 99th time

were it a maid
he would have got laid
that 99th night

on that 99th night

with a maid
he would have been fucking
not freezing

It was said that Captain Fukakusa called on Ono Komachi ninety-nine nights in a row and got nowhere. Each time, he carved a nick into the *shiji* 榻 of the cart. When he froze to death on that last night, he must have already made his mark. The second/third *ku* has various versions and two possible readings depending upon whether it is taken as *the* ninety-nineth evening or *for* the ninety-ninth time. The first reading owes a bit to Solt: *"a maid / will make you do it /all ninety-nine times."* Grammatically speaking, *saseru* means to compell someone to do something, but, idiomatically, it is just how females *do it* (get done?) in Japanese. The ambiguity of the *ku* permits many readings. I favor my last two, but am still awaiting the judgment of those who know Japanese better than I do. （★「も」ではなく、「ハ」となったから、句意が「〜所であったのに」？であれば、全回も今回でいい?).

百夜目ハ三もくもおす気で通ひ 摘 1-25
momoyo-me wa san moku mo osu ki de tôi

on the 100th night
he planned pushing
c̲ three stones

If 3 *go* stones surround an opponent's stone, the one must run or be prepared to abandon it to be picked up by a fourth stone, leaving an open eye [space] behind.

もふ一ト夜通ふと　つをされる所 万
mô hito-yo kayou to ketsu o sareru toko 安四

one more night
and she would've been
butt-fucked

百夜めは小町裏門あけて待ち？
momoyo-me wa komachi uramon akete machi

the hundredth night
komachi waited with her
back-gate open

The draw for the first *ku, "Make it a fad!"* (はやり社すれ *hayari koso sure*), makes us feel less sympathy for it. The second *ku,* with the rare euphemism that also works allegorically, supposes Komachi had yet to hear of poor Fukakusa's death.

百夜めハすまたをさせるつもりて居 摘
momoyo-me wa sumata o saseru tsumori de iru 4-5

on the 100th night
she planned to let him slip
between her thighs

"Bare-thighs-do-let/have" (*sumata o saseru*) means *intercrural* sex. Unlike the scholarly English term, the Japanese one is true vernacular (pink massage parlors advertise *sumata* play, today). *"~ He planned a surprise: slipping / it between her thighs"* would also be *possible,* but the draw was *"just fool [him]"* だまし社すれ *damashi koso sure*).

穴なしといふわる口ハ百日め 万
ananashi to iu waruguchi wa hyakunichi-me 明二
("hole-not" saying bad-mouth-as-for hundred-day-th)

"that ana-nashi!"
the insult was born on day
one hundred

only then did
they say 'the holeless bitch'
the 100th day

百夜目は何を隠そう穴がなし 柳 38
momoyome wa nani o kakusô ana-ga-nashi
(100th night-as-for what[acc]hide-would hole-not)

the 100th night:
but what would she hide
without a hole?

the 100th night:
what's a holeless one got
to hide anyway!

the 100th night:
without a hole she's got
nothing to hide.

もふ一チ夜通ふと　なハ無ひといふ 万
mô ichi yo tôu to ana wa nai to iu 天二桜 3

you could say
she was holess if you went
one more night

The first *ku* (1765) claims the death of the ardent suitor was the start of maligning the poetess as "holeless." I hope I got the rhetoric right for the next two *ku.* Without access to data-bases, I cannot try to check the birth of *holeless* in poetry and share it with you, but *Cuntologia* traces back the 100-night idea at least as far as a Genroku era (1688-1704) ballad 謡曲「通小町」She didn't promise he could *screw* her; just that if he called for 100 nights, she'd *"hear what he had to say"* (百夜通ったら言う事を聞く). Given *that* attitude, the next *ku* does seem persuasive, though the one after it is the only rational response to all of this:

ことわりや穴さえ有らばさせもせめ
kotowari ya ana sae araba sase mo senu 摘 4
(protest/qualification!/: hole even have-if let do-not)

i beg your pardon
even if she *had* a hole
she *wouldn't* have

見た事も無くて小町の穴を云い 新編
mita koto mo nakute komachi no ana o ii 三
(seen-thing even not komachi's hole[acc.] saying)

without seeing it
making pronouncements
re. komachi's hole

all this talk of
something never seen
komachi's hole

Sometime in the 80's or the 90's, I recall seeing a photograph of a mummy on a hanging advertisement for a weekly magazine which stuck in my mind because of the headline about this Silkroad find. Not only was she a *blond* in the Far East but a *virgen!* The next day, Sato Sanpei, lead cartoonist for the prestigious *Asahi Shinbun* (who was kind enough to treat me to sushi when I got some of his work into the *Japan Times*), had her with blushing cheeks – how he did it in b&w I cannot recall – a quote of the "virgen" claim and some words to the effect that she was horribly *embarrassed* that they were so rude as to look.

おしい事開かずに散る花の色
oshii koto hirakazu ni chiru hana no iro
(regrettable thing open-not falling blossom's color/beauty)

what beauty lost
when a flower blows without
having bloomed!

what a waste!
the beauty of the blossom
that never blooms

a thing to regret
the bloom that drops
un-openned

a crying shame
this bud never knew
the birds & bees

The phrase "flower's color/eros/beauty" (*hana no iro*) is commonly found in Komachi *ku* not actually naming her. Another: *"The beauty of / a flower that remains / virgin for life"*(生娘で一生くらす花の色 *73-7 ki-musume de isshô kurasu hana no iro*). They play upon her own *waka* (*"hana no iro . . ."*) regretting beauty lost as she wasted her life on idle concerns. Until I read her poems in Carter's *Traditional Japanese Poetry*, I might have agreed with her self-evaluation. But, when you read *"In my idleness / I turn to look at the sky – / though it's not as if / the man I am waiting for / will descend from the heavens,"* or another *waka* expressing her desire to share with someone the bush clover bloom and chime of the clear-toned cicada★ in the evening glow, you *know* her life *was* well spent.

小町桜を穴のあく程ながめ 65-3
komachi-zakura o ana no aku hodo nagame

komachi cherries
let's drill holes in them
with our eyes

komachi cherries
let's stare until holes open
in their blossoms

staring at those
komachi cherries until
the buds open

Beautiful dark cherry blossoms, a light grey variety (薄墨桜) in particular, was sometimes called a Komachi-zakura. Could they have been a bit slow to open, or was the only point the play on the idiom for gazing intently at something as *making holes*. Regardless, the classy *Willow ku* was reprinted many times (77-2, 88-10, in addition to the above). Reading a *ku* where Issa stares so hard at the sky the night the Star Lovers meet that he rends a hole in the Milky Way, I recall thinking he invented the expression, but the idea of staring until a hole is opened would appear to be common idiom, and fitting here for obvious reasons. Komachi's above-mentioned *waka* includes *nagame* (gazing) in its last line (又小町桜の「ながめにあかぬ」という長唄もあるが、たぶん関係ない).

小町の屁一方口で音の良さ 145-9
komachi no he ippô-guchi de oto no yosa

pudenda acoustics

komachi's fart
with but one way out
a good sound

komachi farts:
with but one exit what
sound quality!

This is a prime example of superb late-period *Willow* and what senryu does best: making a questionable stereotype into a fantasy, as realistic as it it ridiculous. It is a fact that additional mass close to a vibrating string or orifice reduces acoustical leakage. I would *bet* the author of the *ku* was an instrument maker.

弁慶はまだしも小町はから無体 43-25
benkei wa madashimo komachi wa karamutai

chaste benkei
we get, but komachi?
gotta be fake

弁慶ハいいが小町ハ惜しいもの 142-28
benkei wa ii ga komachi wa oshii mono

benkei? so what!
but komachi, ah, that's
a real shame!

Benkei was a mightly warrior who had a love, but was so faithful a retainer, he couldn't find time to sleep with her. In fact, senryu have him sleeping with her only *once* shortly before the battle when he went down with more arrows in him than St Sebastian, or than a porcupine has quills, if you prefer not to use Christian metaphor. The "shame" in the second means a shame to the sex-starved men of the senryu culture, i.e., "a waste of good pussy." In attitude, this late-period Willow *ku* may be the most senryu of the senryu in this chapter.

弁慶と小町はバカだなア嬶
benkei to komachi wa baka danaa kaka

komachi and
benkei? both were fools!
says the old wife

The old wife's comment reflects the fact that holelessness was not the only reason given for Komachi's chastity. It is only the favored explanation of senryu. Komachi as portrayed in the popular drama of the day was an extraordinary beauty, so haughty and full of herself that she wouldn't allow any man to touch her. With her love poems hinting at deep affection, this made her what my generation called a prick-teaser. Naturally, she receives her come-uppance:

小町をつつ通したのハすゝきなり 万
komachi o tsutsu-tôshita no wa susuki nari 安六
(komachi[acc] through/through[poke]-passed-as-for eulalia is)

the one who knew
komachi through and through
a pampas fellow

the lucky one
to pierce her to the quick
mr. susuki

Drama depict Komachi as a homeless hag who dies alone in the barren fields, where she is eventually found, with her orbit (eye-socket) violated by a blade or blades of *susuki,* the tall saw-grass – *miscanthus sinensus* – you have probably seen in samurai movie scenes, often translated as *pampas grass*, for it has plumes). In other words, she is used to illustrate that saying we all would like to be true more often than it is: *pride comes before fall.* Carter, who introduces a dozen of Komachi's poems in his book (1991), writes there is nothing to that legend. So it would seem; her poems are neither naughty nor haughty. But drama, haiku, senryu or folksong all agree on one thing, *she was a beauty*. Issa has numerous *ku* mentioning such Komachi, my favorite of which has petals falling on the ass-print a Komachi left behind under a cherry tree (See *Cherry Blossom Epiphany*: 2007), where it is clearly used that way.

から鮭に小町の果で おもわるゝ 保吉
kara-shake ni komachi no hate de/mo? omowaruru

a dry salmon
comes to mind because of
komachi's end

in dry salmon
the fate of komachi also
comes to mind

Bashô (1644-94) once alluded to Komachi's end. Sitting within view of a picture of skeletons dancing, he wrote, *"A flash of lightning – where there were faces / plumes of pampas grass"* (trans. Makoto Ueda). The later, Tenmei (1780-9) *haikai* poet's less ethereal but still enigmatic version transposes a dried salmon hung up by a straw (or braided saw-grass?) rope passing through its eye sockets. My second reading assumes a mistranscription (hand-written, で and も can be close).

folk-ballad komachi shocker

But, let us skip additional haiku or senryu and end the essay on something *lower,* something that makes most dirty senryû clean by comparison, on what must be the most shocking song Komachi has ever been put into. It is a stanza from the *Akita Ondo* 秋田音頭, or Akita folk ballad, introduced by Takenaka Rô (たけなか・ろう『にっぽん情哥行』ミュージック・マガジン 1986.) Curiously, it does not mention what she does not have. Maybe the holeless Komachi meme did not propogate into the provinces. I do, however, expect to find holeless Komachi in 19-20c kouta 小唄 and other popular songs born in urban areas.

[initial scat refrain skipped]

Akita women are beauties, you say?
You gotta be outta your mind!
Ono-no-komachi was born here, hey,
You either don't know shit or you're blind!
Damn all women! You can't tell by their sweet faces
They're more frightful than demons in other places!
Raw cock, they eat alive, starting with the head,
Regurgitating babies that come out bloody red!

キタカサッサー・コイサッサ　ホイナー・こら秋田の女は何して美人だと・聞くだけ野暮だんす・小野の小町の生れ在所ダお前さま・知らねのぎゃ　／／　こら　女と云うもの尋常な顔して・鬼よりまだ怖い・生でま食らて・似たよなガキこしゃる。 *kora akita no onago wa nani shite bijin da to / kiku dake yabô dansu / ono-no-komachi no umare tokoro[zaisho] da ome-sama / shirane no gya // kora onna to iu mono jinjô na kao shite / oni yori mada kowai / nama na [ママ] henoko o iki de ma kurate / nittayo na gaki kosharu.* Note: Takenaka found this ballad was of a chanting/kidding (*hayashi*) rather than a singing variety, *i.e.*, close to what we now call "rap music." (在日の皆様、これは凄い音頭に違いないが、「穴無し小町」の歌ではない。そういった宴会用歌やら小唄の類をご存知ならば教えてください。再版に加えたい。よろしくお願いします。ところで、たけなか・ろう『にっぽん情哥行』のもっとも面白い指摘は、H な替え歌知ってるから、われわれは破礼の方が後だと考えがちであろうが、本当は、逆に本来地口満々たる音頭・民謡などが、おきれいに直された場合が意外に多い。)

"We" (most readers) are called "Caucasians" because of the legendary beauty of Circassian women, a reputation established by Arab, Persian, Turkish and North African (whomever the harem served) enthusiasm for the white slaves who came from the steppes so named. The beauty of white-skinned Akita women was legendary in Japan, so if *they* were as crazy as "we" were, not only a husky (dog), but *all* Japanese might be called *Akitas*. I spiced up the words a bit, for the last line actually says only "make similiar kids" (*i.e.,*similar to cocks). Since Japanese call babies "red-lings," the consciousness of bloodiness was probably there, though not made explicit in the original. Perhaps the song was written and sung in good humour, but there is more than a trace of spleen in it. Could the high reputation of the women have brought men from around Japan into competition with the locals, who, not unreasonably would resent it? Beauty has complex repercussions on those who have it and those who want it.

envoi

ほめるにも小町きよくるも小町なり 万明五
homeru ni mo komachi kiyokuru mo komachi nari
(praise-even komachi put-down/kid even komachi is)

praise her & she's still
komachi: put her down &
she's still komachi

praise her or
put her down, a komachi
is a komachi

praise komachi
or make fun of her: it's all
the same komachi

praise her beauty
or demonize it: beauty
changes not a wit

Not a rose by any other name, but *a rose whether you like it or not, is still a rose.* The draw-ku was *jiyû narikeri* (自由也けり), or "people are free," to which the poet, with his Komachi *ku,* added "to think what they will, *but . . .*"

~ eddies ~

Other Holeless Ku. The three printed all explicitly mention "holeless." Not all the "holeless" *ku* are so direct. The two *ku* below are from *Pluck.* The first *ku* puts holessness in a positive way. The second is identical to the second *ku* in the chapter for the first eight syllabets, but has a much more understated tail.

哥で見りやけつしてあなはあるとみへ 摘
uta de mirya kesshite ana wa aru to mie 2-16

from her songs
you sure would think
she had a hole

穴もないくせに小町は恋哥也 摘 2-9
ana mo nai kuse ni komachi wa koiuta nari

despite the fact
she had no hole, komachi
the poet of love

Because of the way that later anthologies reprint things from earlier ones, figuring out the order of the scores of holeless Komachi's would be too much work, so I have not done it.

~~~~~~

The Flaw on the Gem. If you have read my books, this will be *at least* the third time you have encountered this expression, *tama ni kizu.* Can you recall it? *The 5th Season* has a haiku expressing Issa's trepidation about releasing smoke into the gem-like blue sky of the New Year. *Topsy-turvy 1585* has a senryu about Kyôto woman being gems but for one flaw, namely, they stood while they peed (it was because of the remarkable enthusiasm of Kyôtoites for recycled fertilizer and their method of collecting it by urinating into troughs). But I cannot recall if I have introduced my favorite usage anywhere. It is in a late-19c or early-20c parlour song *Tsuki wa Mujô* 『月は無情』 where a beauty, bright and kind in every way is called a gem with only one flaw,

. . . but the fact she will not fall for me makes her damaged goods.

僕に惚れぬが玉にキズ *boku ni horenu ga tama ni kizu* (me-with love-not-that[is] gem-to scar)

~~~~~~

Like a Belly Button? An Empress whose consort was demoted while she was deposed because of her affair, lamented: *"If only the vagina were fashioned like the navel, then I would not have ended in such a calamity."* (from 6th story in *Boudoir Tales of the Great Eastern Land of Japan* (*Daitô keigoho* = 1785, trans. M.E. Jamentz, highmoonnoon 2004)

~~~~~~

& Chime of the Clear-toned Cicada. Carter's translation ends "evening light shining / on bush clover in full bloom / as crickets bring on the night." He has a note about the "cricket" having a name (*higurashi*) partially homophonic with dusking (*kureru*). Indeed, even today the name is commonly associated with nightfall. But, to understand how good the *waka* is, which is to say why Komachi longed to share the sight and sound with someone, you must know something about *the sound*. An individual mole cricket, associated with clover in Japanese poetry makes one of the most plaintive sounds in nature. No human singer can match the delicacy of the irregular warble (though young Dolly Parton sometimes came close). Saigyô once made this *waka* about such a cricket:

.

ひとりねの寝ざめの床のさむしろに涙催すきり／＼すかな　西行
hitorine no nezame no toko no samushiro ni namida moyôsu kirigirisu kana

Ah, mole cricket drawing teardrops
from the rush-mat of one who wakes alone!

But it is not a sound that may be shared (unless two extraordinarily sensitive people are fortunate enough to live together). It is too tiny and personal. And collectively they are not particularly impressive, for the grain of the warble is less audible. Finally, they keep chirping into the wee hours of the night when they are best heard. Komachi must have heard a particularly fine chorus of chiming *higurashi,* a light green, transparent-winged *cicada*. Each three to eight-second long song with one to five notes per second starts at medium speed and quickly speeds up as the notes rise, then falls off a bit at a time as the tone drops until fading out with a reluc-tant last note. Anyone with a good ear can immediately feel its similarity to the way something speeds toward you and passing slowly leaves, *i.e.* the doppler effect. The way the notes attenuate is not unusual in classical Indian music, but it is so rare in Western classical music that I find myself wondering whether it reflects a lack of sensitivity to natural beauty on our part, or just the lack of the right singing bugs to educate our ears. The individual *higurashi* are loud enough to be fine in chorus, and the overlapping songs coming from various directions create a sublime musical experience of the type one wishes to share with others so badly it hurts. The attenuation sticks in the mind, so while the clear tone is cheerful, the overall effect of the fading-away while dropping tone is sad, though there must be a better adjective I have failed to find, and it seems the perfect soundtrack for the passing of the light of day. Please pardon this irrelevant aside.
~~~~~~

~~~~~~

Holeless in England. The bountiful and superb notes to Project Gutenberg's e-book version of Mark Twain's *1601,* give us another Komachi closer to home. Ben Jonson in his *Conversations with William Drummond of Hawthornden* had the following to say about Queen Elizabeth:

> *That she had a membrana on her, which made her uncapable of man, though for her delight she tried many. At the comming over of Monsieur, there was a French Chirurgion who took in hand to cut it, yett fear stayed her, and his death."*

~~~~~~

Happy Ending for Captain Fukakusa and Ono Komachi. When looking up the ballad 通小町, I found it was a *yobanmemono* (四番目物), a remake of an older sundry Noh play 雑能 co-written by Kanami (1333-84) and his son Zeami, the most famous Noh-writer+actor. A monk meets and recognizes their ghosts (hers by the pampas grass connection and his by its being so thin) and gets them to accept whatever Buddhist commandments/judgement they deserve and the upshot of it is that they are to simulate the would-have-been hundreth night, after which, all regrets lost, the two hitherto lost souls are enlightened and join the godhead.

十一 11

金玉の寂さ
Balls Gold & Blue

睾丸は極大切な不用もの 145
kintama wa goku taisetsu na fuyomono

the bullocks
two very important
worthless things

Seeking a book to complement *Cuntologia*, I was disappointed to find the closest one available from the publisher (太平書屋) treated *balls* (玩球隠士編撰『岐牟太末学大全』1985). The cock only gets a passing mention. I did, however, discover some things of value in it. One was Mark Twain's *1601* (1882). A passage was cited – *in Japanese* – where the sixty-eight year-old Virgin Queen recalls that, when she was fifteen, Rabelais told her that his father knew a man with *"a double pair of bollocks,"* at which point *"ye learned Bacon and ye ingenious Jonson"* quarrel about the correct spelling of the same, only to be interrupted by the lady of the house: *"Let the spelling be, ye shall enjoy the beating of them on your buttocks just the same, I trow."*

お気の毒だが金玉様は　アーソラソラ　／　オマンコするとき尻なめる
okinodoku da ga kintama-sama wa aa sora-sora omanko-suru toki shiri nameru

Pity your good balls, – ah, sorah! sorah!
Whenever you fuck they lick her butt . . .

Lines from an *omanko-zukushi,* a folk-song (甲州禁哥考上) where each stanza included "cunt," collected by Takenaka (1986), who said old ladies particularly loved to sing it in public. Before finding *1601* at Project Gutenberg, I imagined the verb (banging) was *smack, hit,* or *bang*, but hoped it would be "lap" for we could think of the tide coming in and the dew-lap of a lizard . . . But I should add that after a dozen pages about this phenomenon, including a warning for big-balled men not to turn a woman's face into a punching bag when performing 69, superbly punning 落語 joke-stories about men who tied on huge fake balls to satisfy their wives desire for being well-whacked, the author of *Balls* tacked on a disclaimer (for worried male readers?) to the effect that most testicles rise up to the base of the penis during intercourse, so there is very little actual slapping.

きんたまとさねの間にふどう尊 摘
kintama to sane no aida ni fudôson 1-6

acala

between the balls
and cunt – is that
the god of fire?

If the vulva and testicles are equivalents, then the penis can be seen as an in-between, a bridge across a gap. This God of the gap is literally *called* un-moving-respect/god, but his image is fiery red, as some prints depicted the male member.

睾丸さねに語って曰くつまらねえ
kintama sane ni katatte iwaku tsumaranee

say the balls
to the cunt, how we hate
being out of it

入ッ口に番をしている玉二ッ 三七
iriguchi ni ban o shite-iru tama futatsu

by the entrance
they keep watch
two jewels

睾丸の曰くいつでも露ばかり *120-34*
kintama no iwaku itsudemo tsuyu bakari &164-26

the poor balls
all they ever get
is dew drops

睾曰男根やおいらも這入たい 葉
tama iwaku mara ya oira mo hairitai 別3

say the balls
"hey, big root, we, too
want in!"

if balls spoke
"move over big poker
let us in, too!"

The first *ku* puns on "worthless" and its homophone "crammed[in]-not." *Tama*, in the second, means jewel/gem/ball. Usually modified by "gold," here, "two" does the trick. "Dew" idiomatically means *something of no substance*. The 男根 in the last means "maleroot"(*dankon*), but the syllabet count demands *mara.*

睾丸はいわば小僧の涎れ掛け *145-28*
kintama wa iwaba kozô no yodare-kake

what are balls?
call them a bib for him
the little monk

family jewels?
more like little monk's
drool guard

In Japanese, one word for "bib" is drool-cover. This metaphor is more rare than gate guard – there are countless folk-songs and senryu about the poor balls that must wait outside the gate while the cock has all the fun within – and better, until you try to find something protected from the "drool."

川越はきん玉たこが衿にでき 四五
kawagoshi wa kintama tako ga eri ni deki

river-crossing
collars end up with
ball-calluses

river-crossing
collars all callused
by testicles

睾丸を襟巻にする大井川 五十
kintama o erimaki ni suru ôigawa

the balls make
fine mufflers out on
bigwell river

ôi river
where balls become
mufflers

Most ball-related senryu are not about sex and only obscene to the degree one finds balls gross – let's face it, they are only marginally better looking than the twaddle on a gobbler and that is pretty damn ugly. The above is a blue-collar worker, to be precise, a ferryman/river-porter's perspective on balls. Carry over enough people on your shoulders – this was called a "shoulder-car (*kata-guruma*)" – and all those crotches, balls in particular, wear out your robe-collar.

花見と雪見睾丸が伸び縮み *79-10,13 &*
hanami to yukimi kintama ga nobi chijimi 151-9

blossom-viewing
and snow-viewing: balls
stretching, shrinking

穏かさ実に睾丸も下り切り 161-12
odayakasa jitsuni kintama mo sagarikiri

utter calm
even balls hang down
all the way

halcyonity
even the balls could not
hang lower

The balls are both a temperature gauge and a measure of one's state of mind, which in the second ku may be compared to fruit dangling on a windless day.

ひゃうきんの忠義きん玉つかんで見
hyôkin no chûgi kintama tsukande-mi 80-5

waggish loyalty
grabbing balls for first-
hand testimony

droll fidelity
doing a reading of your
shôgun's balls

大久保も隣をにぎる穏かさ *66-10*
ôkubo mo tonari o nigiru odayakasa

sir ôkubo, too
was calm enough to grasp
another's balls

大久保へ手を洗へとは御高運
ôkubo e te o arae to wa go-kô-un

asking ôkubo
to go wash his hands*: that*
was fortunate

In a legendary tale from the Warring Era, the father of Honda Heihachirô Tadakatsu (本田平八郎忠勝) suddenly reaches for the balls of his son, who was halfway armored up for his first battle. Finding them hanging loose, he smiles/laughs. This event is not famous enough for senryu; but Ôkubo is, for he grabbed the balls of the man who finalized the unification of Japan, Tokugawa Ieyasu. At that time, the Shôgun was in dire circumstances, lying low, when this aide suddenly thrust a hand into his culottes' side-slit (Japanese had openings where we have pockets) and took the measure of his mind. Since having one's balls grasped places one in mortal danger, and this was an age when betrayal was the rule rather than exception, the Shôgun might have shrunken-up immediately even if he had not been relaxed. But, no, he is reputed to have said, *"Hey, what's this horsing around* (巫山劇) *when we face a do or die battle? Go wash your hands and come right back, you dirty old man!"* So Ôkubo knew Ieyasu was calm and collected and stuck by him, and the rest is history.

握った二分金御治世の元手也 *92-12*
nigitta nibu-kin mi-chisei no motote nari

divided balls
a hand on the origin of
a unified land

in split jewels
a first grasp of one who
would unite us

The *nibukin* 二分金, literally *two-part-gold/money*, in the original was half of a larger coin called a *ryô*. The unit postdates Ieyasu and Ôkubo by centuries and is just a pun for the balls, as *gold* (*kin*) is shorthand for the *gold-gems*. Detail makes this senryu: when balls are relaxed and hang low, they separate from one another, horizontally and vertically, becoming noticeably two-part.

御静代我のを握るふところ手
on-shizuyo? ware no o nigiru futokurote

tranquil times
within your robe holding
your own balls

peaceful times
let your own testes serve
for testimony

I recall reading that "we" once held one another's balls in the so-called Middle East, *i.e.,* cradle of the Occident as we might shake hands today, as proof of mutual trust; but, with senryu, my thoughts on ball-grasping have grown more complex. Such *ku* are interesting for they show *peace was not taken for granted.* Another: *"Thankful / to see bedtime pictures / for fun"* (まくら絵をしやうだんに見るありがたさ 万明五 *makura-e o jôdan ni miru arigatasa*). Dirty pictures were carried to battle in the armor, typically the helmet, for good luck. In senryu, the main purpose of that armor was hiding dirty pictures to scare maids who discover them on summer drying day, when everything gets carried out into the sun.

きん玉もぎう／＼といふ供おさへ 万
kintama mo gyû-gyû to iu tomo osae 安七

even their balls
are squeaky tight alright
a daimyô's men

their bollocks
sound out gyu-gyu-gyu
a fine retinue

down the street
they go polishing their balls
the lord's train

We have tightly trussed up loincloths. Issa has a number of *ku* about the discomfort (heat, cold or rain) suffered by the retinues of the daimyô, as compared to his comfortable poor self, sitting indoors. Every year the lords of Japan had to file back and forth to the capital city. The smartly dressed attendants displayed their fancy marching steps when passing through crowds. For common folk, they were quite a show and for senryu poets a good contrast with the old saw of hang-ball peace. – If Edoites disliked war, they loved fights and love:

きん玉が降るように湯の大喧嘩 *121-20*
kintama ga furu yô ni yu no ôgenka

there's a brawl
in the bath-house & it's
raining balls!

土手のかご弐厘五毛もかるいはづ万 明四
dôte no kago ni-ri go-ke mo karui hazu

sedans coming
up the dyke should be
a gram lighter

In Japan, rather than *dogs and cats*, it rained "spears." As balls hang low when warm and are out of their loincloths, they would fly about more than in a fight outside. *Ku* two: the figure in the original is 2 *rin* 5 *ke,* "the weight of a man's semen" (Okada). A *rin* is 0.0375 grams. *Ke* is literally a *hair!* The men got rid of every hairy drop in Yoshiwara. How do we know *where* it was spent? Any sedan not otherwise specified, especially if the route is on a dyke, is assumed to be going to and fro said pleasure quarter. A puzzling *ku* has one of these shouldered sedans (for details on sedans, see *Topsy-turvy 1585*) flying up and down with *kintama*, but we cannot tell if they belong to the sedan men or the party carried (金玉と上へ下タを飛四ッ手かご *kintama to ue-shita o tobu yotsute-kago*). I believe it must mean the traffic was one way on the top of the dyke and one on the bottom (or boats).

きん玉をねらうにこまる朝かえり
kintama o nerau ni komaru asa-gaeri 摘 *3-2*
(gold-gems[acc] target[v]-from troubled morning-return)

when your balls
are in mortal danger
a morning return

a dawn return
when you know she's
after your balls

Near *ku: "Morning return / When your balls will get / gnawed off!"* (きんたまへかぢりつかれる朝かへり 万明七 *kintama e kajiri-tsukareru asagaeri*) *Kajiri* suggests the wife may milk the husband's sin, for it is used in the idiom *sune-kajiri* "shank-gnawing," or living parasitically on someone. *"Morning return / His wife feels like uprooting / his pecker"* (朝かへり女房へのこをひんぬく気 天八幸 2 *asagaeri nyôbô henoko o hin-nuku ki*). The same *hin nuku* is used for "pulling up" *daikon* radishes.

きん玉をお妾鼻へぶらつかせ
kintama o mekake hana e buratsukase

making balls
dance upon the nose
of a mistress

69. I have seen *shunga* (spring-pictures) of it. There is wit in this nose because mistresses were typically depicted as reading the hairs in their master's nostrils.

きんたまをかく頃薬リ箱か出る 万明四
kintama o kaku koro kusuribako ga deru million

right when he starts
to scratch his balls out comes
the medicine box

I first imagined (wrongly) that this was a messenger boy waiting for medicine, because senryu is full of them – their specialty is drawing peckers on walls when kept waiting! – but, come to think of it, we need an older man for the right image here. Okada explains that the doctor's attendant is waiting outside. With Japan's muggy summers, I expected to find more crotch-scratching for ringworm, but loose loincloths, plentiful baths and proper diets (minerals in sea-weed?), or lack of an equally good name for that fungus, kept it out of senryu. Instead –

疝気睾丸褌へ煮へこぼれ 145-20
senki kintama fundoshi e niekobore

ah, lumbago!
balls in loin-cloths
boiling o'er

Lumbago, says my dictionary, is "a pelvic *affection*." From what I have read, *senki* seems more of an *affliction*, but complaints about it were so common in Japan – in haiku, it is a winter theme – that it could not possibly apply to one disease. So *affection* is understandable. The original *ku* has the balls boiling over "into" the loincloths. Perhaps they peep out. But Japanese loincloths could be trip-ably long and could expand like a pelican pouch to hold elephantiasis-sized – or if you believe the cartoonists, elephant-sized – gonads. *Senki* is often called *senki-mushi*, rather than just *senki,* as with this *ku. Mushi* means "bug" (like our flu *bug*), but it is a homophone for *steamed* and brings wit to the boiling.

疝気持西瓜畑で疑ぐられ *145*
senki-mochi suikabatake de utagurare
(lumbago-having[person] watermelon-garden suspected)

lumbago looks
suspicious in a patch
of watermelon

The wit in this *ku* probably lies in its studied redundancy. It pretends there is no saying to the effect that no gentleman will even *approach* a melon patch, for it is a place where anyone spotted is assumed to be a thief. I say "gentleman" for the saying goes back going back to ancient China and, in the Sinosphere, *gentleman* 君子・紳士 is code for Confucian morals). The patch usually mentioned is *uri-batake* 瓜畑 or *kaden* 瓜田. This is the only time I have seen the melon *type* specified. Only the largest would do.

川越シも困る疝気の肩車 *18*
kawakoshi mo komaru senki no kataguruma

crossing rivers
is a pain with lumbago
shoulder-cars

狸閉口大仏の疝気持 *121*
tanuki teiguchi daibutsu no senkimochi

even tanuki
are shocked: a colossal
with lumbago!

Is this a pain in the neck for Mr. shoulder-car, or, in the crotch of his rider? Either way, it is an unpleasant picture! The Colossal is what the Europeans called the *daibutsu,* or "big-buddha." Only such a huge entity with lumbago could possibly impress a raccoon fox with its legendary proportions – balls that could stretch to cover the floor of an average-sized room (The *tanuki* is usually called a "racoon dog," but I became close with three generations of them and can attest to their delicate foxy feet and cleverness. The scrotal skin was used to pound out gold-leaf, someone got confused about what stretched, and graphics artists had so much fun finding uses for enormous balls that the mistake stuck for centuries).

きん__ハかんせいぬひのさいくなり 万 安三
kintama wa kansei nui no saiku nari

the bollocks
are fine kansei style
embroidery

Kansei style embroidery shows the thread on the outside and has some gathering (shirring? 閑清縫). I am unsure how to English it, but do have a seam on the . . . .

睾丸へへのこを包む角力取 葉 *12*
kôgan e henoko o tsutsumu sumôtori

the sumo wrestler
his cock swallowed up
by his ballocks

裸参りの睾丸はくるみ焼き *152-7*
hadakamairi no kintama wa kurumiyaki

the naked pilgrim
his ballocks turning into
roasted chestnuts

Re. the sumo wrestler. I saw the same in my high school locker-room. Thick thighs push the balls up and out from below while a fat pubic area swells out and down from above. (We'll discuss the varying pronunciation of 睾丸 in two pages.) *Re. the pilgrim.* I read of a nude woman whose pilgrimaging was a publicity ploy to draw people into a temple in Issa's *journal* but had not known of men doing such Hindhi-esque pilgrimages. Both *ku*, like the previous one, are sheer image, what many Occidentals and some Japanese consider *the* mark of short-form poetry.

ぶら付きの金褌でしめられる *117-2, 5*
buratsuki no kin fundoshi de shimerareru

his loitering bollocks
trussed up by
loincloths.

bollocks
caught loitering
trussed up by loincloths

We already know balls have nothing to do. A society of busy people can't just let them hang around. In the original, both the balls and the garment are in mid-*ku*. I can only seem to fit them fore or aft. (元句を「とりしめられ」で締め括りたかった。一字余りでも千金でしょう！)

ゆるいふんどし睾丸がばァをする *131-24*
yurui fundoshi kintama ga ba! o suru

loose loincloths
balls with play, play
peek-a-boo!

The game of *ina-ina-baa,* "not [here] not [here] booh!" is abbreviated as simply "baa!"

睾丸のある武士斗り四十七 *95-25*
kintama no aru bushi bakari yonjû-nana

they had balls
all forty-seven of them
were warriors

not one of them
lacked balls, you could count
all ninety four

In the original, "warriors with balls, but forty seven." All Japanese know 47 ex-samurai revenged their master at the cost of their own lives (not to mention those of others who died in their surprise attack). The equation of having balls and having courage may be *assumed* from the story about Tokugawa Ieyasu we have seen, but it is not common idiom. That makes this *ku* significant.

きん玉と徳利のならぶ牛車 50-6
kintama to tokuri no narabu ushiguruma

ox cart outing
sake flasks and ballocks
all lined up

らせつの睾丸小便をしかけられ 144-31
rasetsu no kintama shôben o shikakerare

pity the balls
of a de-peckered man
wet with piss

"Ox-cart," may not be the right word, for the ox-drawn vehicles used by noblemen and/or women going out for fun spanned the gamut from a hayride-like cart to what can only be called a black limousine. Needless to say, the first *senryu* is cleaner than many early *haikai ku* but it is more than balanced by the image drawn by the later senryu, which is disgusting (the "pity" is my addition).

夜ばい仰天睾丸へ猫がじゃれ
yobai gyôten kintama e neko ga jare

night-crawling
a sudden shock: ball-boxed
by a tom-cat

lovers meeting
at night: suddenly his balls
whacked by a cat

Night-crawling was how people in ancient times made love. If romantic literature has it right, noblemen with time on their hands went house to house, visiting lovers like tom-cats on the prowl. Country folk, on the other hand, until recently did their night-prowling to court possible lifelong partners, much as "we" did in New England with our "bundling." In senryu, however, we most easily imagine a town scene with an illicit lover coming when a husband is out of it. Leaving in the dark, robe barely closed – no underwear – stepping off the veranda or climbing through a gap in a fence, he is exposed to a cat intrigued by the motion and maybe a whiff of something fishy: *whack!* Who knows how often this has happened! All we know for sure is that the person who *wrote* the senryu almost certainly got whacked by his own cat at least once. To tell you the truth, it has happened to *me*, to the dingaling, not balls, as was the case for this *ku* published about the same time as the last in another collection: *"Night-crawling / a sudden shock: a cat whacks / a wet cock"* (夜這仰天ぬれイ八へ猫がじゃれ　葉別七 *yobai gyôten nuremara e neko ga jare.*) Either the same poet put different versions in different collections, someone wanted to change the one detail to match *his* experience, or cat attacks were endemic.

睾丸の上り下りで時が知れ *50-17*
kôgan no agari sagari de toki ga shire

telling the time
from the rising & falling
of their testicles

睾丸が長アく成ると時計チャン 葉
kôgan ga nagaaku naru to tokei-chan 別 6

when the balls
get really looong, it's
clock-chan

A few years before the first *ku*, a link-verse jam (of Issa and friends) mentioned *"telling the time by the eyes of a cat."* Years after reading that, a friend wrote a book by that name and I learned it was a Chinese commonplace. But, the real allusion here is to the old-style grandfather clocks – in the early-19c Japan had some – with their balls hanging from chains. The suffix *chan* after the "clock" in the second *ku* is a term of endearment suggesting that "clock" would be a good nickname for such a man. Southernese might make it "Master Clock."

Shiki's (haiku) Balls

~~~~~~

I had not planned on including *balls* in this book because 1) I thought to save them for another book on racoon foxes (I became friends with them in Japan; one ♀ had a crush on me) and 2), because of their relatively low level of obscenity. I changed my mind because I felt the cat senryu was too good to leave out, and because I found a cache of Shiki's balls I carefully squirreled away when reading his complete haiku about a decade ago and thought it might be fun to reveal them to the world before I lost them again and this seemed like as good a place as any.

睾丸の邪魔になったる涼み哉 子規 拾遺 明治二十八書簡 *374*
kintama no jama ni nattaru suzumi kana shiki (1867-1902)
(testicles/ balls'interference/bother-as/into become coolness!/?/'tis)

evening cool
only my balls are
in the way

these jewels
are no help at all
cooling down

These haiku balls belong to the great Shiki and the summer theme of coolness/ cooling-off. Though there is no rule, as a rule senryu and haiku favor the colloquial pronunciation of 睾丸, *kintama* ([gold]balls), but, on page 184, following Syunroan, I used the formal *kôgan* (testicles/gonads) for the clock *ku*. Japanese may always be pronounced differently when judged appropriate. Length is no help, for both words are equally four syllabets (きんたま vs. こうがん).

睾丸をのせて重たき団扇哉 拾遺
kintama o nosete omotaki uchiwa kana shiki
(testicles/ balls'[acc] place/loading heavy fan!/?/'tis)

laying my balls
upon the fan, surprised
at their weight

how heavy
the fan with my balls
placed on it

a fan loaded
with my balls feels
very heavy

To fully appreciate this, one must be familiar with the type of fan called an *uchiwa.* It is a round fan, sturdier than the folding type and has a handle from 4 inches to a foot- long. So there is a bit of resemblance to a shovel. I do not think this started as an experiment. Shiki is lying there ill and beat from the sultry heat of the Japanese summer. I imagine him lying on his side, in a largely open robe, reaching down to lift his balls so air may pass through better. Both the poor leverage and his weak state would have contributed to the heavy feeling. I feel the *ku* should have been put with a selection of his best and not left with the dregs. Note that one is not forced to use "my" in the Japanese which for that and other reasons is better than my translations. Another *ku* impresses less:

these balls
just lay there sweating
it's pitiful!

it's pitiful
seeing my balls sweat
by themselves
~~~~~~

睾丸の汗かいて居るあはれ也 子規拾
kintama no ase kaite-iru aware nari shiki
(testicles'sweating-are pitiful be/come/are)

~~~~~~~~~~~~~~~~~~~~~~~~~~~~~~~~~

秋のくれ祖父のふぐり見てのみぞ 其角
akinokure ôji no fuguri mite nomi zo kikaku
(fall's-end grandfather's balls seeing only!)

winter's near
all grandpa does is gaze
upon his balls

the end of fall
all i can see are my
grandpa's balls

Sweating from exercise, outdoor or sexual is one thing, just lying there and sweating another. I think Shiki is transferring his sadness to his balls. The character 居 lets a reader feel the poet and his balls are not moving, but it would not help with a pure auditory reading. Moreover, while I, too, have seen *mine* as strangers and can appreciate Shiki's feelings, the third person approach is better. It is why Kikaku's *ku* is often encountered but not Shiki's. It goes without saying that the balls of an old person are oddly pitiful. Grandfather could be Kikaku's father, for once one becomes *a* grandfather to someone, one is "grandfather" to all – even to one's son – in Japan, and I would guess, most cultures. But, father or grandfather, I prefer to think the balls actually seen belong to the poet who keeps seeing in them his father or grandfather's balls glimpsed when he was a boy. That second reading to my second reading makes most sense to me, though Kikaku may be nursing his father (★わが勝手な解釈に対し物知る人のご異見を求む!).

夏痩やきん丸許り平気也 子規
natsuyase ya kintama bakari heiki nari

summer thinning
only my jewels are
fat and happy

summer thinning
only my balls float
fat and happy

Shiki, again. Summer thinning is a common dis-ease for the thin majority of the world. His balls are *heiki,* "unfazed." With only the second character of 睾丸 written, I feel them as an entity, even a boat, for "round" (丸) at the end of a word is used where we would use an SS. Hence, the bath image. Reading *ku* such as *"my balls / roll forth from / the shichô"* きんたまのころげて出たる紙帳哉 拾遺 *kintama no korogete detaru shichô kana*) – the *shichô* being a paper mosquito net – I wonder if Shiki suffered from the "lumbago" already mentioned, swollen balls as a result of circulatory problems common with the bed-ridden!

睾丸に須磨のすず風吹送れ 拾遺
kintama ni suma no suzukaze fuki okure

blow cool
send the breeze of suma
to my balls!

blow over
the cooling suma wind
to my balls
~~~~~~~~~~~~~~~~~~~~~~~~~~~~~~~~~

Suma is a place of exile both tragic and romantic by the sea-side. Being to the South, it is warm and humid and *ku* often mention open dwellings with nude residents, but the sea breeze was cool. If only English had a better verb for "blow-send!" That year, Shiki found balls everywhere. One was published in the *Hototogisu*: *"Cooling the balls / of a beggar: the pure / spring water"* (乞食の睾丸をひやす清水哉　ホトトギス 明治 28 *kôjiki no kintama o hiyasu shimizu kana*). Another, presumably a reflection: *"White clouds / emerge from a dark crotch / mountain spring"*(またくらに白雲起る清水哉　*matakura ni shirogumo okiru shimizu kana* 上記の三つ後です). "Pure spring water" and "mountain spring" are the same *kiyomizu* in the originals, but neither impress us like his more personal *ku*.

睾丸の垢取る冬の日向哉 明治二九
kintama no aka toru fuyu himuko kana shiki
(balls' lint/dust/crud take winter sun-face[bath]!/?/'tis)

picking lint
off my balls basking
in winter sun

sun-bathing
i pick long john lint
off my balls

This is *excellent* (『子規句集』にないのがケシカランぞ) but hard to English for one is forced to use "ing" twice or a pronoun, where Japanese is better with neither.

永き日や頻りに股のいらかゆき 病状手記 *30-9-29*
nagaki hi ya shikiri ni mata no irakayuki shiki
(long day! frequently crotch's tingly-itchiness)

a long day!
my crotch going from
itch to itch

That was one loose translation – if the itch was ringworm, it's an understatement. That year he also depicted another's discomfort: *"A blind boy / crotch aflame from below – / Lonely lumbago"* (寂や疝やまた下萌の小座頭や *sabishisa ya mata shitamoe no kozatô ya*). It is followed by: *"Out of demand / the heat of hair growing / on your balls"* (売れずして玉に毛生る暖かさ *urezu shite tama ni ke haeru atatakasa*). If you were actively moving about, would the hair wear off on your loincloth? A new twist on mossy rolling stone? The next year's *"Wolves! a traveler's balls freeze"* (狼や睾丸凍る旅の人 31 拾) is not in the same league with Issa's deservedly better-known goose bumps on seeing wolf scat. This, a couple years later, is slightly better *"A fall mosquito / comes to stab the skin / of a jewel"* (秋の蚊や玉の御膚刺しに来る　明治 33 *aki no ka ya tama no on-hada sashi ni kuru*). In the original, the skin gets an honorific prefix. Finally, the year he died, Shiki joked to a friend who desperately wanted a boy that *"Peach Tarô* (the legendary boy) *comes from Peach-gold* [i.e. balls]*-Tarô, you know!"* (桃太郎は桃金太郎は何からぞ meiji 35 *momotarô wa momokintarô nani kara zo*). That is to say, it depends upon your gonads. Shiki, was well-known for his support of baseball and interest in science as well as poetry. And, here is one of his last *ku*, giving what I think is a macabre portrait of his near future.

墓の木ハ茂り又玉や腐ルラン 明治 *35*
haka no ki wa shigeri mata tama ya kusaru ran
(grave's/s' tree/s growthick/rank again balls/soul!/: rot[+emph.]

grave-side trees
thick with leaves, again
my balls will rot

That's it for Shiki whom many think the first man of modern haiku (*I* think of him as the last man of old haiku/haikai). Let me give a quick summary of the balls in old *haikai* before quitting the essay and heading back up the *eddies*.

1. はるかぜにふらめきわたる松ふぐり 犬筑波
swaying about in the spring=erotic breeze, pine=waiting cones=balls,
永き日門にたてる傾城
a long day standing by the gate a pretty prostitute.

2. 藤が枝のさがるやたんな松ふぐり 犬子
wisteria boughs hang down: ribbons=loin-cloths for the pine cones=balls

---

harukaze ni burameki wataru matsu fuguri // nagaki hi kado ni tateru keisei
↑ inutsukuba 1536. *fuji ga eda no sagaru ya tanna matsu fuguri* = enoko 1633

Early *haikai* are full of pine-cones, which is to say *waiting* balls, for "pine" and "wait" are homophones, *matsu.* Since the *ku* are usually interesting only as part of a link-verse sequence, the reading of which is killed by explanation in a way stand-alone *ku* are not, they are unsuitable for translation. Senryu were not *that* interested in pine cones, but here is one, that may be kept only to gas *haikai:*

ふぐり持松に放屁の沙汰はなし *111-10*
fuguri mochi matsu ni hoppi no sata wa nashi willow
(cones/balls have pine/s-by release-fart/s' episode/hardship-as-for not)

~~*men & trees*~~ *men vs. trees*

~~*at least all those*~~
~~*pine trees with their cojones*~~
~~*don't fart on us!*~~

a pine's cojones
at least they are not gassed
while waiting

On second thought, I am mistaken, for imagining people walking under pine trees is not so senryu as imagining something else, which also puns on pine-as-wait. Do you recall all those balls waiting outside as peter has all the fun within the crimson gates? This is a later senryu's clever paraverse (another good example why it is wrong to put down later senryu) of what had been crude stuff. I used Spanish because *cojones* means both *cones* and *balls*. That dual connotation saved half the wit, but the other half (pine=wait) was lost and the last line dead.

~ eddies ~

The Seven Paradoxes of Balls.

In the shade, they are dark-skinned;
Young, show the wrinkles of age;
Gold, yet they gain not entrance;
Jewels, they shine not at all;
With a seam, they never come apart;
Hanging loose, they never drop off;
Fellow travelers, they must wait outside.

(蔭に居れ共色黒し、年は若くて皺がある、金はあれ共通用せず、玉といへ共光なし、縫目あれ共綻びず) From *Balls* (玩球隠士編撰『岐牟太末学大全』), source of much in this chapter. Eventually, I found balls *gaining entrance*, but it was not in *Balls*. It was in *Cuntologia*, within the discussion of a certain type of vagina, the pull-string, or pouch-purse, which is not as good as an *octopussy,* but pretty good:

巾着という筈金までくくり込み　柳彦生栄
kinchaku to iu hazu kin made kukuri-komi

A draw-purse!
Of course, because ours
are drawn in!

Literally, *"even the gold=balls is encircled and drawn in."* In O.E., a man's purse was his pouch, so we came close, but the wit depends upon "gold/money" meaning balls *and* being homophonic with part of the name for the pull-string purse (vagina), *kinchaku.*

Twain's 1601 (or, CONVERSATION, AS IT WAS BY THE SOCIAL FIRESIDE, IN THE TIME OF THE TUDORS.) I am not amazed to find Twain enjoying obscenity for obscenity's sake, which is to say "giving resounding slaps on what Chaucer would quite simply call 'the bare erse" for the hell of it. But I was surprised I had to find out about it in Japanese! Googling, I consequently found the thing itself at the Project Gutenberg expertly set in an intriguing history and judicious commentary. Secretary of State John Hay who helped to get it known, signed off his first letter commending *1601* to a literary critic, *"Yours, very much worritted by the depravity of Christendom,"* words facetious on one level yet telling, as they show he appreciated Twain's perspective: to wit, our *not* using earthy language was a corruption of the good Elizabethan tongue of the old bards. He made that explicit in a second letter sent with the manuscript:

But the taste of the present day is too corrupt for anything so classic.
He [Twain] has not yet been able even to find a publisher.

Subtler drollery in his other letters also confirm Twain's appraisal, *"In the matter of humor, what an unsurpassable touch John Hay had!"* Four copies were printed in 1880, it's first real printing of fifty copies was done at West Point in 1882, and soon later, *1601* came to be "privately printed in several countries, among them Japan."

*The Chaucer comparison was by C. E. S. Wood, who got the book printed at West Point. The Gutenberg e-book *1601* is produced by David Widger.

One More Lumbago. How did I miss this next one, right in the first book of *Willow!?*

橙八年神さまの疝気所 *1-7*
daidai wa toshigami-sama no senkidoko
(bigerade-as-for year-god-sir's lumbago place)

the bigerades?
the place where the year god
leaves his lumbago

the bigerades
so even the year-god now
suffers lumbago?

The huge yellow citrus, larger than a grapefruit usually balances on top of magical mountains of longevity (*hôrai*) or piles of food (*kuitsumi*) to be ravaged over the course of the New Year holidays. Because of the way it is said that the *senki* bug leaves the body to descend into the testicles, I went out on a limb with "leaves" in the first reading.

~~~~~~

More on the Raccoon-Fox. Perhaps the most senryu thing about *tanuki*, the real *tanuki*, is this: *Thanks to tanuki / animal paths come with / public restrooms.* Which is to say, they make collective toilets every half mile or so along their pathways through the woods. They tend to be perfectly round and when the seeds in their scat sprout turn green.

~~~~~~

& Don't Forget the Navel. The navel can be compared to the balls in uselessness or to holes, if you think of it as one. Navels do not fare so well as balls in senryu and my little collection of navel haiku – many are very good, though there is nothing vulgar, much less obscene – so there is no belly-button chapter in this book. But, one of the obscene/ original Japanese folk songs introduced by Takenaka Rô, who notes it was once a favorite with *goze*, blind female singers who were led from house to house, *must* be squeezed in. After tracing the genealogy of the respective holes back to the Celestial Cave and Mt Fuji's crater, we come to the navel's main complaint, *"The rest of the holed fraternity have all the fun* (deleted), the main details of which follow:

The hole next door is treated well, by all the world adored,
Except when its monthly business grows too heavy to ignore.
It's always bustling with party cheer —
I can't help noticing, living so near:
Sunset to sunrise, seven days a week,
Someone knocking up the gate and when I took a peek:
There, dangling in the air, I saw a hairless head,
A standing cut upon its crown, the whole of which was red.
But when I took a second look, it wore a kinky wig (deleted)

It must be a Main Temple, of what sect I do not know,
To see so many monks, all strangers, going to and fro.
They must polish rice by the boatload down there,
For the milky wash, it overflows, however they take care
To wipe it up with cloth and paper, all is never caught:
It spills into our navel ground where it goes for naught.

With the neighbors always painting up the town
Can we navels help it, if we all feel down?
Life for us is so unfair;
We'd be happy just to have some hair
To help keep out the dust and the lint,
If we can't be plum or cherry, at least we could be mint!

Alas, alack, our neighbor is such a f__ing glutton!
How miserable to be a bellybutton!"

Can you see why I try not to translate songs? The deletions are in Takenaka's rendition, for he first gave it in a short column and felt he could not give it more space. More importantly, he explains that the song shows that obscene songs are not all alike. *This is not heartless obscenity but has a touching quality, just right for the blind women who sang it.* I agree, and would only add that these women encountered in senryu, when not being looked over while peeing are usually worried about being hit, for a horrid superstition made it good luck to hit one when you slept with her!

(The first part of the song, if it is the same song (Takenaka jumps about like flying fish chased by tuna) starts: 「哀れなるかな　へそ穴口説」 and the part I translated, which might be a different song, picks up pages later: 「よその穴衆の　たのしみ聞けば ・俺らが隣の　朋輩穴は・かわいがらるる愛嬌ありて・月に一度の　お役のほかは・毎夜よごとに　そのにぎやかさ・暮の六つから明六つまで・どたらばたらと　玄関たたく・わしもたまげて　のぞいて見れば・光る頭を　ブラブラ下げて　・坊主あたまに立傷はわせ・禿げたる頭に　かずらを巻いて（略）」。If you would see more or sort it out: たけなか・ろう著　『日本情哥行』1986.)

If you find the song's premise, that the navel is a "hole," odd, please note that in Japanese, the navel is not a belly *button.* Lacking that "button," it was more easily thought of as a depression, or hole. Indeed, Blyth introduces a clean navel senryu he describes as "a satire on the dignity, the majesty, the divinity of man" where the navel is described exactly as he Englishes it: *"Until death / It cleaves to you / The hole of the navel"* (*shinu made wa kuttsuite-iru heso-no-ana*). Yep, a parasitic *hole!* Most girls would doubtless tend to be *inners*, because theirs were tied more tightly than male navel chords as it was thought good for assuring they had a tight twat (the opposite was the case for men). And, due to a superstitious fear of cleaning the navel in parts of Japan, they really can look black inside, which makes them seem an actual hole! The *woman's navel* in the song is a close parallel to the neglected *balls of the male*. Aside from the last stanza, where I laid on the English idiom with a trowel (the *mint* and the *glutton* are not in the original), it is, on the whole (excluding the *seven days a week* I could not resist, and the head's being *reddened* for the rhyme), a close – and, therefore, lousy – translation. The *goze* song is *not* found in a 400 pg book of navel lore published in 1929, perhaps because of fear of the censors who came into being largely to protect Japan from the slander of the ever-so-prissy Occident. That book does, however, include a long and boring tale of a samurai who blasted his adversaries with farts emitted from his navel, and a short and sweet one of a town that collected belly-button lint to make soup for an orphaned thunder-demon child (All Japanese children know to keep their navels well hidden lest the thunder demons steal them). Be that as it may, the navel-as-hole idea can come in *useful* sometimes. Take, for example, this brilliant Genroku era (c.1700) proto-senryu, or *zappai*, the first given in Suzuki Katsutada's *Enku no Sekai*:

やかましい・我はへそから出たわいやい
yakamashii ware wa heso kara deta wai yai 綿帽子
(noisy/shut-up! i[the child]-as-for navel-from came-out[+emph])

◎ *oh, hush up!* ◎
you, child, came from
my belly-button!

.

I recall my nephew, when his total vocabulary was maybe a hundred words, proud to proclaim *he* came from my sister's "uterus" (!). I suppose a difficult word like that is one way a parent can flabbergast a curious child – and, as Hofstadter notes in *Le Ton Beau de Marot*, there is joy, even magic, in our difficult names for *dinosaurs* (the roots of the very word "dinosaur" are opaque to many of us) as opposed to Chinese, where it is all so clear, so plain – but, if I ever get married and *my* wife has a child, I think I would prefer belly-button to uterus. After all, it is not a complete fib. The child does "come from" the nutrients sent up his own belly-button and his mother who sent him those nutrients did get hers from her belly-button . . . , so generationally speaking . . . But, that would only hold up for a while. Suzuki gives a follow-up:

ふしんうつ・おれはへそから出たかいのう 削かけ
fushin utsu ore wa heso kara deta kai nô 正徳三

◎ *she has her doubt* ◎
is the belly-button really
where *I* came out?

In most of Japan, he first-person pronoun *ore* is only used by a male dominant today, but was once used by male and female alike in many parts. Suzuki imagines a girl as the most likely to ask her mother this, so I made the first pronoun, – which was not in the original cap-verse draw (just *doubt strikes/expresses*) – feminine.

cooling down
bitten by an ant
on my belly-button

I am unsure who wrote this *haiku* (*suzushisa ya ari ni sasaruru heso no ana* in the original), but I like it (原文求む：頼む誰か、気に入った句ですよ！).

~~~~~~

~~~~~~

o m a k e

~~~~~~

かの「猫じゃれふぐり」といえば、かの本[1]の裏表紙の内に駄句を見つけし

ʃʃ

~~~~~~~~~~~~~~~~~~~~~~~~~~

千摺りにわが手も加える馬鹿な猫

~~~~~~~~~~~~~~~~~~~~~~~~~~

千摺りや猫が勝手にお手を貸し

~~~~~~~~~~~~~~~~~~~~~~~~~~

猫のてが余計な世話ゾ手淫中

~~~~~~~~~~~~

いずれも敬愚

~~~~~~~~~~~~

1. 玩球隠士編撰『岐牟太末学大全』1985

独身の我輩に猫の手を借りようともしなかったが、Catが勝手に
そうした。が、かの慣用語もない母国語に拙句ながら英訳してもつまらん。

驚愕。その後『末摘花』の中（2-11）で、同じ体験をした者の句をば見つけた！

馬鹿なことおえたを猫が狙ってる
baka na koto oeta o neko ga neratteru

how ridiculous!
the cat would catch
an erection!

re-dick-ulous!
the pussy would pounce
on a hard on!

I still do not know where the cat whacking the balls in the text came from, but I found the above in *Pluck*. Forgive the odd punning! 好奇心満々の猫と暮らした、あの頃大変だった。自己防衛のため、籠を逆さまにして、毎晩、大事なところ上にかぶせて寝るという、この世にも珍しい馬鹿なことになりました。猫君にいわすれば、シーツの下にて、コソコソ動くものは、ミンナ、やはり、鼠君になる、という訳です.

松茸＋不動尊＋絵馬＝珍考

Meeting Acala, God of Fire, between balls and cunt (pg 178), made me recall the votive tablet (*ema*) pine-mushroom penises I once saw, and how they were often fiery with lightning-like "veins" on the shaft. Compare their vigorous mortality with our solid phallic symbols and do they not seem dead as a *stiff ?*

十二[12]

和尚や黄巾の賊
Bonzes Wearing Gold

~~~~~~

和尚のへのこ黄巾の賊と成り
oshô no henoko kôkin no zoku to nari 葉 11
(bonze's/s' cock yellow-cloth's gang become)

the bonze's cock
becomes one of the gang:
a yellow-cloth

the priest's tool
has joined the order of
the gold turban

The Yellow Cloth, or Yellow Turban Bandits,[1] wreaked havoc in 2c China. The leader literally clothed himself and his fighters in Taoism, hence the color, and the uprising got considerable support from peasants. So, the allusion would be to a rebellious, allegedly religious member. Taoist-Buddhist connections aside, why *yellow?* In a society where little red meat is eaten, what Usanians assume to be brown or burnt sienna is generally closer to that color, and, in Japan, at least, sometimes called gold.[2]

いい和尚糞の輪袈裟を子にかける
ii oshô kuso no wakesa o ko-ni kakeru 葉八
(good bonze/s shit-ring-surplice/s[3] [acc] child-on put)

a good bonze
puts a surplice of shit
on his child

Senryu sodomy does not *always* mention a *bonze*, as low-order Buddhist priests, were usually Englished (from the Japanese *bôzu* via Portuguese in the 16-17c) before "monk" became the common translation, but, the two went together. The *narrow* (*semai/kitsui*) *path* of pederasty was more acceptable behavior for bonzes than the *wide* (*hiroi/yurui*) *way* of sex with women, as the risk of falling in love was low, and that of fathering a child or committing adultery was nil. Hence, the bonze with ordure on his "child" was, by definition, "good" (*ii*).[4] Yet, Buddhist clergy were supposed to kill their desire, so the verse is not just *bronze*[5] but
~~~~~~

*iron*ic. Joking aside, most of us, unlike many of our primate brethren who do not mind taking feces in hand and throwing them, are uncomfortable with touching shit, even our own. Why a greater number of people in some cultures than others are not bothered by it would require a book to do it justice. For here, suffice it to note that even backdoor enthusiasts might have mixed feelings about having it on their penis. Leupp (1995/7) mentions one scholar, Nishimura Sadao, who thought "feces might produce disease" and, in 1834, provided his readers with a preventative remedy learned from someone who practiced male-color. To avoid having shit, "called a headband (*hachimaki*)," on the head of the penis (*karisaki*),

> when you are about to withdraw your turtle-head, you should strongly pinch [your partner's] buttocks. Because of the pain, he will immediately droop down [sic.] (*omowazu shiri o shibomu*). If you withdraw at that point, you probably will not acquire disease from the headband. (色道禁秘書 in Leupp: *Male Colors* 1997. p.153)

The second bracket with the *sic* is mine. While *shibomu* can describe the *wilting/ drooping* of blossoms, it is most commonly used for those that *shrink*, or *pucker-up* while doing so (*eg.,* the morning glory). If the cock withdraws at the moment the insertee involuntarily *clenches his spincter* not only will it be cleaned on the outside, but some of the fluid in the urethra milked out.

うら門ハじやうがうすいとげんがいゝ
uramon wa jô ga usui to gen ga ii 末 3 - 26
(back-gate-as-for lock's[affection] thin/easy abbot-the says)

with back-gates
the lock is easier to pick
says the priest

the back-gate's
easy: we feel so much less
says the priest

The *gen* is the head of a small temple. The *ku* does not English because we cannot pun *lock* with *affection/emotion,* both *jô* in Japanese. When I first read it, years ago, I rhymed some of its implications into the margin of the book:

Would you eschew attachment on earth?
Defer to the hole that doesn't give birth!
~~~~~~~~~~~~~~~~~~~~~~~~~~~~~~
Since no one falls for a bum-hole,
use it, if you must use your pole!

Of course, my "no one" is wrong: I can't help wondering if *homosexual* bonzes were ever advised to do only women. But for most bonzes, woman was the enemy because they loved her (and children/attachment likely). One *ku* on vagina-love, perhaps drawing on Bashô's *"It is like nothing / made to stand for it / the three-day moon"* (*ari to aru tatoe ni mo nizu mika no tsuki*), may be relevant:

what in the world
can stand for its depth?
the bobo hole!
~~~~~~~~~~~~~~~~~~~~~~~~~~~~~~

其深さ何にたとへん開の穴 葉 三四
sono fukasa nani ni tatoen bobo no ana

Bobo has a light feel to it in Japanese as in English, but it is anything but.

> *. . . thoughts of 1,000 Ryo safe-boxes, and entire mansions being sucked down the hole come to mind. Get wrapped up in the wrong hole and a man can even lose his life.* (Syunroan 犇露庵主人)

This modern (1995) gloss is banal but true. Beautiful courtesans were not called "castle-topplers" for nothing. [6] If we ignore the banal implications and take it as a riddle, *the sea* (*umi*) would be one good answer, for it is homophonic with "birth." *The dark* (*yami*) would be another, for the unenlightened spiritual life was said to proceed from *yami* to *yami*, as the physical one did from *ana* to *ana,* hole to hole. It is unlikely the *ku* was simply an expression of awe at something literally profound, but if it was, let us note that the vagina, placed up front by medical mock-ups from front-biased cultures is usually closer to the *middle*, enough so that, in coital embrace the male may sometimes feel as though he were the *axis mundi*. Lodged at the very center of the sphere – could anything be deeper? That is why (to me) the *bobo* beats the butt, even if evolution has given us tighter anuses than vaginas (it is more important to push out shit than to pull in pricks). Obviously, not all feel that way. Tales and treatises warn of "men who come to financial ruin because of homosexual involvement." (Leupp:1995/7 p.152)

大だわけ陰間をくじる馬鹿和尚 葉 21
ôdawake kagema o kujiru baka oshô

pure stupidity!
a foolish bonze fingers
a bought boy

what a load a crap!
the dopey bonze fingers
a catamite crack

As we shall see, some bonzes developed affection for the anus that reached even to its smell, thus betraying their goal of unattachment to the world; but this *ku* focuses elsewhere. A bonze, either novice, imbecile or both, is at a tea-shop, in senryu, always a place for sex between unmarried couples or with prostitutes, where he proves himself doubly the fool for thinking he must arouse someone from whom he buys sex and not realizing how rectums and vaginas differ in respect to the utility of foreplay. Another *ku* (莫大の難儀陰間に二本指 128-48 *sôdai no nangi kagema ni nihon yubi*), not specifically about a bonze, explains that standard two-finger fingering is nothing but a pain in the ass for a catamite.

心中に和尚陰間のけつをなめ
shinjû ni oshô kagema no ketsu o name 葉 五
(heart-in/faith-proving priest pro-catamite's ass[acc] licks)

his heart's in it
the bonze really licks
a catamite ass

dying to prove
his love, the bonze licks
his boy's groove

Shinjû here is short for *shinjû-date*, proving one's fidelity to a lover. It is most commonly used for courtesans who prove their sincerity to a doubting customer-lover by cutting off a pinkie. We saw it in the devil's tongue cunnilingus senryu (pg. 80), but the nuance here is very different. The bonze sins against his religion for being attached to, *i.e.,* fond of, his love-object, and his society's mores for mixing macho buggery with ass-licking – the vectors of the inserter and insertee were, in Japan, as elsewhere in much of what Burton called the Sotadic Zone,[7] at a far further remove than the slight difference in mindset we call homo- and heterosexual, although the insertee without a gay nature could switch into the inserter when they matured. The word "dying" in the second reading reflects the most common usage of *shinjû,* the double suicide of lovers who typically tie themselves together and jump off a bridge, or, more incredibly yet, jumped or hung themselves simultaneously in different locations if they were prevented from meeting.[8]

To prove his love will ever last —
The bonze licks his boyfriend's ass.

Homosexual affection resembling heterosexual affection would seem to have been laughed at by this and other senryu, but Leupp cites a number of sources to the effect that the love suicides and love-pledges we generally associate with courtesans were actually the invention of romantic homosexual lovers. If we are seeing pretty crude stuff, it is because senryu tend to prefer the prostitute variety precisely because it is vulgar and purely physical, and I have further selected for such. Higher literature focuses on pretty young boys (*chigo,* literally "infant") whose relationship with the older men was closer to the socially accepted boy-love in Greece. Bashô, who admitted being drawn to male-color for a while when he was younger, expressed this beautifully in his well-known *ku, "the moon is clear – / I escort a lovely boy / frightened by a fox"* (*tsuki sumu ya . . .* trans. by Makoto Ueda [9]). We can well imagine the delicate features of the worried boy. The affection for *chigo*, generally orphans or children of poor parents raised or given schooling at monasteries, sometimes grew into love and created intense rivalry for the boy's affection that betrayed the original reason for choosing the narrow way.

和尚さまひざへ来ル子にしゆずを出し
oshô-sama hiza e kuru ko ni juzu o dashi willow 4-4
(bonze[+hon.] lap-to come/ing-child/ren-to prayerbeads[acc] take-out)

that nice bonze
has sweets on tap, for kids
who visit his lap

Ah, so *that's* the bait! The original wit hides in the *juzu,* or, *prayer beads* (no "sweets" are mentioned). Because they are rubbed (*suru*), a suspicious association is evoked; but the meaning lies elsewhere. This *must be* an abbreviation of *juzu no mi* (数珠の実), literally, *nuts or berries of the prayer beads,* but temple argot for *snacks*, most of which were a variety of food and drink carried up the mountain by worshippers (I recall someone carrying up a watermelon, the perfect gift, for money is nothing for those who have it, but labor is *always* labor).

あの人に寺子の時に抱つかれ 寄太鼓
ano hito ni terago no toki ni dakitsukare 元禄 14
(that person-into, temple-child's time-when clung-to)

he grew up fine
the temple-child that
clung to me

the temple-child
that clung tight to me
a family man!

I might have missed this *zappai*, dated seven years after Bashô's lovely boy *ku,* had Suzuki Katsutada not explained it (the ellipsis after the *ni* is so large I thought *ni* meant "[held]by," rather than "[turned] into). As any good-looking little boy at a temple school might become the object of sexual affection, and many little boys who do *not* become homosexual cling to and even turn their butts toward older men, it is hardly surprising that most of the *terago* developed into normal heterosexuals. We cannot say if "a family man" is correct, but "that person to" implies the boy became a respectable adult, a man of substance. Nonetheless, for a man who knew him sexually, the change would have been shocking. Yet, good.

けつをされうんこが内へ這入るやう 葉 21
ketsu o sare unko ga uchi e hairu yô

butt-fucked
"it's just like a turd
coming in"

After Bashô's fantasia, and the sweet senryû, *that* was a rude awakening! This could be the thought of an inexperienced boy with a bonze. Then, again, it could be an empty *sake* keg retriever (a common Ganymede in senryu) sodomized by a samurai, a wife by her husband during her period, or a curious maid. Regardless, so näive and tactile a *ku* is rare.[10] A visual metaphor – which could run either way – is more common,: *"A pickle pulled from rice-bran bean paste looks like a pecker that did an ass"* (胡瓜の溷漬穴ッをしたイ八のやう 葉 別七 *kyûri no dobu-zuke ketsu o shita mara no yô*). Describing a pickle in terms of beshitted cock (more so than the vice-versa) suggests the practice, or consciousness of it, was common.

かげまの屁和尚提灯吹き消され
kagema no he oshô chôchin fukikesare
(shade-space[catamite]'s fart bonze lamp blown-out)

shade-boy farts
and the bonze's lantern
is blown out

shade-boy farts
and the priest blows out
the lantern

His boy drops a fart
And the bonze's wick
Sputters in the dark.

The original is unclear about who or what blows out the lantern. Did the fart blow out the lantern, held close by the bonze to see something ugly? But *chôchin* (lantern) is slang for an old man's penis – paper lanterns fold-up like accordians – could we instead have a weak erection/flame blown out by the fart? The *wick* in the last translation, an off-the-cuff from respondent P.D., saves the possible allusion. It does not *go out*, but is faithfully ambiguous. My preferred reading is the second: if Japanese knew that a flame takes the stink (sulfur) from a fart, we may have a masterful description of one so infatuated with buggery that he relishes every fart! [11] Another *ku* has a bonze y-y-yawn thrice at a catamite's fart (陰間の屁和尚三べんあくびをし *kagema no he oshô sanpen akubi o shi*), presumeably to better take in the smell (though I have yet to find another such use of yawning). The drollest take on bonzes+boy=love+farts I have seen is not, however, a senryu, but a late-Ming Dynasty story about a bonze suffering from enlarged balls (the *lumbago* mentioned in another chapter) who visits a Doctor:

> "This disease may be cured in the case of most patients, but it is difficult for me to do anything for an honorable leave-house (someone who left the secular world behind, i.e., a bonze)."
>
> "Why is that?" asked the Bonze.
>
> "Because, those big bags of yours are stuffed so full with the farts of all your acolytes." (『笑府』憑夢竜撰 found in *Balls*).

In Tantric Buddhism, vital juices might be sucked up from a woman by the well-trained penis, but this was yet another thing! I cannot say if the above tale, found in Japanese, was of genuine Chinese origin, but one thing is certain. For centuries, most Japanese did think of male-color, or, at least that involving little boys and men of the cloth, as *a practice of Chinese origin* brought back to Japan by Kûkai (774 – 835 CE), also called Kôbô Daishi, the founder of the Shingon (Pure-word) sect of esoteric Buddhism, who composed Japan's Fifty Sound (Syllabet) Song – unlike the English Alphabet Song, which merely parrots the alphabet, it arranges the entire syllabary into a single mellifluous poem (possible because all but one Japanese syllabet ends with a vowel sound) on the transitory nature of life – and is sometimes credited with inventing the syllabary itself. When visiting China, this genius was said to have amazed his hosts by painting instant landscapes by hurling ink at paper and writing five sutra simultaneously with as many brushes. A *Pluck* senryu put it like this:

空海はへのこばかりが無筆なり 摘
kuukai wa henoko bakari ga muhitsu nari 2-14

kukai's only
illiterate part
was his private one

saint kukai
only his pecker
won't hold a brush

The original says "only Kûkai's cock is brushless=illiterate." I have seen an Edo era painting showing this. Each hand and foot grips a brush. The fifth is in his *mouth* clenched between his teeth. This *ku* probably alluded to the following one:

弘法の五筆は冬の日也鳧 む 四
kôbô no go fude wa fuyu no hi nari

kôbô's five brushes
it must have been
a winter day

This 1752 *Mutamagawa* 5-7-5 *ku* already has the great teacher's private part in mind and expresses the absence of a sixth brush in a witty manner. Or so I thought. But, when I wrote an man with a site devoted to the *Mutamagawa* – who, believes I over-estimate the sex and body parts in it – to see what he thought of my reading, he cited a researcher who explained it in a different way: Kôbô uses five brushes *because the winter day is so short that he must make up for lost time*. Since the *Mutamagawa* was more *haikai* than senryu in style – indeed, most think its *ku* ought not to be called senryu but *zappai* – the point is well taken, for that certainly is a good seasonal reading. But, someone in Kôbô's capacity should have been capable of writing by lamp-light. In other words, *I am not convinced*.

古ル郷を弘法大師けちをつけ 万
furusato o kôbô daishi kechi o tsuke 宝 11

our home-town
the great saint kôbô
puts it down

What would our home-town be? The *mons veneris*, or, to be more specific, the cave with the entrance on its slope. Japanese slang for the vagina includes "birth-place" (*ubusunadokoro* 産土所), "cave" (*iwaya*), "birth-home-town" (*umare-kokyô*) and "(heaven's) cave-door" (*ama no iwato*) vulva. The *ku* may refer to the catechism of the esoteric Buddhism Kôbô introduced to Japan [12] or the choice of homosexual love as less sinful for the clergy.

名僧のへのこ日ましに細ヶなり 万 明七
mei zô no henoko himashi ni hosoku nari man

day by day
a famous priest's prick
grows thinner

Does doing *chigo*, or lovely little boys, make it shrink the better to squeeze into a narrow place? Is heaven punishing his prolifigate ways by thinning his proud part? Was he castrated? None are realistic, but the first is most likely correct.

羅切した和尚まことの無一物 *128-4*
rasetsu shita oshô makoto no muichibutsu

de-peckered
a have-nothing monk's
the real thing

losing his thing
a have-no-thing monk's
the real mcCoy

A *not-one-thing* (無一物) is a begging bonze without possessions. "One-thing" is slang for the penis. *Rasetsu* (羅切) is having it, rather than the balls, cut off. Chinese feared more than bastards from their harems, so their eunich's were not just deballed but de-cocked. Japanese knew about the Chinese practice and may have used it as a punishment for rape in the Heian era, when capital punishment was suspended. Otherwise, Japanese were not big on castration of *any* sort. Surely, the number of boys castrated for their voices – or *was it just for the voices?* – in South Europe far exceeded all such mischief done in Japan, where even ears were not pierced. Yet, there are any number of senryu depicting it:

羅せつきざしてしほ吹の口のやう
rasetsu kizashite shio no kuchi no yô 葉 19

the erection
of a de-peckered man
like a kiss

へのこにとがハ無キものを羅切ッとは
henoko ni toga wa naki mono o rasetsu to wa

why de-pecker,
when your pecker is
not to blame?

The "Kiss" hides a loss in translation. The original says *"like a salt-blowing/ spouting-mouth."* It refers to a *hyottoko* funny-man mask. The mouth is puckered up and off-center, like someone trying to plant a kiss on the far side of a big nose. The second *ku* (葉 26) is right, but boring. Does it help to *rhyme?*

While the cock itself is not to blame
'tis the one castrated, all the same!

Not much. Buddhism has it that desire came from *within* and not *without*, right?

睾丸の方を切らふと馬鹿和尚
kintama no hô o kirô to baka oshô 103-2

trying to remove
his balls, now that is
an idiot bonze

he'd cut off
his balls, not cock,
that fool bonze

This senryu would seem to contradict the last, implying that castration of the balls is less important than the cock. While lack of feedback would dampen desire and justify a de-cock rather than defrock, going for the balls would be the best way to lessen the sinful desire. Would a *bright* bonze want to keep desire for his antagonist? I am kidding. It is more likely that the author simply did not know as much about castration as any member of a culture with plenty of livestock would. Here is a much more entertaining idiot bonze *ku:*

かたい後家だと馬鹿和尚土砂をかけ
katai goke da to baka oshô suna o kake 102-12/17

a hard widow
the idiot bonze throws
sand on her

the fool bonze
dusts a widow playing
hard to get

wooing a hardy widow's hand
~~~~~ the dumb bonze ~~~~
tries softening her up with sand

(trans. p.d., "~~~" mine)

A fool takes words literally. Do you recall the way a standing cock was brought down in the *Dry Kidney* chapter? That dust – the Japanese is "sand" (*suna*), but dust is more magical to us – was generally used to soften dead bodies by the bonzes (or their helpers?). In Japanese, to be "hard/stiff" was to be chaste or behave in a manner we might call "straight." While it was generally agreed that,

ゆるいのをするのが和尚おちどなり 摘
yurui no o suru no ga oshô ochido nari 1-27

for a bonze
poaching a loose one's
reproachable

'tis a demerit
for a bonze to do
a loose one

– there were bonzes who just *"did not care to be cramped"* (窮屈なことが和尚はきらいなり 末摘 2-23 *kyûkutsu na koto ga oshô wa kirai nari*). Or, maybe, the poet meant not wanting to be cramped was a character of the high-level bonzes/*bôzu* called *oshô,* who generally had the means to buy a woman.

和尚様若集にあきるふとゞきさ 万安二
oshô-sama wakashu ni akiru futodokisa million

honorable monk
how unfaithful can you be?
tiring of your boy!

for crying outloud
we have a monk who's tired
of the young-crowd!

背に腹を替えて和尚は不首尾也
se ni hara o kaete oshô wa fushûbi nari

exchanging backs
for bellies, that monk as
a monk, is sunk!

back to belly,
trading place: a bonze
out of grace

The first *ku* probably was intended to play with the idea of keeping the faith in the religious and romatic sense. Saying the monk is tired of the young-crowd/ gays who entertain him implies he is contemplating a return to women, which would be breaking faith with his religious obligations, and, we might note, breaking the civil law as well, for extramarital sex with women by clergy in much of the Edo era (1603-1857) was a capital offense. Yet, it was generally agreed, by the popular culture, or senryu at any rate, that widows were the exception – bonzes could console them without fear of being executed – but not, of course, if their services were unwanted. And, thanks to funerals and periodic funeral services, bonzes, who were in charge of the end-side of life, had a good chance to console the bereaved: *O*

○

O

the perfect pair
a widow and a priest
they both would most do
what they should the least

~~~~~~~~~~~~~~~~~~~~

bonze & widow, a perfect pair
c̲ their bodies down here
their hearts up there

~~~~~~~~~~~~~~~~

widow & bonze: a match
big prick c̲ big snatch!

~~~~~~~~~~~~~~~~

widow and bonze
two of a kind
united by death
what do they find?

~~~~~~~~~~~~~~

後家と坊様こち／＼とした同士 摘
goke to bôsama kochikochi-to-shita dôshi 2-9
(widow and bonze hardened /stiff/thick fellow-spirits)

kindred spirits
widow and bonze: two
hardened pricks

widow and bonze
hard-boiled & hard-boiled
make a real pair

two of a kind
more wizened than wise
widow and bonze

I did the first four translations *guessing* about the meaning of *kochikochi* about ten years ago. I thought it meant "similar" because *kochi* is "here" or "this one." As it turned out, that was *not* one of the 5 meanings of *kochikochi* found in the OJD. Two of the last three readings are probably right and the other close.[13]

天蓋であろうと和尚後家をほめ
tengai de arô to oshô goke o home 見利評万句合
(heaven-lid [you] are-probably [says] bonze widow [acc] praises)

Two of a Kind
(from one octopus to another)

you're a ciborium
did you know?
the bonze praises
the widow.

On the other hand, this, seemingly more difficult *ku,* is easy. One name for the type of wandering bonze's hat that seems a cross between bowl and parasol, is *tengai*, literally "heaven-lid," *i.e.,* "canopy," "baldachin," or "ciborium." Because it resembles an octopus's head, the bonzes who wore it were called *tako, i.e.,* octopus. A read and lost but well-recalled senryu claimed tea-houses used for sex that employed boys experienced fishing doldrums (*shike*) whenever octopus = bonzes were "out of season." Octopus is also an abbreviation for "octopus-pot" (*tako-tsubo*), a nooky with a grip good enough to be called prehensile. A senryu like this one is out of its element in translation, but interesting as a curio.

毛の生えた尻を和尚は餅につき 摘
ke no haita shiri o oshô wa mochi ni tsuki 4-16

a hairy arse?
for heaven's sake!
the bonze pounds it
into rice-cake

A samurai might sleep with a boy,[14] but *a hairy ass?* That could only happen with a man who lives among men alone, a bonze. As explained before, "rice-cake" is not like cake at all. Freshly pounded and kneaded, *mochi* is closer to play-dough, but pure white and springy to the touch, like, say, blubber, konjak or sea cucumber (Again: English lacks tactile metaphor because we lack variety in the mouth-feel of our food). Marshmallow was tempting, but it is not pounded into being. That pounding is done by a mallet with a long head. Bonzes, well-hung and hard (horny for lack of sex) by convention, or at least senryu convention, would pound whatever they pumped into *mochi*. Or,

茶の泡のためしもあると和尚ぬけ 摘
cha no awa no tameshi mo aru to oshô nuke 3-15
(tea-bubble/foam/froth's try/experiment too is [says] bonze pulls-out)

Foaming Over
(*ceremonious thoughts*)

O ~~~~~~~~~~~~~ O o
O doubtless, it would make O
o O a fine tea whisk O
o says the bonze o
O o O pulling out O o O o
O O O o O o O O

This association is both more delicate and gross than the *pounding* one. Woman-on-top sex was called "tea-mortar/hand-mill" (*cha-usu*) style; and with Zen identified with the tea ceremony, in senryu, bonzes are usually the male party in this position favored by Japanese pornographic prints for showing off male and female genitals (and the woman's frontal body/clothing) in coitus. Both parties sit, the woman's back to the man, legs apart and, ideally, with a mirror in front so they can see what art shows us all. Love-juice tends to drip down the base of the cock-stem and drip over the balls. Another translation:

brain-child

perhaps it could
froth up the tea, too?
a bonze pulls-out

The whisk has a glans-like end. Powdered tea was whipped up to a froth and could overflow. But, frothy or not, it was *light-green*. As another *ku* points out,

茶臼ではなくて白酒臼のよう 摘 *1-25*
cha-usu de wa nakute hakushû-usu no yô
(tea-mortar-as-for not[being], white *sake* mortar-like)

a tea mortar?
not quite! i see a mortar
for cloudy wine

no, it's not like
a tea mortar, it's one
for raw wine

Pestle and mortar (*usu*) means sex in Japan as everywhere, but foam (*awa*), is found in freshly whipped tea and raw (white/cloudy) rice wine. We imagine a man telling a woman that their position was called a tea-mortar, only to have her point out that from what she could see (in that mirror), the color was wrong.

和尚様草履取りに/へも御手がつき 万
oshôsama zôritori ni/e mo o-te ga tsuki 明四

honorable bonze
will even lay hands on
zori retrievers

Because sandals were removed at entrances, it helped to have someone to keep track of your footwear. That someone was a boy. Usually, only youthful keg-retrievers had to watch their backsides because drunken men would poke at anything, but, with bonzes, even a sandal retriever was in portal danger! "*Sama*" is a polite suffix. The last time I faced it, I turned it into "that nice bonze" for it fit the context (giving candy to children to seduce them). Here, it is obvious the intent is to contrast his proper appearance as a man of the cloth with his improper behavior. "Honorable" is a horrid translation; I devote much of the first chapter of a book (*Orientalism & Occidentalism*) to discussing why another subtle Japanese prefix (*o*) is orientalized by turning *it* into "honorable." But, *here*, it works.

囲われの障子に丸い影がさし *70-25*
kakoware no shôji ni marui kage ga zashi

a round shadow
passes through the door
of his paramour

on his mistress's
paper partition a bold
round shadow

The *kakoware,* literally *surrounded,* or "cloistered (one)" is most commonly used to mean the mistress of clergy (otherwise *mekake* is usual). Blyth translated the best high-color senryu of such a *kakoware*. If you read it, you probably can recall that the bonze told her a secret: *hell did not really exist.* Here, we have only a round shadow, the shaven head of the bonze standing for the glans of his erect penis. Because hairless heads look phallic, many names for the Buddhist clergy doubled for "penis." We have already seen one with 小僧 *kozô* ("small monk") in a *ku,* 入道 nyûdô ("enter-path" i.e. novice) is another:

夜な夜なに入道の来る淫の御所 葉末十九
yo na yo na ni nyûdô no kuru in no go sho

night after night
a nyûdô shows up at
the lewd place

While most bonzes kept their heads shaved, the *nyûdô,* or novice, was most clearly so. Though hardly poetic justice, there is something perversely right about the members of a religion that put down desire as the basis for suffering becoming themselves synonyms for the medium by which desire is expressed. The "*in no*," meaning "licentious" or "obscene" implies desire-based *i.e.,* sinful sex . . . *with a woman.* It puns on *hedged/fenced* which, with the honorific expression for place, 御所 (*gosho*), means a temple or house where men might conference in private. The *ku* parodies the martial tales of the Warring ages, when bonzes served as messengers, medics and even strategists for opposing armies. The young messenger would come "night after night" to the war-room.

よし町を気無シに通る宗旨なり 万 明七
yoshichô o ki-nashi ni tôru shûshi nari man

a faith that can
pass through yoshi-chô
without desire

Yoshichô? Another *ku* explains, *"The back-gate of Yoshiwara is there: Yoshichô"* (よし原のうら門ハよし丁にあり 万 安三 *yoshiwara no uramon wa yoshichô ni ari*). That is, this "town" (actually a *street* or *block*) in Edo catered to the rear-end. Bonzes frequented the catamites there (ch.17). But what "faith" – in both meanings of the word, the sect and its tenets – could possibly free its bonzes of desire, so they can pass through the valley of sodomy and feel nothing? See the explanation of the next *ku.*

死ぬ／＼と祝す門徒の姫はじめ 葉 1
shinu shinu to shukusu monto no hime-hajime

propitious words	**first princessing**
i die! i die! cheer for a gate-monk's first-princessing	*i die! i die!* a monk and his wife celebrate life

i die! i die! are words of celebration:
a married monk has his first relation

A *monto,* short for *montoshû* (門徒宗) monk belongs to the greater Pure Land True Religion (jôdô shinshû) faith, the only major sect where marriage was permitted at this time. How the idea of *la petit morte* comes alive with *shinu! shinu!* (I die! I die!) – a common Japanese love-cry! The *first-princessing*, or *princess-start*, which is to say *first sex of the year*, was usually celebrated on the second day, for New Year's Eve was too holy and busy. The first three days, and to a degree, the first week or two of the year were magical, full of metaphysical significance. As a rule, words such as "die" are *taboo* at this time beyond time, when magic is in the air and anything a person does is of consequence (see *The 5th Season: Poetry for the Re-creation of the World* (paraverse press 2007)). But, the Buddhist clergy did not find dying unlucky. Their livelihood largely depended on funeral services. This senryu is one of a small number in this book repeatedly encountered when reading broadly in Japanese. I would not be surprised to discover it has already been translated. Nevertheless, I thought I had to introduce it here to give the chapter a happy ending and not leave my readers with the impression that *all* Buddhist sex is boy-love or back-alley stuff.

よし町てさかさに遊ぶもんと寺 万
yoshichô de sakasa ni asobu monto-dera 宝 12

<はり合にけり>
they're up for it!

monto at play
turn the world upside-down
in yoshi town

in yoshi town
the monto templers play
upside-down

But, if it is too nice, it isn't senryu. Just because the monks are married doesn't mean they behave. This is one of the rare cases where the draw, *hariainikeri,* is a greeat help. *Hariai* means to be stoked for something, and retains some of its literal meaning of a swollen or tense atmosphere coming from a conflict of interest, rivalry or other challenge (such as being illegal) . The implication is that, for *monto,* doing boys would be wrong, and this would make them all the more excited. *Upside-down* used figuratively most often applies to parents outliving their children, which is to say, something that bucks the natural order of things.

しんらんハ世を廣ク見てあなかしこ
shinran wa yo o hiroku mite anakashiko 万宝十
(shinran-as-for world/society widely saw/seeing amen)

祝ひ社すれ
something to celebrate?

saint shinran
saw the world broadly
women, amen!

As Kôbô Daishi was deemed father of clerical buggery, Shinran, founder of the Pure Land True Word Sect, was credited with being the first to allow married clergy. I thought *anakashiko* was how women used to sign their letters, but Okada says it was in Shinran's epistle on the subject and my dictionary gives one word for its translation, *amen.* As mentioned before, *wide/broad/loose* is associated with a woman's recepticle as opposed to a boy's. What adds to the wit in the original is the fact that there is a hole (*ana*) in the *amen* and the whole expression suggests someone being "hole-smart," whatever that means (in *haikai* it was applied to bugs hiding out in their burrows in the winter!).

~~~~~~

~ encore ~

~~~~~~

師の坊へわびハらせつを先キにたて 万
shi no bô e wabi wa rasetsu o saki ni tate man 明四
(teacher-to apology-as-for cock-cut[acc] before stands)

bonze world

to beg the pardon
of his master, he stands up
his cut-off cock

Perhaps such a thing has been done, but it is hard to imagine it would stand unless the decocked bonze found a good taxidermist! This *ku* from Senryû's *Million* was submitted for the draw *maneki koso sure,* or *"Do invite us/them/him/etc!"* or *"Make it an invitation!"* Should all the other bonzes, or the whole world, be called 'round to witness the admirable deed? Or, is the standing object supposed to act like a finger and wave people over. I only know that conceptually speaking, the severed member is an analog of the finger a courtezan would cut off to show the sincerity of her apology. It is also something more meaningful than a pinkie, for it is probably related to his misdeeds. I figure it is good to end the chapter on because we all have our apologies to make.

~~~~~~

★ *We no longer find pederasty to speak of among Buddhist clergy in Japan, or at least do not hear of it, while, in the USA, where it is believed to be a great evil which destroys the lives of its victims, the Christian clergy suffers scandal after scandal . . . . History may not always repeat itself, but it sure does love irony.*

~~~~~~

~ eddies ~

~~~~~~

1. *Yellow Turban Bandits?* Japanese sources speak only of wearing yellow (as we might
~~~~~~

wear green on St. Patrick's Day) or attaching a piece of yellow cloth to the head. Because Japanese did not have the concept of a turban, it might have been lost in translation. Or, conversely, it was just a strip of cloth, tucked in a headband which English having adopted the word "turban" felt obliged to use.

~~~~~~

2. *Ordure as Gilt*. Why do I interchange "yellow" and "gold" in my readings? Here is a passage from a book printed in 1928 describing one of the great strikes of Japanese labor history, the Great Noda (Kikkoman soy sauce) Strike.

> At night, the fighting-party [strikers] formed groups of four or five men and snuck up to the houses of Takanashi and other leaders of the justice party [strike-breakers] and liberally spread about the shit-piss [excrement] they had prepared. One justice-party chief, surprised to hear odd noises outside, rushed out the door and slipping on the scattered shit, turned into a golden Buddha (剥げっちょこの黄金仏となった) . . . day after day, [the strikers] tried new tactics but, finally, they had nothing at hand but golden munitions, so it would seem they had come to the end of their rope." (『野田血戦記』Found in the Diet Library and quoted on pp 131-2 in one of my seven books written and published in Japanese: ロビン・ギル著：『日本人論探検』TBSブリタニカ 1984. I was contradicting the myth of Japanese voluntary peacefulness as opposed to the bloody labor history of the Occident. In retrospect, introducing this childish material probably proved little, but it did add entertainment value to my book!)

Coming across this and other golden shit time again, I once convinced myself that *ordure* was etymologically related to *ore,* which turned out *not* to be the case! On other levels, however, the relationship of the two is legend. No one needs to be told what a tight-ass is.

~~~~~~

3. ***The Surplice*** on a sodomist's tool was also called a golden ring/halo (*konshiki-no wa*), a golden hood (*ukon-no zukin*), a gold-brocade headband (*ôkin-no hachimaki*) and a golden collar-wrap/tippet/stole (*ukon-no eri-maki*). Until reading for this chapter, I assumed the sea cucumber with the laver surplice in *Rise, Ye Sea Slugs!* owed its metaphor entirely to an essay by Bashô's wayward disciple Shikô that turned this placid creature into a Taoist sage (see robin d. gill: *Rise, Ye Sea Slugs!* (2003)). Now, I must also assume the possibility it just had a tryst with a shellfish!

~~~~~~

4. ***Pederasty as Good?*** Falling in love or fathering a child made one *more* attached to the world, when bonzes ought to be cutting ties with it, and committing adultery, while not a sin *per se*, was considered a capital crime against the social order. Compared to that, sodomy was a fleeting affair. The Jesuits who came to Japan in the 16c, dwelled on this "abdomination" practiced by their rivals in religion from the outset (Xavier railed in the streets about it). While their value judgment can be disputed, they may not have exaggerated its prevalence. For a longer presentation, see *Topsy-turvy 1585* (2005).

~~~~~~

5. ***Bronze Irony.*** Respondent P.D. wrote, "Pity American usage doesn't have a word like 'bronze' (though the 3 vol. dialect dictionary might list it), which means 'anus' in Australian slang ('To go for the bronze' was something not only Olympian finalists tried!)."

~~~~~~

5-6. ***Not Catching Diseases***. Here is another senryu: *"The cheater / who caught clap leaves / things undone"* (りんひやうに成ル間男は不首尾なり 万明二 *rinbyô ni naru maotoko wa fushubi nari*). That is, explains Okada, for fear of child or staying longer, his coitus was interupted, which was thought to increase the chance of picking up a dose. There may be something to this as well as the advice on pulling-out while the other puckers up. After all, germs do enter the urethra so it makes sense to try to expulse them
~~~~~~

at the end. (See the same *ku* in the ch. on menstruation. I left it here to show the possible variations in readings. While in an earlier chapter, the other was done later and is better.)

~~~~~~

6. ***Castle-toppler and Pit.*** My Aussie respondent in Italy notes the 傾 in the Japanese *keisei* (傾城) is "more 'tilt' than 'topple'" . . . while associating the image with the tilting of the phallic leaning tower of Pisa." Indeed, the character *is,* but the larger character, or beauty of the *keisei* is, like "the face that sunk a thousand ships," more lethal. Eventually, the word came to mean any pretty prostitute, then any pretty girl (Some such *keisei* are found in *Cherry Blossom Epiphany – The Poetry and Philosophy of a Flowering Tree*: 2007). I was also presented with a translation in the down-under dialect: *Can anything match / The sheer depth of it? / The snatch's pit?*

~~~~~~

7. ***Burton's Sotadic Zone.*** Burton defended his *Nights* with aplomb. Much applies equally to senryu, so I will quote at length.

> Readers who have perused the ten volumes will probably agree with me that the nad've indecencies of the text are rather *gaudis-serie* than prurience; and, when delivered with mirth and humour, they are rather the "excrements of wit" than designed for debauching the mind. Crude and indelicate with infantile plainness; even gross and, at times, "nasty" in their terrible frankness, they cannot be accused of corrupting suggestiveness or subtle insinuation of vicious sentiment. Theirs is a coarseness of language, not of idea; they are indecent, not depraved; and the pure and perfect naturalness of their nudity seems almost to purify it, showing that the matter is rather of manners than of morals. Such throughout the East is the language of every man, woman and child, from prince to peasant, from matron to prostitute: all are as the naïve French traveller said of the Japanese: *"si grossiers qu'ils ne sçavent nommer les choses que par leur nom ['So coarse that they only know how to call things by their real name / So uncouth they only know how to call a spade a spade'[tr. P.D.]]"* (From *The Terminal Essay* in his *Arabian Nights* vol.10, via Project Gutenberg. The translation of the French is by P.D.)

While senryu also never aimed to debauch the mind, I am afraid some are depraved, and Japanese are hardly so innocent as the naïve French traveler thought. Today, we might stop with a defense of language. But, Burton, writing at a time when homophobia was as common in much of Europe as it remains in parts of the peculiarly Puritan Usania, felt he could not end his defense on a general note. Aware some readers might react to certain behavior of the same type associated with bonzes in this chapter, he continued –

> But I repeat (p. xiv.) there is another element in *The Nights* and that is one of absolute obscenity utterly repugnant to English readers, even the least prudish. It is chiefly connected with what our neighbours call *le vice contre nature* – as if anything can be contrary to nature which includes all things." (ibid)

Burton then delineated his so-called *Sotadic Zone*, "bounded westwards by the northern shores of the Mediterranean" and 780-800 miles wide, "including meridional France, the Iberian Peninsula, Italy and Greece, with the coast-regions of Africa from Marocco to Egypt," then, running eastward, "narrows, embracing Asia Minor, Mesopotamia and Chaldea, Afghanistan, Sind, the Punjab and Kashmir," but broadens in Indo-China, "enfolding China, Japan and Turkistan," after which, it opens up, embracing "the South Sea Islands and the New World where, at the time of its discovery, Sotadic love was, with some exceptions, an established racial institution." [1] I.e., *most* of the human race did what the bonzes did, though I would caution that "the third sex" institutions found in the New World are very different from the pederasty found in the Near East or Far East.

> Within the Sotadic Zone the Vice is popular and endemic,[1] held at the worst to be a mere peccadillo, whilst the races to the North and South of the limits . . . practice it only sporadically amid the opprobrium of their fellows who, as a rule, are physically incapable of performing the operation and look upon it with the liveliest disgust. (ibid)

Burton held that pederasty/sodomy was "geographical and climatic, not racial" and though he felt it was bad for the population (growth considered *good* at that time), he conceeded that "we must not forget that the love of boys has its noble, sentimental side." Within the longer survey that followed, a reference to "the modern fashion to doubt the pederasty of the master of Hellenic Sophrosyne, the 'Christian before Christianity' (Socrates)" is followed by a warning somemight well heed today:

> We [2] are overapt to apply our nineteenth century prejudices and prepossessions to the morality of the ancient Greeks who would have specimen'd such squeamishness in Attic salt. (ibid)

---

1. ***How Popular?*** 16c Florentine records "show that something of the order of 70% of the adult male population had been called before courts to answer charges, based on anonymous denunciations, that they engaged in homosexual activity." (P.D., correspondence) *High enough?*

2. ***Are"We"Still "We"?*** My respondent (in Italy) reminds me of the following:

"We are, apart from evangelical freaks, way past this squeamishness, and take homosexuality to be a natural variation in sexual drives, no more 'moral' or 'immoral' than, say, impotence or frigidity (both of which are far more frequent, and militant against the sex-as-reproductive-duty theory of Christian theology). Indeed, we no longer need to justify our remarks with specific references to a 'Sotadic' zone, since homosexuality is universal. In Burton's own England, in its elite colleges and universities, homosexual love was, if not rampant, certainly, to gather from memoirs of the period, familiar to most. The question which we rather ask ourselves to day is, not why sodomy is widespread throughout the non-Western world, but rather, why has the Western world proved so hostile to sodomy that it refused to acknowledge it as anything more than what 'other' races do." *My reply:*

> True, people whose eyes are not closed by religious dogma realize homosexual behavior is natural in humans and many other animals, and the only questions are its prevelancy and the degree to which genes and culture influence it; yet, if I am not mistaken, even the well-educated who acknowledge such natural variation and live in a society with a large percent of acknowledged homosexuals, may well be squeamish about sodomy or same sex fellatio *as part of a generally heterosexual life cycle or parallel to heterosexual relations.* A bonze in Japan who gave up women for boys and later, back in secular society, returned to women, or a macho Mexican who lives for seducing and sleeping with women, yet does not hesitate to sleep with a man when no woman can be found, and the reality of societies where such is considered (and felt as) normal behavior is hard for those of us who grew up in cultures where bisexuality is rare to grasp, much less feel at ease with.

~~~~~~

8. ***Dying for Love.*** I added the "dying" translation after P.D. asked: "Isn't there resonance here with 心中 as a suicide pact, Robin? If so, *Dying for love of it,/The bonze licks the bronze,/His catamite's shit."* The answer is, *yes;* but the primary reading of *shinchû(jû)date* remains *a demonstration of fidelity*. The "shit" for *ketsu*=ass/anus is not wrong, but pushing it. The only English translation of the *ku published* to date – *"to show his love / the high priest licks / her asshole" – is* wrong: a *kagema* is a catamite that might *do* a woman but never *be* a woman, and I have yet to come across *analingus* of any *woman* in Japanese prints or poetry. Coincidentally, "bronze" – *anus* in Aussie slang – in Japanese is *shinchû,* and polishing it (真鍮を磨く) is slang for young-crowd pledging fidelity to one another!

~~~~~~

9. ***Bashô's "Lovely Boy" Ku*** was one of seven themes on love (恋) split between Bashô and six of his students. One of his last poems, Yamada Kenkichi wrote that it showed his attachment to romantic narrative remained to the end (芭蕉名句集). For more commentary on the *ku* by various Japanese critics, see Makoto Ueda: *Bashô and His Interpreters*. Ueda noted that "Bashô himself, recalling his youth, once wrote: "There was a time when I was fascinated with the ways of homosexual love." He does not give a citation, perhaps because it is commonplace knowledge. Leupp, who has no less than six references to Matsuo Bashô in his *Male Colors*, does & gives the Japanese: *ware mo*

mukashi wa shudô-zuki. I have come across some lines of 5-7-5+7-7 link-verse with a good measure of male-color (it was common in haikai) composed by *Peach-blue* , as Bashô still called himself at age 35, in *Edo Hirokôji* (江戸広小路), including a line about *enthralling the enemy with shapely buttocks by turning tail on him* (敵に後を見する尻つき *teki ni ushiro o misuru shiritsuki*). I dare not make a quick translation of the sequence, but can leave you with one more fine line from it neither "haiku" nor male-color: *"The fish's guts / sink into the sea / undisturbed"* (魚の腸そのまゝ海に沈められ).

~~~~~~

10. Like a Turd Coming In. If this naive senryu is surprising, P.D.'s response is nothing short of *astonishing:* "In Australia, having a shit has been occasionally likened in larrikins' speech to being *'bummed off from the inside.'*" Unless one is buggered far more than one poops, wouldn't the direction of this metaphor be bassackwards!

~~~~~~

11. Relishing Farts & Pudendum Smell in general. Unfortunately, I don't even care for the smell of my own; but my learned respondent, PD, noting that "in Australian slang, a 'poon' is a bloke who goes round sniffing the saddles of bikes pedalled by girls, for the crutchy mixture of fanny and cunt," excuses those who *do* with a gorgeous gloss:

> St Augustine famously remarked: *Inter faeces et urinam nascimur*, 'we are (all) born amidst shit and piss,' and some versions of erotic pastoral turn the nostalgia for origins into delectation at the archeological fruits of pristine olfactory memories."

~~~~~~

12. More on St. Kôbô and Male Color in Japan. Explaining a 7-7 senryu with the accompaniment "*Gong! Gong! The bell goes gong! gong!*" ごん／＼と鐘のごん／＼と),

あちらむかする弘法の無理
achira mukasuru kôbô no muri

making them
turn about, kôbô goes
against nature

Suzuki Katsutada explains "It is said that Kôbô *thought up* (考案した) male-color on Mount Takano, where women were not allowed" (江戸上方「艶句」の世界 *italics mine.* 句は、人丸社奉納　延享四). He repeats *one* popular explanation. The other has Kôbô *bring it,* together with esoteric Buddhism, to Japan. Both ideas are bogus. Kôbô may well have encouraged male-color in the monastaries, but it hardly needed to be invented *or* imported from China. It would seem that to the extent homosexual relations were seen as deviant, there was a tendency to attribute it to foreign sources. There was much pedaresty in China, but there is still irony in this, for moralistic Confucianism, also from China, would probably have been the most likely source of the idea that it was "bad!"

おかしさハかけまやかしんごんしうし　万天六
okashisa wa kagemaya ga shingon-shû shi　million
(funniness-as-for shade-boy-shop/s true-word-sect does/is)

that would be funny
a shade-boy tea-room run by
the pure-word sect

funny it would be
if shade-boy shops were run
by the pure-words

That faith was founded by St. Kôbô. In both Japan and Europe, religion was not always, everywhere free of ties to prostitution. In Japan, there was an order of nuns who were not nuns and European churches were loath to forego the income (see *Topsy-turvy 1585*).
~~~~~~

尻からげ・高野の山じゃおろさしやれ
shirikarage, takanonoyama ja orosashare

◎ *a tucked-up hem* ◎
this here's mount takano
you'd better drop it

◎ *mister hem-in-sash* ◎
if i were you i'd drop it fast
this is mt. takano

Issa's *ku* include a number of butt-proud footmen, with no male-color intended. It was normal for men on the road in hot and humid Japan to strip to their loin-cloths or lift up their robes tails and tuck them in their sash (though Issa's best has their butts shining in the cold winter moonlight). Such nudity was fine until we forced Japan to copy us and get ringworm. As Suzuki explains, the *meaning* of this cap-verse *ku* is that with few youths on this famed mountain of esoteric Buddhism, headquarters of Kôbô's Pure Word sect, even a hairy-assed adult male could provoke the residents' lust. A less appealing but very senryu *ku* from *Million* shows what could *happen:*

みそをすってるをつかまへけつをする 万天元
miso o sutteru o tsukamae ketsu o suru

one stirring miso
is caught and
ass done

The "stirring" here is "rubbing/grating," as done in a mortar with a pestle, hence:

miso without miso within

right up the ass
of one caught in the act
of grinding beans

There is an expression for conflating similar things, *miso mo kuso mo isshô* "[putting] miso and shit together." The color and consistancy is pretty much the same range as that of people who eat a low meat diet. Rape is wrong. But, there is something aesthetically right here. Should we call it *poetic injustice?*

高野山犬さへけつでさかるなり 摘
takano yama inu sae ketsu de sakaru nari 3-19

mount takano
where even canis in heat
bares his anus

~~~~~~

13. *Widow & Bonze Similarity in a Ku:* I wanted to squeeze this *ku* into the text but the phallic design of a composite translation that followed would have been truncated, so:

世を捨てた人へへのこも穴も売り 葉六
yo o suteta hito e henoko mo ana mo uri

selling cocklings
and holes to people who
left this world

The shade-boys (see ch.17) served the bonze and widow, both unattached to society.
~~~~~~

14. ***Samurai and Boys.*** For more samurai, whom I have neglected, see Gary P. Leupp, *Male Colors: The Construction of Homosexuality in Tokugawa Japan* 1995/7.

★ ***Rude Awakening.*** For the reader shocked more by the poetry in this chapter than the behavior itself, let me introduce a Martial epigram mentioned at the start of the book. The translation (from an old Loeb Classic) is: *"Charinus has nothing left of his backside, slit as far as his navel. Poor man, what a big sore troubles him! He has no backside; yet he is a pansy."* The original, minimally rhymed – some would say not rhymed like Japanese verse – seems a bit more sprightly. If I were to err on the opposite side of the above,

The Pansy's Dilemna

Poor Charinus has no behind,
his anus is split to his navel –
A running sore, yet he has a mind
to do what he's no longer able!

My learned respondent gives *thumbs down* to my reading, as the *done to* side (*cinaedus*) needs no ability. I *know* that, but think it makes my translation all the better: Charinus, so worn out he can't even attract or hold one even if he could. To twist Twain, even a *candle -holder* does not last forever. Amazingly, we have a senryu using the same hyperbole, but referring to what was usually called *wide* in contrast to the anus: *"Wide is this: / split clear to the edge / of the navel"* (ひろい事へそのきわ迄さけて居る 摘 2-14 *hiroi koto heso no giwa made saketeiru*). The *ku* is more original than might be guessed, for proximity to the navel was usually synonymous with a good cunt. More of Martial's putdowns:

> " [Hyllus] . . . Your poor belly gazes at the banquette of your arse; and the former is always hungry, while the latter gorges."
>
> ". . . if you [Mamurianus] batten on the steam only of a sooty kitchen, and on all fours with a dog drink from dirty puddles, I will not prod that latter-end of your's – it isn't a latter end, which never shits – but I will gouge out your remaining eye. . ."
>
> "Seeing that the boy's prick is sore, and your backside, Naevolus, though I am no diviner, I know what you are up to."

Sorry stuff, but, Martial did それなりに have his moral compunction. He advised men to –

> "Refrain from stirring the groin with poking hand. Toward beardless boys, this is a greater sinner than your yard, and your fingers create and hasten manhood. . . .

I.e., fuck boys but don't play with pricks, for it affects development and is girly behavior. Martial also advises a wife not to compete with boys, but to be grateful for their presence:

> "Slave-boys guarantee more to you than to their master. It's they who cause you to be the one and only woman for your husband; it's they who give what you as a wife don't want to give."

No, she says, "I *do* give all ...." But that, Martial explains, "is not the same thing; it's a good Chian fig I want, I don't want a big coarse one. . .[1] Grant to the boys use of their part, and make use of your own." Lest my gross selections cause the reader to think of Martial as a mere butt-pounder of the stylus so to speak, one more text:

> "So shadowy is the down on thy cheeks, so soft that a breath, or the sun, or a soft breeze, rubs it away. With such a fleecy film are veiled ripening quinces, that gleam brightly when plucked by maiden fingers. Whenever I have too strongly impressed upon thy cheek five kissses, I become, Dindymus, bearded from thy lips." (all same Loeb classic)

I have always thought peach fuzz singularly unattractive, like the acne it may come with. Hormonal mold. Not the Greeks and Romans, they find it *luscious!* Could downy cheeks be so precious because they cannot be captured in a statue, or because they are soon lost, *i.e.,* precious where the one ideal of beauty is neotenous.

---

1. The original, P.D. notes, contrasts a luscious 'Chian fig' and a big and less tasty marisca fig. I am not up on figs. If Martial were writing in Usanian English – I want a peach, not your watermelon? Or Latino – a cherry, not a papaya?

~~~~~~

< 御師匠様のへのこ迄書キならひ > 万 安七。岡田曰く「寺小屋の悪戯っ子」と。しかし「弘法は筆選ばず」といえども、先生の方が選んで持たせた珍筆ではないか？それとも両説は可能か。当の句を英訳したい再版までに、御意見ください。

~~~~~~

オマケ, or Xtra

明星のつかまへ所菊の花　む 十四
myôjô no tsukamae-dokoro kiku no hana mutamagawa
(venus's caught-place chrysanthemum flower)

was that the place
where kôbô caught venus:
chrysanthemum?

Neglected *Mum*. I had thought to leave the above *ku* as-is in Japanese only. Why? Because I have not solved it. I *guess* it unites Saint Kôbô's encounter with Venus at the moment of his Enlightenment with his alleged introduction of male-color to Japan, but a man with a large website dedicated to the *Mutamagawa* believes it only means that Venus is spied by someone out early looking after his mums. (Or, sighting the Gold-star is good synchronicity for one up early to drink the dew at dawn for longevity?) Also, the mum stands for the ear as *kiku* is "hear"– but I thought Venus entered Kôbô's *mouth* Obviously, further research is needed, but when I realized that, despite three chapters on homosexuality (one in ten, about right), the only Chrysanthemum anus in this book was in the heterosexual example of 69 in the Cunnilingus chapter, I decided to introduce it if for no other reason than the fact that the Chrysanthemum is still *the* primary symbol of sodomy in Japan. One constantly finds the flower replacing the anus in dirty cartoons. Here are a couple far less esoteric *ku* (senryu / *zappai*) about *that* chrysanthemum:

裏門へまわって菊の根わけかな
uramon e mawatte kiku no newake kana
(backgate-to go round mum's root-split!/?)

going 'round
to the back-gate to split
the aster root/s

うつむいて・菊の案内する小姓
utsumuite kiku no annai suru koshô
(stoopover mum/s guidance-does page)

bottoms up
the page leads him to
chrysanthemum

(二番目の句は雑俳 天保五笠付類題集) The roots for the fall-blooming plant were split in the Spring. English's need for the/a/nil/his/etc. before a word (maybe *the* would be better for the second *ku*), together with the length of the name for the flower make translation a challenge. Of course, we could tax up a rung to *aster*. With the back-gate" and "chrysanthemum" redundant in the original, the use of the obvious *aster* for the first *ku* seems appropriate. I have come across *three* explanations for the mum-gate idea. 1) The name of the Chinese Emperor's favorite; 2) the small buds of the mum associated with a tight anus; 3) the asterick-like nature of the small-petaled bloom (a way to make an ass-hole seem pretty?) – but who knows! I favor the last. *Caveat*. Please try not to find anuses in all the *asters* you may encounter in Japanese art and letters!

<u>*Making Water Babies*</u>
子を水にながす方法

十三 13

黒鯛、水ガネに、逆日丸
Black Snapper, *Q*uicksilver & The Pill

~~~~~~

唐辛子の力 — *chili pepper*

~~~~~~

唐がらし計って買はおそろしき む五
tôgarashi hakaratte kau wa osoroshiki

chili peppers
how dreadful to buy them
by measure

chili pepper
buying it by design
is dreadful

buying red chili
by the measure, dreadful
beyond measure

At first, I thought this was the reaction of a person afraid of spicy food, or a stab at stereotyping Koreans in Japan. But one senryu does not a stereotype make, and one must beware of one's reading of any senryu which does *not* build upon a stereotype because it is so rare. Gathering senryu on chili peppers, I found this:

子おろしを下女ハ八百屋へかひに行
ko oroshi o gejo wa yaoya e kai ni yuki 万?

The green grocer
a place maids go to get
their abortions

for a drug
to drop a child, maids go
to the grocer

しこたまに辛子を喰ってみなと云う
shikotama ni karashi o kutte mina to iu 万明四

try eating
a whole mess of chili
she is told

Can you guess what is happening yet (I wish I did not have a title on the chapter!)? No direct answer appears. But, keep reading. The answer forms slowly, in the gestalt. 摘 4-6↓

ひどいこと下女三文で子をおろし
hidoi koto gejo san-mon de ko o oroshi

the horror of it
a maid drops a child with
just two bits

女房の植ゑてこはがるたうがらし む
nyôbô no uete kowagaru tôgarashi 13

a frightful thing
when planted by the wife
chili peppers

つまみ喰いして流したる辛子あえ
tsumami-gui shite nagashitaru karashi-ae 74-10
(pinch-eating[snacking]-did flowed=miscarried pepper-sauce)

it cost a child:
too many snacks with
chili sauce

I had always assumed women ate so much less hot food than men in the countries where there is a lot of it because they were not so *macho* or it may have made breast-milk too spicy; but, reading the senryu, it would seem there may have been more to it!

A chili abort:
who says snacking makes
you *gain* weight?

I would bet that I have read of such a use of chili in link-verse but missed the meaning because senryu had not yet taught it to me.

たうがらしにも角文字の陰 む 11
tôgarashi ni mo ~~kaku~~/tsuno môji no kage

~~*Doctor Pepper Is In*~~

~~*the shadow*~~
~~*of a dr's shingle cast*~~
~~*on chili, too*~~

~~*chili peppers*~~
~~*are also found below*~~
~~*a fancy shingle*~~

chili peppers
also have their dark
romantic side

This, like the *ku* with the wife mentioned (right-top), also from the proto-senryu *Mutamagawa*, alludes to chili peppers doctoring women who wanted a miscarriage. Old Japan, like any stable traditional culture not at war with its neighbors, was at peace with birth control. What I strike through is a possible pun-allusion. *Horn-letters* 角文字 pronounced *kaku-môji* mean the script that would be found on a shingle, but the main intent is the same pronounced *tsuno-môji,* which means letters in words associated with romantic love (see pg.164), which usually fears issue.

black snapper 黒鯛の力

喰いようによって黒鯛罪になり
kui yô ni yotte kurodai tsumi ni nari 7-37

it's a sin that
hangs on why you eat it
black snapper

black snapper
is sinful, depending on
why you eat it

Black snapper, or sea bream, was far more expensive than chili and out of the range of maids unless their employer had an interest in helping the maid miscarry to prevent serious repercussions from an affair (黒鯛を命にかけて下女は喰い *kurodai o inochi ni kakete gejo wa kui* 13『女陰万考』によるが柳の索引にない).

黒鯛を辛子で旅の留守に喰い 28?
kurodai o karashi de tabi no rusu ni kui

black snapper
eaten with pepper while
he's on the road

black sea bream
wolfed down with pepper:
he's out of town

A drug cocktail? Chili might have capsaicin, but a fish? Perhaps it is a bottom-feeder, often taken from bays – or a bay – polluted from heavy metals due to mining operations. After all, heavy metals were known to cause miscarriage.

水銀かミズガネ *mercury and its risks*

めったにうらぬはずさと鏡とぎ 万明六
meta ni wa uranu hazu sa to kagami-togi

it's really not
s'posed to be a hot item
says the mirror-man

i don't know why
it's selling so fast says
the mirror-man

水かねで留守の曇りを研いでおく 121 乙
mizugane de rusu no kumori o kagaide oku

with mercury
cloudiness in his absence
polished away

clouding over
in his absence, wiped clean
with mercury

To save two syllables, the "mirror-polisher" became a "mirror man" in English. Like the knife-sharpeners, book-lenders and riddle-leavers (if you like their riddles you could make a donation), he was one of the scores of door-to-door vendors that helped make the economy of old Japan efficient enough to support the growth of Edo, the world's largest city at the time. Mercury was used for work on the reflective backing of mirrors and the mirror-polisher was known, in senryu at any rate, for showing his balls, because, as gems, they associated with polishing, and because he worked squatting in the heat, loincloth loose for the air and was reflected in his own work. The first *ku* suggests either that the mirror-man is pretending he does not know what the mercury is used for, or for some reason, many women were desperate to abort that year (maybe year of the Fire-horse, when any girl born might be unable to find a husband or some other reason). The second *ku* means that a wife has misbehaved during her husband's absence. It alludes to the spiritual mirror of reflection that was supposed to be kept clean of all dust = impurities = desires, and was a homophone of *paragon*, as in various paragons of womanhood, books spelling out what we might call catechism for life as a woman that were written in Japan as in Europe.

汞に片手の消えて生れる子 広原海
mizugane ni kata-te no kiete umareru ko 元禄十六
(mercury-by one-hand's vanishing born child/ren)

just one hand
vanished in quick-silver
the new-born

a child's born
with one of its hands
lost to mercury

We immediately think about Minamata and the images, but this is supposed to be witty. If a proper dosage of mercury aborted the foetus, not enough would make only part of the foetus vanish instead of the whole thing.

気遣いなし・水銀えろう呑んだ後家 三国力こぶ
kitsukai nashi mizugane erô nondu goke 文政二

◎ not giving a damn ◎
the widow chugalugs
her quick-silver

The widow may have received refreshment from a good bonze, but she cares for her late husband's good name and does not mind risking her health by what must have been known to be a dangerous medicine.

~~~~~~

moxa-combustion 三点 灸の七日

~~~~~~

せつなさに下女毛の中ヵへ灸をすへ 摘
setsunasa ni gejo ke no naka ni kyû o sue 4-16

from hopelessness
a maid burns mugwort
within her hair

The maid, seeing no future in her affair, fears to conceive. Like acupuncture needles, but more so, mugwort mounds were usually set far from the place they acted upon, but in this case, three pellets were burned close to it, on the brow of the pubic mound a little more than an inch above the upper end of the vulva. Or, as another *ku* put it, on the head of the mountain wizard (山伏の頭へ slang for a hairy twat). One book dated to about 文政五(閨中紀聞枕文庫 in 女陰万考) warned that doing this for seven days would render one barren for life, but senryu suggest that the efficiency of this particular type of contraception was doubted by many:

ひたひ口やいても同じおとみなり 摘
hitai-guchi yaite mo onaji ototo mi nari 1-13
(brow-mouth burnt-even same brother see is)

burnt dead center
of the brow yet here comes
little brother alive

burnt on the brow
yet the same little brother
pops from mother

~~~~~~

灯心を呑めば — *a lamp wick, quick!*

~~~~~~

燈心を誰に聞いたか嫁は飲み 六
tôshin o dare ni kiita ka yome wa nomi

where'd she learn
of lamp wicks? the bride
drinks it quick

大腰につかい燈心ゆりこませ 万?
ôgoshi ni tsukai tôshin yuri-komase

hips in motion
jiggle-joggling down
the lamp wick

This, like the chili, black sea bream and mercury is an abortifacient. ↑安六礼七. Both *ku* date to the 1870's but seem to record two completely different methods of taking it. The wick in question was evidently made of *rush* (called *tôshin-gusa,* or "wick-grass"), but who knows whether the effect, if there was any, came from the rush or the oil the wick was steeped in.

灯心は火をとぼさせるために飲み 122
tôshin wa hi o tobosaseru tame ni nomi

the lamp wick
she drinks it down to
light his fire

Evidently, some men stopped making love to their wives the minute they knew they were with child. The original does not say "his," but what else could it be?

~~~~~~

朔日丸 — *the pill in japan*

~~~~~~

antidote

the first-day pill
dispels a pine mushroom's
poisonous spore

a first-day pill
so pine mushrooms won't
make her ill

朔日丸で松茸の毒を消し 142-39
tsuitachi-gan de matsudake no doku o keshi
(first-day-pill-c pine-mushroom=penis's poison[acc.] quell)

the calends pill
an end to poisoning by
pine mushroom

Poison? When you consider the high fatality rate of child-bearing in pre-modern times, it is easy to visualize sperm as slow-working poison that swells up the victim's body over a period of nine months (and, I put it mildly compared to what Elaine Morgan wrote on fetus-as-parasite in *Descent of the Child*). This *Tsuitachi-gan* had a good reputation for working – no senryu doubt it – and was sold by female gynecologist/abortionists (仲条). Its name, "First Day Pill," comes from its being *taken once a month on the first day*. I write "it," but a 1699 book 続呪重法記 says the round pills, made from powdered 楊廬 tree (maybe a bush honey-suckle) , were swallowed on the first of the month *thirty* at one time, or if a fifty-day effectiveness were wanted, that number, which makes me suspicious of the information (*Cuntologia*). Common sense dictates more than one active ingredient or the female doctors would not have had a monopoly on its sale and a woman would take a pill a day, starting with a fresh one-month supply at the start of each month.

逆日をまるめて月をおん流し *38*
tsuitachi o marumete tsuki o on-nagashi

rolling up those
first-days so the moons
keep flowing

the first days
rolled up to send the moon
downstream

The "moon" is welcome when one does not wish for a child. If that moon stops coming, it is said that the flow has stopped. That is when that dammed energy builds up a fetus, instead. The metaphor of *on-nagashi,* or politely sending the moon packing, or "flowing" is the same as that used for exorcism of disease or bad-luck by setting scapegoats into paper boats and letting them float down rivers.

ねつ湯の心朔丸にかけ 万宝 11
nettô no kokoro tsuitachi-gan ni kake
(hot water's heart first-day-pill-in lacking)

there is nothing
frantic about it:
first-day pills

hope simmers
in the warm water
first-day pills

The expression "wash hands in hot water" meant frantic behavior, so the first reading guesses the *ku* evokes the calm, collected, well-planned contraceptives prostitutes with means use are very different from the usual hurried measures taken just before and after coitus. The second reading assumes the pills were drunk with warm water by a woman ardently hoping they'll do the job.

みそか事 逆日丸であかるくし 九四
misoka goto? tsuitachi-gan de akarushi

every month-end
thanks to the calends pill
is bright as day!

The Japanese luni-solar calendar kept the moon in the month, for every month began with the new moon (the sliver was usually visible from the second day), hosted the full moon in the middle and ended with a moonless dark night-sky. I think the above must be one of the most cheerful senryu ever composed. It could have been an advertisement for the pills. Maybe it was, or became one. To the extent that they worked (placebo effect included), this medicine, and many others we are only beginning to learn about today, helped save women's lives and reduce infanticide throughout the world long before the belated "invention" of oral contraceptives, the import of which 20c Japanese doctors fought tooth and nail – supposedly because they were in the pocket of the condom companies and benefited from performing abortions, but more likely for fearing the attitude expressed by country music star Loretta Lynn in *"The Pill"* – but, in the Edo era, it would seem Japan was big on giving women a choice.

~~~~~~

the lady doctor 中條・仲条ないし、女医者

~~~~~~

When the Jesuits came to Japan in the 16c, they never qualified their condemnation of the *abomination,* pederasty/sodomy, but abortion and infanticide were rarely denounced without a qualifying sentence about how the women who did it, did so for the kindest of motives, to save their older children from starving and save the baby from having to be sold. The Jesuits suffered enough to learn what mattered in life and understood, though they dared not write it, that Japanese mothers were morally correct to judge that a child had more of a right to life than a fetus or even a newborn. Senryu did not get into such deep moral waters, but simply viewed the women who did that work with detached bemusement.

仲条で娘覚悟の前を出し 73
chûjô de musume kakugo no mae o dashi

at the doctress's
the young lady offers up
a resigned front

無造作に中條股へ手をいれる 安九
muzosaku ni chûjô mata e te o ireru 梅三

how artlessly
the doctress slips her hands
into a crotch

もみくちゃは中條流の道具なり 13
momikucha wa chûjôryû no dôgu nari

for a doctress
messing things up is part
of fixing them

今までのことを中條水にする *19*
ima-made no koto o chûjô mizu ni suru
(now-until things[acc] abortionist water-into make)

the abortionist
spills all that happened
under the bridge

thanks to the doctress
her past is now completely
written on water

The "front," short for "front-hole," in the first *ku* is slang for the cunt. What is "made water" in the third is what English calls "water under the bridge." Ideally, this is so, but women were taken advantage of by Buddhist sales-women who spoke of hells specially tailored for them and of the need to pay for memorial services for their "water babies" (see chapter 2 in *Topsy-turvy 1585* (paraverse press 2003)) and such services were again pushed in the last half of the 20c by some Buddhist temples. (注：名雑学者西沢来によると「中條/条」は「なかじょう」であり、「ちゅうじょう」ではないが、他にどこ見ても、皆「〜ちゅう」なんです。どうしょうか?)

仲條のむすこ気づよく地色をし 万
chûjô no musuko ki-zuyoku ji-iro o shi 明三

the doctress's son
tends to have his way with
amateur whores

coming on strong
with the local girls, the son
of the abortionist

The black humor of senryu did not stick with the relationship of the abortionist/doctress with her patient. We can well imagine an impudent son telling maid-servants and neighbor girls alike that doing it with him was safe because . . .

三人を二人たすける女いしや 万 明四
san-nin o futari tasukeru onna isha

helping two
out of three people
the lady-doctor

draw: むりな事かな *muri na koto kana*
女いしゃ小の虫とハへらすぐち 万
onna isha ko no mushi to wa herasu-guchi 明三
(lady-doctor small[er] bug as-for reduce-mouth/s/population)

A hopeless job?

doctress logic
the little bug is the mouth
that is reduced

abortion logic
little bug – it's about less
mouths to feed

"Letting the big one survive, killing the little bug" is found in the prototypical *haikai* almanac, *Hair-blowing Grass* (毛吹き草 1645). *"Killing little bugs to help*

big bugs" was the more usual version. One horrendous example of this perfectly rational logic has someone (a daimyô, perhaps) saying he loved his grandson more than his own son but had to force him to cut his belly because ~ . (浄・近江源氏先陣館 八). This does not mean the "little bug" was not appreciated – other Japanese sayings attribute *will* and *spirit* to even the tiniest – just that they put things in perspective: they were *reasonable* rather than *religious*. As a corollary saying puts it, *"Both killing the little bug and not killing the big one come from human compassion"* (人情・恩愛二葉草 初). At any rate, judging from the draw, the poet had valid doubts about either the rationalization or whether a family with trouble feeding itself would be helped much by one less mouth.

人をころして世をわたる女医者 再現
hito o koroshite yo o wataru onna-isha 61-11

murdering
for a livelihood
the doctress

the lady doctor
she makes her living
killing people

killing humans
their living is assured
lady doctors

No quibbling here: "people-killing world-crosses woman-doctor." This is as direct as they come. But still, who does not wonder about the poet's intent? I would guess it is purely love for paradox – other *ku* play on the way all doctors must kill some to save other lives (alluding to their first years of medical *practice*) – but I could not swear the poet intends no criticism.

仲條へ男の来ルハ毛切レなり 万明四
chûjô e otoko no kuru wa kegire nari

when men come
to the ladies' doctor
it's hair-burn

We have information on the "hair-cuts/abrasions" which I translate as "burn" in ch.23. Until I came across the above senryu (after writing the rest of the chapter), the word for the doctress used in this *ku,* 仲條 *chûjô,* always concerned gynecological matters, of which 90% was abortion. It is interesting that the men, too, prefer to leave the health of their crotch to a female doctor.

~ eddies ~

First-day Pill History. I hope someone will gloss the *tsuitachi-gan* (research the history and active ingredients, etc.) for a future edition. After finishing this chapter, I came across two more Tsuitachi-gan *ku* in books 5 and 6 of the *Mutamagawa*, which is to say as early as 1763-4. The first, a 7-7, reveals the pill had already been around a while.

.

His present mistress	今の妾も *ima no mekake mo*
Also, drinks The First.	一日を呑 *tsuitachi o nomu*

The second, a 5-7-5 depicts taking birth-control as both natural and normal behavior –

月並の丸薬呑で衣がえ　武玉川 六
tsukinami no maru-gusuri nonde koromogae
(month-order/normal pill-medicine drinking/drunk dress-changing)

Swallowing her monthly pills,
She changes into summer-wear.

~~~~~~

Loretta Lynn's *The Pill* Lyrics. I have put about half of the lyrics below. Besides italicizing *the pill,* I italicized the poultry stuff because it is not a paltry matter. I did it to bring something to your attention: poetry and song is only as good as the bank of metaphor it has to draw from. Of course, the content and overall-style matters, too, but one quickly bores of both if the metaphor is limited. One often hears of *vocabulary* counts for individual authors (Shakespeare commanded a vocabulary of so many words, Hemingway . . .), but what about comparative *metaphor* counts? One could do the comparisons for genre, or dialects, too.

You wined me and dined me / When I was your girl
Promised if I'd be your wife / You'd show me the world
But all I've seen of this old world / Is a bed and a doctor bill
I'm tearin' down *your brooder house* / 'Cause now I've got *the pill*

All these years I've stayed at home / While you had all your fun
And every year that's gone by / Another baby's come
There's a gonna be some changes made / Right here on nursery hill
You've set this chicken your last time / 'Cause now I've got *the pill*

I'm tired of all your crowin' / How you and your hens play
While holdin' a couple in my arms / Another's on the way
This *chicken's done tore up her nest* / And I'm ready to make a deal
And ya can't afford to turn it down / 'Cause you know I've got *the pill*

~~~~~~

More on the *Lady-Doctor*. Anyone who has researched this subject is welcome to send me a supplemental essay, ideally, written so well I can use it *as-is* for a gloss that will both entertain and inform readers of the next edition. Of course, it can be critical, too. Add. note: one source claims 仲條 is pronounced *nakajô,* but all the rest gloss it as *chûjô.*

~~~~~~
~~~~~~

Spendings of Modern Senryu
現代川柳の捨てぬ心

十四 14

ゴムのお見本
Sampling Rubbers

~~~~~~

I found a charming paperback anthology of 20c senryu edited by the patron saint of old (and dirty) senryu, Okada Hajime, for practically nothing in a used bookstore. The *ku* in *Enku* (『艶句』1962), or *Eroverse*, were selected from over a hundred-thousand sent in from around the country every month for five years in the 1950s (contents on pg 458-9). If anything marks post-World War II Japanese sex, it is the condom, or *gomu* ("rubber" from the Portuguese). 下記全句『艶句』より.

ゴムを買う夫を妻は遠く待ち
gomu o kau otto o tsuma wa tôku machi
(rubber[acc]buying husband[acc] wife-as-for far-away waits)

a husband buys rubbers
for the coming night
his wife, blushing
out of sight

he buys rubbers
in the store as she waits
down the street

she waits outside
oh, for a place to hide
while he buys skins

Aren't most people – at least half of every couple – embarrassed to buy rubbers? In Japan, shortly after *Eroverse* was published, that problem was solved. Saleswomen employed by Japan's world-class condom makers started selling them door-to-door (something impossible in backward Usania).

家計簿に「お菓子」と書いて避妊薬
kakeibo ni "okashi" to kaite hininyaku
(house-ledger-in "pastry" as write contraceptives)

the house ledger
where it says "for pastry"
contraceptives
~~~~~~

The woman was typically in charge of a family's books. *Okashi* (cakes/pastries) is homophonous with "funny," or damn close to it (*okashii*).

いつまでもゴムを隔てて他人めき
itsumademo gomu o hedatete tanin-meki
(how long rubber-across separated stranger-like)

how long do we stay
divided by latex walls
strangers in the night?

are we to stay
strangers after all? when
will the latex fall

the berlin wall
who gives a fart? rubber
keeps us apart

latex walls
that, too: call it *strangers*
in the fall

The *"meki"* at the end hints at *aki-meki* or "deepening fall", something seconded by the poet's *nom de plume* Akigusa, "autumn grass." The verse reminds me of *ku* by Bashô, Buson and Issa about Fall as the start of isolation. While I used the first person plural, as a senryu, this ought not to be taken personally.

情熱のこれ見よゴムの消費量
jônetsu no kore miyo gomu no shôhiryô
(passionate this look[+emph] rubber-consumption-amount)

a passionate pair
'just look at what we've
spent on condoms!'

'love you, dear?
just count up the condoms
we used last year!'

The first is the most natural reading, but the second is possible. The words in the middle part, *kore miyo,* "look at this!" make the *ku* good.

コンドーム代を引いた残りで予算組み
kondomu-dai o hiita nokori de yosan kumi
(condom expense[acc] subtracted remainder-with budget make)

far from topeka

she works out
the budget after giving
condoms their due

budget interruptus

after condoms
are taken out, what's left
gets squeezed in

In the battle of the budget, condom expenses are excused from the trenches. This was a hard *ku* to translate without going over budget with the beats. *Topeka, Kansas* is the title of a country number (by Shel Silverstein) that starts off with the dripping kitchen sink and ends up with *". . . and ones on the way"* so we can kiss goodbye all hope for a new refrigerator this year. Family planning played a huge role in Japan's rise as a superpower, and, now, China's.

ボーナスで少し余計にゴムを買い
bonasu de sukoshi yokei ni gomu o kai
(bonus-with few excessively rubbers[acc] buying)

he splurges a bit
on rubbers for his dick
with his bonus

with his bonus
he treats himself to some
extra rubbers

bonus in pocket
free of care he buys rubbers
enough to spare

Having overcome the temptation to put a bone with the bonus, I fell for the temptation to add another rhyme, the third reading.

コンドーム土曜日毎に減ってゆき
kondomu doyôbi goto ni hetteyuku
(condoms Saturday-every-with/on diminish)

every saturday
the condoms' ranks
are thinned

During the work week at this time of post-war recovery, many Japanese men did not get home until 10 or 11 and barely had time to bath and eat before they had to be up again. They usually worked Saturday, too, but not as late.

これきりのサックあいにく穴あり
kore kiri no sakku ainiku ana ga ari
(this-last sack=rubber unfortunately hole has)

wouldn't you know it
the very last sack
has a hole in the front
as well as the back

Life is cruel. If not, why is it always the last item, when you have no substitute at hand, that has a problem? But, that is not enough for poetry, in English, anyway. Compare the direct Englishing and my "translation."

妻の押すダメは昨夜で切れた品
tsuma no osu dame wa yube de kireta shina
(wife's adamant no-as-for last-night-with ran-out good]

more than a headache

the wife's clear "no!"
leaves no room for doubt
last night they ran-out

last night a good
ran out, so now his wife
says "that's too bad."

The above third-person style would fit the pre-20c senryu, but it is hard to say here. The senryu-ness of the *ku* is mostly in not specifying *what* good ran out. It shows us that rubbers were a solid theme. Here is a paraverse ignoring that:

my wife shakes her head
when I try to love her
last night we used it
the last rubber

The good is specified, yet by saving it for the very last word and, with the help of an extra line creating that strong rhyme with "love her," it works. I would be surprised if no one has yet made an ad reading *"If you love her / Wear a rubber!"*

実弾の恐怖をゴムが遮断する
jitsudan no kyôfu o gomu ga shadan suru
(real-bullets' terror[acc] rubber[the] block-does)

i think this says it best
a rubber, my friend, is
a bullet-proof vest

The terror of live ammo, real war:
wear a condom and fear no more!

In the face of live ammo, any cover:
hiding behind a millimeter of rubber.

While pox was carried by man-o-wars in England and muskets in Japan (names for disease-ridden street-walkers, see ch. 5), *live ammunition* usually refers to the possibility of creating an unwanted life. While pregnancy is much more dangerous for a woman than a man, a conscientious man not in a position to be married can be terrified of it. I recall crying with relief when I heard a cricket chirping thirty years ago (sure enough she called me shortly after with the news: *It came!*).

喧嘩した数だけコンドームが残り
kenka-shita kazu dake kondomu ga nokori
(quarreled numbers just condoms remaining)

old quarrels still
count the number of condoms
yet to be filled

First read "still count," and, then, think "count the number." A paraverse:

Each fight we had
with one another
lies in the drawer,
an unused rubber.

It's unJapanese, but some of my elaborated senryu, if they are still senryu, work best in the first-person (either number).

ごみ箱へ昨夜の夢をそっと捨て

gomibako ni yube no yume o sotto sutete

(garbage-can-into last night's dreams[acc] quietly dumped)

after their dreams were spent
into the garbage can
they went

last night's dreams
are quietly discarded
in the garbage

last night's dreams
according to plan, end up
in the garbage can

Have used condoms ever been so lyrically expressed?

she quietly throws away
last night's dreams
today

last night's dreams
after putting a knot in them
tossed in the trash

after screwing
the rubber gets tied up
– dead-end –

the pity of it
hitched yet still tying
half-hitches

The first is my paraverse of the dream rubber *ku*. Minus the garbage can, it really is lyrical. The second two with the added knot – detail found in the best of traditional senryu – are my doing, as is the last. They reproduce evolution in senryu. First, mention a knot, then, in a latter edition, *only* mention a knot, and let the reader guess where it was hitched. I suppose a "dead-end" for sperm is maudlin, but maudlinity is one rhetoric of wit, is it not?

by the seashore
what son of a whore left
his condom tied

on the beach
within reach of the sea
trapped sperm

Of the above, do you prefer the anger [pardon the s.o.w. expression, chosen for the rhyme alone] or the bathetic death-trap? And, is it disconcerting to find your author-translator misbehaving like this? Reading the ancient songs of longing in the *Manyôshû*, I could not help but *write* such poems to someone who, as it turned out, had a father who was a *Manyôshû* scholar (she also had a husband and was in love with another scholar). They are lost, but a description of a self-portrait I took to send her at the time should suffice to give you the picture: *me in a pine tree holding a big-eye red snapper and a sweet potato*. It was the New Year, fish felicitous not only for being red but for name-punning reasons, pine homophonic for "wait" and the sweet-potato with "little-sister," or "sweetheart." This is classic, not senryu symbolism. Like-wise, when I read senryu, I cannot help *writing* them. The above combine memories of growing up on a beach with adult feelings, such as, *why the hell tie one up when you are on the beach!*

どこでどう落としたものかコンドーム
doko de dô otoshita mono ka kondohmu

where and how
was it dropped – the story
of a condom

a story tied up
in each and every one –
used condoms

where in the world
and how was it dropped?
a floating rubber

The first reading is close to the original. The "story of" was added to catch the emphatic *mono ka,* which has no equally nondescript English equivalent but can be matched by "where in the world." Since most rubbers found are found where they were used, the where intrigues. Doesn't that put the condom, or condoms, in a huge trash pile or in a river?

出勤の橋から昨夜のゴムを捨て
shukkin no hashi kara yube no gomu o sute
(commuting bridge from, last night's rubber/s throw)

tossed from the bridge
on the way to work, last night's
rubbers: what a jerk!

The percentage of car ownership in Japan at this time was low. Evidently, some of them were jerks, though that was my value judgment. I only include the blah *ku* because of the better one – by another contributor – that follows.

大川のくらげとなってゴムは果て
ôgawa-no kurage to natte gomu wa hate
(big river's jellyfish into become rubber's/s/s' end/s)

rubbers end up
as jellyfish, jellyfish
in the big river

a condom's end
flowing toward the sea
moon jellyfish

Particulars do magic for poetry. Were the original in English, I might change "rubber/condom" to Trojan for a real senryu experience! Another *ku*, came in for a close-up, describing a condom, or condoms, floating, quivering by a buoy or buoys (ウキのそばゴムがゆらゆら流れゆき *uki no soba gomu yurayura nagareyuki*). Amazingly, someone in the USA who almost surely did not read these senryu, wrote one, too: *"East bound off Manhattan"* I found in Higginson's *Haiku World: "condom / floats with the jellyfish / down the East River"* (Raffael de Gruttola). "*With* the jellyfish" is good. A born scavenger, I can forgive some trash in scenic areas, provided it is interesting. A rusted car bursting with plants is a pleasant sight, and nothing is as amusing as bicycles hanging from a tree (unless it is model fish). Even condoms can add something of visual worth to a river. The only problem is that there are too damn many of them because there are too damn many of us because there were too few of them on too many of us.

sex by a reef
coitus interruptus feeds
an angel fish

sex in the sea
a delight to see nothing
goes to waste

No condom here. I'm at it again. This is a fifteen-year-old memory. A little yellow angel-fish started the feeding frenzy. I do not know if it is a senryu (I hate to categorize myself), but is the type of pleasant memory few people will have if we breed more, consume more and lose our reefs.

from one bag
to another, the sad life of
senryû sperm

spurting out
then flushed right down
senryû sperm

The single life – of responsible bachelors, not those that live for sex alone and father children by the dozen – is not generally spent feeding angel fish. For most of us, most of the time, it is dreary as my last two *ku*. Am I wrong? But, there is a heart-warming, even bright side to the low-life and low-ku, too. It is indirectly captured in the next senryu.

コンドーム気軽に借りる裏長屋
kondohmu kigaru ni kariru ura-nagaya

backstreet flats
where people think nothing
of borrowing skins

where condoms
are easily borrowed or lent
an old tenement

This is important to put the embarrassment at buying condoms found at the start of the chapter into perspective before we finish it. The embarrassment was bourgeoisie. The common folk, now "middle class, but still the poor as of the mid-20c – were not so prissy, at least in the flats in the large cities.

ゴム埋めた土犬が嗅ぎ猫が嗅ぎ
gomu umeta tsuchi inu ga kagi neko ga kagi

the earth below which
we buried the rubbers
dogs sniff, cats sniff

dogs sniff, cats sniff
the earth below which
we buried the rubbers

Nitty-gritty *ku* like this justify the editor's remark that *Eroverse* – together with two sibling books that came before – was the modern version of *Pluck* (1776). The original has the critters *last*. For this chapter, when all the *ku* concern rubbers, that is better for it keeps the surprise for last. But in a different context, as a lone *ku* where the rubbers would be the surprise, I prefer them first, as per my second reading.

~~~~~~

~~~~~~

~ *eddies* ~

~~~~~~

Senryû in This Chapter. All senryu other than the few specifically mine and the one from Higginson's *Haiku World* came from Okada Hajime's *Eroverse* (*enku*). All senryu in the *Eroverse* were attributed to pen names, which I did not give. Some 19c senryu also gave the pen names, but I prefer not to. If you should quote any of mine, you need not give my name, or even my pen name, keigu (敬愚). But, please do give the name of the *book* you found it in: *this one.*

~~~~~~

Door-to-door Condom-sellers. This sounds splendid, but we should not forget that the Japanese condom industry has its sordid side, too. It teamed up with the abortion industry to keep out the pill *for decades*. As so often is the case with evil-doing, this was not without benefit, for it slowed down the inroads of AIDS and genital warts we now know cause cancer. As sheer literature, the condom saleslady cannot be beat. In the first book I ever read by myself in Japanese, Inoue Hisashi's collection of short stories called *Burijetto Borudo* (punning the actress's last name into the wine), one chapter introduces such a business from the inside-out. I cannot recall if that was where I read of the man of the house home when the condom lady came being shamed into buying more condoms then he could use. It may have been in Inoue's *Katei Kôron*, or its sequel, other books by Inoue Hisashi I read and recommend to people who prefer popular culture and puns, not to mention good plots (Inoue is a popular bard) to high-faluting "literature" (in Japan, Inoue Hisashi is probably more famous than Inoue Yasushi, whose *haute culture* novels are far better known here).

.

<u>*Alcoves & Tongue Puppetry*</u>
舌人形ト活花ノ鉢合セ

十五 15

"又舐めなさるか"
Who *Does* It? Who *Likes* It?

~~~~~~

鼻とさね鉢合せして開をなめ 葉 15 オ
hana to sane hachi-awase shite bobo o name
(nose and clit pot-meet[collide]-doing cunt[acc] licks)

licking cunt
while the nose and clit
play eskimo

licking cunt
while his nose & her clit
eskimo kiss

I trust you can see from the direct rendering above that my reading is less a translation than a paraverse. But would the following, seemingly closer translations serve any purpose?

nose and clit
put their heads together
licking pussy

nose and clit
collide in space over
cunnilingus

nose and clit
go noggin to noggin
licking pussy

The wit of the original may not be reproduced. It lies in the use of an idiom meaning *collide* that has "pots" in it and may be taken to mean pots arranged with respect to one another, as with *ikebana* flower arrangements in the alcove called a *tokonoma*, built into all Japanese-style houses, that might be called 'an altar to fine art.' Accordingly, the wits of Japan called this position of cunnilingus *"tokonoma* position" (床の間体位 *tokonoma tai*)! I would have guessed the name came from the reverential posture assumed toward the *tokonoma* by a guest viewing its art, but, the explanation provided by Syunroan is much better: in this position, the male proboscis would tend to touch a woman's pubic hair, and the natural Japanese expression of that, rapidly pronounced – and in parts of Japan *"e"* and *"i"* tend to merge – sounds like *there's a flower arrangement.*

鼻へ毛が入る = <u>*hana e ke ga hairu*</u> = nose-to hair-the enters
花活がある = <u>*hana-ike ga aru*</u> = flower-arrangement-a is/has

Such art would be displayed in the *tokonoma.* Even Cockney cannot beat that!
~~~~~~

筆細工ぼぼをなめたを思ひ出シ
fude saiku bobo o nameta o omoidashi 葉 4 オ
(brush/es-handiwork cunt[acc] licked [acc]remembered/ing)

finishing off
a brush, he remembers
licking pussy

I owe this chapter to John Solt, or to AK for reminding me I really should see his six page presentation *Willow Leaftips* (1996), or to MMcM for finding it at Tuft's library and e-mailing me a copy. *Why?* Because Solt pointed out that

> . . . we rarely find cunnilingus performed in *shunga* [erotic pictures], and if we had no other evidence upon which to base a judgment, we might conclude that Edo Japanese found it unappealing not only to depict in a picture, but also to use as the subject of a poem. One look at *Yanagi no hazue* and we are disabused of the notion, leading us to wonder conversely why *shunga* ignore the subject.

Thus, *"bareku"* [dirty poems] provide

> a literary corrective to some of the artistic conventions . . . that otherwise might be interpreted as social conventions. . . . recognizing that the culture drew the line at pictures rather than words, we can avoid . . . believing that merely because a sexual practice is absent from one genre does not preclude its presence in another genre or its existence in the society at large.

Amen. We can observe something akin with respect to the lanky models filling fashion magazines that might make the proverbial Martian think we worshipped bones on the one hand and the fleshy women in strip-joints and porn videos revealing what most men really desire. Still, the number of *ku* on cunnilingus in *Willow Leaftips* is *particularly* high, even for collections of *bareku* and may reflect a desire to shock and the paucity of *cunnilingus* (frontal & 69) in *shunga* – far rarer than fingering (usually accompanying rather than preceding coitus) to be sure – seems natural *for work intended to arouse readers*, mostly male (few men get aroused imagining licking). The poetry, while lewd is *not* pornographic, for it is not intended or read for *arousal,* hence. . . Be that as it may, Solt's translation:

making calligraphy brushes
is reminiscent of
licking quim

While the original does not specify "finishing off," as per my translation, that is when the brush-maker puts his lips around the brush hair and, with the help of his tongue, brings the hair tips together into the fine point you see on new writing brushes. Not uncommonly, a Japanese woman's generally straight and thick pubic hairs clash in front of the *mons,* just above the vulva, with each side, right and left, pushing the other up from the skin surface, like what happens when incoming and rebounding waves meet. As they also point somewhat down, disengaging from cunnilingus can indeed leave a moistened brush-tip of hair.

鼻が邪魔舌が子宮へ届きかね 葉28
hana ga jama shita ga ko-tsubo e todoki-kane

the nose blocks
the tongue from reaching
the baby-room

毛が鼻へ入ってどうも舐めにくい
ke ga hana e haitte dômo name-nikui 葉 55

hair enters
the nostrils making it
hard to lick

ばかの剥身の気でしゃぶる実の先 葉36
baka no mukimi no ki de shaburu sane no saki

feeling like it's
a shelled surf-clam he sucks
the tip of the clit

Nose as culprit and nose as victim. With the first, I think it likely to have been inspired by reference to a Tenmei (1781-9) dog story called Chin (「チン」『間女畑』『女陰万考』出典), where a teenage girl enjoys daily cunnilingus with her chin whose long tongue reaches in so far it licks the mouth of her baby-urn, which is to say cervix, which inspires her nanny to try the same, but instead the frightened dog (all that hair, etc., see ch. 3) only barks. At any rate, this type of dog has a snout that does not stick out and get in the way. The second *ku* may have been somewhat funny to people exceedingly conscious of nostril-hair (pp.98-100), but is still a good example of a bad (far-from-literary) senryu. The hair is the same that becomes a brush-tip. The last includes untranslatable wit, for the name of the shellfish that looks like a long vulva in Japanese is a "fool-shell" (*baka-gai*), so we feel the licker may identify his foolish self with what he licks.

極ずいの好開ッ子をベエろべろ
gokuzui no suki bebekko o bêro-bero 葉 *20*
(extreme's liking pussy[acc] *bero-bero* [mimetic])

a bero-bero for bebe'kko

he gives the pussy
he loves to death
a good licking

Gokuzui is *extreme;* but it is hard to tell if this is a man who is infatuated with all pussies or finds a particular one too adorable not to lick. Probably the former.

股倉でべろ／＼をするぼぼんのう
matagura de berobero o suru bobonô 玩宮隠士？
(crotch-store-room-at *bero-bero*[licking] do: *bobonô*)

bero-bero

the bo-bon-no-oh
licks clean the walls of
the crotch godown

The above *ku* was in *Cuntologia,* within a definition of a Bobonnô as a man who likes to lick pussies. (「舐めるのが好きな男を『ぼぼんのう』といいます。」『女陰万考』) The author also provided the following dialogue from an early 19c book:

Woman – *"You like licking something terrible, don't you! Isn't it dirty?"*

Man – *"What are you saying! I don't think your pussy's dirty, not at all!"*

(参考：女「お前は舐めるのがきつい好きだねえ。汚いじゃないかね」男「なんの、お前のぼゞはちっとも汚ねえとは思わね。。。」(『紅の花』天保のころ))

I have not seen the bobonno (a word that calls to mind the most highly sexed ape) in any *ku*, but, then again, when I collected them I did not know to look. . .

又舐めなさるかと女房嫌な顔　葉 15
mata name-nasaru ka to nyôbô iya na kao

"do you please to
lick me again?" says his wife
looking revolted

Mata, "again" is a homophone for what is licked, the *crotch*. Finding a good match for *iya-na, yucky/glum/repulsed*[at]*/troubled*[with]*/sour*, which modified the wife's face, was hard, but *revolted* does it. As the Cuntologist explained, with the above prose and this *ku* for examples, it was often the woman who was reluctant to receive the favor. Yet, we do find two *ku* implying that was not always the case. One we saw with the konjak masturbation (pg 80), where a man was supposed to prove his love by going down on a woman and cheated.

馬鹿な婿いいあんばいとなめて居る
baka na muko ii-anbai to namete-iru 葉 30
(foolish groom/married-in good taste [says] licking-is)

the fool groom
saying that the taste's just right
while he licks

mr married-in:
a fool with quim in his face
praises its taste

The wife, of higher status than her husband who, marrying into her family, remains the "groom," evidently doesn't feel *hers* is dirty, while he experiences a most interesting sort of cognitive dissonance. As Syunrôan puts it, "the taste is generally somewhat salty, so he is a "fool" for thinking it well-seasoned." I might add, that good *anbai* implies the right balance of sweet and salty flavor.

極ずいの浅黄舌人形が好き　葉 3
gokuzui no asagiura shita-ningyô ga suki

the asagiura
sex maniacs just love their
tongue-puppets

hic samurai
like their country theatre
tongue-puppetry

These are masterless samurai (an oxymoron, for the latter cannot be the former) portrayed in ways reminiscent of the way "hillbillies" were treated in Usania, but worse. Senryu have them wiping off the smell of a cheap whore's pussy with regret, stepping on dog doo when intent on viewing dogs in congress, fingering assholes to warm them up and so on and so forth, literally *ad nauseum.* By saying that *they* like cunnilingus, the senryu indirectly implies that although men may do the act to please or keep a woman as necessary, only a real sex maniac, or pervert would love to do it. This is not to say that no respectable men liked doing it. I have seen a shunga print where a fine looking samurai or magistrate and a courtesan are enjoying 69 (again, the man is getting it, too). I just have not seen the proof in senryu.

神農もさすが開をもなめて見ず 葉別 4
shinnô mo sasuga bobo o mo namete mizu

even shinnô
failed to try giving
pussy a lick

even shinnô
didn't test out bobo
by licking it

That is to say, the ox-headed father of Chinese herbal medicine (漢方薬), inventor of musical instruments and the I-ching overlooked one medicine. Actually, Chinese alchemy, which focused on longevity rather than gold (their heads were screwed on better than the Occidental gold-cravers) probably did not. Indeed, the only frontal cunnilingus I have seen in a Japanese painting – by the most prolific and skilled graphic artist of all time, Hokusai, no less – is done for such medical life-prolonging motives. In this print (c. 1830), predating the above Leaf *ku,* a clitoris-licking gentleman holds a flask under one of the woman's butt-cheeks (ample enough even from the front to prevent any liquid from flowing into the tight crevice completely blocking the anus from the picture) to collect the precious liquid he draws. One is reminded of collecting spring water dripping from a boulder. It is like the poet, seeing Hokusai's print thought, *Hey, hey, hey! Herbs are not the only medicine to be collected!* And, now for the rest of the story. I cannot recall where I first came across Hokusai's print, but just a week before paginating this book, I got Timon Screech's book of erotic images in Japan and it had not only the same print, but two older prints, one c.1810 and one 1822, showing Occidentals collecting such "vaginal juices!" One was sucking it up through what looks like a long reed and the other had four fingers up the woman. Did Hokusai think *we Japanese can do better with our tongues?* Japanese were familiar with Chinese legends about long lives attained by partaking of this human fountain of youth. Now, with interest in the West supplanting that in China, they were licking (trying out) *their* medicine, but what an odd transposition!

深更に猫の水呑む音がする 21
shinkô ni neko no mizu nomu oto ga suru

in the wee hours
there is the sound of a cat
drinking water

猫が水呑むかと姑声をかけ 86
neko ga mizu nomu ka to shûto koe o kake

thinking a cat
was drinking water? shûto
calls out to it

Mr. Cuntologist (玩宮隠士) thought this sound of a cat referred to that of cunnilingus, but I would guess we are talking of the little wave-lapping noises wet coitus is more likely to create than oral sex. The *shûto* is the mother-in-law of the fucking couple and also the accepted wife/female head of the household – I wonder if I could get away with *"Is that a pussy / lapping water? Mother superior / calls out"* ? She typically drives her son and his wife, but mostly his wife, crazy by listening to what they do – senryu have her faking snores, getting up to take a piss whenever they are going at it, and castigating them for taking a chance on giving birth to a thief (doing it on Kanoezaru night, when they should abstain) – so, if the idea here is that she was really fooled, it is pretty funny!

行平ハ塩物迄も喰ちらし 摘 4-26
yukihira wa shio-mono made mo kui-chirashi

that yukihira
even left half-eaten
salted goods

yukihira even
chewed & left his souse
strewn about

なめたらしょっぱいおめこだと行平
nametara shio'ppai omeko da to yukihira 葉 9
(licked-if/when salty cunt/s is/are [says] yukihira)

after licking 'em
"these cunts are salty"
said yukihira

upon licking it
yukihira said, "this *is*
a salty cunt"

"if you lick her beaver
you'll find it salty"
declares Yukihira (Solt)

Yukihira, brother of the playboy of the *Tales of Ise,* Narihira, was also an enthusiastic lover of women. Exiled to Suma, he found his consolation in a pair of beautiful brine-scooping maidens (潮汲女), *i.e.* salt-gatherers. The declarative *"da to"* fits a man with so much experience he can speak authoritatively about the taste of one (or two. This is the first senryu I have seen with the vulgar word for 'cunt' still common today, *omeko.* Another Leaf *ku* has Yukihira doing the sisters simultaneously with a portmanteau verb *shi+kujiri, do(fucking)-fingering,* (二人リ並べてしくじるの中納言 葉 10 *futari narabete shikujiru no chûnôgon*).

鵺の開蛇ハ我物顔でなめ 葉 別 六
nue no bebe hebi wa wagamonogao de name
(nue's cunt snake-as-for mythingface-with licks)

◎ *nue sex, or how a tail*
in a tale gets some tail ◎

nightbird pussy
the snake licks away looking
like it owns it

chimera snark
is half the ark: yes the snake
is circumcised

snaketail bird
licking a tiger a cock makes
a monkey of it

The *Nue* is a creature from Chinese mythology with the head of a monkey, body of a tiger and tail of a snake. It is known to most Japanese for being banished by a hero in the 16c *Tales of Heike*. I like the Japanese pronunciation too much to look for the Chinese. Despite the translator's desperate paraversing, the *ku* is better in the original because "lick" means to treat as one likes, have sex with, etc. and "mythingface," meaning, with *a proprietary air*, is perfect, because the snake is part of the chimera and is, thus, technically speaking, practicing the inalienable right to masturbate. I was tempted to change "licks" to "flicks." The *Leaf* senryu uses a night+bird 鵺 character for Nue, but the other, equally common one is sky/emptiness+bird 鵼. That better reflects the connotation of Nue-as-snark.

What about *the smell?*

In case, you have read senryu one might *think* support an *extraordinary love* for cunnilingus, I must regretfully point out that, aside from the filth-loving Asagiura, those I have seen are equivocal. On the whole, they show the poets found the act *ludicrous*. In case you have seen it, one *ku* Englished as *"nothing like / the taste of quim / to make you dizzy"* really meant, as we saw in the *Dry-kidney* chapter, that he/you has/have *a cunt-hangover* from too much sex. Likewise, for *"nothing whatsoever / approximates the taste / of pussy"* (ぼぼの味じ凡たとふる物ハなし 葉 11 *bobo no aji oyoso tatou(e)ru mono wa nashi*). One cannot preclude the *possibility* of literal taste, but *aji* probably means the *overall feeling a man experiences* with/in it. Another example, not yet mis/translated to my knowledge: *"A wife's taste: / it's neither great nor / a total waste!"* or *"A wife's taste: / nothing that's especially / good or bad"* (女房のあぢハ可もなくふかも無シ 摘 4-24 *nyôbô no aji wa ka mo naku fuka mo naku.*). This "taste" question is a good example of how metaphor, without which description would be so boring we would all prefer drawing to writing, can be a double-edged sword.

.

花娵のイ八をくハへる無言の場　葉
hanayome no mara o kuwaeru mugon no ba 30
(flower-bride's cock[acc] bite/suck/hold no-word-scene)

a silent scene
that night the bride is
full of cock

This one had me fooled at first reading. The verb *kuwaeru* means *to hold something in one's mouth*, a pipe or cigarette being the most common usage. *Hoh*, I thought, *the groom's penis has finally shut her up* (I, too, talk a lot, so *please* do not take this as misogyny). Indeed, a machine-translation would surely put the cock in her upper mouth. But *cunnilingus* right after marriage seems unlikely.

As Syunroan explains, she is finally – after a talkative day – speechless, savoring what fills her nether mouth, perhaps for the first time. Like "flavor/taste" (*aji*), we have an oral metaphor for coitus. On the other hand, the following *Willow ku*, almost surely concerns the act we are looking for:

かぐ事もならずさし身をへろり喰
kagu koto mo narazu sashimi o berori kuu 10-6
(smell[v] thing too be-not sashimi[acc] licking-eat)

you mustn't sniff
when wagging your tongue
you eat raw fish

when sticking out
your tongue to eat raw fish
man, do not sniff!

It is still considered impolite to sniff – a fish shop owner in Japan once became *infuriated* when I did it – but real *sashimi* is not eaten *berori to,* which is to say, tongue-out-of-mouth (usually it means sticking out one's tongue at someone), and *sashimi* can also mean either kissed lips or the female genitalia. So, the *ku* from Willow bk 10 would seem to say that if you lick quim, it should be done in a big way – by a man somewhat drunk? – in order not to notice the smell, speaking of which:

源氏名も開は大かた匂ふ宮
genjina mo kai wa ôkata nioumiya 葉 一
(genji name too cunt-as-for most scent-temple)

with genji names
"perfumed prince" is fitting
for most vaginas

Ladies-in-waiting in the Daimyô castles and courtesans often had nicknames from the chapter titles of the *Tale of Genji.* Chapter 42 features Nioumiya, Scent-temple, a prince who became a master of perfume-making to compete with his friend (probably Genji's child) Kaoru, the Fragrant Lord, whose scent welled up from within. I borrowed Solt's fine "fitting," which punfully (*niou/niau*) supplies the absent verb, and some more. The fragrant connotation of "*niou* = smell," as *written* here 匂, is belied by the fact that, phonetically, it could *stink.* And, even if it is not taken that way, an ironic, or *reverse-reading* (as when a fat man is called "Slim") seems far more than likely than a straight one.

釈迦如来嗅い穴から出たでなし 葉
shaka-nyorai kusai ana kara deta de nashi 12
(shakyamuni stinky hole from came [emph] not)

shakyamuni
didn't come out of any
stinking hole

大こくの好くまたぐらハきれいなり
daikoku no suku matagura wa kirei nari 万明 五
(big-black likes crotch-storeroom-as-for clean is)

the crotch godown
loved by the god of grain
is a clean one

The Incarnation of Truth Shakyamuni Tagatha. But Buddha is Buddha. Other *ku* testify he was delivered by C-section. The God of Grain is sometimes drawn with a forked daikon (*futamata-daikon* 二股大根, a ra<u>d</u>ishing crotch?) 'seated' on his shoulders. Why? I assume because grain (like beans) was born from the goddess's vagina. The *ku* is a very witty response to the draw "Just eat it up!" くらへ社すれ *kurae koso sure*). We *know* what the clean exception goes to prove. Further comment on these two *ku* and the following one is unnecessary.

いい女開もきたなく思われず 葉
ii onna bobo mo kitanaku omowazu 28
(good=beautiful woman pussy also dirty think-not)

with a beauty
even her cunt doesn't
seem dirty

a pretty girl
you feel even her cunt
is not dirty

What About Fellatio?

淫乱歯がゆく小へのこをしゃぶっている
inran ha-gayuku ko-henoko shabutte-iru 葉 *20*
(insatiable-teeth-itchy small-cock/s[acc] sucking)

crazed with desire
her itchy mouth is sucking
a small pecker

insatiable venus
her mouth finds and sucks
the small penis

Syunroan's standard explanation is that the widow or lady-in-waiting is not satisfied with vaginal intercourse with the slender penis of the young "shade-boy" (ch. 17) and her frustrated desire spills over in this way. The original has "itchy teeth," but Japanese often has teeth where we might have "mouth" ("mouth-feel" is "tooth-reply/response" (*hagotae*) etc.), but the indirect rendition where her mouth *finds* his penis in my second reading works better, doesn't it? I would add that an older woman might be drawn to the pretty smooth white penis far from the gnarled limbs (or hard dildos) she was used to. This is, surprisingly (for me at least), the only clear cock-sucking senryu about a Japanese – why "Japanese" in a moment – I have seen. Others are indirect:

嬶が口延ビあがらねば吸へぬなり
kaka-ga-kuchi nobi-agaraneba suenu nari 摘 *3-33*
(oldwife's mouth stretching-give/raise-not-if suck-not-be)

his old lady's mouth
unless he stretches south
he cannot suck it

his wife's mouth
he must stretch out and up
if he would suck

I imagined woman-on-top coitus, but Nishizawa says the *flea couple* (big woman + little man) are doing 69 with her on top and her "mouth" is the one not already fellating him. Since husbands and wives not specifically newly married were not big kissers – remember, kissing is "sucking" in Japanese – he must be right.

唇の毛切れは髪のこわい客
kuchibiru no kegire wa kami no kowai kyaku

for hair burn
of the lip, a john boasting
pubes like wood

hair-burnt lips
stiff pubes mark
a hard customer

~~*labial hairburn*~~
~~*that's what makes stiff pubes*~~
~~*a hard customer*~~

"Stiff" and "scary" are both *kowai.* I thought the lips were labia, but differ to sexologist Nishizawa, who believes it is about fellatio, on this one. He also opined that tongue-puppet or harping (*hamonika*) was more popular in literature because of being intrinsically more *kokkei* (滑稽), i.e. outlandish, droll, ridiculous, absurd.

へのこをなめろと魚へ書いて入れ 摘
henoko o namero to sakana e kaite-ire 4-17

suck my prick
he writes on a fish and
slips it within

lick my prick
says the note pushed
into a fish

Were the words on paper slipped into the fish's mouth or belly? Or were they written *on* the fish – brushes could do that – and left in a message-box? Regardless, it is harassment, not gag, by a young man turned down by a maid. *Nameru* is most commonly "lick," but can also mean sucking with tongue-contact (as a lollipop or the breast). But what should interest us here is not who is insulted or the nature of the verb. It is the negative connotation of cock-licking/sucking.

稀な事まらをしゃぶって四百取 葉 12
mare na koto mara o shabutte shihyaku tori

a rare thing
sucking a cock he gets
four hundred

越王はふさふさしくも拝味する
kô-ô wa fusafusashiku mo haimi suru 49-39

king koh
overwhelmed still
takes a taste

越王は喰い切ろうかと度々思ひ 113-38
kô-ô wa kui-kirô ka to tabitabi omoi

king koh
now and then considered
biting it off

In the Spring-Fall Era 春秋時代 of China, one generalissimo cum-monarch, the Japanese call Kô Ô and we, following the Chinese pronunciation, call the King of Yue 越王, Guo Jian 勾踐,was captured in battle and enslaved by the King of Wu 吳王, Fu Chai 夫差. That much, name pronunciation aside, early 19c senryu and Chinese television dramas see eye to eye. Then, they diverge. Senryu assume he sucked the penis of his enemy generalissimo cum-king, curing his cock of a long-time ailment (clap) in the process and was freed as a reward, while the modern Chinese have him licking a 胆 = gall bladder he kept in his room every night before going to sleep to keep himself motivated while living a slavish life of menial work. Hence, *"lie on faggots, licking bladder"* 臥薪嘗胆 for *biding one's time.* I do not yet know whether the gall-bladder idea – one wants to keep one's spleen up? – was misunderstood by a Japanese story-teller, or the Chinese doctored their history, but bladder-licker or cock-sucker – and some Japanese explanations include *both* – Guo Jian eventually not only won back his kingdom, but united China's 400-plus *countries* for the first time. Someone not knowing the legend would think that 400 was money for a blowjob. Gary Leupp notes the *extraordinary absence* of male-male fellation in the otherwise thriving homosexual culture of pre-modern Japan and elsewhere might be due to a skilled component (learning not to gag) of the *action* contradicting the *active-passive* categories. I *doubt* that, for skillful loving by women was appreciated. Is it not because most men fear putting their lives in the hands/mouths of other males?

~ *eddies* ~

Mother Superiors and Not Hearing the Cat. More about the *shûto*=old-wife, dictator over her daughter-in-law, in the *Fart* chapter. Just note that stereotypes may be qualified. In the *Tale of Genji* (c1000), we already hear that the bad stepmother stereotype is unfair and in senryu we hear of *good shûto*, though they may not be called by that term. Eg.:

すいな母そら寝入してはじめさせ 葉六
sui na haha soraneiri shite wa hajime sase

the kind mother
fakes falling asleep
to let them start

the smart mom
plays possum for her son
and the pussy

猫であろとは母の慈悲也後チは後 折句いろは引
neko de aro to wa haha no jihi nari nochi wa nochi 文化中

"it's probably a cat"
is a mother's mercy: what comes
later comes later!

The first *ku* is almost certainly about a shûto called by the more familiar and affectionate word, mother (*haha*). *Sui* means wise+kind+sensitive=knowing. The second *ku* is probably not about a *shûto* nor even sex noise. A mother protects her daughter and the "night-crawler" (caller), who inadvertently tripped on something (Suzuki), or otherwise made a noise, from the potential wrath of the father. We strayed a bit from cunnilingus, but I thought the overall picture of who is listening for what might be helpful to know.

* This *ku* has previously been Englished as: *"the good mother / fakes being asleep / while stimulating her man,"* a misreading made for lack of familiarity with senryu stereotypes.

~~~~~~

Playboys. **Narihira** by one account (others differ) enjoyed with 3,333 women, from the highest to the lowest, oldest to the youngest (and that doesn't include hundreds of boys).

業平はイ八へさねだこいつか出来　葉 25
narihira wa mara e sanedako itsuka deki

sooner or later
narihira got cunt corns
on his cock

Perhaps corns would best be left to feet, but "calluses" are not bumpy enough and *knobbies* (like on surfer's knees) would be even more specialized. There is a *ku* calling Narihira "a sea cucumber" in *Rise, Ye Sea Slugs!* (2003) The common explanation of it, which I gave, was that ladies men are *soft-spined*, because they will stoop to do anything in order to get what they are after. Yet, reading this, and recalling the bumps on Japanese sea cucumbers, I wonder . . . Be that as it may, here is a less appreciative view:

色男くふにゃたりぬ(な)と相模下女(いゝ) 摘 4-18
iro-otoko kuu nya tari(na)nu to sagami gejo(ii) 万明八
(color-man eat-for lacking [quote] sagami maid/says)

'a playboy is
just not enough food for me'
says the sagami

sagami maids
say 'those playboys are not
filling enough'

As mentioned elsewhere, a Sagami maid wants lots of sex, while a lover-boy, of which Narihira was the prototype, waste a lot of time and energy on sweet talk.

男でなりひらほどしたものハなし 摘
otoko de narihira hodo shita mono wa nashi 2-33
(man-as narihira amount done thing/person-as-for not)

as a man
no one has done
so many

Actually, the original says "As a man / none have done so many / *as Narihira,"* but a better poet would have left out his name. Note that the only Chinese character in the *ku* is "man." That is the best part of the *ku* for it implies, "but, when it comes to *women*, any number of street-walkers have Narihira beat many times over."

~~~~~~

Collection of Juices. Screech gives a senryu or *zappai* claiming "we" ("hairy-Chinese"= Occidentals) put vases under women's butts. Here is the original c̲ the correct Romanization & source: 毛唐人女ナの尻へ鉢を置キ 摘 3-20 *ketôjin onna no shiri e hachi o oki*).

~~~~~~

Angry Pecker ku. These are older than the fish: *"The maid, delighted / cuts open the letter: it's a cock"* (下女ハうれしくふうをきりやへ＿こ也　万安七 *gejo wa ureshiku fû o kiri ya henoko nari*) and *"Within a letter on scrap-paper he draws her a cock"* 切レ文の中カへへのこを書てやり　摘 1-32　◎ やめられぬ事 ◎ *kirefumi no naka e henoko o kaite yari*). And I have seen one from a man upset at a girl marrying another. What's odd is this: Japanese penises are less spear/weapon-like than Occidental ones, so why this usage?
~~~~~~

Where Men are Wood & Women Water

男木女水で来ル出合茶屋

十六
16

すっぽん笑ふ
Tea-*less* Tea Shops

何も 無ィ 茶やを尋ねる二人リつれ 万
nani mo nai chaya o tazuneru futari-zure 安元
(what-even-not tea-shop[obj] visit two-together)

pure turnover

visiting a tea shop
with nothing whatsoever
to sell: a couple

"To sell" is not specified in the original, but what else could "a shop with nothing" *not* have than items for sale? I guess the draw, *sukui koso sure* (すくひ社すれ), means "going for turn-over," which is to say profit made on the entrance fee to the place where sex was refreshment enough: "*Where they joust / without food or drink / rendezvous tea-shops*"(くひのみもせずにたゝかう出合茶や 万安八 *kui-nomi mo sezu ni tatakau deai-jaya*), but with phonetic letters I cannot tell for sure.

男木女水で来る出合茶屋
otoko ki onna mizu de kuru deai-jaya
(man/en tree woman/en water-as come dating-tea-shop)

the men as trees
the women as water come
to this tea-shop

the tea-for-two
where men come as trees,
women as water

The *deai-jaya*, is a *chaya*, or "tea-shop" for *deai*, or "dates," "trysts," "assignment," "rendezvous," etc.. So, what shall we call them? "Date tea shops?" "Rendezvous tea shops?" My J-E dictionary unkindly skips the word, either because it is obsolete or because the editors were also stumped. Japanese today describe a *deai-jaya* as the Edo era equivalent of a *rabu-hoteru*, the "love hotel" of the late-20c, for those without other places to go, or seeking facilities tailored for sex (The outlandish fittings, manifesting the exhuberant bubble years, got worldwide attention in the 1980's). The obvious sexual metaphor plays on the Chinese concept of five-elements 五行説where male=wood, female=water.

さねかしら木のやうになる出合茶や 万句合
sanegashira ki no yô ni naru deai-jaya 安永 2

tea-for-two
where clits also turn
into wood

where the clits
become like wood
date tea shops

Sane is usually "clitoris," sometimes "vulva." The overall content and pegged on "head" (*~kashira*), make it 100% clear this is about what the Chinese call the *lucky-tongue* here. My "also," guesses a play upon the elemental male = wood.

出合茶屋女は蛇なり男は蚊 摘 *4-18*
deai-jaya onna wa ja nari otoko wa ka

date tea-shops
the women become snakes
men, mosquitos

A snake *swallows*, a mosquito *stabs*. That beats the birds and the bees, doesn't it? Though men and women joined in these shops, senryu sought out the differences, even to the extent of having one descend to do "small-business" and the other "to go *shi-shi*" (出合茶屋小便に降おりしゝにおり *deai-jaya shôben ni ori shishi ni ori* 摘 1-3,柳 5-35). Different words for urinating? We have a *whole chapter* (27) on it.

おごの白あへ一種也出合茶屋
ogo no shiroae isshu nari deaijaya 摘 2-15
(ogo's white-sauce one-type is/become date-tea-shop)

just one dish
ogo with white sauce
the date tea-shop

it is a sort of
seaweed blancmange
date tea-shops

Lacking knowledge of various types of seaweed, English cannot describe many things. The closest thing to pubic hair would probably be spanish moss, but it is grey . . . The type of white-sauce mentioned does not bury condiments completely, but drips down over them. I used the name of a famous old European white-sauce to get a name in there, for if I used the proper name of the seaweed in question, the *ku* would have become a biology lesson.

たゝかう事二十余合出合茶や
tatakau koto nijû jo awase deaijaya 万安九
(fighting thing twenty-plus matches date-teashop)

it's a fight thing:
twenty-odd matches at once
the date tea-shop

date tea-shops
arena for a score or more
of gladiators

The enemies, which is to say men and women, face off in hand-to-hand, *cock to cunt combat.* We will soon see which side usually won, but first a rule:

出合茶屋ほれたほうから払いする 摘 1-14
deai-jaya horeta hô kara harai-suru (o shi 万)

date tea shops
the one with the crush
pays the bill

A more concrete earlier *ku* specifies the pock-marked party as the one who puts out the money (出合茶やあばたつつらが金を出し *deaijaya abatatsu tsura ga kane o dashi* 12-23). Payment by the infatuated party seems more natural than boy-pays or Dutch; but, whatever the assymetry of love, they were equally there for sex:

お　しなからさうしをする出合茶や
oeshinagara sôji o suru deai-jaya 万 天四

cleaning-up
with a hard-on
the date tea-shop

Since even noble Japanese were known for cleaning up at their lodges (*Topsy-turvy 1585*, item #11-17), I first imagined a customer between rounds, but came to settle on an employee. A man surrounded by sex either experiences a state of horniness that might be called rutting, or loses his desire altogether (As a grad. student in Hawaii, I responded to an ad for a job paying double-the-minimum wage for speaking Japanese: selling porn to Japanese tourists (hidden under chocolate-covered macadamia nuts to fool customs). I lasted only two weeks.) This man would be one of the former. The "cleaning" is mostly picking up wiping paper (ch.28).

出合茶やへ　こをわたし切ﾘにする 万
deai-jaya henoko o watashi-kiri ni suru 安八

date tea shops
where i get a penis
all to myself

date tea shops
where each one gets
her own pecker

Among the women going to these tea-shops, the proverbial lustful widow and horny *oku jôchû,* ladies-in-waiting if you would think high, harem chambermaids, if you wish to think low, figured in heavily. The latter were depicted as having to share one penis with scores or more (3,000 if the Chinese trope is counted) other women (ch.4). *Watashi-kiri,* or "all mine" – with a first-person pronoun used by a female speaker – suggests the subject, but the first-person can be used as third-person, also, hence the second reading.

出合くたひれい__つたりにぎつたり
deai kutabire ibittari nigittari 万天四

the rendezvous
all that teasing, all
that squeezing!

出合茶やへ＿こにちつともたれきみ
deaijaya henoko ni chitto motare-gimi

date tea-shops
where cocks feel like they
ate too much

へのこにげつふうをさせる出合茶や
henoko ni geppû o saseru deaijaya 摘 2-38

they will make
your old pecker belch
date tea-shops

出合茶やへのこのありつたけハする
deaijaya henoko no arittake wa suru 摘 1-35

date tea-shops
where cocks are milked for
all they're worth

date tea-shops:
where you use your cock
until it runs-out

ありつ切男をしぼる出合茶や
arikkiri otoko o shiboru deaija 摘 2-36

where ev'ry ounce
of manhood is wrung-out
date tea-shops

かつ水に成ルとわかれる出合茶や
katsumizu ni naru to wakareru djy 万明六

when the water
runs dry, then its goodbye!
date tea-shops

根をしはってももふいけぬ出合茶や
ne o shibatte mo mô ikenu deaija
(root binding even already can't datetea-shp)

even torniquettes
won't keep the blood in them
date tea-shops

even root-bound
no more wood's to be found
date tea-shops

出合茶やばくやかつるぎ折レるなり 万
deaijaya bakuya-ga-tsurugi oreru nari 安六

date tea-shops
where even excaliber
would break

出合茶やのちハへ　このこしかぬけ
deaijaya nochi wa henoko no koshi ga nuke

date tea-shops
the pecker ends up with
a pulled back

万天五↑

出合茶屋男ハ半死はんしよなり
deaijaya otoko wa hanshihansei nari

date tea-shops
where men are left 'twixt
life and death

↑万安四

It was obvious that date-tea-shop senryu were full of hard sex, but only after reviewing many *ku* for this book did I finally notice something more interesting: most tea-shop *ku* depict the relative weakness of man vs. woman! "Excaliber" is the female of a pair of famous Chinese swords 干将+莫邪/耶(Kan Chiang & Moyeh/ jp.: *bakuya*) which, used loosely, means a magical blade, as it was the better known name and part of a saying: *"Even the sword Moyeh depends on who wields it."*

わかれ際そろそろ開のあとねだり 葉
wakare-giwa sorosoro bobo no ato-nedari 36

just when the time
comes to part, the bobo
begs for more

出合茶や何か男のわびるこへ 13
deaijaya nani ga otoko no wabiru koe -37

date tea-shops
what's this! do we hear men
begging pardon?

出合茶やゆるせの声は男なり 万
deaijaya yuruse no koe wa otoko nari 安 2

date tea-shops
the "have mercy! voices
are all male

Moderns might find a *man* wanting one more round in the first *ku*; but, having read hundreds of tea-shop *ku*, I think we must go with Rembrandt's *before* and *after* of Joseph and Pointar's Wife, and make the *bobo* the greedy party.

あるひて行くかと出て見る出合茶や 万
aruite yuku ka to dete miru deaijaya 安五

going out, he sees
if he can make it home
on his own two feet

going out, he sees
if he can make it home
on his own two feet

This is exceptionally good for the imagined detail. If the man finds he is just too tired – his back out of joint? – he will call for a sedan.

女の跡トからよわりはてたおとこ 万
onna no ato kara yowari hateta otoko 安六

trailing after
a woman, an utterly
spent man

Images of salmon, drained of their life-force, gasping and slowly turning over in the stream. One would expect this on the Isle of Women, but in macho Edo?

出合茶やすもものような顔で出る 摘
deaijaya sumomo no yôna kao de deru 4-11

pink tea-shops
coming out with their faces
plump as plums

出合茶やあんまりしないつらで出る 摘
deaijaya anmari shinai kao de deru 3-2

leaving with her
i-don't-do-it-much face
a date tea-shop

Pink? Why not? I just do not like the sound of "date tea-shop." Others could be changed, too, if you wish. The plum in question may be a relative of the prune, but it is not dried. A man coming out into the sunlight after hours of love-making will be dry and wrinkled as a raisin, while a woman only gains humour and energy. She could check in for a new battle the next day while *for four or five days / a man's useless* (出合茶や四五日おとこ用だゝす万天三*deaijaya shigo-nichi otoko yô datazu* (★ in Japanese, "useless" is "role stand-not" & puns c̲ not erecting).

もふ女見るもいやだと出合いい
mô onna miru mo iya da to deai ii
(ever woman see even yuck is date says)

late in the date
"i don't care if i never see
another woman"

"i don't even want
to see a woman" he says
after the date

It could be after the date talk with a buddy, or it could be man-to-man banter in the restroom at the tea-shop.

出合茶や二つにわれてかへるなり万
deaijaya futatsu ni warete kaeru nari 明三

date tea-shops
and splitting in two
they go home

pink tea-shops
they split in two for
the return trip

ひそひそと繁盛する出合茶屋
hisohiso to hansei suru deaijaya 26-15

flourishing
in a hush, hush way
pink tea-shops

This took me to Plato's original sphere, but the draw-verse was a bit more down to earth: "*keep it under wraps!*" (かくれ社すれ *kakure koso sure*)

其跡へ貝殻残す出合茶屋
sono ato e kaigara nokosu deaijaya

pink tea rooms
they leave behind their
empty shells

leaving behind
a mound of empty shells
the deaijaya

Issa has a *ku* with piles of oyster shells. But *these* shells had no fish. They contained stamina-enhancing medicine (証句：丸薬の貝殻残る出会茶屋 *ganyaku no kaigara nokoru deaijaya*). The female part is called by a dozen types of shells, depending upon its development and characteristics; one unfamiliar with senryu, not knowing the voluntary (the horrid Usanianism "pro-active"comes to mind) nature of the sex at these shops might mistakenly read abandoned women into this. The *ku* was so lyrical, I *had to* use the *pink* translation and original *deaijaya.*

Lotus Blossoms & Snapping Turtles: *the* Tea Shop *over the* Pond

ねないのは銭にならぬと池の茶や 万
ne nai no wa zeni ni naranu to ike no chaya 安七

rootlessness
brings us no money jokes
pond-tea-man

"no money comes
from those who don't sleep"
mr. pond tea shop

"the money comes
from the roots" says the host
a pond tea shop

The reference is to the lotus blossoms with their roots in the mud. "Root" is a homophone of "sleep," which in Japanese, like English, means fucking. A place and its owner or manager can be called the same thing in Japanese, at least if the place name ends in *ya* (屋). I regret the syllabets wasted for "man," "mr" and "host," but it could not be helped. ↓ 摘 3-19

根が好で蓮飯二人喰に行き
ne ga suki de hasu-meshi futari kui ni yuki

liking their root
the couple goes to eat
a lotus lunch

出合茶や蓮を見にきて立テ込める
deaijaya hasu o mi ni kite tate-komeru

a tea-shop room
coming for the lotus bloom
they hide inside

The first is not "root hog *or* die," but root hog *and* die. The most formidable word for penis next to *mara* was *dankon,* or "man-root." Evidently, lunches were on sale at the tea shops, but we know what these couples are after.

手の音トにすつぽんのうく出合茶や 摘
te no oto ni suppon no uku deaijaya 3-22

the suppon rise
to the sound of hands
date tea-shops

up pop turtles
to the sound of hands
pink tea-shop

手を打つとすっぽんが浮く出合茶屋
te o utsu to suppon ga uku deaijaya

clap your hands
and up pops a *suppon!*
date tea-shop

Soft shelled turtles, not the ferocious alligator turtle but a type of snapping turtle all the same, have long springy necks from where, after decapitation, blood flows for men to drink. The way turtles are killed recalls the punishment for adulterers, but I assume they were sold as a potency enhancer. 'Scientific'evidence of the correctness of the correspondence is used to sell the same today, in liquor, pills or in the raw (promising a 'dreamed for second-round' to old men c̲ demanding wives in an ad I saw). As Buddhists, there was some *guilt* involved here. I recall a story of a slow woman working in the pleasure-quarters, who had a bit too much drink and failed to recall someone pushing jingle-balls (*rin no tama* pg. 89-90) up her twat the night before, feeling them plop out at her toilet and panicking because she was convinced the karma of her parents killing snapping turtles for customers at the pond tea-shop had resulted in her emasculating a man with her lower mouth!

すっぽんの度／＼たまされるふいた紙 摘
suppon no tabitabi damasareru fuita kami 1-16

snapping turtles
are fooled now and then
wind-blown paper

the poor suppon
are fooled now and then
love-wiped paper

The verb *fuku* can mean blow or wipe, but the former requires passive tense here, which it is not. I leave "wind-blown" anyway because the fooling need not be deliberate; the wind might blow such paper to a *suppon*.

其下ですつぽん首をおやしてる 柳
sono shita de suppon kubi o oyashiteru 28-15

beneath them
the snapping turtle necks
have hard-ons

池で鳴ルやうだと二人リ首を上 摘
ike de naru yô da to futari kubi o age 1-23

it seems the bell
sounds from the pond: two
raise their heads

Turtles, straining their necks to reach for food, do indeed seem to erect. Japanese enjoyed the theme of *suppon* so much there are even *ku* seemingly but not really about them. Re. the second *ku,* there is no *bell* specified in the original. Because the conjugation of the verbs with the character 鳴 are not specified in some versions of the *ku*, it is often made out to be *naku* 鳴く and this "cry" made out to be the calls of the turtles. One round-robin discussant of *Pluck* wonders if *naru* is not more likely (as it was so specified in the older *Million*, suggesting the Goddess of prosperity and beauty, Benzaiten (who has a shrine on an island in said pond), shouting at an adulterous couple; but, finding no precedents for such behavior by said Goddess, he switches to the *roar* of turtles jumping into the water. Another discussant, points out the parallel behavior of turtle heads poking up from the water and lovers: *"A suppon's come! / two faces poke up / [from the futon]"* (すっぽんが居やすと顔を二つ出し　万？明四智一 *suppon ga iyasu to kao o futatsu dashi*). And, yet another cites a work on popular culture which points out that this refers to the bells of Ueno marking nightfall, time to close the lover's heaven. That makes sense because it is the most natural usage of the verb and because sound does travel along water. The turtles are only a light evocation.

秋お前おきなと払う池の中 万
aki omae okina to harau ike no naka 安二
(fall, you. thanks and pays pond-middle)

"'til next fall!
thanks, bud!" paying
in mid-pond

"'be here in fall!"
"much obliged!"paying
in mid-pond

A widow or chamber-maid has footed the entire bill because she had both more money and desire than the man. Such crisply expressed familiarity – helped by the Kinki (Kyoto-Osaka-Nagoya area's direct "you" and graceful "thanks" – has a pleasant ring to it. My reading is based on the idea that women tended to have the most energy after the battle, that men were more likely to be away for part of the year and a man wouldn't say *thank you* like that; but a guess is only a guess.

おそろしくしたとはき出す出合茶 摘
osoroshiku shita to haki-dasu deaicha 3-7

After frightful things are done,
the date tea shop is swept out.

After they do frightful things,
the date tea shop vomits them

We cannot tell if it is 吐き出す (throw-up/disgorge) or 掃き出す(sweep-out). The latter seems most likely, but the former is more than possible, for the tea-shop easily becomes the subject, rather than place, and many customers/lovers do suddenly leave at vespers.

~~~~~~
~~~~~~

~ *eddies* ~

***"Clits like Wood"* got me to thinking.** Were I in Japan and received a grant to do the clit justice, it would not be hard to come up with a senryu collection titled, say, *One Hundred Clits*. I have not enough for a good chapter, but considering the neglect the clitoris – has suffered at the hands of English speakers (to think we do not even have a native word for it!), some more *clit ku* will be introduced:

実頭の玄関の破風造り 葉末
sanegashira no genkan no hafu-zukuri leaf
(berry/nut-head=clit's frontgate's blockwind-make)

the clitoris is
the wind-block of the
portal of love

the clit stands
the spitting image of
a gate's hafu

A Japanese *genkan* is a roofed-entrance+vestibule. That roof has what looks like a small corner of a rooftop stuck on it so water and wind spilling over the larger roof is directed to both sides. It might be described as a miniature gable or a fake short dormer without windows. If English has a better word for such a *hafu*, I do not know it.

開中の重役らしいさねがしら 葉
bobo naka no omoyaku rashii sanegashira 22
(cunt among's director/important-role seems clit-head)

all the bobo crew
must take their orders from you
captain clitoris

Since *sane* at this time came to be used occasionally to mean the labia minora as well, there is a nuance of being head (*kashira*) of that in the name, but it also may have been seen as the functional head because the spring-prints (*shunga*) often show men stimulating the clitoris manually, not for foreplay but *while* their penis is *in situ*. I cannot recall seeing that in European erotica, though I cannot imagine that no one did that!

小便が鼻づらかするさねッ首 葉18
shôben ga hanazura kasuru sanekkubi

pee grazing
the tip of the nose
of the clitoris

As Syunroan points out, this is probably painted from the imagination – but what things men do imagine! I think it likely this may be one upmanship of a print showing a blind woman's piss grazing a peeking man's nose, but, be that as it may, the presence of the clitoris is more strongly felt with this simple ku than with sexual ones.

読みかけて娵笑い出すさねかづら 新編24
yomi-kakete yome warai-dasu sanekazura

starting to read
his name the bride cracks up:
sanekazura

She is playing a card game where one poem each from a hundred poets . Having just learned the word *sanekashira* or *sanegashira* from her husband or a sex-instruction book presented at marriage, she suddenly finds something sexy in the name of the poet. In Japanese, the two words are only one letter apart (さねかしら vsさねかつら). *Cuntologia* has a stanza from a 19c or early-20c song (魔山人『赤湯文字』1979 出典) with another name for the clitoris which it shared with the cunt in general, *mame* or "bean."

Mr. Flea took a seat on the head of the bean –
Hoh, the hole's deep! And he threw himself in!

(mame no atama ni nomi ga koshi kakete
fukai ana ja to mi o nageru)

~~~~~~

Toilets at Deaijaya. Advertizements in restrooms are a phenomenon far less studied than W.C. graffitti but, with the passage of time, equally interesting. If I am not mistaken, the following *ku* concern toilets at a date-tea-shop.

子おろしやけいこ上るり見てハたれ 万
ko oroshi ya keiko agaruri mite wa tare 天四

cheap abortions
and lessons in this or that
all seen pissing

小便をしながらおろす思案か出 万
shôben o shinagara orosu shian ga de(ru?) 明五

while pissing,
plans to abort begin
to take shape

The draw-verse for the second is *"What a scary thing!"* (*kowai koto kana*). That is not so much the idea of having a child or an abortion per se, as thinking of it immediately after sex. With Japanese toilets, women as well as men face the wall when urinating, so it is harder to say to whom the ads are addressed. (「あがるり」?)

~~~~~~

Turtles & Possible Allusions to Turtles. Some one could do a whole book on turtle senryu.

かむやうに成たと笑ふ出合茶屋　摘 2-28
kamu yô ni natta to warau deaijaya

Pink tea shop –
'You've finally learned to nip,'
says he, laughing.

Love bites? Because of the location, I cannot help thinking his lover has learned to better control her vaginal gate from snapping turtles – call it sympathetic magic – after several visits?

蓮池でへのこくわへて引こまれ　摘 2-24
hasu-ike de henoko kuwaete hikkomare

At the lotus pond,
sucking on peckers,
they pull you in.

The turtles' revenge? Alluding to the water sprite, *kappa* – though they were commonly believed to attack through the anus? Could they do that? Or, is this simply the hyperbole to beat all hyperbole, where the door of the date tea-shop is conflated with hungry cunts conflated with snapping turtles submerging with their prey? After all, we *do* have the *snake* as swallowing tube as woman, so, why not the same for the *turtle?* As I learned reading Lacquer's overly simplistic (esp. with regard to the clitoris) yet entertainingly written account of the shift from seeing women as men inside out to seeing them as a different animal so to speak in the West (*Making Sex* 1990), to the ancients – was it Aristotle? – and, later, Vesalius our 'father of anatomy,' the vagina was considered the penis pulled outside-in and the penis the vagina pulled inside-out. Well, with this turtle, you get the inside and the outside all in one long neck and head, don't you!

細工は流ゝ亀がへのこに成り　摘
saiku wa ryûryû kame ga henoko nari 4-14
(detail-work-as-for style-style turtle/s-the pecker are/become)

the detail-work
for each dildo differs
as do the turtles

whate'er school
of art, the turtles all turn
into peckers

the detail work
of a trademark turtle is
pure pecker

turtles turning
into peckers according
to their makers

But *this* turtle *ku* has nothing to do with the date-tea-shops. I would have put it with the masturbatory aids of chapter 4 had not the oxen taken up so much space. It is either about penile armor, the most expensive dildos or both. The turtle in question is not a soft-shell *suppon*, but I do not know whether it was a sea turtle or galapagos tortoise or . . .

<u>*Shade-boys at Work*</u>
陰間の小人生劇

十七 17

後から前から
Foes Fore & Aft

~~~~~~

生酔に成て陰間を壱度買い
nama-ei ni natte kagema o ichido kai

pissed out of his mind
just once, he buys
a boy's behind

The boy in the original is a *"shade/shadow-space."* I first assumed *"kagema"* described the cubicles in the so-called tea-rooms where the catamites plied their trade, while a respondent associated it with the female principle, the *yin.* Actually, it derives from 17c *kabuki* where it referred to the aspiring or apprenticing kabuki actors who hung out in the shadow of the stage and were known to sell sexual favors to the audience. The name beat out synonyms including "shade-guy" (*kagerô*) and "shade-dance" (*kagemai*). As a *catamite* is not necessarily a pro, while the *kagema* was, and we lack a common English term, we must be inventive. Meet "shade-boy," "shadow-boy," etc..

あんまりな嘘はかげまのよがりよう
anmari na uso wa kagema no yogari yô 88-19

a lie of a lie
is a shadow boy's lie,
his love cry

a lie beyond
all belief: the love cry
of a shade-boy

Yogari includes all expressions of excitement verging on and including orgasm, but generally means the cries/yelps. Even coming from a woman selling sex they are suspect. From a man, or, rather, boy, they are doubly suspect. The bald-lie seems the subject, but my second reading, where his cry shares our attention, seems better. The pitiful image of the *kagema* in senryu contrasts with the *wakashû,* the gay and/or transvestite "young-crowd," loved by *haikai*, who, showing off their finery at cherry blossom viewings, etc., openly strut their stuff.
~~~~~~

雪隠へ二度来たかげまなぐさまれ
setchin e nido kita kagema nagusamare 5-38

a shadow-boy
who visits the wc twice
is consoled

高年の陰間みごそいものを食い
kônen no kagema migosui mono o kui

an old shade-boy
eats something that won't
stay down

The toilet in question, *setchin*, is for the bowels. The boy suffers a client who comes repeatedly, or worse, suffers from piles or the runs. In the second, a boy whose butt has grown hairy must do something else which he evidently is having a hard time with. One might think this *wretched* stuff, but the *mae-ku,* or refrain that elicited the first was *rippa narikeri (x2),* or *"How splendid he's become!"*

馬鹿陰間床入まえに行く屁用
baka-kagema toko-iri mae ni yuku he-yô
(fool-kagema, bed-enter before going, fart-use)

before it starts
a foolish shade-boy goes
to take a fart

The substitution of what normally would be a *piss* or a *shit* (小用 small-use, 大用 big-use, respectively) with a *fart* intimates that the *kagema* may have been so nervous he thought the former was coming, when it wasn't. Or, did he even more foolishly believe his clients minded farts?

其の時は五臓にまとうかげまの屁
sono toki wa gozô ni matou kagema no he 94-9
(that time-as-for five-organs-to/on cover shade-space's fart)

at that moment
it sinks into the bones
a shade-boy's fart

coming in a swoon
he cops the boy's fart &
swells like a balloon

Apparently, the catamite farts right when his customer is coming and, as a result, the smell is felt in a different and deeper way than the usual. Reading #2 is a shortened P.D. paraverse. In the chapter on bonzes, the same farts give us trouble. The hard part is deciding whether to take them *positively* or *negatively*. Senryu really does make you, the reader do most of the work. It goes without saying that sodomy asks for scatological (fart or shit) humor. In reality, the pressure put on a woman's belly by a "missionary" not gentleman enough to use his elbows might be as likely to force a fart, but who knows!

仏縁が有りてかげまの繁盛さ
butsu-en ga arite kagema no hansei sa 67-31

buddha helps those
who help bonzes? shade-boys
are flourishing

buddha's good graces:
how those boys flourish
in shady places

Yoshichô. We saw the relationship of bonzes with sodomy and Yoshichô with boy-brothrels in chapter 12, but here are a couple more banal confirmations: *"The ones showing their hand in Yoshichô are the diligent priests"* (よし町てうつハりちぎな和尚也 6-15 *yoshichô de utsu wa richigi na oshô nari*); *"The good bonze, erect all the way to Yoshichô"* (よし町へ行にハ和尚たちのまま 18-27) *yoshichô e yuku ni wa oshô tachi no mama*). As mentioned before, *oshô* is a high-level bonze, so I make them *priests* or *good.* Yoshichô costs too much for poor bonzes. There is a better *ku* about Yoshichô I read and lost long ago. I cannot recall whether Yoshichô was at the start or end of it, but that makes little difference, for I often change the order in translation. If you recall, octopus=bonzes (p 205-7).

when octopi are
out of season, the catch is
down in yoshichô

yoshichô suffers
a dry spell when octopus
is out of season

The *ku* included a word I still recall looking up: *shike,* a long period when rain or wind keeps fishing boats from going out and/or getting large catches. "Dry spell" is for chuckles. My father spent just such a time with Japanese fishermen and was impressed with how they drank rot-gut – "like fish" – the whole time.

地者だと陰間の笑う寺小姓 152-6
jimono da to kagema no warau tera koshô

local molly boy!
a shade-boy pokes fun at
a monk's helper

'amateur tail'
the shade-boys laugh at
the acolytes

Little boys, seven to eleven, of commoner parents often boarded at temples while doing odd jobs for schooling. They were stereotypically screwed by the bonzes. The shade-boy as a pro, puts them down. "Local-guy/gal" *always* meant a rank amateur in the trade. Whether a boy who accompanied a priest to Yoshichô, to mind his sandals, etc. is addressed or such boys in general is not clear.

かげまと逃げて尻を喰う屎たはけ 96-33
kagema to nigete shiri o kuu kuso-tawake

licking ass, he
skeedaddles c̲ a shade-boy
mr. shit-stupid

a shit-for-brains nut
flees c̲ shadeboy & ends up
scoffing his butt

The accepted way to abscond is to be a poor bachelor in love with a courtesan who, having been bought by her owners, has a huge debt to work-off or be paid-off early by a wealthy patron. Then, you do it, maybe getting yourself killed (for it is illegal) and turned into a romantic play. The top shade-boys in the elite establishments demanded courtesan-class prices, but most were cheap in both senses of the word and only a total moron would abscond with one. The *shit* before the "stupid" is an intensifier. To be overly sincere is to be *kuso-majime, shit*-sincere, too honest, *kuso-shôjiki, etc.*. Both readings owe something to P.D..

よし町ハせまい所てはんじやうし 万明三
yoshichô wa semai tokoro de hanjô shi

yoshichô town
where prosperity's found
in narrow places

Love it or hate it, the ordure shaft was mined for ore in Yoshichô. But, as we shall see, that shaft was not the only source of income for the boy brothrels.

中條てたび／＼おろすかけまの子 摘
chûjô de tabitabi orosu okama no ko 1-31

the abortionist
sometimes sees to the child
of a shade-boy

sometimes the child
of a catamite is dropped
by the abortionist

How could this be? In many cultures, the line between *hetero-* and *homo-* sexuality was not drawn in indelible ink. Japan was one of them.

よし町ハ和尚をおぶい後家をだき 万
yoshichô wa oshô o obui goke o daki 安六

in yoshi-town
they piggyback monks
& hug widows

後家出家かげま前後に敵をうけ
goke shukke kagema zengo ni teki o uke

widows & monks
the shade-boy has a foe
in back, in front

monks! widows!
a shade-boy has foes
front and back

よし町でとしまの分ハ弐役し やわらかな事
yoshichô de toshima no bun wa futayaku shi 2-26

in yoshichô
the older ones have to
play two roles

For the first *ku,* I write "monks" for the beat, though *oshô,* prosperous priests, are likely for the first and prosperous men who have retired for the robes in the second. The first *ku* is better for turning society upside-down, as babies are piggybacked by women in Japan, but the additional wordplay (*goke*=after= home/ family=widow+*shukke*=leave-home/family/monk) in the second *ku* is splendid. The third *ku,* with the draw *"flexible indeed,"* is more of an explanation. We will return to those widows soon, first, let us see just what is happening to the boys:

まらが半むくれかげまの中どしま 葉20
mara ga han-mukure kagema no chûdoshima

his cock half-peeled
a shadow-boy's
middle-age

両めんに成ルとかけまハやすくなり 万
ryômen ni naru to kagema wa yasuku nari 天ニ

a shade-boy
is cheaper with both sides
in circulation

with both sides
in use, a shade-boy
grows cheaper

十九廿歳陰間にすれば老の坂
juku hata sai kagema ni sureba oi no saka

nineteen, twenty
for a shade-boy it's called
over the hill

けつござれへのこござれと売ってやり 末摘
ketsu gozare henoko gozare to utte-yari 4-3

"we have asses!
we have cocks!" just so
they hawk 'em

they are sold
just so: "asses for you!"
cocks for you!

Unlike girls who tend to have their first menarches within a year or two of their friends, the age at which the erect male glans emerges from its hood varies tremendously. Many come out by the time they get their permanent teeth, but an equal number wait for puberty. Because Japanese were not circumcised and bathed in public, they knew the process well (ch.19), hence, the first senryu describing boys in their pre- or early teens. As the second *ku* makes clear, the main demand for the *kagema* came from men, so the added versatility of being able to do women, too, did not offset the loss of youth. "Old-age hill" is the original idiom in the third *ku.* Once that hill was crossed and shade-boys started smelling like men, with hair sprouting around their chrysanthemums, they were expected to serve the needs of the female cliental, typically wealthy widows, more rarely, the partially cloistered chamber-maids, or ladies-in-waiting of the daimyô's/ nobles' residences who frequented the better kagema establishments.

よし町ハ化ヶそうなのを後家へ出シ
yoshichô wa bakesônano o goke e dashi 3-21

yoshichô: where
the morphing boys go
to the widows

in yoshichô
the changelings are
fed to widows

The Japanese verb *bakeru* (*bake-*) means changing into something spooky, usually not on purpose. We know about it – take that kissed frog for example – but have no choice other than the plain "change" or "transform," or the too-new "morphing." I *love* that Japanese verb and I hate translating it (for better or worse, I am writing under the influence of whiskey in chocolate milk). 万安五↓

女客陰間をえらい目にあわせ 摘
onna kyaku kagema o erai me ni awase 1-7

female customers
leave the shadow-boys
in a real pickle

申のこく無いとかげまはこしがぬけ
saru no koku nai to kagema wa koshi ga nuke

without curfew
shade boys would throw
their backs out

Female customers want to see a lot of spending for what they spend, and that means wearing out the shade-boys, who may or may not have had to *come* when poked by male customers. In respect to the first *ku,* the word *erai* in Edo generally meant splendid (偉い), but many if not most of the shade-boys harked from Kansai, especially the Osaka area, where the expression even today can mean something *troublesome* or *awful*. This was no laughing matter. As discussed in *Dry-kidney* (ch.7), Japanese (and most men in the world?) genuinely worried about losing their vital humours. The literal translation of the symptom noted in the second *ku* is "hip/s pulled-out (of joint)," i.e. *throwing ones lower back out*. Even today, when that happens to a man in Japan, he is kidded about overdoing it the night before. The senryu plays against another *ku* I recall where the "jaw"of a woman's cunt is thrown out of joint by too much fucking. The "curfew" is literally the "hour of the monkey," the last hour of the afternoon. The chambermaids had a strict curfew, so I think it refers to them, though it might have been for sodomy with bonzes and other boy-lovers. But overdoing it was but half the problem with female customers. There was mental duress.

芳町で牛蒡を洗う女客 末 摘
yoshichô de gobô o arau onna kyaku 1-4

yoshichô, where
the female customers
wash burdocks

よし町で御菜せん香折レといふ
yoshichô de on-na senkô-ore to iu 4-19

in yoshi-chô,
they call madame greens
joss-stick breakers

Some of the *kagema* may have been homosexual all the way down to their pinkies, in which case, performing with the other sex may have been torture, while others, at first happy to do so, may have been ashamed to find their toys *inadequate*, for these women with money to play were generally old (one old 7-7 points out *"The women's voices are the low ones in Yoshichô"* 女の声は低いよし町 武玉七 *onna no koe wa hikui yoshichô*), with slack ones, in which moving a slender member would be, as the above *ku* makes explicit, *rinsing a burdock root in the sea* (大海に牛蒡). Japanese, like Celts – I recall reading poems by proud, sex-loving women insulting scrawny penises, but the name of the book is in one of my journals, from which poverty (lack of space) separates me – noted how boy-cocks grew bulkier *after* adulthood. "Honorable green" is standard for a woman from the palace, *i.e.* chamber-maid, perhaps because ancient poetry had them out digging for greens in the spring for their souvereign. Joss sticks set the customer's (and sex-worker's) time. Instead of punching in a time-clock the courtesans or shade-boys got their supply of incense-timers and customers had to get off before theirs burned out. Here, the joss does double duty: these wonmen tended to overstay their time and were too much for the boy's thin members. That is not to say some of the women did not appreciate pretty little things:

女客白うほなども聞て出シ 20-38
onna-kyaku shirauo nado mo kiite dashi

female customers
asking about white-bait
are shown some

A picture of a "whitebait" (*Salanx microdon*) in a haiku *saijiki* shows why it is used as a metaphor for slim white fingers. When young they are translucent. These would be women wanting to see the boys, all of the boys, on sale.

女客後架がよいで目にかかり 摘
onna-kyaku kôka ga yoi de me ni kakari 3-18

female customers
you see them because of
the good toilets

female customers
the toilets are good so
they come around

Have I focused too much on the sad side of the *kagema?* With the location of Yoshichô not too far from the theaters, the tea shops were far from dingy. The atmosphere, at least from the perspective of the customers, was probably bright as can be. I do not know if the above *ku* describes the customer toilets in all the shops on the block or only those, or even one shop, that catered to females, but when I found it, I knew I *must* translate it, for some things never change from age to age or place to place and one of them is the relationship of women and toilets.

よし町をかへる女中の大またき 万
yoshichô o kaeru jochû no ô-matagi 宝九

palace women
with manly strides return
from yoshichô

from yoshichô
back they go, stretching their
palace crotches

The draw was *"they're counting but"* (かぞえ社すれ) the trick is guessing what. Is it the number of women who went to Yoshichô? Strides? The number returning to the long-flat before the night curfew? No, *probably, the strokes of the bell*. And they rush because they stayed up to the last minute to satisfy their pent up lust for male flesh. I almost dropped this *ku* because the wit walks with that "big-crotch-stride," which may mean just *walking quickly* but is literally erotic. *Manly* (vs mincing lady steps) and my other tricks only half-work.

スズメ殿はく下駄も芳町狭き 敬愚
suzumedono haku geta mo yoshichô semaki

high on stilt-shoes
stylishly narrow, chipper
yoshichô sparrows

芳町雀箱せこと輪けさ也 柳 118
yoshichô suzume hakoseko to wagesa nari

yoshichô sparrows
surplice and tissue boxes
a narrow de rigor

A man who frequented Yoshichô was called a Yoshichô *suzume*, or "sparrow," and among the fashions born on that block (the name says "town" but it is really a street) was the extraordinarily narrow Yoshichô *geta*, the stilted shoes with a sandal-like top. If shoes are symbolic of concavity (perhaps a stretch for sandals), could these *geta* reflect the "narrow" straits of anal sex? I made up the first *ku*. The genuine one does not actually have the word "narrow," but that is how the *hakoseko* tissue box, usually carried by samurai and their wives or daimyô maids, is described. The "ring-surplice" (I was tempted to drop the *sparrow* and start "yoshi-chô things" for the *ing* chime) is a surplice narrowed down to a circular band worn over one shoulder circling the torso diagonally. But, for all the attention given to Yoshichô in senryu, the numbers for male prostitutes on that block given by a 1768 guidebook cited by Leupp, were *67*. If that was the case, I think it safe to say there were ten senryu written for every shade-boy there!

◎ *playing with stereotypes* ◎

~~~~~~

ごぜの客四十ぐらひのかげまか出 万明二
goze no kyaku yonjû gurai no kagema ga deru

a blind singer
out comes a shade-boy
of forty or so

While there were wealthy blind troupe leaders, who were men and also money-lenders, the female blind singers and/or masseurs called *goze* were probably not wealthy enough to buy *kagema*, but if they could, they would have no trouble *feeling* age. This plays on a shade-boy trait we have already discussed, their age limits. Were it not a shade-boy, one might fool the blind woman with a white-haired partner of sixty or seventy. Forty for a *kagema* is like a hundred. Here is another *ku* playing on a stereotype about shade-boys and another about wet-nurses. I would guess you can read it without difficulty:

よし町をふらつく乳母は不人相
yoshichô o buratsuku uba wa funinsô 6-7

a wet-nurse
walking about yoshichô
out of place

The original says "not-physiogyny," that is, her *wide* member would not match the *thin* members of the boys for sale. Two stereotypes re-enforcing each other.
~~~~~~

a wife's perspective

よし町へ行キなと女房かさぬなり 万天元
yoshichô e iki na to nyôbô kasanu nari

)))))
(((((
)))))

"Why don't you just go
to yoshi-chô!" His wife
won't lend hers.

Lend her *what?* Okada Hajime gives a hint: 釜を. That is her *kama,* or "kettle," which is slang for ass, as opposed to 鍋 *nabe* or stew/pot, meaning cunt (and "honorable kettle," or *okama* means a catamite). One likes the mettle of the wife who not only tells her husband to bug-off but literally *where to go!*

a reflection

芳町でする水あげのゑらひどさ 摘 4-8,
yoshichô de suru mizuage no irahidosa 万明四
(yoshichô-at do water-raising's extreme horror)

how horrific
the launch ceremonies
in yoshichô!

If you would find out how a Courtesan was "launched," it should be easy as many take an interest in the Pleasure Quarters. For a pleasantly humorous 20c geisha *water-raising*, see the egg-sucking account in Liza Dalby's *Geisha.* The reality of the indentured boys, made to become sexual objects at a much younger age than girls, must have been just what the senryu says, *horrific.*

錐もんで野郎に売た子を思ふ 鬼がはら
kiri monde yarô ni utta ko o omou 寛保中
(gimlet-kneading guy-to sold child[acc] thinks)

caressing his awl
thinking about the boy
sold to the yarô

gimlet in hand
a carpenter remembers
the boy he sold

Parents did not sell boys to the "yarô" (a *guy* who deals in shade-boys and may himself be an old one) out of greed, but to ensure the survival of his siblings. Suzuki thinks the carpenter father imagines the pain (of being sodomized?) as something like being rubbed by the gimlet or awl (Japanese ones have square or triangular-edged like foil blades). I think it more likely the tool suggests a little boy's tiny penis and self-inflicted pain (typically it was jabbed in the thigh to keep scholars awake). Moreover, this tool makes one feel the long time it has been used. The way a palm pushes against the rounded butt of the handle puts a patina on them that makes them plaintive in a way no other tools are. "Caressing" is too much," "rubbing" would be meaningless, "wringing" or "kneading" wrong for the material, and "in hand" too little. English lacks the right verb. Perhaps, had he been able to raise the boy, he would have inherited the tool. The accompaniment, probably a *maekuzuke,* or draw, was *"sari to wa sari to wa,"* a fatalistic yet not utterly resigned and hence touching unspecific conjunctive, which in this case might be fleshed out as *"it couldn't be helped but . . ."* A touching *zappai.*

boys unofficially used

Pederastry was typically associated with Buddhist priests with their helper/acolyte/pupils, samurai with their pages and boy-brothels with their wealthy customers. But boys from poor families were not only sent to temples for education, apprenticed to nobles/samurai or 'sold' to shady establishments; they could be indentured to emplowed for a pittance by commercial firms.

穴ッをした小僧を手代叱りかね
ketsu o shita kozô o tedai shikari-kane 葉 23
(hole/ass[acc] did small-monk[boy+acc] clerk scold cannot)

a clerk has trouble
scolding the little boy
he butt-fucked

it bugs the clerk
he cannot scold the boy
he buggered

Syunroan explains that in shops employing many clerks and boys, it was dis-advantageous for the former to become involved with women (distracted by love, children & budgets?), so homosexuality was common. Several decades before the above *ku*, we find the present-tense, reverse side, that is the boy's mental state.

けつをする内ハ番頭こわくなし 万
ketsu o suru uchi wa bantô kowaku-nashi 天三
(hole/ass[acc] doing while-as-for head-clerk frightful-not)

nothing to fear
so long as the head-clerk
butt-fucks him

Note that the boy who is the subject is not actually named. The head-clerk may be homosexual, but he is more likely holding out with women so he has a chance at the boss's daughter. In other words, the boys in these *ku* serve a function similar to aimed masturbation (pp.67-8). Considering the training said necessary to be safely sodomized, one wonders how these things happened so easily, if they really did. Were these literally half-assed sexual encounters? I write lightly, but this must not have been something easy for those living out the senryu. The next chapter should reassure readers that not all male color in Japan was exploitive.

~ *eddies* ~

English Equivalents to Shade-boy. I considered *rent-boy*, but felt it more applicable to *wakashu,* or young-crowd (next chapter) entertainers than these boys bought on premises or coining *molly boy* (England's molly houses were probably more adult than boy), for the word *molly* with its light sound and perfect etymology (which Defoe put to best use with the name Molly Flanders: *soft-lowland*) makes it very attractive to the word-lover.

My first translation* of the First *Ku was *"piss drunk / just once he buys / a catamite;"* but P.D. suggested *"Pissed out of his mind / Just for this once / He shops for a boy's behind."* I liked the rhyme, but it was long and "shops" too deliberate for a drunk, so . . .

Male Cries. The shade-boy who cries out making love is suspicious, but what about *this?*

底が知れぬ・声あげて居る男妾　水加減
soko ga shirenu: koe agete-iru otoko shô　文政一

◎ you never know ◎
how deep it goes:a male
mistress moaning

◎ infinite desire ◎
a kept man is raising
high his voice!

A "male mistress" is a man kept by a wealthy woman. They must have been rare indeed, for this 1818 *ku* was my first encounter with them. It uses the words "voice raises/ing" rather than the common verb for love-crying, *yogaru* associated with women, perhaps to make the idea sound more plausible. The Japanese "bottom-the know-can not" (*soko ga shirenu*) usually refers to the depth of human greed for sex or money, so I believe the implication is that such will cause a man, too, to make love cries. But, love cries, like sexual proclivity are hard to pin down. How much of whether and how much a woman cries out in intercourse is genetically determined and how much culturally influenced?

The Making of a Shade-boy. Leupp (1995) writes that "destitute parents offered sons to teahouse propietors . . . as early as age eight" and the "slave-like indentureship" could last up to ten years. He describes the conditioning of a new boy that parents, like the pensive carpenter in the senryu, were probably not aware of:

> His rectum would be dilated by insertion of wooden implements of increasing dimensions several times a day for a month or more. (Leupp: *Male Colors*. Referenced to 西山松乃介：「衆道風俗に就いて」in『性風俗史』vol.3 社会編 1959)

In his translation of commentary on line *ku* 38, *"Some people / call it perversion,"* of Tantan's *haikai* love sequence in *Divine Wagtails Mating* (1717), Chris Drake writes –

> "Some, a man remarks, consider homosexuality unnatural, against the Way. They point to the suffering of boy lovers, who must practice with

pine or cedar poles for a month or more before their anal passages can accept adult males. But this pain, he believes, can make male lovers fiercely and romantically loyal." ("Haikai on Love" in *An episodic festschrift for Howard Hibbett*, highmoonoon: 2000)

~~~~~~

A Senryu Already Englished? In Leupp (1995), I encountered the following sentence:

> It was said, "The one thing the Eight Buddhist Sects agree upon is the [fun to be had at] male brothels"

The Romanized Japanese in the footnote is : *hasshû e kuchi o awaseru kagema jaya,* so I suspected it was a senryu and googling did bring one hit. It was in a dictionary, under a heading defining the shadeboy teahouse at a suspicious site (www.call-girl.jp/kojien/b044): 八宗へ口を合はせる陰間茶屋, but, *still* had no attribution. I'll try one translation:

.

eight sects agree &
in one voice sing, catamite
teashops are the thing!

It is common for Japanese books on sexy themes to cite senryu as evidence without giving a source+date for the same. It would seem the practice has made it across the Pacific!

~~~~~~

Young Boy Cocks vs. Adult Male Cocks. With respect to the "over-sizing of organs" in *shunga* (spring-prints), Screech, finding "more realistically sized ones appear, mostly on younger people or the very old," opines that

> "*shunga [spring-prints] abet the fantasy of the adult male who wishes to imagine himself larger than a youth to compensate for the latter's greater potency and stamina . . .*" Timon Screech (1999 *my italics*)

There may be something to this, but I would call the "realistically sized ones" intended as examples – by comparison to the huge standard ones – of the stereotypically slim-cocked kid and wonder if it is not possible that the pictures, and senryu with the same message, exaggerate a real difference which our culture ignores. Maybe most penises *do* gain girth year by year until old age.

~~~~~~

Senryu Coping with Change: As Male Color Retreated. Screech (1999, p.85) mentions an 1833 source which "calculated that, compared with the 1750's, the number of *nanshoku* [male color] prostitutes in Edo was down by 90 per cent." Not having the later volumes of *Willow* on hand, I cannot check to see how closely the greater river of senryu flowed with reality, but only 7 *ku* (about 1% of the total) in *Leaf*, dated 1835, mention *kagema*, of which two mention them going both ways and the one recommending Yoshichô as the place to go to buy peckers (*henoko*), not assholes – playing on a haiku of Yoshino as the place to go for blossom-viewing – comes from the mouth of a widow (まらが仕たくばよし町へござれ後家　葉 5 *mara ga shitakuba yoshichô e gozare goke.*), two we've seen poke fun at a bonze's analingus and fool absconding with a boy, and one we've seen treats development of the prepuce of a *kagema.* The Yoshichô presence is not what it was in *Pluck*. The remaining one may speak to the plight of an older shade-boy or one suffering from the recent government clampdown on male brothels. It is classic nitty-gritty *Leaf* style and I am amazed that I missed it until now. A prose translation: *"A shade boy with as much time on his hands as a widow is also itchy"* and a poetic one:

後家程にひまな陰間もむづがゆし 葉 *14*
goke hodo ni hima na kagema mo muzugayushi

a shade boy, free as a widow
also itches down there
~~~~~~

<u>*The Young Crowd*</u>
若衆も天晴れ

十八[18]

お洒落はゲイか
Strutting Their Stuff

~~~~~~

くどかれて若しゆしりこみいたす也 万
kudokarete wakashu shirigomi itasu nari 天五

propositioned
the young-crowd beats
a smart retreat

Most Japanese today have never heard of a *kagema,* the working catamite that was such a big presence in senryu. *Wakashu,* literally "young-crowd," despite its tiny presence in senryu, is now synonymous with Edo era male-color. To me, this one *ku* indirectly sums up the *wakashu*: they are all show.

若衆は夜食ひかえるうれひあり 卯の花かつら
wakashu wa yoshoku hikaeru urei ari 宝永七
(young-crowd-as-for nightfood refrain woes are)

free of care?
gay boys do not dare
snack at night

even gay boys
have the blues: snacks
at night are out

refraining from
night snacks: who says
gay is carefree?

they must refrain
from snacks at night:
young crowd blues

The refreshing picture of the young-crowd found in *haikai* is felt indirectly in this senryu – more indirectly in the original, for I have fortified the rhetoric. It comes from a collection with a 7-7 post-verse rather than the usual pre-verse: "In summer, thin hemp, in winter *kenbô* robes" (なつはあさぎに冬はけんぼう *natsu wa asagi ni fuyu wa kenbô*). The former recalls Sei Shônagon's description of how ugly some men look through the gauze-like cloth and the latter was a pale yellow and
~~~~~~

gray and thin for a winter robe. How interesting to have young men worried about gaining weight and losing their figure in a culture which generally did not give a damn about figures, *male or female!* In fact, the male generally tied his belt low so his belly hung out and showed him a man of substance. Are we seeing something of the fastidious attention to looking trim and prim found in a homosexuals and cross-dressers throughout history? I always assumed it might be unconscious compensation for the dirtiness of anal intercourse, but with boys considered the ideal insertee, and the young almost uniformly trim, could it, rather, stem from the nature of homosexual desire?

若衆こんしやうが出たがる江戸家老 12-36
近カよりにけり（x 2）*wakashu konjô ga detagaru edogarô*
(young-crowd spirit-the/his/their come-out-wants edo house-elder)

his gay spirit
wants to come out, an edo
major-domo

~~*their gay spirit*~~
~~*is sorely tempted: an edo*~~
~~*major-domo*~~

~~*an edo major-domo*~~
~~*brings out the fighting spirit*~~
~~*of the young crowd*~~

Is this elder in charge of house affairs, or at least moral matters, whom we saw eyeing girls for possible violations of their moon-duty, a closet gay entering his second childhood or, by being such a fuddy-duddy, an ideal target for the young crowd to bait? As there are better ways to express the second, the first reading is far more likely (enough so that, on second thought, I'll strike the other). Yet, his "gay" spirit might only be a "youthful" one, for *wakashu* could mean *youth who have yet to go through the coming-of-age ceremony*, the *ku* is from *Willow*, which is not all dirty, and 家老~*garô* house-*elder* invites *youthful* contradiction.

若衆にほれたをしりめと申なり
wakashu ni horeta oshiri-me to môsu nari 22-20
(young-crowd-with smitten [hon.]buttocks[+denn.]" call-is)

getting a crush
on a young-crowd, he says
"my bad tushy"

to a young queer
it is put thus: "my dear
boy-buttocks"

The combination of an honorific "o" before and denigrating (but sometimes oddly endearing) *"me"* after the *shiri*=buttocks translates poorly. Though not obvious in my translation, this language has the inventive quality of gay-speak.

箸紙に若衆の唐名薬くひ 嘯山 (1717-1801)
hashigami ni wakashu no karana kusurigui shôzan
(chpstick-paper-on young-crowd's chin. name medicine-eating)

on the hashi sheaf
a young-crowd's chinese name
– medicine eating –

With this last *ku* we have moved from senryu to *haikai*, not the old type that only makes sense in sequence, but the type we call "haiku." The seasonal term would be medicine-eating (*kusurigui*), getting together to cook and eat meat for warmth and vigor to survive in the early winter. It was done by the literally thin-skinned sex, men, and never by women. The third usage of the term in the OJD is *sexual intercourse* – a usage example has carefully regulated coitus as a good medicine – but that is not an option here, for the seasonal meaning would be nullified. The young-crowd would probably be one of a group providing entertainment at the all-man barbecue (the meat was generally venison or boar and eaten outdoors). Japanese (and all who learn the language) love to have Chinese names of their own making which often must be written down to be comprehended. We can imagine the young man had a fancy name and a deft touch with the brush, so the older poet pocketed the sheaf in his sleeve and took it home as a memento.

春駒や若衆をつくる玉くしげ 嘯山 shôzan
harukoma ya wakashu o tsukuru tamakushige

spring ponies
a fancy comb box makes
a young-crowd

Nobles, wearing their spring finery, traditionally went out on their ponies and rode abreast in the spring countryside. It was a rite popular to *waka* poetry but might be wrong here, for *harukoma* also came to mean performers who went house to house with toy-horses. The youngcrowd hairstyle was more like a woman's and higher upkeep than a man's. I can not guess the relationship between the first line and the next two (*maybe* by the next edition), but the mood is, well, *gay*. The mark of a *wakashu* is the smart dress and perfect grooming, the sort of perfectionism with respect to looks we find with more gays than straights in the USA. I think that was one reason why *wakashu* were respected.

小若衆に念者きはまる巨燵哉 李由 d.1705
ko-wakashu ni nenja kiwamaru kotatsu kana riyû

a little gay boy
his lover gets heart-burn
at the kotatsu

at the kotatsu
a little gay boy's would-be
cannot help himself

a little wakashu
admiring parties party
round the kotatsu

The *kotatsu*, if you recall from the wet-nurse chapter, is a table with a skirt to hold in the warmth from a heater that serves as a theater for playing footsie. It is also the best, possibly only place, people sat that close together, for Japanese did not generally eat at common tables like Europeans, but had trays carried out. A *nenja* is someone with a crush on a *wakashu*. In the specialized vocabulary of Japanese, hetero- or homosexual love may be *koi,* but thinking about or longing for someone of the opposite sex is *omou* (思う), while that for someone of the same sex is *nensu* (念す). We can imagine the boy sitting prim at the table. It is hard to tell if he is with one high admirer or a number of contenders.

若衆の髱を辷る雨たれ「とくとく清水」
wakashu no tabo o suberu amadare む 2-29

raindrops gliding down
the wakashu's chignon

若衆の肘の袖笠に出る「とくとく清水」
wakashu no hiji no sodegasa ni deru む 3-17

the elbow of the wakashu
appears in his sleeve-hat

When I read through the proto-senryu *Mutamagawa* I was not looking for *young-crowd*, so I did not find them; but the above was on the internet with comments, including female novelist Tanabe Seiko on the first: "What beautiful passion." A sleeve hat is an *ad hoc* solution for a shower. The nape of woman's neck is not as erotic to me as to Japanese of this era, much less a *man's* white elbow (!); but, *so it is described* as a "voluptuous scene" by the internet host, and, as the Roman said, *taste is indisputable*. A slightly later *Mutama ku* admitted *"Reaping with gratitude the plot of seventeen letters"* (十七文字 の恩の田を刈 mu 5). That means 5-7-5 *haikai*. It a sure bet that someone with access to a good data-base (例えば、岩波日本文学大系) could put in the word "rain" and "wakashu" and come up with a dozen antecedents for the above. Lacking such access, I must instead give you something more interesting:

恋はたゞはだかかたなのごとくにて
をよばぬこひをするぞおかしき

Love's nothing but a bare sword, take a swing:
Unattainable love is a crazy thing!

われよりもおほ若衆にだきつきて
うちはあかくてそとはまつくろ

I'd grab hold of a gay boy, a big one at that:
Inside it's red, outside it's black!

しらねどもをんなのもてる物に似て
こひはゆみおれ矢こそつきぬれ

Who would know it, but, it's like a woman's,
With love, bows break, arrows run out.

This is from the *Inu[dog/pseudo]-tsukubashû* (1553), an early-*haikai* classic, edited by the top *haikai* master of the age (the one Bashô grew up in), Sôkan. We already see the *wakashu,* here translated "gay boy." The *ô* in the line we may romanize as "*ware yori mo ô-wakashu ni dakitsukite*" is "big," but one annotator thinks it *means* "adult." I suppose an adult *wakashu* would be less coy, less unattainable, but elsewhere in the same classic we find:

くびをのべたる　あけぼのの空
きぬ／＼に　大若衆の口吸ひて

Stretching out his neck, against the dawn sky – *kubi o nobetaru akebono no sora*
For his sweet good-bye, he kisses the big gay boy *kinuginu ni ôwakashu no kuchi suite*

Sexologist Nishizawa imagines a short man hanging from a tall young-crowd as he reaches up for a lip-sucking ("kiss" in Japanese) goodbye after a night of homosexual love. It fits the *mae-ku* (previous verse) and is properly ludicrous for this classic setting the tone for *haikai* to come. I forgot to write down which version of the *Inu-tsukubashû* I used, but another, probably later version found in an excellent article/chapter on "the eroticism of classic *haikai*," has the following two lines instead of *bows breaking and arrows running out.*

.

いのちしらずとよしいはゞいへ
君ゆへに腎虚せんこそ望みなれ

It can cost your life, i know, but i can't let it be
For you, my only desire is getting dry-kidney! *kimi yue ni* <u>*jinkyo sen*</u> *koso nozomi nare*

Already, the "empty-kidney" that will become so popular in senryu (ch.7)! It replaced those b*reaking bows and spent arrows*. We find much more in *haikai* linked-verse but your author is out of energy and just wishes to finish the book before hurricane season, so let us only note in brief a couple more interesting sequences. One, in the *Enokoshû*, the 1633 classic anthology with the white salty buttocks we saw on pg 32, includes this line (若衆のむりをいふこそ本意なれ *ku* #1794 犬子集 *wakashu no muri o iu koso honi nare*), which might be inter-preted in a number of ways –

Love-spats for a wakashu is what they do.
or, *Young-crowd bitching comes from the heart.*
or, *Making unreasonable demands is very wakashu.*

The Iwanami edition notes that *wakashu* knew how to take advantage of an admirer's love by starting quarrels of a type where unreasonable demands are made (all that from the phrase *muri o iu!*). These *wakashu* could be recognized in 21c U-sanian gay situation comedies! A more outrageous sequence from the 1675 Sôin-edited *Osaka Dokuginshû* (大坂独吟集 *ku* # 957-961) suggests all was not roses:

Smoke never stops rising from the funeral site of Birdside Field.
Don't all the kites and crows ever sneeze? [carrion eating birds, sneeze → curse]
Hateful curses for the vendor who sold them the rotten octopus. [birdlike beak]
Running piles, the diseased mouth, too, out of control [octop. an anti-coagulant]
He makes up his mind to quit the Way of the Wakashu. [which gave him piles]

The original for the last line: 若衆のみちはすたりし心だて *wakashu no michi wa sutarishi kokorodate*. Were I a young man in Osaka three centuries ago, this is the sort of wild verse-jamming that would have appealed to me. Some, not all, links between verses are added in brackets. To explain the relationship of *sneezes* and *curses* alone would take a paragraph, or page if I included example *ku* of what Japanese might say when they sneezed. So I *won't*.

いやがるをだいて念者の無理所望・前髪つたふ涙はらはら 貞徳正章千句
iyagaru o daite nenja no muri-shobô / maegami tsutau namida harahara teitoku
(disliking[despite/one] hugging attentive-one's forced-possession // bangs transmit tears shower)

unlovely loving

embracing one
who does not want it
a pushy admirer

by way of his bangs
a train of tear drops

Only boys have bangs. With a 5-7-5 followed by 7-7 by the same poet, a link *haikai* sometimes seems to demand the full treatment, rather than being translated in single lines, as I did for the other *haikai* sequences. While there is a concept of forced love later requited, the so-called 和姦, or "gentle/soft-rape," in Japan, I doubt the kind Teitoku (1570-1653) was sympathetic with it and would guess this *ku* is sympathetic for the unwilling boy, who would be a young *wakashu*, or *chigo* (not a *kagema,* or professional catamite, because a *nenja* is not a john).

年忘昔念者と若衆哉　春来 (c 1760)
toshiwasure mukashi nenja to wakashu kana shunrai

year-forget party
an old admirer drinks with
the young-crowd

the year-forget
a young-crowd and his
ex-lover drink

Here is where I miss Blyth with his sure comments on male vs. female ways of facing the world and each other. Sure, some were off-mark, even sexist, but most were entertaining and some made points gender research has yet to pick up on. Had Blyth not steered clear of male-color, we might have been treated to similar psychologizing on homosexual relations. I cannot do it. There is something particularly poignant, or perhaps, refreshing about the atmosphere of the year-forget party between a male and his-ex lover, also male, but I am not sure what it is.

若衆公事けつだん所とわおもしろし 万
wakashu kôji ketsudansho to wa omoshiroshi 明二

wakashu court
settling civil matters
gay means fun

wakashu court
the judgments concern
their arrears

Open courts for sundry civil matters were set up in 1333 and modernized a few hundred years later. They were called *ketsudansho,* or "decision-places." Gays quibbling *are* entertaining. They like words and the words like them. Gay wit reminds us of the most famous wits of Japan, the geisha. I think this is the main point of the *ku.* We also have a homophonic pun on *ketsu,* or decide, it means ass/anus. My second reading is wrong, but gets the *ketsu* pun in.

抱合へば二人おかしき女子なり 千枝分銅
daki-aeba futari okashiki onago nari 宝永 1
(hug-meeting-if/when two[people] funny, girl is)

after embracing
the two have a good laugh
'why, you're a girl!'

making love
both find it very funny
that he's a girl

A Suzuki find. The *wakashu* were so popular with men seeking to be stylish, that young women, especially if they had boyish features, were said to have pretended to be young-crowd, for fun or business (若衆女郎). How nice they *both* laugh!

若衆見事に恥をかゝせる むち十二
wakashu migoto ni haji o kakaseru

the young crowd shame
themselves, splendidly.

I am unsure what this *Mutamagawa* 7-7 means, but it seems perfect to end this chapter (that I hope someone else can expand) on the right note.

~~~~~~

What Makes Young Crowd Scary?
若衆はなぜこわい、こわい？

~~~~~~

There was to be a whole chapter on the *chili pepper*, but after the chili-as-boy's-penis and chili-as-abortifacient *ku* were moved to their respective chapters, I decided to move the remaining *ku* to H.I.C. (*Haiku in Context*). There was, however, one *ku* I really wanted to include in this book, and, as it happens, it is about the *Young-crowd*. So, I give you the subtitle above, the lead *ku* by Issa, with some explanation, two of the *ku* Issa (1762-1827) improved upon, two senryu commenting on the same, and *that ku,* the senryu (if a *Mutama zappai* can be so called) which depending upon one's reading of it may be hardly dirty at all or one of the most obscene *ku* in the book.

男といはれて涙ほろ／＼たうがらし 一茶
otoko to iwarete namida h/poroh-h/poro tôgarashi issa
(man as said/called tears tricklytrickly chili-pepper)

chili-pepper:
his tears pouring down
called 'a man'

called a man
as his tears pour down
chili-pepper

This is one of a score of *ku* I did *not* read in the standard selection of Issa's haiku (ed. Maruyama Kazuhiko, publ. Iwanami bunko) that made me realize *I no longer wished to read selections* when it was possible to find a full collection of someone's work and choose *for myself*. How could it be left out! How *dared* the editor skip it! True, the *ku* is too long, unless we give *otoko* (man) an odd reading (*eg.* "o"). Moreover, *chili* is only nominally seasonal in-doors. But, the trouble may lay elsewhere. When I tried out the *ku* on Japanese friends, I found they, unlike me, did not immediately get it! Because Japanese are no longer big on hot (*picante*) foods, they cannot even *imagine* what is going on. Maybe that's why the editor overlooked it. Having engaged in such contests in Mexico and Korea, I had *personal interest,* he did not. . . . [*abbrev.*] a couple paraverses of Issa's *ku*.

◎ chili peppers ◎

"what a man!"
the whole room cheers
as his face begins to run with tears

◎ honky-tonk ◎

he is a man,
after all, man-sized tears
begin to fall: red hot chili-peppers

A literal translation of the chili is "chinese peppers." Japanese, at least in some parts of the country, were evidently more like Koreans than today: they ate hot food and, with those hot tongues, were, doubtless, more argumentative (Any anthropologist with free time? *Please* check out this intuitive correlation!). . . . [*abbrev.* Let me add only that *ku* suggest that the bars were the location for the matches]

賭にして唐からし喰ふ泪哉　几董
kake ni shite tôgarashi kuu namida kana

making a bet
eating hot chili pepper
flowing tears

金平を泣せた種に蕃椒　素丸
kinpira o nakaseta tane ni tôgarashi

and it has made
red-haired tomboys cry
the chili pepper

Kitô's *ku,* on the left, antedates Issa's by about a hundred years. I have read and in my unfortunate moves, lost another *ku* even closer to Issa's, by Shirô, one of his many teacher/employers. Somaru, who composed the *ku* on the right was also Issa's teacher/employer. The "red-haired" is a reddish tinge that dark hair may get with much exposure to the sun. It is clear to me that Issa, especially in his old age, consciously or not, paraversed his own *ku* and those of others. I do not mean this as criticism. Issa almost always managed to improve them. Compare his "called a man" tears with the description of the betting situation by Kitô, a somewhat obscure but highly rated student and successor of Buson. Issa, country bumpkin, was a consummate literary stylist to the end. [*abbrev.*]

とうがらししたたか食ふも下卑たもの
tôgarashi shitataka kuu mo gebita-mono

chili peppers
vulgarity eats them
too easily

たてひきでとうがらし喰う馬鹿な事
tatehiki de tôgarashi kuu baka-na koto

a stupid thing
eating chili peppers
on a dare

[*abbrev.*] These last two *ku* (川傍柳 4, 初代川柳) both predate Issa's chili tears, but do not go back as far as Kitô's on eating chili on a bet. And, now my excuse for making you suffer through haiku and senryu that are *not* obscene, this *ku:*

たうがらし喰へば若衆も怖くなり むハ
tôgarashi kueba wakashu mo kowaku nari 1755
(chili eat/ate-if/when young-crowd even scary become)

even catamites
are scary after eating
chili peppers

after chili
even a pretty youth
can hurt you

chili pepper
after eating them beware
gay power

At first, I was *sure* this meant that the senryu writer, A) having experienced a burn coming out as well as in, considered what would happen *if* . . . . or, B) that one appeal of *wakashu,* their effeminacy, would be belied by this macho act that a man would lose his confidence of being in charge. But, considering the way *wakashu* were said to come on strongly in some towns, it could also be read C) "if you eat chili, even the *wakashu* will shy away (from you)." Unfortunately, I have not received a comment from a senryu specialist about this. One Japanese respondent (learned, but not especially in this field) voted for A).

~ *eddies* ~

Thin Winter Robe. My dictionary does not say if the *kenbô* (same *kanji* as the Constitution!) is thin or not, but a *ku* (降る霜に若衆の夜着の薄さ哉 *oru shimo ni wakashu no yogi no ususa kana*), with a preface mentioning a scene out the second floor window, by Ichiku (移竹 d.1760?) suggests that it was:

Jack frost comes –
How thin the night-robes of
The young-crowd!

Dirty Haikai. Please note that I did not go looking for the dirtiest *haikai*. My examples come from the most commonly encountered collections. Here are some lines from one sequence (lost source, sorry) more explicit than the examples given in the text.

The one whose body crumbles is the ejaculator,

身をくだきてはせいを出す人 *mi o kudakite wa sei o dasu hito*

His ass-hole's so tight, you feel like quitting,

しりのあなこそせばくあきたれ *shiri no ana koso sabaku akitare*

The young-crowd whose sympathy wears thin hides it with his tight one,

うすなさけかくる若衆はすばりにて *usu-nasake kakuru wakashu wa subari nite*

All these are from 7-7⇒ 5-7-5⇒ 7-7⇒ 5-7-5 sequences tricky to jump into. I will not bother to try to make sense of them. At any rate, *haikai* did get down and dirty,

~~~~~~

Year Forget Parties. When I worked in Tokyo in the 1980's and 90's, we had to go to so many of these parties, the last two weeks of the year passed in a hang-over! The final year-forget party became, in essence, a party to forget the damn year-forget parties!

~~~~~~

Additional. Positive Image of the Wakashu. My impression of the totally refreshing person of the wakashu in senryu coming from *haikai* is backed up by things within a book written by an early (pre-Bashô) *haikai* master, Tokugen (1558-1647), namely, the *Reasonable Book* (*Motomo-no-sôshi*) of listing mentioned in the Introduction (pg 442). Among the *"Pretty and Clean Things,"* with its *"water cast upon the road," "freshly cut lengths of green bamboo"* and, *"if one exists, a person without greed,"* we find –

"the whiteness of a young-crowd's (gay youth's) teeth."

Tokugen also mentioned "the whiteness of a woman's body." (参照：きれいなる物の品々　路地に水うちたる　青竹のぬれ縁　若衆の歯の白き　女の身の白き　もしあらば無欲の人). And, among the first of the *"Gentle/soft Things,"* we find –

"the heart/mind of a noble young-crowd." Followed by,

"the same for a woman's heart/mind." And an addition, *"~ skin."* (参照：やはらかなる物の品々　やんごとなき若衆の心。同じく女の心。付　肌。)

I will not try to explain, for I do not think any explanation is needed. Instead, let me add some items from one of my favorite listings, *Scary Things:*

"A person who's lost his mind," "laundry with too much starch," "under-boiled dried sea-cucumber," "over-boiled octopus."

(参照：こはき物之しな／＼　理非を知らぬ人　　糊のつきすぎたる洗濯物。なま煮なる煎海鼠。ゆですぎたる蛸。)

Perhaps I'll figure out what is so scary about under-cooked trepang (the octopus may be the bad type mentioned elsewhere) before doing the revised edition of *Rise, Ye Sea Slugs!* (2003). The starch puns on *stiffness* and *loud sounds* – too much to explain here – but it is true that such can be scary and this is one place where Tokugen's sensitivity approached that of the diva of discrimination, Sei Shônagon.

~~~~~~

What Happens to Old Young-Crowd? An Unresolved Question. Reading Martial's LVI and LXII one can see a difference between Japanese and Classical homosexuality. "We" cruelly stigmatized the insertee (Japanese did not).

> You think you fool us, Charideme, because your legs and chest bristle with hair . . . Why not testify to your clean-cut nates by depilating your whole body! You ask "*Why* do you say this?" The whole world is talking, we *all* know you're *poked.* (in my loose and abbreviated translation, likewise below)
>
> That you pluck your chest, legs and arms, and even your prick is barely haired is known even to your girl but (does she know) who borrows the ass you pluck?"

The "pluck" might actually be "strip," for LXXIV mentions resin or Venetian clay, but the unresolved question is, *why do we find no ass-hair depilation in senryu?* We have
~~~~~~

seen that the professional catamites retire from sodomy when they mature, but what about young-crowd? Were they, by definition, not allowed to be "old?" Were there no old insertees, not because of any stigma, but because the poked is supposed to be cute?

~~~~~~

Were All Young Men Wakashu? **Reading Mack Horton's *The Journal of Sôchô*** (Stanford 2002), I found our *wakashu* was consistently translated as "young men" or "young man." Eg.:

> ◎As I tarried there, some young men gathered, bringing things on hand nearby to eat or drink, as well as flutes and drums, and we made merry."
> ◎Young men from the shrine, monks and others went ahead . . . From time to time there was singing and dancing to drums and flutes.
> ◎. . . a dozen or so boats lay ready for me and the young men and monks in my company. . . on the way we danced, sang, and played pipes, hand drums and large drums, "beating in time on the boat sides."
> ◎ He arrived with many people including some young men.
> ◎ To see Shôzôbô off, I invited two monks from Shôrin'an and some young men. . . . . [At Miidera] He must be quite happy there, what with all those young men!
> ◎The scribe was a young man; his calligraphy was beautiful.
> ◎. . . a linked-verse session at my lodgings at the shrine . . . There were many young men in attendance, which was pleasant.

While it is true that the "Young Man" (YMCA) song became a sort of gay anthem in Usania, so I was not completely unfamiliar with young-man-as-gay, I found this use of "young man" for *wakashu* a problem when reading the journal, for how could one tell what was happening? True, the Japanese *wakashu* is ambiguous, too. But, its *first* meaning in *haikai* and *senryu* alike is attractively dressed youth or groups of youth knowingly attractive to other males. That connotation is not in "young men." Like all too many university press books, you must play footsie with the notes in the back of the book to know what you are reading in the front (and not all these youngsters were footnoted). We have seen enough *wakashu* in *haikai* linked-verse to belie the common idea of young-crowd culture arising from *kabuki* in the early 17c (one confusing factor is that there were wandering players before the formal kabuki plays as we know them) but, translation/note quibbles aside, the *Journal* (1522-27) adds something I have not seen expressed well elsewhere. It shows us that *wakashu* were in attendance at verse-jams – *haikai* had many monks for temples and education went hand-in-hand and one needed to be a monk to travel freely – and that they were, more than anything else, *entertainers* and *road companions*, as Japanese expected entertainment while traveling and appreciated the protection against brigands that numbers brought. I do not know to what extent they performed this function for people of means who were *not* monks and to what extent they formalized relations with shrines and temples. Unfortunately, Leupp starts his in depth discussion with the 17c and Horton did no more than define them (*wakashu*) ambiguously as "youths who were often made prostitutes." (made?) Leupp does touch upon the military relationship with pages and the clerical one with their little helpers, but if anyone has written any thorough on the more independent wakashu in English, I have not read it. A careful study of the roots of *wakashu* (i.e. their role in society before the Tokugawa created and solidified the stereotypes), it would be especially useful in showing how additional genders add life to cultures, as was the case with many if not most native Americans before the Europeans murdered their cultures in the name of the sexually immoral religions of the Near East (Judeo-Christian-Islamity). [Don't get me wrong: I am not a relativist and think it worthwhile to try to help good cultural practices and hinder bad ones. Not all was or is good with any culture. When it came to sex, however, these religions had and still have particularly unnatural and harmful ideas.]

~~~~~~

People Borrowed or Rented. Screech (1999) writes that

> *Saikaku's Great Mirror* [男色大鑑] mentions a rent 'boy' still as being pene-

> trated at the age of 38, although that was regarded as too old and provoked laughter upon discovery. No male rented to be so penetrated.

I am a bit puzzled by that last sentence (without seeing the Japanese, I think it should be either "no male *that age* rented to be so . . ." or concern the wishes of the *penetrator*), but my interest is elsewhere, in the word "rent-boy." I can find no Japanese for it (the book has no index to check whether I missed an earlier usage) so I cannot tell if this means a *kagema* or a *wakashu*. I checked the OED, for Screech introduced a beautiful old English word, *molly-house* – had I known it early on I might have invented *molly-boys* rather than *shade-boys,* but found *nothing* (then again, the OED, unlike the OJD, is short on off-color words, which are delegated to slang dictionaries though good clean words that survived less time are allowed in). My OJD has only little girls who did chores for their mistresses in the pleasure district in Osaka: *kariko,* 借り子 which is to say "borrow/rent-child." But there is this:

女のハ取る若衆のハ借りる也 摘 4-31
onna no wa toru wakashu no wa kariru nari

A woman's thing, you take,
a young-crowd's, you borrow.

I had relegated that *Pluck ku* to a note before reading Screech as I was unsure where it came from. A mere aphorism is usually not enough. Now my guess is that Saikaku used the word "rent," and the *ku* means "Haven't *you* read *The Great Mirror of Male Color?"* I must answer, with embarrassment, *no*. I should read it, but have so much else to read or write first that I am afraid it will have to be in another life. But, I have read enough elsewhere to know I exaggerated when I wrote *wakashu* were all show and no sex in explaining the first *ku* of the chapter. My aim was to separate the *wakashu* from the *kagema* for the sake of clarity. Now, I think we could say the *wakashu*, as an entertainer, or a group of entertainers were *hired*, which is like rented, and any sex that might arise from it was consensual, while the *kagema* was *bought* to do with as one liked. And the woman you [male senryu reader] *take* – what about her? The poet would probably defend it with something along the lines that all is fair in love or war. (★ a day later: "rent-boy" was used at least as early as Oscar Wilde and today in England means a boy who sells his sexual services).

~~~~~~

Conflating Young Crowd and Shade Boys? One synon. for kabuki-related young-crowd, *kageko* (陰子) shade-child, is close to *kagema* (陰間) shade-space, our shade-boy. The following *ku* may show that one cause for confusion was the latter passing for the former.

かりに若衆とあらわれて寺へすみ 摘
kari ni wakashu to arawarete tera e sumi 3-6
(provisionally wakashu-as appearing temple-to live)

pro tempore

who's appearing
at the temple to live as
a young crowd?

The glossary in the back of my *Pluck* edition that has the following note in the glossary by Okada Hajime: *wakashu*: another name for *kagema* (若衆 陰間の異称（三 6）). Okada would not have defined *wakashu* like that, so my guess is that in an earlier edition the note was on the same page as the *ku* and intended to explain it alone. I may, however, be misreading, for the *ku* is ambiguous even for a senryu.
~~~~~~

Ms. Dowry & Mr. Phimosis
持参は痘痕、越前は包茎

十九 19

女の命と男の命
Face-value vs. Tool-value?

~~~~~~

It is said there are infinitely more types of ugliness than beauty, but ugliness in senryu tends toward stereotype, pockmarks, or the lacking proboscis, which is to say bridgeless nose common to those (peasants) who ate little protein. It is also limited by sex; ugly males are few and far between. The typical ugly human in senryu was described in a 7-7 *ku*: *"Her dowry 1000 ryô / Her face 1000 pits"* (持参千両あばた千粒 む十 *jisan sen ryô abata sen tsubu*). Blyth called this: "one of the cruelest and truest of all the verses of Mutamagawa." (*Edo:* 1961) Perhaps, but compare *that* ugly girl to one who has no dowry to ensure she could marry and experience motherhood. As Herodotus admitted, there is something to be said for the Babylonian Marriage Market (see the *Eddies* at chapter's end). Blyth also introduced *"The pock-marked girl,/ Resigned / To going to Heaven"*(極楽へゆくとあばたの諦めて む *gokuraku e yuku to abata no akiramete*) explaining it as follows: "The point of this is not the pathos of the un-beautiful girl, but the revelation of the unsatisfactoriness of "revealed" religion" (ibid). While I do not doubt that most men who wrote senryu were what Europeans might have called "free-thinkers," he may be reading too much into a plain poem. *Pluck,* published a bit after *Mutamagawa*, brought the talk down to earth with this *ku:*

しりからハいやと持参をはなにかけ
shiri kara wa iya da to jisan o hana ni kake 摘 *1-12*
(rear-from-as-for no/yuck is says special-dowry [acc] nose-on placing)

i may be a dog
she says, but no doggy style
on *my* money!

no doggy style
for me, says dowry, noseless
nose held high

no doggy style
she says, knowing a dowry
has face value

no, not doggy-style,
you better do me right!
her dowry makes cruel
demands at night
~~~~~~

In Japanese, the idiom "to stake on one's nose," meaning "to be proud" sounds the same as "lacking a nose." Japanese were very conscious of the relationship of frontal intercourse with attractiveness. A similar *ku* from *Willow:*

持参金はなはあれどもすじがなし
jisankin hana wa aredomo suji ga nashi 18-25
(special dowry nose/flower/money-as-for is-but bridge [missionary position]-not)

her dowry's her nose
but missionary position
demands a bridge

dowry has one
to pay through but who rides
a saddle-nose?

Untranslatable. First, she has a nose but *it lacks a bridge*; second, the dowry is also called *hana=flower* money and, third, despite paying it *up front, i.e. on the nose*, she is not granted frontal intercourse. Amazingly, English lacks a decent word for such intercourse and must drag in the missionary, who seems to prove that we had no name for that position precisely because it was the only one allowed. We have the idea of giving a horse its nose, and "nose" in Japanese also implies that, too, so we might say, she has her will, but not her way, despite her parents paying through it. Why not? A *Leaf* senryu explains:

持参開イ八にあたまを上ゲさせず 葉 別三
jisan-bobo(kai?) mara ni atama o agesasezu
(bring-gift cunt cock-to head[acc] raise-not)

dowry cunt
can't raise her head
to the cock

if dowry cunt
raises her head, cock
will lower his

My second reading fills in between the words. *Ugliness can not insist.* A cock may be paid, but it can not be bought (though there are *ku* implying otherwise about men married into wealth: *"the cock is not his, he sold it"*). Moreover, the cunt is literal. Of course, there are exceptions, such as the girl with *skin like a shark wasted on an octopus cunt* (pg. 138), but *dowries* were generally thought to have as little fortune in their cunts, as their faces. And, if the man rises above his revulsion, when orgasming, they look like "monsters" and their love-cries sound like *shichiriki*, an awful classical wind instrument that sounds like a cross between a bag-pipe, a kazoo and a fistful of fifes (持参金しちりき程によかる也 摘 4-30 *jisankin shichiriki hodo ni yogaru nari*). For them, marriage was a different thing than for your usual virgin: *"Only when the seal is finally broken [on the container of money and her hymen] can the dowry sigh with relief."* (持参金封を切られて安堵する 38 *jisankin fu o kirarete ando-suru*). And, heaven forbid, they propagate easily:

あいそうにしたの=持参はらむ也 摘
aiso ni shita no ni jisan haramu-nari 4-17

Though he does it, trying to be nice,
Dowry's knocked up, on their wedding night!

There is no *wedding night* specified in the original, but I feel confident adding it for reason as well as rhyme. But it was not just "trying to be nice" –

持参の内取リのこりハはらむまで 万
jisan no uchitori-nokori wa haramu made 天元

the dowry bride
the rest of it received
after conception

針だこのかわりさねだこ持参也 摘
haridako no kawari sanedako jisan nari 1-14

the dowry bride
from sewing callous
to cunt callous

The contracts sometimes called for the husband of the ugly to get half the payment at marriage and the other half after she became pregnant. くらへ社こすれ↑

Beauty on the Other Hand

There are a far smaller number of *ku* on pretty brides/wives coming with nothing. I believe these *ku* were thought up as foils to the numerous dowries.

絵のよふな女房なんにも持て来ず 万
e no yô na nyôbô nannimo motte kozu million 安四
(picture-like wife anything-not bringing comes-not)

A wife, who is as pretty as a picture,
Brings nothing whatsoever with her!

まことなりけり
ain't that the truth!

In many books a senryu has a short accompanying phrase. I left it in, above. The most common versions have her coming to her marriage buck-naked as it were:

花よめのはだかははぢにハならぬなり 万
hanayome no hadaka wa haji ni wa naranu nari 天五
(bride's nakedness-as-for shame-as-for is/becomes-not)

a naked bride
is nothing to be
ashamed of

the nakedness
of a bride is nothing
embarrassing

Hoods Who Were Laughed At

While senryu treats some men suffering from summer thinness or noses opened by syphilis, ugly men are not a *theme*. This is probably because male fortune in love depends more upon wealth or cock than face. Thus, the closest male equivalent of the unloved dowry, is probably the despised *phimosian*. Most

Japanese today have never heard of the *dowry* we have been discussing, or even the early-20c term for ugly women "graduation faces" (principals and teachers introduced beauties to wealthy families – presumably for a fee – so they usually married and dropped out of school leaving the *sotsugyô-men*); but 99.9% know what the penis problem we call *phimosis* is, and what to call someone with it. These unfortunates are common in Japanese cartoons today and I have even seen a young woman accuse a youth who was rude to her on a TV game show of *being one!*

ゑちせんはつるの出そうなへのこ也 摘
echizen wa tsuru no desô na henoko nari 1-30
(echizen-as-for vine appear/sprout-seems/would cock is)

what's an echizen?
a prick that looks like
it could grow a vine

mister spear-cover
given water, this prick
would sprout a vine

Echizen province was famous for its spear-blade covers, which came in all shapes and materials (but, especially bear). *An* Echizen was an adult male with *phimosis*, which is to say, an unretractable prepuce. As if one metaphor won't do, the Echizen spear-sheath turned into a potato with pointed ends, *satsuma-imo*. A long foreskin can look a bit like a vine growing from such a potato.

ゑちせんて嫁人しらぬふたのしみ 摘
echizen de yomebito shiranu futa no shimi 2-31

An Echizen – The bride's party knows not: her lid's cracked.

Woman-as-pot and *man-as-lid.* An old metaphor. On the eve of the wedding, her/his cover is not yet blown. I made the original "stain/blemish (*shimi*)," a *crack*, as it seems better for a lid. A foreskin is also a cover of sorts.

ゑちぜんハへのこくらべをいやといゝ 摘
Echizen wa henoko-kurabe o iya to ii 3-11

The Echizen says this about cock contests: *"No way!"*

Japan was big on all sorts of contests – called comparisons – and one finds many old picture scrolls of men contesting the size and power of their equipment, the latter generally tested by balancing things on, or hanging things from, *it*.

越前ハ壱本もない長つほね 摘 1-13
echizen wa ippon mo nai nagatsubome

Not even one Echizen among them, the chambermaids.

The chambermaids or ladies-in-waiting in the daimyôs' or Shôgun's palaces commanded a large stock of dildos, all with smooth, rounded ends, but oddly enough, there is one more *ku:*

ゑちぜんハ致シにくいと小間ものや 摘
echizen wa itashi-nikui to komamonoya 3-7

'an echizen is
a hard order to fill' says
the haberdasher

'an echizen cock?
we've none in stock,' says
the notions man

The poet surmises that at least one chambermaid wants a dildo with an exceptionally narrow tip rather than the usual round-headed variety and the notions man replies politely that he cannot comply with the order. Neither would he want to keep a good in stock that someone might call inferior.

越前ハゑみわれさうにおやす也　摘 4-23
echizen wa emi-waresô ni oyasu nari pluck

a phimo erect
looks like he/it is holding
back a smile

Pardon the sudden "phimo," but this absence of words for things in English is driving your translator crazy. Why borrow words like Echizen, when we should be making our own? This is about a post-pubescent man whose head cannot manage to push through the turtleneck. Compare it to the next *ku* about perfectly normal development:

ちんぽこの皮を剥たらイ八が出た 葉
chinpoko no kawa o muitara mara ga deta 18
(weeny's skin[acc] peeled-when cock/dick appeared)

coming of age

peeling back
the wee-wee's skin,
out comes dick

when his peewee
flap peels back, it's *cock*
a-doodle-doo!

Our culture's ignorance of the foreskin is astounding. According to an excellent summary found & lost on the web, even today, "many physicians . . . are unable to distinguish between normal developmental tightness and clinical phimosis." Until recently, the most frequently cited literature was mistaken. Based on poor surveys, it grossly exaggerated the developmental curve so that 92% of boys had fully retractable prepuces by the age of 5 while more recent, careful studies, show only 20% of boys are fully fledged by that age, 44% by age 10-11, 60% by 12-13, 85% by 14-15 and 95% by 16-17. With faulty findings making double-digit percentages of boys out to be abnormal, the Usanians of my generation were probably lucky to have been circumcised as infants. As a premature baby, slow to develop in every way, I am sure I would have spent my youth worrying about when I would be fully out. To give you an idea of the difference between a civilization where sex is really looked at and one where everything is hidden away because of superstitious ideas of sin, look at this *Willow Tip* senryu:

越前ハ一生おさな皃うせす 摘
echizen wa isshô osana kao usezu 4-21
(echizen-as-for one-life infant-face-thins-not)

about echizen
you can say this: they look
young for life

mr phimosis
will never lose this:
his baby face

I do not think this only refers to the penis. Neoteny, which is more developed in the undeveloped, i.e., prematurely born, probably does effect one's health and appearance even as an adult.

~~~~~~

Today, "Echizen" is obsolete, but Japanese still have several common names for a man whose foreskin doesn't allow his glans to emerge when erect: *hôkei* = 包茎、*kawakamuri* = 皮被り、*hôkamuri* = 包被り。Compare that to *phimosis*, a word I only learned when I looked up one of the Japanese terms (包茎 *hôkei*) in my Japanese-English dictionary while writing this chapter! When you consider how important a smoothly functioning apparatus is to the male, is this not odd? At the same time, it bears mentioning that a clitoris too tightly covered is also said to suffer from phimosis: it is hard to find a problem that affects only one sex.

~~~~~~

~~~~~~

~ *eddies* ~

~~~~~~

Blyth's Two Examples. *"Her dowry 1000 ryô / Her face 1000 pits,"* from Bk 10 of the *Mutamagawa*, is a paraverse of another in Bk 7, *"the face exchanged for a chest c 1000 ryô"* 千両箱と 取替た皃 む 7-34 *senryô-bako to torikaeta kao*) . Blyth commented as follows about the same "thinking she'll go to paradise" *ku* only a year before in *Japanese Life and Character . . .* (1960), as follows: *"It is so. If there were a paradise, a pock-marked woman would go there without fail, and whatever her sins."* Sweet words. Needless to say, the lean mean newer ("cruelest and truest") version beat that. I hope to be equally outrageous if I ever redo *this* book.

~~~~~~

Nose Paradox. There is something odd about the frequency of lacking noses + dowries.

持参金よくよく見れば鼻もあり・持参金よく見りゃ鼻も有りハ有 安元梅4
jisankin yoku yoku mireba hana mo ari • jisankin yoku mirya hana mo ari wa ari

taking a close,
close look at the dowry,
a nose, as well!

if you look,
real carefully, the dowry
does have a nose!

Blyth, who translated version one, *"Looking carefully / At the girl with the dowry, / She did have a nose, but . . .",* I am not sure if his implication, "but something else is ugly/missing," or "though it was hard to tell with the face so bumpy and pitted" is the point of the *mo,* which could be *also* or *even* as well as *emphatic*. My guess is it plays against the flower-money, *hana-kin.* The man gets the flower/nose=*hana* as well as the money=*kin*. But, I also like my second reading, which plays between two connotations of nose, one of which only deems a bridged nose *a nose*, and one which admits anything
~~~~~~

with two holes in mid-face the same. I do not want to nitpick with Blyth but to introduce his observation: *"The Japanese admire a prominent (high) nose, but many rich girls seemed to have lacked them."* I vaguely recall thinking the same, but failing to write it down. I think that we have merchants who, unlike the samurai, who generally had hawkishly high-noses, might have the typical peasant's porcine saddle-nose, passing on their genes, rather than that of the beautiful wives and mistresses their wealth attracted, to their daughters, but, regardless, it does show that a simple high-nose = high-class, low-nose = low-class equation did not work in Japan as one might assume from the art alone.

~~~~~~

Babylonian Marriage Market. One of two Babylonian practices highly lauded by Herodotus, the other being a public obligation to provide medical advice in the street to others suffering from the afflictions one has gotten over. When a Marriage Market is held, prospective brides are put on an auction block, starting from the most beautiful, who are "bought" for enormous sums of money by prospective grooms, then working slowly down until the point is reached where the men must be *paid* to accept the plain-looking women as a bride. That money, or dowry, paid to the men, who, needless to say are poor, comes from the bride's price obtained for the beauties; the sum gets higher and higher as the women get uglier until even the blind and deformed find a husband and a home. When I related this story to one of my sisters, she thought it *barbaric* and reprehensible. But, I wonder. Don't many if not most beauties in all cultures manage to find someone wealthy to "fall in love with"? Don't ugly women and poor men suffer from remaining single in societies where marriage is the norm? And, isn't it good for there to be a progressive tax on money and looks accomplished at one fell swoop? (Actually, I am not completely happy with the Babylonian system, for I dislike the great disparity in wealth upon which it is premised. The best social system to allow people of good and bad appearance, and good and bad sexual function, to enjoy a measure of equality and, consequently, contentment in life, that I have come across is found, or was found, among the Muria of North-Western India with their rotating sex communes, called *ghotal*, for teens. Check them out, if you would think about deep social justice.)

~~~~~~

Phimosis. Wiki has a fine summary that starts: *Phimosis is a medical condition in which the foreskin of the penis of an uncircumcised male cannot be fully retracted. The word derives from the Greek phimos ("muzzle"). The term is confusing because it is used to denote both a physiological stage of development, and a pathological condition.*

There are degrees of foreskin development from phimosis to tight prepuce to not fully separated to separated but non-retractable. Japanese clinic advertisements (my collection) for circumcision operations, show 4 types, ranging from "true phimosis" (a tiny hole open in the hood) to "false phimosis" (half of the glans peeks out) to Canton phimosis (the skin pinches tightly around the chin of the glans) and normal (head out and smiling).

A fine article (not Wiki) explains: "The false diagnosis of phimosis in boys is very common in the United States and the United Kingdom." And it taught me something new: "There is a phase of development during which some boys may experience "ballooning." Ballooning is the inflation of the prepuce during urination by the pressure of urine inside. This can occur if the inner layer of the prepuce is separating or has separated from the glans, which typically happens around three years of age, . . . Ballooning is an indication that the normal separation of the foreskin from the glans penis has occurred. . . " Finally, it explained why parents need not fear delaying: "If a narrow or non-retractile prepuce becomes a problem, a wide variety of conservative alternative treatments to circumcision are now available. Circumcision is an outmoded, radical, traumatic, disproportionate, unnecessary surgery for a minor problem." What is unbelievable is that we put men in rockets and sent them to the moon before we realized the first thing about the workings of our own little rockets.

~~~~~~
~~~~~~

The Female Equivalent of Phimosis? The Eggplant. This is a good example of the rhetoric of cross-sexual similarity found for most stereotypes in senryu.

どう見ても茄子は女の皮被り　葉 九
dô mite mo nasubi wa onna no kawakaburi

by any standard
the eggplant is a female
skin-hood boy

The *eggplant* tends to be the lowest ranked cunt in the listings. Drawings show various sized blobs of flesh, sometimes hanging down enough to block the vaginal opening. As there are far fewer "eggplants" in senryu than involuntarily hooded men, I skipped them in favor of the more numerous "dowries" as the better complement, but, as pointed out in *Cuntologia*, there would still seem to be more senryu than the number of "egg-plants" actually encountered should warrant. Perhaps the name attracted the poets:

植えぬのにひょんな茄子のなり所 万
uenu no ni hyon na nasubi no naridokoro 明三

not planted still
odd eggplants pop up
in odder places!

蒔かなくも何を種とて開は茄子 葉 25
tane ga naku mo nani o tane tote bobo wa nasu

though you don't
sow them what seed grows
pussy eggplants?

The adjective in the first *ku* could apply to eggplant &/or place. If you choose place *"Not planted, still / Don't eggplants pop up / in odd places!"* might be a good translation. The second *ku,* from the allegedly not-so-literary *Leaf* is the more poetic for borrowing the first 12 syllabets from a *waka* wondering what seeded the floating plants on the undulating waters by Ono Komachi, herself thought to be blocked up below (see ch. 10).

茄子は女の疝気だと山家医者 新編 40
nasu wa onna no senki da to sanka isha

the aubergine
is female lumbago says
the hill doctor

If you recall, lumbago *in senryu* refers to what happens when the lumbago bug takes refuge in the testicles: they swell. The eggplant is also confusing for it is a grab-bag of irregularities, from oversized dangling clitorises, labia, swollen perhaps from glandular problems or extremely long to vaginal prolapse. The description used was often a dried persimmon (the type hanging on the tree), for the dangling thing was not always shiny and swollen and at least one doctor pointed out that the prolapse tended to occur at childbirth because there was too much furniture/ equipment (*dôgu*) in the vagina, so, contrary to the low-ranking of the eggplant, such women tended to be *good* in bed. (さて、かの「山家医者」が辞典にでない。やぶ医者の変形でしょうか)

~~~~~~

Men With Pockmarks. I thought pockmarked men were OK, for looking scary is one male strategy for gaining respect, but Saikaku reminds us that at least girls can find a mate with the help of a large dowry, while similarly disfigured boys "are doomed to go through life unloved by men" (in Leupp:1995 from Schalow *Great Mirror.*) and that *"a youth with no male lover is like a maiden without a betrothed – i.e., the object of pity."* (Leupp notes this line is quoted with approval in Yamamoto's *Hagakure*). But, when adulthood is considered, the premise of this chapter ♀= face-value ♂= penis-value is not overturned.
~~~~~~

<u>*Why They Hate Senryû*</u>
川柳嫌ひも御尤も

廿[20]

下女臭ィ下女ハ
A Stinkiness *of* Maids

~~~~~~

下女よんで見て川柳はにくいやつ/ねへ
gejo yonde mite senryû wa nikui yatsu/nee 91-9
(maid read/ing-tries/sees, senryû hateful guy/thing)

after reading it
the maidservant says
"I hate Senryû"

trans. ueda

The above *Willow* senryu – in two slightly different versions of which Ueda's is the best ★ – is a marked improvement of another *ku* written decades earlier: *"Yanagidaru / after reading it the maid / gets angry"* 柳樽下女読んで見て腹を立ち 37-17 *yanagidaru gejo yonde-mite hara o tachi*). It is because we feel the humanity of the maid more in her own words, invented or not. But *what* upset her so much? On the whole, the maids (always meaning *maid-servants,* and not "maidens," in this chapter) in Ueda's selection are sweetly depicted. The only *ku* one could *possibly* find demeaning would be the description of her writing as "warped Sanskrit letters." Read this chapter and understand why *"I hate senryû."*

どうもつまめぬは子宮と下女の鼻 葉
dômo tsumamenu wa kotsubo to gejo no hana 16

what you just
cannot pinch: the cervix and
a maid's nose

鼾ではひくそふもない下女の鼻
ibiki de wa hikusô mo nai gejo ga hana 137-31

from her snores
you wouldn't think it small
the maid's nose

Ancient Japanese pictures tended to show *all* women virtually noseless, either because they followed Buddhist morality more than men and even as girls did not eat animal protein (needed for building bridges), because the nose represented a strong character considered bad for a woman, or for both reasons. Yet, by the time of senryu, the aristocrats of both sexes tended to have noses with a bridge (look at the prints) and all the high-class courtesans and other idealized beauties
~~~~~~

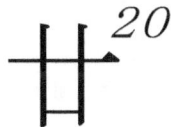

boasted beaks. Most maids came from localities and families that could afford so little animal protein that almost all went to the men. Most really had little more than a button with two holes in it for a nose. When I first came to Japan in the 1970's (and I knew one such maid!) the nose was *still* a major class indicator.

下女目立とこはほうぺた尻っぺた *86-11*
gejo medatsu toko wa hôpeta shirippeta

where the maids
stand out: the cheeks of
their faces, asses

where a maid
stands out: her cheekiness
above and below

I do not think "cheekiness" is idiomatic in Japanese, but Europeans who visited Japan in the last half of the 19c were surprised at the spunkiness of Japanese servants who presumed to do things *their* way if they thought they knew better than their master or mistress and that Japanese expected them to do so. This might owe something to the broadspread literacy. The pejorative description of the maid's handwriting, above, in international context, is rather testimony of the high level of culture among the menials in Japan that the Russian Captain Golownin (held captive by the Japanese in the early 19c) first made clear. But there may be other causes. One of my pet theories is that Japanese felt more at ease with their servants because they had a more clear-cut language of superiority and inferiority than Europeans, or at least English speakers. But all of this did not free the servants, from outlying rural regions, mostly under half-year or year-long contracts, from becoming perhaps the most popular butt of black humor.

しゝよけをしても麦ばた下女あらし 万 安二
shishi yoke o shite mo mugibata gejo arashi million
(boar-protector[+obj] done-even wheat/barley maid storm)

you may protect
your fields from boars but what
about the maids?

stop wild boars
the wheat's still beaten down
a storm of maids

The wheat or buckwheat fields were *the* place for blue-collar love. When the maids had a holiday, they were crushed. We will see more of this raw animal sexuality, but not outdoors.

下女が開ぼぼと思ってすれバ開 葉別
gejo ga kai bobo to omotte sureba kai 5 オ,138-23
(maidservant's *kai, bobo* as thinking, doing-if *kai*)

the maid thinks
her twat's a quim, sorry
that's a twat!

maids think that
they've pussies: but tried
a twat's a twat

at night all cats
are gray, but the maid's pussy
remains a twat

An often encountered literary chuckle has the maid's humming – which, in Japanese has connotations of self-contentedness, which may be why so few of them do it – bring down soot in the kitchen (下女が鼻うた台所のすゝがおち 14-20 *gejo ga hana-uta daitokoro no susu ga ochi*) – a contrast to a classic song where a beautiful (and operatic?) voice makes dust "dance" in the rafters, but we are looking lower in this book. The maid in the above *ku* is slapped back into her place when she over-rates her most popular part. Syunrôan guesses that the implications of *kai* were not so good as *bobo* back then, but I cannot help wondering whether 開, which was itself often pronounced *bobo* as well as *kai,* may not have had other pronunciations besides and here stands for the worst of them (*bebe* or *meme* or something). So, what is the problem with them?

毛虱も鼻つまんでる臭い下女 *146-14*
kejirami mo hana tsumanderu kusai gejo

even pubic lice
are holding their noses
a stinky maid

In Japanese, *pubic* lice are "hair-lice," a name that fits what a microscope shows: how finely adapted they are for holding tight to hair (like sloth toes). In the world of senryu, they were believed to live in a littoral zone, breeding or drowning from the water of life (seminal and vaginal emissions). In other words, uncleanliness, specifically, insufficient wiping after sex, was believed to breed them. And, note, unlike the maids, who tended to lack bridges on their noses because of low animal protein intake as well as genetics, these lice can hold *their* noses!

.

開ハ皆くさい物だと下女恥ず　葉 *27*
bobo wa mina kusai mono da to gejo hajizu
類句：誰がぼぼも臭い物だと下女思い

all pussies
stink says the maid
unashamed

Another *ku,* playing on a proverb, says "*'Keeping a lid / on something that stinks'* – that *is* / a chaste maid!" (くさいものふたをするのハかたい下女 万安六 *kusai mono futa o suru no wa katai gejo*). Most probably *did.* Maids did not get to take many baths.

下女うぬがうつり香だのに臭エイ八
gejo unu ga utsuriga danoni kusee mara 葉別 4
(maid conceit-the/is transfer-scent is-though stinky cock)

a maid's conceit
knows naught of transferred scent
"that stinky prick!"

And, couldn't we say that when something can't be helped, it is smart to have enough brains to fool oneself? To continue, it *looks* as bad as it smells. One *ku* speaks of shitty seaweed (下女寝糞おご) down there. Another declares that when a saint fell down for a *maid* doing her laundry, he fled right back up to heaven (下女のせんたく仙人も逃上り 124-90 *gejo no sentaku sennin mo nige-agari*) referring to a classic Chinese legend of one who fell off his cloud for a laundress who was not a maid). And they *sound* as bad as the smell and look: *"When the maid / really comes / she squeals like a pig"* (trans. Solt. 下女将によがる時其声豚葉 1 *gejo masa ni yogaru toki sono koe buta*). That is to say, when her *love-cries* are for real – not as she imagines they *should* be – they sound as swinish as she is.

下女よがる拍子にイ八へ屁を仕掛 葉
gejo yogaru byôshi ni mara e he o shikake15

c/ each love-cry
the maid cuts upon his cock
another fart

cutting a fart
on his cock c each love cry
a maid's art

The Coming of the Maid

c each cry
she cuts a fart
upon her master's
private part

Barnyard humor, but the original did have one fine word I failed to fit into the translation, *byôshi*, meaning *rhythm* or *beat*. It is like the maidservant is a one-woman or one beastie band. *Yogaru,* here, *proves* what I have observed, but the dictionaries fail to note: *it can mean the cries rather than orgasm*. The last translation is twelve years old. At that time, I was not shy about using four lines.

豆は豆だが下女の豆は納豆 26
mame wa mame da ga gejo no mame wa natô

natô nookie

a bean is a bean
but a maidservant's bean-toy
is fermented soy

Her bean is her clit, her cunt or both. I happen to love *natô* both for its unique flavor and for being the most digestible of all soy products. Stir a few beans together and they get exceedingly slimy and sticky and, to most Usanians, at least, downright nasty looking. When she took a noon nap, a less polite *ku* opined that the flies gathered 'round her "spoiled bean/s" (下女昼寝蝿の集るすえた豆 新編 14 *gejo hirune hae no atsumaru sueta mame*). Another very odd new metaphor: *"It can make even the tip of a spear shrivel up: a maid's dry-sardine boat"* (鑓先もなえるは下女の干鰯船 108-2 *yarisaki mo naeru gejo no hoshika-bune.*) It became popular and was repeated in *Willow* 110-? and 162-5. The Japanese sardine has a huge oily gut: the stink would rise to high heaven. And, worse yet, a maid out in the country was said to taste like a hinged-flounder (ざいご下女てうし平目のあぢがする　摘 1-6 *zaigo gejo chôshi-birame no aji ga suru*), a small flounder dried cut open and spread, that Edoites found particularly stinky. A generation later, the stereotype is literally summed up: *"Adding above & below, she's just eighteen: the maid's mouth/s"* (上エ下タで十八さいの下女が口 柳 88-32 *ue shita de jûhachi-sai no gejo ga kuchi*). "Nine" is pronounced *ku* and "years-old" *sai.* Each mouth must be nine-years-old, *ku-sai,* or, *"stinky"*(*kusai*). Now, *ku* about her dirty *behavior:*

下女の恋地ひゝきのする時も有リ 万
gejo no koi jihibiki no suru toki mo ari 宝 12
(maidservant's love earth-echo does times even are)

せわしない事
< *hasty pudding* >

the loves of a maid
sometimes we even feel
the earth shake

An earth-echo is a thud made when a tree falls on the ground or a heavy book on the floor. The maid is crashing down with her lover in total abandon.

いぢるとよがる猫の喉と下女の開 葉 32・*ijiru to yogaru neko no nodo to gejo no bobo*

1. *Stroke them, and they purr, a cat and ... a maid's pussy.*

下女じたい開にけちけちせぬ生れ ・ *gejo jitai bobo ni kech-kechii senu umare*

2. *The maid by birth・ never was one to starve ・ her cunt.*

下女か恋夜だひるだのしや別ッ無シ 万明四 ・*gejo ga koi yo da hiru da no ja betsunashi*

3. *A maid's love ・ draws no line between ・ day and night.*

立て居てもちぎりをこめる下女が恋 変種多い・*tatte ite mo chigiri o komeru gejo-ga-koi*

4. *Though overworked ・and beat, a maid makes love・on her feet.*

せっかちな下女逆寄に這て行 121 乙 24・*sekkachi na gejo gyakki ni haite-yuku*

5. *The hasty maid・ turns the table, crawling・ to get laid*

丁稚へも福分けをする下女が豆・*decchi e mo fukuwake o suru gejo ga mame*

6. *A maid's bean ・she shares her good luck ・with the boys*

いけ好きな下女お馬でもいい乗んな 88-12 ・*ikezuki na gejo o-uma demo ii norun-na*

7. *The dirty maid– ・ even if i am a horse ・ climb right on!*

引ッたてざねで聞て居る娵の下女 葉 30・ *hikittate-zane de kiite iru yome no gejo*

8. *Listening ・with perked up clitoris ・ the bride's maid*

下女が核人こそ知らね沖の石 紅の花・*gejo ga sane hito koso shirane oki no ishi*

9\. *A maid's clit – ・ that rock in the ocean ・ unseen by men*

~~~~~~

下女が色まき部屋などへ閉じこもり 明四義 8 ・ *gejo ga iro maki-beya nado e toji-komori*

10\. *A maid's sex: ・ she takes herself to ・ the woodshed*

~~~~~~

雪隠へやっとおさまる下女が尻 161-52 ・ *setchin e yatto osamaru gejo ga shiri*

11\. *In the toilet ・ he finally pacifies ・ the maid's ass*

~~~~~~

下女のはらこころ当りが弐参人 y 21-9 ・ *gejo no hara kokoro-atari ga ni san nin*

12\. *The maid's belly ・ – she can think of two ・ or three men.*

~~~~~~

総割にして出す下女がおろし代 ・ *sôwari? ni shite dasu gejo ga oroshi dai*

13\. *They chip in ・ for the fee to cover ・ the maid's abortion*

~~~~~~

仲条で下女よがって叱られる 摘 1-35 ・ *chûjô de gejo yogatte shikarareru*

14\. *At the abortionist ・ the maid gets scolded . . . for coming!*

.

There are so many dirty-minded maid *ku* not worth a full presentation that I changed the format. In respect to the above: 1) "Purr" here is not the usual (*nodo o narasu*), but *yogaru*, the verb for love-crying English lacks. 2) Literally, "to be "stingy (*kechi*) " *to* her bobo. The wit is in the "to" rather than the usual "with." (「ご自愛を／＼」と前句したい！). 3) Big deal? It is only natural if maids are as easily made by day as by night. Similar *ku* have them do what should be done lying down standing up (とんだ下女寝てすることを立ってする 摘 2-3 *tondu gejo nete suru koto o tatte suru*). Why not? (前句＝どふそ／＼と) 5) In China, the girls could call on boys, too, but in Japan it was thought unseemly (alt. version: 待かねて下女こっちから這て行 明五義 5). 5) Beans were thrown outside in a seasonal ritual to rid one of bad luck and ones tossed inside and/or eaten for good luck. And *bean* was... 丁稚 comes from China where boys had pig-tails: (丁). In Japan, *decchi* were boys hired to do odd jobs around shops. It is kind of the maids to share with them. 7) The "horse" is her period (ch.2). 8) Ears are *perked up* in Japanese, too. 8) The rock in the sea alludes to a classic poem (one of the famous 100) that no one saw because it was "always wet" with tears of unrequitted love. It is common clitoral trope. 10) Actually, it is "locks herself up" or "holes up in" in the woodshed. I could not resist taking advantage of an idiom. 11) Or, is she pacifying her own ass, by masturbating there? 12) Another version ups it to *five or seven* men! 13) Self-explanatory. 14) *Abortionist* is an ugly long word, but English lacks another. The original uses that missing love-cry verb, *yogaru*. Another version has *hana o narashite, i.e.* "sounds her nose," for Japanese associate noses with sexual excitement even if maids aren't supposed to have them. Solt cleverly makes the *yogaru* version "~ *brings herself off* / and gets scolded" (my italics), but explained only that she was given "erotic prints to take her mind off the pain." *The idea was to induce sexual excitement to help get open the vagina and the cervix enough to insert an abortificent* (Could "our" priests have done the same to baptize babies in dying mothers with syringes?), which might be done for several days in a row. So, it is not so much coming, as doing so *loudly*, that was uncalled for.
~~~~~~

ふんどしを上へと下タとへ下女ハ〆
fundoshi o ue to shita to e gejo wa shime 万宝 13
(convince-not-if maid even ass-as-for do/allow-not-be)

the maid cinches
her loincloths one above
and one below

くどかねば下女でもけつはさせぬ也 葉
kudokaneba gejo demo ketsu wa sasenu nari 8
(convince-not-if maid even ass-as-for do/allow-not-be)

even a maid
must be talked into giving
up her ass

The first describes what a chaste maid is up against. The sign 〆 is written on the corner of a sealed envelope. The second responds to decades of dirty maid stereotypes to say *unless she's persuaded*, she won't let you *that*.

恋の闇下女は小声でここだわナ 121 乙 33
koi no yami gejo wa kogoe de koko da wa na

love in the dark
the maid's voice is soft
"it's right here"

The maid's voice in the original is touching with its straightforward *"da"* (is), open feminine emphatic "wa" and assertive suffix (?) "na." We think back to our first magical gropings in the dark. Such a *ku* beats the fancy mythological allusion: *"In the bed-dark / what shines is the cave-door / of the maid"* (床闇で明くは下女の岩戸なり 41-13 *tokoyami de akaruku wa gejo no iwato nari*), itself perhaps a parody of a classic senryu about a king's sweetheart who could more than liquify her robes: *"Shine-through-Clothes Princess pierces the darkness with her hole "* (くらやみへ衣通姫は穴をあけ 10-11 *kurayami e sotôri-hime wa ana o ake*).

手と足で来るのを下女は待ッて居ル 摘
te to ashi de kuru no o gejo wa matte-iru 4-5

the maid awaits
a man who calls on his own
hands and feet

下女へ這い先ンがあるので這い戻り
gejo e hai mazun ga aru no de hai-modori 6-11

crawling to the maid
"somebody's already here"
so back he crawls

板の間に有ル夜手の跡ト足の跡ト 万&
itanoma ni aru yo tenoato ashinoato 宝 11

◎いやしかりけり◎
how lowdown can you get

left one night
on the wooden floor
handprints, footprints

In classic times, even nobles spent their nights sneaking about like tom-cats to visit their mates (who generally stayed in *their* homes), so this was called "night-crawling." If you think of a jar of fireflies lighting the way it is romantic; if you think of the mosquitos and watch-dogs, it is not. With the maid, her men probably really had to crawl, for if there was any light, shadows would show through paper partitions. With respect to the second *ku,* we feel sorry for the man – it is a touching *ku* – but the maid was only being pragmatic (trying them out). With the last *ku,* I may have over-translated the draw. Maybe *"Ignoble indeed!"* or *"How Beastly!"*would be better.

もふしてハやらぬと下女はおどされる
mô shite wa yaranu to gejo wa odosareru 摘 1-35

how to threaten
a maid: tell her "i won't
do you anymore!"

"i won't do you
anymore!" – threatening
a maid servant

Black humor. From high-school in Miami, Florida, I recall: *"What happens when you quit paying the garbage bill in Poland?" "They stop delivering."*

下女胡瓜何にするのか一本買い・ *gejo kyuri nani suru no ka ippon kai 別下 36*

1. *the maid-servant buys one cucumber – whatever for?*

~~~~~~

そった胡瓜をつくずくと下女眺め ・*sotta kyuri o tsukuzuku to gejo nagame 90-37*

2. *the maid stares, transfixed by a cucumber with an arc*

~~~~~~

つくづく胡瓜の疣に下女見とれ・*tsukuzuku kyuri no ibo ni gejo mitore 63-18*

3. *the maid, utterly enthralled by the bumps on a cucumber*

~~~~~~

ふかしたて握って下女の余念なさ・*fukashitate nigitte gejo no yonen-nasa 55-19*

4. *just roasted, now gripped – the maid totally engrossed*

~~~~~~

丸焼きを下女おし込んで開火傷・*maruyaki o gejo oshikonde bobo yakedo 葉別 4*

5. *a baked yam, pushed in whole: the maid's burnt bobo*

~~~~~~

焼芋逆カ手目をすへて下女よがり 葉7 ・*yaki-imo sakate me o suete gejo yogari 葉 7*

6. *a hot yam held ninja style, eyes rolled back, the maid yodels*

1. Buying *one* is suspicious. 2. An up-bend penis was considered classy. 3. There is something endearing about innocent desire for self-pleasure. 4. And isn't it enlightened to lose oneself? 5. Perhaps, not entirely! 6. These *[satsuma]imo* are the color of of roasted chestnut and the mouthfeel between a baking potato and a yam. They are generally roasted between hot river stones. Solt's translation, *"the maid inserts / a roasted sweet potato / and her eyes roll back in climax,"* is accurate – I captured the love cry with the "yodel," while he chose to name the physiological state accompanying it – but the wit is in the martial imagery of the reverse-hand grip (*sakate*), one where the blade sticks down from the butt of the hand. That is how *ninja* are typically depicted. I suspect the combination of said grip and eye-rolling may be found in some dramatic character. While the above vegetables are the mainfare for maid masturbation, senryu could only digest so many pickles and potatoes. How about something different, like . . . fish?
~~~~~~

すばしりて命を捨てた下女も有り　万
subashiri de inochi o suteta gejo ari　明五

there are maids
who have lost their lives
for a mullet

Oddly enough, the more explanatory *ku* come decades later: *"An emergency! / The maid can't pull out / her mullet!"* サァ事だ下女鯱がぬけません 葉7 *saa koto da gejo subashiri ga nukemasen.*) Another *ku* further explains she got in trouble using the *subashiri* where the *ina* was correct –the navel of the latter being the cap to the cervix (すばしりをイナものにして下女困り 73-18 *subashiri o ina mono ni shite gejo komari*). Both fish are just *young mullets* to English. With round cross-sections and blunt snouts, these fish are phallic, but scales would make hell to pull out, even if they did not have gills. If only the maids were more literate, they might have noticed the danger (危) lurking in the fish's very name (鮠)!

あかぎれのかかとでしめて下女よがり 摘
akagire no kakato de shimete gejo yogari 1-15

with chapped heels
finally clinching it,
the maid cuts loose

皆入れて紐のこそばい奥女中 名付親
mina irete himo no kosobai okujochû 文化 11

all of it pushed in
the string tickles
the chambermaid

Tying a dildo to the heel seems odd for a maidservant because it was a Chinese-derived practice associated with ladies-in-waiting and chamber-maids (ch.4). Their heels would not be chapped and their cries would be stiffled in their long sleeves. Compare that chapped heel with the delicacy of string brushing tush.

下女工夫糸こんにゃくを指に巻き 61-28, 88-32,
gejo kufû ito-konnyaku o yubi ni maki & 160-2

a maid's cunning
wrapping the devil's tongue
'round her finger

the ingenuity
of a maid: wrapping konjak
'round her finger

a maid's invention
wrapping her fiunger with
strings of konjak

下女たすきかけてあきれた事をする 万
gejo tasuki kakete akireta koto o suru 安元

the maid she
does outrageous things
c/ a tasuki

A springy starch *bar* made from *Konnyaku*, *konjak* or devil's tongue, that men masturbated with is described elsewhere (pp.78-81). It was also sold in string form. The maid is imitating the practice of wrapping another type of root-starch ribbon, *higo zuiki*, around the penis to give it more breadth and tickle-power. It is possible she is doing the same with a *tasuki.* Or else she is tying a vegetable dildo to her heel. But, what is a *tasuki?* It is a strap used to gird up ones sleeves. When sleeves are extremely wide as they are in some traditional Japanese clothing, the sleeves can get in the way or get dirty, so people doing chores, but not wishing to take time to change to workclothes with narrower sleeves just take this thin but strong cloth ribbon and wrap it around and under their shoulders so it makes an X over the chest. When a pregnant woman wears one of these is the only time one notices breasts in Japan (or, noticed, for this is no longer true).

せんやくをいたゝけば下女ついと逃
zenyaku o itadakeba gejo tsui to nige 摘 *1-2*
(steeped-medicine[acc.] receive[humbly] maid flees)

he raises his cup
of tea in the air & suddenly
the maid's not there

the maid bolts
the moment his herb tea
clears his head

The *draw-ku* is, "s/he's on the ball!" or "that's clever indeed!" (*kashiko-kari-keri*). An innocent reader might think she avoids an old man soon to have a hard-on. That is the teaser reading. The maid sees him raise his concoction into the air *and thinks he is offering some to her*. Another senryu translated by Blyth has a maid flee when offered a *koban,* a large unit of money (さあ小判欲しかやらふに下女は逃げ 明和 *saa koban hoshi ka yarô ni gejo wa nige*). He writes "she runs away because she wants the money"(1960). I would say, because it could be forced on her and the maid is afraid one thing can lead to another. In the case of the above *Pluck ku,* she was too clever for her own good. The tea was raised up high out of respect (目八分) for the medicine and doctor and from the wish that it work its miracles on the man receiving it. The *Pluck* round-robin team mentions joking stories (江戸小咄) where a similar mistake is made for collaborative evidence. Yet, I found a later *Pluck ku* that shows why maids need to stay on their feet unless they want a fall:

四ッ目やの心見に下女される也 摘
yotsumeya no kokoromi ni gejo sareru nari 4-21

as a test run
for the four-eye cream
a maid is done

As mentioned elsewhere in the book, but where I forget, the four-eye-shop sold aphrodisiacs and, most of all, salves to increase a man's staying power, including the patented Nagamochi-maru, the SS Long-Last.

gang-banged maids

ねこい下女初手の人たと思つて居 万明七
negoi gejo hatsude no hito da to omote-iru million

a heavy-sleeper
the maid thinks he is
the first one

割て見りや下女夜たかより安クつき 万
watte miriya gejo yotaka yori yasuki tsuki 明五

pool your dough
and a maid can be laid for
less than a whore

もうおれハいやだと下女を替わり合
mô ore wa iya da to gejo o kawari-ai 摘 4-33

"i've had enough"
he says, giving the maid
to the other

These are all disrespectful to maids. The *draw-ku* for the second *ku "An embarrassing thing"* (はつかしゐこと) implies the maid should be ashamed to be so cheap. Only the last hints at shame on the part of the men, *"That's beyond the pale!"* (あんまりな事) but it may just mean the maid can wear them all out. Regardless, it would be less than honest not to own up to the existence of many *ku* that are truly beyond redemption. The above three are probably about the sex-starved men taking advantage of the maid's being fine with taking care of many men, but maids are clearly the victims in the majority of clear *rape* senryu.

大の字に引ッはられてゝ下女__れる 万
ô no moji ni hippararete de gejo sareru 安六

a crime written 'large'

stretched out
to make the letter 大
a maid's done

手に弐人足に弐人リで下女ハされ万
te ni futari ashi no futari gejo wa sare 安四

two for each hand
and two for each leg
a maid's done.

半分ハしらない人と下女ハなき 万
hanbun wa shiranai hito to gejo wa naki 安六

"and half of them
were men i didn't know"
cries the maid

前後あらそひにて下女をとりにがし
zengo arasoi nite gejo o tori-nigashi 万安九
(before-after fighting-in maidservant[acc]catch-flee)

quarreling over
who goes first, their catch
the maid escapes

These four *ku*, all from the early *Million*, show Karai Senryû was partial to this *theme* from the get-go. At least the last one makes it clear that the men were considered as beastly or more beastly than the maids.

むごい事下女してハのき／＼ 摘
mugoi-koto gejo shite wa nokinoki 1-35
(horrid thing maid doing-as-for leaving/fleeing)

something horrendous
making the maid, they flee
one after another

a horrid thing
one at a time leaves the maid,
leaves the scene

a horrid thing
one by one they get
off the maid

how many the maid no longer knows
as soon as one comes . . . off he goes

The last, from Senryû's more selective *Pluck,* starts with the phrase that came to mean *rape* in senryu, usually, but not here, in the draw-ku: *"mugoi koto,"* or "horrendous thing." That term suggests no one countenanced the *practice*, but the draw, "so long as there's life" (命なりけり／＼*inochi narikeri*), seems fatalistic: ". . . men will do these things."

娘は死出のだんまつま次ギャアおれだ 葉
ko wa shide-no danmatsuma tsugya ore da 別四
(girl-as-for death-road's throes-of-death next-as-for me is)

the girl's soul
is halfway gone – "hey,
my turn's next!"

a girl near death
their concern: "me next!"
"me next!"

the girl is knocking
on heaven's gate: the cock
'fraid of being late!

I cannot tell if this last *ku,* from an 1839 supplement to *Leaf,* should be taken as black humour of the worst type or criticism of male selfishness and cruelty.

むごい事十番迄ハ下女おぼへ ・*mugoi koto jûban made wa gejo oboe* 万安四
Something horrendous – the maid remembers up to the tenth.

~~~~~~

いち／＼ハおほへませんと下女ハなき・ *ichi-ichi wa oboemasen to gejo wa naki* 万安七
"I can't recall this or that detail," says the maid, crying.

The draw for the first, "horrendous" *ku,* is *"hold a grudge"* (*urami koso sure*). In Japan, the woman's most dependable weapon was her *grudge*, especially if she took it to the grave so she could exact revenge as a ghost (in the Sinosphere, some even killed themselves to speed that process). Would not belief in this sort of vengeance-by-grudge – logically more reliable than a curse because it does not rely upon God but upon one's own spirit to personally punish the evil-doer – be a bigger check on bad behavior than a belief in Heaven and Hell?
~~~~~~

死ヌまねをしろとおしへる下女が宿 万
shinu mane o shiro to oshieru gejo ga yado 安七

"just pretend that
you're dead," they teach –
the maid's lodge

てんば下女寝床へ薪を一本持ち *4-3*
tenba-gejo nedoko e maki o ippon mochi

the tomboy maid
keeps one large faggot
right by her bed

With the "draconian" law of Tokugawa Japan, I doubt such instruction was necessary – it is probably a fiction, invented to cope with (?) the common occurrence of gang-banged maids *in earlier senryu*. Still, the advice is familiar. It fits the usual one for an urban civilization: *don't fight criminals, leave that to the authorities*. Call me a barbarian, but, bravo for the tomboy.

極重く極く早いのハ下女が尻 *39-32*
goku omoku goku hayai no wa gejo ga shiri
(extremely heavy extremely fast-as-for maid's ass)

very heavy
yet light indeed, the ass
of a maid

as slow as can be
yet too fast to see: the ass
of a young maid

slow as molasses
yet fast and loose, the ass
of a young maid

なめた下女叱ればぺろり舌を出し *37-17*
nameta gejo shikareba perori shita o dashi

The maid, who was taken advantage of
sticks out her tongue when she's scolded

Slow/fast s*ass*iness is most common in teens, so I made the maid "young." *Ku #2* is about poetic justice: in Japanese, to be "taken advantage of" is to be "licked!" *Perori* is one of my favorite of the many adverbs of psychological mimesis Japanese boasts. It helps one visualize that tongue stuck out and moving a bit. Maids may have liked sex, but they did expect *something* from their partner. A less poetic earlier *ku* put it like this: *Even a maid / won't take you twice coming / empty-handed* 手ぶりてハ下女も弐度とハ承知せす 万安元 *teburi de wa gejo mo ni do to wa shôchi sezu*).

ちょつ／＼としてくんなよとさがみいひ
cho' cho' to shite kun-na yo to sagami ii 摘 *1-17*

now don't you
come 'round for a *little* sex
says the sagami

The existence of the stereotype of clearly nymphomaniac maid-servants from Sagami makes it clear that maids in general were simply exuberant, full of animal spirits, blessed with healthy sexual appetites. I can't begin to mimic a semantically identical senryu in a much thicker country dialect: *"Tain't right to halp yerself to a tad o' pussy"* (おちゃぴい少しまくってあかんべい 摘 3-40 *ochyapii sukoshi makutte akanbei*). It does not mention a Sagami, but if it isn't Sagami dialect, then, *ben trovado*, it should be, for there are *hundreds* of *ku* about the insatiability of Sagami: *"Come, come and / come for me again / moans the Sagami," "If you can come ten times, / then, come on! / says the Sagami."* – as they say in Sweden, *"One time is not a time"* (*en gong er inte en gong*). It is claimed that merely *"The sight of a mushroom / suffices to turn on /a Sagami."* They are so horny they turn the usual way of men with maids upside down. To wit, they threaten their masters to fuck them *or else:* But, hey, they are alright! "*Aside from making [men do it],a Sagami has not a bad bone in her body"* (させる外さがみわる気の無イ女 摘 1-31 *saseru hoka sagami wa waruge no nai onna*), as one fine *Pluck ku* I could not at first manage to parse into a poem, put it.That is to say, their bedtime manners may be a bit pushy, but they have absolutely *no ulterior motives unless it is the sex itself.* The *Pluck* Round-robin could not agree whether the *ku* had a slight barb –

They show no mercy to a man's private parts –
Otherwise, Sagami have very kind hearts.

– or was facetious criticism by some one really grateful for the existence of such giving girls:

.

A Sagami, what luck!
All they really want is a good fuck!"

These maids are not loose of morals or psychologically deranged, that is just their nature that comes from their place of birth. As one senryu put it, "The lower mouth of a Sagami woman and the upper mouth of a Shinano man." Both are gluttons (Issa, by the way, comes from Shinano and his numerous *fart ku* suggest he was a big eater). The typical *young* woman in the world of senryu is happy to get a break from male demands for sex. A Sagami wants all she can get. *"To think that there are chastity belts! / A Sagami stays open year-round"*(original, alas, lost) A "battle" with a Sagami doesn't stop *"until both ships are sunk"* (original lost to my regret for *now* I realize the rarity of the ship metaphor . . .).

そう泣カばぬくぞと下女をしつし (ち=万) かり
sô nakaba nuku zo to gejo o shicchikari 摘 *2-28*

if you keep on
crying like that, i'll pull out
he tells the maid

This combines two stereotypes 1) the maid makes loud animal-like love cries (which might catch his wife's attention?) and 2) the maid likes doing it so much she can be manipulated by holding back. The second shows us that the difference between the generic maid and a Sagami was not always pronounced.

~ eddies ~

Versions and Readings of the Lead Ku. The version I took from a collection of all *Yanagidaru* senryu ends in "is hateful, right!" (*nikui nee*). Ueda's version ends in "is/are [a] hateful guy/book/poems" (*nikui yatsu*). It is clearly better, and a bit ambiguous because "yatsu" can mean a guy, or simply anything that one feels critical about. Since it increases the humor to think of the maid blaming one person, Senryû, for the sins of all *ku*, I favor Ueda's version in his reading of *gejo yonde* . . .. But please note the irony in this. Ueda, like most who have written about senryu, puts down the late-period senryu as lacking originality; but he chose *Willow* 91-9 over 37-17. Copycat or not, it *is* better.

Servants with Minds of their Own. It is possible that the Japanese servants employed by European visitors were extraordinarily bold characters who gave an exaggerated impression of their independence of mind, but 19c Europeans (including Usanians) found that Japanese accepted servants as equals in ways their own cultures did not. Good quotes may be found somewhere within my 740pg *Topsy-turvy 1585* (2003) monster.

Golownin and Japan's High Level of Culture. Captain Vasilii Mikhailovich Golownin and some of his men were captured and held by the Japanese from 1811-13 as a result of ill-feelings that arose as a result of pillage by rogue Russian "traders." Learned and patient, he turned his imprisonment into an intercultural opportunity. Among other things, he noted that most officials were free-thinkers (rational and atheist, but appreciative of the uses of religion), that Japan had a more thoroughly developed market economy (with advertizements and price tags) than anything he had seen in Europe, and, relevant to my comments re. the maids, that jailers, soldiers and others who were neither officers nor gentlemen generally read at night and played difficult board games (not checkers, but *shôgi*, the equivalent of chess, or the even higher board game of *go* that can still beat up Big Blue *et al*. (More from Golownin, whom I think the world of, in *Topsy-turvy 1585* (2004))

Why We Segregate Classes. Additional to my hypothesis that the more clear-cut manner in which Japanese treat language between unequals serves to make unequals more comfortable in each other's presence than they would be speaking the more socially ambiguous English, I wonder if our ideology of equality (already wide-spread in the 19c) and blind faith in capitalism made us and still make us uncomfortable to be with those whose presence reminds us of the inequality we depend upon and shows that the market (our excuse for amoral behavior) does not reward most people fairly for their work.

Hair Lice & Cunt Lice** (the same thing)* ***Senryû. Just a few from *Leaf* (葉末) –

つびじらみ人と成べき水のはし 葉16
tsubijirami hito to narubeki mizu no hashi
(cunt-lice man-into-become-ought water's edge)

pussy lice
on the shore of the water
bearing man

毛虱の曰く素人のが味い 146-12
kejirami no iwaku shirôto no ga umai
(hair-louse/lice say/s amateur one's tasty)

hair lice know
the so-called amateurs
taste best

淫水の津波毛虱おぼれ死 葉九
insui no tsunami kejirami obore-jini
(lascivious-waters's tidal-wave hairlice drown)

a tidal wave
of lechery: for pubic lice
death by drowning

a tidal wave
of lechery: the lice drown
clinging to hair

コイツ無宿だ土器のつび虱 葉別九
koitsu mushuku kawarake no tsubijirami

this one's homeless!
a cunt louse on
a bare pie

~~~~~~

Why Maids are Adorable. Reading the senryu translated by Blyth, after I stopped admiring sheer intelligence (maybe in my thirties?) but years before I could read them well myself, I realized I had grown very fond of the maid-servants.

どのくらいから美人だと下女まじめ
dono kurai kara bijin da to gejo majime 66-2
(how much from beauty is [says/asks] maid earnest)

'just how beautiful
makes one a beauty?' the maid
asks in earnest

I have no complaint with Blyth's expansive translation – *"How beautiful must one be / To be called a beauty" / The maid-servant asks quite earnestly.* – which is easier to read than mine. But, his comments are another matter:

> The question is a very foolish one, and admits of no answer, but it is not therefor to be scorned and scoffed at by a mere man. It reveals the woman's soul, its longing for adulation and love, its vague, unintellectual, inarticulate nature, the nature of Nature itself. (In "Women" in *Japanese Life and Character in Senryu*)

Blyth's broad-brush genderizing is not so unctious as that of D.H. Lawrence and Nietzsche; but, here, I wanted him to say instead, *blessed are the naive*, for they are open and not afraid to admit to not knowing everything. This is not about *woman*, but *maid-servants*, or some of them, at any rate. If one grew up in a rural village, met very few people and saw few pictures, and those you did see idealized appearance so the faces were either saddle-nosed peasants or well-beaked samurai and nobles, the variety encountered in Edo might have been hard to make sense of. The senryu may be chuckling at the maid for asking that, but it really is not a foolish question. It is a *good* one. I am so tired of ignorant know-it-alls and pretentious fools. Perhaps, had Blyth lived in late-20c Usania he would feel the same. I recall with fondness the few truly naive country souls I have had the good fortune to meet in my life – one was a girl-friend – and regret that, with the spread of Usanian culture, they are fast becoming the most endangered species on earth. The maid-servants of senryu – whose image I am afraid this chapter, concentrating on the part below the belt fails to do justice to – are a record, the very memes of the meek of the earth who, unfortunately, are far from inheriting it. *Amen* (apologies for preaching)*!*
~~~~~~

Persuading Words?
下手も口説き

廿一[21]

「オレのが小さい」等々
"Mine's Small" & Other Bad Lines

~~~~~~

おれがのハちいさいともりくとかれる 摘
orega no wa chiisai to mori kudokareru 1-26

mine is small
he says, trying to make
the baby-sitter

小むすめをあたま斗とくどく也 摘
komusume o atama bakari to kudoku nari 1-12

just the tip
he says coming on to
the little girl

Pluck has been called literature, but this is crude stuff! I recall a joke with the "tip only" come-on from my early teens in South Florida. I know not if it is *realistic*, for I have never tried to talk a woman *of any age* into sex. If a woman wants to, she wants to, if not, not. What makes this theme interesting is that modern Japanese, or at least Tokyoites, seem boringly unverbal *except when drunk* (far from Scots, who enjoy exchanging quips, Cubans who enjoy the same with insults, or Koreans, who argue ferociously). Using reason to cajole or convince was frowned upon: a superior should not *have to* explain himself and an inferior was not *supposed to*. That might not have been true in more egalitarion parts of Japan, but having experienced all too much of it in person and in the literary criticism of traditional poetry which never fails to call *logic-based wit* something insincere and foreign to Japan, namely, *Chinese*, I was *delighted* to find people using words to try to have their way in folk-song and senryu, genre hard to saddle with the charge of being "foreign." And, not only did Japanese *talk* people into doing things, they had a good word for it, *kudoku* (口説く) that serves well in the active or passive form. The baby-sitter above is *kudokareru,* but the English passive form "being made" does not work, "solicited" is lawyer talk, "seduced" a different matter (seduction is not *what* but *how* you say it),"persuade" too general and "come-on" too crude. I was tempted to use the 19c "ruin" for the first two *ku.*

おれも能イ男とごぜをくどくなり 摘
ore mo ii otoko to goze o kudoku nari 1-8

i'm handsome, too
he claims, trying to make
the blind chanson
~~~~~~

Again juvenile humor. A blind balladeer called a *goze* sometimes sold her body with her voice. 摘 1-20↓ 摘 2-6↓

おれにばかさせぬと下女をくどくなり
ore ni baka sasenu to gejo o kudoku nari

i'm the only one
not getting any, trying to
make the maid

してやるも大きな事と下女へいひ
shite yaru mo ooki na koto to gejo e ii

doing it to you
is risky for me, too, he
tells the maid

While, "I'm the only one" is a pitiful argument that degrades both parties, maids *were* sympathetic souls with the strong sense of fairness that comes naturally to people who spend their lives serving others and getting the short end of the stick; the line may have worked sometimes. The *"risky for me"* in the second *ku* is more like *"is a big thing"* in the original. It, too, is a true line. Even if he – the master of the house or his son, for the verb used for "doing it" (*shite yaru*) implies he does so as a favor, as someone might throw a dog a bone – does not risk getting pregnant, or losing his job, he can get hell from his mother or his wife. There are senryu which made such things clear –

おろす沙汰女房高みで見物し 摘
orosu sata nyôbô takami de mimono-shi 4-29
(dropping[abort] report/affair wife heights-from spectator-does)

The Abortion

husband and maid
it serves them right – his wife
sits cool that night

The Spectator

the abortion doctor
makes a call – his wife alone
above it all

There were high stakes involved in love play, for even without Christian morals, people got jealous because they were people, and people felt compassion for others because they were people. The wife is still fuming and the husband torn between compassion for his maid lover and fear of his wife. No, that is still too simple, he would have also felt some sympathy for his wife's situation. Please excuse the diversion. The senryu is a good one and had it not been introduced here, I would have slipped it into the chapter on abortion. Back to those lines:

したいときやいつでもいへと下女にいひ
shitai toki ya itsudemo ie to gejo ni ii 摘 *2-10*

if you should ever
want to do it, just tell me
says he to the maid

if you ever want
to be laid, just say, he
says to the maid

As embarrassing as it is to admit it – especially after writing that I did not use lines – I have faint memories of using this one, which I did not think of as a line, but just a fact, somewhere, sometime in a past that seems increasingly like a foreign country as I age. But I would never have said anything like the next.

見た事があるにといやなくどきやう 摘
mita koto ga aru ni to iya na kudoki yô 2-16

'afterall, i saw
you doing it' is no way
to get a lay

'you know i once
saw you nude' is very rude
for a come-on

Seeing lines like this, one becomes aware that senryu are not giving us the best lines, but the *worst*. This is like a bad writing contest. Indeed, I think that when it came to lines, it was. But, the vagueness of the original, of not knowing *what* was seen (no "you" need be specified), makes it a *slightly* better in the original.

跡トがらくだよと道鏡くとくなり 万 明三
ato ga raku da yo to dôkyô kudoku nari しんしつな事

"a kind thing"

after me, the rest
will be easy as pie: that's
dôkyô's line

Dôkyô's huge member could hardly have fit anyone but his likewise bountiful Empress, but this senryu imagines him trying to make a girl. The line's meaning? Thanks to that broadening experience, she will not have to suffer the pains of giving birth. My title is the *draw* of the original. I have seen the same line in a modern cartoon, coming from the mouth of a white man hung like a horse trying to seduce a Japanese girl. More rarely, it was used for pacification:

うむ時はどうするものとがまんさせ 摘
umu toki wa dôsuru mono to gaman sase 1-7

"then how will you
ever give birth?" he says
making her bear it

That would be a married couple doing it for the first time, so it is not so much a come-on as persuasion to continue doing what they started. Presumeably, it was a combination caused by her having little experience and his being well-hung.

かたづけて遣ルはつにして合点させ 万
katazukete yaru hazu ni shite gatten sase 明三
(tidying-up-send-should-with doing agree-makes)

with some words
about fixing her up he gets
her to give in

she sees the light
when he says he'll make her
someone's wife

The draw, *suki na koto kana* (something [you] like, right?) implies these are people who like to do it and the ambiguity of *hazu* (should/ought) implies a far from formal promise. Together it means the possibly insincere master of the house's line worked on the half-believing maid-servant. Be that as it may, we are out of lines. Here is something a bit different, a senryu *about* a line:

口説かれて娘は猫にものをいひ
kudokarete musume wa neko ni mono o ii 4-38

single daughters

when she's fed
a line, she tries feeding it
it to her cat

when a man
comes on to her, the girl talks
to her cat

This is an example of an excellent, but not at all dirty *ku*. It is in the Iwanami selection of top senryu, a good portion of which are identical to those translated by Blyth (which is why I do not give many good clean *ku*). Typically, the *musume* + *neko* (cat) combination means a daughter/girl who is a virgin, stays home and wastes away from consumption unless shocked out of it by a physically complete love affair. The cat, especially a black one, was thought to be of some help for her condition. But this is not *necessarily* about such a girl. It could be read more cheerfully. We may imagine a sassy young thing, making fun of her would-be lover, perhaps right before his face.

へのこゆへぶちのめされる色男 摘
henoko yue buchi-nomesareru iro-otoko 3-26

his pecker
gets the lady's man
beaten up

the lady's man
takes a good beating
for his cock

木娘をくといたつらにみみずはゐ 万
kimusume o kudoita tsura ni mimizu hai 安四

the face of the man
who seduced his sweet daughter?
feeding maggots

One can lose by winning. The first *ku* is there simply to set the scene. Reading the second, far better *ku* – *Pluck* clearly did not get all the best *ku* from *Million* – I recalled a line from a country song about a sweet-talking suitor: *"... and there will be one less Philidelphia lawyer."* The verb is the same *kudoku,* meaning to persuade someone by words to do something. Here, "seduced" seemed right.

give it to me
and be orderly about it!
a wacky line

ちんじやうにさせろはとんだくどきやう
jinjô ni sasero wa tonda kudoki yô 摘 *2-39*
(tamely do/let[imper]-as-for shocking line-style)

"be a good girl
and let me do it" – talk
about a bad line!

"just surrender
your body to me" – that's
a wacky line!

Judging from the *next ku,* the above comes from the mouth of a samurai who thinks he has a right to a maid-servant or other commoner's body. The adverb was often used with verbs appealing for criminals to come out peacefully and surrender. The verb here is none of those, but the third reading provides it nonetheless.

くどく間がなくて理不尽つかまつり 摘
kudoku ma ga nakute rifushin tsukamatsuri 1-11
(persuade period/time not, logic-not-exhaust did [in honorifics])

too busy to woo
he was forced to force
himself on her

having no time
to wine and dine i had to
make her mine

too busy
to make her he just
made her

According to the *Pluck* round-robin, this last *ku* was inspired by court records (奉行所の口書) of interrogations and testimony by the accused and all involved. While the euphemism "logic-not-exhaust" is used for *rape*, the round robin feels the draw-verse, "a delightful thing" (*tanoshimi no koto*) means the *ku's* focus is not on the crime or conviction, for capital punishment was taken seriously, but on the pretentious language used by the samurai defendent. In other words, it pokes fun at the warrior class, disliked by the townsmen for their overbearing nature. That leaves me a bit confused, but it is interesting to see how a senryu can be a miniature ballad, a sort of digest of the news.

くどきよふこそあらふのに手を合
kudoki yô koso arô no ni te o awase 摘 2-19
(persuade-seems[emph.] should though hands uniting)

when she might
be talked into it why
resort to prayer

though she could
be fed a line he puts
his hands together

Would your will be done?
Why clasp hands and bow your head,
when you have a tongue!

from woman to man

あいたあなだからしなよとむごくいひ
aita ana dakara shina yo to mugoku ii 摘 1-21

my hole's open
so why not do it! that ***is***
a brutal line

brutally put:
the hole's unemployed
so let's do it!

While it is said that Japanese women in ancient times propositioned men, the mythology seems to show that at some time (with the ascendence of a different culture?) that became unacceptable. At any rate, in the heyday of senryu, men were supposed to be the active party. I think that is why the vector of persuasion or proposition is so lopsided. The exception is, of course, the street-walker. I know they made little mousey squeeks to catch a man's attention because of an odd sea-cucumber haiku (a *holothurian* is a "sea-rat/mouse in Japanese: 海鼠) in *Rise, Ye Sea Slugs!* And, thanks to senryu, I now see they *spoke up*, too. This would have to be an old hussy, a street-walker over-the-hill hoping for enough money to buy some noodles. Maybe I should have ditched the original phrasing (*do it*, without the "it" is Japanese) and made it more colloquial, say, *"Come-on mister / plug my hole . . .* but that would not have fixed the main problem with Englishing the *ku*. It is in the metaphor of being "open" (*aita).* We reserve it for appointments, but Japanese use it to mean they are not engaged in work. *Unemployed* is too much for an old street-walker, but what else can we say?

女房をなぜこわがると土手でいひ
nyôbô o naze kowagaru to dote de ii 22-39

"why fear
your wife?" they say
on the dyke

A comeback line from a cheap outdoor whore propositioning a man who uses his wife as his reason for turning her down. Roads on embankments were common around Edo and especially traveled by people going to or coming from places of entertainment such as the Pleasure Quarters or Blossom-viewing. If there was a street culture *in* the city, there was a dyke culture along the boundaries.

女房の枕こと葉ヲゝ寒 類似折句集
nyôbô no makura-kotoba o o samui

His wife's pillow words,
"My, it's chilly!"

婆寒いかと何事もなし　折句袋
baba samuika to nanigoto mo nashi

Old wife: "Chilly isn't it?"
leads to nothing.

These *ku,* dated respectively 1762 and 1771, are acrostic *zappai.* I don't get the folded-in words, but they make an interesting pair of *ku* (wed by Suzuki) and bring us down to earth. Be that as it may, I'd like to find more ♀→♂ lines.

men who don't want to

ころぶ気だのにおどらせるやぼなやつ 万
korobu ki da no ni odoraseru yabo na yatsu 天三
(fall-to mood is though dance-making brutal guy)

though the dancer
wants to trip, the barbarian
makes her dance

Reading "lines" one feels that all men are perpetually horny, when such is not the case. This is for balance. *Yabo* means *uncouth, unrefined, vulgar, bad form.* But combining that adjective with "guy" (*yatsu*) is boring, so I made him a barbarian, though it is usually another word. The *dancer* is not mentioned in the *ku,* but she is there for all who know senryu because her aim was to *trip/fall* for the right customer and earn more money than her strumming and singing got her.

おばゝへこ／＼の気あるでむづかしい 摘
obaba hekoheko no ki aru de muzukashii 4-18
([hon.] baba hekoheko feeling is/has-so difficult)

grampa's in a fix
the old lady's in the mood
for some hekoheko

the old dame
feels like some hekoheko
but the men . . .

The old bag wants to rattle her bones;
Grampa wishes she'd leave his alone!

Equality in sexual congress is not the rule. When the women want it, men are not so sure. We cannot tell who she has eyes for. Heko (凹) by itself means the female part in Akita and doing it means coitus. Doubled, it means something weakly done and the examples in the OJD all start with an old lady, but that is all. But the context seems clear enough to supply the meaning.

あの娜手入らずといふふしつけさ 摘
ano musume te irazu to iu fushitsukesa 4-29

he must be a rat
not to take advantage of
a girl like that

'tis a faux pas
not to reel in a piece
of tail like that

The character 娜. The syllabet count suggests *musume,* a daughter, or an unmarried woman, while the right side radical 朗 suggests she is *slutty.* Yet, in Japanese, as in most countries, a man is expected to eat what he is offered.

winning hearts (cunts, anyway) folk style

On the whole, senryu did not excel on this theme. Senryu can not match the naive beauty of the line given by the mythological first man to the mythological first woman, namely that *as he seemed to be stuck with an extra thing and she had something missing, maybe they'd best put them together and found a nation*, on the one side and can not match the *glorious vulgarity* of the come-ons filling old folk-songs (*bawdy ballads*, if you prefer) such as those in a "mortar-grinding songs" (臼挽き唄) sung by groups of young men and women verbally sparring before partnering up at song-wall=fests (謡垣). Take this one from Kôshû (Yamanashi prefecture), where a man points out the *be* べ sound in "night-pot" is the same as that in *bebe* べべ or "pussy," even includes a brutal supernatural threat,

If you do not give it to me
Your clit will end up bent
With maggots breeding all around

俺にさせぬと　その核曲る　サネのまわりに蛆がわく
ore ni sasenu to sono sane <u>magaru</u>, sane no mawari ni uji-<u>ga waku</u>
(me-to give-not and / that clitoris bends / / clit's vicinity-in maggots boil-up/swarm)
(たけなか・ろう（『にっぽん情哥行』1996）の　甲州禁哥中「したきゃ させましょう」という章から)

I failed to match the fine vowel-rhyme in the original, but the content speaks for itself. It makes the well-known line in Marvell's "To His Coy Mistress" *"and thy quainte* [= cunt] *honor turn to dust"* seem downright effete by comparison. Speaking of which, a song from Tsugaru（津軽吹きよせ）that starts with the trite metaphysical 101 observation that *you better use it here for you can't take it with you* – as a *Leaf ku* explains *"First, a ghost / must leave its bobo / behind in Hell"* (幽霊は開を地獄へ置て出る　葉末 30 *yûrei wa bobo o jigoku e oite deru*) – surprises us by ending on a note so brutally artless it is refreshing by contrast:

.

姐コこっちやきて・穴出せどうだば
aneko kotchi ya kite ・ ana dase dô daba
([older] sister, here! come, hole out! how 'bout is?)

So, come here, sister!
Out with your hole!

I was a bit disappointed to learn that the version recorded by Japan's top spring-song collector, Sonoda Tomomichi, did not have that "hole" specified. Instead it of *ana,* it was *are,* a rude word for *it* or *that.* I hope that Sonoda's singer or his ears were wrong. But, regardless, I trust this sampling of lines from song suffices to show why I pursue senryû lines no further.

unspoken lines

~~~~~~

There are, of course, ways to seduce without words. Here are two examples, one
~~~~~~

material and one pictorial, both rude, respectively.

おへきつたのをさしつけてくどく也 摘
oekitta no o sashitsukete kudoku nari 1-32

the extent of it

pulling out and
pushing a boner on her
his kudoku-ing

Lack of a specific verb for *trying to talk a woman into it* is even a problem for translating a *ku* about not doing it.

むくつけな・後家を絵本でそゝなかし 安政三
muketsuke na / goke o ehon de sosonakashi 実意金石集

◎ *that **is** gross!* ◎
seducing a widow with
a picture book

◎ *just disgusting* ◎
to seduce a widow c
spring pictures!

Another word for widow, hated by feminists, *mibôjin* 未亡人 (pre-death-person) is found in far less *ku* than this one, *goke*, literally "afterhouse," and suggests she should be putting mind and house together in order to pray for her dead spouse's soul. It is wrong to take advantage of her newly experienced sexual hunger, as pictures of sex for her would be like pictures of food shown to the starving.

~ *eddy* ~

Bobo Left in Hades? I had no notes for this chapter, but thought I better add a word about "Hell," lest the senryu sandwiched within a sentence on page 314 causes confusion. Japanese artists depicted Hell as a place more horrific than even the most terrible Christian hells, but the nature of hell and its King was nonetheless completely different from the Christian concept. The Chinese or Japanese Hell only keeps and punishes people who do really bad things, unlike the Christian one, which (according to many Christians, not all) tortures people merely because they do not share their particular mythology. The King of Hell does the work some Christians give to St Peter at the Golden Gate, he sorts out those *deserving of punishment*, decides what type of torture is fitting and oversees it. As elaborated upon in *Topsy-turvy 1585, he is not a bad guy like the Christian Devil.* It pains him to have to give pain even though he knows it is done for justice and to make people behave better on earth. He even tortures himself out of guilt for torturing bad souls, though he knows they deserve it and the punishment is for the good of all. Unlike *our* Devil, who is a bag of contradictions (if he is punishing bad people, he is only doing what God wants – and, according to the Old Testament, did himself – and why does he want to tempt people to be bad and get *more* people down there to torture, anyway? Is he a workaholic?), the Japanese – and probably Chinese – King of Hades makes perfectly good sense. I ended up explaining this somewhere else in the book, but will leave the redundancy for it is an important point). But, why does the senryu have a *bobo* and we do not find a *henoko* left in Hell? The penis, after all, is more likely to become unattached. I would guess it is partly mysogeny. The cunt, like Pandora's box or Eve's apple(?)-eating mouth, was often blamed for bearing all the ills of the world. Mostly, however, it is because Japanese ghosts, which had only tops emerging from their gowns and no legs – I guess the logic is that if they had no legs, they had no crotch *and* if they have no crotch . . . – were more often than not *female.* Why were more ghosts female? I think it is because women were more likely to have to resort to supernatural means to get justice and command respect (see pg 302). Be that as it may, the *Leaf ku* left me wondering whether the woman who wrote a haiku of the sea cucumber leaving its eyes on the sea floor (*Rise, Ye Sea Slugs!* 2003) could possibly have read the senryu. And all my logic-mongering may mean little or nothing, for the poet may have mentioned a ghost with a missing vagina rather than one with a missing penis simply because he saw a certain print by Hokusai – I am pretty certain what *I saw* but cannot relocate was by Hokusai – of a succubus in action. We see a skeleton, from the hip-bones up. There is no vagina, but no matter – the dreaming man's penis is so large it seems find stimulation enough bouncing off the inside of her rib bones!

<u>*Shy Weenies & Cleaven Cuties*</u>

ちんぽことよきで割ったの

廿二 22

子供のアソコ
Innocent Privates

よきで割ったようなが湯屋でらんがしい
yoki de watta yô na ga yuya de rangashii 万 安4桜3
(hatchet-by split-like one/s warmwater-shop[baths]-at rambunctious)

cleaver-split
little ones in the baths
so clamorous

at the baths
the little cleaver-cuts
tear about

その憎さ・指似子隠してふろへ入り 宝十三
sono nikusa / shijiko kakushite furo e hairi 類似折句集
(that spitefulness! finger-resemble-child hiding bath-into entering)

◎ *how spiteful!* ◎
to hide his pinkie thing
climbing in the tub

◎ *of all the gall!* ◎
hiding his little wee-wee
to join our bath

Private parts, unlike bamboo, which sprouts from the ground boasting its full diameter (big bamboo or small bamboo) – you must see this to believe it, for that is different than any tree – start small. And all, well almost all, tiny things are cute. Look at the baby banana tree shoots. The little boy had his "chili pepper" and a little girl had her "hatchet cut" (note: the *yoki* hatchet is finer than ours: and does not make a "hatchet job," but if the connotation of *hatchet* is irredeemable, "cleaver" might do) or *"line drawn on a peeled hard-boiled egg."* The second *ku* takes it for granted that people want to see or even play with the wee toy – Louis the XIV, with his tiny teapot "spout" and, later, "draw-bridge" that his nurses reputably liked to tinker with, represents *what was once normal rather than exceptional* – and the little one is being a cad for monopolizing himself rather than sharing his prettiness with the world. I de-italicized the second two lines in the *ku* to emphasize that this *ku* was a capped, or "crowned" verse (*kamuri-zuke*), which incorporated the draw as the first line. Such capping could also be called a *kasa-zuke,* but when you consider that *phimosis* (normal on little boys) was colloquially called a *kawa-kamuri,* or skin-*crowned*, I found the poetic form and the poem's content a delightful fit. The next *ku* puts the boys and girls together:

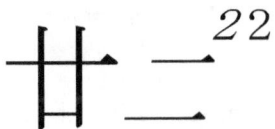

にきやかな事・とうがらしよりそら豆か湯に来てハ 万
nigiyaka na koto // tôgarashi yori soramame ga yu ni kite wa 宝十一
(noisy thing // chili peppers more-than lima-beans bath-to come/ing-as-for/?)

how noisy it is!

Because more
lima beans than chilies
come to the baths?

I am no lima-bean lover. To me, they are to beans what brussel sprouts are to cabbage (a flavor i am still *trying* to like). But I have a very clear image of the lima bean my cat brought back to its kittens while crying as if it had stolen a fish for them. They are large and have a clearly defined indention, a fine line that goes around them. That is what bears a resemblance to the thin line of a little girl's vulva. This *ku* precedes the clamorous girls-in-the-*bath* by almost a decade. It is a solution for the draw I made the title. It is a provided in a quizzical, oddly tentative way (*kite wa*) that is fascinating. As a stand-alone *ku* (one without the *draw*) however, it is lacking, so the later version made the noise explicit. So, what explains the difference between the sexes observed in this double pair of *ku?* Since little boys generally accompanied their mothers into the woman's side of the bath, it is easy to imagine the little boy embarrassed by the attention, particularly that of older women, who tend to be vocal about dear little things they can see and touch. The little girl, on the other hand is running about enjoying the water completely oblivious to her self and her sex which as yet is just the location for tinkling and has not caught the attention of others as the boy's has. If there is a penis envy, she does not yet have it, while the little boy is shy for having something that catches the attention of the bathers. Some readers might find all this silly, but I find the *attentiveness* of the poets interesting.

.

ちんほうハていしゅの方へ引ッたくり
chinpô wa teishu no hô e hittakuri 万宝 *12*

けんどんな事
doling it out

and the pricks
are tugged over to
the father's side

The above refers to a divorce settlement and, judging from the *draw,* is an example of the heartlessness of things done roughly rather than to fit individual circumstances. I just put the *ku* here because it suggests another reason for the silence or absence of boys. Women were more likely to go to the baths with children, and this meant they were more likely to take their daughters with them. Yet, their years of innocent abandon in the baths ends soon enough. A little girl learns she, too, must cover up and take more care than her brothers. She comes to feel it when people look at her, especially after her first period. There is a senryu about a girl's first step toward the mindfulness which is a woman:

恥恥しさ知ッて女の苦のはしめ 1-19,
hazukashisa shitte onna no ku no hajime 73-1

a woman suffers
from the first time she feels
embarrassment

a woman's woes
begin when she knows
that she blushes

I came across this twice published *ku* not long ago, and thinking it too subtle for this book, misplaced the original, but coming across a translation – *"When a woman / discovers / her degraded lot / her suffering begins"* (S. Rabson) – in a packet of books received from Highmoonoon, decided I better find and include it. The *"suffering"* is real, but I doubt we are talking about the *shame* of being a woman – a sort of sinfulness taught by some sects of Buddhism. Is this not about something that lies between nature and culture, either abstract, as I translated, or, as a correspondent believes, the impact of the girl's first period?

割り箸の身で生娘は湯へ這入 新編?
waribashi no mi de ki-musume wa yu e hairi

with a body like
splitable chopsticks, virgin
enters the bath

a virgin steps
into the bath, her body
like waribashi

A great *ku.* To think that the split-chopstick of the fast-food restaurant was already used in Japan hundreds of years ago! I dared not use the English word for them, as that would ruin the metaphor. Unfortunately, the word "chopsticks" *itself* is ludicrous and embodies the prejudice of those who fail to realize they are more, not less "developed" than our fixed utensils (see *Topsy-turvy 1585*). Such chopsticks snap apart crisply, releasing a fresh scent. This plays on *ki-musume,* a word with a truly *pure* rather than the repressed, religious "virgin." Yet, connotations of virginity and metaphor hinting at the next step, means a girl who has already reached puberty, and that is getting ahead of the story. Back to the boys!

the wish of a boy

~~~~~~

川中でへのこを出して神たのみ
kawanaka de henoko o dashite kami tanomi

in mid-stream
he petitions the gods
pecker in hand

in mid-river
he pulls it out as he
prays aloud

Now, this *could* be a prayer to get rid of a sexually transmitted disease, but for that, there were other things to be done like dropping a loincloth on the crossroads or having sex with a menstruating woman (pp 44-5). The location favors a different, more wishful request by a boy or young man who has not yet come to
~~~~~~

terms with his manhood. To help you see why I feel that way, let me share with you some song lyrics. The answer is in the final Summer stanza, but I will show you *all* because songs (the type meant to be actually sung, not just old poems called songs) are the least translated genre of writing – from Japanese to English, at any rate – and I thought that even in my poor translation, you would enjoy it.

.

チンチンチンチンチン・チンチンチンチンチン・
ヤーヤーヤーヤーヤー・チンチンチンチンチン
chinchinchinchinchin chinchinchinchinchin
yahyahyahyahyah chinchinchinchinchin
~~~~~~~~~~~~~~~~~~~~~~~~~~~~~~
Weenie, weenie, wee! Weenie, weenie, wee!
Yahoo, yahoo, yahoo! Weenie, weenie, wee!

So much for the opening/closing scat! The mid-20c pop song *"Oh, Chinchin"* (lyrics by Satoyoshi Shigemi, ©Astro-music) is what country music would call *a novelty number*. It was a big enough hit to find its way into party-use songbooks, something that may be found at most bars in Japan. The *"Oh!"* in the title is borrowed from English, and sounds somewhat ludicrous in the original, too, while chinchin is the most common term for a child's penis. I prefer the livelier "chinpoko," but the song says "chin-chin," so *chin-chin* it is. Regardless, they beat English, where *penis* is too formal, *pecker* too local, *cock* too adult, *prick* and *dick* too rude, *wee-wee* and *pee-pee* too close to urine, etc..

子供の頃の雪の朝　白く積もった庭に出て
kodomo-no-koro-no-yuki-no-asa / shiroku tsumotta niwa-ni dete /
(childhood's snowy morning / whitely piled garden-into went /
チンチンつまんでオシッコで　雪に名前を書いたっけ
chinchin tsumande oshikko-de / yuki-ni namae-o kaitakke
wee-wee[penis] gripping pee-with / snow-in name[acc] wrote-did)

When I was just a little boy, one winter morn so bright,
I went out to the garden where the snow was thick and white;
Then, with a stream of weewee, I scribbled my whole name,
And if I misspelled it, well, my weenie warn't to blame!

Simplicity is fine *if you can match it*. I failed and compensated by adding the possible misspelling. *You* have the word-for-word above, and *are welcome to do better* if you can. This, and all verses, is followed by a refrain:

オーチンチン　オーチンチン　あのチンポコよ　どこいた
oh chinchin oh chinchin / ano chinpoko yo doko-e itta
(oh wee-wee! oh wee-wee! / that pecker [+emph] where-to went?)

Oh, weenie, my weenie! Does anyone know –
Where in the world did . . . that little pecker go?

Are there actually men in Japan who are so nostalgic for their lost childhood that they actually look back with fondness at being small? *Stanza Two:*
~~~~~~~~~~~~~~~~~~~~~~~~~~~~~~

夕焼け空が　燃えていた　トンボつりした　帰り道
yûyake no sora ga moeteita / tonbotsuri-shita kaerimichi /
(sunset sky burning was / dragonfly-fishing-did return-road /
チンチンつんまんで　オシッコで　日暮れの町に　水まいた
chinchin tsumande oshikko de /higure no machi ni / mizu maita
weenie gripped peepee-with / day-falling town-on water sprinkled)

All dragonflies with relief sigh, our hunter's going home;
His net against the sunset sky, he's on a hill alone,
When he pulls out his wee weenie and showers the whole town,
Shouting out "Wee-wee!" "Wee-wee!" – as it was falling down!

One could probably collect a memorable piss story *from every male in the world* except the one-in-a-million who do not pop out until puberty. According to Jonathon Cott, the best known writer about Japan in history, Lafcadio Hearn, scaled the famous steeple jack of Cathedral of St. Peter in Chains (the highest structure in Cincinnati), accompanied by a foreigner, Rodriguez West, and "later confided to a friend that he omitted mentioning in the article [*'Steeple Climbers'*] the Mephistophelian delight," he felt when from his cathedral aerie, he 'piddled on the universe'" (*The Wandering Ghost:* 1991). The "universe" no less! I guess that is the difference between adult and child. To the latter, his town *is* the universe. Please pardon the second-person in my translation of the lyrics in this stanza – I tried a version that ended "and the little boy was me" but line-three failed – you can see why I stick to haiku and senryu. I will return to first-person in the final, salient stanza, my main excuse for including this song with the senryu:

夏の河原の　水遊び　小さくちぢんだ　チンチンを
natsu-no kawahara-no mizu-asobi / chiisaku chijinda chinchin-o /
(summer's river-field's water-play / tinily shrunken weewee /
つまんでのばして　ひっぱって　大きくなれと　泣いたっけ
tsumande nobashite hippatte / ookiku nare to naitakke
gripping stretching tugging / become big! [said] cried[+emph])

Goosebumps in the river, playing on a summer day,
I saw my wittle weenie had turned blue and shrunk away;
How I tugged it, and i pulled it, but it didn't do no good
So I prayed it would grow up real big, like daddy said it would!

"~ nare to," or, *"become ~!"* (*~ big!"* in this case) is a simple and conventional Japanese way of actively wishing for something, which is to say it is a cross between a prayer and a charm, or spell. I first learned of it when a 20-ish Japanese woman of farm-upbringing told me in 1972 how she used to stroke her bridgeless nose and make almost an identical request for it to grow "high" (*takaku nare!= high become!*). This is partly because Japanese can sing-song more emotion into fewer sounds than English can, and partly the result of the verb coming last. English requires more, at the very least a short couplet, such as, say:
.
Become a limb! Oh, little twig!
Grow! And grow big!

The river, where sin and disease are washed away. But, *change is change.* If bad things can go, good ones can come. It is a place for wishing, too. Prayers may be helped by an ordeal – letting your bare head be battered by a freezing cold waterfall, or, if you lack ready access to one, bucket after bucket of cold water drawn from a well are the typical examples – but cold water is *especially* cruel to immature male parts and most boys already fear they are too small. In Japan, I often came across magazine articles with diagrams showing how a sidelong glance at a urinal makes the other guy look bigger than you. Girls may have penis envy, but most lose it when they realize they are different rather than lacking. Boys are the ones who worry for years. That is why a song like *"Oh Chin-chin"* is touching. As an aside, let me confess that I do not know the melody. While it once was a well-known song, *I* never heard it. But, I have sung it myself to great applause at a Japanese bluegrass+old-time music festival. *How so?* I sang it to *Ghost Riders in the Sky.* The grandiose melody of the classic Hollywood country & western hit brought out the poignancy of the wee weenie, the *chinchin,* so well that I saw, and still see no reason to even *try* to find the "right" way to sing it!

蛤の肥しちんこがイ八となり 葉 *18*
hamaguri no koyashi chinko ga mara to nari

fertilized by
the clams, the chinko grows
into a mara

all fattened up
by clam muck, dingaling
becomes a dong

This would be a co-developing couple. A *chinko*, like a *chinpoko*, is a boy's twig, a *mara* a man's limb. A clam is a plump young, cleanly split (labia minora hardly visible) but fully developed cunt

toys are for playing with

隠れんぼうと油断した母 銀の月
kakurenbô to yûdan shita haha 元文五

the mother who lost track of them
playing hide-&-go seek

mothers who let down their guard
for hide-and-go-seek

まま事は蜆ッ貝に唐辛子 *71*
mamagoto wa shijimikkai ni tôgarashi

playing mama
and papa: corbicula
and chili peppers

The 1745 *zappai* (前句は鈴木 1996) is cryptic, but an erotic book of the 1760's (『水のゆく末』明和頃) gives the game away, "Now-a-days," you must watch what your children are up to (今の子供遊び油断がならず. . .), for what starts as hide-and-go-seek might end in "practice to be husband and wife" (女夫事のけいこ).

Mamagoto, in the second *ku,* means *playing house*, *playing cook* and, more rarely what we call *"playing doctor"* (So, is *that* why so many soap operas take place in hospitals?). The tiny shellfish (*shijimi*) that Englishes as *corbicula* is common argot for a tiny girl's part, while the chili pepper stands for a little boy's. Both metaphorical parts, in turn, stand for the person.

ちんぽこをあの子の口と姉の声 葉七
chinpoko o ano ko no kuchi to ane no koe leaf
(weenie[acc] that child's mouth[quote] older-sister's voice)

"he's put his wee wee
in the baby's mouth"
the older sister cries out

trans. john solt

It's bad enough how babies put things in their own mouths. They hardly need little brother's help. To most Usanian readers this might seem a serious matter, but to Japanese readers, it would only be something to chuckle about and savor for beautifully bringing out the essence of baby and boyhood, and slightly older, more responsible sisterhood. Since it is found where it is found (an anthology with much black humor), we cannot say that genitals had *no* shock value for Japanese, only that they were not taboo, or should we say Puritanized? Solt includes another, somewhat similar *ku* in his sampling of *Leaf* senryu:

.

イ八を子にもたせ女房にどやされる 葉一
mara o ko ni motase nyôbô ni doyasareru leaf

he gives his prick
to the kid to hold
and gets shouted at by his wife

trans. john solt, with one change

Syunroan depicts a domestic scene, where the father is sitting and his *cock* – *mara* has a larger feeling than *prick*, more like a *yard* or *tarse* (an old Scott word) – which has peeked out from the side of his loosened loincloth, and attracted a baby or tiny child's attention. The kid reaches for it and the man lets it play with it, until the wife spots the fun, and says "Stop it, right now! That's disgraceful!"

He lets his child play c̲ his cock,
and gets an earful from his wife.

Motase has elements of allowing someone to hold something and presenting someone with a gift. The right translation is somewhere out there between Solt's and mine. This is a funny *ku,* but it makes you think. In Usania, we can imagine the wife calling the police and having her husband thrown in prison for something that would only mean something to any involved if it were made into something. And, how about this next from the same collection?

人形の着物をイ八べきせて見る 葉
ningyô no kimono o mara e kisete miru 17

seeing how
a doll's kimono looks
on a cock

and why not?
trying on a doll's dress
for his cock

In one sense, the *dressed* Japanese doll is far from a penis: its head, rather than costume is replaceable. But, Japanese dolls are notably missing in clear facial features, so a cock dressed up might just pass. This is also from the "dirty" *Leaf* collection, but, to me, it is as far from dirty as a poem, if it is a poem, can get. It is testimony to the sanity of the poets. A culture where a man (or his woman) cannot dress up his penis and laugh about it could only be called sick, right?

bare pots that are pies

~~~~~~

On the other hand, the Japanese fascination for what used to be called *kawarake* or bare (unglazed) pots, and are, now, called *pai,* which is to say "pies," seems somewhat perverted to any modern who is not a pedophile. (I say *somewhat* because I think of once hairless *sumo* bodies – now, some are hairy, but old illustrations show they were not – and the folds of healthy infants that, promising much growth to come, tie into fertility worship. *Plump hairlessness has its place in nature and culture.*). Things are somewhat confused because cunts that lose their hair because of disease or depilated ones may be called the same, but for old senryu, 99% of the *kawarake* are about little girls, or . . . the real thing, pots.

土器の豆喰いたがる隠居鳩 159
kawarake no mame kuitagaru inkyo-bato

the retiree's dove
hankers for that bean on
the unglazed pot

55 土器の豆をつっつく鳩の杖
kawarake no mame tsutsukku hato no tsue

pecking the bean
on the bare pot, the dove
grip of the cane

"Retiree" sounds modern and, as a matter of fact, is written in a manner to suggest a sage, "hidden-residence" *i.e., hermit*; but well-off Japanese traditionally retired early and turned over their fortune and affairs to their children, so the term became synonymous with virtually all old gentlemen. One common style of cane has a grip carved as a dove. Senile old men sometimes try to have their way with boys or girls. We call the police. Japanese and Classical civilization laughed.

風呂でよがりなきをするハ皆おやじ 万
furo de yogari-naki o suru wa mina oyaji 安六
(bath-at orgasmic-crying do-as-for all old-men/pops)

the ones who
get all excited at the baths
always old men

the only ones
who gurgle at the baths
are old men
~~~~~~

only old men
get off at what they see
at the baths

The missing English verb for noise made in sexual excitement strikes again. This *ku* is right. Dirty old men are a reality. It is common in dementia for men to lose their inhibitions. Old women slobber on good-looking men, but old men get sexy.

土器を好くのも隠居虫のせい
kawarake o suku no mo inkyo mushi no sei40

love for bare pots
that, too, can be blamed on
the retiree bug

土器へ手を出し隠居投げられる
kawarake e te o dashi inkyo nagerareru48

laying a hand
on a bare pot, the retiree
is thrown

土器に投げられているへぼ隠居
kawarake ni nagerareteiru hebo-inkyo57

thrown but good
by an unglazed pot
the dirty retiree

A "bug" is a habit one can't lick. Senile old man are often like that; luckily, girls can usually lick *them*. But, in an obscenely unequal world, money buys honey. Sometimes old men probably did get to actually lick girls. A *ku* I did not translate says they would lick bare ones, but the "light/thin hair" *ku,* about a bare pot with a wee bit of glaze on it, seemed more interesting. Other *ku* report(?) that the idea of absorbing juices from virgins to rejuvenate oneself sounds good, but the reality is more sordid:

御隠居の涎薄毛へひんなすり
o-inkyo no yodare usuke e hin-nasuri 73

master retiree
his drool lightly brushes
some fine hair

冷や水は皆かわらけに吸い取られ
hiyamizu ya mina kawarake ni suitorare 69

the cool water
is all absorbed by
the bare pot

Instead of remaining cool and getting the benefits of the virgin water, the old geezers get turned on and end-up losing what little juice remains in them. There are three words, unexpressed but found throughout senryu and most popular black humor, that come to mind: *Serves them right.* But, I am afraid it was not *just* old men who were either senile, hankering after rejuvenation, or both. The Toy Temple Hidden Master (if I English the pen-name of the author of *Cuntologia*) presents two senryu that suggest that sexual relations could occur. One notes that even if a pot is persuaded to go along (crumble-dropped) it will crack (be damaged), which seems a reasonable warning that consent can not make a child adult – the language (かわらけもくどき落とすと割れるなり *kawarake mo kudoki otosu wareru nari* 40) is untranslatable.

土器の割れるも花の盛り也 *40*
kawarake no wareru mo hana no sakari nari

the bare pots
their breaking, too, is part
of blossom rut

though bare pots
break it's part of the cherry
blossom carnival

Actually, I think Toy Temple Hidden Master was suckered on this one. It is a facetious metaphor, a fine example of a seemingly dirty but actually clean senryu. There were concessions selling bare saucers – the word *kawarake* does not specify any shape, for 器 could be any *vessel* – on a few mountain tops where visitors were most abundant when the cherries bloomed. The idea was to throw them far, or through something, to make wishes come true and for the sheer pleasure of it. Needless to say, they broke on falling. I know of this because I wrote a 740 pg book on blossom-viewing, but most Japanese do not and probably did not know of the game.

土器の哀れ割れずに元の土 153
kawarake ni aware warezu ni moto no tsuchi

the saddest fate
bare pots to dust return
without a break

the sadness of
a bare pot never cracked
yet dust again

Once, somewhere, I read that girls who had never slept with a man were buried under roads with heavy traffic to placate their lonely souls.

土器へ毛生え薬を付けて見る *73*
kawarake e ke hae-gusuri o tsukete miru

trying a slip
of hair-growth medicine
on her bare pot

I hoped to find a girl's equivalent for the boy's wish for a big one. This was as close as I could get. A folk song (添田知道『日本春歌考』1963 より) puts it like this:

かわらけチャンコに　墨塗りつけて *kawarake chanko ni sumi suritsukete*

On her bare pot chanko, she tried painting with black ink –

早く毛になれ　そりや無理か *hayaku ke ni nare soriya muri ka*

'Hurry up and turn to hair!' – and if that is impossible . . .

While courtesans shaved down there, most women had hair, so girls wanted the same. Because little girls have no idea how their sex within shapes up to that of others, it would seem their wish focused on the secondary sexual characteristics. What about breasts? You find almost nothing except in so far that relates to the color of the nipples (pregnancy). Japanese men, Japanese women and Japanese fashion cared nothing for breasts, so little girls did not even think about them.

その昔シほしがりし毛に斧が入り　万　宝十三
sono mukashi hoshigarishi ke ni yoki ga iri　million

below the hair
she longed for long ago
a lost hatchet

now the hatchet
is buried below the hair
once longed for

At first reading, I imagined a dense underbrush put to the axe – there may be a hint of in the original – but, then, realized the *iri* (enter) is being used in the sense it is used for the *moon* which "enters" rather than "sinks behind" the mountains, sea or whatever, when it goes down. This would be a woman who got more than she wished for. One last, after *ku.*

へりハせまいけれとも廣くハなろう 摘
heri wa semai keredomo hiroku wa narô 4-33

wear down
for sure, it won't,
but wide it will become

The argument that wife-lending or borrowing was fine for it didn't diminish what remained for the husband came from the mouth of ancient Japanese poetry as well as Chaucer's Wife of Bath. This would be the counter-argument, based on the fact that if the male member tends to grow heftier with age, many women slacken.

~ *eddies* ~

☆ ***Two major developmental matters***, the retracting or not retracting prepuce of the boy and the first menarche of the girl, are taken up in other chapters (19 and 2, respectively).

Boys in the Bath? Here is one reason mothers might prefer not to take their boys to the bath:

男の子はだかにするととかまらず 3-35
otoko no ko hadaka ni suru to tokamarazu
(male-child/ren's naked-into make and/when catch-not)

male children
without their clothing
are uncatchable

when little boys
are stripped, boy is it hard
to catch them

"Make them naked" can mean only for a bath or for pedophilic purposes. I prefer the former idea but if one were to find words to that effect in a book of instruction for boy-lovers, then the latter would have to be taken for the correct reading.

~~~~~~

Singing Songs To The Wrong Melody. Any one with courage and a command of many melodies should try it. There is some of the same joy one gets with more complex improvisation and demonstrates how melodies and words relate, to create, or fail to create, moods.

~~~~~~

I have many fond memories of bathing in Japanese public baths in the early 1970's, but the best of all was a little boy who had gathered all the tiny plastic stools and plastic wash buckets he could find and used the stools to couple them into a long train, probably a steam locomotive for they became very popular at the eve of their demise, which he pulled about on the tiled floor of the washing area (one washes thoroughly before getting into the hot water of the bath) – I recall not the boy but my painting of the scene published with my column in an ecoradical magazine. That is the type of thing I might have done had I grown up in Japan.

~~~~~~

Ad-hoc Bawdy Theater. It is too late for this book, but a new category of *ku* has started to grow in my mind. We have the pecker in a kimono, here. We have the konjak (devil's tongue) shaped into a cunt and men popping themselves through paper partitions and putting bad pictures into fish elsewhere. Here is one more:

すりこ木でふたまた大根突て見せ 万宝十一
surikogi de futamata daiko tsuite-mise million

he shows off
the forked radish poking it
with a pestle

By radish, I mean the huge white radish called a daikon. Those with a third root are, of course, male. Those with two are female. I bought one such in Japan and she was quite shapely. Particularly shapely daikon, or ones boasting a short third root in the appropriate place were sometimes donated to shrines. Be that as it may, a hundred or so of these *performances,* with illustrations, would make an artsy book.

~~~~~~

The Loneliness of a Hairy Pot. We saw the sadness of the bare pot that returned to earth unbroken, well, here is the sequel:

.

遠藤さ草だらけだにまだ明き地 *156*
endôsa kusa darake dani mada akichi

unmarried still
the grass thigh high
& never tilled

~~~~~~

Two Ku Difficult for Me. But I did not want to cut them, for they seem to be *significant.*

みの輪から雇蚕豆唐辛子
mi no wa kara yatoi-soramame tôgarashi

lima beans and
chili peppers farmed out
from the red zone
~~~~~~

The edge of a Japanese lima bean bears resemblance to the thin line of indention of a little girl. The pleasure quarters were known for *employing* cute little girls from age 6-7 to 13-14 to assist and apprentice to the courtesans – one fine senryu translated by Blyth mentions a wife who visited to see what her husband was up to and fell for these cute little *kaburo* or *kamuro*. Or was there a sadder practice I have read nothing of? *Could the children of the courtesans and workers at the pleasure quarter have been leased out as workers cum sex toys to people outside? Or, were they simply fun to have along blossom-viewing?* The accompanying stanza is *It's become a fad!"* (*hayari koso sure*).

蜆に松茸釣り合わぬ急養子
shijimi ni matsutake tsuriawanu kyû yôshi 143
(corbicula-with pine-mushroom matches-not sudden adopt.)

a sudden adoption
a *corbicula* proves no match
for a pine mushroom

If the last *ku* seems close to a celebration of child abuse, this seems even more unpleasant. From ancient times, we find nobles adopting little – even infant – girls with an aim to culture them into the perfect second, third or whatever wife, when they come of age. Judging from poetry and tales, the men did not always wait for puberty to switch from father into husband. I suspect this refers to an incident in one such tale, whichever was best known. The reason these men jumped the gun was not so much because they were infatuated with young girls, as because they feared, not without reason, that some handsome young man might succeed at sneaking in and winning the affection of the girl before they did. Since women were given more freedom to go out than was the case in much of the Far East and Europe (see ch.2 of *Topsy-turvy 1585*) at that time, and all it took was a glance for love to spark and . . . So reading 1 of 2 (the same translation can be read two ways) is that the man of the house tried to consummate his child-bride marriage-to-be and his highly ranked penis – a *matsutake,* or, "pine mushroom" is a lusty cock with a broad *glans penis* – became his misfortune; it just would not fit. Failure in first-sex can be traumatic even without the shock of finding the person you think is your father has other designs, so the poor thing is transferred to another house. Reading 2 is more innocent: an old married couple with a business and a prepubescent girl want a son to inherit their name. Usually a chief clerk would be "adopted," *i.e., married in*, but the couple worry that a man with a fully developed cock would be too much for their young daughter to take, so they instead adopt a boy to groom for her. The "sudden" favors the first reading. I suspect there may be another reading altogether, and if I can find a sexpert on senryu to weigh in, the next edition will have it.

~~~~~~

***The Hair-wishing Folk Song, One More and a Geisha Surprise*.** Sonoda's rare book of "spring songs" 添田知道『日本春歌考』1963 was with me for decades, but finally disappeared in my last unavoidable move. *Cuntologia,* which was the indirect source of most of the bare pot *ku*, did not give details for the song. Detailed work in nonfiction depends upon having at least one of the five following 1) a settled existence 2) affiliation with a good university 3) having money (to hire researchers), 4) a photographic memory, 5) abundant time (one can camp out at various libraries or take years on a single book). Your author lacks all of these. So, please be happy with what you get! In Takenaka's book, which *did* stick safely with me, there is a similar stanza from a song in a chapter mentioning Sonoda's work in the same cold north-east coast region (Tsugaru).

My *ane* has a long-clit,	姉は実長	*ane wa sane-naga* (older-sister as-4, clit-long)
My *imoto* has long hair,	妹は毛長	*imoto wa ke-naga* (younger-sister as-4, hair-long)
But I alone am *kawarake* bare.	わたすひとりはかわらげだ	*watasu hitori wa kawarage da*
~~~~~~

Without words for older and younger siblings, they do not appear in English music and poetry as in language cultures with them. But, it is odd that the middle sister should be without what her younger sister had. One wonders how much this desire for hair is based on fact (pubic hair is a far more significant sign of female sexuality than it is for a male who has the size of his dingaling to be concerned with) and how much on male fantasy. Liza Dalby translates a "conversation" found in a titillating *"'Primer in Geisha-ology'* ostensibly to instruct tourists not yet savvy in the art of having fun with geisha," about a song and dance number called *"Shallow River,"* where the dancers had to raise their kimono hems bit by bit with each new stanza, while guests "watched with big grins, saying *'Where's the hair? Where's the hair?'"* Here are the last three lines:

> *Geisha D:* The poor young girls – some of them didn't even have any grass grown in yet.
>
> *Interviewer:* So what did they do?
>
> *Geisha D:* Before a party, they took a brush and black ink and drew grass all over their mounds.

It is not common for geisha to show that much. As Dalby explains, the establishment with this booklet was at a hot-springs (*onsen*) tourist spot and geisha parties at these hot-springs towns "reek with prurience." (*Geisha:* 1993/98). I would only remind readers the fact that geisha were identified with hairy ones (eg. pp 30, 36) might have added poignancy to the embarrassment of the (probably imaginary) girls training on the job to eventually be geisha.

~~~~~~

An Alternative to Bare Pot: The Transparent Biidoro (Port. *vidrio:* glass). If the idea of an unglazed pot to represent a prepubescent *Mons Veneris* is hard to appreciate, how about that of the *biidoro,* or *popin,* a small noise-making glass toy resembling a paper-thin martini glass with a hollow stem and covered top, which made clicking sounds when blown lightly into because the glass was thin enough to function as a membrane, for a vagina, or, at least, a tiny one with a tiny opening? (It went *popin-popin* or *poko-pon-pon* or *poppon* or *poppen* or *pohin-pohin* or *ponpin* or *pokon-pokon* according to the OJD, and could be called most of these). At first, it came to represent a beautiful young women, for fragility and transparency (透き通る様に美しい) were key characteristics of "short-lived" true beauty. But, by the heyday of senryu, it came to stand for virgin pussies as well (at least 7 such *ku* in *Willow* alone). If a bare pot easily cracks, fine glass shatters.

新しいびいどろを割る果報者 50
atarashii biidoro o waru kahôsha
(new popin[acc] break/crack luckyone)

a new popin
whoever breaks it is
the lucky one

a new popin
whatta break 2 b d 1
who breaks it

硝子へ白酒をつぐ祭り事 165
bîdoro e hakushû o tsugu matsurigoto
(popin-to white-wine[acc] inject/pour fest.thing)

a sacred fete
when a popin's injected
c̲ white spirits
~~~~~~

廿三 23

毛切石等々
Hair-cut Stones

傾城は臍の下まで不二額 103
keisei wa heso no shita made fujibitai
(tip-castle-as-for, navel-below-until fuji-brow)

the castle-toppler
had another mount fuji
below her navel

the pretty whore
had one more mt. fuji
below her navel

Castle-toppler is so common a term for pretty prostitutes in Japanese that the etymology tends to go unnoticed by Japanese, so the second is the more responsible translation. Mt. Fuji, with its crater top, is what we call *a widow's peak*. The area around the crater (?) on *Mons veneris*, kept bare of hair, would be white as the mountain's snowy peak. One reason for this was the relationship of hair and age. The less hair, the younger the appearance. The pretty old whore who mows her lawn becomes a "new mint" (傾城の年増まくれば新造也 46 *keisei no nensô makureba shinzô nari*). "Plucking her hair, the old tart (*night hawk*) becomes new tail" (毛を抜いて夜鷹新造開と見せ 葉別 4 *ke o nuite yotaka shinzô bobo to mise*).

売り物になると毛を引く籠の鳥
urimono ni naru to ke o hiku ori no tori 74
(selling-thing/goods-into become when hair[acc] pull caged bird)

put on sale
the caged bird must pluck
her own tail

I *added* the "must" – the other improvements are stylistic – for young women did not enjoy having to sell themselves, not for easy money, as is common today, but for the sake of their families. The reality of her new circumstances must have been felt like never before as she shaved, plucked or burnt (more details, below) her pubic hair off for the first time and, then, the second, and third . . .

売り物は毛をばむしってよく洗い 四六
urimono wa ke o ba mushitte yoku arai

goods that move
keep their hair removed &
wash, wash, wash!

The reason given for removing hair was not wanting to look young but fear of *"hair cuts"*(毛切れ *kegire*), abrasions made by hair rubbing against the penises of over-active men and prostitutes who took too many customers. Perhaps *hair-burn* (following the wrestling term, *mat-burn*) would be the best translation.

草深い池で蝮蛇かすり疵 *167-30*
kusa-bukai ike de mamushi kasuri-kizu

lying by the side
of a grassy pond a pit viper
with abrasions

by grassy pond
one water moccasin
all scuffed up

A cock is poisonous for it can impregnate. The *mamushi* is Japan's only poisonous land snake, but it still hangs out in bogs. A fiendishly persistent bad guy would be a *mamushi* and hair-burn only happens when men overdo it.

山伏と仕合い虚無僧眉間疵
yamabushi to shiai kyomuzô mayu-ma kizu

fighting the wizard
a mendicant monk ends up
with a scraped brow

The fighting monk-wizard of the mountain is the woman's part, while the mendicant monk whose name translates as "Empty-nothing-monk" is the man's. This is because the vagina is compared to an esoteric shrine tucked away back in the mountains, while this variety of monk wears a hat of the mushroom-head sort considered especially phallic by Japanese. The location of the wounds in the original are between the eyebrows, *i.e.,* just below the hat=*glans*, where the skin is most delicate.

とっさんは湯屋でかちかちかちかちし
tossan wa yuya de kachikachikachikachi shi 明三孝 2

that's father
at the bath going *kachi*
kachi, kachi!

"i saw pappa
at the bath going *kachi*
kachi, kachi!"

Pubic hair has no sex, but the types of men and women who removed it differed. With women, hair-removal was mostly by prostitutes. The man mentioned above is the equivalent of our blue-collar worker, whom we might call a loin-cloth worker, for doing much of his work wearing nothing but a loose jacket-like top and a loin-cloth. With the hot and humid summers in Japan, anything more than a loose loin-cloth would have invited ringworm, but that is probably not the main reason many of these men attacked their pubes. The loincloths were just strings when viewed from behind and you would see not much more than a pouch in front when the flap blew to the side. The men probably had the same aesthetic concerns women do with their bikinis today. Hair hanging out of a cloth-delineated border *looks bad*. The *kachi-kachi-kachi* sound is one typically made by striking stones together to make sparks. It may be a bit too dry sounding here. The reason Japanese commonly rubbed together stones to grind rather than cut-off hair is that the edges of the hair were duller that way. It must not have been easy, but I do not know if we will ever find a historical re-enactment where participants not only shave their heads but their pubic hairs like this!

女湯へ蛙きこゆる毛切石
joyu e kaeru kikoyuru kegireishi 161-18

the sound of frogs
heard from the women's bath
hair-cut stones

石榴口蛙啼くなり毛切石 74
zakuroguchi kaeru naku-nari kegireishi

frogs croaking
by a pomegranate mouth
hair-cut stones

The sound of the stones rubbing together was likened to frogs *croaking/singing/chirping* (蛙鳴くように毛を切る石の音 91 *kaeru naku yô ni ke o kiru ishi no oto*) – the Japanese verb *naku* lacks the ugly connotation of "croak," but includes many animal sounds. Male and female baths were generally – not always – separate, though the sexes might be able to see one another dressing and undressing over the low partitions. At first, I thought the pomegranate mouth was a metaphor, odd to be sure, for the female part; but, no, it is the entrance to the part of the public baths where the bath itself is. The owners economized by keeping the bath rooms warm enough not to cool the water, so, unlike today, customers had to crawl in. These doors were so tiny they were compared to the mouth of a pomegranate. Back to sex:

いさゝかなけがほね迄もからむなり 万
isasakana kega hone made mo karamu nari 安元

a superficial
wound goes right down
to the bone

just some hairs
but they can kill bones
like vines a tree

Without Okada's laconic explanation – "from a hair cut, a grave matter" (毛切れから一大事) – I probably would have missed this. A direct rendering might be, "~ gets the bone *involved* (in a complex bad situation)." Yes, *bone* has the meanings it does in English. The second reading picks up on the *ke* in "injury" (*kega*) doubling for hair (*ke*) and a connotation of *karamu* (involves/wraps). The draw is こほ(毀)れたりけり *koboretarikeri* means "sometimes they break off." Was this urban myth? I think not, for abrasions can develop into deadly staph infections.

度々怪我をさせても女房髪惜ミ 葉4
dodo kega o sasete mo nyôbô kami oshimi

though it cuts him
from time to time, his wife
treasures her hair

though she injures
her husband sometimes, her
hair is her hair

石で切るのをあぶながる女の気 *7-38*
ishi de kiru no o abunagaru onna no ki

a woman is
more afraid of getting cut
by the stones

While men, or at least men who did it a lot but used their fingers too little would want that dastardly hair out of there. But not only did wives not cut their pubic hair, they did not *want* to. The above *ku* give two reasonable reasons why. Whatever the reasons, some husbands evidently did get burnt and it affected their love life: *"After the hair cut / he only took his business / to his mistress"* (毛切レ已後お妾へ斗カいらつしやり 摘 1-14 *kegire igo omekake e baka irashiyari*). The honorific "o" before mistress and the polite verb for going, *irashari,* indicate a *bushi* (samurai) husband and wife. "Business" is word added to regain some of what was lost in translation.

女房ハ毛切れのろんに出シて見せ 万
nyôbô wa kegire no ron ni dashite-mise million 明四
(wife-as-for hair-cut/burn argument-as/during extract-show)

だてなことかな
That *is* flashy!

re. hair-burn
his wife says whip out
your proof

I think the draw (*date-na koto kana*) might be read to include an allusion to a woman who behaves in ways generally thought of as male (*onna-datera*), as well as acting in a cool way. Judging from senryu, not all men favored hair-removal.

いらぬこと女房石にてサネをぶち 摘 *1-34*
iranu koto nyôbô ishi nite sane o buchi

not needed
a wife beating her sex
with stones

undesirable
a wife who would stone
her own sex

The round-robin annotator points out that *since they would not have had stones at the woman's side of a bath*, the wife was probably trying it at home with incorrect equipment simply to copy the cool prostitutes. My guess is the wife either is thinking of playing around or has already played when the husband was away and has lice to lose. Committing or having committed adultery, she is stoning herself. The *buchi,* or "beat/hit," is not to be taken literally, but as an idiomatic way to describe such a lithic depilation.

おしい毛をけいせいみんなひんむしり
oshii ke o keisei minna hinmushiri 摘 *2-20*

what a shame
the pretty whore pulls out
every last hair

Even with prostitutes, there was no call to remove *all* the hair. Only a low-class street-walker or cubicle-shop whore (切店 *kirimise*), where lice might be a problem, would have good reason to do *that.* You might note that the above *ku* mentions *pulling* rather than cutting or rubbing off the hair with stones. Pulling out hair, whether it was on the head or pudendum, was often likened to pulling out weeds, but was, in reality, much more painful. One compromise was to leave a coppice on top of the merry mount and only remove the hair near or on the *labia majora* that could actually get entangled. *"Pro mountain wizards pluck their foreheads"* (くろう人の山伏額抜いている 37-36 *kurôto no yamabushi hitai nuiteiru*), that is, they leave it on the head, the peak of the venerated Mons.

おつな音毛を抜く度に開ぱくり 葉 23
otsuna oto ke o nuku tabi ni bobo pakuri

a funky sound
c each hair pulled, her
vulva pops open

毛をぱくり／＼と女郎ひんむしり 五六
ke o pokuripokuri to jorô hinmushiri

weeding hair
by hair, the whore goes
pakuri pakuri

Think of a penny purse. That is how something opens with a *pakuri*, as mentioned here. The mimesis *pakuri* is related to the *paku* of the Pakuman (Pacman) game, with its gobbling mouth. The detail in these *ku* is of the sort that may well be peculiar to senryu. Imagine the *labia minora* being pulled apart when a hair on the *labia majora* is tugged, than popping shut when the hair gives, and the repetition of the same. Compared to this, the following observations are a bore:

毛を抜くととんだ大きな口が開き 摘 2-37
ke o nuku to tonda ôkina kuchi ga hiraki

after her hair
is plucked, it's in the open
her big mouth

毛を焼いてみれば中／＼長いさね 葉
ke o yaite-mireba nakanaka nagai sane

after burning off
her hair, her eyes take in
a very long clit

I took some liberty with the translation trying to re-create a modicum of wit. The second is a paraverse of an older *ku "Burning her hair / she looked long at / & to herself* (毛焼きして我が身ながらも長く見え *ke-yaki shite wagami nagara mo nagaku mie* 摘 4-23) the wit of which rests on a pivotal use of the adverb/jective "long" that is hard to translate because of English's need for prepositions (at/to). At any rate, pulled or burned, women found their sex exaggerated. So did men. Indeed, one can find male and female versions of many of these hair-removal *ku.*

毛を剃るとイ八 二三寸長く見え 葉別二
ke o soru to mara ni san sun nagaku mie

shaved, his pecker
looks two, or three
inches longer

Shaved. Japan had the sharpest blades in the world, so why so little shaving of the privates? Probably, because the edge on blade-cut pubic hair is so sharp it would need to be redone every day or two. Generally, pubic hair was shaved to get rid of lice. For reference, a *ku* on a naturally or diseased hairless *mons:*

コイツ無宿だかわらけのつび虱 葉
koitsu mujuku da kawarake no tsubijirami 別九

homeless
that cunt louse resting
on a bare pie

call that sucker
a hairless bobo hobo
the cunt louse

A sloth can barely walk on limbs made for hanging upside-down from branches and a hair louse is made for clinging to hair. Without it, he or she are lost, or as this senryu puts it, homeless. Lice, by revealing an affair can also make people homeless – I vaguely recall such a senryu translated by Blyth. But, when it comes to observing lice, haiku does much better, so let us leave them and return to the hair. Did you know there is one professional woman who lets hers be?

地女は龍のひげ程はやして居 万明二
ji-onna wa ryûnohige hodo hayashiteiru

as for the locals
they grow it as thick as
dragon whiskers

毛をぬかぬ斗りが芸者地もの也 葉六
ke o nukanu bakari ga geisha jimono nari

in this one way
geisha are like locals
their hair stays

素人に成ルとそのくせ熊のかわ 万明七
shirôto ni naru to sono kuse kuma no kawa

an amateur now
wouldn't you know it
a bear's pelt!

Amateur whores, usually called "earth-ones" (地者 *jimono*) where "earth" has the "local" nuance, were contrasted to professional ones in the pleasure quarters. To really appreciate the first *ku* you must *know* two things and *not* know one more. You must know *locals* were equated with hairy beavers and that dragon whiskers are thin long and single-stranded. *Then*, you look up the word (in Japanese) and discover that dragon whiskers mean *mungo grass*. Why did I not put *mungo grass* in my translation? Because most Japanese must not have known the plant's name either. In other words, *the explanation doesn't kill the wit, it makes it, just as is the case for any riddle.* The draw is *"really puffed out but"* (ふくれこそす

れ) – her loincloth would bulge, softly. Geisha, despite their heavy make-up, were natural women below. While these skilled mistresses of the performing arts, as a rule, did not sleep with customers – hence did not worry about lice and hair-burn – they could have one, or sometimes more patrons, so the insinuation that they are otherwise identical to the courtesans is not utterly without basis. The 'amateur' in the last *ku* is not the same thing as the locals, it is to an ex-courtesan what returning to the secular world would be for clergy. The *draw* was *"You laugh but"* (わらひ社すれ). And now, for some contrast, the opposite type:

かわらけハさっぱりとしたかたわ也 摘
kawarake wa sappari to shita katawa nari 1-34

hairless pie
is a very slick-looking
deformity

a bald cunt
a refreshingly clean
deformation

A *kawarake* カワラケ is an unglazed piece of pottery and a hairless Mons veneris. Generally, it refers to an undeveloped girl, but it sometimes is used for an adult's plucked, shaven, ground-off or burnt-clean mound. *Katawa* means a cripple and by extension a deformation. I cannot help but think of a certain essay in Kenkô's 14c *Tsurezuregusa,* or Idle Grass, where he suddenly came to think of the love for oddly formed or deliberately misshapen bonsai as the equivalent of a fetish for abnormal, or crippled humans, and gave them up. In the 1980's, when the presence of pubic hair was the main reason given for censoring in Japan, I recall coming across photos of shaven *montes veneris* on magazine covers in book-stores and even outdoor vending machines. They did not seem *deformed*, but impressed me as *far more obscene* than the controversial hair.

開のもみ上げけつ近カにはへ下り 葉
bobo no momiage ketsu chika ni hae-sagari 11

the side-burns
on a pussy grow right down
to the a-hole

growing down
clear to the a-hole, pussy's
mutton-chops

Once *andaheya* (underhair=pubes) was liberated, Japan's "sports" papers and other cheap tabloids made up for lost time with mound after mound of beautiful venereal woods. The detail was like nothing I have seen in the West where beaver is beaver, just a pelt. Senryu and *shunga* (spring-prints) show the attention to pubic hair detail preceded the taboo.

小僧の月代銭湯へ石二つ 73-38
kozô no sakayaki sentô e ishi futatsu

sakayaki

the little monk
for his tonsure, two stones
at the public bath

the moon-bare
for his little monk? two stones
at the pay-bath

"Tonsure" is not right for the partial shaving of the head was not for religious reasons and Japanese haircuts do not make them look like Friar Tuck. Moon-bare is a word I just made up, for the original 月代(*sakayaki*) is written "moon-representative" and I thought it enough to note the *moon* alone and add what it is, *bare*. At first, I did not get it. I imagined a father brought his little boy with him to the bath and tried out the stones on his head, for real little boys were sometimes given an adult-looking moon-bare haircut. Then, I recalled that the "little monk," like a "son," was a nickname for the cock. Still, the type of haircut I have seen on the TV Easterns did not seem right. Men did not remove *that* much of their pubic hair. Further investigation revealed that in the Heian Era when the moon-bare was invented, it was for the purpose of preventing hair on the forehead from peeking out around the tall phallic hats the nobility wore – as women did in Europe when they wore similar (but more pointed) hennin! – and that made it a perfect analogue for keeping the pubic hair perfectly within their loincloths. The poet knew his history.

土器で切った毛切れは自切なり *92-14*
kawarake de kitta kegire wa jiketsu nari

the hair-burn got
from a bare pot
is self-inflicted

At first , I thought of pieces of a pot used as a razor, but on second thought, it is about sex with a woman suffering from alopecia or a prepubescent girl, whose pudenda were called unglazed-pots (*kawarake*). That is an unpleasant picture, but the idea of being burned by one's own hair is good, especially if you know that "self-inflicted" is "self-cut (*jiketsu*)" in the original, and suggests its most common idiomatic meaning: suicide by self-evisceration.

a refresher after all that hair

湯屋の石なめるところをふんだくり
yuya no ishi nameru tokoro o bundakuri

as the child starts
licking the bathside stone
it's yanked away

~~*a child is cuffed*~~
~~*on the verge of licking*~~
~~*a bath-house stone*~~

Bundakuru ぶんだくる– having a valuable one is carrying wrested away (usually by a highway robber) is a verb so rare it gets only two lines in a 20 vol. dictionary and none in a 2000 page one, while *bunnaguru* ぶんなぐる, "to give someone a whaling" is in any dictionary. As you can see, da だ and na な are similar enough that handwriting might be misread. Since Japanese were known for not whipping or otherwise punishing children since the 16c, when the Jesuits were delighted to find support for the gentle treatment of children in their schools, I thought, that if the latter were the correct reading, it would be a reflexive response to the child licking something gross and not punishment. Meanwhile, looking for the source of the senryu, I found another version in *Pluck* using a common verb for wresting something away, *hittakuru/i* (湯やの石なめる所ロを引ッたくり 摘 3-22 *yuya no ishi nameru tokoro hittakuri*) that supports the first-reading above. Since there were no stones on the woman's side of the bath, so we may assume a husband or widower is caring for the child. 19c European visitors to Japan (or at least those who wrote in English) were surprised to see men holding children sometimes as this was considered unmanly in the Occident (more on men and children in *Topsy-turvy 1585*).

~ eddies ~

Removing Hair. Pubic hair removal only caught my eye because of those stones sounding like frogs! I would welcome a short global survey. I read somewhere that 16c French nobility copied Mohammedans and removed all their pubic hair for a while, but it was done by a professional barber, as was facial hair. Japanese were evidently more dexterous, for they generally did all their own shaving.

Men Shaving Fully. It is one thing for a man to shave outside his loin-cloth line and quite another when this happens: *"The base of the mast is also beat-mowed with stones"* 帆ばしらの根草も石で叩キ刈リ 137-21 *hobashira no negusa mo ishi de tataki-gari*). Using a stone would probably not be for lice, so might be a male prostitute or a monk who might be putting his pole in a dirty place.

Hair-burns in English. The only hair burn I recall learning about in my youth was deliberately caused by wrestlers who shaved their heads a few days before the matches and ground them into an opponent's side and underarm when trying to roll someone over for a pin. But a friend who saw the chapter titles alone wrote: *"Hair-burns in Bed?* Is that anything like the *"brillo-pad burns"* we used to kid guys about when they bedded negro lasses?" *Hmmm*. Other factors equal, hair-type might correlate with the spread of stds . . .

Pornographic Mimesis. Sometimes, it seems a senryu exists for no other reason than to titillate readers with graphic onomatopoeia. We saw the *pakuri, pakuri* of a vulva opening and closing. It had some value as a poem for describing a behavior, removing hair, in an unusual way. But what about the following?

引張ッて放せばさねはぴちり言ヒ 葉四
hippatte hanaseba sane wa pichiri ii

pulling and
releasing it, 'pi-chi-ri'
says her clit

Is that not purely gratuitous mimesis? The mimesis of pudenda-in-motion might form a whole category of senryu. *Weaving* was a favorite, because the girls moved the warp with their toes, utilizing groin muscles. See if you can catch the action of the loom separating the threads and tamping down on them in the mimesis:

機織のぼぼキイパクリトンパクリ 葉九
hataori no bobo kii-pakuri ton-pakuri

the weaver's cunt
squeak 'n puckery thunk
'n puckery!

And They Wore Kettles on Their Heads
すりこ木を差すべき筈を鍋かぶり

廿四 24

筑・摩・祭
Tsukuma Festival

If the festival of Tsukuma in Ōmi would just come early
so I can see the number of pots on that bad girl's head!

(A prosaic translation of a poem from *The Tales of Ise,* early-10c)

近江なる筑摩の祭とくせなむ つれなき人の鍋の数見む 伊勢物語 120段
ômi naru tsukuma no matsuri toku senamu tsurenaku hito no nabe no kazu mimu

Oh, when will the festival of Tsukuma be here? I cannot wait,
and, yet, i fear to count the pots upon her faithless head!

(A wild translation (*fear* added) of a mid-10c paraverse of the same)

いつしかも筑摩の祭り早せなん つれなき人の鍋の数見む 拾遺和歌集 1219番
itsu shika mo tsukuma no matsuri hayasenan tsurenaku hito no nabe no kazu mimu

The Tsukuma Matsuri/Festival, is a theme of common interest to haiku and senryu, for the former because it is held at a certain time of the year, making it seasonal, and for the latter because it touches upon sex. Held at a Shrine in what is now called Maihara Town, Sakata County, Shiga Prefecture, at the start of the 5th month (the start of mid-summer in the old calendar) this pot-w/bearing festival is one of the three top "weird-festivals" (珍祭*chinsai*), the other being a carnival-like *Kurayami Matsuri* (Pitch-black festival) where part of Kyoto went into darkness and sexual license was permitted, and a buttocks-whacking festival which will bring up the rear of the chapter. With festivals where men risk death riding huge logs down hills or wallowing in mud, etc., I do not know why these were chosen, but so be it. I had imagined that the pots representing lovers that year were carried on the woman's head as women anywhere carry them, rightside-up, but the verb used is usually *kaburu,* the same as for hats, so when I finally saw photographs of them worn upside-down, half-covering the face, I was not *that* surprised. Because the enshrined deity at Tsukuma is a *food god*, one theory is that the original practice was for newly wed parishioners to make offerings of the first food, in which case those pots could once upon a time have been rightside-up. Enough background. The poems.

竈に鍋の数見ん猫のつま　不卜 江戸蛇の介
hetsui ni nabe no kazu min neko no tsuma futo 1679

Just count those pots on the stove!
One for each of our pussy's loves!

誰か猫そ棚から落す鍋の数　沾徳 *c. 1690*
daga neko zo tana kara otosu nabe no kazu sentoku

Whose cat is that? That is a lot
of pots knocked off the shelves!

These two *haikai* are for warm up. They are not about the festival *per se*, indeed, not about it at all. They do, however, depend upon the reader's knowing of it. and were probably written in linked-verse, in response to mention of Narihira, the lady's man of the *Tales of Ise*, or Tsukuma. They are typical *haikai,* in that a romantic – or, at any rate, human sex-related – theme is handed over to the cats, whose early spring (now, winter) love-making would become a top-five-hundred, if not top-hundred seasonal theme by the 19c. As *tsuma* can also be a snack, the pots on the stove may contain food for the cat, but the point is that merely mentioning the number of pots tells us it is the season for cat love because they are associated with human love because of the festival. This next *ku,* from an anthology Bashô participated in, is often the first one found under the Tsukuma festival theme in haiku *saijiki*.

君が代や筑摩祭も鍋一つ　越人 猿蓑３巻
kimigayo ya tsukuma matsuri mo nabe hitsotsu kôjin *1691*
(lord's-reign/era!/&/: tsukuma festival even/also pot/s one)

In our lord's time, just one pot each,
even for the Tsukuma Matsuri!

For the Tsukuma Matsuri, too
in our lord's time, one pot must do.

Kimigayo usually implies a favorable comment on the times/ruler, and was common in *haikai*. Issa has scores of them. Like Usanians in the last half of the 20c, Japanese in the middle part of the Tokugawa Era often exhibited a smug sense of superiority vis-à-vis foreign countries, and that could include the foreign country within, their own past. Note that because Kôjin's *ku* is seasonal and true, it *is* haiku – when I skip articles, I use *haiku* like one might use the word *kosher* – but, the implied social criticism (and criticism can be positive, as we saw with the relaxed balls celebrating Tokugawa peace), not to mention sex practice also make it a proto-senryu. The first "even" reading assumes that sartorial laws encouraging frugality were in the poet's mind, the second that there was a campaign to promote monogamy or Confucian morals (relatively chaste), or a general awareness that people were less promiscuous than their ancestors.

つくまの鍋の我をいくつめ　む八

tsukuma no nabe no ware o ikutsu me mu 1755

(tsukuma's pot/s' me[acc. +ellipsed verb] which ordinal)

A head of Tsukuma pots, how far
From the top is the one that's me?

~~~~~~~~~~~~~~~~~~~~

Tsukuma pots, how far
From the top is he?

If the 7-7 *haikai* snippet from Mutamagawa is called senryu, it is the oldest one on Tsukuma. *I/me* is rare in linked-verse and senryu but the Japanese first-person, like the English second- person, includes multitudes or individuals, such as, say, the *Tale of Ise's* protagonist, Narihira. A much later 19c *Willow* senryu would strike back at this Don Juan, presumptuous enough to criticize a would-be lover for *her* possible loves, when he averaged four-score a year, followed a few contests/volumes later by a me-too *ku* potting the far more gracious romantic hero of what some have called the world's first novel. Respectively,

業平に冠て見たき筑广鍋 *140-11*

narihira ni kabusete mitaki tsukuma nabe

We'd like to see
Narihira wear them himself
Tsukuma pots!

源氏にも筑广の鍋を冠せたし *159-20*

genji ni mo tsukuma no nabe o kabusetashi

Prince Genji, too!
You'd like to have him wear
Tsukuma pots!

Both postdate this more radical 7-7 Mutamagawa *ku:*

をとこに鍋を着せて見たがる　む十四

otoko ni nabe o kisete mitagaru mu 1760

(man/men-on pot/s wear[make] try-want)

She'd like to try putting
Those pots on the men!

I'd like to try making
the men wear the pots!

Radical because not just playboys, but *all* men are targeted for equal treatment. When you think about it, upside-down pots on *male* heads does seem symbolically a better fit. The next *ku,* a senryu dated 1786, suggests resymboling.

すりこ木を差すべき筈を鍋かぶり *21ス10*

surikogi o sasu beki hazu o nabe kaburi

While it should be a pestle . .
She wears a pot, so it is not.

While it should be pestles,
What they wear is kettles!

"Kettles" is there for the rhyme, later we will see why it should be *pot*. Japanese didn't need Freud to tell them the implications of the *concave* and *–vex*. We know what upside-down pots mean, but pestles would indeed make more sense,
~~~~~~~~~~~~~~~~~~~~

especially in the case of multiple lovers. The original uses the verb *sasu,* or, "stab" for the pestle. It is used for hair-pins, so the idea would be wearing huge phallic hairpins! *Why not?* An 1830 senryu either seconds the idea or favors a phallus-parade: *"Pestles rather than pots make a better god-thing [Shinto rite]"* (なべよりもすりこ木でいひ神事なり 35-22 *nabe yori mo surikogi de ii shinji nari*).

摺粉木の数鍋で知る御祭礼 73-7, 12
surikogi no kazu nabe de shiru omatsuri-fuda

How to divine the number of pestles?
From the kettles tallied by the shrine!

Counting the tags tallying the pots handed out, will provide the number of cocks. Or, is the *ku* an indirect dig at the contradiction of 凹 used to represent 凸?

鍋冠る祭りも人がにへこぼれ 72-17
nabe kaburu matsuri mo hito ga nie-kobore

~~*A pot upon head festival where people boil-over*~~

People boil over for pot-wearing festivals, too.

Wrong symbol or not, the festival was popular. My first translation caught the metaphor but dropped the point, which *must* lie in the *"mo,"* meaning "even" or "too." Could it refer to the far more common and always popular festivals where float-size phalluses are paraded through the fields and villages? But enough phalluses for now, the best (and most horrendous) phallus is saved for last.
.

男だと釜をかぶせる祭り也 58-20
otoko da to <u>kama</u> o kabuseru matsuri nari
(man is and/then kettle[acc] wear-make festival becomes)

If men took lovers, would the Gods
Of Tsukuma settle for iron kettles?

Kettles not *pots*. Homosexuals, which in Japan did not mean the heterosexuals who sometimes slept with them, but *only those on the receiving end* (the attitude was Greek or Spartan), were called O*kama,* or *Honorable Kettle.* Never *nabe* (pot). The difference between a *kettle* and a *pot* is so small that I have conflated them in translation when rhyme and rhythm demand – but, in Japanese, where one is female while one is gay, the metaphors can not be mixed. They are, however, similar enough that the above is funny in the original (see direct rendition).

今一度婆々もかぶれよつくま鍋　一茶
ima ichido baba mo kabure-yo tsukuma-nabe   issa *d.1827*

Auntie, too, show us your mettle!
Take an encore, a Tsukuma kettle!

This is sweet. Old ladies in most cultures, including Japan, are beyond shame (in a good sense). They find sex amusing rather than embarrassing. If only English did not insist upon number, the *ku* could be personal and collective at one time.

Now, all together, show you're hot:
Old biddies, too, put on those pots!

Though *ima ichido* (now-once) is puzzling for meaning either doing something once more, all at once, or even *en masse*, the power of the *ima,* or *"now,"* is what makes the *ku* effective. Before explaining *why*, let's see Issa's first and least known Tsukuma *ku,* where he came close to "now" with an emphatic "today."

けふこそは鍋かぶり日ぞ百合の花　なにぶくろ
kyô koso wa nabe-kaburi-hi zo yurinohana issa

Hey, lilies! Today is it;
Your day to wear pots!

Lily, hey, today's the day,
For you to wear your pot!

His *ku* was in a fairly risqué verse-jam. *Lily* is standard trope for a beautiful walker. Talking to lilies about it is a very classy way to admit to being a woman watcher isn't it! A century later, Santôka was to haiku *"A maiden with a pail on her head walking voluptuously"* むすめ盥をあたまにうらうらあるく　山頭火 *musume tarai o atama ni <u>ura-ura</u> aruku*). The adverb (*uraura*) suggests Spring, but I would not be surprised to find it dated to within days of the Tsukuma Festival, which came at Summer's start by the new (Gregorian) calendar. Real lilies would also be in bloom at this time in Issa's cold mountain region and we can imagine someone joking about covering one. That is why the "now" or "today" is important. It brings the festival home (or wherever he was) with Issa, making the *ku* real instead of an imagined happening off in Maihara. Then, years later, when he was almost sixty, finally, the missing age group:

小わらはもかぶりたがるやつくま鍋　一茶
kowarawa mo kaburitagaru ya tsukuma nabe issa

Little kids also want to wear them!
Tsukuma pots.

A very senryu *ku. Children copy us*. It's called wanting to grow up. A senryu encountered many times by all who read senryu has samurai children teaching commoner playmates how to self-eviscerate; another, less often encountered, has children pretending to commit romantic (and illegal) double-suicide. *Children enjoy costume*. What is a bowl over the head if not that? It is ironic when you consider that the original purpose of the festival was to reveal. I cannot help wondering the age and number of the participants in Issa's time. 250 years earlier, a shrine document records they were *up to 15 years-old* (*jûgo-miman*). Today, they are *eight!* That is right. Eight of them parade on the 8th day of what was the 4th month, *i.e.,* Buddha's birthday! (Another source says 4-3). Once, the festival was held at a more appropriate time: the dark of the moon, on the first day.

つくま人かざしの花や真鋳鍋　彌平 東日記
tsukumabito kazashi no hana ya shinchû-nabe bihei 1681
(tsukuma-people [head/hair]adornment!/?/: brass-pots)

Brass kettles! In Tsukuma,
They call it dressing up!

Cherry blossoms on their head?
in Tsukuma brass pots, instead

"Dressing up" is a creative translation. The original *kazashi* means "ornamental (for wearing on the head) flowers." This "brass" would be shiny but thin, like tin rather than thick as the fittings with which we now associate it. The typifying cast of the *ku* marks it as the sort of *haikai* soon be called *senryu*. Originally, the pots were earthenware. Today, they are paper meche. Over a hundred years after the above, Issa wrote –

土鍋もけふの祭りに逢ひにけり
tsuchinabe mo kyô no matsuri ni ainikeri

Running across earthen pots, too, in today's festival.

If the 1681 *ku* was referring to the festival pots, Issa's journalistic *ku* may mean there are unofficial entries in the parade with real earthenware on their heads in addition to the official brass ones, unless the 1681 *ku* was pure fantasy and paper meche already the official pot headwear. Issa may also have found and eaten from earthen ones in the streets, for Festival aside, the area was known for its stew, though it is a less likely reading. One thing is certain, this was a potty town. A senryu jokes about there being more pot than hatchet stores in Tsukuma (斧屋より鍋屋の多いつくま村 113－18 *onoya yori nabeya no ôi tsukuma mura*).

一つさへ重きかうへや筑摩鍋 仙茶 芭蕉庵再興集
hitotsu sae omoki kôbe ya tsukuma nabe sencha *1771*
(one even heavy head!/?/: tsukuma pot)

Even one makes a heavy crown
The earthen pots in Omi town!

~~~~~~

Tsukuma girls find even one pot a heavy cross to bear.

Because this *ku* was in a Bashô-school *haikai* anthology, I am tempted to take it literally. Perhaps all the girls only wore one pot in that era yet still when Sencha held a pot, he found it surprisingly heavy. So maybe they *were* brass. The word he used for head, *kôbe*, something like "noggin" supports that, but there is still room for a more figurative, senryu reading. We will see examples of psychological burden soon.

shame, shamelessness and the gods
~~~~~~

筑摩祭鍋は恥かき道具哉　一雪 洗濯物
tsukuma matsuri nabe wa hajikakidôgu kana issetsu
(tsukuma festival pots-as-for, shame-scratching-tool! 1666)

Tsukuma Festival: Those pots with names
Fine tools to display a thing called shame!
~~~~~~~~~~~~~~~~~~~~~~~~~~~~~~~~~~~~~~
Tsukuma a festival of fame, where pots
as pillories display their shame!
~~~~~~~~~~~~~~~~~~~~~~~~~~~
Tsukuma Festival – so even a pot
can be a tool for disgrace!

The original, from an early *haikai* collection the name of which translates as *Laundry*, points out that the pots are the equivalent of being forced to do one's laundry in public. Believe it or not, this odd "shame-scratching-tool" (恥掻道具 *hajikakidôgu*), the means by which shame is stirred up, if it were, in public, is actually in the dictionary! It reminds me of an imaginary tool in a book I have long wanted to translate (別役実『道具尽し』) – one side is a scratcher made from poisonwood, the other a spongy head with powerful itch relief cream! The idea is to always have a *scratch* for your *itch* and vice-versa. It is a sort of perpetual motion machine of animal pleasure. But, to return to the *ku.*

tsukuma festival
where pots rub their noses
in their love!/?

If it were not for the astonishment indicated by the *kana*, the *ku* could be a senryu a hundred years ahead of its time. It also raises what is, for me, the central question about Tsukuma's custom. But, first one more *ku:*

あた人よ嘘なつくまの鍋の数　鶴郎　古今句鑑
adabito yo uso na tsukuma no nabe no kazu kakurô 1777

Fair liars who laid around come true,
Or Tsukuma's pots will tell on you!!!

Heartless girls, you had better not lie!
And I'll tell you why – Tsukuma pots!

This early-*haikai*-style *ku*, puns an obsolete literary grammar for a negative request (*na*+verb[usually *so* follows, but not here]) into the name Tsukuma. Alluding to a Christmas song in my re-creation – and, heaven forbid, a cross the page before – I hinted at why the girl/s might hesitate to lie. A Shrine report dated 1568 (「筑摩大神之記」永禄十一年記) declared that if the maidens had violated their chastity 犯淫の輩在るとき (committed lewdness), they would "surely be found out when their pots fall" (必ずその鍋落ちて発覚す). To me, this suggests that by this date, multiple pots may already have been a thing of the past and the whole idea was to use religious belief to shame teenage girls to keep chaste until marriage! Not knowing this when I first read about Tsukuma in the *Tale of Ise* and in Issa's ku, I naively thought the Festival reflected old – or, rural – Japan's free attitude about sex, with women out there proud to strut their stuff. Maybe it *once* was like that, but it surely was not so at the time haiku and senryu were born. *Coming of Age in Japan*, like in Samoa, probably never was simple, even if it might have been slightly saner than it was in much of Europe at the time! Before working down to the more oppressive *ku,* let us see some ironic ones:

.

なべの数いただきまつるつくま哉　三征　境海草
nabe no kazu itadaki matsuru tsukuma kana sansei 1660

Tsukuma! Where we're given
a number of stew-pots to fest!

~~~~~~~~~~~~~~~~~~~~~~~~~~~~~~

By the Grace of God, we learn the Number
Of pots to celebrate! Ah, Tsukuma, so odd!

If I am not mistaken, this typical pre-Bashô-style light and logical *haikai* pretends that something as unreal as a number, and that of an exceptionally humble utensil, is worshipped in this festival. God and his rhyme in the second reading are indeed *odd*, but English has no good verb, like *itadaku/i,* for *receiving something as a gift is received from on high* and "celebrate" is not as meaningful in English as in Japanese, where it includes an element of *worship* and *roast* (as one would a celebrity). In other words, the poet ridicules the festival.

結ばぬを神の吟味やつくま鍋　そまる発句集
musubanu o kami no ginmi ya tsukuma nabe somaru 1712-95

Where the gods check over
Virgin girls? Tsukuma pots

One of Issa's teachers/employers, Somaru. The word used for "check" *ginmi,* implied the careful scrutiny of people, usually indentured women, attempting to sneak out of pleasure quarters or cross other checkpoints in disguise, or dealers in women giving their equipment a once over. This *ku* seems like a senryu in its satirical slant, but if we take the *ya* as not only a caesura but a rhetorical question, it points at the incongruity of the Festival *as it is explained* and *as it appears*. At this time, I would bet there were no longer any women with lots of pots but only a parade of innocent little girls, halfway between the fifteen-and-under maidens of the 16c and the eight year-olds of the 20c. Most poets (senryu or haikai), never could let go of the titillating and/or misogynist fiction – any more than we can give up the ostrich with his head in the sand – but here is one more exception. Of course, it could also be by Somaru, for he certainly had the right touch for senryu.

鍋一つ貞女がかむる神事なり 39-2
nabe hitotsu teijo ga kamuru shinji nari ya?

Call it a sacred rite, where virgins
carry a pot which says they're not
~~~~~~~~~~~~~~~~~~~~~~~~~~~~~~

Recalling a Japanese version of Lady Godiva (on foot) drawing vast crowds into an understandingly popular Buddhist temple (before the authorities cracked down, probably at the instigation of the competition), mentioned by Issa, in his journals, I really overdid my first translation, where I had *"hot women chaste / through the streets wearing nothing but one pot."*

鉢かつき落ての後は沙汰もなし むセ
hachi katsugi ochite no ato wa sata mo nashi

What happened after the pot
she bore dropped? Nothing.

Is that not right in the face of the religious establishment (though probably a century or two late)? This *Mutama ku* predates Kakurô's punning *ku* by a decade or two is interesting for giving one of many instances of deliberate or incidental testing of superstitions in Japanese history and the use of the verb *katsugi* rather than *kaburi* is witty, for a *katsugiya* means a person full of superstition. I was tempted to title the *ku "Testing Tsukuma,"* as Tsukuma is not mentioned in it.

思ふまゝ・天窓の上に大かつき　万
omou mama // atama no ue ni ôkatsugi 宝九

< free love >
upon her pretty head
a big load

This is a 7-5 cap on a built-in draw (*kamuri*). *Omou* means "think" and *omou mama* generally means doing things as you want to, but *omou* also means to "long for" or "love." "As you please" might be the better as a stand-alone, but it would not fit. *"What she longed for"* would be closest, but far too precise.

つくまなべへのこをかへておもく成リ 摘
tsukuma nabe henoko o kaete omoku nari 3-25

Tsukuma pots are a sort of levy –
Change cocks, they grow heavy!

If the last *ku* was neutral or even positive, this seems negative. But I cannot help wondering how many multiple pots were found at this date, or if even the multiple pots in early *haikai* were imaginary. The following number seems real enough:

ものいはて着るや筑摩の鍋二つ 成美 d.1816
mono iwa de kiru ya tsukuma no nabe futatsu seibi

Saying nothing, she wears them
Two Tsukuma pots

She never said a word, just puts on
Her two Tsukuma pots

Or, did Issa's teacher Seibi simply pick a properly concrete yet moderate post-Bashô sort of number out of the air? If so, it works. We wonder. *Did she have one boyfriend, then marry someone her parents thought better? Did one die?* If it were any more, our thoughts would be less. I will have to test out my two readings on an educated Japanese audience. While my second reading seems too dramatic for haiku, who knows! (A ku from *Haizange*, an anthology by Oemaru to which young Seibi contributed also has two pots: *"Wiping off sweat / It starts in Tsukuma after / the second pot"* (汗ふきやつくまの鍋の二つより　大江丸？ 俳懺悔 1790 *ase fuki ya tsukuma no nabe futatsu yori.*) Is there some budding two-pot tradition here? Silence or sweat, with haiku, the judgment, if there is one, is not explicit.

我が恋を人にしられる御例祭 27-8
waga koi o hito ni shirareru oressai ya?

In public, our private loves
are weighed – a pot parade

This senryu takes back to the "shame-scratching tool" in the 1666 *haikai* collection, *Laundry.* There are countless *zappai* and senryu versions of this idea.

あたまへ恥のふりかかる鍋　む 14
atama e haji no furikakaru nabe 1760

Those pots pouring shame down upon the head.

~~~~~~~~~~~~~~~~~~~~~~~~~~~~~~~

わか恋をみなふちまけるなべの数 万
waga koi o mina buchi-makeru nabe no kazu 天四
(my/own/personal-love[obj] all strewn-about pots'#)

Every ounce of private love in public cast – count the pots!

~~~~~~~~~~~~~~~~~~~~~~~~~~~~~~~

つまみ喰いしたが祭りの鍋で知れ 158-6
tsumamigui shita ga matsuri no nabe de shire
(snacking-did but festival's pots by known)

You may not swell, but if you snacked, the pots will tell.

~~~~~~~~~~~~~~~~~~~~~~~~~~~~~

幾人にさせたも知れる祭りなり
ikunin ni saseta mo shireru matsuri nari

A festival, this, to know how many men knew them.

~~~~~~~~~~~~~~~~~~~~~~~~~~~~~~~

鍋祭り他人の口に蓋は無し 123 別三
nabe matsuri tanin no kuchi ni futa wa nashi c.1830

Pot festival – where peoples' mouths have no lid.

Call Tsukuma a cross between a parade, wordless Public Confession – perhaps bringing some absolution for those who had doubting relationships, or at least preventing a dangerous build-up of suspicion – and what might be called a Love Inquisition, though the only punishment was mental. The last *ku* straddles two idioms 1) keeping the lid on something (like gossip) and 2) a "lid" as a mate or husband for a woman=pot. Note how we had pots pouring shame down on faces in the older senryu – an image that fits there being worn upside-down.

鍋の数かぶって顔に火がもへる 27-24
nabe no kazu kabutte kao ni hi ga moeru (1791)
(pot's number wearing face-on/in fire [is] burning)

Numerous pots! How red her face
how hot her flaming cheeks!

~~~~~~

顔に火を焚いて祭の鍋の数 30 (1804)
kao ni hi o taite matsuri no nabe no kazu

Kindling fires upon faces
the festival with pot upon pot!

This metaphor, however is odd once you know the pots are upside-down, for fire should go under the *butts* of pots, right? But flames and love have long been a pair in Japanese for punning reasons (*longing=omoi=omohi=hi*=flames/ fire) – we have breasts afire that would burn holes in kimono if tears didn't put them out and whatnot going back millennia. Reading *ku* like these is one reason I wrongly thought the pots were rightside up until finding images showing otherwise. The blushing, i.e. flaming faces, is different from classical fires in the heart, for they were kept under wraps, unless one were to say, where there is fire, there are tears. *Nabe no kazu,* literally, "pots' number" may be the most common phrase found in all the Tsukuma *ku,* senryu or haiku – do you recall the cats?

初鍋は重ねたよりも出にくがり
hatsunabe wa kasaneta yori mo denikugari
(first-pot-as-for stacked more than appear[in parade] difficult)

More ashamed with that first pot
Than older girls (who boast a lot)

First-pot girls have a harder time
Coming out than those with nine

The first pot makes a girl blush more
Than stacking them high as a whore!

A new angle? The marginal decreasing returns of embarrassment. than doing it.

女に業をはたかせる神事なり
ona ni go o hatakaseru shinji nari 24-7

A sacred rite to pound a woman's karma into her.
~~~~~~

At first, the verb *hatakaseru* (*hataku*), which in sumo means slapping an opponent down, and one Buddhist view of woman as particularly sinful, made me think this was *"A sacred rite to slap down woman's karma;"* but that would not work with the postposition *ni: "to/on women."* So, 業*go* or *"karma,"* in this *ku,* means *a woman's place in life*, largely *defined* by Confucian morals but *justified/ rationalized* by the Buddhist idea that *one is born to and must accept it because it came from one's behavior in a previous life.* Still, the syllabet count is a bit off, suggesting errors in transcription (Could it be, perhaps, a rite making the woman's karma – meaning both place in life and *sins – naked to the eye* (*hadaka ni saseru*), i.e. *patent to all?*) Regardless of such detail, the wit lies in a Shintô rite (神事, or "god-thing") aimed at making women good Buddhists!

鍋冠る翌の祭りが嫁頭痛
nabe kamuru asu no matsuri ga yome zutsû ya?

Tomorrow's pots give the Tsukuma bride a headache.

Needless to say, the burden of shame in this festival was lop-sided, unfair for women. That women, or some women, at any rate, were (imagined to be) not only ashamed but unhappy with such treatment is made clear from this *ku* and the next:

お祭りがいやさに美濃へ嫁入する
omatsuri ga iyasa ni mino e yomeri suru 25-29

Hating that festival, she marries into the rival town.

The original gives the name of the town, Mino. It lies next to Omi (now, Maihara?), home of the Tsukuba shrine. The wit lies in an allusion to a saying about the closeness of the two towns divided by administrative fiat: *"Mino and Ômi's Sleeptime Tales."* With the paper-thin border, the residents of one town can hear those of the other talking through the walls as they lay in bed. In a sense, those pots told "tales of sleeping" (*nemonogatari*) so there is a secondary reason for the allusion. Evidently, girls in Mino were not pressured into participating in the festival.

.

二つめの鍋を隠して髪を切 む 14
futatsu-me no nabe o kakushite kami o kiru
(second pot[acc] hides/hiding, hair[acc.] cuts)

she cuts her hair
to conceal an affair
her second pot

A woman has decided to leave her husband and become a nun so she won't have to reveal a lover, but the logic in the original (see direct rendition) is hard to follow. If I am not mistaken, calling the lover a pot tells us the woman lives in Tsukuma, where she would be found out in the parade and that forces her to go to a convent.

鍋の数親の顔まで墨をぬり 91-19
nabe no kazu oya no kao made sumi o nuri c1830
(pots' number parent's/s' face/s-until ink[ac] painting)

So many pots! The soot even shows on her parents' faces!

~~~~~~

So many pots, her sins are apparent, even to . . her parents

Though senryu are largely the literature of single men, they had parents. "Soot" (*sumi*) is written here with the character also used for all black ink/paint. It was commonly marked on faces to show mistakes or loss of points in party games.

親心ひとつは鍋もかぶせたし
oyagokoro hitotsu wa nabe mo kabusetashi 98-77
(parent's/s' heart one-as-for pot-even wear-would-want)

A parent's heart: if it's one, they want her wearing a pot

~~~~~~

Pot-luck festival: Both parents prefer one . . . to none!

This *ku* is clear enough, though I found it discussed (but ruled out) as a possible reference to the custom of burying children who died of certain diseases with their heads in pots on a webpage linking senryu to cultural anthropology.

from haiku, light pots and sweet

~~~~~~

ころんだを絵にみて久し鍋祭 乙二
koronda o e ni mite hisashi nabe matsuri otsuni d.1823
(fell[one][acc] picture-in seeing/saw [a]while, pot festival)

Again you see
her tumble down that hill
the kettle festival

Recalling our love
for the first time in a while
That pot smiled

here again to see
fallen women made concrete
the pot festival

Otsuni is a well-known *haikai* poet and his actual metaphor, which translated too long to use is that he could see [her] tumble as if seeing a picture of it. Maybe, I should add a "clearly" to the "see" to match its meaning. To *tumble* was idiom for sleeping with someone and standard for dancing girls sleeping with their clients. For the first reading, I thought of "take a spill" but tossed it out and kept the rhyme-found *hill*, so at least anyone who read about the roots of Jack and Jill could chuckle with me. For the second reading, "fallen" has too much Christian baggage and "concrete" sounds too modern, but the general idea that the poet has found a way to poeticize his seeing the Festival for the first time in say, five
~~~~~~

or ten or twenty years is more likely than the last, erotic reading. While senryu can be as hard to crack as a riddle, haiku ambiguity is often such that only the poet knows/knew which meaning was his or her intent, so one must rest content with a number of solutions/readings rather than one. Note the more cheerful nature of the haiku approach.

破鍋の縁もめでたき祭哉　成美　谷風草 1790
yaburi-nabe no fuchi mo medetaki matsuri kana seibi

such a festival
joyful even to the rims
of the broken pots!

This *ku* by Issa's best known teacher-employer, Seibi, is the last of eleven Tsukuma Matsuri *ku* found in Shiki's huge *Categorical* anthology. Following the largely critical takes on the pot festival we have been reading, such a savoury is just the thing, is it not? I believe the festival is already a remnant and girls too young to have to worry about anything. But broken pots does not seem like paper meche. Could there have been some short plays on the side? If historians need poems, poems need historians and I will have to find someone in Japan (or with access to "public" resources I lack) to make more sense of these things. All I can say is that Seibi's approach is reminiscent of a New Year *ku*, where Chiyo found even the dust from the Lucky Straw something worth celebrating, but deeper, for finding good even in the "bad" of life.

鍋脱て聞けや筑摩の時鳥　大蟻 d.1800
nabe nuide kike ya tsukuma no hototogisu taigi
(pot/s remove/ing hear! tsukuma's cuckoo)

Take off your pot and bend an ear!
Is that a Tsukuma cuckoo I hear?

Off with that pot, girl, bare your ears!
A Tsukuma cuckoo is coming near.

undoff your pots
and listen well! A tsukuma
cuckoo cuckoos!

This haiku would be famous if the poet were (Note, *this* Taigi is "big-ant," not the better-known Taigi 太祇). The cuckoo once was trope for a lover who flew from nest to nest if it were, but with the young age of the girls at this time, we may imagine an older poet, sympathetic to the girls with their heads buried in their bucket-sized pots. *Sumer is icumen in*. It might actually be hot and Japanese cuckoo didn't sing as *lhude* as ours.

七夕や二千余年のひとつ鍋　大江丸 俳諧袋
tanabata ya nisenyonen no hitotsu nabe ôemaru *1801*

The loving stars . . .
Over two millennia with one pot.

Oemaru is a humorous and unpretentious poet Issa worked for / studied under. Like many of his *ku,* it is hard to say if it is brilliant in its simplicity or worthless. The Herder and Weaver Stars are said to cross the Milky Way (in China, the woman travels, in Japan, the man) and renew their vows once every year, on the seventh day of the seventh month, which was the start of Fall but is now in the summer, at least in Japan. Most thought once-a-year sex a lonely proposition, but Lady Ukyo Daibu (12c) confessed to being envious as she was involuntarily chaste, which is to say, going to waste (after a decade of the same, I can see her point!). While this *ku* reflects upon the Stars, it might best be understood as a celebration of monogamy via the Tsukuma Festival.

.

& finally, light tsukuma senryu

~~~~~~

相州に筑摩祭りがあるならば
sôshû ni tsukuma matsuri ga aru naraba

Now if there were a Tsukuma Festival in Sôshû . . .

The senryu on this pot festival tend to be excessively serious and even plodding. This one and the next are not. I would not be surprised if this *ku* with one-of-a-kind grammar (「あるならば」で終わる句ほかにご存知？) came from a humorous print, or became one, for Sôshû is also known as Sagami, and Sagami was, according to the world of senryu, home to *nymphomaniacs* (p.303-4.). The pots would be piled sky-high! One rarely if ever hears of *the Sagami* in haiku, nor, for that matter, another of my favorites, *the Ikebukuro*, maids (sometimes brides) from that locality, blamed for what parapsychologists call poltergeist effects! Imagine *them* with all those pots! And, now, let's take them all away:

かぶらずに筑摩祭を小町する 77-8, c1820
kaburazu ni tsukuma matsuri o komachi-suru
(wearing-not tsukuma festival[acc] komachi-do/does)

S/potless!

No more pots: So Tsukuma festival is Komachified?

~~~~~~~~~~~~~~~~~~~~~~~~~~~~~~~~

Bare-headed, A Komachi does her stuff at Tsukuma.

~~~~~~~~~~~~~~~~~~~~~~~~~~~~~~~~

Bare heads at Tsukuma – Girls doing the Komachi?

Komachi, Japan's most famous poetess of love. There are scores of senryu about her; almost all concern one thing. Or, rather, *no* thing. The Elizabethans made a big ado about *nothing* – a euphemism some feminists, who rightfully think it *some*thing, resent – but in Komachi's case, there was literally nothing between her legs! I cannot tell if this *ku* means 1) the authorities forbade pot-wearing at this time 2) a potless girl was in the procession, 3) many such were, or 4) a special virgin contingent was added that year. Perhaps historians can resolve this.
~~~~~~~~~~~~~~~~~~~~~~~~~~~~~~~~

in the aftermath

c.1830 髪の毛に癖も筑摩の祭り過 138-43
kaminoke ni kuse mo tsukuma no matsuri sugi
(hair-in quirk/wave-also tsukuma's festival passing/ed)

Her hair indented for days
after the tsukuma matsuri

The festival left a permanent –
The pot is off but not the dent!

This senryu puns on the name *Tsukuma* in a manner most common in *waka* and *kyôka* (crazy-verse): it makes it a pivot-word. A *kuse* is a vice or quirk in something, the hair in this case, and *to acquire* such a *kuse* is to have it *tsuku,* or "stick"(stay). As you read Tsukuma, the *tsuku* part sounds like, that is, becomes that verb before the last syllabet makes it the place. This poet and the next noticed all that concentration on numbers of pots and shame left aspects of the festival untended. The fine detail came from the imagination alone, but one finds some of that in haiku, too.

翌日祭り一と村洗う鍋の尻
yokuhi matsuri hitomura arau nabe no shiri

The real party comes the next day,
a whole village cleaning pot butts!

No comment. Just, I wish I had a date on this senryu, which, if a real observation, might have been a haiku and makes a perfect ending.

.

an unprintable ~~senryu~~ interpretation

Sorry to ruin it all, but this *is* a book of *dirty* senryu. And there was *one* that piggy-backed on to the Tsukuma Festival. Do you recall the idea of having woman sport pestles rather than pots? That was still light stuff, the sort of thing found in classic *haikai*, too. Here is black humor only found in senryu:

つらい事へのこをかぶるまつり也 21-ス12
tsurai koto henoko o kaburu matsuri nari 1786

A trying thing: a festival
With a cock on her head

This does not refer to the fertility festivals with enormous phalluses shouldered about town, because everyone enjoys that. Even little children shout with glee –

they do not know why, but, like good dogs, catch the moods of the adults. (Can you imagine what would happen if such were paraded in the USA? Macy's would be the perfect place – skyscraper meet phallus!). No, it alludes to Tsukuma, where pots stand for cocks and, according to senryu, women suffer, but, I would bet that is the *fooled-you reading* and the senryu is really about a horrific event, which was reported by Carletti around 1600, that is, on the tail of the savage warring era, where an adulterous woman was made to parade around town with the severed penis of her partner in crime on her head (while he wore her vulva – the parade must have been brief, for they should have been bleeding to death). Carletti added, lest his readers thought the Japanese barbarous, that the Portuguese were far worse, for they killed their women at whim, based on mere *suspicion* of adultery. Considering how an astute 18c German traveler (Kaempfer) offered up something that happened in the early-10c *Tale of Ise* as recent news (breaking a pledge of chastity, an adulterous couple got locked, like a dog, in intercourse), one can never tell about such stories, but if the fiction was believed by foreigners, in many cases, it was because it was believed by the Japanese who told it to them, so I cannot help thinking the senryu was about that incident or one like it. And if I am wrong, it is still clever to call cocks pots.

.

extra: a sibling festival, or butt-whacking on cormorant hill

Having seen people beaten by relatively thin but by no means twiggy branches with green leaves (maybe pine needless, I stood at a distance), I assumed the butt-whacking also was a charm, or boost for fertility and only discovered the truth when checking the festival's location today, while indexing and paginating. I suspect there may be *senryu, zappai* and *haikai* to be found, but it is too late for that, as it is too late to squeeze this into the first page, for the rearranging would set the book back by hours, so it brings up the rear of necessity, not pun. The festival at the Cormorant Hill Shrine in Lady-within Town, Lady-defeat County in Rich Mountain prefecture (富山県婦負郡婦中町鵜坂), like Tsukuma's pot festival took place every summer, and the women had to confess the number of lovers they had (Kôdansha 日本大歳時記, which introduces it with no sample haiku, does not say, but during that year, like Tsukuma, would be my guess) – honestly, or the gods would punish them, of course – after which they were "whacked on the butt that many times." Though the festival was called a 尻打祭 or "butt *beating* festival," the word used by the Kôdansha editor, "being *whacked*" 叩かれる, is the same one used for beating the dust out of *futon.* I would guess split bamboo (something like a kendo *shinai* used for fencing practice) would be used for the spectacular echo at little pain. In the modernizing/Westernizing late-19c (Meiji era), the practice was discontinued and the shrine horses were instead made to run thrice around the shrine with people whacking? slapping? their rumps. And, in the early-20c (Taisho era) that, too, was abolished. I hope I can at least restore it to poetry in a future edition.

~ eddies ~

This Chapter, with the exclusion of the new-found butt-whacking section, is based almost entirely on an article for my column HIC (haiku in context) in the online haiku magazine *Simply Haiku.* I have rearranged much, but kept all *waka,* excepting the historically relevant chapter-head pair, out of the picture, to better focus on haiku and senryu. Here are two more *waka* and a line from a song for broader perspective.

おぼつかな　筑摩の神のためならば　いくつか鍋の数はいるべき
obotsukana tsukuma no kami no tame naraba ikutsuka nabe no kazu wa irubeki

What'll we do?
I haven't the foggiest take
on how many pots

we are supposed to make
for the god/s of Tsukuma!

This *waka* by Fujiwara Akitsuna 藤原顕綱 was poem #1098 in the *Goshui-wakashû* 後拾遺和歌集, published c.1005, about ninety years after the *Tales of Ise,* when the festival first appears, and contemporary with *The Tales of Genji*, 1005. If the on-line explanation and my quick read of it are correct, the poet ran the office for supply & requisitions, entrusted with supplying the women in charge of the Imperial kitchens earthen pots to the number of one for every man the women in the palace had slept with, which would later be presented to the Shrine. It was important to get the numbers right because a correct votive offering would bring good health to the woman, while a mistaken one would endanger the same. But it was not easy to guess how many pots would be needed and the women were not eager to open up ahead of time. So he was stymied. Some of the language suggests that women made their own pots. If so, why exactly was the poet's forecast needed? Did he need to supply the clay? Or, as the involvement of the head of the kitchen, was food stock the issue? Is this proof the pots were originally carried right side up and bearing food? If so, I'll bet dried sea-cucumber was in those pots! *The missing pestles!* Hah! (Hopefully, someone will supply a gloss for the next edition.)

うらめしや 筑摩のなべの 逢ことを 我にはなどか かさねざるらん
urameshiya tsukuma no nabe no au koto o ware ni wa nado ga kasanezaru ran
(envious!/: tsukuma pots' meet/ing-thing[acc] me-as-for-etc. overlay/repeat-not!)

Jealous, damn straight! All those pots the likes of me

never get to go to Tsukuma to see, much less repeatedly!

That is my best guess at a line from an early-16c poem/song (『七十一番職人歌合』の六番に *nanajuichiban-shokunin uta-awase*) about various workers. I do not know what worker it represents, but I suspect Narihira's free travel, his leisure is the source of the jealousy. Unfortunately, English cannot stack-up trips, so the original wit cannot be re-created. If the protagonist is a woman in circumstances not permitting her to take multiple lovers, it could mean

.

~~*How envious to learn of Tsukuma, of pots stacked high!*~~

~~*Me and mine have no such luck, our race is run, with one.*~~

But, I put lines through that reading and the next, which was my first, because a close reading of the grammar does not allow it (しかし読みに自信ない。全くない).

~~Jealous, you bet! And the gods are too blame~~
~~Not a pot in Tsukuma bears a poor boy's name!~~

And, in Bunsei 3, which is to say 1820, the same year Issa joked about little kids wanting to wear Tsukuma pots, a famous actor 三代目坂東三津五郎 at the 江戸中村座興行 sang a song (*naga-uta* 長唄 *Asazuma-bune*「浅妻船」) from a woman's point of view, with a line that questions –

.

筑摩祭の神さんも　何故に男はそれなりに
tsukuma matsuri no kami-san mo naze ni otoko wa sorenari ni

But why should the Gods of Tsukuma, too,
Allow men to get away with what they *do?*

To fully understand where haiku and senryu come from, such sources outside of conventional poetry also must be studied (and I have hardly begun) and/or interpretation done by teams of scholars well-versed in the respective genre.

Difficult (for me) Haikai. There were also some *ku* I was, and still am, far from confident about:

鍋ずみやはげをかくせし筑广姫　言水 東日記
nabezumi ya hage o kakuseshi tsukuma hime gonsui 1681

< the old shrine maiden >

Kettle black! The Tsukuba princess
Has no trouble hiding her baldspot!

Pot soot! – How the Princesses
In Tsukuba cover their baldness!

My best guess for this *ku* by a well-known *haijin* is provided in my title. The women who worked at the Shrine handing out charms and telling fortunes and so forth are sometimes called "princesses." They are usually young but sometimes include old women. We might imagine one borrowing the soot for her crown, but weren't they brass or paper meche already? Who knows! The only other reading I can come up with is to take the inverted pots themselves as bald heads with soot for hair.

.

七重八重細道強し鍋祭　蘭更　d.1799
shichie yae hosomichi tsuyoshi nabe-matsuri ranko
(seven-layers/folds eight-*ditto* narrow-road strong pot festival)

Seven, eight – hairpin turns invigorate the pot festival!

On the winding way to the pot festival we find our second wind.

The winding paths of lovers bear heavy traffic: seven pots, eight!

Winding paths encourage lovers, now we see the pot parade!

This is also by a well-known *haijin* poet. But I have no idea what *"piling up seven or eight, the narrow way is strong, pot festival"* means! I can hatch a dozen or so interpretations, from Tsukuma Festival mimicry by young-crowd (gays), as the "narrow-way" could be male-color, to an old poet who likes walking winding roads, to allusions to the "night-crawling" path of the lovers who became pots. If I had to guess, it would be that a straight path would seem like punishment, but a winding parade route would not, though I am not sure why this would be.

~~~~~~

Solving the Mystery of Tsukuma Festival. Once, standing up in the Kitazawa bookstore in Jinbocho, Tokyo, reading from the Loeb classics, which I could not afford to buy, I recall coming across some fragments about the relationship of crows, marriage and, perhaps, special slippers or something, definitely some odd charm-words that the author, probably Plutarch, confessed to not understanding. He wrote of going back to the oldest mention of the practice in Greek and finding that author himself said that the practice originated in ancient times so the meaning of the words was lost . . . All of my readers have doubtless come across the expression "turtles all the way down" – if not, you are not reading enough – explaining the final ground upon which the Cosmos stood; but, here I am thinking of something far more nebulous, and it is *a world of nonsense without end.* And yet, we can always make *some* sense of nonsense. Isn't that why we continue to culture it?

~~~~~~

Top Weird Festivals. As mentioned at chapter's head we noted that the Tsukuma Festival is one of the three top weird festivals. I would guess most foreign residents in Japan would probably select the festival where Sumo wrestlers scare babies and the baby who cries loudest wins a prize for *weird festival number one*. I know about it because of the outrage expressed in the letters published each year in the *Japan Times*.

~~~~~~

The "Shame-scratch Tool" (恥掻道具 *hajikakidôgu*). The OJD gives the kabuki play called 浮世柄比翼稲妻 (うきよづかひよくのいなづま) for its usage example, but that is little help for understanding where the term came from, as it dates to 1823 and the haikai with it I introduced is almost two centuries earlier: 「洗濯物」の一雪の句より古い使用例又は造語の話を求む.
~~~~~~

Making Love with the Wind
男なければ風と共に

廿五 25

女護島物語
The Isle of Women

~~~~~~

アアもっと奥を吹いてと女護島
aa motto oku o fuite to nyogogashima 67-21

aah, deeper!
blow in deeper!
the isle of women

I have yet to sort out the various fictional isles of Japan. For a start, there is the Japanese take-off from *Gulliver's Travel* that seems to have been written based on the general idea of Swift's book but not actually translated from it. There is some poetic justice in this, for if I recall correctly Swift has the Mikado of Japan forcing people to lick the floor (I guess he didn't know about *tatami*). It would have served the English right had the Japanese done similar things to them. The Isle of Women is one of the two best known fantasy isles (the other being The Isle of Long-armed Men), but I cannot recall if either are in that Japanese Gulliver book. The Isle of Women (like so much, going back to China) captivated me, for I have seen *very* erotic depictions of these women lying about with their thighs spread wide, inviting their lover the Wind – or, is it *lovers,* the Winds? – to fill their longing cavities. Seeing those pictures, a man can feel something that might be called *elemental envy*. The "deeper" used in the above senryu is not the most common one used to refer to vaginal depth, but one used with *topography*. That is not to say it is wrong for the vagina, for one nickname for said sheaf is "the inner shrine" (*oku no in*) and that "inner" – the same idea as, say, "Inner Mongolia" – is the "deep" here. Anyway, we get the idea.

.

色気づき団扇ほしがる女護の子 65-9 &
iroke-zuki uchiwa hoshigaru nyôgo no ko 72-20

coming of age
on the isle of women a girl
wants a fan
~~~~~~

A *fan,* not a *man.* There is a nice unstated rhyme relation in the translation not found in the original.

大風のうわさ女護の乳母は待ち *75-42*
ôkaze no uwasa nyôgo no uba wa machi

typhoon coming!
on the isle of women eager
wet wet-nurses

typhoon coming!
on woman's isle wet-nurses wait
with open legs

The second reading combines the above senryu with the one mentioned in the wet-nurse chapter which has them telling the typhoon *"Come on!"*

女島鼈甲の場を扇でし
onnajima bekkô no ba o uchiwa de shi

the isle of women
where fans are more fertile
than the turtle

women's isle
where fans fill the shoes
of tortoise-shell

isle of women
where fans replaced
the carapace

Luxurious dildos were turtle/tortoise-shell. There is irony in an isle of women who forgo a marine animal. My first reading plays with Ogden Nash's poem that ends "*. . . I think it clever of the turtle / In such a fix to be so fertile.*"

南風女護島では舟を出し
minami kaze nyogogashima de wa fune o dashi

a south wind
on the isle of women
welcome-boats

I recall my visit to the Ogasawaras, tropical islands officially part of Tokyo though hundreds of miles due South. How the locals (& hostel owners, local or not) came out in boats to welcome our big boat and, later, gave us a great send-off. But, here, it is more important to note that "boat" was a common nickname for the vulva, a conception odd to Usanians perhaps, but natural enough to Australians, as one of their old slang words for the clitoris is *"the boy in the boat"* (PD).

春風に春水を出す女護が島
haru kaze ni haru mizu o dasu nyogogashima

spring breezes
prime the spring water
on women's isle

the isle of women
spring water wells up
for spring winds

またぐらのしめる女護の南風 *79-36,7*
matagura no shimeru nyogo no minami kaze

crotches dampen
a south wind is blowing
on women's isle

crotch godowns
grow moist on woman's isle
a south wind

Have you ever read a better example of erotic topography than the first of the last two *ku*? As the wind picks up, can you hear the moaning on the ground as well as treetops? The second plays on crotch-as-underground-storehouse and the way walls can dampen. "Crotches dampen" loses that wit. I hope the *godown* works.

女護が島惣開帳は南風
nyogogashima sôkaichô wa minami kaze

the south wind
brings open treasure day
to women's isle

Open treasure day, literally, open ledger (*kaichô* 開帳), is the day a temple opens the doors, which in Japan can mean walls, to show off all of its Buddha statues, paintings and whatnot to all visitors who show their appreciation by throwing donations (coins) into the grill-covered offertory troughs. This religious term is also used to describe a woman revealing her privy parts. The untranslatable 惣 (*sô*) stuck on the *open ledger* makes it clear this is a hamlet-wide, or island-wide collective occasion.

女護の張がた拵えてる御影堂 葉四
nyogo no harikata kosaeteru mieidô

mieidô fashions
dildos for export
to women's isle

on woman's isle
dildos fashioned
by mieidô inc.

the isle of women
their custom-made dildos
from mieidô

Mieidô, *mi-e-i-do-o,* was Kyoto's top fan-maker. I added "export" and "inc." to make-up the syllabet loss in English pronunciation, where vowels are given short shrift and not the individual treatment they get in Japanese. This *ku* is far better than the more explicit late *Willow* effort: *"For a dildo / they use fans / women's isle"* (張形に団扇をつかう女護島 117-14 *harikata ni sensu o tsukau nyogogashima*). John Solt has a slightly different translation of the classy *Leaf* senryu:

Dildos for the Isle of Women
are lined up on display,
in the Hall of Shadows.

The difference comes from the rare word *kosaeteru*. In the book I have, it is written with the character for "make" (拵). In his, it may have been phonetic or 御座えてる, a rare usage of *gozaru,* or "[we] have [in stock]," which, with poetic license, could become "lined up on display." The "Hall of Shadows" is a direct rendering of the name of the shop. *Why not?* All is fair in love and translation.

女護島ふいごを使う長局
nyogogashima fuigo o tsukau nagatsubone

women's isle
the ladies in waiting use
their bellows

women's isle
chamber maids bellow
for the wind

Before the *bellow for* pun hit me, I had *"fan their fires /with bellows."* If this *ku* can be dated, I would like to know if it ante- or post-dates the *fans*. Living quarters for women monopolized by the shôgun or daimyô makes little sense on said Isle, but the idea of their being used to artificial intercourse is fun to play with. Because they supposedly liked big dildos, a fan would not do so . . .

北枕して死にますと女護島
kita-makura shite shinimasu to nyogogashima
(north pillow doing die/ing and/says women-isle)

her pillow north
the words "i die!" come forth
it's women's isle

I clever *ku* indeed. People only lay with their heads to the North in Japan when they are at death's door and to do so otherwise was thought to be most unwise. Even today, people take care about this. But, if the wind blows from the South, the receptive woman will have her head to the North and what women cry as they come takes on a new shade of meaning.

やんだのおなへたと笑ふ女ごのしま 万明 2
yanda no o naeta to warau nyôgo no shima

oh, what a pity!

when it dies down
they kid it for going limp
on women's isle

the isle of women

when the wind
dies down they laugh at it
for going limp

The draw to this early senryu is *oshii koto kana,* which can mean *"Oh, what a pity!"* from the point of view of the women or poet, who would be happy to replace the spent wind. The original makes us guess from the verb *yanda,* or stopped (not quite as specific as "died down," for it can also be used for *rain*) that *it* is The Wind. I think it might be more interesting to mention the wind and not the location. Regardless, this is the riddle quality that makes most senryu senryu.

凪だ日は子壷の眠る女護島 葉九
naida hi wa kotsubo no nemuru nyogogashima

the isle of women
on a calm day all the wombs
are fast asleep

on a real calm day
one can hear wombs snoring
– the isle of women –

The Fruit of the Wind?

女ごのしま風を引てもばゝを呼ヒ 万宝 11
nyôgo no shima kaze o hiite mo baba o yobi million

the isle of women
catching a cold they call
for the babushka

the isle of women
they call babaloo for
a case of the flu

This is what might be called a Humpty-Dumpty translation, for first you must read the "cold" as "wind" as that is what Japanese call them or root out the same in *influenza* and, second, you must pretend my terms for old women mean they might be midwives. I could not use midwife, as such directness (not in the original) would ruin the poetry, but I was afraid "auntie" would be too vague.

& Its Extended Metaphor

長つほねうき名のたゝぬ南風 万
nagatsubone uki na no tatanu minami kaze 宝 9
(chambermaid floating[bad]name's rise-not south-wind)

たのしみな事
pure enjoyment

ladies-in-waiting
no gossip waves will rise
with a south wind

a lady-in-waiting
keeps her good name, using
"the south wind"

the chambermaid
i think i'll name it, she says
"the south wind"

The original treats the relationship of a this lady/ies and her/their dildo/s. Sadly, a *bad reputation* is not a "floating name," and *gossip* and *waves* do not both "rise/stand" in English. Frustration gave rise to the somewhat changed second and clearly different third reading, a paraverse. (Finally, I hope to find *zappai* about the second meaning of the Isle in Kansai, a Pleasure-Quarters, for the next edition.)

~ eddies ~

1. ***The Isle of Women in English & Saikaku.*** Can you guess the source of the following?

> The erotic literature of the Chinese and Japanese is highly developed and their illustrations are often facetious as well as obscene. All are familiar with that of the strong man who by a blow with his enormous phallus shivers a copper pot; and the ludicrous contrast of the huge-membered wights who land in the Isle of Women and presently escape from it, wrinkled and shriveled, true Domine Dolittles.

It is Richard F. Burton: *The Book of the Thousand Nights and a Night*, Volume 10. A "wight" is a supernatural or brave human. Un/fortunately, I have yet to come across a Domine Dolittle. The hero of Saikaku's 1682 novel, 好色一代男 (the sex-lover of his age – translated as *An Amorous Man*), Yonosuke caps his life dedicated to love-making by a trip to said Isle at age 60; as sex was his religion, I would agree with the aozora.gr.jp/cards website's summation: *"It was his Pureland, his Paradise."* That is, the place to end his life in this world. Here is how Yonosuke – 世之介 literally, the-world's-guy – put it:

> *Now, crossing over to the Isle of Women, I'll find myself women to be had at will* (抓みどりの女を見せん)*. . . . Though I should get dry-kidney* (腎虚 see ch.7) *and turn into the dirt of this land, it is the way this man, fated to be born to love out his entire life, wants to go.*

I do not recall what happens when and if the good ship *SS Sex-loving* (like-color 好色丸) arrives. If the women were so stuck on the wind, why would they love to death any men who happened to land? At any rate, Saikaku's famous long-selling novel is doubtless the cause for the interest in the Isle shown by senryu. Saikaku sited his isle near Hachijoshima (八丈島). Put the guy 介 right under the 八 and *bingo!*), known for maintaining a matrilineal society up to modern times, though it was less absolute than that of the Moso (also Mouso) people of Southwest China, who, until the Great Cultural Genocide did not even have a name for "father" (*"That's something to make a feminist drown in her tears of joy"* = Takaki Atsushi 鷹木敦), as lovers snuck in and out at night. The English-speaking reader may well shake their heads over the way the Isle became all about sex, but that sure beats "our" Amazons-of-lopped-off-breast as pugnacious as those who dreamed them up!

According to Minakata Kumagusu, some of whose writing is made public by aozora. gr.jp/cards, Pliny mentioned horses that bore extremely fast colts when impregnated by the West Wind near what is now Lisbon. Meanwhile, in nearby Spain, Pliny observed there was a breed of horses that moved their front and hind-legs in parallel, in the manner of camels, giraffes and llama. Kumagusu does not make clear whether or not they, too, are windlings, and doubts it is a genetic proclivity. He points out that horses were trained by hobbling them in a way to require the front and back legs to move in tandem with the result that one "could carry a cup of water without spilling a drop while running like the wind." Kumagusu would have been amused to know that decades after he wrote, some Japanese claimed that *they*, the ancient Japanese, were unique in the world for being ipsolateral runners, that is the arms and legs moved in tandem rather than offsetting as is usual (google for the pmjs log thread on it). But to return to the horses, my horse-savvy sister says "most people call it *pacing*" and that it is not always taught, for horses who have been injured may do it naturally, etc. In respect to the folk credulity that gave rise to ideas of fatherless birth, Kumagusu pointed out how the benighted owner of a female cat in the backwoods of Kumano, failing to realize how athletic and devious a cat in heat can be, was sure she could bear without mates and claimed it was enough to brush her behind with the broom! At, any rate, we in the West have *West,* not *South* wind.

~~~~~~

John Wilmot, Earl of Rochester and master of obscene poetry indirectly touches upon wind-loving women in *A Ramble in St James's Park* (1672), which starts,

> *Much wine had passed, with grave Discourse*
> *Of who fucks who, and who does worse.*

and develops into the most vitriolic diatribe against an unfaithful lover ever written, and ends, as follows:

> *May stinking Vapours choke your womb*
> *Such as the men you dote upon*
> *May your depraved appetite*
> *That could, in whiffling Fools delight*
>
> *Beget such frenzies in your mind*
> *You may go mad for the North Wind;*
> *And fixing all your hopes upon't*
> *To have him bluster in your Cunt,*
>
> *Turn up your longing Arse to th'air*
> *And perish in a wild despair!*
> *But cowards shall forget to rant,*
> *Schoolboys to frig, old Whores to paint;*
>
> *The Jesuits' Fraternity*
> *Shall leave the use of buggery;*
> *Crab-louse, inspired with grace divine*
> *From earthly codd, to Heaven shall climb.*
>
> *Physicians shall believe in Jesus,*
> *And disobedience cease to please us.*
> *Ere I desist with all my power.*
> *To plague this woman, and undo her.*

Note the posture. Most Japanese illustrations show *their* wind-loving women lying on their *backs*, which leads me to believe that they, unlike ours, are not horsing around. I do a longer quote than necessary because there may be readers of this book unfamiliar with the bawdy poetry of their native tongue. (Also, note that the Jesuits, though well-versed in classical culture, were not particularly prone to sodomy. The English were prone to put them down, as agents of the Pope. "Physicians" would be meta-physicians.)

~~~~~~

Animals Impregnated by the Wind and The Isle of Women. Conway Zirkle wrote an article published in *Isis*, Vol. 25, No. 1 (May, 1936), pp. 95-130 called "Animals Impregnated by the Wind." It includes the following words

> *The Isle of Women in the China Sea. Women are found there and not a single man. They conceive by the wind and bring into the world females like themselves.* (ibid)

I wish I could share more from the article with you. Perhaps we could find some rhyme or reason in the direction of the wind and choice of animal or woman as a wind-lover; but I cannot see it myself. ***Why?*** Because even though the article is *over seventy years old,* it is only found on an online data bank reserved for people who are belong to the top universities and wealthy prep-schools who can afford the "public" service (J-stor). Today, the internet is the cutting edge of discrimination, and your author is among the *billions of have-nots denied access to what should be a common information bank for all.*

~~~~~~

John Solt's translation (pg 363) was left-margin with no initial cap or a period. Such is common in modern translation and would not bother me, but for the way capital letters are used for proper nouns. We can either do it the Japanese and Chinese way, **no** caps (not even for "I"), or use them properly. But, I apologize for centering to match my style.

~~~~~~

Why Such an Isle? One of W.H. Hudson's many books of essays has the best description of a woman in the wind, or, rather, suffering from the wind, I know. As my own life and library have pretty much gone with the wind, maybe a reader can find it for me. I can clearly recall he depicted women and the wind as natural enemies, one trying to reveal, and one to hide. I recalled it when I came across this early *Million* senryu, one of a small number of 7-7 *ku* in it: *"Japanese women are shy / when it comes to the wind"* (日本の女ハ風にはつかしゐ 万 宝 11 はれな事かな *hinomoto no no onna wa kaze ni hazukashii*). Why? "Their hems are disordered" (Okada). In other words, unlike Chinese women who tend to wear pants and leave robes to men, Japanese women could be exposed. Is it possible this *wind-consciousness* (nemesis=lover) helped give birth to the Isle of Women?

~~~~~~

A Modern Haiku Possibly Influenced by the Isle of Women. I found it among a two page selection of *ku* 船笛 by Sawai Yôko 澤井洋子（貝の会）in one of two haiku magazines『俳句研究』2001・9 号 a Japanese friend kindly sent me a few years ago.

女岩の陰処吹き抜けて夏の風
onna iwa no hoto fuki-nukete natsu no kaze sawai yôko
(woman-rock's shade-place-blow-pierce/passing summer-wind)

the summer wind
blowing through the hoto
of woman's rock

There are two rocks that emerge side by side – slightly separated – at low-tide in the Futami Okitama Shrine near Ise (capital of the native gods, or at least the sea-related ones) one male and one female. The former is phallic in the Japanese hyper-cephalic manner while the latter has the requisite hole. Several times a year, the vows, or ties between these wedded rocks (*meoto iwa*) are literally renewed with new connecting festoons, thick spiral-braided straw rope (weighing hundreds if not thousands of pounds) called *shimenawa* (you may see smaller ones hanging over Sumo tournament rings). Sawai Yôko's haiku does not necessarily allude to The Isle of Women, but she may have thought of it when the warm wind caressed her skin. *Hoto* (the pronunciation for "陰処 shade/yin-place" was given) is an archaic word for *cunt*, that can also mean a hollar, and is most commonly written phonetically or with the single character 陰 shade/yin. Two etymologies given in the OJD harken to an "inclusive place," two an "oven," & one the "front-door." To translate "cunt" would have been too blunt, "twat," too twitty, and "hole," lacking eros. So I went with the original *hoto*. Sawai has a Male Stone *ku,* that seems Aegean, yet takes me back to Korea, with its shamanism, next to the female one:

男巌に通へる小鳥夏深む
otoko iwa ni tôeru kotori natsu fukamu
(male-rock-to commute small-bird summer deepens)

summer deepens
a bird flies to and fro
the male rock
~~~~~~

<u>*Nothing as Bad as "1601"*</u>
トゥェーン程じゃないが

廿六 26

へのへのへ

There *R* Farts & there *R* Farts

~~~~~~

屁をひつておかしくも無イ一人者
he o hiite okashiku mo nai hitorimono 3-6
(fart-cut even if, funny-not singleman/men)

Bachelor Blues

What good is breaking wind
when you've no one to
shoot the breeze <u>*c*</u>*!*

a sorry sight

looking for all the world
like he'd sooner fart than not
a single man

association

a single wino
whenever he cuts the cheese:
his empty life

boredom

single life
even farts are never
a surprise

even farts
never get a laugh
living alone

living alone
even our best farts
are wasted

letting rip a fart
it doesn't make you laugh
when you live alone

(g. bownas & a. thwaite, trans.)

This *ku, included* in Iwanami's top senryu selection and probably translated many times (the last from *The Penguin Book of Japanese Verse* 1964) is representative of the dominantly negative senryu fart. Here's a cheerful haiku fart for comparison:
~~~~~~

屁くらべが又始るぞ冬篭 一茶 1762-1827
hekurabe ga mata hajimaru zo fuyugomori issa

comparison is odorous

hey, hey, again
the fart contest begins!
wintering in

again the time
to compare our farts!
wintering in

Kurabe means both *compare* and *contest* (*match* in the sense of the verb & noun). Kikaku, whose *ku* I have lost, *pioneered* the real fart *ku* – as opposed to older *haikai*, where they tended to be metaphorical. Issa not only paraversed him in a folksy way (*zo* is rough talk), but developed fart *ku* for every season. Between Kikaku and Issa, we have the great Shôzan (1717-1801), whose *ku* are so easy he is under-estimated to this day, and Ôemaru (1719-1805), for whom Issa worked.

時となく快き屁や冬こもり 嘯山
toki to naku kokoroyoki he ya fuyugomori

wintering in
there's no time like this
for pleasant farts

冬篭嬉しきまてに夫の屁 大江丸
fuyugomori ureshiki made ni otto no he

wintering in
delighted with the farts
of her husband

Haikai masters were on the road a lot judging contests and offering lessons. A wife would be so happy to have one home for a while that . . . While Issa had a handful of variations on Kikaku's missing (a free book to the first who finds it for me) ground-breaker – I suspect he was hoping to make *Comparing Farts* a *fuyu kigo,* or "winter seasonal word/theme," which, I am afraid, has not happened – he also recognized that Spring and Fall were probably the fartiest seasons of all, even if one was not so aware of one another's production as when shut in for the winter, and cut dozens of farts into them. When Spring came people were eating gas inducing *daikon* pickles and other salted greens that outlasted the winter and were metaphysically full of pep and ready to go. Issa confesses or boasts to mixing his stink with the scent of the plum (using the double verb *koki-mazete* more than once). He did it when he had a young wife and babies, so one feels the plum blossom stands for his wife with her breasts full of milk. Plum is written 梅. Can you see the 母 mother in it? And can you see the tits in the mother? He draws out his idea more clearly in a *kyôka,* or crazy-verse than a haiku, so here one is:

梅が香に御ならの匂ひこき交ぜて　草の庵も春辺なりけり 一茶
ume-ga-ka ni onara no nioi kokimazete / kusa no iori mo harube narikeri issa
(plum[bloom] scent in hon.fart's smell mixing // grass[stinky] hut too spring[swollen] is!)

GrAsS hut airs

what wind i break
into sweet plum's bouquet
spring has finally come
to this old fart

the scent of plum
in bloom and smelly farts
mix together

How my old grass hut
swells with the spring!

Issa's original lies somewhere between those two translations. He is feeling both his oats and his age. Issa wrote a few crazy-verses every year, mostly when he had emotions he did not feel like expressing so clearly in haiku. His best uses the characters for *silverfish* as an *adverb* (紙魚／＼と *shimijimi to*) to express how much he hated his townsmen for letting some of his papers be destroyed; but, let us stick to farts (I am collecting silverfish *ku* for another book). Issa's home-made dialect and usage dictionaries include the most famous crazy-verse on farts. It puns on two homophonies, 1) *Nara* (the old capital) and *fart*, and 2), the "eight" in "eight-fold cherry" (double-petalled varieties) in the old pronunciation where *e* "え" can be written *he* "へ" and the *other* common pronunciation of "fart." It may be found in the chapter on said blossoms in my 3000-*ku* 740 pg. monster, *Cherry Blossom Epiphany*. Nara, by the way, was not only known for such blossoms, but for the picture scrolls called *Nara-e-hon*, which have been reproduced around the world and include the infamous *Battle of Farts* (放屁合戦 *Hôhi-gassen*), in which bonzes "shoot" their "fart-balls" back and forth at one another while shouting out things like *"Call me the Windbag!"* (referring to the bag carried by the God of the Wind) or *"I'm going to shoot me down a nun!"* Now, back to haiku reality, a fall *ku* Issa composed a half year before his marriage when suffering from an extended illness convalescing at a student's house.

十ばかり屁を捨に出る夜永哉　一茶
jû bakari he o sute ni deru yonaga kana issa
(ten just farts[acc] throw-out-to go-out night-long 'tis)

just ten farts
is all i go out to dump
this long night

growing for what
so i can go out to dump
ten farts a night?

a long night
ten times out i go
to dump farts

Seven years before, Issa had lamented "Frost on my head and now wind, too, blows through my body!" (霜風も常と成たる我身哉 *shimokaze mo tsune to naritaru waga mi kana*). The original is not that clear, but knowing he suffered from alopecia, it was clear enough what he meant. Still, that was old-style *haikai metaphor*. Those ten farts are fresh even if Issa may have been playing on a *ku* of separation 留別 by Shikô (d.1731) *"The memento / of a short night, just / ten snores"* (短夜の名残や鼾十ばかり *mijikayo no na-nokori ya ibiki jû bakari*). Later, after he got married, an exuberant Issa would develop the idea of going out to dump farts further by naming the wall where he cut loose, the *"Geezer Stink Bug Wall."* A less creative poet would have come up with a mere "farting wall."

さま／＼に音をなく中の屁ひり蟲　む 20
samazama ni oto o naku naka no heppiri mushi

among the many
sounds that may be sung
a farting bug

That is a 5-7-5 part of a 1760's linked-verse from the *Mutamagawa*. What makes Issa's series of cheerful stink-bug *ku* different and new is that they are *personal* – he either address the bug, describes it in a way that you *know* he really pays attention to it, or compares himself to it. I have done that series up in style for another book (*A Dolphin In the Woods*), so no more bombardiers, here.

屁籤なかまに猫も入りけり　魚淵
he-kuji nakama ni neko mo iri-keri

he adds the cat to those
playing 'who-cut-the-cheese?'

This 7-7 by Mabuchi, one of Issa's students and closest friends, is in a link-verse session Issa presided over. *Kuji* is usually translated as a "lottery" or "draw," but this was more like spin the bottle. People (and cats) made a circle and someone spun a piece of twisted twine with a bent-over top between their palms (with eyes-closed?) and whomever it pointed at was held responsible. From what I know about Issa and his cat/s, I bet it is about him. But, while Issa's notebooks were full of fart *ku* (some horses, I should add), the earliest fart *ku* of his I found in a link-verse jam comes relatively late (when he is over 60). It is a 7-7 part:

屁を引いたことも負けぎらい也 再現
he o hiita koto mo make-girai nari

even when it comes to farts
s/he hates to take second place

English's addiction to pronouns makes good translation impossible when we don't know if Issa means himself, his spunky recently departed wife or someone else. I realize these *ku* are a bit tame compared to the rowdier senryu, but they seem virtually identical to the *zappai* of *Mutamagawa*, some of which are senryu. Perhaps, I will gather enough for a small book some day to prove that point.

.

屁くらべや芋名月の草の庵　一茶
he-kurabe ya imo-meigetsu no kusa no an issa

comparing farts, for smell, for tune,
a grass hut below the yam full moon

Actually, that is a 5-7-5 by Issa to which I added *smell* (punned in the grass), *tune* (implied) and rhyme (why not?). Haiku-wise, it is significant for the way it links yams and farts. Somewhat older *ku* mention bonzes digging, eating and farting yam, but Issa brings it home. Yam – and not beans (actually, *cabbage* was once *our* fart scapegoat) – is still *the* fart food of Japan. A more proper translation.

what a fart-fest!
my grass hut pungent below
the yam full moon

Over a decade later, the year before Issa's death, he copied into his journal a stanza from a folk-song that epitomizes that brave old country world ignored by the clean-minded haiku poets and dirty-minded senryu poets alike:

かはい男は芋喰て死んだ　屁をひる度に思ひ出す
kawai otoko wa imo kutte shinda // he o hiru tabi ni omoidasu
(cute man-as-for yam-eating died // fart[obj] cuts time remember)

lover boy choked
on sweet 'tato tarts
she still recalls him
whenever she farts

This is the type of folk-song mentioned by an early senryu: *"Songs of a kind / in no songbook you find / in the WC"* (哥書にない哥を後架に張ッて置キ 筥 2-17 *kasho ni nai uta o kôka ni hatte-oki*) We know it goes back 200 years at the most. *Why?* Because these yams were introduced to Japan by the Portuguese. And Issa did not neglect the classical food for farts in the pre-yam *Nara picture scrolls' Battle of the Farts.* Can you guess? *Chestnuts.* Green ones in particular had literally explosive results. In a link-verse jam he participated in decades earlier, someone 7-7'ed *"Renowned for farts, too / roasted chestnuts"* (*he mo hyôban no arishi yaki-kuri*). In Issa's late fifties, he would try have a *hero-hero-god* (also called *bero-bero no kami*), the spirit of the same twirled paper we saw incriminate the cat, point in their direction and another (*let's do a double-header*).

yakikuri ya heroherogami no muku hô ni
(roasted-chestnuts! the hh-god's facing way-at)

roasted chestnuts
right in the direction
the youdidit points

herohero no kami ga hina ni tsunmukinu
(herohero-god-the doll/s-at face[+emphatic])

the god spins
and herohero points
right at our doll/s

Even before they are eaten chestnut farts can do serious damage. I have fond memories of being cussed out by my father the first time I roasted chestnuts, not knowing one had to cut a vent in them. It was in a tiny stone cabin and everyone hit the floor as they ricocheted from the walls. Issa had a shelf with dolls on the wall separating his part of the house from his brother's and they took a lot of grief – *scapedolls?* – so it is hard to say if he means one doll, like the cat included in the circle, or the doll-shelf. The same month Issa wrote the above, he brings farts into yet another season:

oya to ko ga he-kurabe nari kado-suzumi issa
(parent and child fart-compare/contest becomes gate-cool)

parent and child
compare farts by the door
cooling at dusk

The date of his notebook suggests early fall, but *cooling down* is a summer theme.

This is the most refreshing of all fart-ku, is it not? But the best – if most poignant is best – of Issa's fart *ku* was composed a few years before, after Issa was married, he had his cheerful farts. This is not one of them. I would say he had one of those nights when rotgut and whatever he ate disagreed.

屁くらべが己に始る衾かな　一茶
he-kurabe ga onore ni hajimaru fusuma kana

comparing farts
first, between me and myself
the worn futon

the fart match
starts within my winter quilt
all by myself

As Japanese did not have central heating, they needed cover when awake, too. These futon called *fusuma* had sleeves, so they were *worn*. But the relevant point here is that they not only hold in heat but gas. The sulfur build-up is impressive. If odor could be seen, one might make indian smoke-signals from his or her farts! *I have heard the best strategies for holding or releasing such gas discussed on Japanese talk radio.* Some soon-to-be-married brides dwell on this problem!

he o hitta koto o mo chô ni tsuke-kerashi issa
ôrosoku no pah pah to tatsu nabuchi

Issa: *The fact he cut a fart was taken down, or so they say –*
Mabuchi: *The large candle, sputtering, flares.*

Issa composed the above in a mixed-verse jam the same year he had the cheerful farts of parent and child. When Issa was sick he tended to be wild, but when he was in decent shape and kept his cool, he tended to do stuff by the book, which is to say, *use allusions,* for they were more certain to gain respect than novelty. Note this early senryû:

御屁まで帳面に付御大病　筥 2-33
on-he made chômen ni tsuku ondaibyô 天明四
(hon. fart until note-page-on mark hon.big-disease)

his august illness
even his honor's farts
are recorded in the log.

The similarity is closer in the original than in my translation. Who knows whether Issa read the senryu or both poets allude to a common source! My point is only to show that farts passed freely between genre. And Mabuchi's 7-7 response to Issa is *pah! pah!* perfect. Was there a secretary (other than the doctor) sitting across the room who watched a candle near the bed for indications of flatulence? Mabuchi indirectly confirmed my reading of a sodomy *ku* (pg.199).

Now, back to Issa. A couple years before his death, he had the final word on those dolls:

雛棚や隣づからの屁のひびき 一茶
hinadana ya tonarizu kara no he no hibiki
(the doll-shelf neighbor-from's fart's echo)

My dolls passing gas once more?
no, the farts come from next door!

~~~~~~~~~~~~~~~~~~~~~~~~~~~~~

The sound of a fart, cuts through the wall —
My alcove of dolls have been cleared after all!

Odd ways to translate a haiku, but I am not sure it is a haiku. Issa's doll shelf was up year-round (or, am i wrong?), so, unless wondering about a neighbor makes it a Fall *ku* because Bashô had one asking what the neighbors were up to, it might better be called a *kyô(crazy)ku*, which would mean a close relation to the senryu, which is a type of *kyôku*. I like it with my improvements, for even in Japanese, the context is needed. For a senryu, the "my" would have to be killed:

right behind
the doll-shelf, farts
from next door

a doll shelf
and right behind the wall
farty neighbors

Issa also has plenty of rhetorical farts, for the Japanese equivalent of *not giving a fart for* something was *not thinking a fart of* it, and doing no great harm or good was *neither farting nor burning incense* (Issa has at least half a dozen *ku* with this!), but they are like the whiney gospel songs of Elvis Presley, better forgotten. Rhetorical and allegorical farts were especially common in crazy-verse, *kyôka*. You have seen one of Issa's (the *GrAsS Hut Aires*). Here is something slightly older (徳和歌後萬載集 1785) and utterly unseasonal:

すかし屁の消え易きこそあわれなれみはなき物と思ひながらも 紀定麿
sukashi-he no kie-yasuki koso aware nare mi wa nakimono to omoinagara mo
(slip[silent]fart's vanish-easily especially sad is // substance-as-for not thing knowing-while)

how sad a thing
the silent fart, so quick
to disappear

i get no cheer in knowing
'twas nothing from the start

While I know longer care for this type of purely logical (which is to say ludicrous) poem in my old age, reading one takes me back to the time I was crazy for the metaphysical poets and I find I cannot help joining in.

pity the silent fart
vanishing without a trace
though nothing of substance
in the first place
who is?
~~~~~~~~~~~~~~~~~~~~~~~~~~~~~

The last line is mine. If life is but a fart, is happiness making it trumpet?

断食の屁の音も香もなし む
danjiki no he no oto mo ka mo nashi 11
(fast's fart's sound and scent [are] not)

A fasting fart has no sound,
And, just as well, no smell!

This *Mutama* 7-7 is more like a miniature crazy-verse than a haiku or senryu.

乳の下て屁の音トのするおもしろさ 万
chichi no shita de he no oto no suru omoshirosa 宝 *13*
(breast/s/tit/s' under-at fart's/s' sound does interestingness)

those little things

how interesting
the sound of a fart from
under a breast!

There may be less farts in senryu than in *haikai*, for they are only dirty in a culture where all below the belt is. The above, from the early *Million* shows how far one poet went to find a senryu in "farts." After wavering between dropping the *ku* as worthless or keeping it as good in a childish sort of way, I noticed the draw was *inochi nari keri,* one of the most troublesome phrases ever invented, which Japanese-English dictionaries avoid like the plague. It could mean *"That's my love!" "That is what life's about!"* or *"How good it is to be alive!"* and, after thinking, kept the *ku,* gave it a title and recalled another for a movie: *The Unbearable Lightness of Being*.

大腰につかって開に屁をひらせ
ôgoshi ni tsukatte bobo ni he o hirase 葉 15
(big-hip-with poking pussy-to/by fart[acc]cut-make)

long-stroke art
can make a pussy
cut a fart!

c/ long strokes
the bloke makes her pussy
cut some cheese

c/ long strokes
he makes her pussy start
passing gas

stoking her pussy
mr long stroke makes it
a blazing saddle

And, to tell the truth, another reason I kept the boob-fart *ku* was to compare it with the above. Despite a quadruple-bypass translation, the *Leaf ku* says nothing. It just describes something anyone who fucks around discovers sooner or later.

Martial did much, much better with his Gallena (hen), *clucking*, of course, from both ends. And, the fifth story of *Boudoir Tales of the Great Eastern Land of Japan* is better yet. After Hon'in no Jijû allowed Taira no Sadabumi to take her from the rear, and *"the vigor of the comings and goings of his manly penis caused a curious sound to issue from her vagina . . . something like a fart and yet . . . not a fart,"* the wit, not losing a stroke, piped up: *"What need is there of string and bamboo instruments? Marvelous musical tones reside within your vagina"* – this a reference to a Chinese poem seeing no need of such instruments when mountains and waters sound as they do. You might think the woman would be delighted with such graceful contextualization, but *"Jijû suddenly twisted her rump and repulsed his penis. She never permitted him to take her from behind again."* (orig. 1785. trans. M.E. Jamentz, 2004. Part of An episodic festschrift for Howard Hibbet published by highmoonoon.). With truly bawdy tales like this – and it is better when the fat is not gouged out to shorten it as I did – we can see why senryu is not so much bawdy as off-color, or dirty.

へをひったより気のどくハおなら也
he o hitta yori ki no doku wa onara nari
(fart[acc] pulled=cut-more-than feeling-poison-as-for [hon.]fart is)

passing air
is more regrettable than
cutting a fart

This sort of aphoristic *ku* is not a very typical senryu, but it indicates the place where most senryu farts came to be found: *emotional pain*. The contrast of the vulgar *"he"* and the more elegant *"onara"* refers to either 1) the different circumstances of men and women – *Farting with one's buddies in the open air is fun / But pass gas in the inner-chambers and a woman is done!* – 2) likewise for ladies and their maids, or 3) ditto for high and low society – *A fart among equals may turn your face red / But do it before the shôgun, and lose your head!*

屁をひって妾は下女に壱歩やり 末
he o hitte mekake wa gejo ni ichi-bu yari 1-11
(fart[acc]pull=cutting mistress-as-for maid-to one bu gives)

a mistress farts
the maid gets a penny
just for starts

Now we are getting senryu. A *bu* is a pretty penny, but I could not decide on "pound" or "crown," so *for starts* . . The *ku* probably does not mean only this:

the farting mistress is far from dumb:
she pays her maid to hold her tongue.

She probably expected her maid to do more, to actually claim her stink, or behave in such a way to give that impression to her master, for Japanese even has a word for a servant specializing in passing off a mistress's farts as her own!

the farting mistress
winks: a bu for her maid
to cover her stink

paying her maid
a farthing, the mistress
passes off a fart

I was not joking about the fart-changer, though it is possible the literature which passed down information about such people was joking. Such a servant was called a "fart-bearing nun," or *he-oi-bikuni* (屁負比丘尼).

たいこ持安ス金て屁はひらぬ也
taikomochi yasukin de he wa hiranu nari 万？明七
(drum-carrier[hanger-on]/ cheap-money-for fart[acc] cut-not becomes)

a pro ass-licker
for a bargain price
un-cuts a fart

the whore's clown
asks for almost nothing
to uncut her fart

A drummer would seem to be a rodeo clown for the Pleasure Quarters. The existence of this *ku* is why we can be sure what the *ku* about the mistress farting and the maid means. The *Pluck* round-robin team observed that the payment was extravagant. One *bu* was a maid's monthly salary. They ask: "For a woman who made a living by being sexy, was a fart *that* damaging?" I suspect the amount of money was decided by poetic fiat. In Japanese, the sound of a fart is just like the coin but with a touch more emphasis: *"booh!"* (ぶっ) instead of *"boo"* (ぶ). This was indeed a trade! However, let it be noted that Japanese, as any sensitive people, were aware of the damage associations could do to romantic relations.

菊慈童屁でもひったらしばり首 摘
kikujido he demo hittara shibari-kubi 4-25

little mumsy
had he farted, would have
lost his head

had little mum
but farted, head & shoulders
would've parted

"Chrysanthemum-merciful-child," a boy favorite of an ancient Chinese Emperor, committed the unpardonable sin of stepping over His pillow. He should have been executed, but was instead exiled to *the mountains*, in Chinese also meaning "wilderness" (as "desert" did in the West, thanks to the Near Eastern Bible), where he lived 800 years thanks to sipping the dew from Chrysanthemum petals. The execution term *"shibari-kubi"* has no English equivalent. 1) It means to be decapitated with one's hands tied behind the back, then have said head put on display. Perhaps, it plays on the way prize 'mums were grown tied to posts and had their heads cut-off for display. A rarer meaning, 2), is execution by strangulation, the common way of doing in Imperial rivals and lovers in China. This *ku* playing on a classic tale of *lése majesty* is not about odor and attraction/repulsion, but farting as rudeness. (Before moving on, one note to balance this account of a Chinese Emperor who banished some-one for what was probably an innocent slip of the foot. Another Chinese Emperor was so attentive to his little boy love that he cut off his own sleeve rather than risk waking the child when he had to get up for business. Because of this pederasty in China came to be called "cut-sleeve.")

屁をひって嫁ハ雪隠出にくがり
he o hitte yome wa setchin denikugari 摘 1-15
(fart[acc] cutting bride-as-for toilet leave-hard-fear)

a fart escapes
and the bride is stuck
in the restroom

(in other words)

that fart in the crapper was heard beyond doubt
a young wife is lost for a way to sneak out

The above reading, where the young-wife is embarrassed to come out of the restroom is 99% certain. But there is 1% chance it could be read as follows:

A restroom fart
the shy young wife:
now she cannot shit
to save her life!

Were it not for the draw-verse being "it's clear as can be," (*hakkiri to suru*), I might have considered the even less unlikely (1%) chance reading:

ashamed to shit
the young wife lets out
a hell of a fart!

The stereotypical "bride" is a young wife who must live under the critical eye of her mother-in-law, the official "wife" of the house. A marriage was not followed by a honeymoon, as in the West, but *an initiation* that lasted for years. The young man can do no wrong and his wife no right. A simple senryu, parodying a well-known supposed Confucianism "to hate the sin and not the sinner" (その罪を憎んでその人を憎まず) – doesn't Christianity share this? – puts it thus:

.

母其つびを憎んで其イ八を憎まず 葉 29
haha sono tsubi o nikunde sono mara o nikumazu

his mother
hates the cunt but hates not
the cock"

With this attitude – that reminds us of not only the hazing young wives received, but how the newly married man's mother liked to listen to their sex – we can imagine young wives living with their husbands would be hesitant to let it out!

嫁の屁は怒り自分の屁は笑ひ　きち坊
yome no he wa okori jibun no he wa warai　kichibô

the bride's fart
makes her mad, her own
make her glad

Knowing the censors would allow gas to pass, Blyth translated some good senryu fartology, of which this is classic. His translation is a bit long – *The farting of the daughter-in-law / Makes her angry. / Her own is for laughter.* (1960) – but clearer than mine. Translating *yome* as "daughter-in-law" is masterful. She, after-all, is the odd one out. Other senryû depict the bride/daughter-in-law eating her dinner *"as if she is counting each grain of rice"* (花嫁ハめしをかぞへるやうに喰イ 9-29 *hanayome wa meshi o kazoeru yô ni kui*). The poor thing *"cannot scratch her can even though it itches"* (花嫁ハかいくもしりハかゝぬなり 末摘 1-28 *hanayome wa kaikumo shiri wa kakanu nari*). In fart terms, we get this:

花嫁ハ壱つひつても命かけ 万？明七
hanayome wa hitotsu hitte mo inochi-gake
(flower-bride-as-for, one pull/cut even life-risks)

the young wife
cutting but a single fart
fears for her life

each fart cut
by the-daughter-in-law
a mortal blow

To fart was, as a figure of speech, *to do something bad*. A senryu (misplaced) saying that an archbishop is unaware of his own fart (*he-ni oboenashi*) brings that out in a bassackwards way. The powerful can fart but the powerless who can, after all, do nothing but fart, fear doing even that. The trials and tribulations of the young wife at the hands of her husband's family (especially his mother) were, until recently, the most popular theme for tear-jerking drama in Japan.

居眠って下女ほそ長く屁をすかし 37-19
i-nemutte gejo hoso-nagaku he o sukashi

dozing off
the maid passes a long
thin fart

下女おならかゝとで潰し／＼ひり 112-6
gejo onara kakato de tsubushi tsubushi hiri

the maid cuts
and cuts the cheese
upon her heels

a maid's farts
squeezed through her heels
pass bit by bit

a maid's farts
squashed over & over
by her heels

A bestial maid who cut a fart on her master's cock with every stroke they made is introduced in the chapter on *Maids;* these two *ku* are much more human. They remind me of an innocent one translated by Blyth where a maid-servant eats a serving of noodles with active buttocks – remember, no chairs, so she would be bent over eating it, while seated with her legs folded under her upon the tatami mat. That method of sitting is often mistakenly translated as *squatting*, despite being the most elegant and, in Japanese terms, "proper way of sitting" (正座*seiza*), while squatting, with its shades of defecation, squaws and squashes, has primitive connotations. It is sitting on top of your feet, which is to say with the top of your feet (and shins) resting upon the mat, rather than your rump, which, instead, rests upon your heels and that explains the second *ku.* And why didn't she just get up? Because, unlike European servants who tend to stay up while their masters sit down, servants in Japan (and many other cultures) must sit lower than their masters or mistresses. Moreover, the maid often needed to bend her body forward to be lower yet and that would impact on the bowels so . . . The first *ku* is a happier one, for a long thin fart would be dry, reflecting good muscle tone and a healthy digestive tract. As ridiculous as this may seem for so insubstantial a *ku*, I believe it reflects quiet observation, equal to that of the best haiku poets. And, as classic haiku observations were rarely pure, but rather fitting to their theme as developed over time, the fart was proper to the stereotype of the *gejo,* literally "low/under-woman," which is to say servant, or "maid" in one sense of the word.

下女と屁の対決をする居候 37-22 &
gejo to he no taiketsu o suru isôrô 79-14
(maid-with fart showdown does hanger-on)

the hanger-on
has a fart showdown
with the maid

the maid-servant
pushed to exchange farts
with a parasite

An *isôrô* is someone without work, typically, but not always a distant relative, who hangs around the house – in Usania, today, black (African-American) comedy is full of such characters, usually depicted as a threat to wife or girlfriend – and one can imagine how hard it must have been to a maid-servant to be plagued by one such character. One can imagine any number of damned if you do and damned if you don't type situations. Because of idioms where farts stand for the last defense in a hopeless situation – making a stink as you go down, this *ku* might be about a serious end game; then again, it might be a relaxed open house. Either way, the casting for the confrontation is correct.

下女の屁をかぶった晩にくどくなり
gejo no he o kabutta ban ni kudoku nari 末摘 2-31
(maid-servant's fart[acc] covered evening-on persuaded)

on the same day
he covered the maid's fart
she's talked into it

he took the blame
for the maid's fart and later
that evening made her

The *Pluck* anthology is said to be the more literary of the obscene senryu collections, but this last *ku* falls short.

屁ひとつになる説法をおやぢとく
he hitotsu ni naru seppô o oyaji toku 柳多留拾集遺 巻 14
(fart-one-in become lecture[acc] gramps/geezer solves)

~~*his old man*~~
~~*figures out that lecture*~~
~~*like one fart*~~

his old man
explains how a lecture can
become a fart

~~*the old geezer*~~
~~*solves the riddle: preaching*~~
~~*with one fart*~~

I just read the explanation for a saying "hundred days of preaching, fart one" (百日の説法屁一つ). It means *though one does many good works, all may be undone by a single slip-up*, *i.e.* a fart. Before learning that, I assumed the saying meant long lectures weren't worth a fart (another old saying compares a parent's lecture to cow piss: long and good for nothing). Now, I am unsure *what* the senryu means. I added the middle reading as my best guess, and imagine the old-man is using the fart to lecture his kid about keeping his nose clean .

lost at the start
a senryu where buddha
becomes a fart

I could *swear* I read a *ku* where the ぶっ = *booh!* sound of a fart and the ぶつ = *butsu* sound meaning the Buddha = 佛 = are f/used to teach the nature of the emptiness, for what is a better symbol of "all is vanity" than a fart? Then again, I might have dreamed up the existence of such a *ku*, for I have always done much of my best thinking in bed asleep or half-asleep. Now I must get up before I have time to read my mind, chew my cud and arrange my thoughts, in order to fetch the paper (through the spider webs and over the railroad track) I don't read, feed the cows I don't eat and clean the pool I don't use – poverty and family circumstances demand it – so, for better or worse, you are not getting the benefit of my dreams in this book. Ah, I have found *prose* with the idea in a book Issa encouraged and sold: *有なし草：*「ぶつと放つ屁は仏陀のめうかんにいたる」

~ eddies ~

Issa's Farts. I thought to pack Issa's farts into a book someday, but fearing my 100 pg. water-soluble manuscript might be lost first, cannibalized it for this chapter, leaving out all the horses. I will restore a summary of something contemporary (1994 or 5) included to prove an "infatuation with flatulence," as I put it, for the record. A TV variety show fed a dozen or so young women in bikinis various food and drink, especially bananas so they could eat them lasciviously, encouraged to do so-called fart-priming exercises and promised awards for the first fart, most farts, loudest fart etc.. When a girl felt one coming on, she would call an announcer who would run over and shove a microphone in her crotch. Meanwhile, I translated a children's book about farts for family and mailed it to the USA, where parts were read to a conference of medical doctors. Unfortunately, nothing was done with the book and someone else ended up making millions (!) from it.

~~~~~~

Japanese Farts in a Nutshell. While Japanese do not seem quite so full of beans as the Chinese and Germans, they do, like the French, have their great flautists of a single hole (both legendary *and* historical) and *haikai* (including *kyôka crazy-verse*) is as farty as any of poetry (there is even a collection of a hundred fart *kyôka*) in the world. Japanese do have one advantage over their competitors when it comes to literary farts. It is the letter へ or *he,* which is one pronunciation of fart. Imagine, one letter makes a fart. Poets got much mileage from it . Issa used へ to describe mountain tops when he was feeling empty and senryu, perhaps following a haikai *ku* about a rooftop of a lone house in a withered winter field, noted that most outhouse rooftops were "shaped like the farty letter" (雪隠の屋根ハ大かた屁の字形 1-32 *setchin no yane wa ôkata he no jikata* willow). And even today Japanese draw disgruntled farty faces with the へ for eyes and mouth.

~~~~~~

Between the Boob and Deep-stroke Farts. I found the missing link between the *Mutamagawa* breast and the *Leaf's* vaginal farts – among Suzuki's *zappai* – but could not squeeze them because the textual peristalsis, or flow of the essay was too satisfying to break.

両方が上手汗で腹鳴る　宝暦 13　類字折句集
ryôho ga jôzu ase de hara naru

both are good:
their sweating makes
their bellies sing

"They are both so good at it / their bellies fart with sweat" might be a closer translation of the 8-7 *ku.* The last verb is a problem. *Naru* means the ring/clang/toll/dong of a bell, the buzz of a buzzer, the roar of thunder, and many things that sing-out if it were, including *farts*, which Suzuki specified (*onara no yô-na oto*). A slightly later capped verse starts with 5-syllabets suggestive of rain.

降り頻る・汗で腹鳴る上手同士 鼻あぶら 天明 2
furi-shikiru //ase de hara naru jôzu dôshi

◎ *it's pouring down!* ◎
their bellies thunder with sweat
two who can love

The rain turns out to be sweat, but the weather metaphor may be developed in English even better than Japanese because of our fine verb, or noun-turned-verb, *thunder.*

闇中戦・馬の深田の音もあり 伊勢冠付
anjûsen // uma no fukada no oto mo ari 文化 10
(pitchdark mid-battle // horse'/s' deep-field's sound also is)

◎ *a battle at night* ◎
one sound that horses make
in deep paddies

does pony truck
through a field of muck?
◎ *the night battle* ◎

Suzuki capped the farts with this *ku.* In English, Japanese caps/crowns often seem better at the *end* of the poem they are supposed to start.

Farts and Romance. One might not think it necessary to explain *why* farts matter to a mistress or courtesan, but readers who have swallowed too much 20c psychology could use a refresher. D. H. Lawrence on Swift is an example of such unnatural naturalism:

> "It was not the fact that Celia shits which so deranged him, it was the thought. .... Great wit as he was, he could not see how ridiculous his revulsions were...... He couldn't even see how much worse it would be if Celia didn't shit. His physical sympathies were too weak, his guts were too cold to sympathize with poor Celia in her natural functions. His insolent and squeamish mind just turned her into a thing of horror, because she was merely natural and went to the w.c. It is monstruous! One feels like going back across all the years to poor Celia, to say to her: It's all right, don't you take any notice of that mental lunatic. And Swift's form of madness is very common today. Men with cold guts and over-squeamish minds are always thinking those things and squirming....... ." ("Introduction to Pansies"(1929) in *Sex, Literature and Censorship*: edit. H.T. Moore)

Swift adverse to excrement? Wasn't he the one who distinguished the shit of Englishmen and Scotch-Irish by the tell-tale points on the end of the former (fundamental tight-asses), and who had the Yahoo shower Gulliver with ordure, etc.. No, D.H., for better or worse, the Dean was Mr. Scatology, himself. Deranged to have an unfortunate lover discover that *"Celia, Celia, Celia, shits!"* Come off it! Swift was warning against snooping too much into other people's business. Especially those we love. And more important, he was just reworking an old saw inherited from Classic times. (Did D.H. stop reading Ovid before arriving to his *"remedies for love?"*) Moreover, one finds revulsion for and/or the concealment of excrement in cultures around the world. Did we not have a natural interest – the prevention of spreading parasites – in feeling repulsion? How ridiculous to call the natural "yuck!" reaction a "form of degraded taboo-insanity!" Moreover, Swift was writing in a hyperbolic vein. Here is our hero half way into the poem:

> *"Dear Gassy, though to ask I dread,*
> *Yet ask I must, Is Caelia dead?*
> *How happy I, were that the worst;*
> *But I was fated to be curs'd."*

After a hundred or so lines that only once hint at the nature of the catastrophe –

> *"Oh Peter! Beauty's but a Varnish,*
> *Which Time and Accidents will tarnish:*
> *But, Caelia has contriv'd to blast*
> *Those Beauties that might ever last"*

– the Dean finally lets the punch line hit the fan:

> *"Nor wonder how I lost my Wits;*
> *Oh! Caelia, Caelia, Caelia shits."*

If D.H. Lawrence didn't chuckle reading this, than he is the one who has really lost *his* wits! And, in case you think the Romans whom Swift improved upon, were themselves uniquely sicko, let me add that an ancient Japanese Tale in the *Ujihiromonogatari* (c.1220) shows us that Ovid and Swift were hardly unique. To summarize:

> A noted lady's man fell head over heels for a court lady. Being used to having women in love with him rather than the vice versa, and horrified by his failure to control his own feelings, he desperately sought a remedy, a way to fall out of love. Finally, remembering that she must be human and answer the call of

> nature once a day, he devised a scheme to get hold of her excrement before it was disposed of, the idea being that a good smell of it would, to use modern polymath Aramata Hiroshi's wording, "instantly blow away a love powerful enough to last a hundred years." *Free at last!* Unlike, Swift's laughably naive lover; this worldly man knows what women do. But, he also knows that knowledge and experience are not the same thing. So he has a henchman bring him her honey pot. He rips open the cover and plunges in his nose . . . only to encounter the sweet bouquet of cloves and other spices! Someway or another, she had gotten wind of his plan and preferred to keep him enthralled.

Aramata opines that this story marks a new chapter in Japanese toilet practice, the end of the ancient nobility's "river-house" where shit dropped directly into the river and lovers often rendezvoused, and the beginning of what was later to become of agricultural use, a toilet where waste is collected. One wonders what Lawrence would have made of this story! (Aramata's essays are not translated, but you may find the tale and many others suitable for adults in Royall Tyler's *Japanese Tales:* (Pantheon 1987)).

~~~~~~

***Hate the Crime** and not the Criminal (or hate the sin and not the sinner)*. The attributions to Confucius may be confused.「その罪を憎んで、その人を憎まず」. 孔子とその門人の言行を記した『孔業子』（くぞうし）孔鮒の著といわれたが、後世は偽作とみた（莽露庵主人）。又、『忠臣蔵』では、「孔子」と言わず、そのような言及にした。曰く「*君子は*、其の罪～」と。

~~~~~~

***Kichibô?** きち坊。Blyth being one of very few writers – or his publisher being one of a very few publishers – willing to put up the original Japanese with the translations, I hate to complain about a thing, but with this senryu, and all too many other *ku*, he gives us the name of the author rather than the name of the work in which it was published. With senryu, the latter is what matters.

~~~~~~

Mark Twain's *1601.* About half of Twain's bawdy small edition work concerned *farts*, or rather one large one:

.

> In ye heat of ye talk it befel yt one did breake wind, yielding an exceding mightie and distresfull stink, whereat all did laugh full sore, and then –
>
> > Ye Queene. – Verily in mine eight and sixty yeres have I not heard the fellow to this fart. Meseemeth, by ye grete sound and clamour of it, it was male; yet ye belly it did lurk behinde shoulde now fall lean and flat against ye spine of him yt hath bene delivered of so stately and so waste a bulk, where as ye guts of them yt doe quiff-splitters bear, stand comely still and rounde. Prithee let ye author confess ye offspring. Will my Lady Alice testify?
> >
> > Lady Alice. – Good your grace, an' I had room for such a thundergust
> > within mine ancient bowels, 'tis not in reason I coulde discharge ye same and live to thank God for yt He did choose handmaid so humble whereby to shew his power. Nay, 'tis not I yt have broughte forth this rich o'ermastering fog, this fragrant gloom, so pray you seeke ye further.
> >
> > . . . . .
> >
> > Ye Queene. – O' God's name, who hath favored us? Hath it come to pass yt a fart shall fart itself? Not such a one as this, I
~~~~~~

> trow. Young Master Beaumont – but no; 'twould have wafted him to heaven like down of goose's boddy. 'Twas not ye little Lady Helen – nay, ne'er blush, my child; thoul't tickle thy tender maidenhedde with many a mousie-squeak before thou learnest to blow a harricane like this. Wasn't you, my learned and ingenious Jonson?
>
> Jonson. – So fell a blast hath ne'er mine ears saluted, nor yet a stench so all-pervading and immortal. 'Twas not a novice did it, good your maisty, but one of veteran experience – else hadde he failed of confidence. In sooth it was not I.
>
> Ye Queene. – My lord Bacon?
>
> Lord Bacon. – Not from my leane entrailes hath this prodigy burst forth, so please your grace. Naught doth so befit ye grete as grete performance; and haply shall ye finde yt 'tis not from mediocrity this miracle hath issued.
>
> . . . . .
>
> Sr W. [Raleigh] Most gracious maisty, 'twas I that did it, but indeed it was so poor and frail a note, compared with such as I am wont to furnish, yt in sooth I was ashamed to call the weakling mine in so august a presence. It was nothing – less than nothing, madam – I did it but to clear my nether throat; but had I come prepared, then had I delivered something worthy. Bear with me, please your grace, till I can make amends.

I cannot help wondering what Twain would have thought of senryu. Would he have found them kindred spirits for their free way with words, or found them too dark for his taste? He certainly would not have minded their obscenity (*1601* is not all farts – there is sex-related discussion including a fine little story of how a smart maid outwitted a dirty old man). You may find the book at Project Gutenberg.

~~~~~~

The Best Fart Ku of All. There are *two*. One is a *haiku*, or, perhaps a *kyôku,* the last by a poet whose pen name Englishes as "leaving-sound," that I found in Joel Hoffman's fine anthology: *Japanese Death Poems*. It took two full pages of my book on composite translation *A Dolphin In the Woods* to do the subtle pun-filled but deeply significant poem justice; I could not bring myself to include it here, where it would be among more vulgar farts. The other is a senryu captured by Blyth in his *Japanese Life and Character:*

.

音も香も空へぬけてく田植のへ
oto mo ka mo sora e nukete-ku taue no he 秀乃助？*58-16*
(sound/s and scent/s too sky-toward piercing-go paddy-planting-fart/s)

sound and smell
head straight for the sky
rice-planting farts

Blyth's *"Farting while planting rice; / Sound and smell / Rise away to the sky"* probably beats mine. The *nukete-ku* is tricky. It is not just that all is absorbed and harmonized in nature, as Blyth explains, it is as if the farts, in their two packets, escape this world.

~~~~~~

p.s. Blyth has chapter headers on the left page and individual headers on the right. *"While there's fart there's life"* is found above this *ku*. Few people notice headers. My *"Rise, Ye Sea Slugs!"* has *outlandish* individual headers on *every* page, yet they were not mentioned by a single reviewer!!!

From Wee Tinkle To Woeful Torrent

シィシィ から ザァザァ まで

廿七[27]

小便の音

The Sound of Piss

~~~~~~

娘シイ年増のはじゅゥ?乳母のはザア 一五六

musume shii toshima no wa juu uba no wa zaa

daughters go *shi~i*
experienced women *ju~u*
and wet-nurses *za~a*

a maiden *tinkles*
mother *showers*, wet-nurse
just *pours* down!

This is very late *Willow ku* (bk 156) is poetry if *Old McDonald Had a Farm* is. Yet you can bet it made its author and editor happy, for chances are no senryu (or haiku) before it contained more than *two* piss noises in 17 syllabets. Such is the nature of competitive short-form literature. Moreover, onomatopoeia *itself* takes on the nature of a word game in Japanese where one may find whole dictionaries devoted to matching sounds both physical and psychological with their proper subject (or, is it object?). Perhaps the closest English equivalent would be the collective nouns of venery (as in *hunting*) assembled after Sir Arthur Conan Doyle, who did it in a novel (where a young man was quizzed as to the proper terms for various groups of game), and thoroughly but not exhaustively supplemented by James Lipton (*An Exaltation of Larks, or the venereal game:* 1968). It turned into a parlour game. Old McDonald aside, English keeps the lion's share of its extraordinarily good sound sense (it suffices to consider *stop* and *shrimp*) under wraps – I call it *built-in* as opposed to apparent mimesis – so such games combining aspects of matching, collecting and guessing, do not work.

an
Edo
observation:
girls go *tinkle,*
their mamas *shower,*
but wet-nurses can power
a hydro-electric plant !!!
~~~~~~

Pardon the hyperbolic anachronism or anachronistic hyperbole as you wish. This example of one of the oddest themes to ever chapter a book come from *Cuntologia* (女陰万考) whose page on the subject starts with an explanation about why a woman's urination was said to sound like a cataract (「女の小便滝の音」), namely, it gushes so powerfully for being far closer to the bladder than a man's nozzle. I think I would call it oxygenated, for the sound sometimes resembles that of water coming from a tap with a filter. But such spigots were not around back then and because we moderns generally piss into water (I guess this makes us closer to raccoons, who do the same), males now sound as loud if not louder, in a less hissy way, for the longer distance to splashdown and the sound-box effect of the bowl.

しのをつく様にお乳母は小便し 摘 四
shino o tsuku yô ni uba wa shôben-shi

like a torrential downpour
the wet-nurse's water
is an ear-sore

raining cats and dogs?
well, a wet-nurse
pisses hogs!

The wet-nurse, proverbially slack, as we see in another chapter, pisses true to character, or rather, stereotype. The *shino* in the original is a small variety of bamboo that combined with *tsuku* (stick/stab) denotes, as far as I could make out, a big bundle of slender projectiles flying together into something "downpour" literally translates as "sticks shino" and that idiomatically means a torrential cataract of a rain, what we might call "raining cats and dogs" but in Japanese is usually "raining spears." I added "ear-sore" in one reading because this rain doesn't always strike the ears as music (see Mother Goose: *It's raining, its pouring, the old man is snoring* verse) and to bring out the insulting quality intrinsic to wet-nurse senryu. Directly after the above *ku,* Mr. Cuntology introduced a 7-7 epigram that transliterates as "affection-exhausts/ing piss/ing-sound" (*aisô no tsukiru shôben no oto*).

Where went the lovers' bliss?

falling out of love to
the sound of piss

Love's dead, the proof is this

you suddenly hear it
the sound of piss

love's dirge

the sound of piss
from one who
no longer
cares

The verb in the original leaves room for ambiguity. I think it means that awareness of the sound of piss marks the death of love, but it may mean that the pisser is no longer trying to piss in a manner to please, or, at any rate not alienate the other, so the sound really is different.

cupid flown
discretion ceases
now she pisses as she
damn well pleases!

But most women in senryu *did* care:

なりつたけ娵小べんをほそくする
narittake yome shôben o hosoku suru 摘 2-21

just married, she
would do all her pissing
through a pin-hole

a young wife
does her best to keep thin
her stream of piss

the bride tries
her best to keep a bridle
on her piss

the new wife
keeps her piss as narrow
as possible

The dietary joke in the second reading is an anachronism. In Japan, brides (young wives living with their husband's family) had to struggle not to grow *thin*, for, if senryu are right, mother-in-laws preferred growing hair in closets (mold on hidden dumplings) to satisfying the appetite of their son's wife. The bride is both struggling not to sound gross to her husband and, I would think, not to challenge her mother-in-law with a bold display of sound.

たしなんた尼ハ小便しわくさせ 万宝
tashinanda ama wa shôben shiwaku sase 13

prudently
the nun works to knit up
her pissing

decorously
the nun puts pleats in
her sheet of piss

to be discreet
sister puts pleat after pleat
into her piss

Shiwaku sase is "to wrinkle" or "put folds in." This nun is embarrassed to reveal her gross humanity rather than one trying to sound demure and feminine.

小便をいきめば器量がどっとせず 五
shôben o ikimeba kiryô ga dotto sezu
(urine/piss[acc] strain-if/when looks/beauty plenty-does-not)

straining at pee
for all the world knows beauty
does not gush

squeezing her pee
for cats and dogs would mar
her beauty

a careful piss
her beauty won't mean shit
if it bursts out

beauty's boudoir
strains her pee lest it belie
her fragility

Usually the verb *ikimu* is used for straining at stool; here it means trying to restrict it rather than push it out faster, but both activities involve squeezing and breath-holding. First, I imagined a maid-servant who presumes to be a beauty, then a pretty mistress, a "Celia *Pisses!*" I took the Japanese from *Cuntologia*, but *alas*, it and, hence, my readings are probably wrong! A 1995 reprint from a prestigious publisher (岩波文庫), and a 1927 reprint (日本名著全集版) have one less syllabet – making it proper, for the above version was a syllabet over, something rare in the middle part of a senryu. *"I<u>ki</u>meba,"* or "strain-if/when" becomes *"imeba,"* to have a strong aversion for, or "loathe-if/when." In this case, the allusion would be to a popular scam –popular in senryu at any rate – called "the piss team" (小便組*shôben-gumi*), where an exceptionally beautiful woman becomes a mistress on extraordinarily reasonable terms, and within a week or two starts pissing in bed, then demands a high settlement fee to break off with her patron, i.e., the victim. Unfortunately, the final five syllabets, *dotto sezu,* have a number of readings. Using the same one used above, a figurative translation might be: *"If they hate piss / they are not blessed with / drop-dead looks,"* a round-about way of saying that one rarely gets lucky with beauties. But another idiomatic reading of *dotto sezu*, gives us –

小便をいめば器量がどっとせず 五
shôben o <u>ime</u>ba kiryô ga dotto sezu
(urine/piss[acc] <u>loathe</u>-if/when looks/beauty <u>cares-for-not</u>)

if you loathe piss,
beauty is something
you can miss!

fear piss enough
and you will not dare
care for beauty

these beauties
will find nothing amiss
if you hate piss

The first and second readings seem weak of wit, so I prefer the last, which takes the "looks" (*kiryô*) for the person – something possible then, but not today. I.e., the beauties want someone who hates it so they can lose their job and gain that severance package. What's funny is *how* attention is called to a perfectly normal dislike of piss *in bed*. But I am beginning to feel like a fool for wasting so much time on one stupid senryu – I even had one more reading: *By definition he hates pee / A woman who doesn't gush is a beauty!* – and leave it only as an example of how a lack of pronouns can make some poems horribly polysemous. While all three *imeba* versions may be wrong, chances are that Mr. Cuntology misread. I went along with his *ikimeba* reading because it was surrounded by other *ku* about that same idea. As Laurence Sterne's *Tristam Shandy* (1759-67) once explained:

> *"It is the nature of a hypothesis, when once a man has conceived it, that it assimilates everything to itself as proper nourishment; and, from the first minute of your begetting it, it generally grows stronger by every thing you see, hear, read, or understand. This is of great use."* (Go read this old post-modern novel if you have not!).

If you listen for strained piss, you will hear it. *Enough*, one last *ku* to get rid of the piss-team and we will get back on the main path of this essay.

小便は古イと妾あわをふき 万
shôben wa furui to mekake awa o fuki 明七

piss is old
so this mistress
spews foam

piss is old hat
so now mistresses are
foaming over

A confidence trick must be new to work. With *bed-wetting* so well-known, it was time to move on . . . to *epilepsy*. I suppose the poet invented this, for I encounter no more of these *ku,* while the piss-team continues in senryu for generations!

めつきりと・小便ほそふする娘　かぢ枕 宝暦六
mekkiri-to shôben hososuru musume

a young maiden
all too obviously
thins her pee

Coming of Age in Senryu, or at least a 1756 *zappai.* I will not explain how the 7-5 plays on the letters of the adverb めっきり (obviously). Suddenly self-conscious, a young girl squeezes her piss. Do her parents *hear* that their daughter is no longer innocent? The sound is not given in the *ku,* but we are conscious of it. So women of various ages and professions all worried about how they sounded pissing. The author of *Cuntology* also gives a *ku* about a woman in the Court, I cannot understand, though I *imagine* it means someone has the job of covering the sound, as a radio might do for bashful moderns, and concludes his "Sound of Pissing" section with a word of sympathy for the high-stress lifestyle these women led, when even the natural pleasure of release in urination may not be enjoyed *chibiri-chibiri* (in drips and drabbles), when one is afraid to let it all out.

欲心の無い小便を下女は垂れ
yokushin no nai shôben o gejo wa tare
(desire/greed-heart's not urine[acc]maid-as-for drip)

the maid-servant
lets loose a stream of piss
without avarice

Nor *artifice*, for it is the same thing. The verb, *tare,* normally used for male pissing, suggests a real stream of piss. But maids are generally reserved for *sex* in senryu. It is the wet-nurse who cannot piss without becoming a target for senryu:

あいくつわむしさと乳母ハたれて居る摘
ai kutsuwa-mushi sa to uba-wa tarete-iru 1-28

"it's only a giant katydid"
says the nurse-maid
making water

あいくつわむしさと乳母ハたれて居る摘
ai kutsuwa-mushi sato-uba wa tarete-iru 1-28

a giant katydid?
the country wet-nurse
is taking a piss!

Without the Chinese characters, we have yet another ambiguous reading for the first *ku.* The *sa* is an emphatic which I made "it's only," and the *to* means that what came before it was spoken (a verbal quote-mark, lacked by English), but together *sato* means "country." Regardless, we may assume the "giant katydid" (*Mecopoda elongata*) does not say *"Katy did!"* but sounds like a cataract.

乳母たれる向ふでくろがほへて居る 万 安四
uba tareru mukô de kuro ga hoete-iru

nurse-maid pisses
and, over the way, hark!
blacky is barking

That is enough attention paid to the sound of piss in senryu, though I am sure there must be much more, and better, for Japanese prose was full of it – there are *entire lines* of onomatopoeia following a piss from start to finish! Honest to goodness, purely verbal musical scores that read like jazz scats. Here is one I recalled reading in Inoue Hisashi's personal grammar+reader in Japanese (井上ひさし著『私版日本語読本』), kindly looked up & economically transcribed by Y, the partner or doppelganger of O (I don't have it straight yet) who works in a NY bookstore – for I am currently exiled from my books – which has it in stock: シヤリ（+くりかえし記号４回）ザラ（+４回）シヤア（+４回）チウ（+４回）シイシ（+１回）トツクリ（+１回）ポトン、チヨビン (I forgot to ask its *original* source)。

.

sharisharisharisharishari, zarazarazarazarazara, shashashashasha,
jujujujuju, shiishishiishi, tokkuri tokkuri, poton, chobin!

It seems the mimesis picks up in mid-urination and the sound is altered by the varying thickness of the flow – maybe something was going on within sight of the pisser – and, possibly by what the piss strikes, and it ends on some notes that indicate the manner in which the flow is shut-down, though I dare not try to read it.

サホ姫のしと／＼降るや春の雨 貞徳 崑山
sao-hime no shito-shito furu ya haru no ame teitoku 1570-1653

princess spring is out again
making flowers bloom
fine pizzling rain

A original is only *"Princess Sao's is falling shito-shito: spring rain."* The idea of *making flowers bloom* comes from reading Alexander Pope on women-as-clouds & vice-versa and from reading a *ku* by Issa, in whose sundry collection of dialect

(方言雑集：全集七) I found Teitoku's *ku*. Issa's *ku* may already be in another of my books and, lacking mimesis, does not really belong here, but it is my favorite of Issa's half a dozen Goddesses pissing *ku,* so here it is:

さほ姫のばりやこぼしてさく菫 一茶
saohime no bari ya koboshite saku sumire 文政三

where princess sao
spilled her urine, there
bloom the violets!

Classic poetry credited rain and mist with dyeing flowers and leaves. But what a beautiful complement to Ben Franklin's observation that eating pine nuts could make urine smell like violets – the scent of ideal urine (?) – in his Letter to the French Academy of Science suggesting study be given to improving the smell of farts! And, so long as we are off-subject, let me say that there are older pee poems in Japanese than Teitoku's. The earliest I know is in the *Manyôshû* (9c). It is not *about* pissing but a rare example of something famously rare in Japanese, *cussing*. A lover upset at another's unfaithfulness used piss (*shiko*) to modify this and that (one *that* was a *bed*, if I recall right) three times in a tiny 31 syllabet complaint – ancient Japanese used it as British did the word "bloody." But Teitoku's is the first clear piss mimesis of the type that would soon become ubiquitous in Edo era literature. that I know of, and, right next to it, Issa jotted down (*bassackwards*) the most famous of all, or the only *classic* pissing poem:

サホ姫の春立ながらしとをしてかすみの衣裾はぬれけり 一茶記 犬筑波集
sao-hime no haru tachinagara shito o shite kasumi no koromo suso o nurekeri [sic. ★]

Princess Sao
tinkles with the coming
of the spring
Wetting the hems
of her misty robes

With her spring
Princess Sao makes water
standing tall
Wetting the misty
hems of her robes

The standing=arriving [Spring] does not English. Reading the original, one thinks of Kyoto, where women, like men, *pissed into collection troughs while standing*. Neither this nor Bashô's well-known late-fall shower (*mura-shigure*) that wanders about like a dog whizzing a wee bit here and a wee bit there (*inu no kakebari*), or Issa's many pissing *ku,* use *sound* words. *Usually*, Issa uses plenty. Could he hold back when dealing with crude material lest his high *ku* be considered low?

雨だれは只さほ姫の夜尿かな 犬子集 (1633)
*ame dare wa tada sao hime no yobari [*or *yojito]kana*
(rain drops-as-for just sao princess's night-piss!/?/'tis)

those rain drops?
just little princess sao
wetting her bed

The rude metaphor used in this *ku*, dating to about the same time as Teitoku's, *feels* senryu, but is haiku in direction (nature described by the human).

つみ草に来てハこらへるいなた姫 万
tsumigusa ni kite wa koraeru inada-hime 宝九

draw-verse: *it's so scary!*

plucking herbs
she holds it in all the while
a princess inada

princess inada
comes to pluck herbs but
must hold it in

There is no sound here but the chuckling of the poet. The main themes in pissing (or not pissing) by women in senryu are 1) wanting to sound feminine, or sounding otherwise, as explained above; 2) the gorgeous piss-gang (小便組 *shôben-gumi*) mistress who wets her bed on purpose to make a man dislike her and gain a severance fee; 3) men pissing somewhere they shouldn't; 4) Things that happen when pissing – thoughts, civilities, observances of nature; 5) women, mostly blind, unaware they are being spied upon by a man, generally their servant; 6) fear of being violated by snakes if they do it in the country, and 7) Fear of doing it on worms (like snakes vindictive?). If I did not fear creating yet another 740 pg worst-seller (I already have *two*), I would have introduced more of each, but this wee sample must do. Pissing evidently did not piss-off the censors, for Blyth catches enough of 3) – perhaps the most amusing category – and 4), so I was able to let them go and instead chose to concentrate on sound, for its raw quality makes it *sound* senryu. The above *ku*, from Karai Senryû's earliest major collection, is one of the wittiest examples of 6). Princess Inada, more commonly Kushinada-hime, daughter of an ancient King, bound to be the next victim of the Leviathan, Yamato no Orochi, was saved when a suitor got the serpent drunk and cut it/him to bits. Please note that without the use/non-use of particles, in Japanese, the princess in the poem may be *the* princess, i.e. an imagined happening after the mythological princess was married to her brave suitor (for noble women went out in the Spring for herbs), AND *a* Princess Inada, which is to say a clever idea for a name for all women who tend to hold it in on field trips (more likely fearing chiggers or leeches or poisonous plants than snakes). In English, the *ku* cannot have it both ways; it must be OR, one or the other, as determined by the use or non-use of an "a." That is far more important than whether the syntax puts the Princess in the first line or the last, as it is in the original.

しゝの出ル穴ハ別さとさゝめこと 摘 3-16
shishi no deru ana wa betsu sa to sasamegoto pinch
("peepee's leaving hole-as-for different [+emph]" whisper-words)

pillow talk:
telling him the pee hole
is different

"you know, the hole
for pee is not the same"
sweet nothings

"so you thought
the pee hole was the same!"
young lovers

I can recall an argument with friends in primary school about this same problem. Boys just do not know. Moreover, if women really worried about how they piss (as senryu would have it), you might think it reflected on the diameter of their vaginas, and one word for vagina in Japanese was the ninth hole 第九穴 (when anyone who counts the urethra separate would come up with *ten*, or twelve, counting tits). *Shishi* is a colloquial term with good sound quality. I did not do a chapter on *holes* as I save them for a whole book I will probably never write.

~ eddies ~

Other Onomatopoeia. More mimetic senryu in this book may be found in passim, but here, two fine examples should suffice for *the sound of things other than pissing*.

悪ふざけ障子をスポン／＼抜き 85-22
waru-fuzake shôji o supon supon nuki

a bad prank:
popping out from
a paper wall

horse-play
pop! pop! through
a paper wall

Or, is *it*, rather "popping *in*" ? The original mimesis, *supon,* cannot be matched by English unless we add a moving *s* to *pop*, making it *"spop!"* or *"spopping."* It does not allude to but evokes the *suppon,* a long-neck soft-shell snapping turtle identified with the penis and eaten or drunk (the blood) as a fortifier for men. This mimesis is not one of those commonly repeated, so I imagine two men, either doing it on a dare possibly to surprise a maid, or else, in their own rundown pad after painting a woman or women on the paper. Another reason for *two* or more men, rather than one, poking multiple holes is that cock-matches (*mara-kurabe*), contesting size, erective power (lifting strength) and hardness (punching through paper) were common, at least in picture scrolls of such fun (who can speak for reality?). There would be an old paper door, window or room partition – *shôji* can be any of these, and doors that slide *are* often nothing but partitions, *ergo* "wall" (scene of our pecker-through-the-mouse-hole jokes) – that is, easily *spopped* paper to make it tempting. Since Japanese tend to be neatnicks, such activity would take place at years-end, when the paper would be replaced anyway.

がさ／＼といふととんぼうつるむ也 摘
gasagasa to iu to tonbô tsurumu nari 4-30
(rustling say and dragonflies mating is)

what makes
a rustling sound? mating
dragonflies

a dry sound?
it would be the fucking
dragonflies

This is a senryu often reprinted and probably has been Englished elsewhere. It starts in a manner that reminds us of *listing*, where one might be challenged to supply examples of *"things that rustle,"* but some readers might recall Saikaku's gay(!) dragonflies as well.

Issa's Goddess/Violet Ku. Because this chapter concerns pissing I emphasized the Goddess but please note that Issa's *ku* is, at heart, a violet (*sumire*) *ku*, excellent because it indirectly describes the place where violets are found, ground so damp another Issa *ku* explains, *"I sit after / spreading out tissue paper: / violet-viewing"* (鼻紙を敷て居 (すわ) れば菫哉 *hanakami o shiite suwareba sumire kana*). Issa did not actually say "viewing" and the tissue is literally "nose-paper," but you get the idea: he didn't want his seat to get wet. It was a mistake for the editors of Issa's ALL to only include the *ku* in question under "Princess Sao" and forget to at least mention it in under the theme "violet."

~~~~~~

More Pissing *Ku type 3 and 4.* The "Pissing on the Moon" chapter of *A Dolphin in the Woods* (in progress) has men pissing where they shouldn't and my *Fifth Season* has them pissing while engaged in civilities. Please note, I do not have particular interest in making water; it just happens to be a favorite theme of the haiku master I know best, Issa.

~~~~~~

Pissing Type 5, or, Watching Blind Women Pee? I have half a dozen such before me now, of which my favorite has someone, almost surely the blind singer's attendant, so eager to get a peek that he is tip-toeing (*nuki-ashi*). I also have a picture, with a poor senryu and hundreds of words of prose, showing a man legs spread wide like a giraffe at a waterhole, bent so low to get a good view that his chin is all but grazed by the jet of urine, while the fingers of one hand rest in the rivulet created by the same! The fingertips of his other hand are barely visible reaching around his massive cock in mid-ejaculation. The message for us? Even in a culture with a relaxed view of nudity, men got off by looking.

~~~~~~

Huge Serpent Lovers. If you find such myths and the way they are used in poetry today interesting, Yamato no Orochi appears in a number of translated sea cucumber haiku you may find in *Rise, Ye Sea Slugs!* (Paraverse Press, 2003)

~~~~~~

★ ***Issa's Inu** (Dog) **Tsukuba Princess Pissing on her Robe.*** Since Issa, with his word-book, was concerned with the term used for *pissing* (*shito suru*) in the old *haikai*, he put the 5-7-5 that followed the 7-7 first, simply because it had the phrase. The original order is better. Hiroaki Sato skillfully precedes it with a linked verse from the slightly earlier *Shinsen (new) Tsukubashû* (1495), some call the start of honest-to-goodness *haikai,* where Monk Sôzei wonders "whether he's looking at the inside or outside of the robe because the day has not fully broken." Then he gives the opening linked-verse of the *Inu (dog=pseudo) Tsukubashû* (1536): *"the robe of haze is wet at its hem / Princess Sao of spring pissed as she started."* He passes over the *standing* connection, but his "started" is itself a good pun – I use it several times in *The Fifth Season* with respect to Spring's starting/standing – and his broader explanation is elegant:

> The *maeku* (initial part) is innocuous enough; but, instead of explaining conventionally why the robe is wet, the respondent – it could have been Sôkan – says it is because the goddess of spring inopportunely succumbed to the call of nature. (*One Hundred Frogs:* 1983)

Other Japanese explanations where the haze stands for the vanishing *waka* replaced by the wet (full of bodily humors?) *haikai*. Then, in the heyday of *haikai*, in the 1633 *Enoko* (dog/puppy) collection, we have the more outrageous pissabed goddess we saw in the maintext. But so long as we are off-subject, a few more examples from Issa's word-book, or "vernacular miscellany" (方言雑記) as it is called. On the same page as the pissing Princess: *"Shiritasuki* [*shiridasuki*]," a butt that looks like it has been criss-crossed by a *tasuki* sash/chord (see page 299). The OJD explains this means someone is so *thin* their butt gets folds. Pages before we learn the fine line between the privates and the anus is called "ants' gate-crossing" (蟻の門渡り), i.e., a single file from gate to gate. And, before that, we find *"chopenashi:* when an old man etc. pinches a woman's butt"(一茶全集七巻).

~~~~~~
~~~~~~

One Meta-mimetic Senryu. The following is so simple an observation that only an extraordinarily alert poet could catch it.

家毎に風は違った音を立て　素人
ie goto ni kaze wa chigatta oto o tate

the wind makes
a different sound
at each house

I found this *ku* in Blyth's *Japanese Life and Character . . ,* with no source given (Change "at" to "Round" & uncenter for his translation). Blyth writes "This is yet another example of how the poetry of senryu is different from that of haiku." It is also an extraordinarily poetic *ku*. ◎*What I mean by the title of this eddy, "meta-mimetic,"* is that I wonder if people might listen more carefully to sounds other than the human because of their tendency to turn so many of them into onomatopoeia. The *ku* does not itself contain mimesis, but it may have been born of it. (Note: Japanese intellectuals can get quite conceited about their mimesis and, since I hate collective boasting as much as I hate individual boasting – unless it is damn funny hyperbole ala Davy Crockett – I have also pointed out that the existence of settled upon onomatopoeia for so many sounds may dull ears to the real thing. That argument and what I wrote above may both be true.) ◎ *And, why so much use of mimesis/tic rather than onomatopoeia/tic?* 1), it is shorter; 2), it includes psychological sound effects which are clearly recognized in Japanese but not in English; 3) it is easier to spell and remember if you only know what *mime* means. Try using the word. If others mimic you, soon we may be able to discuss sound more easily.

~~~~~~

～　蛇足　～

仮章題には、「シイちゃんからザアザ・ガボール迄」の方が良かったかしら？
~~~~~~

<u>*Paper Before & Paper After*</u>

紙鉄砲から犬張子迄

廿八 28

八百万拭乃紙

Picking up God with your Toes

~~~~~~

かみいます女郎の開の奥の院 葉
kami imasu jorô no bobo no okunoin 10ウ

<u>*paper/god*</u>

"the kami is in"
her innermost shrine:
the whore's quim

Many *ku* take advantage of the coincidence, if it is coincidence, of god/s and paper both being pronounced *kami* in Japanese. The eccentric monk Sengai (1750-1837) *used* it to promote Enlightenment. He removed the toilet paper *kami* from his outhouse so a visitor had to *kami-danomi,* which is to say *call for paper* or *call on the gods*, for help (He probably wrote a *ku* about it, too, but my Sengai is in a box in a warehouse in Shizuoka). In respect to the above *ku,* the god/s, or idols – to use a word I *hate,* for lack of another – in Japan were generally not up front for easy-viewing. The shrines or temples with them showed them to the public on rare occasions, called *kaichô,* or "open-ledger" (also a synonym for the cunt), but here, the customer is not being so openly treated. *Jorô* covers a broad range of prostitutes, but this paper that "is in" was typically used for birth-control and hygienic reasons by the most proper women of pleasure. Carefully folded and rolled up into a wad, covered with spittle (or medicine) and pushed deep into the vagina, it bore a resemblance to something all boys love –

.

まずい事紙鉄砲にしてさせる 摘二
mazui koto kamideppô ni shite saseru pluck
(poor thing paper-musket-as/into making made)

his bad luck
she makes a pop-gun for
him to fuck
~~~~~~

The OED's oldest usage example for the pop-gun is by Hobbes (1662). Considering the rapidity with which guns spread in Japan the previous century until they outgunned any country in Europe or, for a while, perhaps all together, it is possible the device was a Japanese invention, but the principle probably was discovered by the Chinese, as they loved both noise and children more than any other civilization. There is an ironic tone to the *ku,* for the disappointing harlot was an expensive one, not one of the night hawks who were called loose guns (actually, just guns, *teppô*) for being dangerous purveyors of disease. Another *Pluck ku, "The courtesan / rolls it up just like/ a Chinese ball"* (しな玉のやうにけいせい丸メこみ　摘 1-32 *shina tama no yô ni keisei marume-komi*). For more on the balls which were inserted in the vagina, see pp 59, 89-90, 117. The pop-gun metaphor is far wittier.

梅干親父上げ底を買いに行き
umeboshi oyaji agezoko o kai ni yuki 65

ole dried plum
daddy goes out to buy
a raised bottom

Thoreau, in *Concord* (a book I got translated into Japanese for the first time – there were maybe 19 of Walden!) noted that old folk either dry up like they are cured or bloat like pickles. Japanese dried plum is something like dried prune or raisins and the standard metaphor for a crinkled face. No, the dried-plum geezer is not after a boy. This is a different metaphor for the same practice we have been discussing. A "raised bottom" means a *false* one in Japanese. By not being readily apparent from outside, this wad of paper had something in common with that type of common mercantile fraud. Because inserted paper was common with pros but rare with local amateurs, this meant that poor men, mostly young, who could not afford the pleasure quarters like that old man, had something to be happy about, at least if they were lucky enough to not to catch anything.

はづかしい・紙に音あり新枕 青木賊
hazukashii / kami ni oto ari nimakura 天明 2
(embarrassing // paper-to/in sound has new-pillow 鈴木)

◎ *embarrassing* ◎
paper is far from silent
their first night

◎ *embarrassing* ◎
paper has a paper noise
their first night

While I have no quarrel with prostitution, thinking about it is depressing because all the amusing metaphor in the world cannot erase the cruel inequalities that create it. Newlyweds and their paper for sopping up love juices are a relief. Still, the middle part of this capped-verse is tricky. Directly translated, *"paper has sound."* It evokes a saying: *kabe ni mimi ari,* "walls have ears;" and, that is the point. The match-maker who only collects the second half of his fee after confirmation of consummation of the nuptials is in the next room, listening to all. If it is a high-class marriage, the bloody proof might also be required later.

新世帯恥ずかしそうに紙を買い
arasetai hazukashisô ni kami o kai 31

the newlyweds
look very embarrassed
buying paper

Buying this paper, used used where Europeans would use cloth or moderns tissue, would have been as embarassing in 18-19c Japan as buying condoms today. Why these things are embarrassing, I do not know. But, I think everyone feels it.

冶に乱をわすれず相模もんだ紙 葉別九
ji ni ran o wasurezu sagami monda kami

in peace forgetting
not war, a sagami brings
crumpled paper

forget not war
in times of peace, sagami
bring soft paper

しばし言葉もなかりけり紙をもみ 54
shibashi kotoba mo nakarikeri kami o momi

for some time
nothing is said as she
softens the paper

for a while
even their words stop:
crumpling paper

I had assumed the paper in Japan was so good that, like tissue paper, it was soft and absorbent from the start but, evidently, there were many varieties and the cheaper ones were more absorbent and/or softer if they were crumpled before being applied to the wet genitals. The nymphomaniac Sagami, whom we met in the Maid-servants' chapter, are so well-prepared for doing battle – the allusion is to a phrase in the *I-ching* (易経) – that they carry in her bosom or sleeves pre-crumpled/softened paper, so they can lose themselves completely in the sex and glide from orgasm to orgasm with no pause to soften the paper as per the second *ku*. Sorry for more complaints about English, but once again, we do not have the verb needed for a good translation. Our *kneaded* would work if paper were clay or flour, but paper is paper and we have nothing for it between *crumple* and *soften* such as the Japanese verb *momu/momi/monda* found in both *ku.*

唇で紙とる娘すれて見へ　壬生の雨
kuchibiru de kami toru musume surete mie 享和一

taking the paper
with her teeth, a maiden
looks worldly

taking up a piece
of paper with her teeth
she looks jaded

Finally, the act in which the prop is used. Perhaps you have noticed the paper in ukiyoe love scenes. It may be clutched between the teeth of the woman, whose curled toes show she is about to come, or dabbed on the genitals in mid-sex. If, in the above *ku,* her lover thought she was inexperienced, this might give him cause for concern. Perhaps, she – a *musume*, someone's daughter rather than someone's wife – thought it would look cool because she saw it in a print. I was tempted to use the word "picking up" rather than *taking,* but pulling a piece of paper from her paper box or bosom, while both hands are occupied making love, to have it ready, would not be imagined from that verb. The English-speaker would imagine that paper is only picked up when it is cleaned up.

女房がなくたびにいるふくのかみ
nyôbô ga naku tabi ni iru fuku-no-kami 失出典
(wife-the cries time-at needs/is wipe/happiness's paper/god)

there each time
the wife cries, the god
of happiness

needed each &
ev'ry time the wife cries
tissue paper

Now, we're cooking! Besides *god/s=paper* (*kami*), we have *wipe=happiness/ wealth/fortune/luck* (sorry for the polysemy, but *fuku* in Japanese covers a range of meanings not found in any English word, though *fortune+fortunate* would come close. For once, the specialized verb for orgasmic crying (*yogaru*) is unnecessary; with the "wiping paper," I translated as "tissue paper," the shorter generic cry (*naku*) suffices. The *ku* is so effortlessly charming in the original, where *both* of the above readings are intended and coexist *without any strain whatsoever*, so it reads like an aphorism. Yet, it can only be re-created in composite translation. And, that wife *had better wipe*, especially if she is with child. Citing the *Leaf ku "After a night / of sex, her bobo's foaming / from the mouth"*(宵越しの開は口から泡を吹き 葉 別九 *yoigoshi no bobo wa kuchi kara awa o fuki*), the author of *Cuntologia* quotes a passage from a Bunsei 5 (1822) booklet of advice for married folk claiming that not sopping up all that stuff invites 癲癇 *i.e.,* meningitis and epilepsy to a fetus, or, in everyday language, might make the child to come peevish and fitful. Yet, he also noted, one was not supposed to overdo it. *"Unlike modern times, in the old days even paper was used frugally."* Of course, the proof of that, too, is a senryu:

帆柱をつかんだ紙で舟をふき
hobashira o tsukanda kami de fune o fuki

with the paper
that gripped the mast she
cleans the boat

She used the paper on *his* mast first, then *her* boat. And, who knows, a real boat may be in the picture, too, for most senryu mentioning masts being taken down (which, was actually done at night), involved prostitutes who made their living on boats called "boat-dumplings" (*funamanjû*) or "boat nuns" (*funabikuni*): *"The boat-nun / would lay to rest all / standing masts"* (帆はしらの立ったをねかす船比丘尼 摘 1-3 *hobashira no tatta o nekasu funa-bikuni*. For more about the *bikuni* "nuns," see *Topsy-turvy 1585* (2004) , item #2-43 and 2-44).

腹に浪打ッと抜手で紙を取 葉
hara ni nami utsu to nukite de kami o tori 別*10*
(belly-in/on waves-strike and/when removed-hand-with paper[acc] take)

while waves lap
over their bellies she swims
for the paper

when the waves
break on her belly, she back
strokes for paper

her belly heaving
she throws up her arms
for pillow paper

To borrow the watery metaphor of the original, much drowned in the translation. *Nami-utsu* means either/both waves dashing on a shore or into rocks, and an undulating movement. *I.e.,* the overflowing sexual juices *and/or* the dying contractions of her orgasm. And, we have a type of swimming the OJD defines as "the ancient national style of swimming where the arms are removed from the water between strokes." Here *Kenkyusha's J-E* helps: "the (double) overarm [trudgen] stroke . . . swim overarm [hand over hand]." Since the paper may be kept in a compartment in the lower=box part of the pillow, there should be a backstroke variety of this stroke, too, but if there isn't, then she took her arm from around him and reached into her bosom – call it a breast stroke – for, as you may have seen on prints, Japanese appreciated strip-teasing, but were not big on stripping all the way down for sex (though the artists who enjoy painting clothing may exaggerate the extent of clothedness in sex).

おゝしんき・延紙へとゞかぬ四本の手
o o shinki / nobe e todokanu shihon no te 天神花

ヲゝしんき・延紙へ背中で這ふ妾
o o shinki / nobe e senaka de hau tekake 水加減

◎ *oh, heavy stuff!* ◎
all four hands cannot reach
the tissue paper

◎ *oh, heavy stuff!* ◎
a mistress crawls for tissue
upon her back

These two *zappai* capped *ku,* 宝暦三 and 文化十四, respectively, were side-by-sided by Suzuki. With the emotive "oh, oh," I would guess the *shinki* would be the one (of dozens) charactered as 心気・辛気, with a meaning hard to define. Let us just say it is a feeling arising from a difficult situation and I apologize for having to resort to the slang of my generation to catch it. With the second *ku*, I *also* think of 新奇, which is to say "How novel!" The poet, too, may have thought to get double-duty from the cap. *Nobe* is short for *nobegami,* paper bought by the stack.

挟み紙碁を打つような指で取り *121*
hasamigami go o utsu yô na yubi de tori

after the match

twat-paper
pinched as if she were
playing go

This *hasamigami* or scissored/squeezed-paper is the pop-gun or raised-bottom paper mentioned at the start of the chapter. Now, she is removing it. Forgive the neologism, *twat paper!* I wanted to make it clear that this was not about tissue for superficial wiping. For most people it is somewhat tricky placing the discus or lentil-shaped smooth stones upon a crowded go board, or removing them. They are not held between the thumb pad and a fingertip pad in the natural way, but between the middle-finger tip's pad and the finger-*nail* of the index finger, an odd necessity which could only be done without if the stones were drastically redesigned – I have played with roofing nails upside-down and it is a lot easier. However natural the person with go experience makes it look, for others, it is an awkward way to handle some-thing and, at first, I thought the person removing the paper was doing so in an oddly self-conscious way, keeping it at fingers length because it was yucky with spendings, but lifting my fingers from the keyboard, I just noticed that how wide the space between thumb and index finger is. Using the fingers in that way would be the only way to reach the bottom of the vagina. A *Leaf ku* published another variation of go-style loving about the same time as the above: *"Even fingering / the go master keeps / his palm down"* (くじるのも本因坊は下へ向け 葉 11 *kujiru no mo honin-bô wa shita e muke*). While late-period *Willow* twat-paper *ku* is real, this go master *ku* is a mere head-trip.

紙くずを足のゆびにてはさみすて 神子の臍
kami-kuzu o ashi no yubi nite hasami-sute 宝永七

sometimes this way, sometimes that (其時によるへ)

used papers
pinched & disposed of
by her toes

using her toes
to pinch & throw away
crumpled paper

The beautiful high quality paper pulled from the bosom, or held between the teeth to stifle a love-cry or be at hand for patting wet members, ends up flung upon the tatami where it is picked up by the same toes curled in ecstasy minutes earlier (who hasn't seen those toes in erotic prints!). Using lowdown digits to pick-up the paper may seem disrespectful to the paper and the lover; but that is definitely the easiest way to pick things up if you are exhausted or gassy yet blessed with prehensile toes. I (menial for my sister's four old dogs – three dalmations – as I write this) even pick up large dog bowls twice a day that way.

のべの紙せんにかうのが仕廻なり 摘
nobe no kami sen ni kau?kô? no ga shimai nari 1-6

with some tissue
to cork it, the exchange
comes to an end

Cork is a noun and a stopper in the original. With scores of *kô's* to choose from, a character would have helped. 交う= v. *intercourse*. 交=coitus? Euphemistically, 講= event? 功= duty fulfilled ~ 終わる? 好 amity? Regardless, we get it.

みす紙を上と下とへくわへて出 105-13
misugami o ue to shita to e kuwaete de

then out she goes
tissue clenched in her lips
above & below

This *misugami* may not be quite the same paper as the *nobegami* mentioned earlier, and we should remember that none is quite so soft as the "tissue" I translate with, but it held up better (important, for tissue is so weak it tends to leave pieces which turn into dingle-berries of the front) and, thus, could be left in place and walked out of the room like this. Perhaps, you have seen it. The mistress of the charming money launderer and tax-cheat in *A Taxing Woman* (called *Tanpopo*, or "dandelions" in Japanese!) does just that and you see the paper peeking out from behind as she walks to the restroom (all of that director's movies show his familiarity with Edo-era sex). An earlier *Pluck ku* had explained "It is called *misu* because it is sandwiched はさむによつてみす紙と名づけたり 摘 1-28 *hasamu ni yotte misugami to nazuketari*), but the allusion to the fancy rattan blinds (a type of *sudare* called *misu*) with a piece of partially transparent paper between two screens is too studied even for Japanese readers. The late-*Willow ku's* action is far more effective, and more realistic than the cork.

花嫁のうちは紙屑気にかかり 万安三
hanayome no uchi wa kamikuzu ki ni kakari

while newlywed
she can't get used tissues
out of her head

In other words, the young wife is self-conscious of the paper, whether they are using too much or too little and what his mother or the paper recycler or whomever might encounter it might think.

した跡を皆かんなめに犬はりこ
shita ato o mina kanname ni inu hariko 98
(did mark/traces[acc] all plane-marks-as dog-papier-mâché)

that they did it
as plain as a plane's mark
in papier-mâché

all their loving
left a mark within a dog
of papier-mâché

Who knows how or when it began, but by the early-19c, any decent trousseau had to include one item: *a papier-mâché dog* to feed that paper to. As one *ku* put it, *"A classy basket / for paper rubbish? A dog / of papier-mâché* (品のいい紙屑籠は犬張子 51 *hin no ii kamikuzu kago wa inu hariko*). One could not feed them crumpled up manuscript, for it was not *kamikuzu* but had a completely different loftier name, *hanko* and might be used for wallpaper or heating baths. It was considered good to leave clear plane marks on the back of a mask, as a subtle signature of the craftsman. I guess a chisel would be too obvious or these planes were so narrow they left marks like peelers do on a root vegetable, but the point of this odd metaphor is that there is a trace of what was *done* out of plain sight.

犬張子祭の紙を喰いにくる 104
inu hariko matsuri no kami o kui ni kuru
(dog papier-mâché festival's paper[acc] eat-to comes)

a painted dog
comes to eat paper from
the carnival

a painted dog
comes to eat paper left:
their shrine fete

a painted dog
comes to eat what's left
of their jubilee

The last *ku* was full of so much information and the English word for hariko so long (papier-mâché) that I really needed to composite translation. This was much simpler – after I came up with the "painted dog" – and no number of translations could fix the one problem, but I couldn't resist trying. It is the *matsuri.* I made it "carnival" rather than the usual "festival" because the former word at least has some flesh/meat=eros in it, then, because these festivals took place at shrines and the female genitalia was, as we have seen, a shrine, I *feted* it that way; but nothing can re-create the dynamic *matsuri* with frenzies of men and, often women, too, shouldering shrines through crowds and the fact that *matsuri* can mean "sexual congress" and *matsuru* is one verb for doing it. The paper in the *ku* lightly suggests the gods found at a shrine (implied by the *matsuri*). We return to such a god/paper pun which, you might recall, takes us back to what started the chapter.

福神を乗せた娘がたからふね 摘
fukugami o noseta musume ga takarabune 3-13
(wipe/wealth-god/paper [acc.] carried/boarded daughter/girl-the/is treasure-ship)

a young lady
loaded with tissue – that's
a treasure ship!

*the young lady c_*
the god of fortune aboard,
a treasure ship

his daughter with
the paper god of wealth
his treasure ship

The God/s of Good Fortune homophonous with *tissue-wipe* were on the painted or printed treasure ships put under the pillow or bed for propitious dreams on the second night of the New Year. At first, I imagined paper strewn over the girl proving she was a treasure in bed, for such rumplings of spent desire scattered on the *futon*, *tatami*, and even bodies are found in so many prints one might call it *the measure of love*, or that portion spent, at any rate. But, the wording favors a girl *equipped* with tissue. A treasure ship was also an affectionate term for the cunt and for a high-earning courtesan. *Musume,* strictly speaking, a "daughter," but usually used to mean a maiden is *the* problem. The last reading is favored by another *ku* not far before it in the same *Pluck* volume that comes right out and says: *"He plugs up / his growing hole of debt / with his daughter's"* or *"Deep in debt / he fills in his hole / with his daughter's"* or, *"Deep in the hole / he pays for his debts / with his daughter's."* (借金の穴を娘の穴でうめ *shakkin no ana o musume no ana de ume* 3-3). I am unsure if the metaphor Englishes, but what is as worthless as a father who would dig out of debt by selling his daughter's hole?

紙の音日本国が寄るといふ 梅柳 天保二
kami no oto nippon koku ga yoru to iu 1831
(paper-sound sun-source-nation near/convene &/when say)

the sound of paper
it's called 'japan the country
coming together'

From all the attention given to paper, one might think that if Japanese ever ran out of it, they would stop fucking altogether. I first thought this *ku* meant you could tell you were nearing Japan from the sound of wiping and crumpling paper, but the final "say[it's said]" did not allow that. Checking a dictionary of sayings (ことわざ大辞典 小学館), I found a stock-phrase for couples in the acme of their pleasure-making used by pillow-novels: *"[the] Japanese Country/ies convene on one-place"* 日本国が一所へ寄る (*nippon-koku ga hito-toko e yoru*). The couples in the example passage were in bed snug within folding partitions pulled tightly shut and I could not help wondering if there might be an analogy (intended or not) between this pleasure and the orgasmically high culture of Edo, hidden behind checkpoints within a country proudly separated from the world by the ocean. Suzuki oddly passes over this phrase, calling *nippon koku ga yoru* one expression of pleasurable sensation based on the country-birth myths. True, Japan was *procreated*, not *created*, and some philologists claim a woman's part is called a bean because beans were born from a goddess's vagina and all the gods were gathered by that vaginal grotto the Sun would not leave. Moreover, we can *hear* the gods excited by the world's first striptease (pgs. 435,455) because the *sound of paper* puns as that of the *gods*. But, the idiom would seem to express how pleasure makes its location the epicenter of the world, does it not?

紙が損伊勢屋するのも加減をし 葉
kami ga son iseya suru no mo kagen o shi 14

paper's a loss
iseya even cuts down
on doing it

what a waste
of paper! iseya says
to do it less

The employees of Iseya, a mercantile firm based in Mie-ken (Between Osaka and Nagoya), trustworthy and frugal, operated so many outlets in the Edo that it was said the city was full of *"Iseya shingles, Inari (Fox-god) shrines and dog-shit"* (「伊勢屋、稲荷に犬の糞」). There are countless jokes about their frugality, which, in this case, extends even to usage of a product they were known for.

eddies

God and Paper, or Translating Homophones. The reader may have felt irked to find me put the Japanese *kami* in my translation and give its meaning, paper/god as the title. John Solt did a very different translation

god and paper exist
in the sacred interior
of a whore

To me, *presence* rather than existence seems closer to the connotation of *imasu*, but what matters here is the creative substitution of both words for a punning homophone. *Why not?* (I cannot recall if I have tried it. If not I should!) The wit is lost, but the idea, slightly upgraded, is translated. To re-style it my way:

god and paper
both present in the bobo
of a whore

Syunroan's slightly modernized spelling clearly gives us 開, or *bobo,* plain and clear. Solt either used a different version with "sacred interior" (*oku no in*), or added it rather than explain that the cunt *could* be called such things and, hence, was properly cultured for the god/paper pun. It is also possible that 開 was misread as 閨, which is close to that meaning (though usually just the *boudoir*) I have seen the latter mistakenly explained as commonly used to mean "cunt" or *bobo,* by someone else, so one never knows.

The God of Happiness Out of Bed. As even Sasama, in his *Eropedia,* points out with "an Edo era senryu," spendings were not the only thing paper could wipe:

.

雪隠や黄金の山に福の神
setchin ya ôgon no yama ni fukunokami
(snow-hide[wc]!/: yellow-metal[gold]-mountain-on fortune-god)

out in the privy
there's a mountain of gold
with a god on it

The Chinese characters say "wealth/fortune/happiness-god," though we *know* it is toilet paper. Since solid waste was traded for fresh vegetables and even subtracted from a tenant's rent, there was indeed gold in them thar hills (see *Topsy-turvy 1585*, item # 11-21 and #11-22.)! As explained on pg. 210, poop in Japan was *gold* rather than burnt sienna. I vaguely recall a saying, probably Englished first by the Lord Chancellor (Bacon), and recycled by Poor Richard (Franklin), to the effect that *money, like shit is only useful if spread around.* Well, Japanese shit, at least, *was* (Today, in the USA, neither is: hence, we are in deep shit.). I am unsure about "privy," but rest- or bathroom would have been worse. *Setchin* says the 2,000-page Kenkyusha's Japanese-English dictionary, is slang for *benjo* (toilet/ bathroom) but "slang" connotes a vulgar usage, while *setchin,* lit. "snow-hidden" (from using something soft, like feathers to immediately swallow the bm, as water does, so it would not assault the senses) comes from a *high*-usage. I recall it used for tasteful toilets associated with tea ceremony architecture, and even today it is a classy, though archaic word. In senryu, it is curiously common, either because it was the fashionable term – when the euphemism became popular – in the 18-19c, or because the contrast it made with the vulgar actions within heightened the humor, or both. (For more on Japan as a "feces-friendly" (Leupp) culture see Leupp:1995 and the scato. ch. of my *Rise, Ye Sea Slugs!* 2003)

~~~~~~

Mast Encore c̲ Boat Nun. The *ku* in the text is boring as hell for anyone who already knew about boat nuns. The later *Willow ku* below is a big improvement.

帆柱を寝かしてあるく舟びく尼 104-19
hobashira o nekashite aruku funabikuni

putting a mast
to bed, the boat nun
takes a walk

The masts were not stowed away but laid fore to aft over the cabin and served as the ridge-pole for a tent made of the straw mats used for sails under which travelers slept (for reasons given in *Topsy-turvy 1585*, Japanese boats were not allowed to sail at night). The 'nuns'' boats were small and usually sculled, so the mast is clearly the customers and the above *ku* implies she docked ashore and went to spend that money on food or something. But not all masts were on boats or anchored in them: *Feeling empty, a single man knocks down a mast* (帆柱をむなしく倒す一人もの 摘 3-37 *hobashira o munashiku taosu hitorimono*). One feels like Helen Kellering it: *Would a mast / toppled by a man alone / make a sound?* None of these work well because the mast must be preceded by a/the/his in English and being forced to chose one makes it harder to imagine the other.

~~~~~~

A Fuku God Not Paper & a Folksy Treasure Ship & a Girl's Treasure Ship

ふく神のするを見給ふ二日の夜 摘
fukugami no suru o mitamau futsuka-no-yo 3-4
(wealth-god's doing[acc] watching[+hon.] second day's night)

the second night:
the god o' good luck watching
as they f__k.

the god of wealth
looking on as they do it
the second night

the god of luck
watches over as we fuck
the second night

After a chaste night waiting up for the rising sun, the first-fucking was officially underway on the night of the second day of the year, when a treasure ship lay below. The God here would be a New Year doll on the god-shelf. The treasure ship is *not* mentioned, but we think of it and, perhaps the tissue, too. One final New Year's Treasure Ship:

たから船しわに成ほど女房こぎ 摘 2-22
takarabune shiwa ni naru hodo nyôbô kogi

the wife sculls
so much the treasure ship
is all wrinkles

This treasure ship is not her part but the charm under her bed. She was especially active for their first sex of the year. The treasure-ship/cunt, like the god/paper already introduced, is also found in folk-song.

The honorable cock at our home is black as soot ・ *kono ie no omara wa susukemara*
Wash him in *bebe* (cunt) and he turns real white ・ *bebe de araeba shiroku naru*
Lying pillow by pillow in the still of the night ・ *makura narabete shizumaru yoru wa*
The sculling oar jolts our treasure-boat into motion ・ *gui-to kogidasu takara-bune*

My notes in the *Issa Manuscript* say the song (Probably from Sonoda: 1965, lost in my last move) is about the pleasures of a poor household surviving on the magic of love and that it is from Nigata, the prefecture of the ex PM Tanaka Kakue (a cross between Daley, the Kingfisher and LBJ). He may even have sung it in public, for unlike a certain Southern governor (JD) who denied his earlier recordings of dirty blues and pretended to be all *sunshine* and no shade, Tanaka is said to have sung dirty songs on the radio, *with pleasure.*

宝船／＼ ・ 小指を入れてみる娘　鼻あぶら 天明二
takarabune takarabune ・ *koyubi o irete-miru musume 1782*
(treasure boat treasure boat / little finger insert-sees maiden)

'Treasure boat, what treasure boat?'
The maiden slips in her pinky to see.

This Suzuki find, an oddly presented *ku* with a 5-5 subject repeated like a draw, but incorporated into the ku, like a crowned or capped verse, is extraordinary. *To see what?* To see what all the excitement was about, to see why people called it a treasure ship.

~~~~~~

The Sins of a Chaste Widow. The following is not as good a *ku* as most we have seen, but is *so* senryu. Does the *mugoi koto* usually reserved for gang-bangs show the chagrin of the horny single man at the waste of a good hole or sympathy for the widow's plight?

むごいこと後家のべ紙で鼻をかみ 24 *mugoi koto goke no nobegami de hana o kami*

A terrible thing! That widow blows her nose c̲ love-paper

~~~~~~

Paper Far from Obvious. See if you can guess where the paper hides within the poem:

蛙釣る女郎のそばに薬鍋 宝 13 柳多留拾遺採録記号有
kaeru tsuru jorô no soba ni kusuri-nabe

by the whore
fishing for a frog, a pot
of herbal tea

by the side
of the frog-fishing harlot
medicinal tea

This woman is in the Pleasure Quarters, though the original uses *jorô*, a word covering anything from a street-walker to a courtesan. The frog is a charm made of folded paper, *origami,* with the name of a customer whom the courtesan wants to come back written on its back. "Frog" in Japanese is a homophone of "return" (kaeru) – when I was in Japan, men calling home from the office said *"I'm a tadpole,"* meaning *I'll be home soon.* The frog was hidden in a drawer or somewhere no one would notice it. The man has not come back, for the "medicine pot" (a pot steeping herbs) indicates that love sickness has broken down her health, and she cannot recall where the charm that didn't work lies.

Unplaced &/or Unsettled
章がないヤツ斗り

廿九 [29]

迷子句・雑魚句
Orphans & Small-fry

seasonal

~~~~~~

若水でざこねのへのこ洗ふなり 摘 3-21
wakamizu de zakone no henoko arau nari

with young water
a cock that slept like a net
of fish is washed

sleepathon cocks
clean off the last year
in young water

A *zakone* or "sundry-fish-sleep" is when a whole mess of folk lie together like a netful of fish, or, say some dictionaries, *small-fry*. These sleep-overs were held at shrines or temples on the last day of the year, which was always the dark of the moon. Perhaps some hosts encouraged abstinence, others sexual license. *Young water* is the first scooped up for washing and/or drinking on New Year's Day (see *The Fifth Season* (2003) ch.15). I have come across sections in senryu anthologies that treat the seasons, and know of books with chapters on them, but *dirty* season-related senryu treat so many subjects that only a whole book could do them (and the reader) justice. I do have a favorite, though; it is this:

暑気見舞たって裸にされる也 柳五
atsuki-omimai datte hadaka ni sareru nari

'a dog-day treat!'
he says as she is whirled
from her dress

In Japan today, there are New Years cards and visits as an Occidental might expect. And there is something else unexpected. There is *a mid-summer card*, presents of something cooling (food, drink, wind-chime, fan, etc.) and, sometimes, a visit to alleviate the heat in this the hottest part of the year. The word *omimai* is the same as that for the visit one might make to someone who is ill or recovering from an accident to wish them well. The original, which made me crack-up, does not say "whirled" – just "made naked," *i.e.,* stripped – but I imagine an *obi* (sash of a kimono) pulled like one pulls the string on a top (they are wrapped around several times). Someday, I must do a flipbook of it!
~~~~~~

sans cérémonie

ぶれいかうへのこをかくししかられる
burei kô henoko o kakushi shikarareru
(~~rude child~~ impolite-party prick[acc] hid/hiding [is]scolded)

~~a mean trick~~
~~the boy in the bath is hiding~~
~~his prick~~

~~don't be rude!~~
~~a little boy is scolded for~~
~~covering his toy~~

a sans cérémonie
a man is scolded for
hiding his prick

anything-goes-party
where you get chewed out for
hiding your cock

a sans cérémonie
for rich, poor, young & old
stripping's de rigór

the rude party:
a little boy is scolded for
covering his toy

This was to be the very first *ku* for the *Innocent Parts, i.e.,* the little chili and lima beans of chapter 22. I liked it better than the one specifying the site of the boy's bashfulness, a *bath*. I assumed *kô* was some sort of slang for *ko* 子 "child" I did not know, but eventually ran into a word I had not known, *bureikô* 無礼講, literally, "no-politeness-lecture/festival/party," a traditional practice of holding a party (which always meant a feast c drinking) open to people of all classes and sexes – the original block party! I cannot count the times I ran into sundry-fish-sleep, the promiscuous sleep-overs, so it is odd I missed this for decades; but I did. The one who won't show it *could* be a *chigo*, i.e. "lovely boy" sought by men, or, who someone older. Who knows. Here are two more *ku* on the same from *Pluck*, that I read right over without noticing a dozen years ago.

無礼講おやかしたのがぶっさらい
bureikô oyakashita no ga bussarai 摘 4-20

the rude party
the man with a hard on
draws all eyes

the rude party
a man who got it up
is lionized

無礼講衣通姫の給仕なり　摘
bureikô i-tôri-bime no kyûshi nari 4-33

the rude-party
waitresses shine through
their clothing

a rude-party
c pass-robe princesses
for waitresses

Those *bureikô* must have been great parties! The first *ku* is obvious. I would only add that Japanese found erections fascinating. After all, they paraded huge models through town. The second *ku* assumes knowledge of a legendary beauty. The white skin and original cave door of the "clothes-through-princess" were said to shine right through her clothing. Here, I think the women were wearing gauze-like robes of wide-weave linen or crepe-like *chiri-men* slips. I have come across dozens of *ku* mentioning *chirimen* and how it makes a woman's private parts prettier for half-covering them. I regret not collecting them, for combined with the lady who put snakes into her cavity, they show the antiquity of the "strip-tease" in Japan.

the blind boss

~~~~~~

女にはいつそ目の有る座頭の坊 摘
onna ni wa isso me no aru zatônobô 1-13

he has an eye
for women like no one else
the troupe head

for womanflesh
none boast eyes as he
the troupe head

やく座頭杖をころして帰る也 摘
yaku zatô tsue o koroshite kaeru nari 1-34

a jealous zatô
returns home c
bated cane

間男をやみうちにする座頭のほう
maotoko o yamiuchi ni suru zatônobô 摘 1-5
(lover/cheater[acc] dark-strike does troupe-head-monk/boy)

in utter darkness
the troupe head surprises
her paramour

his cane is not
a shot in the dark, blind boss
beats her lover

A *zatô* may simply mean "a blind-man," but the literal meaning "troupe-head" is not simply a figure of speech. The blind joined nation-wide unions at an early age and competent blind men bossed troupes of women who did musical performances, massage and prostitution while also serving as money-lender. Or, some were just work-alone acupuncturists or massage givers. Almost all blind men in senryu are assumed to combine wealth, bad tempers and the ability to judge a woman's ability in bed by touch. The "bated" cane is "killed" in Japanese, where breath is usually "killed." The "her" in the third *ku* refers to his mistress. The original is witty for taking advantage of the Japanese idiom for a surprise attack happening to be a *yami*=dark(utter darkness)-*uchi*=strike. This could, of course, be a realistic depiction of something which could happen, but the juxtaposition of idiom, the circumstance of blindness and the zatô's
~~~~~~

reputation for using that cane are sufficient. As the Round-robin explained, realism in senryu was not quite there at that date. There are hundreds of senryu about these blind "troupe-heads" who are interesting for many reasons. I recall reading about a university press book about them. Perhaps it has some of them.

kinky girls

ちじれ髪十ぶん床をみそで居ル
chijiregami jûbun toko o miso de iru 摘 3-37
(crinkled-hair/s enough/many bed[acc] forte/pride is/have)

ms kinky-hair
knows that she is fair
indeed, in bed

Crinkle-hair referred to a woman of marriageable age who had hair that was not considered attractive but was considered a sign of being a good bed partner (we find other *ku* where the match-maker suggests the young man should withhold judgment and try her out). Before I knew that, I assumed the reference was to pubic hair and mistranslated the above as:

The number of pubic hairs in their bed
– a source of pride for the newly wed.

bachelor blues

へのこから朝おきをする一人者 摘
henoko kara asa-oki o suru hitorimono 2-33

bachelorhood
you wake each morning
after *it* does

single men
awakening every day
to your cock

you get up
cock first every day
living alone

寝おきからきげんのいゝハへのこ也 摘
neoki kara kigen no ii wa henoko nari 4-32
(sleep-wake-from mood's good-as-for cock is)

the only bird
who wakes up happy
is your cock

one wakes up
in the best of spirits
it's your cock

ready to go
as soon as you wake?
you're a cock

There must be hundreds of *ku* about morning hard-ons. While appreciating (as a fellow suffering single) the pathos of the first *ku,* I like the second more for the metaphorical possibilities (as per my last reading). My son's fine, but *I* need caffeine.

むつくりと・息子は起きて朝参り 笠付類題集
mukkuri to ・musuko wa okite asa-mairi 天保五

◎ *lickety-split* ◎
his son was up and paying
the shrine a visit

The first 5-syllabets means "abruptly," is usually applied only to something that *lurches awake* or *jumps up* and also can mean *embonpoint* (healthily plump, like Tinkerbelle). The responding 7-5, cleverly did not put the awakening right after the adverb but let it lag behind the "son," a common nickname for one's penis. A "shrine" is not mentioned in the original, but a morning-visit using the humble word for visiting, *mairi,* can only be to a Shintô shrine. In other words, this man is not a bachelor but married and gets to put his morning erection to work.

ひやめしとおへるにこまる壱人もの
hiyameshi to oeru ni komaru hitorimono 摘 1-34
(cold-meal/rice and erecting-by troubled single-one)

leftover rice
and erections: a plight
of bachelors

the singleman
troubled by cold meals
and erections

As Watanabe Shinichirô wrote in a book I have not read, *"dirty poems are a manifestation of the sadness of men"* (「バレ句は男の悲しみの発露」渡辺信一郎著『江戸バレ句恋の色直し』集英社新書).

discipline

開修行先ズ辻君をはじめとし 摘 3-39
kai shugyô mazu tsujikimi o hajime to shi

cunt errantry
first, you take on a lord
o' the crossroads

The "crossroads-lords" (*tsujikimi*) were the tough streetwalkers ruling these strategic spots. They stereotypically sold sexually transmitted diseases with their favors. The idea of *shugyô,* or ascetic discipline, which I *knighted* so to speak, covered almost anything imaginable in Japan, where people were and still are highly respected for taking the time and effort/suffering to really become expert about something. In Usania (I can not speak for the entire English-speaking world), I believe expectation of and appreciation for such superhuman effort only extends to athletes and, even then, to certain sports. It is no accident few learn difficult foreign languages or other sciences requiring cumulative effort for little reward. "Cunt errantry," if we may so call cunt *shugyô*, is not found in the OJD, but its parent word is: *iro shugyô, i.e.* "color" or "sex-shugyô." The preface to the floating world novel (*ukiyo-sôshi*) *"Sex-shugyô through 3000 Worlds"* claims *this* is a subject none yawn to hear about and none tire though reading of it on a long Autumn night. A German ethologist has written that each animal lives in its own world and I would guess the reference is to the worlds of 3000 women Narihira the great lover slept with or the even larger number of women and men Saikaku's protagonist knew. I do not know if the latter ever took on a crossroads lord. Seduction-wise, a crossroad's lord would be an easy start, but living in an age of syphilis, it would make more sense to leave her for last!

war zone

濡れ開でさわぐ夜討の白拍子
nurebobo de sawagu youchi no shirabyôshi 葉 22
(wet pussies-with clamor night-strike's white-rhythmlings)

running about
c̲ their wet cunts dancers
in a night raid

a night-assault
dancing girls run about
c̲ wet pussies

a night raid
commotion of wet-cunted
dancing girls

The dancers stayed over with those they entertained sleeping with whomever they "tripped" over. While attacks by night were common enough to have a name (*youchi*), and could be against a house, the scene is probably a military encampment because troupes of dancers tended to follow troops of fighters. One could compile war or dancer *ku* but I have not. This scene can stand alone.

pleasure Qs

めゝつてう四五人つれるいゝ女郎 摘
memechô shigo-nin tsureru ii jorô 4-18
(cunt four five-persons trail good=pretty harlot)

~~*'Pussy, pussy!' all the men call*~~
~~*But they follow her, enthralled.*~~

~~*A ½ dozen johns pulled in the wake*~~
~~*Of a shapely whore on the make*~~

~~*4 or 5 twats*~~
~~*accompany a whore*~~
~~*who's pretty*~~

~~*pussies, 4 or 5*~~
~~*trail a gorgeous feline:*~~
~~*the man-trap*~~

With kittens, four or five, her pack
a drop-dead gorgeous pussy cat!

Trailed by cuntlings, three or four,
A beautiful woman called a whore

The first two lined-out readings are in the margin of my *Pluck* book. I thought the *ku* either broke after *memechô* so the *memechô* belonged to the pretty harlot, or stood for her plain-looking companions who used her for bait. The OJD failed to note what I later found in the more thorough *Cuntologia, memechô* is not just a pussy but an unfledged one, in this case the *kaburo,* prepubescent cutie-pies who help a courtesan with her dress (and loneliness), entertain waiting customers, run errands and so forth. Since we have no name for cuntlings, I adopted feline terms for *neko* or cat was slang for courtesans (or was it geisha?). Another *ku* (in 神の田艸) has a chinese phoenix accompanied by several cuntling birds (めゝっ鳥). This just goes to show why I steer away from the Pleasure Quarters in this book. It needs a book all to itself, with plenty of invented/re-created vocabulary for the *ku* to be interesting.

gross & maybe

生酔にさせてむねから下吐だらけ 摘 3-22
namayoi ni sasete mune kara shita hedo-darake

doing it c
a drunk, puke-plastered
tit to toe

はやる湯ややたらへのこをほうばらせ
hayaru yuya yattara henoko o hôbarase 摘 2-9

popular baths
how they cram in all
those cocks

The first *ku* is about as unpoetic a "poem" as can be imagined. I put it here to prove that *Pluck* includes *ku* as bad if not worse than the worst in *Leaf*, despite the fact the latter is considered the bad boy and the former "literature" because it was selected by Karai Senryû. In respect to the second, also crude, I first imagined oral sex drawing customers, but now think it's pure dirty metaphor as there was a tiny waist-high entrance into the baths proper to hold in the warmth better with a resemblance to the topography of the female lowlands and customers *were* crammed in, but what is curious here is why *men.* Did men travel about searching out good baths while women stuck to whatever bath was closest? A Japanese respondent still believes it *is* about blow-jobs – there were attendants at bathhouses who sometimes . . . I will reserve judgment until I get expert opinion.

asagiura

gimme some
of that *buku-buku* says
the asagiura

let's do slap-stick
you and my dick says
the asagiura

ぶく／＼をしてくれおれと浅黄いひ 摘
bukubuku o shite kure ore to asagi ii 2-25

The mimesis *bukubuku* generally means sagging or floppy things. I have never seen it used for sex, but it *sounds* possible – maybe even the rare b.j.! Does the Asagiura samurai hick, dirty to the heart, think of sex as a sloppy and loose thing? If I had written this book a few decades ago, I may have given a large chapter to these paragons of innocent filth, but now I am perfectly content to stop with one more, which I mentioned but failed to give in another chapter:

あさぎうら犬のつるむにくそをふみ 摘
asagiura inu no tsurumu ni kuso o fumi 3-21

watching them mate
the asagiura steps
on dog shit

mushrooms

数千本へのこをかえす材木屋 摘 4-27
sûsen hon henoko o kaesu zaimoku ya

where they hatch
several thousand cocks
the lumberyard

the lumberyard
where several thousand
cocks incubate

the lumberyard
where they turn peckers
by the thousand

As we saw in ch.4, the dildos in senryu are generally made from water buffalo horn or, more rarely, tortoise shell. Could this be *models* – shaven idols? – for the prayer shelves of the courtesans? Or, are these really *mushrooms? Kaesu* can mean "hatch" *or* "turn-over." A respondent favors the mushrooms just growing there, but from what I read of the efficient use of space in the Edo era, I would, on the basis of this senryu, *bet* that left-over logs or wood that was aged for some reason in lumber yards *was routinely used to grow mushrooms*. In the next edition this will go with the mushroom *mara* in ch.6. For now, they're stuck here.

& more morphing

作用姫の開の毛直に苔と成り 葉 31
sayôhime no bobo no ke jiki ni koke to nari

Instantly, the hair on Princess Sayô's pussy
turned to moss.

Princess Sayô was favorite mistress/concubine (愛妾) of Satehiko. How a princess can be called a mistress, I don't know, but Japan had lots of princesses (I follow Syunroan). According to the 8c *Nihonki*, or *Chronicles of Japan*, Satehiko was made the general of a force that sailed from Kyushu in Month Ten of the Christian year 537, when Shiragi invaded Mimana. We will let the details (like their full names and whether they are in Japan or Korea or China) slide, and just point out what counts. And that was that she loved him so much that standing on a peak overlooking the shore shaking talismanic strips of cloth or strings of it tied to the boat – I'm not sure of what was what – seeing his boat off, then standing in place as he sailed off, she turned into a boulder. Dead lovers sprouting trees that unite above their graves are a dime a dozen in the song and legend of England, Japan, and probably scores of cultures, but I cannot recall a metamorphosis like this not done to avoid rape. I guess she was crying so much she instantly dried up! And, odder yet, he came back from the war alive. Now, we are ready for the second *ku* (which was published earlier in *Leaf*), and describes the reunion as you might expect senryu would:

佐手彦の男根も石屋の鑿のやう 葉 9
satehiko no mara mo ishiya no nomi no yô

And Satehiko's cock
like the chisel of a stone mason.

Pygmalion, we usually imagine kissing or gently fondling his statue. Here we have a hard-on pressed into a crevice of a big rock. One reason this *ku* preceded the pubes-to-moss one is that it is an improvement of an older *Pinch* one:

さよ姫がまたかなてこでくじつて見 摘 4-17
sayôhime-ga-mata kanateko de kujitte mi

Princess Sayô's crotch
He tries forcing his way in with a crowbar.

Or her quim which he tries to bore into with a jimmy. Either word, crowbar or jimmy, sound irrevocably Occidental. This *ku* first appeared with insignificant differences in Million (明八). The Leaf *ku* is, I think, far better. One could do a whole book of senryu with nothing but erotic historical figures.

first night

皆母の知恵と見へたる新枕　折句会所本
minna haha no chie to mietaru niimakura 宝暦中

mother's wisdom
saw everything all right
their first night

The original's "new-pillow/bed" always means a bride and groom's first time. A girl with no experience whatsoever would have only whatever sex education her mother gave her. Suzuki, who found this *ku*, put right next to it another one about a new bride too afraid to open up though she really wanted to (ちゝかまる・気はありながらにいまくら 神酒の口 安永四 *chijikamaru ki wa arinagara niimakura*). Such would suggest to me that there was considerable pressure on girls, or some girls, at any rate, not to engage in premarital sex, despite Japan not being a culture that worshipped virginity. On the next page, Suzuki introduces a *ku* providing the point of view of the groom trying to deal with such a bride:

痩馬に針立る様な新枕 折句題林集 (鈴木)
yase-uma ni hari tatsuru yô na niimakura 宝永五
(skinny-horse-into-needle/s-stand-like new-pillow/bed)

びくしやくとする
starting starting

like sticking
needles into a thin horse,
their first night

a first night worse
than sticking needles into
a skinny horse

A skinny horse was known to be a trying acupuncture patient; they were thin-skinned in both meanings of the word and would *start* when stuck. The entire content is a single modification of "new-pillow/bed," what I call *Japanese-style*, for I have never seen it in any other language (though I do not doubt it is found *somewhere.* I put all those hyphens in the direct rendition to make that point. To keep that connection, the second reading roughly reverses the word-order, putting the new pillow first rather than last (the "worse," is a minor difference, added for the near-rhyme with horse) . To keep it last, where it is best for the wit, the English must be weakened by cutting the modifying phrase from the subject as can be seen in the first-reading. You might note that these two *ku* are sweeter than most in this book. That is because the *zappai*, or near-senryu selected by Suzuki are indeed more wholesome than the dirty-senryu that form the heart and most of the body of this book.

marrying in

Since women married in as a rule, this is *not* about them. It concerns the *irimuko,* or "enter-groom," a man who joins his wife's family. We mentioned him briefly in the chapter on *Masturbation*, because that was often all he was allowed to do.

入聟のじんきよハあまり律儀過 摘
irimuko no jinkyo wa amari richigi sugi 4-32

the dry kidney
of a man married-in:
he was diligent

a married-in man
c̲ dry-kidney: call him
faithful to a fault

doing his duties
is how mr married-in
gets dry-kidney

Dry kidney is wasting away from too much sex. Does that seem to contradict what I just wrote? Well, some wives want *more* than their husbands, and for the same reason a married-in could not demand sex, he could not beg out of it.

入むこはきかすにぬいてしかられる 摘
irimuko wa kikazu ni nuite shikarareru 1-33

mr married-in,
scolded for pulling out
without asking

mr married-in
pulls out without asking
and is scolded

I gave ample space in Topsy-turvy 1585 to *discussing* the adoptive-marriage, as it is sometimes called, because it shows that the different rights accruing to the parties in marriage were not so much a matter of gender as of economic power, but nothing *illustrates* the circumstances of the powerless man so well as senryu!

入聟は下女と一所におん出され 摘
irimuko wa gejo to issho ni ondasare 2-33

mr. married-in
is sent packing together
with the maid

For all practical purposes, he was, if not a wife himself, a male maid. As I write this, I am reading Gertrude Stein's *Three Lives* for the first time. Two days ago (I read on the john), I came across: *"Anna knew so well the kind of ugliness appropriate to each rank in life."* Well, so did those who wrote senryu, in a different sense but, still . . .

conjugality

もぎ放しあれおかみさんだなさんが 摘
mogippanashi are okamisan dana-san ga 3-34

You say he goes on and on?
Madam, your husband is . . .

Of course, *dry-kidney* is a possibility, but such men generally do little moving, while *mogippanashi* is piston-like, non-stop. I have another guess:

He goes on and on
to come? Lady, your husband
is seeing some one

The husband either longs for someone he cannot have or is coming slower because he did it with another. Either way, a newly horny husband is suspicious.

A less creative earlier version has the wife in a fine mood saying *"My! Aren't you keeping it up!* (よくつづきなさると女房大きげん　摘 *yoku tsuzuki nasaru to nyôbô ôkigen* 2-13). I forget what I might have already given as my excuse for skipping husbands and wives in this book, but one reason is the stereotypes are too complex and the readings too subtle for the payoff (humor). But I will give you some quickies here and hope I get them right. This next is easy:

我女房でもひるするはぬすむやう 摘
waga nyôbô demo hiru suru wa nusumu yô 2-14

even a wife
done in the day, feels like
stolen love

one's own wife
in the daylight delicious
as stolen love

The Japanese, a hard-working people, seldom had sex in broad daylight. This *ku* I have seen around. A born aphorism I expect it will end up a saying.

よがり泣キ以後物置キに錠 摘
yogari naki igo mono-oki ni jô 3-37

Ever since the love-cries,
the pantry has a padlock.

The wife heard the maid's love-cries, but this is not so much a *ku* about the maid as one about the husband and a calm and thoughtful wife's relationship.

someone heard

So opportunity could not knock,
the pantry was sealed with a lock.

The above reading, or the title at any rate, circumvents English's lack of a word proper to yodeling and whatnot in bed.

して行ハよく／＼好キな夜盗なり 摘 2-32
shite-yuku wa yoku yoku suki na yo-nusumi nari

He who does it, then goes out,
loves night-cheating beyond doubt.

Good for his wife and for his lover: one can sleep, the other will have a long first round. The original doesn't rhyme but it does seem almost a definition.

我すきにさせないと妾カさせぬなり 摘 4-1
waga suki ni sasenai to mekake ga sasenu nari

~~*if he won't let her do as she likes*~~
~~*she won't let him keep a mistress*~~

> quim per quo <

unless the mistress gets her way
she will not let him have his

My wife who coolly used her husband's love for his mistress to her own ends was betrayed by the grammar but I'll leave it here, anyway, for it still contrasts the nature of the sexual contract between man and mistress and man and wife.

cock-pictures

へのこ書キ入レにし後家の金をかり 万安七
henoko kaki-ire ni shi goke no kane o kari

leaving a cock
image in hock: borrowing
from a widow

leaving the widow
a sketch of his pecker
for an i.o.u.

A witty I.O.U.? Or, has she been left c the bird? Drawn cocks deserve more study.

cheating

One sub-category of husbands and wives would be the backdoor man. For varied situations and plots, senryu cannot match the best musical genre I know on this subject, *country music*. Just off the top of my head: *If loving you is wrong, I don't want to be right* (as if it is a crime not to obey love); *God will, but I won't* (forgive you); (We'll do it though we really don't want to) *one last time and sweep out the ashes in the morning; I just started hating cheating songs today* (after learning his own wife was and throwing a beer bottle at a jute box). All of this stuff is sung well and the lyrics do not give it all away at once, but build up beautifully for the punch. People convinced opera or the blues are the only poetry in music don't know what they're missing. Where country loses to the (urban) blues and senryu is in the nitty-gritty of the affair. Here is a bit of the latter:
.

其まゝのへのこで逃ヶるつまみくひ 摘
sono mama no henoko de nigeru tsumamigui 3-13
(that as-is pecker-with flee/ing snack-eater)

A cheater almost caught in the trick,
Runs just behind . . . his fleeing dick!

◆

The backdoor man looks preposterous:
Who's ever seen a fleeing rhinoceros?

The snacker, here, is most commonly called a *ma-otoko,* or space-man 間男, "space" as *between/among/interval*. He sleeps with wives and, since Chaucer, has been Englished as a *paramour*, as if cheating (to use the country music expression) was an import. Let us see a few more of these "space-men," who, like the mistress, might be seen as a sub-category of husbands and wives.

間男と亭主抜き身と抜き身なり 摘 1-35
maotoko to teishu nukimi to nukimi nari

the paramour
and the husband both c
drawn blade

her lover and
her husband: bare blade
meets bare blade

A drawn sword and penis erected from its foreskin are both *nukimi* in Japanese. In this situation, the most common ending was not a bloodbath but the payment of a 5 *ryô* (equivalent of $500? $5000?) fine in exchange for the paramour's life.

間男を切れろと亭主惚れている 摘
maotoko o kero to teishu horeteiru 1-22

'break with your lover!'
the husband's really
stuck on his wife

If it were *kirerô* rather than *kirero,* the husband would be trying to cut the man down as in the last *ku.* As it is, imperative or not, this is an example of the despised foolish husband begging his wife to separate from her paramour.

間男の外へでて拭く運のよさ 摘
maotoko no soto e dete fuku un no yosa 1-16

the paramour
lucky to be outside
wiping himself

間男の不首尾はこぼし／＼逃げ 摘
maotoko no fushubi wa koboshi-koboshi nige 1-9

spurting as
he runs away, no lovers'
afterplay

Perhaps, I could do a bit better with the last *ku,* catching the paramour's failure to do what lovers do and husbands often fail to. But, my heart is not in these cheating *ku.* Perhaps the subject is too banal. I felt the same in the chapter I least enjoyed doing, the one on *lines*. There is little exotic about such goings-on other than the prevalence of the drawn-blade metaphor. Even the confidence game where the "wife" turns out to belong to a gangster husband who comes in with the sword to milk lover-boy of his 5 ryô was surely matched in, say, London. Give me something new, like *octopussy, dry kidney, & blue spots!*

~~~~~~

1 4 U 2 TRANSLATE

位の高下何に論ぜんや生ハ開
kurai no kôge nani ni ron zen ya shô wa bobo 葉 25
(rank's/s' high-low why argue-would!/? birth=commoname-as-for cunt)
~~~~~~

added ku — *scarlet crepe*

緋縮緬白い所ロをなめるやう 摘
hijirimen shiroi tokoro o nameru yô 4-23

scarlet silk crepe
it seems to be licking
her white places

Yes, this is the same crepe used for flashing or strip-teasing men that I regretted not gathering *ku* about it a dozen pages ago. The original does not specify silk, but it was, and it was imported from China. Looking for a page to photo-copy in an old book (see the appendix), I bumped into two good *ku* to add to the sensual one above – which will help you "read" erotic prints showing this cloth against white inner thighs – and thought it enough to come back and expand the chapter, though I still cannot locate my favorite (about how it *upgrades* what's behind it).

衣屋で見ても気のうくひぢりめん
koromoya de mite mo ki no uku hijirimen 30

we get excited
even to see it in the store
scarlet crepe

Like sexy underwear, it was a semi-transparent gauze. This *ku* attracts us mostly because it makes us feel how little time and place changes human nature.

緋ぢりめん虎の皮より恐ろしい 柳
hijirimen tora no kawa yori osoroshii 拾遺八編

more dreadful
than a tiger's coat:
scarlet crepe

There is some fear of woman's power over man vested in the vagina found in Japan, as elsewhere. In this book, the most powerful expression of it – which can border on misogyny – we have seen was in the bloody Akita folk-song (pp.173-4). The above *ku* extends a less creative one *"More dreadful than a tiger's mouth: the one below the navel"* 虎口よりこわいは臍の下の口 新編二 *kokô yori kowai wa heso no shita no kuchi*). The dread was not necessarily about the thing itself. It was more apprehension for what falling for the wrong woman might bring:

傾城のゑくぼにはまる家やしき 柳
keisei no ekubo ni hamaru ie yashiki 拾遺八編

~~*a pretty harlot*~~
~~*crams a mansion into*~~
~~*each dimple*~~

each dimple of
the pretty courtesan
fits a mansion

~~*a castle-tipper*~~
~~*crams a turret into*~~
~~*each dimple*~~

Namely economic ruin. That danger lurks in the very name for a gorgeous courtesan, and now just a *beauty,* the *keisei,* or "tip-castle." And for a man, that was – and, to a degree, still is – tantamount to castration, as women have a way of falling for men with money and avoiding those without it.

erotic ku

いいのいいのを尻で書く大年増 卍
ii no ii no o shiri de kaku ô-toshima

writing いいの
いいの *with her ass*
a mature lass

a grown girl
she writes love-letters
with her tail

"Ii no" in the wrong tone of voice means "Forget it!" but here I think it means "it's alright." But, now, imagine the letters written with a fanny (something I saw done more than once on Japanese television variety shows by girls in bikinis). There are many senryu (and stories) about writing the letter の with the behind, for such stirring is one thing all skilled lovers learned, but I have never come across い's. That い, the horn letter, as we have already seen (pp 164, 218), was associated with romance (sexual urgings). My impression from trying to write it with my rear is that the い letter requires a sexy loose ass – one whose hemispheres have the independent suspension required to move radically up and down – to do it well. This is all exceptionally visual and reminds me of a poem I wrote, partly influenced by drawings by the great erotic cartoonist Tsukikage Ken of the ample rear end of a woman in a kimono walking.

When she walks, my love makes X's
Lines converging on her nexus

I write this because the いい *ku*, one of the minority of old senryu with a known author, happens to be by none other than the most prolific and talented graphic artist in the history of the world, Hokusai (1760-1849). Hokusai drew women with bountiful asses (a rare commodity in Japan) and contributed 182 *ku* under his most used senryu pen-name (柳号), 卍 alone, from bk.84 to bk.125 (as 錦袋,百姓,百々爺,万字,卍 etc. he contributed more to bks 23-125) and, in 1825 (two years before Issa's death), he wrote the introduction for bk 85 and served as one of the judges for it. Most of the examples of Hokusai *ku* I have seen are too difficult for me to crack, but some such as *"Who smelled it, / to turn into metaphor / a kappa's fart?"* (誰が嗅で見て譬たか河童の屁 *daga kaide mite tatoeta ka kappa no he*) are easy enough – a *kappa's fart* means something inconsequental (they live underwater) still today: this follows the idea of an older *ku* wondering who counted the 48-folds in the vagina. Perhaps some day I will read all of his senryu and about them (西山新平著「謎解き　北斎川柳」河出書房新社H13 年版) and make a small book with pictures, which is to say a very different one than this.

<u>*How The Japanese Got Their Spots*</u>
わが子の尻を馬鹿にする親

三十 30

青痣の説和
Blue Ass Mystery

~~~~~~

たい内イである夜赤子ハけつをされ 摘
tainai de aru yoru akago wa ketsu o sare 1 - 28
(body-within one night baby as-for ass[acc.] done)

One night inside the womb, baby gets butt done.

If I do not give this *ku* a poetic, *i.e.* parsed, translation, it is because the original is but a snippet of prose, a far cry from the witty language of the closest English equivalent I know, the Earl of Rochester's description of a precocious fetus:

Written Under Nelly's Picture

She was so exquisite a Whore
That in the Belly of her Mother
She plac'd her ____ so right before
Her Father _____ them both together

These scenarios, impossible, but not *as* absurd in pre-modern Europe or Japan, when illustrations generally depicted babies squatting upright, as today, when we know babies do not do a last minute somersault, are equally disgusting. But, the senryu, which followed the draw *"An outrageous thing!"* (とんだ事かな), is not quite what it seems. The idiom *butt-done*, which *usually* means sodomized, actually refers to something perfectly innocent.

尻っぺたの痣を聞かれて母困り
shiripetta no aza o kikarete haha komari 61-39
(rear-cheek's birth-mark[acc] asked [about] mother troubled)

asked about the mark
on his tush, mom's hard pressed
for an answer

questioned about
that blue mark on her tush
mother turns red
~~~~~~

Innocent, but there is embarrassment, nevertheless, the reason for which comes from the just-so story:

尻の痣親父男根でつめったの
shiri no aza oyaji dankon de tsumetta no 葉 2
([your] buttock's birth-mark: poppa's man-root pinched=fucked)

that blue-mark
on your butt? papa pinched it
with his putz

that mark upon
your rear? papa's roto-rooter
did it, hear?

the mark on your tush?
your old man's wood-pecker
played in the bush

At first, I thought the mother was explaining, but the slangy word for father used suggests the father's elder brother or self-reference (mother would use a more polite term for the father in front of a child). If obsolete English is allowed, "putz" could be changed to "nut," the old English word for the glans, and "pinched" could then change to *stamped.*

十月めにへのこの細工出して見せ 摘
jûgatsu-me-ni henoko-no saiku dashite mise 4-22
(10th-month-on prick's handicraft [=detail-work=adornment] display)

the opening

a work is born
the neighbors laugh to see
dick's handicraft

month ten one day
peter's fine detail-work
is put on display

finally, full term
it's time to learn the extent
of dick's handiwork

I had to *name* the cock here! Many cultures find neck-folds the most precious beauty mark of all because they show the god/s took just that much more time to detail/adorn/finish his/her/their work. *Saiku* is a word generally reserved for fine craftwork, but is purely facetious here, for Japanese did not, as far as I know, make much of the shape of their blue marks, which, like a young animal's protective coloration, fade out and usually vanish with age. Most of us know how facial characteristics vary between races or sub-races of people. But, how many blacks or whites are aware that the yellow and the red have a *mark* we lack, and that it is blue and situated on their buttock? Today, this mark is generally called a "Mongolian blue spot/mark" in English and a "blue mark/blemish" (青痣) or, in modern times, "Mongolian spot/mark" (蒙古班) in Japanese. If the only statistics I could find on the web are valid, 95% of Mongolian babies, 80% of East Asian babies, 40-50% of Hispanic babies and 1-10% of Indo-European language babies have the mark – needless to say, there is some contradiction in the last two terms ("Hispanic" may mean central and south Americans surveyed in the USA), but we get the idea: it is not a black and white thing.

うハばみの毒気赤子の尻へかけ
uwabami no dokki akago no shiri e kake 48
(python[=drunk]'s poison/malice red-child[infant]'s butt-to putting)

an anaconda's
poison tossed on the tush
of an unborn

the poison bite
of a python's spite left
on baby's bum

Because a python/boa/anaconda swallows its prey whole and a giant mythological snake (Orochi), who demanded maidens to eat (remarkably similar to "our" Dragon), was killed because he loved drink and was tricked into becoming drunk, someone who chugalugs drink after drink is called one. I wondered if *uwabami* included cobra, but, no, the poison, here, refers to something we might call *venomous spite*. Snakes, perhaps because of their intense eyes as well as poison, were identified with terrifying vindictiveness. If the product of such "poison" were only an unusually large birthmark, we might laugh; *but medical books of the time specifically warned about "torturing the baby" by coitus after the fifth month. They taught that it not only left marks but could literally be "poison" for the baby's development* (参考：枕文庫　初編文政五 1822). So the senryu treats a serious matter. Despite knowing it was wrong, a drunken man, perhaps mad at his wife for criticizing the money wasted on drink, for sleeping with other women during her pregnancy or, worse, totally fed up with his life, has forgotten about the poor fetus and is pounding out his frustration on poor Mt Veneris.

あざの有る子の母おやのうつくしさ
aza no aru ko no haha-oya no utsukushisa 6-18
(mark-has-child's/children's-mother-parent's-beauty)

kids with marks
tend to be blessed with
beautiful mothers

a child boasting
a big birth mark: the beauty
of the mother!

a big blue-mark
how beautiful the mother
of that child!

Since most Japanese children have the birthmarks, the implication here is a child with an especially large or vivid mark, or one out of place that draws the attention of others. This senryu shifts the blame from papa to momma, for what man can resist the desire to plunge into of beauty? The syntax of the original senryu is what I call Japanese style: the "beauty" at the end is the subject and the rest a continuous flow of modification, leaving no place for what we might think of as a full sentence.

one odd thing

さか子うみそれから茶臼とんとやめ
sakago umi sore kara chausu tonto yame 摘 4-26
(upside-down-child bearing that-from tea-mortar abruptly stopped)

born feet-first
from then on she never
rode backwards

a breech birth
after that, she stopped
grinding tea

After bearing a breech baby, she would have no more to do with the tea mortar, *i.e.,* seated sex with the woman on top, facing away from the man. I know there are no blue marks here. So why do I introduce this *ku?* Because in the early-19c illustrations that I have seen, the fetuses sit rightside-up in the womb, which makes them upside-down for birth but places their butts in a position to get poked. But, if coming out feet-first, *sakago* (upside-down-child) was known to be rare, *how in the world did the butt-poking explanation for blue marks ever get started?*

~ eddies ~

Senryu that Should be Here (and were!). I recall reading two excellent *ku* which would be in this chapter if only I knew *where* I read them. I can only recall general ideas and not words, so I must flesh them out myself. Here they are reincarnated:

changing diapers
she chuckles: a blue mark
on baby brother

husband & wife
boasting that their baby
has no blue mark

The first would *prove that big sister has matured enough to know what it means*, so it is about the blue mark and of coming of age. The second means that the two are so proud of having refrained that they forget such pride only proves (by the senryu way of thinking) *the wife is very ugly* or *the husband very short-sexed!* ★ I found the missing *ku* and I am glad I lost them, for it made for an interesting experience! *They were in Suzuki.* My gestalt memory for the first was perfect, but the only way you could guess the "older sister" was cognizant was not in the *ku* itself but the accompanying 10-syllabet draw which gives us "one-cheek smiling x3," a smirk, I guess, for such are often lop-sided (弟の尻の青いをかへす姉（片ほにこ／＼／＼）宝暦中・大江山 *otôto no shiri no aoi o kaesu ane (kataho niko niko niko).*). The other also was close in the gestalt. It actually said that *"the baby was born without a poppy's worth of blue"* (生れ子の身に芥子ほどの青みなし　宝永中秀吟三百番 *umare ko no mi ni keshi hodo no aomi nashi*) and the draw (とかくうちばにかまへしはよし *tokaku uchi ba kamaeshi wa yoshi*), if I read it right, means "at any rate, *we* took precaution." The difference between these and the other senryû we have seen is that one had to know the draw in order to catch the point of the *ku.* These were not stand-alone *ku,* but because I have mostly read senryu, which *are*, I turned them into just that!

The Blue Spot *Today.* Before reading senryu, my impression of the birth-mark's significance came from television, where I saw Japanese sympathizing with Native Americans for centuries of maltreatment by whites – at the time "we" were Japan-bashing over the trade imbalance – excited to find the same Mongolian marks on the opposite side of the world, happily proclaim "Proof, proof, we *are* blood brothers!" So, naturally, I would like to know *if the Amerindians have any interesting just-so stories for it, too.* Anyone?

~~~~~~

Medical Matters In some New Guinea cultures, a father's continued intercourse with the mother during her pregnancy is considered necessary for fattening up the fetus (later, in at least one highland tribe the boys – all of them – perform fellatio on the adult men, also for their own sake). Japan was at the far extreme of that, as the father's cock was considered the nemesis of the little captive. Even today, Japanese cartoons often show *sex from the perspective of the child* inside the womb, frightened by the intruder. Since there are many animals (horses being the best known example) where intercourse serves to disrupt pregnancy so the "intruder" can father his own child, it would not be surprising if there were *some* pscho-biological basis for this Japanese womb-centric apprehension.

~~~~~~

Googled from English (my underlines)

Blue birthmarks, blue bruise skin, blueberry, blue-green algae, B-lymphocyte ... ◎ Not all birthmarks are brown. The Mongolian blue spot is a blue colour, which looks like a bruise. It's more common in people with dark. .. ◎ It says that mongolian spots usually disappear by adolescence, ... you are referring to is the Mongolian Spot, visible at the base of many asians spines. ... ◎ I have blue birthmarks all over my lower back, a common physical feature in Asian ... I wonder if there was some Mongolian in me sneaking in through the ... ◎ Koreans or those with mongolian descent get a blue birthmark on their bottom at birth. ... YoMAMA does not have blue birthmarks on his (quite large) ass! ... ◎ My sons also have these blue birthmarks. I am native american. ◎ The blue birth marks are called Mongolian marks which ... Yes they can have red or blue birthmarks. ... [In Japan it is always blue] ◎ Mongolian Spots - Term for grey-blue birthmarks. [Mousy] ◎ Medical Column Questions most frequently raised so far have been about Mongolian spots (normal black and blue birthmarks found over the back of buttocks), ... [Like bruises?] ◎Shatel'Nogothrim: The Religion of the Living Dragon .... with blue birthmarks called "Sha'carava."... The Japanese know it as. "Reiki" and the Indians know it as "Atma." ... ◎ Venous malformation (blue birthmarks, glomuvenous malforma-tion ...Venous malformation (blue birthmarks, glomuvenous malformation). ... ◎ WHAT TYPE OF BIRTHMARKS ARE ALSO CALLED STORK BITES? SALMON PATCHES ...? ◎I like the moon best when it is white with blue birthmarks. and not yet full. ...

Comment: Notice that the location of the marks is not only on the buttocks, that there may be an odd medical/biological explanation, and the stork!

~~~~~~

Googled from Japanese (and translated)

Tsungoose Connection? Some think particularly dark blue-marks on Japanese babies is proof of Northern Tsungoose genes (a loose translation of (契丹＝北方ツングース系といわれ、日本人で、蒙古斑＝青痣の濃い嬰児は契丹系という説があります)

Forget the Silk Road, Follow the Blue Mark? The actress and fashion model who personified the aesthetic 松岡正剛 Matsuoka Seigow promoted as *Japanesque* in the 1970's and 1980's, and influenced the appearance of the slanted-eye beauties found in *anime* (as opposed to the round-eyed ones) Yamaguchi Sayako 山口小夜子 and another woman I do not know 高木由利子 have a project to resurrect genuine Edo era drama – reproducing even the lighting – just to see what it was like with their own eyes. That project is named: 蒙古斑革命 – *Môkohan-kakumei:* **The Mongolian Mark Revolution** (If I find the reason for the name – love for neoteny+homo-ludens+sinosphere maybe? – I will add it to a later edition.). Can you recall Yamaguchi's razor-sharp straight-edged, single-fold eyelid eyes, perfectly even bangs reaching and canceling out her eyebrows,
~~~~~~

that jet-black long straight hair, snow white makeup, ruby-red lipstick and purple=blue and even green eye-shadow? www. mokohan.com/

We, Who Were Sumerians? A book by Iwata Akira considers the possibility Japanese originated as Sumerians, the founders of civilization as we know it, who, after a millennium and a half of glory, suddenly disappeared in BC 2004, an idea originating with Englebert Kaempfer in the 18c (岩田 明：十六菊花紋の謎—日本民族の源流を探る). The reasons given include physical similarity and the explanation gets complex with various peoples and seemingly contradictory characteristics involved, but many Iraqis, who inherit much of those genes, it is pointed out have – you guessed it, the Mongolian blue mark, whereas Arabs do not. The ancient Sumerians and the Japanese also share almost identical fertility god statues (a couple, with the male placing his right hand on the shoulder and clasping her right hand with his left).

Blue mark proof of medical efficacy? A pr article from saji-ya.com points out that both Japanese and Mongolians think sour drinks good antidotes and their medicinal tea from Mongolia should work equally well for all sorts of diseases I will not list, and why not, for *"Aren't the Mongolians the great ancestors of the Japanese with our Mongolian marks on our buttocks!"* Silly? Yes, but if blacks have a higher chance for sickle-cell, who is to say Mongoloids do not suffer from common ailments and, hence, would not benefit from common medicines?

And, What About Finnish Beer? Judging from the blogs, a Finnish beer or Japanese beer with something Finnish about it, kicked up quite a controversy by claiming that Finns shared their Mongolian Blue Marks (「東郷ビール伝説」). I suppose the idea was that their tongues, which is to say taste would also be similar, so . . . But, despite the language sharing many characteristics with Japanese, a blogger pointed out that as a matter of fact the Finns had no more blue-marks than was usual for Caucasians. I do not know where such knowledge came from, but the blogger went on to clear up stereotype after stereotype about Finns. I only recall one. Men and women rarely if ever bathed together in the nude, for that was stopped by the Finnish authorities in 1931. So the Germans, Swiss, Australians and others who call such baths "Finnish style" are all wrong. I would ask, *are they?* Maybe, when the Finns eventually reintroduce their ancient style of mixed bathing, they will thank the foreigners for preserving their style.

Blue Spots and Finns, again? A blog affiliated with a travel-tour company talks up the Finns as "having the Mongolian mark, they share with Japanese a tendency to see the world in fuzzy rather than black and white terms.(フィンランド人には蒙古斑があって日本人に通じる白黒つけないファジーな部分が.)

Q. How can one tell apart Ainu [from Japanese]? A. Their features are deeply chiseled, eyes hazel, head long front to back, hair wavy, body-hair long [profuse?] and the incidence of Mongolian marks is low.

The Survival of the Prettiest? "Unfair? Favoritism? *Don't be a fool!* Of course, teachers are unfair. They are going to be nice to kids who are bright, want to improve themselves and empathize with others. Even a parent doesn't love a kid who mumbles and grumbles from the day he is born. *The lazy attitude of wanting others to "just accept me as I am" only works when your Mongolian mark is still shining bright blue on the cheek of your ass.* Even a baby will be treated roughly if it does not turn on the charm. Wasn't there a book called *The Survival of the Prettiest?"* (my italics: www.aynrand2001japan. com/ akira/)

Summation: Aside from the last entry, a unique usage example, it is clear that the blue-mark is now a sort of pan-Asian navel, or sign of common identity and used as such.

~~~~~~

★ **The Picture on the Next Page** (from a book published in 1822) is one of a series illustrating why sex in late-term pregnancy is *bad.* The reason (as mentioned on pg.429) was primarily possible damage to the health of the baby. But the words right above this this illustration mention the blue mark on the buttocks! I had resolved not to include any illustrations, but how could I not share with my readers, who have plowed through page after page of irregular, rocky print, this baby jovially beating back a monster cock?
~~~~~~

へゝとりそう

へのこ
男根小児の尿をつく
ときハ出生して尿よ
めさる〜ゝゞ有るもの
腹中めてく〜まゝむ
もへ毒どくとるとる
気を男と死ぬくの如くよ

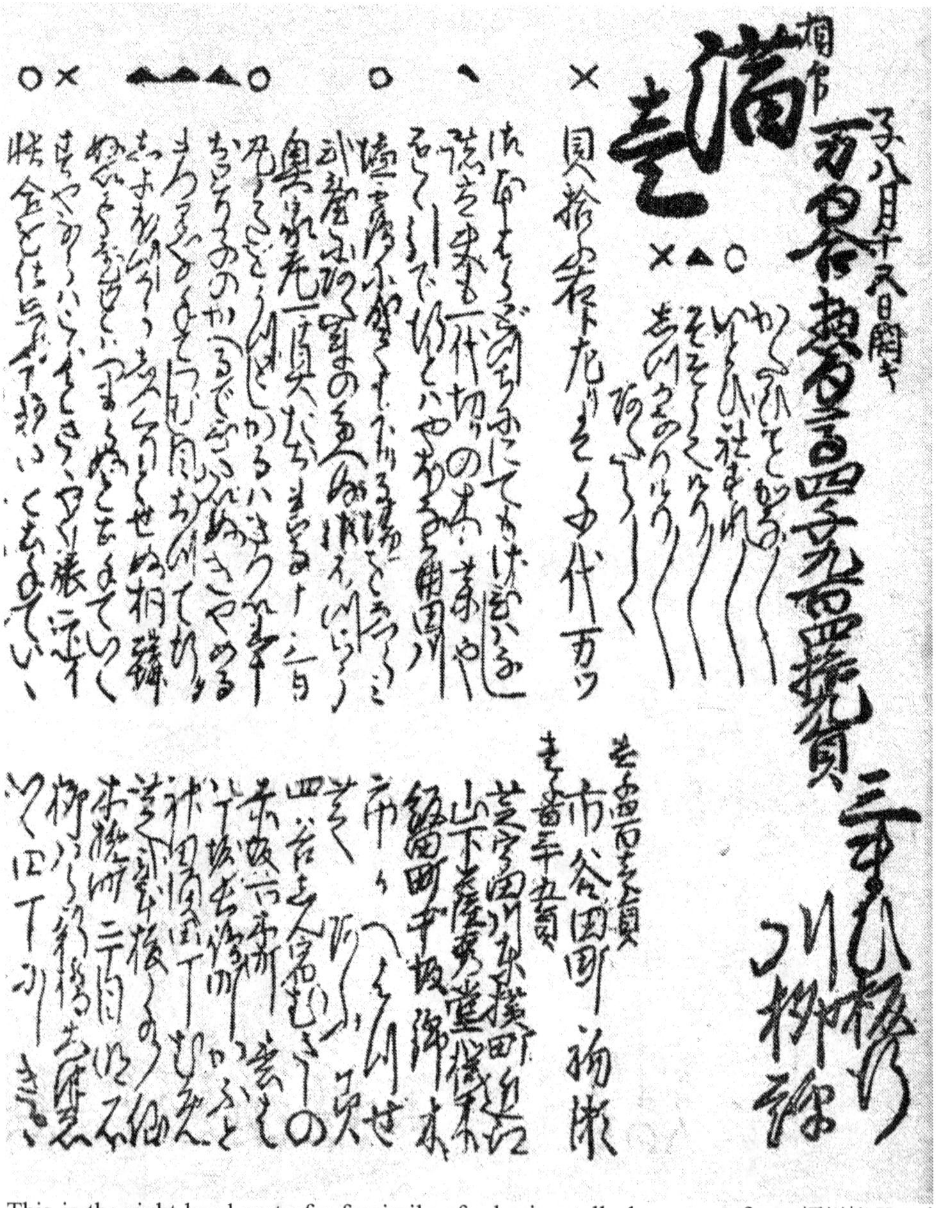

This is the right hand part of a facsimile of a horizontally long page from 柄川柳 Karai Senryû's *Million* (万句合 mankuawase) folded into Okada Hajime's selection (古川柳艶句選) from it. The first page of one of the booklets given to all participants/subscribers, it first lists four draws, respectively nil, ○, ▲, **X.** You can see a dozen or so *ku* on top and the address+pen-name of the participant-contributors on the bottom. According to Okada, 60 *ku* are packed in each long page. From the facsimile, I calculated more like 50, but it is possible that the end of the page was not included. I believe that one-line one-ku, which is to say the compact nature of the single line entry is an important factor behind the spread of poetry contests, for it made the low-cost high-volume business lucrative enough to engage the full-time attention of point-judge+promoters such as Senryû and gain the cooperation of tea-shop owners, etc. to spread the word and gather the poems. I did not use script books at all in my research. For a print sample, see pg. 490. Blyth also borrowed this facsimile from Okada and used it on the flyleaf of his 1960 work.

前がきのひひひき続き

*T*he Foreword

. . . continued from page 12

Japanese earthiness goes back to the beginning. Rather than ribs and snakes and apples, we have an august halberd poking about in the sea with "foamy" islands growing from the stuff dripping off its tip, [9] a Sun Goddess holed up in a cave drawn out by the commotion caused by another goddess doing lewd dances, the world's first striptease – to draw something *out* of a hole rather than into one! [10] – and the first truly human gods, noting each other's extra and absent parts, deciding to unite them to found the commonwealth, *i.e.* Japan was *fucked* into existence (*born* = natural), rather than created from *design* (made = artificial).[11] There is much more – the reverence given to rocks c holes and phallus parades being only the most obvious survivals. Some of the (retroactively) obscene ancient folk tales related in this book when relevant to the senryu reflect this.

While examples of dirty poetry are found earlier, for whatever reasons, the early-16c, also called the Warring Era, seems to have been particularly ripe for it. [12] The *Kangin-shû*, a 1518 collection of folk-song/poems, includes not only some salacious exchanges but one "poem" which is nothing more than a list of synonyms for *cunt!* The 1536 *haikai* classic *Inu-tsukuba-shû* (dog=pseudo tsukuba collection) has numerous verse-sequences playing with coarse subject-matter, such as *boy's asses, balls*, *farts*, *lice*, *pissing* and so forth. [13] With a strong tendency toward allusion and parody, it is hard to tell how much of this came of delight with obscenity for its own sake, and how much from meaner reasons, i.e., sticking it to the romantic ancient canon or contemporary rival schools. After the internecine and international wars ended and the rising classes of commoners became literate in the 17c, the vulgarity (recorded in poetry – such songs have always existed everywhere) becomes increasingly puerile. In the 1633 *Enoko-shû* (puppy-collection), likewise a *haikai* classic, we have love metaphored as puss-filled boils needing lancing, love-forsaken men who would commit suicide in ponds of her piss, etc. (see pp. , 32). Don't get me wrong, even some of the worst lines are interesting, if for nothing else because of the deft punning and extra-ordinary jumps of the imagination. In the often convoluted chain of association created to maintain the flow of this link-verse (*haikai-no-renga*), there is already the riddle element that we find at the heart of old *senryû*.

history

Ueda may be right when he claims Matsuo Bashô (1644-94), the sage who "transformed *haikai* into serious poetry by refining its sportive elements, making it deeply reflective of man's relationship to nature," was probably, more than anyone else, responsible for the divergent evolution or polarization of *haikai* poetry into high and the low *ku*. Then again, who can say. Bashô was not the only poet striving to be serious, such splits had always existed (*haikai* was the low-style pre-Bashô) and more splits were inevitable. Judging from the 16, 17 and 18c *haikai* I have read, and from the preface to the *Mutamagawa* (full name *Haikai Mutamagawa*) first book: 1750) – a collection of witty *ku* both 7-7 and 5-7-5 taken from haikai linked-verse contests, half-way between *haikai* and senryu, today, usually called *zappai,* but also called senryu because many *ku* in it are similar to what would later be known as senryu – there was so enormous and vigorous an upwelling of regional personalities and schools of poetry competing to be the trendiest of all in the urban culture that grew with leaps and bounds over the preceding century, or enthusiastically pushing their regional styles in competition with the exploding new capital of Edo, that plenty of interesting poetry for posterity would have been written in Japan whether or not Bashô existed before, Senryû after, or the *Mutamagawa* editor, Kei Kiitsu (慶紀逸 1694-1761), who wrote that preface (If you think my sentence long, you should see Kiitsu's one-sentence preface!). When we discuss the influence of the great, we must always remember that because they flourished, others who might have influenced the culture somewhat differently did not. Moreover, even the influence of Bashô-ism – like Darwinism, not to be perfectly equated with the man – which is almost universally thought of as good, was actually mixed. Contrary to the usual understanding, it hurt the development of haiku as well as helped it. [14]

Pardon my insufferable iffyness and burgeoning qualifications, but what little I have read of history in fields where I know something has taught me to be skeptical. For example, the history of what came to be called *haiku* (I know a bit more about it than senryu) rarely gives Sôgi (1420-1502), a celebrated linked-verse poet and teacher (*renga-shi*), more than a glance. Bashô, they always say, thought highly of him. Yet, look at the 100-odd *ku* of his included in *Cherry Blossom Epiphany* (i.e., 3% of the 3,000 *ku*) and *then* tell me he was not already writing what we would call *haiku* (not just *hokku*) today! [15] *Why is that?* I believe it is because the clear histories we see are taxonomies of schools of poetry, i.e., lineages, as opposed to chronologies of *what* is first written *when* and by whom. Some day, *that* is the type of literary history I'd like to write. Meanwhile, you'd best look at Blyth, Ueno and, for one collection, Solt, for more history and Gilbert for a regional, *i.e.,* broader but sketchy overview [16] – there were many regions and just one Edo – of the world of *haikai* and sundry verse (*zappai*).

maeku, or *the draw*

Definitions of what made senryu senryu typically focus on a formality, the *maeku,* a 14 or 17-syllabet *ku* that literally translates as a "pre-verse" or "before-verse." As Ueda points out, long before "senryu" proper came to be, the *maeku* was used by *haikai* teachers to elicit a responding verse called a *tsukeku,* literally "attached *-ku,*" which the teacher could then critique; and, "when the teacher had more than one student, this teaching method would easily turn into a verse writing contest." Eventually, it went public. Contests of the *maekuzuke,* or *ku* written in response to *maeku,* became so popular in the 17c, that one held the year before Bashô's death "received more than 10,600 entries sent by residents of fifteen different provinces." (Ueda) [17] These contests could grow so large (and, needless to say, profitable) for several reasons. 1) The cheap printing material and technology (Europe lagged in literacy and paper-making skill), 2) The highly developed networks of word-lovers (federations of local poetry groups could distribute the *maeku,* collect the responses/entries and receive and distribute the books with the winning entries and new *maeku*), 3) The shortness of the poems, and charm of the *maeku*, or draw, that elicited them. With *renga,* or *haikai* sequences, the required content of the *ku,* including but not limited to its proper associations with the other *ku* (not only the immediately preceding verse) followed many rules, while the *maeku* became simpler and simpler until becoming what often amounted to a single adjective with just enough dressing to become a phrase rather than a word (examples below). Participation being easy, the numbers of entrants soared. And Senryû himself was easy on the judging side, too, so much so that, for a bright poet, it must have seemed more like filling in a blank, a blank which had more than one possible answer, than capping a verse.

Most *maeku,* which we will call the *draw* from now on, the better to show their purpose – *bait,* or the *come-on* might also be apt – were 7 syllabets repeated twice. Because Japanese has various repeating signs, the repetition does not *look* as bad as it would in English, and in the cases where senryu were written at gatherings, calling out something twice would be helpful (I doubt it was kept just for perfunctory reasons, *i.e.* pretending to be a traditional 31-syllabet duet). Since an entry fee accompanied a verse, the broadest possible participation was desired, so, I repeat, the draws are simple as pie. *But, in translation, that is, sadly, not true*; they can be very hard to English. What, for example, can be done with one of the most common phrases found in a senryu draw, the 4-syllabet *koso sure,* which, added to a 3 syllabet verb, implies something is very *such*, yet there is something contradictory, paradoxical or odd about that suchness? [18]

kazari koso sure 飾りこそすれ (x 2) ・ 武蔵坊とかく支度に手間がとれ 1-5
Adornment for sure but . . . ⇒ *Musashi-bo must have taken forever to get ready!*
(The powerful warrior Benkei depicted as a walking armory, a watermill of weapons.)
hanare koso sure 離れこそすれ／＼ ・子が出来て川の字形なりに寝る夫婦 1-4
Separated for sure but . . . ⇒ *Blessed with a child they sleep like a river* (川)
(The child lying between actually brings them closer together. An old conceit.)
warai koso sure 笑ひこそすれ／＼ ・御勝手はみな渇命におよんでゐ 1-12
You may laugh but . . . ⇒ *In the kitchen they are all fighting for their lives.*
(The longer guests laugh up a storm enjoying a banquet, the harder cooks must work)
narabi koso sure ならびこそすれ／＼・親戚がにわかに増える通夜の席 雑俳つ花連
All together but . . . ⇒ *The number of relatives briefly spurts at the wake.*
(Assembled for food & drink and possible inheritances, kinship is felt less than ever)
susume koso sure すすめ社すれ／＼ ・あま寺へ来テハせきれい尾を振テ
You can show them but . . .⇒ *Paying a call on the convent, wagtail wags his tail.*
(This bird, called a *sekirei* in Japanese, taught the first humans how to have sex 万宝七)
nozomi koso sure のぞみ社すれ 能女見たい所か一ッあり 万宝九
You might as well hope! ⇒ A pretty woman: there's *one* place you want to see.
(Not that anyone has ever found a relationship between facial and vulvic beauty.

The device "______ *for sure, but . . .*" often works but not always. A combination of "sure" and italics elsewhere can do the trick without the obvious "but," in some cases. In the last translation, I do it with "you might as well," for, with hope, it implies you have little hope of being so lucky. Indeed, a freer translation might be: *"To be so lucky!"* (So, *that's* it! *Koso sure* is Yiddish!) Another of the most common, if not *the* most common, draw phrasing has a 5 syllabet adjective followed by *koto,* or "thing." It, too, presents a dilemma to the conscientious translator:

wagamama na koto わかまゝな事／＼・月の内たつた七日をふつつくさ 万宝七
Talk about spoiled! ⇒ *Grumble, grumble! Though only seven days each month.*
(the length of her period (see ch.2) – but is it the sex or the cooking the husband misses?)

osoroshii koto おそろしい事／＼・うつくしい顔てしまいハ灸を治へ 万宝八
A dreadful thing! ⇒ *So beautiful a face that he ends up branded by moxa.*
(moxa-combustion treatment for empty-liver (ch.__), because he did his wife too much)

kimi no ii koto 気味の能事 ・茸狩リに脉の高ぶる奥女中 万 宝十
It doesn't *feel* dirty ⇒ *Chambermaids, mushroom hunting how their pulses race!*
(The phallic mushrooms (ch._) are cleaner (?) than dildos associated with such women)

arigatai koto ありかたひ事 ・きん玉ハ今の御代迄やわらかい 万 宝十一
Things to be thankful for ⇒ *Our balls clear down to present times, still soft.*
(Soft means relaxed, hanging down. Shrunken by fear, they'd feel hard. Peace was not taken for granted. (Ch.11 for the legend behind this *testi*mony))

While not as tricky as *koso sure,* "thing" is still a problem for translation because it is rhetoric as well as a thing. The first draw in Okada Hajime's selection from Karai Senryû's first major collection, *Million* (*manku-awase*1757-1789), *wagamama na koto,* provides a case in point. After deciding whether to English *wagamama* as *selfish, self-centered, self-serving, capricious, egoistical, self-indulgent, or spoiled*, the translator faces a dilemma, whether to go with *"A ____ thing"* or, *"How _____!"* The *thing* seems fitter for drawing responses, but the exclamatory reading is otherwise closer to the tenor of the original. Also, note that no single rendition of the draw will necessarily have the connotation demanded (in retrospect!) by the response. Another response poem might have demanded "capricious," rather than "spoiled." The penultimate draw-verse above is trickier. *Kimi no ii koto* literally means *"feeling-good thing,"* but the word used for "feeling" (*kimi*) is more commonly found in the negative sense of *kimi ga warui* (yucky/disgusting feeling). So the positive use has the contrary connotation. It is a good example of why it often takes more understanding of senryu (and Japanese) to translate the seemingly simple draws than the poems themselves. Finally, please note that *thing* could always be *things*. As we shall see in the next section, where I will try to explain what makes draws interesting, a syntax that does not require number or person – indeed, subjects or pronouns are not needed even for active verbs – has its advantages. First, a few more suffixes often found in draws lacking an English equivalent, that are often found in haiku, too.

koishikarikeri こいしかりけり／＼・化ヶ物か出ねハ寝かねる長つほね 万宝八
How dear it is! ⇒ *Unless the monster comes out the lady in waiting cannot sleep.*
(the chaste ladies with their beloved dildos will be introduced in ch. __)

fushigi narikeri ふしき也けり／＼ ・にくらしい程能中てなせ出来ぬ 万宝八
It really is strange! ⇒ *So lovey-dovey it's disgusting – why have they no kids?*
(Too much intercourse was thought to thin the seminal fluid, which, of course, it does)

ukiyo narikeri うき世也けり／＼・見物の方にハ本ンのぬれかあり 万明八
Life *is* but a dream! ⇒ *There are some who really do get wet in the audience.*
(A *love scene* in a drama was a "wet-place," while *being wet* is to getting *very aroused*.)

ki o tsukenikeri 気をつけにけり／＼・さきんずる時は女房ふそく顔 万安一
S/he had come to notice ⇒ *When you beat her out, your wife looks unsatisfied.*
(To *come* first was to lose the fight and your life-juices, but longevity was not everything!)

tetsudainikeri 手伝にけり・御虫干おや／＼／＼と下女ハにけ 万明五
S/he'd been helping ⇒ Dry-out day – *"Oh my! Oh my! Oh my!"* The maid flees.
(Dirty picture books surfaced on this day when books, pillows, etc. are taken out to dry.)

homerarenikeri ほめられにけり・せんべいてやっとまくら絵取りかへし 万明四
All buttered-up! ⇒ *With a cracker, at long last, they got the picture book back.*
(A child is buttered up with praise "what a good kid you are!" but seeing how much his or her parents want the "pillow-pictures" back – children and pets feel such desire – holds on all the harder, until being bribed with food to surrender the treasure).

The verb suffix *keri* is extremely common in haiku and is, it is usually explained, a *kireji,* or "cutting word" (*caesura*); but, as Bashô pointed out, *any word* can be a *caesura*, hence, I think it more important to remember that it functions as a particularly elegant, even classy *exclamation* (as opposed to the ebullient *yo* and rude *zo*). With English, we must take these *~keri* draws one by one, and apply appropriate *hows* and *whats* and *reallys* and exclamation marks. And even that may not work. Consider *"Life is but a dream"* as a creative translation of "floating-world is + *keri." Ni-keri* is close, but stresses the action was completed "for good," which is to say possibly for the bad. With draws, it tends to provoke a "but, *then*, this happened response. The English language's addiction to pronouns makes it hard to keep those draws open-ended yet understandable, much less poetic.

oshii koto kana おしいことかな ／＼・人参てよふ／＼出来て御姫様 万宝八
Ah, what a pity! ⇒ *With ginseng, at long last the child, a little princess.*
(Men needing such potency drugs tend to be old and father girls, but a boy would be better to stay with the mother after the man becomes incapacitated or passes away.)

muri na koto kana むりな事かな／＼・ちんほうの無イハ女房へなすり付ケ 万明三
That's pushing logic! ⇒ *The lack of a prick, he tries to stick upon his wife.*
(Pinning the blame for bearing a girl on his wife, as if her sex prevailed . . . [19])

The *kana* is the most common cutting-word+exclamation/emphatic in haiku. It is used a lot when the theme/subject has three syllabets, the better to fill out the last two of the last five syllabets of the *ku*. My collection of sea cucumber haiku had a far higher percentage of *ku* ending in *kana* than my collection of fly-ku for no other reason than that the former creature is called a *namako* (ナマコ) and the latter a *hae* (ハエ). For draws, too, it serves to fill out as it adds, either a touch of astonishment or interrogative wonder. So it is *possible* the poet took the first of the two *kana* draw-verses above to mean, *Is it a pity, or not?*

(5 + 7-5) *nikurashii* にくらしい ・あの小男て大天狗 万宝七
It's galling ⇒ *That little man, a big tengu.*
(Tengu goblins, or their masks at any rate, have proboscises large enough to serve for dildos. A well-endowed shorty evidently upset a less-endowed tall poet.)

(5+ 7-5) *tsuyoi-koto* つよい事・障子に向ふ大わらい 万宝八
Powerful indeed ⇒ *Toward the paper screen, their guffaws.*
(The original does not say "they," but laughing alone is uncommon and popping pricks through paper screens was generally associated with show-off group behavior. See pg.395)

(7 + 7-5) *chirari-chirari to* ちらり／＼と・ちんほうも名を改メル 万宝八
Spare and sparsely ⇒ *His penis also ready to change its name.*
(with pubic hair starting to sprout, the weenie, like the boy are ready to be renamed. See *Topsy-turvy 1585* for "name-parents" and other details of Japanese re-naming.)

While the *maeku* always functioned as a draw, the draws were not all called *maeku* nor the result a *maekuzuke.* A 5-syllabet draw included with the 7-5 response to create a 17-syllabet *ku* was called *kamuri-* or *kasa-zuke* 冠 / 笠付 (*crown*/*hat*-attached/following). [20] Since one-person haiku or senryu could pause after the first 5 syllabets – and the 5-syllabet draws (the above in minimum translation, *"galling," "strong-thing,"*) are less substantial than they appear in my translation – the result might be taken for a 5-7-5 *ku*. The last example, with its 7-5 finish to a 7-syllabet draw-verse is rarer. All of these were mixed among the 7(x2) draw + 5-7-5 *ku* in Karai Senryû's *Manku-awase* (10,000 Verses), the collection – or, rather the judging/selection of which – made him famous and fixed the fortunes of the genre. Ironically, it was not Edo, but Kyôto and Osaka where the use of various draws for contests had long flourished,[21] but thanks to Karai Senryû's *10,000 Verses*, and his more famous *Willow* (*Yanagidaru*) and *Pluck* (*Suetsumuhana*) series that followed and drew from it, these *maekuzuke* that settled on the 7(x2) draw + 5-7-5 *ku* arrangement and became more or less standard for witty urban verse, by both content and location, ended up synonymous with the new capital culture of what was the world's largest city.

monowatsukushi or *listing*

As to the general nature of the draws that helped make senryu become what it became, it is usual to go way back to ancient *waka* (31-syllabets) examples of a 17-syllabet *ku* capping a 14-syllabet *ku* (or the vice-versa). But to my mind, such *formal* similarities – similar if we pretend the senryu draw is 14 syllabets, when it is really 7 – do little more than confirm the obvious: people play with poetry. It would be far more interesting to consider *meaningful* precedents. *Listing* is one.

Things Unpleasant at Heart 不快意 Li Shang-yin (812-858)

Cutting something with a dull knife 鈍刀切物
Wind on its way when your sails are torn 破帆便風
Trees growing up to block a landscape 樹陰遮景致
Building a wall that shuts out the mountains 築墻遮山
Having no wine for blossom-viewing 花時酒無
A mat between the back and breeze on a hot day 暑日背風排莚

While listing items according to one's taste in China preceded Li Shang-yin (李商隠) by centuries, French scholar Jacqueline Pigeot, probably the world's leading authority on listing, judges his work (李義山雑纂), with 41 different lists, the first to have significant aesthetic merits, i.e. the eclectic yet tasteful sensitivity marking the *Pillow Book* (枕草子 *makura no sôshi*) of the greatest lister of them all, the extraordinarily creative miscellanist Sei Shônagon (fl. 1000), who may well have read his work. Shônagon, however, took the art to a new level by creating far broader variety of categories and playing more freely within them. Her precursors had a moralistic or pedagogical bias, while Shônagon, thanks to being so discriminating (hyper-critical) she gained the reputation of being a bitchy diva, was *purely personal and aesthetic* and covered a broad spectrum of categories. Translations of her work abound, so I will keep my examples short:

> *Depressing Things (susamajii mono)*
>
> *A dog howling in the daytime.*
> *A lying–in room where a baby has died.*
> *An ox-driver who hates his oxen.*
> *A scholar whose wife has one girl child after another.*
>
> *Adorable Things (utsukushiki mono)*
>
> *The face of a child drawn on a melon.*
> *A baby sparrow that comes hopping up when one imitates the squeak of a mouse.*
> *A baby . . . crawling rapidly on the ground . . . catches sight of a tiny object and . . . takes it to show to a grown-up.*
> *A little boy of about eight who reads aloud from a book in his childish voice.*
> *Duck eggs.*

About the last item in the *Depressing Things*, Ivan Morris, whose translation (in my parsing, with some items skipped) I quote, notes there were professions where only sons would do and that Shônagon's "things" (*mono* in phonetic letters) might also be translated "Things and People;" but, I think "things" covers it well enough. My comment would instead be that *susamajii,* translated "depressing," includes a touch of the *dreadful*. I only took a quarter of the items in the *Adorable [in Japanese, "pretty!"]Things* list and shortened them, too. Scores of such categories comprise the best part (to me) of Sei Shônagon's *Pillow Book*, and I hope the above suffices to give anyone unfortunate enough not to have read her an idea of the charm of listing, though it is not sufficient to show her broader genius, the artlessly artful way Shônagon arranged her items from concrete things to abstract ideas, or from other things to the human, etc. (Pigeot introduces such examples – she writes as a scholar, I, as an entertainer).

Japanese has a term for listing, *mono-wa-zukushi* (物尽), "things-exhausting." Unfortunately, it is not reserved for aesthetically meaningful styles alone – should we call them *Shônagons?* – and commonly refer to *name songs* or *place songs*, which are not even as interesting as *counting songs*. Shônagon herself had some relatively uninteresting lists of that type, titled simply by the type of thing followed by *wa,* a particle with no English equivalent usually glossed as "as-for." Ivan Morris wisely gives just the name of the thing, such as "flowering plants," "insects," etc.. This type of listing of physical properties (*short, long, white ,black,* etc.) was prominent in the 16c *Dog Pillow (Inu Makura)*, the title of which is less parody, as usually explained, than humorous self-disparagement, as a *dog-* is a second-rate or *pseudo-* item (a *dog*-cherry would be one with substandard bloom, as a *crab*-apple or *horse*-chestnut...) and, in the 17c *Reasonable Book (Mottomo-no-sôshi),* which visually parodies the 犬 (*dog*) in its predecessor's title with 尤(reasonable/ warrantable) and echoes Shônagon's *sôshi* (grass-paper)草紙 with the homophonic 双紙 (double-paper = book). The lists in both – *shinajina* 品々 = *goods/items/ qualities,* rather than Shônagon's *mono* or the senryu draw's *koto,* but basically the same "thing/s" – include plenty of risqué content. The first has sharper "adult" humor, while the second, written for a 14 year-old son of the Shôgun, is more informative. Both also include material expanded upon by senryu. From the second, *Reasonable* (on my desk), a few minutes of searching found that the first of the *"Narrow Things"* (狭き物之しな／＼) was "a catamite's ass, a virgin's hole" (すばりの尻、うゐ穴), *Long* items include the pubes of a seven-disaster-woman (七難女= surviving seven disasters was lucky, so temples kept them for charms) and Ainu nostril hair (ゑぞが鼻毛); among *Stout Things* (太き物の品々), we even find 弓削の法王, which is to say the ancient Buddhist 'Pope' identified with his humongous member so beloved by senryu (see ch.1), followed by the bone/r of a whale (鯨のたけり) and, of course, the proverbial horse.

Pigeot, who did not mention these particularly sexy examples (it had nothing whatsoever to do with her book), was *thrilled* by how Tokugen pulled even wilder stunts than Shônagon in his listing because of his experience with linked-verse, which included both reasonable associations and utterly kooky ones based on homophones or other puns. She noted how he played with the first item in the second part of his book, "Things You *Hiku,"* (forgive "you," I just want to show *"hiku"* is a verb), drawing out the disparate connotations. *Hiku* in its root meaning is "pull," but it *means* anything from *tugging* on clapper-lines (noise-making devises on strings used to protect gardens) to *plucking* musical instruments or *catching a* cold (a "wind" in Japanese). If I may turn Robert Frost inside-out,[22] I suppose that this is *proof of the poetry of listing*, for nothing is less translatable than the span of connotation a single word has in a language. It goes both ways, of course. One could not *pull* an all-nighter, *pull* out of an engagement and *pull* strings, much less have eggs, deeds and women equally "well *done*" in Japanese, either.

The content of *Reasonable* was about one third objective physical attributes (*weight, color*), one-third attitude and behavior (*passing, circling*), and one-third emotional, or subjective/abstract categories (*delightful, hateful*) according to Pigeot but, unfortunately for us, her survey did not continue on to Karai Senryû's *draws* (not surprising since none relate them to listing) and I have yet to see a careful analysis of them.[23] Surely they played a major role in his success in drawing millions of responses over his decades of work.[24] It would be interesting to know if his evident awareness of how abstract draws/categories elicited fine observation linked to feelings came from reading Shônagon, Tokugen and/or other miscellaneous listing. If someone listed listing categories from various miscellany and did the same for senryu, perhaps we would know. That is the only way the relationship between listing and draws I hypothesize might be proven.

But, it would be far *more* interesting yet to compile the best *ku* for each of the most popular draws from all collections of senryu. Such a presentation would put the draws at the center rather than periphery of the work, and we could for the first time see how the collective intelligence of 18c and 19c Japan compares to the genius Sei Shônagon's classic one-woman show or Tokugen's link-verse-influenced one-man show. I am puzzled no one has yet compiled such a draw-based anthology, and may do it myself some day, if no one else does it first.

Withholding the *draws* does not necessarily detract from the authenticity of a collection of senryu. The bold editor of Karai Senryû's *Willow* anthology, Goryôken Arubeshi (-1788), determining that the draw-verse added little or nothing to good *ku* (mostly true for Senryû's collections but not for all *zappai*) dropped them to give more space to the *tsuke-ku, i.e.,* accompanying verse;[25] and, by the time *haikai*-style (俳風) crazy-*ku* (*kyôku*) became known as *Senryû-style* crazy-*ku*, 1770 or 80 – "senryu" by itself was not used as a name for the *ku* until the mid-19c – most collections did not print them. There is a parallel here with *haikai,* where individual *ku* collections came to replace link-verse.[26] This is not to say that either the stand-alone *haikai*, which we now call *haiku* or the stand-alone response to the draw we call *senryu* were appreciated in isolation. They both came to be appreciated in a different context. For the former, the seasonal themes called *kigo* came to assume a life of their own, for the latter, something else I would call simply *stereotypes* did; and these concepts inspired the lion's share of *ku* in the respective traditions. To my mind, even if the draws had continued to be printed, this would have happened to senryu, for, with insufficient coherence in the *ku* received and printed for each *draw* for them to be interesting collectively as examples of this or that abstraction – it would require editing too tight to make money off entrants – the natural desire to make sense of, i.e. classify things that is built into animal intelligence could not help but push readers and writer-participants alike to recognize categories and contribute to their development as stereotypes. The only difference is that seasonal themes became official for *haikai* – ordered, defined, and exampled in haiku almanacs called *saijiki*, they came to provide the structure for most anthologies of *ku* – while senryu stereotypes remained, to all practical purposes, unrecognized.[27]

In *this* book, with senryu arranged according to subject matter rather than secondary similarities, draws would only confuse matters and clutter up already cluttered pages. Some are included in this book, but only when they entertain or happen to bear upon the interpretation of an otherwise ambiguous *ku.*

stereotypes – are they really all bad?

By *stereotypes*, I mean subjects with one or more characteristics so well known that coming across the latter is sufficient to identify the former. If, for example, someone well-versed in senryu were to encounter a huge penis or one that gained a man great power, he would immediately know it was about Dôkyô, the first Buddhist "pope" of Japan (ch. 1); for an equally huge vagina, he would recognize the Empress who loved him. In the case of someone raped by many men – usually elicited by the draw "a horrendous thing" (*mugoi koto*) – or uncertain which of many men impregnated her, we would recognize a maid-servant (ch.20). Ox-horn or tortoiseshell dildos meant a *nagatsubone,* or lady-in-waiting/ chamber-maid (ch.4). The diagnosis for a dead man embarrassing his wife by staying hard, a bed-ridden husband with a pretty wife, or a wife asked about "him" by a pharmacist-doctor, could only be *jinkyo*, or empty-kidney disease, where the sex-addict husband has dried up his vital juices by over-spending (ch.7). And, when these stereotypes are actually mentioned, in almost all cases, the person and his or her condition become one. The above sex-addict is *a* dry-kidney (*jinkyo*), some one with large balls caused by lumbago is *a* lumbago (*senki*), one suffering from a restricted foreskin, *a* phimosis (echizen, from a province famous for spear-covers, *kawakamuri,* etc), maidservants from Sagami famous for being nymphomaniacs, simply *sagami*, and those known to be poltergeist from Ikebukuro, *ikebukuro*.

Coming on the tail-end of a millennium of poetry in a Sinosphere culture that preserved and built upon the past, much of the stereotype in senryu is inherited. I include legendary or literary figures with special characteristics or achievements, locations linked to certain events or modifiers through poetry (called *uta-makura* or "song-pillow") and all other trope about things that would be capitalized in English. To fully appreciate most *haikai* linked verse, one must be a walking encyclopedia of such. But senryu arose in a faddish era where people vied to be knowledgeable about the latest in Edo culture, and was itself one forum for being so. Naturally, that meant novelties were introduced that eventually became new stereotypes classic *haikai* scholars would not recognize.

How did stereotypes form? Karai Senryû did list some of the stereotypical characters (mostly blue-collar types) he was looking for in a poetic way toward the end of volume 2 of *Willow*, but that was long after they appeared in the *10,000 Ku*. The stereotypes would mostly seem to be spontaneously seeded and grown. We can imagine that first there was one *ku*. Whether its main idea came from the head of the poet, a Saikaku novel, the earlier *Mutamagawa haikai/ zappai,*[28] or an ukiyoe print, does not matter. It gets into print as a senryu. Some stop with that, remaining one-of-a-kind. Others are not alone from the start. There is a similar *ku* or two in the same volume. Or, in the next volume. That's all it takes to encourage others to put in their two-bits on the same subject. Before long, the common denominators work their own way out and evolve into a recognizable entity. And this occurs simultaneously with dozens, scores, and, eventually, hundreds if not thousands of ideas. Or, to use plainer metaphor, the content of most *ku* comes to coalesce more and more around a slowly growing number of themes, or stereotypes. At any rate, this process was helped by the removal of the *draws* from the published books and further encouraged by the increased popularity of dirty or obscene themes, where working a stereotype was less risky than writing something completely fresh, because one did not need to actually write out the obscene details when the readers already knew what they were (while Japan was far from Puritan, Confucian moralists occasionally had their way with authorities who cracked down on pornographic excess) and, the editors may have had a hand in this for poetry, unlike folksong, seems better, for the most part, when it does not depend upon words to be obscene.

As a caricature may pick up on more than one feature, some stereotypes are broad enough to include more than one characteristic. The always-interesting servant-maids (who deserve a book of their own), never to be confused with the palace chamber-maids or ladies-in-waiting, are one of two prime examples. They are unlettered, slow-witted, conceited, or clever but generally good-hearted in the clean half of senryu translated by Blyth and Ueno, and sex-loving but literally stinky sex objects in the other half, which I present. The other prime example, monks, are for the most part hypocrites in Blyth, but literal sodomists and ass-lickers in the senryu he called "unprintable." But, we see enough stereotype by way of example in this book – see the Table of Contents – so I will give no more examples here.

The need for short-form poetry to minimize word-waste and wit to play upon stereotype shake hands in senryu. If I have addressed *stereotype* at length it is because others, while mentioning it, have failed to give it sufficient space, perhaps because they feared that calling attention to the abundance of hackneyed themes would be tantamount to admitting one was about to waste the readers' time with a poetry that was worthless. Moreover, the anti-stereotype attitude is probably shared by most editors and critics of senryu in Japan who would agree with Ueda that senryu went downhill after the death of Karai Senryû when it became increasingly "over-intellectualized, pedantic, or enigmatic." To me, what grew naturally from the semantic ellipsis stereotyping allowed is not a *minus* or proof that senryu had taken itself into a dead end, but the natural flowering of a popular genre's development over time, and no more to be regretted or criticized than the cycle of life itself.

Or, to switch from ontogenetic to phylogenetic metaphor, we might say that like the long-haul of evolution, where fundamentally diverse possibilities are lost while the limited number of surviving ones diversify in wondrous ways, senryu's loss was also its gain. Stereotyping may be crude and distasteful. It may limit the imagination. But, actively pursued, stereotyping cultivates a fine eye for *the idiosyncrasies of type*, and when this goes on for decades, the end result is *a splendid gallery of types*. This is why senryu, for all its short-comings, is ideal for depicting selected parts of a singular culture during a period of history when Japan was famously isolated from the outside world. Late-period senryu may be "less poetical" (Blyth) than their exploratory predecessors, but many, perhaps most, of the senryu used as examples in the world's greatest dictionary, the *Nihon Kokugo Daijiten* (日本国語大辞典), which I call the OJD in this book, are late-period, which is to say, post-volume 24 (1791) of the *Yanagidaru*.[29] Not a few examples even come from the very late triple-digit volumes of the 1820's and 30's. May this not be considered objective confirmation of their value to Japanese culture, though not necessarily poetry?

There is one more factor contributing to the enigmatic stereotypes of late-period senryu – or, the tendency of senryu to become *trivia*, as a critic might put it – and that would be the extraordinarily high participant/reader ratio. With up to 60 *ku* published per page, a slim hundred page booklet could boast 6,000 *ku* and almost as many poet-readers. This could not have been matched in early-modern Europe with the greater length of the poems, higher cost of paper and, I dare say, lower rate of literacy. With the results of senryu contests, i.e., these books, printed month after month, year after year, for decades, we had hundreds of thousands of participant-readers familiar enough with senryu to enjoy making, or recognizing in the *ku* of others, minute additions, elabora-tions, changes and *subtractions.* By *subtraction*, I mean *ellipsis of the subject*, not grammatically speaking (for Japanese does not require a subject with active verbs), but *semantically speaking.* This allows the reader the pleasure of filling in the blank for himself. Obviously, such *ku* would make as little sense in translation as they do to Japanese who are not familiar with senryu. But, to criticize such *ku* for being enigmatic (i.e. unreadable by an outsider) is *wrong.* One might as well attack wit itself.

But *who cares about the minutia of inbred poetry?* That is a good question, a paraphrase of reasonable doubt about the value of senryu expressed by a friend. My reply is this: *I* like senryu though *I* am no lover of *trivia.* Proof? I have not subscribed to a newspaper for years and lived more years *without* than *with* a TV because, to me, 99% of the news is old. But, as the Japanese say, *ushi no kuso ni mo dan ga aru = Even cow pies are not uniform.* There is trivia and there is trivia. Only a fool would want to know the names of thousands of movies or even the capital of every country. Huxley was right to call those *"eaten up by an itch for mere facts and useless information . . . the wretched victims of a vice no less reprehensible than greed or drunkenness"* ("Accumulations" *On the Margin* 1923). But, I think it matters who first stuck a hard fist into the air when winning a sports competition rather than waving a hand, or corollary to that, who started doing the same (& shouting "yes") rather than squealing and jumping for joy as humans have always done, who first attached a pick-up to a guitar with no sound box, invented the frisbee, or proved that adding salt to sugar water would make it easier rather than harder to absorb. As to the value of the trivia in senryu, which is to say, *what is in this book*, that judgment is *yours,* not mine, to make.

collecting – a new angle on hyper-shortform poetry

While reasons may *justify* a position, they do not necessarily explain its origin. If my feelings about senryu differ from those held by others, it would probably be due to years of reading the major Japanese poetry anthologies, entire, starting with the oldest. Those intensive studies taught me that major innovation was much rarer than one might think from reading selections focusing on major poets, and that spotting minor novelties even a "specialist" might miss, if he tended to read selections rather than entire works, is surprisingly satisfying. Unfortunately, I lacked the memory to make something out of what I ostensibly learned, so all that remains now are vague recollections of the joy I felt, the many marks made in the few books I managed to keep with me, and the certain knowledge that there is more delight in *little things that are related* than commonly understood.

In retrospect, my delight may have been less that of a *reader* than of a *collector,* and I probably became one because of the unique character of Japanese poems: their *brevity*. While individual *ku* may, in the case of *haiku*, and sometimes, in the case of *senryu*, be enjoyed on their own merits, for many if not most *ku*, no small part of the pleasure felt by the enthusiast comes from placing it (their find) within a number of *ku* sharing the same theme (*seasonal* for haiku, *stereotypical* for senryu) or, perhaps, another property (Some collect haiku or senryu with onomatopoeia!). I would guess that most people who persevere in reading short poetry become serious collectors, because tiny things, whether stamps, sea shells or poems, may be gathered quickly and, once viewed together, one cannot help categorizing, comparing and contrasting them. Soon, we learn to seek details where we did not even recognize difference before. We begin to wish to round-out categories, wonder about yet-to-be-found sub-categories and dream of digging up missing links. We begin to appreciate examples for being rare, where someone who knew less might only find them ugly. We may rejoice simply because a poem, however poorly written, fills in a hitherto unnoticed lacuna. Such a reader-collector would not share a critic's low opinion of work not stunningly new. Rather, he would understand the advantage of working a stereotype – that addition and subtraction mentioned in the last section – over time to collectively gain a fuller picture of things. Each little poem is a puzzle to be fit into a larger overall puzzle. As crazy as this may sound, I only came to realize this when I began to select and translate haiku and senryu. It was not enough just to write them (I had written thousands in Japanese).

Being unschooled in literary criticism, I was not aware of just how *different* my method of selecting poems was until 2003, when I asked a Japanese editor and host of an online haiku forum for a blurb respecting my first book of translated haiku, *Rise, Ye Sea Slugs!* Astounded at my juxtaposition of famous and unknown poets, master-piece and found-piece, he (天気) called this 480-page book with almost 1000 holothurian haiku, "an exhibition" or a "museum of poetry." There, I was, wondering only whether anyone might notice the novelty of categorizing poems on a single theme in *metaphor-based chapters* – imperfectly, I am afraid, so perhaps it is good that no critics have noticed – and instead, was being credited with inventing a new way to *curate* literature, or at least one comprised entirely of short work. Would *museological* be the right word?

Whatever I managed to do, it just happened. Full coverage of limited themes (*sea cucumbers, flies, cherry blossoms*), meant paying close attention to *ku*, good or bad, *by anyone*. I even requisitioned a handful of *ku* from rejected entries for haiku contests on the web. One of those rejects was actually *very* good and probably misunderstood by the judge. But, most were not. I knew that, but felt it did not detract from their value for building what my *haiyû* (friend in haiku) would later call my "exhibition." I did not feel obliged to explain myself, for there were enough good *ku* in the book that I was confident only a fool would take umbrage at the poor ones that served to round-out the metaphors and put the other *ku* into context the better to appreciate them. This book of senryu is different in that not many, but *most* of the *ku* you will see are not only poor poetry but barely poems, yet, still, the *themes* are so interesting that I am not sure it matters!

But, lest I sell senryu short, let me add a few words more about why I find many fun even when they are "barely poems." It is not just the information and collecting suitability. It is the puns, the apparently clean but really dirty or the apparently dirty but really clean double-readings, the allusions and the joy of being able to answer the puzzle they pose or even the pleasure of knowing that I am not alone in not knowing for sure how to read the trickiest ones (I know because I read round-robins where Japanese themselves collectively admit defeat). You might think one would grow quickly bored with word-play, but such is not necessarily true. I find puns by the score, as one finds in Joyce, hard to chew, much less digest, but taken 17-syllabets at a time, they are a joy. One gets just enough pun and conundrum to chew a few times, swallow and reach for another helping. The fit of poetic style and length is so good that I would not be surprised if Japanese poems shrank over the millennia to fit the needs of a language whose syntax, phonology and system of writing combine to favor puns over rhyme.[30] By selecting excellent senryu that are, for the most part, relatively easy to translate because the humor is intrinsic to the content, previous translators have avoided the need to deal with the types of wit that are harder to re-create in translation than poetry. As I seem driven to try to bring as much of the original experience of senryu to the reader as possible, I am afraid I often attempt the impossible. To my mind, such failed attempts provide the context for appreciating the successes, and often have more to teach us about our language – in particular, what it lacks (a verb specific to love-cries, active-voice pronounless ambiguity, visual puns, etc.) – than successful translations do.

on doing the dirty stuff

> To be honest, I am grateful that Blyth *could* not and Ueda *would* not introduce the dirty stuff. That allows *me* to make a clean sweep of it. With haiku, Blyth and others, but mostly Blyth, have translated so many of the best ku, that one never knows when to quote him, with the risk of running into copyright infringements, or not quote him, with the risk of being thought ungrateful or worse. How relaxing, even luxurious, to select, translate and explain without giving a single thought to what another has, or might have done! So long as I stick to the real dirt, I need not raise my head, nor bow it.
>
> — Happy words from the first draft of the foreword.

Oscar Wilde once wrote of not reading a book before he reviewed it, lest he be prejudiced as to its content. He had a point, if nothing else, it does *complicate things* if you are an attentive reader capable of real discrimination, which was and still is not the case with most reviewers, for whom it makes little difference whether or not they read the book anyway. Lacking a broad context because they have not read enough other good books and sufficient depth because they have long since lost the desire and ability to stop and think – it is hard to find time to read when one is in demand and excessive facility with words can fool one into thinking one can think – they can only manage to praise and/or criticize the few things they understand, which probably have little to do with what really matters about the book.

In other words, writing *this* book became more complicated because there was *one* article out there, clearly about the type of senryu I would introduce. And it was one of only eleven "Works in English" in Ueda's Selected Bibliography:

> Solt, John. "Willow Leaftips." In Sumie Jones, ed., *Imaging/ Reading Eros*. Bloomington, Ind.: East Asian Studies Center, Indiana University, 1996.

My memory is as fuzzy as a puppy and equally playful, but knowing that senryu takes a long time to learn to read even for a Japanese, and vaguely recalling that John Solt, whom I had met in Japan in the early 90's because I helped with the translation of a book (*Learned Pigs and Fireproof Women*) by his friend, the great sleight-of-hand artist Ricky Jay, seemed far too involved with avant-garde poetry and arts to have even partially mastered the genre, I was puzzled to say the least. Being out in the sticks of Florida without a car, I had no way to get to the paper (first read at a conference on Japanese eros), so I asked the finest scholar of Japanese literature I know if he could find the time to locate and send me a copy, and the good professor wrote back that I should not bother for I surely knew far more about the subject than its author. Meanwhile, another younger, but likewise brilliant scholar, with a book recently out from Harvard, advised me that I really should see the same, though he did not have it at his fingertips. At this point, I wrote the author of the paper, and John, after considerable time had passed (he had been in the cultural gardens of Thailand), replied that he agreed with the professor that I need *not* see it; but, for better or worse, he was too late: someone else had located a copy and sent me a pdf which I had just finished reading and . . . – the rest of the story in a moment.

First, Blyth. True, under the Occupation, a Tokyo Court ruled in favor of the defendants in a case (参考：末摘花裁判) brought against the best of the dirty senryu anthologies, the *Suetsumuhana* (Englished as the *Safflower Princess* by Solt, and probably others, but, for brevity's sake called simply *Pluck* in this book) and the Occupation authorities did not over-ride them, but that would not mean "our" Censors would have permitted translation. Moreover, English language publishers were still not ready for it in 1960 and 1961, when Blyth's senryu translations were published. I do not know the situation in England or Australia, where people seem less hysterical about such matters, but, in the USA, the publishers did not *dare* to publish material as dirty as the aforesaid senryu until the late-1960's or 70's. So, what Blyth wrote about some senryu being *unprintable* because the *censors* would not allow it makes perfect sense.

Professor Ueda is another matter. I am a *tremendous* fan of his book *Bashô and His Interpreters – selected hokku and commentary* (1992) which I have praised to high heaven as the best book ever published about traditional haiku in two of my books on the same. But, his excuse for neglecting the earthy or obscene *senryû,* rightly or wrongly, strikes me as mildly disingenuous.

> Many of these senryû violate our sense of decency – or, at least, I lack the skill to translate them without perhaps offending some readers. – Makoto Ueda: *Light Verse from the Floating World*

With help from J. Michael Edwards (mentioned in his foreword), Ueda does the best job of re-creating wit in translation of Japanese poetry that I have ever seen. Amy Vladeck Heinrich's back cover blurb – "Ueda hits on such a perfect rendering, in colloquial English, that it is startling" – is true. Modesty is a virtue, but skill is no problem here. We are left to *guess* what the *real* problem is. Mine is that Ueda was 1) not well-versed in *obscene* senryû, which not only has its own argot but, but relies heavily upon ellipsis of the same in order to keep readers guessing, and/or 2) was *afraid.* With respect to 1), I confess there was a time in my life when I read many books of obscene senryû; but I cannot imagine a respectable scholar of Japanese with the time or inclination to do that. Indeed, Ueda's explanation for *"the beautiful wife / boiling his herb medicine / that doesn't work,"* namely, that it is "very likely the medicine is an aphrodisiac," shows that he did not recognize one of the top dozen or two stereotypes of dirty senryu, *empty-kidney*, where the husband is bed-ridden yet literally *semper paratus* so to speak (ch.7). So, he probably did lack something but it was less a matter of skill (the ability to translate well), than of comprehension or a lack thereof. With respect to 2), I can *sympathize* with his trepidation. We may no longer have censors and are free to publish whatever we want, but there are still "consequences," at least, in the United States of America.[31] With guardians of moral correctness lying in wait on the right, and political correctness on the left, a line about a pair of powerful fists in Tennessee Ernie Ford's *Ten Tons of Coal* comes to mind: *If one doesn't get you, the other one will.* Things were simpler in the merely hypocritical Victorian Era when Latin was one's ticket to all the obscenity one could possibly wish to read. But, am I wrong to want and demand *courage* from our learned professors in the face of philistine Christians and illiberal feminists? [32]

an introduction, defense and qualification of bareku.

There is much to be praised in Solt's presentation of a selection of *ku* from what may well be the dirtiest of the dirty senryu books, the 1835 *Yanagi no Hazue* collection, or "Willow Leaftips," which I abbreviate as *Leaf* in this book. For one, the man has chutzpah:

> Contemporary sensibilities may be offended by implications of sexism, classism, agism, or child abuse, but I present them anyway. Not to do so would be to indulge in self-censorship (which is one of the few indulgences that I do not allow myself). Solt:1996

I *like* that. Solt also laid down an indirect preventative defense against knee-jerk feminist critics by pointing out that the poems mis/treat both sexes equally:

> We discover not only the pathos of exploited women, but also of

> exploited men, such as those poems that refer to the Yoshichô district in Edo where women could buy male prostitutes, usually men in their early twenties who had been discarded as too old by their samurai lovers. Solt:1996

And, he notes the unsolvable problem of translating the various names for the male and female parts because "in our culture that politicizes the landscape of the body, connotations of cuteness and intimacy have for the most part been drained from words depicting the genitals." He is right, especially in respect to women. For all that rediscovery of "our body, our selves," we still have no word for the *cunt* that all would agree sounds sweet.

As far as I know, Solt was the first person to introduce the word *bareku* "literally 'violating propriety verse'" (破礼句) to English. He was right to use it to describe *the type of senryu* particularly common in *Leaf*, or *Pluck* (*Suetsumuhana*) – the term was used by Okada Hajime, the leading 20c scholar of senryu and is in common use today; but I would like to note that *bareku* was not used by Karai Senryû, himself, who called the verses he selected for *Pluck* the same thing they were called in *haikai,* namely *koiku* (恋句), or love/sex-*ku*. And, I would want to stress the fact that not just Karai Senryû's *Million-ku* series (1757-89) from which he selected the *Pluck* (1776-1801) *bareku,* but his (and his successors') most well-known collection, the *Yanagidaru* series that ran from 1765 to 1841, called simply *Willow* in this book and considered by all *the canon of the genre* we call *senryu* today, mixed *bareku* with clean *ku* from start to finish. (I am not contradicting Solt here, just shifting the stress a bit.) And, finally, it needs to be said that just as not all senryu are *bareku,* not all *bareku* are senryu, so it might be wiser for scholars to call them in English what I do, simply . . . *dirty senryu.*

> Bareku perform the important function of providing a literary corrective to some of the artistic conventions found in shunga ["erotic woodblock prints"] that otherwise might be interpreted as social conventions. Solt: 1996

We must read a wide variety of literature and see a wide variety of pictures to understand a society. Solt's example is *cunnilingus*, encountered more frequently in *Leaf* (and perhaps other books of dirty senryu) than in the spring-prints, as the erotic pictures were called. I decided to give cunnilingus, or "tongue-puppet" (*shita-ningyô*) as it was once, most delightfully, called, a short chapter in this book because I found Solt's point interesting, and, if truth be told, because I felt his command of senryû terms and Japanese sex-related slang in general was as weak as I had feared might be the case, and that meant that not a few of his 66 selected senryu, including a couple of those touching upon the subject in question, were a bit off. In other words, while his thesis had more than a measure of validity, some of the *ku* that seemed to concern cunnilingus among his translations actually did not. I wanted to set things straight. And, let me add that I do not mean to be critical (as I am with Ueda's reason for avoiding dirty senryu), just factual. Solt was not naive about what he was up against, either. He noted that even in the relatively less literary collection, parts of which he chose to translate, the *ku* were –

> subtle in expression and dense with literary allusions. They comprise a subgenre that requires familiarity with the vocabulary of the highlife and lowlife of a century and a half ago." (Solt: 1996)

Indeed. But he was unlucky enough to attempt his survey of *Willow Leaftips* just before some inexpensive popular books with easy-to-read explanations were published, and was simply not up to translating *ku* packed c̲ senryu argot. Perhaps, Ueda noticed some of Solt's mistakes and decided he best not risk doing the same. Then, again, maybe he did not, for the Japanese original, even Romanized, did not accompany the translations (the university publisher's editors' fault, not Solt's [33]), and *Yanaginohazue* itself was not included among Ueda's sources.

Finally, I must credit Solt's paper with correcting one mistaken impression I had long held about senryu. A month or so before reading it, the same learned and brilliant scholar who in a subsequent letter pooh-poohed senryu as trivia, wrote that he hoped I would hurry up, finish this damn book, and return to my higher literary endeavors (selecting, translating and explaining *haikai*) because senryu was "the type of thing a bunch of drunken men compose at a party that is better forgotten the next day." I reacted with, "What do you mean *drunken men in groups!* I've never heard of such a thing. Senryu were not impromptu doggerel. They were written alone and sent in for contests." For *most* senryu, what I wrote was probably true; but, reading Solt, I had to eat my hat.

> *Yanagi no hazue* was compiled from four poetry composition sessions ("kukai") in which participants gathered to compose senryû. [and later in the article] One can imagine that the poets, who were predominantly male, gathered, drank too much sake, laughed a great deal, and enjoyed literary parties using the medium of senryû to bond. Solt: 1996

At least one major work was composed largely as my friend had imagined. While I had read all of the *ku* in *Leaf* and noticed a higher proportion of simple, even boring *ku* (lacking second readings and puns) than usual, offset with an equally higher proportion of exciting, even shockingly direct *ku* than in the other collections of senryu, I naively attributed it to the editor, Senryû IV's taste. As Japanese would say, *naruhodo!* Drunken men. It had to be. (The same may explain the many free-wheeling *ku* in the proto-senryu *Mutamagawa*, which were selected from link-verse, though they were, on the whole, cleaner. Poetry composed on the spot has both pluses and minuses.) Yet, let me add that there is *another* genre with equally shocking (to most of us) direct dirtiness, with no relationship to either drunken composition or a mostly male environment: folk song.[34] I have slipped some good examples into the text to put senryu dirtiness into perspective.

And a final apologia

But, *caveat lector,* especially those of you who may not know that "lector" means "reader" and have read nothing bawdier than the *Ballad of the Sea Crabb* (that "catcht her by the cunt" and later joined it to her husband's nose). I am not joking when I say most *senryû* here will be *PG* and some even *X-rated,* which is to say as obscene as Martial, Rochester and honest-to-goodness cowboy songs.[35] John Solt stated what was what elegantly and diplomatically. I will be blunter. We encounter *bloody cunts* and *shitty cocks* and worse – for genitalia are but physical things – *some of the humor is pretty sick.* It is not as scurrilous as the *ad hominem* attack common to Classical and English poets who seem to have no shortage of enemies to insult by splicing them into their obscene poems (see examples of the latter in *Bawdy Verse: A Pleasant Collection*, ed. E.J. Burford), but it is still too noxious – or is it obnoxious? – to be excusable.

I know not how to excuse the manners of bad Romans and mad Englishmen, but senryu, like cowboy songs, came of age in a sex-starved culture of men. In the heyday of senryu, Edo was 60 to 80% male, due to the enormous number of samurai from the various *han* stationed – make that, held hostage – there without their families and the influx of male workers from the country to take advantage of its rapid growth into what had become the world's largest city.[36] As if this inequality was not bad enough, women were largely monopolized by the wealthy or otherwise privileged minority (Nobles from around Japan forced to stay in Edo[37] and the samurai serving them, local merchants, representatives of merchant firms from other parts of Japan on assignment without their wives, etc.). Women, excluding those married to nobles or samurai, who committed adultery at risk of their lives, could get *refreshment* (to borrow a Twainism) whenever they wanted it. They could experience the joys of motherhood, of being with little children. Men who were not wealthy, on the other hand, could not partake in refreshment unless they paid for it, and many could not afford to do that more than once in a blue moon, and at great risk for their *noses* (ch.5). Some were migratory workers, with wives and children back in the country, but all too many lived and died without ever enjoying fatherhood. So, when you run across misogyny, and other unkind humor in senryu, please bear in mind those circumstances.[38]

But, again, *what is the good in this? Why waste time on questionable poetry most Japanese would rather hide, on impersonal poems with little stylistic merit?*

First, let me give the arguments of others. R.H. Blyth, in his largest single book, *Japanese Life and Character in Senryu,* recommended reading senryu over haiku as "the best way" to know what is "the essential Japaneseness of the Japanese" for 1) more men appreciate humor than poetry, 2) senryu was good on things human, and 3) Japanese "are more human than most other featherless bipeds." (I am not sure I got the logic quite right, but the argument was odd to start with). Ueda, like Blyth, stressed the value of humor and analyzed it, but, as a modern scholar did not mention anything half so titillating as "essential Japanesesness." He soberly noted that "pre-modern senryu" contain "a good deal of insight into the society and people who produced it," who were of all classes but had a larger proportion of plebeians and, among them more lower status types, "including plasterers, fishmongers and day laborers," than the other plebian literary genres of the day. And, as mentioned, Solt posits the value of multiple information sources to counter misperceptions and form a balanced understanding.

As readers of my books already know, there is far more humor in *haikai* than generally realized, and it is a good bet that minor collections include as large a percentage of lumpen contributors as senryu, and as much local color, even if it is not that of the capital. But, senryu, for reasons explained in our discussion of *stereotypes*, may have polished this information particularly well, and, as a stand-alone hyper-short form, they present it in an exceptionally convenient way. Who needs to make *notes?* Senryu *are* notes. As mentioned previously, this would *seem* to be proved by the inclusion of so many senryu in Japan's, and, possibly the world's, best dictionary, what *I* call the OJD (日本国語大辞典) in this book.

And yet, it was probably not such *information* that Blyth was thinking of when he recommended senryu over haiku. His guts told him that *haute culture* is not the best way to translate hearts across the enormous divide between tongues/ cultures as exotic to one another as English and Japanese, for even when we share a language, emotions are not conveyed so much as *granted* to others on the basis of *a presumption of common humanity,* and this humanity of the other is most felt in the vulgar, for it, unlike specialized skills or more discriminating behavior, is something we can all grasp.[39] By *vulgar*, I do not mean only obscene things in the proper sense, such as the above-mentioned members filled or covered with yucky corporeal substances, but vulgarity in the broader emotional sense of unconcealed *pride, glee, greed, envy* or *hate*. The draws make it clear at a glance that description of raw emotion lies at the heart of senryu. Could *that* have been what Blyth was driving at when he oddly called the Japanese "more human" than the rest of us? There is no small irony here, for Occidentals have, since the 16c, observed that, for better or worse, Japanese repress their emotions,[40] while they are, at least in senryu, more honest about such feelings than we are, or, as P.D. reminds me, at least more open than the Englishmen of Blyth's era were, in poetry (*Punch & Judy* might be another matter!).

Notes の引き続き . . . *continued from page 13*

9. *Erotic Beginnings.* In case other Japanese were not conscious of the sexual implications of their myths of the beginning, the famous apostate Jesuit Fabian spelled it out. After pointing out how odd that a God with a halberd that dripping on the crotch of the letter 大 (for dainichi, "great sun/Japan") could make an island, had to subsequently thrust it down into the ocean and poke around on the seabed to find a foundation for more land, he concluded,

> What this is really about is something you and I would be embarrassed to even talk about, so let us skip the details. What is that halberd? What is that dripping substance. Please guess for yourself.

One can imagine the Jesuits laughing at the facility with which their rude young prodigy tore to pieces Shinto mythology and Buddhist theology and their shock – though they should have seen it coming – when twenty years later, he turned his rationalism on *Christianity*, two centuries ahead of Thomas Paine! You may find some more in *Topsy-turvy 1585* (2004), here, let me note only that the island in question, according to Fabian, was called Awaji-shima, and the *awa* is homophonic with foam, which can also mean scum, and I cannot help but think that is what inspired the following senryu from *Leaf:*

はね後架浮島に成るちぎれ糞　葉六
hanekôka ukishima ni naru chigire-kuso
(rebound wc floating-isles-into become loose-shit)

shit floating
in splash-back crappers
baby islands

This *ku,* representative of *Leaf's* best, fit no chapter and was doomed to wait for another book until these notes found it a place. For ten years, I used *just such a hole* over a cesspool. Luckily, the glop was low enough that splashes rarely reached me, but the stench was so bad I kept a clothespin by the door. Come to think of it, had I read Leupp (*Male Colors*) – trying to find a *reason* for the sodomy-friendly culture of old Japan, he pointed out that the mythology is rare for its literally excremental fertility – earlier, I might have been able to put it into the chapter on bonzes. (The Sundry ch 29 was conceived even later.)

10. ***Amano-Uzumenomikoto's Striptease.*** is often related to the etymology of 面白い (*omoshiroi*: interesting), literally "face-white," coming either from Uzume's invention, make-up, necessary because, with the Sun inside the cave, she had to be seen by starlight (I have read that *cosmology* and *cosmetics* were related, but how about this!) or from the bright faces of the gods illuminated by the emerging Sun. (★Rereading my observation on striptease drawing something *out* of a hole, it *just* dawned on me that, considering the debate on the sex of the Sun God/dess over the course of Japanese history, She could be seen as the *glans* penis and the cave its foreskin, in which case the striptease . . .)

11. ***Izanagi and Izanami.*** If you have missed the charming, childish exclamations about an extra part and a missing one it is because most translations of the encounter between Izanagi and Izanami leave it out, use euphemism or hide it in Latin. Victorian era translations are still copied by people who do not read Japanese, and Japanese, who might complain, are still ashamed because "we" taught them to be. A black blues song (I heard on the blues channel on a 440-channel cable radio in Japan) independently came up with the same idea. *Adam has a thread end left hanging while Eve has a seam left un-sewn!*

12. ***Obscene 16c.*** I can only guess about what gave rise to so many dirty haikai. The end of a long warring era broke down social mores? Increased international intercourse and trade? The rise of literacy in new classes of people? Poets fighting for attention?

13 ***Inu-tsukuba-shû.*** Blyth (JLCS) goes so far as to say the editor of this raucous anthology, Yamazaki Sôkan (1458-1546), "may be thought of as the founder of haiku, senryû and *kyôka* (comic *waka*)." As far as haiku go, I prefer to credit Sôgi (1420-1502). If the reader is a scholar who finds this hard to believe, please check out the 100 *ku* by Sôgi included among the 3000-odd haiku in *Cherry Blossom Epiphany* (2007, equinox).

14. ***Bashôism Damage?*** See part V (*The Bashôism Problem*) of the preface to *The Fifth Season* (2007). Issa, &, later, Kyoshi, unwittingly provided perfect examples of the harm.

15. ***Sôgi, Haiku & Hokku*** (A comment for those serious about haiku). I use the word *haiku* rather than *hokku* deliberately. Many if not most of Sôgi's 15c *ku* that I have translated are definitely not *hokku,* for a *hokku* was supposed to have certain qualities making it a good start for a sequence. Though most of these were published as *hokku* in an early 17c book with *hokku* in its title (「発句帳」 古典文庫 456), they include many of the sort found in mid-sequence of linked verse called *hira-ku* (平句 plain or peon *ku*) or *tada-ku* (只句 simply *ku*). Obviously, not only '*hokku* for instruction' were compiled. Shiki (1867-1902) was right to make or adopt the use of the term *haiku* as a grab-bag for all of these, and note: he includes *hundreds* if not *thousands* of Sôgi's *ku* in his twelve-volume categorical anthology, 分類俳句全集 *bunrui haiku zenshû, still* the largest collection of *ku* ever printed. Use *haiku,* and leave the word *hokku* to specialists (though they over-use it, too, for the same reason we over-use "bawdy" – the word sounds classy)!

16. ***Regional as a Broader View?*** With many regions and one capital (Edo *was* senryu), a regional view of poetic development is a broad one. *The Distinct Brilliance of Zappai: and the Need to Reconsider its HSA Definition* by Richard Gilbert and Shinjuku Rollingstone (on line at *Simply Haiku,* spring 2005) is worth a slow read, though it comes down a bit too hard on those who use *zappai* in a derogatory sense, when one considers the fact that most of it *is* shallower than most post-Bashô *haikai/haiku,* a serious art-poetry born of what might be called a longer-winded discipline. But, I agree with Gilbert and SR that *zappai* includes more of literary value than Tokyo leads us to believe. For example, the zappai *ku* on pg. 428 (from Suzuki, who was more concerned with the content/sex than the form), shows a use of the *maeku* far more intelligent than anything Karai Senryû did. With respect to the development of senryu, however, I would like to set some things straight. 1) *Mutamagawa* was *not*, strictly speaking made from *tsukeku* split from *mae-kuzuke* competition. Participants in the *tentori* (point-taking)-*haikai* link-verse composed *ku* when their turn came in a fixed sequence. Later, their *ku* were judged against other participants' responses, not made to the same *mae-ku,* but to whatever preceded *them* in the sequence. Because they were judged for the excellence of their response to the previous *ku*, their *ku, as a response*, was indeed a *tsukeku,* but it was *also* the *maeku* for the next person's *ku,* which could be considered its *tsukeku* and so forth down the line (That is why some of the *Mutamagawa ku* are 7-7 and some 5-7-5. And, it is why, some of the *Mutamagawa ku* leave even experts stymied as to what the poet was driving at, and the editor, Kei Kiitsu, himself, admitted to reservations about his publishing them out of context, while Karai Senryû's *Yanagidaru,* where the idea was to create and choose stand-alone *ku,* is easier to read *if* only one knows the argot and stereotypes, as I discuss in the text. If you do *not* know them, *Mutamagawa* may be easier to read). I take pains to point this out because it shows how *haikai's* influence on senryu was not only via the use of *maeku-zuke* for practice and the *zappai* contests it spawned. Also, 2) Karai Senryû abandoned *maeku* much later than usually realized, continuing to use them for soliciting purposes, but just not printing them with the *tsuke-ku.* And 3), the worst obscenity and the nearly identical verses, etc. did not wait for the use of *kudai* ("set topics"). You find them from early on. According to the editors of the *Senryû-Zappai-shû* (「川柳雑俳集」日本名著全集: 1927), there were about 500 *ku* in Senryû's *Willow* very similar to ones found in the *Mutamagawa.* Indeed, my impression is that the *Mutamagawa* has more off-color material than its supporters, who tend to dislike senryu obscenity, like to admit.

17. ***The 1692 Maekuzuke Contest.*** The earliest *mae-ku* or *draw* I have seen that resembled the 7-syllabet (x2) senryu draw is in the *Haikkai Yosedaiko* 俳諧寄太鼓 , dated 1701 (examples given in the explanation 解説 of the Iwanami classic *Senryû, Kyôka-shû*). The earlier examples were real 7-7 *ku* of the sort one finds in *haikai* link-verse sequences and which are published as separate poems in the *Mutamagawa*. It would be interesting to learn what exactly the draws (*mae-ku*) were in that popular 1692 contest.

18. ***Koso-sure Draw***. The first draft of the *Introduction* had almost nothing on draw-verses. Then, rereading Ueda, I saw: *"it goes on forever" (tsuzuki koso sure)* repeated twice, followed by *"because of the blossoms / another visitor today / at this grassy hut (hana yue ni kyô mo kyaku aru kusa no io)."* Ueda said the simple *maeku*, published in 1702, gave "maximum freedom to each prospective entrant's imagination," but I, not lacking an imagination, had trouble connecting the draw to the *ku*. So, I redid it in a way that made sense: (*Let it go on!*) *Because of the blossoms, today, too, my hut has a visitor.* Further study made it clear that the grammar would *not* support my "Let it" idea, but that *koso sure* was indeed far more subtle than Ueda's simple reading let on. It means that whatever is mentioned is how something might appear to be, *but*. It calls for a response that is fitting yet contradicts it. Here, the scene is so beautiful, you'd think the blossoms would bloom forever and the hut could be a place of conviviality rather than loneliness. So I thought some more and came up with *You'd think it would go on!* Then, I checked other examples of *koso sure* to be sure I was not deluding myself, and the result was a new awareness of the trickiness of the draw, which I, then, felt obliged to share.

19 *Cause for Sex of Child: Senryu Roots.* *" < That's pushing logic > The lack of a prick, he tries to stick upon his wife"* is an early mid-18c senryu (*Million*). In the early-16c *Inu-Tsukuba-shû*, ed. by *haikai* master Sôkan, we find the following 7-7 + 5-7-5 sequence:

.

あながちなりと人や笑はん *anagachi nari to hito ya warawan*
まふくるも又まふくるも女子にて *mô fukuru mo mata mô kuru mo onago nite*

when it keeps happening
men will indeed laugh
◆
again & again
once again the outcome
is a baby girl

when the cunt triumphs
men will indeed laugh
◆
again & again
once again the outcome
is a baby girl

The adverb *anagachi,* "generally," starting the *maeku* (not *draw* but *pre-verse* for *haikai?*) is a homophone for "hole-win," or, so it becomes after the 5-7-5 is read. The husband is being laughed at for being pussy-whipped, though not in the meaning of the English expression! (&, from this logic, had Macbeth's wife been Japanese, her "undaunted mettle" would have born "nothing but" *fe*males!) Is it not fun to compare the different attitudes – the older one conscious of a public, the newer one a private debate? While continuity in theme from haikai to senryu is obvious, we need many more comparisons to claim this (public ⇒ private) was a pattern. It could be the opposite. (上記の和文は西沢 1985 より)

20. *Sundry Forms with Draws.* With *kamuri-zuke or kasa-zuke* the first 5 syllabets of one's poem come from another. I practice, or rather, have for years *played* a related form (in Japanese, on the internet) where *something* from the last part of another's *ku* is taken for the start of the next *ku.* Because, beginnings and ends of sentences tend to be different, one usually cannot put the entire last 5-syllabets of the previous *ku* into one's own, but enough is taken that the form is called *shiri-tori,* literally "rump-taking." I supposed it could be called capping tails or simply *rumping*. What I would like to see, would be *kamuri or kasa-zuke* where the first 5 syllabets were taken from fine old haiku.

古池や *The old pond –*

けふも数へる日なた亀 *Today, too, i count turtles sun-bathing.*
ここにすむ亀いくつ代 *How many generations of your turtles?*
時おり礫なげてもらふ *I'd hire a boy to chuck in a random stone.*
我借景になる太郎ヶ礫 *The stone-throwing boy improves it for me.*
老犬生きているかごと *Like an old dog, you wonder if it's alive.*
浮キ抜音も河童の屁 *Things are quiet even when it farts.*
白鷺も息ころしけり *A great white egret also holds its breath.*
水泳プールどうおもう *What do you think about swimming pools?*

I would bet my *shirikotama* that this sort of thing is old. The only trouble with it is that haiku often start with a seasonal term, so there are thousands starting with the exact same 5 syllabets. In my New Year haiku selection, *The Fifth Season*, the index shows 64 *ku* starting *ganjitsu ya* (one of many names for NY day) and in *Cherry Blossom Epiphany*, 28 *ku* start with *yamazakura* (mountain and/or wild-cherry/cherries [bloom or tree, not fruit]). I never thought of it before, but seasonal-terms = *kigo* might be considered "draws." Obviously, old haiku used for the type of contest I envision would have to avoid starting with a common seasonal theme alone!

21. *Draw Contest Taxonomy.* Kyoto and Osaka were said to have adopted it from inventive *haikai* teachers in the outlying provinces, but, as the editors of the Iwanami Senryû-kyôka-shû admit, the first examples given show *maeku*/draws that are more or less identical to what one finds in linked-verse (*renga*), so the main innovation would have been in the unlinking of the verse and not the draws *per se*.

22. ***Frost Allusion.*** "Poetry is what is lost in translation." For more discussion, see *A Dolphin In the Woods* (2007 or 2008: proofing etc. for this book has eaten up too much time).

23. ***Surveys of Mae-ku.*** I have not found them, but the time I have spent researching senryu is miniscule compared to the time I have spent reading senryu. Indeed, I have not read a single book *about* senryu, as opposed to *of* senryu. I can only say that no one who *has* that I queried thinks it has been done.

24. ***Millions of ku.*** The figure for *ku* judged given in Iwanami's *Senryû Kyôka Shû* is 2,300,000 (in Japanese, 230,0000, or 230 man), but I have more than once come across the figure of three million. And when you recall that Senryû was not the only judge out there, you get an idea of how big the poetry games must have been.

25. ***Senryû's Editor***. Karai Senryû prepared the draws and selected good/winning *ku* from the entries, but for *Willow*, (first vol.1765) at least, Goryôken Arubeshi selected *ku* from those *ku* selected by Senryû he felt most suitable for being read without the *maeku,* or draw. He clearly explained that policy in a preface. Senryû's work as a judge by itself was legendary. Imagine holding thrice monthly contests, selecting hundreds of winners from thousands or tens of thousands of entries and putting them into print ten days later, and this for six-months a year for decades – *that* is a galley-slave! Yet, it is likely senryu would not have become *the* name for the genre without that editor to whom Ueda (1999), in his introduction, gives over a page of well-deserved attention. However, Ueda and others need to give more – or at least *some* – attention to what Senryû and Goryôken's precursor, Kei Kiitsu, did. His *Haikai Mutamagawa* (first vol. 1750) was the first substantial stand-alone *ku* collection with an urban senryu-like touch to be published as a book and it was a big step in bringing us closer to both senryu and haiku as we know them. (But I would not go as far as some *Mutamagawa* fans do in crediting it for being the first book of *haikai* with stand-alone ku that were not *hokku* for reasons given in note 15 and the next note.)

26. ***From Haikai to Haiku.*** I have yet to read a convincing account of the birth of the individual *ku* as a literature. The first are said to be booklets of *hokku* for students of link-verse, but seeing the examples in the *Hokkuchô* (see n.15, above), I find it hard to believe it stopped at that. Then, we see stand-alone *ku* in *saijiki*, from the mid-17c which, while instructional, are also good reading (where do we draw the line between instruction and literature?). I do not know if anyone has checked to see whether those *ku* were all *bona fide hokku* or included some/many that were not. In the early-18c, the school of Bashô's student (but independent from the start, so the usual word "disciple" seems odd to me) Kikaku is said to have published stand-alone *ku* and, content-wise, Kikaku wrote many *ku* that might even be considered senryu even when Bashô was still alive.

27. ***The Neglected Stereotype.*** Willow began to collect *ku* without using a draw in 1787, twenty years after it began. By this time, most of the main stereotypes in senryu were already well-solidified. As the society evolved, this meant a sort of literary subculture had developed. After this, most solicitations were probably – my studies of this are only starting – by subject (*kudai* 句題). Since these subjects tended to be stereotypes themselves, this discouraged the natural conception of new stereotypes, but, helped round out those already begun. After senryu renewed in the Meiji era, magazines called for a broader variety of subjects or left it up to the poet. In other words, senryu never settled on an order – which could have been around stereotypes or could have emotions – such as we find in the haiku *saijiki*. Let me give two examples. In a book of sexy senryu titled simply *enku* (艶句 erotic ku) published in 1962 that supplies the condom *ku* for the only modern chapter of this book, the senryu are arranged by Okada Hajime as follows:

◎ *Adolescence: pubescent awakening, bachelorhood, dating* ◎ *Marriage:engagement, the first-night, new living conditions* ◎ *Family: married love, birth & children, contraception, discord and divorce, as the years pass;* ◎ *Seasons: new years, spring, summer, fall, winter [note: five seasons]* ◎ *The Body: entire, head, upper body, lower body;* ◎

Personal Life: clothing, food and drink, dwelling; ◎ *Social Life: work place, profession, places, things, entertainment.*

The other book is one of a series of best-selling books of *Sarariman* (salary-man: white-collar workers) senryu published by Japan's largest publisher (Kôdansha: 1997) and backed by one of its largest life-insurance companies:

哀 Sad, Pitiful, Unrelenting (among the 25 categories: middle-aged men, one-sided love, over-work, reality, child-rearing, last-train, making it, retirement pay, commuting, post-bubble(economy), my home, my workplace); 楽 At ease, Without worries (among the 32: after-five, dozing-off, parties, smoking stations, no smoking, a man after-five (with bar-maids etc?), sekuhara = sexual harassment, travel, irresponsibility); 嘆 Complaining, Helpless (29: analog-minded, fear of OA, keyboards, stress, productivity, daughters); 耐 Enduring, Putting up with (30: bosses, internal revenue, serving tea, strong wives, losing it, overtime, longevity, working in pain, window-seat (pre-retirement lame-duck worker); 呆 Beyond Help (love, heavy make-up, telephone lies, English lessons, money, presents, kanji (Chinese characters), wrinkles, diets, life-plans, tardiness; 超 Overcoming, Beyond words (building a house, meddling, the male mind, match marriages, karaoke, gyaru (girl: sassy young things), diagnosis, workaholicism, big families, new-workers, generation gap, shaved eyebrows (young men do it!), wives drinking, nature, shakey-voiced calls, grandchildren.) 『平成サラリーマン川柳傑作選七光り』 山藤章二 他

The second book does take a stab at emotion-centered major categories, but things are still pretty confused. You can see why I stick with old senryu and haiku.

28. *Mutamagawa Ku in Yanagidaru.* The editor of the *Senryû Zappai-shû* (1927) wrote that he easily found 440-450 *ku* that were identical or almost identically written or perfectly identical in their meaning. He said a more careful reading would raise that to over 500 identical *ku* but he need not give examples, for this and that magazine had many articles on this. Though the *Mutamagawa* (1750 ~) began fifteen years before Willow (*Yanagidaru* 1765 ~ 1841), most of the early *Yanagidaru* comes from Senryû's *Million-ku* (*Mankuawase* 1757 ~ 1789) , which started four years before the *Mutamagawa* series ended, so there may be some copying going the other way and both may be copied from a common haikai renga, or written by the same person, etc.. The difference between similar *ku* – what I call "paraverses" – Willow *ku* tend to 1) add information to fill the extra 5 syllabets ; 2) make a simple sentence-like ku into something more aphoristic and 3) find a wittier way to say something. On the whole, they improve.

29. *Statistics on Example Ku* in the OJD (*Nihon Kokugo Daijiten* 日本国語大辞典). The website for the online version gives the number of poems cited from the various waka anthologies and canons of literature such as the Tale of Genji, or more recently, Soseki's various novels, but fails to provide information on senryu and zappai. When I was still in Japan I called the editorial section and was left with the impression that the current editors do not appreciate what the last generation did. It is easy to boast about classics, but senryu . . . I will add statistics to a subsequent edition *if* I can find them.

30. *Why Japanese Poems Shrank.* Yet Chinese has end-rhyme *and* many short poems.

31. *Consequences in the Land of the ~~Free~~.* Indeed, Solt lost his position at a good university partly because he was savaged by a Christian member of a board of trustees who took umbrage at the sex. While I have received enthusiastic support from one female editor in California (see Acknowledgment), my mother, despite having been hip from before the hippies and interested in bawdy literature (esp. Shakespeare's body-words), was very upset with my liberal use of the C word and, as I write, worries about the consequences of publishing this book on my future. Who knows! As the Third Millennium starts, Usania is clearly insane. People are horrified not just of obscenity but completely innocent words. There are those who would prefer to step in *dog shit* than be warned of it (*Honest to God!* In Columbus, Ohio, I was chewed out for using the "s word," warning my nephew of it.) This piddling word, regardless of context, is thought to be *so evil*, *so damaging* that a regulatory agency can fine radio stations up to $100,000 for a slip of the tongue. "Shit happens!" *Indeed.* Meanwhile, we have whole communities where *most* men and many women pepper every sentence with *real* expletives. Stand-up comics on cable TV compete to gross-out their audience with dirty words and pantomimed sex of all varieties. *Bipolar* is the term that comes to mind.

▲ ***An independent classicist*** living outside the USA informs me that "many American scholars have written marvelous articles on and editions of Greek and Latin writers of smut," so my sympathy/worries are out of date. *I wish it were true.* But, if I am not mistaken, classicists are a extraordinarily enlightened breed of scholar and the classic world gets away with things no other culture is allowed – eg., those nude statues (though some complain about them, too) granted exemption from the usual public censorship. Classicists do not run our universities where academic server-based e-mail programs often insist upon automatic checking of bad words for fear the administrators will be sued for something you write (this began in the 1990's); they do not control the mass media (television and radio, using what was once the public airwaves, and major magazines and newspapers) which operate in terror of enormous fines for words that would surely be considered innocuous in any reasonable nation-state. At this time, it is hard to tell whether Usania – as I call my country, for it has no right to sole ownership of "America" – will ever collect/correct itself and regain its sanity.

32. *Philistine Christians and Illiberal Feminists*. Don't get me wrong, not all Christians are prudes and not all feminists language gestapo. The first person to appreciate Mark Twain's obscene writing was one Rev. Joseph Twichell, pastor of the Asylum Hill Congregational Church of Hartford; and we all know hearty, open-minded feminists.

33. *All the More So for University Presses!* All publishers of translated poetry from an exotic tongue *have an obligation* to publish *at least* a Romanization of the poem, better yet, the original. I can think of only one book (including my own) with a significant number of Japanese-English or English-Japanese translations that I have read without finding errors (its translated poems had all been translated many times).

34. *Japanese Dirty Folk Song*. Japanese in the late-20c generally believed traditional ditties were wholesome, while sexy ones were rare and probably examples of change-songs (*kae-uta*), or parodies. This is a natural assumption, as most Japanese know a number of dirty versions of folk or popular numbers (eg. *Seven Colors of the Rainbow* 七色の虹 turned into seven-colored *panties*, a trip *All the Way to Hakodate* はるばる函館まで ending, up mired in what Shakespeare called country matters, etc.) – but, according to Takenaka Rô, a man who traveled the country doing thorough research on the roots of Japanese folksong, this ain't so (たけなか・ろう『にっぽん情哥行』ミュージック・マガジン 1986). The majority of folk-songs (民謡) were *originally*, I repeat, *originally* bawdy, and the clean versions came *later*. In other words, they were Lomaxed over the past 150 years or so. I believe him, because most of the clean folksongs are *boring*; and only smug-faced culturally insecure middle-class and nouveau riche moderns – it is amazing how similar they are throughout the world! – are content with boring lyrics (and music). The great number of change-songs for pop hits in Japan would seem to reflect an unconscious effort to return to the still recently cut-off folk roots. We will see some of Takenaka's examples of the real folk music in this book when they touch upon one of our themes.

35. *Honest-to-goodness Cowboy Songs.* I doubt if one of a thousand of my readers has ever come across *raw* lyrics of the type found in Guy Logsdon's *"The Whorehouse Bells Were Ringing and Other Songs Cowboys Sing"* (University of Illinois: 1989). If you find the sort of poems *Japanese* bachelors could write eye-popping, be sure to peek at this book to see what "ours" sang. There is a tendency to equate bowdlerism with the Victorian era, but it was still very much alive in the 20c. For example, our most well-known collector of folk-songs, changed *"she could fuck and she could suck"* into *"she could smile and she* *could chuckle,"* and *"to slip it up her water works"* to *"I'll carry her to my dugout."* I suppose censorship once could have been justified as an incentive for boys to study their Latin so they could share all the juicy stuff with their professors, who thought readers of the vulgar tongue could not handle vulgarity.[A] My main quarrel with the Establishment of then and now is that I cannot abide dishonesty. I could forgive Lomax had he only prefaced his anthologies with something like this –

> The world of the real folk is not allowed into print by the prudes in charge of the nation, who believe that anything below, and including, the navel must not see print in any language the common man &/or woman) can read. Unwilling to risk our reputations, not to mention imprisonment, we collectors must offer you a deformed picture of folk reality or none at all.

Instead, the scholar helped create the Roy Roger reality of the so-called Golden Days of the American century, as artificial a creation as any of the virtual realities we see today, but far more ambitious an undertaking for an entire nation was stuffed into it.

> ***A. Re. Paternalistic Old-school Intellectuals.*** I would have written more, but it has been said already and better than I could say it:
>
> The first duty of a modern editor of early literature is to reproduce the old texts without bowdlerizing or omitting verses because they use language unacceptable to the unco guid or deal with sexual activities in explicit terms. Gone are the days when such were regarded as tidbits to be privately published in small editions for the delectation of the few wealthy cognoscenti, or printed in a foreign tongue - usually Latin - so that ordinary men or women could not read them even if they had access to them. Moreover it is not fair that only classical scholars should enjoy the privileges denied to ordinary people. These ballads and verses have therefore been chosen because they reflect the standpoint of those ordinary people who were our ancestors, and are in the language used and understood by them. (*Bawdy Verse* ed. E.J.Burford (Penguin, 1982) *Buy it!*).

36. *Edo's Population Guestimate.* The figures vary by decade and time of year. I have not found any from the heyday of senryû (late-18c) but decades ahead and after.

37. *Forced to Stay?* The thousands of nobles, tens of thousands of their samurai and hundreds of thousands (?) of their help from all around the nation were said to serve as hostages discouraging revolt/civil-war, while the cost of maintaining that presence and parading back and forth every year supposedly prevented the accumulation of provincial wealth and potential competition with the central power. This and the fact all big growing cities draw men as they are more mobile (and expendable) than women explain the gap.

38. *Sad Circumstances of the Men in Edo & the Nature of Senryu*. I leave the analysis of senryu humor to others, but Peter Dale found something too good to keep to myself: *'The secret source of humour is not joy but sorrow; there is no humour in heaven.' Pudd'nhead Wilson's New Calendar*. And, add to that the joy of living in the exciting capital of the world and we see why exuberance *also* bubbles over in senryu.

39. Emotions *Granted* to Others. This is taken almost word for word from *Orientalism & Occidentalism – Is the Mistranslation of Culture Inevitable?* It is the gist of what my seven books published in Japan/ese conveyed. The idea that low culture, not *opera* or *kabuki* brings understanding may also be found in Ricky Jay: *Learned Pigs and Fireproof Women*, when he discusses the Japanese Pêtomane (he played the flute by cutting cheese).

40. *Repressing Emotions.* Even the Jesuits, known for their superb discipline (the English called it *duplicity* and *guile,* but England was at war with Catholics) were awed by Japanese mental reserve. But, to a degree, the difference was Sinosphere vs. the Occident and it has been best expressed by Mendez Pinto, who felt "we" acted like out-of-control children compared to the Chinese and Japanese. (See *Topsy-turvy 1585* (2004))

~ *qualifications and continuing questions* ~

★After writing the *Foreword*, I reread Okada's dirty *Million* selection and found myself adding dozens of *ku* to this book. I also realized that many of the stereotypes I imagined *evolving* were *borrowed whole* from *haikai* and/or coalesced much more rapidly than I had thought. Someday, if I can afford the 13-volume Yanagidaru anthology that continues to book 167, I *may* be able to come up with definitive things to say about the evolution of senryu but, as it is, I must take my first analysis as I do that of others (esp. parroted putdowns of late-period senryu by people with precious little reading hours), with a grain of salt. Reading *all* the haiku by Issa and Shiki *start to finish* taught me that one cannot differ judgment to specialists (The late *ku* of the former were given short shrift and the "objective" *ku* of the latter exaggerated attention). The same probably holds true for senryu, but I am afraid my reading is still too incomplete to allow for authoritative statements.

★★ ***Is There Anything Beyond the Pale?*** While perhaps the dirtiest *genre* of literature in the world, senryu only grosses us out or angers us. It rarely horrifies. I refrain from quoting De Sade's *Justine* and *120 Days of Sodom* or Aleister Crowley's *Necrophilia!*

★★★ ***Limited Listing.*** If the added sections on the draw, listing and collecting were not already too long for what is supposed to be a light book, we would have also discussed the following: 1) *mono-awase*, "matching things," and *awase-mono*, "things-matched," from nature's scents, roots and shells to human artifacts like poems and songs. Pigeot thought matching helped prepare the ground for the birth of Shônagon's miscellaneous lists. 2) Some of the limited listing in the *Manyô-shû* and other ancient Japanese poetry/song anthologies. Tending to be religious, they list awe-provoking places, metaphors for this transient world (bugs crying in withering woods, flashes of lightning on fall fields ready for harvest, morning glories shrivelled up before knowing evening dew, . .) etc. as Christians in Europe would later do the same in paintings of "Vanities" (chess-boards and skulls and spilled glasses and flowers, etc.). (In 20c Usania we have all come across *"Love is ~"* listings; again, a single item fixation). 3) Examples of *mono-wa-zuke* (物付), an open-ended (for there is no one right answer) riddle game linking listing and the draw popular in Edo in the 1740's (shortly before the *Mutamagawa* proto-senryu anthology was published), where prizes were given for the wittiest answers about some of the same types of things (eg. "red things," "white things") we have discussed, but not in poetry form. 4) Listing in songs (not just counting).

★★★★ ***How Free Was Japan?*** According to Blyth (1960), draw-verse and capped-verse contests were *outlawed* during the Kyôhô era (1716-35) because they became such a big "racket." The word "racket" suggests that too many poor would-be-poets were being bilked out of their hard-earned money by the *Maekuzuke* promotors. It is delightful to think there so many word-lovers that poetry could become a racket, but this is decades before senryu. ◎There would be occasional suppression by authorities when senryu stepped on *their* toes. I recall reading somewhere, perhaps Ueda, that a *ku* (which I have seen, for it was a remake or reprint of an older one) where the clutching reflex of baby hands was said to start early for children of officials (as if to say *gimme! gimme!* a bribe), was censored but, otherwise, senryu was free to wag its poison tongue even where religion – criticism of which could cost one's life in Europe where even apostasy was a capital crime – and revered historical figures were fair game. Confucian moralists *did* made *some* effort to clean things up every few decades, but the censorship was never so thorough as in much of the West, so poets could pretty much be as dirty as they desired (with some limits, just what I have never figured out) until the so-called Tenpô Era (1830-43) Reforms, which even saw ancient stone statues of literally loving gods removed from their time-honored locations by roads. Soon, this repressive mood was given material and moral support by Christian nations with their blue law mentality. When Perry "opened" Japan, his sailors were delighted with the dirty picture books Japanese fishermen threw into their ships but their officers and ship-borne clergy only thought it proved Japanese were damned. So, to gain "our" respect, the Japanese had to become *pruder than thou* and this charade, which received a booster shot by the Occupation, became real (in much of the country), and continued into the 1990's. In the 70's, when I first lived in Japan, dirty senryu were not burned (as, books of biology are in parts of Usania), but were still clearly *marginalized.* Excluded from 20c anthologies by leading publishers and only available in old books lacking the notes most readers need for comprehension, they only barely survived, thanks to the perseverance of small publishers and one man, 岡田甫 Okada Hajime, and all he inspired. With increased toleration for the obscene in the late 1980's, by the mid-1990's, when pubic hair was finally permitted in photographs and movies, mass market (cheap) books with the real thing fully explained were finally published and available at major bookstores. Today, dirty old senryu is no longer an endangered species of literature.

to be blunt – a word about cunt
A • P • O • L • O • G • I • A

Mon cher lecteur, pardonnez-moi la propriété de cette expression; et convenez qu'ici comme dans une infinité de bons contes . . . le mot honnête gâterait tout.'

Dear reader, I beg your pardon for the (im)propriety of this expression, and hope you will agree that here, as in an endless fund of good stories . . . .the proper/decent word would ruin everything. – Denis Diderot (*Jacques le Fataliste* 1796: trans. Peter Dale)

注 Dale, who knows I value transparency, explains: "The problem is that word 'propriété', where Diderot is playing on the dual sense of propriety (what is proper to the truth, to a thing) and propriety, what social custom deems as sayable."

I realize you are writing for Americans. English and Australians don't have that much trouble with 'cunt', any more than the French have with 'con'. You can say, over the table, 'ah he's a lovely old cunt', and the sense is complimentary. (Peter Dale, correspondence)

While no one minds what I call the *male* sex, the *female* counterpart is another matter. Women have their guards up. I do not want to hurt the sensibilities of any readers, who, like my mother, find the c word offensive, but see no way to avoid it. The word is made for senryu because it is the same length as *cock*, that is, only one syllable, and consonant. While I may use the equally compact *twat* and *quim* for their rhyme at times, the former, like *prick*, seems too sharp for the content of many poems, while the latter, like *yard,* is archaic if not obsolete. *Beaver* is too specifically fixated on the pelt – and cannot yet be divorced from the term "beaver shot" – *snatch* will only do in Australia, and so forth, etc. So, for most translations, the somewhat obnoxious (to the Usanian ear) *cock* and *cunt* will have to do, though an odd *rod* or *pole* may occasionally replace the former and a *snatch* or *hole* the latter, as rhyme and rhythm dictate. With poems where the translation allows two or three syllables, the Japanese original, *mara, henoko* and *chinpoko* for the male, *kai, bobo* and *tsubi*, for the female may sometimes be enlisted (see the list). I try to avoid *penis,* for it sounds like a medical term and only becomes poetic when mightier than the sword. *Pecker* is far better and I may find a place for the recently learned, pleasant sounding *willy* as well. While appreciating the visual concavity and sound of *vulva*, the eye-teeth must reach way out and press down the bottom lip *twice* to say it, so I prefer *pussy* or *cunny*, words more pleasant on the tongue. Unfortunately, one has bad connotations and the other is not in general usage. Where the translation can squeeze in three syllables, I occasionally use *vagina,* which once meant "sheath/scabbard," but, as a rule, try to avoid it for the same reason I avoid *penis*, though the sultry, seemingly Indian-sound and rhythm (combining the pronunciation of the Indian *pajama* with the *jai,* as the *gi* is properly pronounced) of *vagina* make it somewhat more poetic for one attuned to the sound of words (think of holy cows if you must and you can escape from the anatomical *vagina*). There are also the cute terms – who can hate *a little nookie* or *some hoochie-coochie?* – which I am tempted to use occasionally. But senryu, as a pop poetry, generally used conventional – i.e., the most *common* – words. Other things equal, it is best to do likewise in translation. So, "cock" it is, and "cunt."

Moreover, if the truth be told, I am one of those insanely rational souls who holds that *context counts* when judging verbal behavior. Sure, "cunt" in English is often used as a degrading explicative. Yes, many Canadians and Usanians take that usage for granted and either misuse it themselves or avoid it as "a radioactive word, impregnated with hostility" (Beatrix Campbell). But there is no reason in the world we must follow Francis Grose, who, in 1796, found it "a nasty name for a nasty thing" (*Classical Dictionary Of The Vulgar Tongue*). In Chaucer's *Canterbury Tales* that sassy first feminist, the Wife of Bath, who was right proud of hers (*"And trewely, as myne housbondes tolde me, / I had the beste quoniam mighte be"*) spoke freely of what her author dared not spell freely:

> *"For certeyn, olde dotard, by youre leve,*
> *Ye shul have queynte right y-nough at eve."*

And, increasingly, in modern England, "cunt" is used as *a term of endearment.* That, too, is perfectly natural. After all, most of us like it, right? If one hears someone *use* cunt in a hostile way, just ask him (or her): "What do *you* have against "cunt?" What did *you* hatch from, anyway!" I strongly support the so-called liberal feminists who would literally *take back their "cunts,"* as African-Americans did their color when they embraced that different but equally problematic word, "black." Euphemism, in the long run, is a losing game. It is defeatist to call *cunt* "vagina" or some other fancy term. "Cunt Power" is not an ideal but a reality. *Cunt* has not been called *"the A-bomb of the English Language"* (Walter Kirn) for nothing. The only question is whether that power works for good or bad. So why change *words* when you have one already with the clout to change *minds?* And "minds" begin with the woman's. What can only be called the *"Cunt Beauty"* movement, which has graphically depicted vulva in their glorious variety, has improved the self-image of many women. At the same time, I must confess that my personal favorite is *cunny.* Without the "t" at the end reinforcing the "k" sound at the beginning, *cunt* softens up. *Softness* is a good thing in my book, where buns of steel and six-pack bellies represent a vile hard-muscle fetish, *destructive* not only because it affirms Usania, a society so sick it even encourages violent criminals to "bulk up" in prison (something Japanese and other somewhat saner societies find horrific) but because gyms waste energy better put to use doing things otherwise done by resource-hogging machines and muscle burns an obscene quantity of calories coming from over-farming at the cost of the environment or the starving bellies of people without the luxury of "body-building." For somewhat similar reasons, I prefer "willy" – a euphonious word I had not even known was used in that capacity until a poet in Belgium sent me a haiku with a fly on *his* for *Fly-ku!* a couple of years ago – to the obnoxious "cock" and "prick." But I shall not push my politics (= *morals* = *aesthetics*) on you. I will go with that common couple, Cock & Cunt, except where rhyme and reason dictate otherwise. (★As it turned out, I am afraid I ended up using *cunt* more than intended in both the text and index. It is short, my book too long, and inclusive, saving time otherwise lost to choosing among alternatives. *Mea culpa.*)

Afterword

R.H. Blyth's *Japanese Life and Character in Senryu* ends with the following words: *"But will they not call me "the foreigner who praised senryu too much"?* Because, my interest in themes means that I include senryu about which I had only mean things to say, I doubt I run *that* danger. But it is possible some who might prefer my talent for translation be used on higher poetry (such as haiku) will lament that this book is a prime example of *materium superabat opus*, which is to say, that I outdid myself in the dressing up of doggerel; and, I, a fool with *scores of books* on various subjects well-underway (not to mention a revolution in musical instruments & animation) and little chance of finishing most in my lifetime, must admit to worrying that, unless this book does well enough to help me make up the eight months spent on it by the improvement of my circumstances in the near future, I will ever regret the opportunity-cost, which is to say, possibilities lost, just as I do the dreams I must feed to the cows every morning.

Circumstances dictate what we can do. Could I have afforded help to scan in thousands of pages of my thematic selections from Thoreau's Journal – it would take weeks or months – I would surely have finished *Aurelian Harps & Mountains in Space, The Surreal Thoreau* (see booklines at paraverse.org), and four other, completely different Thoreaus – what Borges said about biography may also be said about selections from journals – *before* doing this book. Or, I would have continued on my haiku *saijiki,* of which I have only published the first twenty of two hundred themes, without worrying about the reward for my effort coming decades later, if ever. But, I needed something weird enough to have *a fighting chance of free publicity* – as I lack time/money to make or buy much on my own – a book I could write in far from ideal circumstances, and this was it.

That is not to say I wrote it in the style required for a best-seller. I *could have*, for even though my English skills eroded over decades of writing in Japanese, I still snap like an alligator turtle. I have yet to meet my match in turning out catch-phrases. If anyone with a major publisher is reading: I would be happy to do an illustrated half-length *pure wasabi* version of this book and my earlier *Topsy-turvy 1585,* so long as you give me a decent five-figure advance and promise a large run for each. So why didn't I keep *this* snappy and sell it myself? Because, given the type of printing (POD), publicity (*none*) and distribution (*no return*) Paraverse Press (*I, myself*) can afford, such a book would be less marketable than a wild monster. Meanwhile, I write to *amuse myself* while living under difficult circumstances such as, having nothing to listen to but conceited right-wing radio blow-hards because I cannot afford the new HD radio that would give me more interesting NPR shows – forget Air America, *rich liberals do not think people living in poor rural areas worth reaching* – not eating in a restaurant for ten months because none are in walking distance, taking out a senile old dog (one of four) I must care for, once every two hours because he is incontinent. I have worked on freighters – months at sea – but, believe me, it is easy compared to being landlocked in the sticks of Usania. &, *some* readers (*Thanks, N.*) actually *like* books to be a handful!

Acknowledgement

「ほっておけない気持ちが良く分かりますよ。でも敬愚さんも罪ですよねえ」 美代子.

My debts to those I've read are acknowledged in the *Foreword* and *Bibliography* and will not be repeated here. Here, I thank all who responded to my book title survey and –

My Mom for sharing knowledge from her collection of slang dictionaries, suggesting I not give away too much in the *Table of Contents* and repeated concern lest I write anything misogynist. On the former count, she should be content. On the latter, I am not sure.

Jane Reichhold, to whom I sent an early draft of the first two chapters – still, the first two in the book – for her enthusiastic reply gave me the courage to proceed:

> *My old printer is giggling as it grinds this book out. I have read snatches of it and am completely delighted. Here your breezy method of writing completely fits the material. But most important, FINALLY someone who knows Japanese to tell the truth about what the Japanese have been writing. . . . Go for it! Make your fame with this one and someone will be glad to use your name for the honor of printing all your other haiku books!*

Peter Dale (whose gutsy book, *The Myth of Japanese Uniqueness,* and essay on the same, ~ *Revisited,* I criticized so sharply in my wee book *Orientalism & Occidentalism* that my own mother criticized *me* for being *mean* to him), for reading most chapters when they were 80% done and making good suggestions, some of which I am afraid I have not taken (I *tried* real footnotes, but decided they were not for me). His Australian nonchalance with topics we Usanians are taught to fear – & what stories! His aunt advised the boys, still in high-school, to be sure and *use their elbows* when they got married – helped me relax and just *write* rather than apologize all the time. What an extraordinary coincidence that my fellow iconoclast (my books published in Japan/ese in the 1980's demolished stereotypes of Japaneseness) and collector of exotic lore off the beaten tracks of academe should likewise be interested in obscene poetry and translate thousands of poems by the ribald Roman poet Giuseppe Gioachino Belli (1781-1853) at roughly the same time that I was learning to read Japan's laughing (erotic) poems. He is the only person to have read more than two or three chapters of this book before publication.

My *haiyû* (friends in haiku) for trying to help with what is far from their favorite type of poetry! Especially, Tenki, for answering a few questions in a letter and getting the Q & A bbs up and running, Yukari, actually the *nom de blog* for a male respondent (Miyoko, if you read this, please do not tell anyone else!) for succeeding in answering some of the questions at said bbs. And, Miyoko, herself, for valiantly trying to answer a few questions and her charming remarks – sympathy for fellow sufferer Yukari, whom I think she thought was a woman, too, – submitted to the haiku bbs (*Satin Doll*) where we play:

> *"Yukari-san, good day. That must not have been easy for you. As a gentle person, I can well understand why you would not just let it [my questions about senryu] pass. But Keigu* [my pen name] *is the one to blame! Where in the world did he find those senryu! I've been around for over twenty years* (笑 [joke]) *and never saw any of them. There must have been many dirty old men in Japan from way back. Or, is the whole world like that? Anyway, it beats war. Let's all ero-up to create a peaceful world!"*

Et alia. Kenjiro Goto, who runs a *Mutamagawa* site, for taking the time to respond carefully to my questions about specific *maeku* (draws) – especially the tricky *koso sure* – and some *ku* despite the fact the draw and some *ku* were not *Mutamagawa* & too dirty for his taste; 苔花堂の Gohongi Hiroko and her husband for putting #'s on late-Willow *ku,* MMcM for chasing down a few Chinese-related matters & CZ for *trying* something else.

This book was finished over a hot and muggy summer. Sometimes, recalling the fragrant green switches used in a proper sauna, I found myself wishing I had one. r.d.g.

香り発つ枝打ちながら歩く暑さ　敬愚

B • I • B • L • I • O • G • R • A • P • H • Y

main sources (all **1750-1841**) in chronological order

◎ *Mutamagawa* む 1750-1761. Warrior-gem-river. See Mutamagawa, below.
◎ *Million* 万 1757-1789. Myriad-verses-gathered. See Mankuawase, below.
◎ *Willow* や (or just #) 1765-1841. *Willow Barrel.* See Yanagidaru, below.
◎ *Pluck* 摘 1776-1801. End-pluck-blossom = *The Safflower Princess.* Suetsumuhana.
◎ *Leaf* 葉 1835/6. Usually translated as *Willow Leaftips*. See Yanaginohazue, below.

◆ ***Mutamagawa*** (む) – Published from1750 to 1761, the precursor and the odd-guy out of senryu. *Mu* is a splendid editorial experiment with 5-7-5 and 7-7 *ku* picked out of context from *haikai* link-verse (*renga*) jam – I call them *jams*, for I imagine an atmosphere like a jam-session – contests (the best verses were awarded) with themes of interest to the Kikaku (Bashô student + independent drinker into courtesan culture and riddling *ku*) school of *haikai,* c a new Edo flavor. Though usually called *zappai* (mixed *haikai*), they are sometimes mistakenly, *but understandably*, called *senryu*, for about 500 of the *ku* are similar – some identical – to ones found in senryu's flagship *Yanagidaru* (*Willow*). The editor, Kei Kiitsu 慶紀逸 (1694-1761), selected both 14 and 17-syllabet *ku* from *haikai* link-verse sessions more urban than nature-oriented. Blyth, acknowledges *Mutamagawa's* priority by giving it 207 pages vs. 36 pages for *Yanagidaru* in his *Edo Satirical Verse Anthologies.* While む has the seeds for many of the themes found in this book, it is the least dirty of the collections, so I use it relatively little (but far more than most books about senryu do). The full name is *Haikai Mutamagawa*. My source is a 20c reprint:わが『俳諧武多摩川』出典：日本名著全集版行会の『川柳雑俳集』1927. 現在印刷顔負の珍書.

◆ ***Mankuawase*** (*Million* or 万) – Printed from 1757 to 1789, *Senryû-hyô Mankuawase* means 'Senryû-evaluated-ten-thousand-*ku*-match'『川柳評万句合』c *Man* = ten-thousand meaning *myriad* (a very common word for a large, large number, so I use "million") and *awase* both a contest and gathering together. A *manku-awase* was any booklet full of selected responses (*tsuke-ku*) to a draw (*mae-ku*), *i.e.,* the results of a *maekuzuke* contest, mostly read by participants. Karai Senryû (柄井川柳 1718-90) crammed 60 *ku* per page into his *mankuawase* and eventually published close to 100,000 of the millions he adjudicated. These *ku* became the main source of *ku* for the *Yanagidaru* (willow) and *Suetsumunohana* (pluck). The character 万(*man*) c a date is the minimum citation (申し訳ないが、スペースのため「万」という文字＋年付しか掲載しない). While I translate some found elsewhere, almost all come from Okada Hajime's compilation of the best dirty *ku* from the *Million* booklets that were not later reprinted in *Willow* or *Pluck.* Because he avoided redundancy, this makes the small book the perfect complement for the two classics: 岡田甫『古川柳艶句選』有光書房判（欠年付）*本を呉れた星野CZさん有難う！*

◆ ***Suetsumuhana*** (*Pluck* 1776-1801) – Dirty *ku* selected by Karai Senryû. Widely acknowledged as the best dirty senryû collection, it probably *is*. The name, *"end-pluck-blossom,"* means a type of *safflower* the tips of which were pinched off to create rouge (*beni*). As the collection plucked the most colorful *ku* from earlier *Manku-awase,* the allusion is perfect. And, it evokes an aura of ludicrous sexuality because *Suetsumuhana* is the name of a woman whom handsome Prince Genji wooed in the dark only to discover she had an outlandishly long nose with a red-tip! Rather than English the collection as *The Safflower Princess*, I abbreviated it to the senryû-salient *Pluck.* I have favored vol. I (1776) because I own a round robin discussion of it (Saibara et al. 1995), but include many *ku* from all 4 volumes: 出典：『定本誹風末摘花』岡田甫編　太平書屋　第二版 1967. (この本に、「万句合」の年付もあるが、ここでは省きました。)

◆ ***Yanagidaru*** (*Willow* 1765-1841*) – A series of 166 or 167 books published between 1765 and 1841 that are synonymous with *senryu.* The title, made by the editor Goryôken Arubeshi, who selected the best stand-alone *ku* solicited and selected by Karai Senryû for *Million,* is written with characters meaning "willow-much-remains." Senryû means "river-willow." The editor's succinct preface dubs the same title with different characters meaning "willow-*tub,*" and explains that it (full of *sake* drunk at nuptials) symbolizes his hope that the superior stand-alone *ku* within contain the passion of the fashionable *haikai*-style so the book be truly a marriage of the *maeku-zuke* (draw-verse-derived contest *ku*) and *haikai* (当世誹風の余念をむすべる秀吟あれば、いもせ川柳樽と題す). The full name of the book is <u>*Haifû*</u>*-Yanagidaru*, or haikai-style *Willow*. After Senryû's death, contributors started calling their *ku* "Senryû-style." Eventually, *haifû* was dropped and the continuing series became the <u>*Senryûfû*</u>*-Yanagidaru.* A half-century later, the *ku* themselves became *senryu.* This series was so prolific, so dominant a presence that just a number following a *ku* means it came from *Willow*. In that, I follow the Japanese practice. Most of mine come from the Iwanami pocket book reprint of the first 24 volumes (山澤校訂『誹風柳多留』岩波文庫 全四冊 1995) or an index to the poems of all volumes read in a library over a decade ago. (岩波文庫には、「万句合」の元の年付もあるが、ここでは省きました。)

◆ ***Yanaginohazue*** (*Leaf*) – This 1835 collection of 675 (more, but some repeat) *ku* composed at several parties for that purpose under the guidance of Senryû IV. The name literally means the "Willow-leaf-tips" and plays on both the *Willow/Yanagidaru* and the *Pluck/Suetsumuhana* titles. The *zue* is the same as the *sue* and with a tree usually means the top, but with a willow is in the dust, mud or river. And, as the editor joked in his preface, with a name like this (clever and suggestive of Senryû I), it sounds classy and should sell well! Actually, it contains the best and the worst of what might be called not just dirty but *raunchy* senryu. It is a good complement for *Pluck,* from which, I might add, it pinched a few of its "impromptu" *ku!* 出典: 莽露庵主人全解釈『江戸艶句「柳の葉末」を愉しむ』三樹書房 1995. 「柳の葉末」の木来の編集は川柳四代目。別編は 1838 の五代目によるものという岡田説に従う).

---

selected (★★★ very often, ★★often, ★ less often ○ seldom cited) references

---

○*Aubrey's Lives – Aubrey's Brief Lives* ed. Oliver Lawson Dick. Penguin Books (1949). Miscellanist John Aubrey (1626-97) should be read before reading about old Japan, etc.

★★★ *Balls* – 玩球隠士(pseudonymous) 編撰『岐牟太末学大全』#188 of 300 limited edition 太平書屋 1985. The source of many of the senryu and other snippets on testicles without which I probably would not have had a chapter dedicated to them. A book with nothing but balls, from the physiology to the literature.

★★★Blyth, R.H. *Edo Satirical Verse Anthologies* Hokuseido: 1961; *Japanese Life and Character in Senryu* Hokuseido: 1960. With about 3,000 *ku* between them, the majority of *zappai* and senryu translated into English until the publication of this book are in these two. I didn't star them until counting mentions of Blyth in my index. He barely gets three stars because I mostly discuss rather than cite him. The latter book is mostly *Willow.*

○*Boudoir Tales of the Great Eastern Land of Japan. Daitô keigo* 1785 An *ehon* attributed to Hirayasu Kin. Translated by M.E. Jamentz. #15 of *An episodic festschrift for Howard S. Hibbett*, compiled by John Solt (Highmoonoon: 2004). The combination of wet pornographic stories of the famous (The Empress & Prelate in our ch 1 included) and dry wit coming as Chinese aphorism/morals punned or alluded in the text, as well as layers of odd commentary will make this an erotic classic if a publisher would put in the dirty pictures and, for the sake of students, include the original Japanese and more notes. I only cite it once or twice, but thought the tiny booklet deserved a long mention.

○ Carter, Steven D. *Traditional Japanese Poetry* (Stanford 1991) offers a full – excluding dirty senryu & folk song – overview of poetry from ancient times to the modern age, tastefully selected & introduced, including *waka* by Ono no Komachi I cited.

拙★著 ***Cherry Blossom Epiphany.*** The 3000 haiku on blossom viewing in this book include dozens by Issa about drunkenness and bodily functions as the blossom-viewings were closer to Woodstock than tea parties. Also, scores of ku by Sôgi 宗祇 show that haiku-style playfulness verging on senryu may be found in an elegant and proper poet.

★★★ *Cuntologia* – 玩宮隠士(pseudonymous)著『女陰万考』太平書屋 1996 An encyclopedic labor of love with hundreds if not thousands of *senryû* spicing up the text. The original title (female-yin-10,000-thoughts) is a good pun (actually two) that does not translate, so I coined *Cuntologia.* I call the author Dr Cuntology.

★ **English - Japanese Dictionary.** My 3000+pp *Shogakukan-Random House English-Japanese Dictionary* was used most often to check etymologies, for it is good that way. Because Microsoft Word's spell-check dictionary is not worth a damn (it does not even include the poet-philosopher who is the best known exponent of atomic theory, Lucretius, and the essayist who has been called the first modern man, Montaigne!), I have had to waste hours with the SRH dictionary proofing this book. The fact that it is torn in five parts and is missing a hundred or so pages does not help things.

★★ *Eropedia* – by SasamaYoshihiko 笹間良彦著『好色艶語辞典』雄山閣出版 平成元年. A literal translation: "salacious erotic word dictionary." Uneven, but most of the long headings (where he really did some research) are very good, at least for beginners.

★ *Enoko-shû* 『犬子集』 (1633) This raucous haikai link-verse anthology edited by Shigeyori 重頼 (dozens of his *ku* are in my haiku books) is full of dirty and irreverent material, some of which became senryu themes. 出典『初期俳諧集』岩波, 森川他 1991.

★★***Eroverse***『艶句』有光書房 1962 The source of *Condom ku* – the only modern senryu chapter. Selected, edited and introduced by Okada Hajime.

★ *Inu-tsukuba-shû* 『犬筑波集』 1536. The first major anthology of down and dirty haikai, edited by Yamazaki Sôkan. Used various sources, none at hand.

○ *Gilbert. The Distinct Brilliance of Zappai: and the Need to Reconsider its HSA Definition* by Richard Gilbert & Shinjuku Rollingstone, in Simply Haiku spring 2005. Informative, but a bit harsh on one whose main point was not to put down *zappai* but exalt haiku.

★★★ *Issa.* Haikai master Issa did not shy away from bodily functions and, to a limited degree, sex; my first translations of senryu were juxtaposed to his boldest work. I have his entire works (『一茶全集』信濃毎日新聞) but most *ku* may be found in 全集第一巻 (ただし、特定の句を見つけるために『発句素引 (全集第一巻別冊)』も必要) .

★**Japanese-English Dictionary.** I tend to quote it when the definition is funny, or off, and fume when all 2000-odd pages fail to include a word given far more space in the OJD than others they have simply because the word is so hard to English (or so I imagine), so I feel a bit guilty to mention it by name, but I have an old Kenkyûsha's New Japanese-English Dictionary (1974). I'd prefer using the new one c̲ its large supplement, but cannot afford them. I wonder if *mara* is still included and *bobo* left out in the cold.

★★ Kei Kiitsu 慶紀逸(1694-1761). Editor of top proto-senryu collection => *Mutamagawa.*

★★ *Leupp, Gary P. Male Colors The Construction of Homosexuality in Tokugawa Japan* U. Calif. 1995/7 reads much better than its deconstructionist construction in the subtitle and includes some bold hypotheses. I wanted more development of some areas, but read it to see how Japanese sexuality does not fit our clear-cut hetero-homo sexual categories.

◎ *Makura no Sôshi* 『枕草子』c1005 See *Pillow Book.*

◎ *Mottomo no Sôshi* 『尤の双紙』徳元 1634/73. 出典: 渡辺 校訂『仮名草子集』新

日本古典文学体系　岩波。See *Reasonable Book.*

★*Nishizaki Kitaru* essays what might be called sexual miscellany. I cite one of his best known books: 西沢來『雑学艶学』(miscellogy, erology)文春文庫 1985 (1979 新門出版社).

★★★★ *OJD* stands for the *Only Japanese Dictionary,* a name I invented (a play upon the OED) because 80-90% of the old words I look up are in this dictionary, which is not the case with all other dictionaries I have tried. When I think of how many *ku* I would mistranslate or give-up on without it, I shudder. Moreover, the plentiful folk-etymologies and poems, many senryu, for usage examples in this 24-volume set make Shogakukan's *Nihon-kokugo-daijiten* (*Japan-national-language-big-dictionary*) the world's most interesting dictionary. Some day, I plan to do a book with nothing but a hundred of its more interesting etymologies. 手持ちは小学館『日本国語大辞典』十二冊の縮制版

★★★ *Okada Hajime.* Senryu's 20c patron saint, Okada edited and annotated the *Millions* selection and *Pluck*, above (not to mention scores of books I do not have). He selected for and compiled books of modern senryu, including 艶句, Eroverse, above.

○ *Ôsaka-dokugin-shû* 『大阪独吟集』1672/3. Haikai link-verse from the Osaka area edited by haikai master Sôin. Found in『初期俳諧集』岩波　森川他 1991.

○ *Pigeot,* Jacqueline. Her book about Japanese listing/ miscellany (ジャクリーヌ・ピジョー著　寺田＋福井訳『物尽し － 日本的レトチックの伝統』平凡社 1997) sent me back to *Mottomo no Sôshi* (Reasonable Book: a 17c book of listing by Tokugen, haikai poet of the Teikoku school) Good as Pigeot's book is, I would like to see another work concentrating on the aesthetic variety, represented by Sei Shônagon's *Pillow Book*, alone.

拙★著 ***Rise, Ye Sea Slugs!*** My book c̲ 1000 trans. haiku on sea cucumber (paraverse 2003)

★★ *Round-robin* – A six-person interpretation of all the *ku* in the first book/section of *Pluck*. 西原亮他『川柳末摘花輪講初篇』太平書屋　1995. Expensive, but I had a salary when I bought it (and *Cuntologia* and *Balls*, all from this brave publisher). Wish I could have afforded the following volume as well!

◎ *Saibara et al.* See Round-robin. ◎*Sasama.* See *Eropedia*, above.

★★ Screech, Timon *Sex and the Floating World – Erotic Images of Japan, 1700-1820* (U. of Hawaii Press: 1999). This was the last work I saw before finishing this book. The attention given to the *uses* (masturbation) of dirty pictures and effort made to conceptualize where picture-centered books fear to tread is refreshing, but some of the details of interpretation made me realize how important this (my) book could be for those engaged in such work – more familiarity c̲ senryu terms would improve reading of pictures and suggest other areas to investigate – so I added a dozen pages (and lost a week of pre-xmas sales, for it is hard to adjust an almost finished book) all because L. thought I should see the book (as already mentioned?) and Amazon had a copy I could afford.

○ *Sei Shônagon* 清少納言(fl.1000) diva of good taste, queen of listing, mother of mischievous miscellany. I hypothesize that the listing (*monowazukushi*) in her classic work, *The Pillow Book* (*Makura no sôshi*『枕草子』1005?) may ultimately have influenced senryu through its influence on the *draw*. I have the Ivan Morris translation.

★★ *Senryû.* 柄井川柳 Poetry judge *Karai Senryû* (1718-90) => *Million, Willow, Pluck.* I occasionally mention his draws but the *ku* he selected stand for themselves.

★★ *Shiki* 子規 1867-1902. Put the word "haiku" into circulation and, together c̲ Kyoshi, is considered the father of modern haiku. Famous for advocating strict objective/ photographic realism, but those who have read all his work find him an imaginative poet unafraid to put his feelings into a *ku.* I introduce his overlooked testicle *ku* here, for I have never seen them outside of his complete works and because, like Issa's *ku,* they show that the body is part of nature, seasons and haiku. 子規全集はアルスだったか講談社だったか、全集は全集で、どうでもいいが、各々句の年付、きちんと書き留めた。オンライン雑誌「週間俳句 2007-7-22」にも和文記事として纏めて掲載しました。

★★ *Solt, John.* “Willow Leaftips.” In Sumie Jones, ed., *Imaging/ Reading Eros*. East Asian Studies Center, Indiana University, 1996. A well-written and gutsy presentation of the history of the book I call *Leaf* and a selection of sixty-six *ku* from it. These are the only dirty senryu translated prior to this work that I know of. Wait for the revised (some translations were premature) reprint, upcoming as part of *An episodic festschrift for Howard Hibbett*, published by Solt’s Highmoonoon Press. The festschrift is full of lusty short work by talented translators tastefully done but too sparely annotated for my taste.

○ Sonoda 添田知道『日本春歌考』1963. His book on “spring songs,” as bawdy songs are called in Japan, is *the* classic. I lost my copy from having to move too much, or this book would surely have borrowed much from it rather than just mentioning it.

○ Sugimoto 杉本長重『川柳狂歌集』日本古典。。岩波 1958 This standard anthology includes a selection of the best *Yanagidaru* senryu (many of which are translated by Blyth). The introductory remarks, c egs. + chronology of *maeku,* is helpful, as are the annotations (unlike the bare-bones Iwanami bunko) but lacks an index, fine for academics who can search within Iwanami’s books online, but not for me.

★★★★ *Suzuki* 鈴木勝忠 Comments by Suzuki Katsutada. Sometimes his annotations are a bit too subtle for me to follow, but the sex-related *zappai* he compiled from various minor collections, often in complementary pairs – thematic juxtaposition – reflects editing backbone rare to the timid world of print. Many of the *ku* in this book from minor collections come from his book:『（江戸上方）「艶句」の世界』三樹書房 1996. As they are not easy to find, I give the name of the collection as well as the date (in Japanese).

★★★ *Syunroan* 葬露庵主人 While I take issue with a number of comments by *Syunroan Syuzin* in his annotated reproduction of *Yanaginohazue*, many if not most were very helpful. If his name seems odd, it is because he chose to use an old-fashioned way to Romanize his name. Today, most would write “Shunroan Shujin.”『（江戸艶句）「柳の葉末」を愉しむ』三樹書房 1995 was my only source for *Leaf ku*.

★★ *Takenaka Rô* たけなか・ろう collected bawdy Japanese folk songs by region, supplying local color and context in a remarkably free manner. After Sonoda, above, my second favorite book on “spring/dirty songs,” but the only one with me, so I am much in its debt for this book. たけなか・ろう『にっぽん情哥行』ミュージック・マガジン 1986

拙★著 ***Topsy-turvy 1585*** – a translation and explication of Luis Frois S.J.’s *TRATADO listing 611 ways Europeans and Japanese are contrary* (paraverse press 2004 and short version 2006). One of my books. As it is 95% my words and 5% Frois,’ I, and not the 16c Jesuit, am the author, though TT*1585* is a full translation of his work. I cite it often for, like Chamberlain’s *Things Japanese*, it covers a broad spectrum of culture, and unlike Chamberlain’s book, I know exactly what is in it and have a copy right here to check.

○ Tyler, Royall. *Japanese Tales.* Pantheon: 1987. You will find much as “dirty” as the content of senryu, but told in a classier/classic way in these 1000 year-old tales that have not received as much attention as they deserve, perhaps because tales are mistakenly considered juvenile literature today. If I did not quote Tyler’s translations, it is only because I am separated from my copy of his book.

★ Ueda Makoto: *Light Verse from the Floating World* Columbia Univ. Press (1999). Good history and excellent translations of about 500 classic senryu, but nothing dirty. Unlike Blyth, who worked in a time when we had official censors, Ueda could have introduced it, but chose not to. Still, following Blyth, it is our main introduction to senryu in English.

○ Ueda Makoto: *Bashô and His Interpreters.* Stanford Univ. Press (1992). No book in English demonstrates the polysemy of haiku read by Japanese like this one compiling and translating critics’ comments on a selected number of Bashô’s *ku* presented one at a time. By extension, it should help you understand how much is lost in translation.

*M*issing? <u>I am sorry but this is all I have time or space for. More of *my* books are on the last page</u>.

G • L • O • S • S • A • R • Y

㊤ selected Senryu, Haikai, Zappai, Poetry & Translation terms ㊤

S◎S ***Bareku.*** 破礼句(lit. break-etiquette-*ku*). Lewd haiku, *kyôku*, senryu or *zappai*. Many senryu are *bareku*, but *bareku* need not be senryu, so they are overlapping, not equivalent.

P◎P ***Beat.*** "Mary had a little lamb" has 4 beats, most haiku/senryu 7 or 8.

T◎T **Composite Translation** – Multiple translations of a single poem or bit of prose intended to be read together. Especially *useful* for translating exotic tongues where so much is lost that it may not be restored in one reading. It is particularly *pleasing* for haiku, senryu or other hyper-short-form poetry, where the readings may fit in a single page and be arranged in clusters. I think it best done by a single translator. The word (not necessarily defined as *I* define it) probably was first coined by Liz Henry (on the www).

▲ ***Capped.*** See *Kasazuke.* (This and the next are the same, just from different dialects of Japse.)
▲ ***Crowned.*** Like *capped* verse. See *kamurizuke.* (To be plain, I end up 'capping' most)

S/H/Z◎S/H/Z ***Draw.*** My word for a short phrase soliciting a poem called a *maeku* in Japanese. Blyth (1961) called it "a fourteen syllable subject." Ueda (1999) uses the Japanese term, as is. Gilbert (2005) calls them *"a previously given verse."* See *maeku* heading.

H◎H ***Haikai.*** Wild and witty 14 and 17-syllabet link-verse (commonly 50 or 100-*ku*), generally following the seasons, but sometimes playing with romance (*koi*) in an irreverent manner, which, c the birth of the *saijiki* (seasonal almanac) in the 17c, began to get serious, and was developed into a higher calling? by the haiku saint Bashô (1644-94).

H◎H ***Haiku*** – A *ku* of about 17 *syllabets* (below) in Japanese, or 7-8 beats in English, expressing a heartfelt connection to a seasonal or calendar phenomenon so good you want to read it more than once. Like Shiki (and practically no one else) who first popularized the word in the last part of the 19c, I think *haiku* should be used for haiku-like poems going back *at least* to Sôgi and the other 15c link-verse masters.

H◎H ***Hokku.*** The first verse of a link-verse sequence and what the *ku* in the first collections of stand-alone 17 syllabet *haikai* were called. Because most collections of *hokku* were not really all *hokku,* but *ku* from other parts of a sequence (平句 *hiraku*) or composed with no reference to a sequence (只句 *tadaku*), I prefer to reserve the term to what I *know to be a first ku* and use simply "haiku" (or *haikai ku*) in all other cases. If that bothers you, just call them *ku* so there can be no mistake.

T◎T Honorable 御. *"Honorable"* is an affected translation, the result of English lacking a less exaggerated honorific, such as the prefixes *"o"* or *"mi"* or *"on."* As it can simply mean the item pertains to the other party, I only use "honorable" when it adds to the wit. If you would know how such things must be lost in translation, please read *Orientalism & Occidentalism*, one of my many worst-sellers and see *Lost in translation / examples* in the *Idea Index,* for some of the words, though not "terms" *per se* in Japanese, are so common in senryu that lack of an equivalent prevents good translation.

P◎P ***Japanese-style.*** My term for a poem (*ku* or *ka* = waka) which is nothing more than the modification of a subject that comes to a head at the tail of said poem. It is better in Japanese than in translation because gerunds can be active in Japanese, but it is nonetheless a stunning phenomenon – imagine, no plot/story/sentence? to speak of! – and I can not for the life of me see why it is not *the talk of the town* so to speak among scholars of Japanese. It is a concept I introduce in all my books of translated haiku. With senryu, said subject itself may be left off and that is the wit/riddle of it.

Z/S◎Z/S ***Kamurizuke*** 冠付。 A capped verse, where the first 5 syllabets of the *ku,* the "crown" or *kanmuri,* is provided and the contestant finishes it. These are common in minor early senryu (not necessarily called senryu), such as collected by Suzuki (1996), and found in the first books of Senryû's *Manku-awase* (*Million*).

Z/S◎Z/S ***Kasazuke*** 笠付。The same as *kanmuri,* used in Osaka, Kyoto, Nagoya & South.

H◎H ***Kyôku*** 狂句。 Any wild, free spirited 5-7-5 *ku* from the renga/haikai tradition. It was used for what was to become senryu when it was in the process of defining itself away from formal haikai which liked to claim its collections were all *hokku.*

S/H/Z◎S/H/Z ***Ku*** 句。 A haiku, senryu, zappai or any Japanese poem of 17 syllabets or less, or parts of a poem of 31 syllabets or less. I use *ku* a lot in my books because it is short. Japanese also use *ku* for the parts of a *ku:* a haiku might have a first 5-syllabet *ku* and a second 7-syllabet *ku;* but using it that way, too, would be confusing, so I try not to.

P◎P Listing 物は尽し *monowazukushi.* I believe the *maeku*, or draw, in senryu, shares something of the elements, if not the spirit of *listing,* after the style of Sei Shônagon via Tokugen et al. Prime examples of a subject would be *adorable things* or *horrible things*.

S/H/Z◎S/H/Z ***Maeku*** 前句。 Literally, pre-*ku,* or previous-*ku,* the *maeku* in early senryu solicited, or drew *tsukeku, i.e.,* "attached-*ku,"*or verses that psychologically responded to or completed the idea posed by the *maeku* from many people in contest situations. While the *maeku* was used in *haikai* as a teaching aid before senryu came into being, in *haikai* link-verse the *maeku* is just the *ku* that comes before the *ku* in question, which will, in turn be the *maeku* for the next one. Also, in *haikai,* the *maeku* itself was a genuine poem or poem fragment, but by the time senryu came to be, the *maeku*, while ostensibly a 14-syllabet *ku,* was in reality just one 7-syllabet phrase repeated twice, and much of that was formulaic. Clearly no *ku* in the sense of being a verse, it was not a subject in the usual sense of it, *i.e.* a theme, either, so I decided to call it a *draw* (see, *draw,* above), instead.

S/Z◎S/Z ***Maeku-zuke*** – Contests putting up *maeku*=draws to get many responses and the result, *the draw+response together.* The best known selections of these draw+responses later became known as senryû. While most *Mutama* (below) *ku* were written in response to the *ku* before them, they were not written as *maeku-zuke,* but for link-verse, while senryu in *Yanagidaru* were, at least until 1778.

T◎T ***Multiple Translation.*** Like *Composite Translation* (above) but not necessarily intended to be read as a single multi-faceted poem-object. D. Hofstadter's Le *Ton Beau de Marot* is the most thorough exploration of it. For more, see my upcoming *A Dolphin In the Woods, In the Waves a Boar*.

T◎T ***Number.*** Japanese words should only be pluralized when they are proper nouns, eg., "The Tanakas are coming over." Words such as haiku, senryu or *ku*, not to mention *geisha*, sound better if you do not add an "s" for the plural. To me, Japanese words with an added "s" sound as horrid as "yous" for the second-person plural would to you.

Z◎Z ***Oriku*** 折句 An acrostic *ku,* usually *zappai*, spelling out a given subject or taking a word from the preceding *ku,* etc. c̲ the first syllabet of each break of the 5-7-5 or 7-7 *ku.*

T◎T ***Paraverse.*** Once an alternative universe, I use it for an alternative poem or line, with more play, or separation from the original than in a responsible multiple translation.

P◎P ***Paraversing*** – My coinage for the art of composing paraverses. See *A Dolphin In the Woods* or the paraversing page at paraverse.org for examples.

H◎H ***Saijiki*** 歳時記 A detailed calendar-based parade of themes, or "season-words," (*kigo*) for haiku going back to the mid-17c, but building upon over a millennium of poetry presented in rougher seasonal order. Each theme, natural or cultural, is defined and examples of *ku* are arranged chronologically. Large *saijiki* have thousands of these *kigo.*

S◎S ***Senryû*** 柄井川柳. Karai Senryû (1718 - 90), the point-judge whose name became synonymous with the genre and the poems. While "senryu" has been naturalized – why I do not italicize it – the man is not, so I leave the diacritical mark on that "û."

S◎S ***Senryu***. The Yanagidaru first claimed to be *haifû,* or *haikai* style, but after Senryû died, the *Yanagidaru* (*Willow*) came to be called Senryû-style to differentiate it from other *haikai-style maekuzuke* collections. Senryu, the *ku* itself, is defined in the Foreword. Let me add one more definition here to reward the persistent reader: *Senryu is the most unromantic, unmystical, unlyrical and unmusical, which is to say unpoetic poetry in the world.* It is opposite to, say, the following lines from the poet Hafiz, *"Ah, could I hide me in my song, / To kiss thy lips from which it flows"* which would be poetic no matter how translated (in this case, by Baron Von Hammer-Purgstall & found in Emerson's essay, *Persian Poetry*).

P◎P ***Syllabet.*** Because each syllable in Japanese can be a letter and is the counting unit for poetry, and *mora* is opaque, I use and recommend this word of my coinage that is naturally understandable.

S◎S ***Tsukeku*** 付け句. The *ku* capping another, which in link-verse can itself become the *maeku* or draw for the *next* person's *tsukeku.* In senryu, there was one *maeku,* or draw to which multitudes responded with *tsuke-ku* from which what became senryu were selected.

P◎P ***Waka*** 和歌 The 31-syllabet traditional poem that tends to pivot on a pun or other change in perceived meaning between the 17-syllabet first half and 14-syllabet second half. They tend to be about romance, celebration, and mourning but include novelty, too, and came to be arranged for the most part seasonally long before *saijiki* were invented.

Z◎Z ***Zappai*** 雑俳 Sundry forms of *ku* on the periphery of *haikai* that are, strictly speaking, neither haiku nor senryu for either content or formal reasons. It is commonly used to refer to *ku* in the *Mutamagawa* collection. Zappai includes capped verse, acrostic verse and more. Some day I hope to set forth in the wide world of *zappai* and discover what I do not know. This book includes scores of examples, mostly from Suzuki (1996).

㊦ body parts, main characters, important props & ■ dates ㊦

▲ **Ana-nashi** 穴無し Holeless => *Komachi.*

凹 **Aonyôbô** 青女房 Pale(ill)-looking wife, from sex with over-endowed husband.

凸 **Asagiura** 浅黄裏 Samurai from the country in Edo, hicks naively filthy in body & mind, somewhere between a dirty joke and a moron joke.

凸 **Ategaki** 当挊・当掻 Masturbating/stroking while faithfully keeping a certain person in mind. The expression even became well-known enough to be used as a metaphor!

凹 **Ateiri** 当入り. Masturbating/inserting [a dildo] while keeping someone in mind. I have only seen one example usage for this female equivalent of *ategaki* but OJD admits it!

凸 **Balls** 睾丸 Hanging loose because the country is at peace, or sad to wait outside the swimming hole. Usually pronounced & sometimes written 金玉 *kintama, gold gems.*

凹 **Bobo** 開 One of many pleasant-sounding names for the *cunt. Pussy*, if you like cats, *cunny* if you like rabbits; but more upbeat yet, so I sometimes retain the Japanese. Simple to write phonetically ぼゝ, the common use of the character simply meaning "open" may have served partly as something we might call a visual euphemism.

凸凸 **Bonze.** A Buddhist monk. From *bôzu* 坊主, a run-of-the-mill monk vs. a better-off priest, *oshô*. They were used loosely enough to partially excuse my loose translations.

凹凸 **Blue-spot** 青痣 Blue-*mark* is the correct translation for this birthmark found on the rear of most Mongolian race babies (it fades later). *Spot* sounded better in the book title *and* rhymes with its supposed cause, *cocks* that cannot stay out of a pretty pregnant wife.

▲ **Bride** => Sometimes brides are brides but usually in senryu they are =>*Young wife*

凹 **Castle-tipper/toppler**. 傾城 *keisei.* A courtesan fortunes may be lost on , ∴ a beauty.

凸凹 **Chili** (-Pepper) *tôgarashi* – 1). The penises of little boys and those boys. 2) A cheap, early-term abortifacient. 3) A tool for men to contest their masculinity.

凸 **Chin-chin, Chinpo, Chinpoko** – Wee-wee, dingaling, prick, etc. A boy's penis, though all the words are sometimes used by men referring to their own member.

凹 **Clam** 蛤 *hamaguri* – a young-adult cunt and/or its owner. Japanese clams are sleek with clean edges. In *haikai* they are basted on pine-cone *balls*, in senryû slurped twice by the groom (in the soup and later. . .) and metaphor for cunts *spitting*.

凹 **Corbicula** 蜆 *shijimi* – A tiny shell standing for a little girl's vulva, or her self.

凹 **Chambermaid** 長局,お局 – Women serving in the Edo residences/palaces of the Daimyô (rulers) of the fiefs in the Tokugawa Dynasty (1603-1856?). In senryu, mainly identified with *masturbation* and *dildos*. In the original, they are named after their "long" living quarters. Also, *Lady/ies-in-waiting* or *jochû*. See *nagatsubome*.

凸 **Chigo** 稚児 Little boys, beloved by Buddhist clergy and samurai, translated by some as "lovely boy/s," though at temples they might be called *acolytes*.

凹 **Courtesan** 遊女 *yûjo* – Though the most popular seem to have lived like queens, the "court" misleads: these women are indentured prostitutes of the Pleasure Quarters. I would use the Japanese as is, "play-girl," but that would make the girl the player rather than played-with. There are too many ranks and names for me. The Pleasure Quarters argot (and practice) requires an entire book or none. So you'll see very little here.

凹 **Cubicle whore** 切り店. The kirimise, or "cut-shop" is a cheap, partitioned brothel.

凹 **Cunt** – See the *Apologia* if this 'quaint' word bothers you. *Cunt* is a fine match for *cock* and, being short, both fit haiku well. It's odd that only one is controversial.

凸 **Daimyô** – These "big-names" headed feudal domains under the Tokugawa dynasty. The word is often used retroactively for the rulers of those domains before Japan was fully united (when early European visitors called them *kings*).

凸 **Dankon** – "Male-root," not to be confused with *daikon* – "big root," the large radish!

▲ **Dildo** *harikata* 張形 => *Ox*.

凸 **Dôkyô** – A Buddhist prelate (d. 772) synonymous with the colossal cock that made him "Pope" (法王) of Japan. See *Empress*.

凹 **Downer** 下開 *shitatsuki* "down-attached." A *low-cunt*, near the anus. Opp. of *Upper*.

凹 **Dowry** 持参金– An ugly bride or wife betrothed by a large gift of money to a groom from her wealthy parents is called "a dowry," literally, 'specially-given-money' = *jisan-kin,* or just 'specially-given' *jisan).* Rarely, "thousand-gold/coins," *sen-kin*.

凸 **Dry-kidney** (*jinkyô*) – A horny, if not priapic man, usually with a pretty wife, bed-ridden by over-spending his vital juices. The original is "kidney-empty," but poetry demanded "dry" rather than "empty."

凸 **Echizen** – Echizen, a province famous for spear-covers became synonymous with phimosis. => *foreskin*.

■ **Edo era** – From 1603 when Edo, now Tokyo, came to be the capital of Japan (and soon, the world's largest city) until 1857, when the governing Shôgunate was replaced by an Imperial state with more than a touch of democracy. See *Tokugawa*.

凹 **Empress** 女帝 *jotei* – There was more than one "woman-emperor," but only one c̲ a huge cunt requiring Dôkyô c̲ his huge cock. Most commonly called Kôken Tennô 孝謙天皇 (8c), sometimes Shôtoku Tennô 称徳天皇, not to be confused c̲ 聖徳太子.

■ **Era of Seclusion.** Foreshadowed in the late-16c, complete by the mid-17c and lasting until Perry arrived in the mid-19c. See *Topsy-turvy 1585* (2004) for more details.

凸 **Foreskin** – A man with *phimosis*, *i.e.,*, a foreskin that doesn't allow his *glans* to see the light of day. Invented to match Japanese terms, such as *Echizen* and *kawakamuri*, though I use Echizen as is sometimes and joke about *hoods*.

▲ ***Golden gems*** 金玉 *kintama.* => balls.

凸 **Goose-high** 雁高 *karidaka.* Literally, "goose-high" (consider the way the top of a goose's head rises up over the line of its neck), a highly regarded cock c̲ a huge glans jutting up and out over the shaft. In most of the Occident, a penis is primarily a shaft, with the head barely differentiated from it, or considered a mere spear-tip, but in some cultures, like Japan, it is a veritable *head*, emphasized so much there are many common names for it and, today, plastic surgery to enlarge it. =>*Pine-mushroom.*

▲ ***Hanakuta*** 鼻腐=> *Noseless*

凹 **Harem** – I refrained from calling the *Nagatsubone* (daimyô castle) women *a harem*, because of the middle-Eastern image, but I was tempted. After all, the circumstances of the women seems akin to that of Solomon's concubines whose plight so troubled Twain.

凹 **Hatchet** 斧 *yoki (de watta yô na)* – Little girl's vulva, from looking like a hatchet blade left an indentation (Japanese hatchets are very thin).

凸 ***Henoko*** への子 – A grown-up penis but not so awesome as a *mara.* The sound-sense is close to "pecker," but I sometimes call it a "cock" or even "prick" if the rhyme wants it.

凹 **High-cunt** 上開 *jôkai.* – A woman favored with a vaginal opening, particularly close to the navel and/or such a cunt. Opp. a low cunt. (All translation is quite optional, it could be up-cunt vs down-cunt as well, though to me that would be more suggestive of the angle than the placement of the opening, so I went with high/low).

凸 **Higo zuiki** 肥後随喜 – A long strip of dried taro root wrapped around the erect penis to make it more stimulating to wide women.

凹凸 馬 **Horse** *uma.* 1) Menstruation, for gear is required to ride. 2) A large male.

凹 ***Isle of Women*** 女護島 Nyogogashima, where women lived without men and had intercourse (and children) with the south wind.

▲ ***Jinkyo*** 腎虚 See *Dry-kidney.*

▲ ***Kagema****(ya)* => *Shade-boy*

凹 ***Kai*** – The Chinese derived pronunciation of 開, "open/ing." *Cunt.* I thought it medical if not elegant until reading a *ku* (pp 292-3) that showed *bobo* was the classier word. The same character 開 is *supposed* to be read *bobo* in most *senryû,* so one must guess!

▲ ***Karidaka*** => Goose-high.

凸 ***Kasa*** – A parasol, umbrella hat, mushroom cap, corona (overhang) of the glans. Japanese, unlike Usanians (all Occidentals?) are *very* conscious of this shape.

凸 ***Kawa-kamuri*** – skin/hide-crown. Phimosis (a restrictive or closed foreskin) or someone with it. See *Echizen, foreskin.*

凹 ***Keisei*** => Castle-tipper/toppler. ▲ ***Kirimise*** => cubicle whore

凹 ***Komachi*** – 1) Ono no Komachi (fl. c 850), the Sappho of Japan, most famous in senryû for lacking a hole. 2) Any pretty prick-teaser. 3) a beauty.

凹 ***Lady/ies-in-waiting*** – Women in the Edo residences of the Daimyô (rulers) of the fiefs in the Tokugawa Dynasty (1603-1856?). In senryu, mainly identified with *masturbation* and *dildos.* In the original, they are named after their "long" living quarters. Also *nagatsubome, chamber-maid, jochû.*

凹 ***Lima beans*** – A little girl's pudendum.

凸 **Lovely boy** – Pretty little boys loved by priests and samurai, more common in *haikai* than in senryû. See *chigo.*

凹 **Low-cunt** 下開 – *Gekai.* A woman with a vaginal opening, particularly close to the anus and/or such a cunt, considered a poor one. Opp. a high-cunt.

凹 **Maid** – English for *gejo,* literally "below-woman," a *maidservant* (and never a maiden) in this book. Abundant in senryû, some are clever and fast and some are slow, but all have robust appetites for sex, despite being common victims of rape, and masturbate with comestibles (some with roots, some with fins).

凸**Male Color** 男色 *nanshoku* – The varieties of male-to-male love and sex and the eros there-of. "Color" is a sexy word in Japanese.

凸 Married-in 婿入り *mukoiri*. Because of the sorry existence – judging from senryu that made fun of them, any way – of many men, who, marrying into their wife's (more wealthy) family, found themselves the picked-on party, we know that money=power, not gender, spoke loudest in Japan.

凸 **Mara** 魔羅・イ八 Senryu use it to mean *a big thick cock.* When translating, *cock* beats *"prick,"* but still rings hollow. "Dick" might work (if only I could tell if it is sinister due to itself or a certain ex-president), but, like "peter," seems culture-bound by coming from a proper name, so I rarely use it. I may have used the obsolete *yard* or odd *dong* a few times out of desperation. OJD flops defining *mara*. We learn it was 1) a demon and 2) used by Buddhist clergy to indicate their member because of a relation with *maru*, meaning something excrement/al (?!), and are treated (?) to a 古今著聞集 quote about someone cutting off his *mara* and tossing its "turtle-head" from a bag . . . But the dictionary missed its general meaning even though it included the odd Chinese character senryu uses for it イ八. Microsoft Word lacks it, so I combine and narrow two characters.

▲ **Matsudake** => *pine mushroom.*

■ **Meiji. 1868-1911.** When Japan quickly modernized, in some ways surpassing the USA (evolution could be taught). It might well have ended with Japan safely on the road to democracy, but the seeds for future confrontation were already planted by England's reaction to Japan's whipping the "white power" Russia. *Shiki* and his *balls* are Meiji.

▲**Monk,** a => *Bonze* who didn't rhyme. ▲**Mother-in-law** => *Old Wife.* ▲ **Mukoiri** => *Married-in.*

凹 **Nagatsubone** 長局 – Literally, Long-bureau, the living quarters for the ladies of the palace and they, themselves. Since some look after their mistress, a wife of the fief or national ruler (the shôgun), in a manner that makes them more her companion than a maid, while others do more physical work, I use *chambermaid* and *ladies-in-waiting,* or occasionally *palace women,* arbitrarily. They are all those things and there is no good word for translation. See *harem* above. Also called *tsubone, otsubone* and *chûjo* 中女.

凸 **Narihira** – 825-880 a prince & poet who spent his life in the pursuit of women supposedly bedding 3000 – or was it 3333? – of them, became the playboy protagonist of the *Tales of Ise* (early-10c) and synonymous with an inveterate womanizer or, hopelessly (according to a haiku in *Rise, Ye Sea Slugs!*) invertebrate lady's man.

凸**Narrow** きつい、又 狭い。 Anal sex, permissible for bonzes. Opp. *wide* (vaginal).

凹 **Nighthawk** 夜鷹 *yotaka* – The low class, generally old and diseased street-walker.

凹 **Noseless** – Someone with a nose lost to syphilis was said to have had it drop off (*ochita*). Whether entirely lost or eaten up within but still there, the sufferer was usually called a *hanakuta,* 鼻腐 or "nose-rot."

▲ **Nyogogashima** => *Isle of Women*

凹 **Octopus** 蛸・章魚（壺） Short for *octopussy* ↓, or a Buddhist priest/bonze, so named for his shaved crown and/or his round upside-down punch-bowl-like hat resembling it.

凹 **Octopussy** A prehensile vagina and/or a woman blessed with one, usually a mistress. The favored etymology is octopus *pot* (the octopus within the trap grabs you), but octopus-potty would not do, would it?

凹 **Old wife** *shûto* – The wife of the master of the house. She is not called old in Japanese (though it's in the character 姑) but compared to the "bride," or wife of her son, also in the house, she is. If she were not in her own house, she would be the *mother-in-law* of the young wife of her son, whose life she typically makes miserable. While she "loves the prick and hates the pussy," she bothers both because her main nighttime interest is listening in on their sex and they know it. Maybe the young wife called the "bride" should be called the daughter-in-law, as done without ado by Ueda (1999), instead, for she is the outsider though living in the house.

▲ **Ono Komachi.** See *Komachi.* ▲ **On the Horse** – See *Horse.*

凸 **Oshô** 和尚 A polite term for a monk or head of a temple too small to be called an *abbot*, whom I would call a priest more often but for the Christian smell it makes.

凹 **Ox** 牛 *ushi* – Short for 水牛 or, water buffalo and in senryu, by itself usually referring to the horn dildo typically used by the *nagatsubone*/chambermaids/ladies-in-waiting.

凹 **Palace**. Only used with respect to "women of the palace," the *chûjo* 中女 literally middle-woman/en. The same as the *chambermaid, ladies-in-waiting, nagatsubone,* etc.

▲ **Penis.** Avoided as too clinical in this book => *Mara, Henoko, Chinpoko*

凸 **Pine mushroom *matsudake*** – A fungus that looks not only phallic but ideally so from the Japanese viewpoint. See *Karidaka* and *Kasa*.

凹 **Pot-wearing festival** 筑摩祭 *tsukuma matsuri* where woman wore a pot for each man she slept with during the year.

凸 凸 **Samurai** – Dangerous when drunk and captive to their etiquette, which includes self-evisceration and boy-loves.

凸 凸 **Shade-boy** 陰間 *kagema.* Indentured male prostitutes who worked in boy-brothel establishments 陰間屋 (lit. shade-space-shop) in Yoshichô (below) serving men before puberty and men *and* women after that.

▲ **Shûto** 姑 => Old wife.

凸 **Sori** 反り – The *arch* (noun or verb) of something, usually used to refer to the *curve* of erect penises or swords, where an elastic tension is felt.

▲ **Tako**(-tsubo) => *Octopus* & *Octopussy*

■ **Tokugawa** 徳川幕府 Tokugawa Ieyasu of-the-relaxed-balls founded the Shôgunate, or shôgunal dynasty that would rule Japan for the entire Edo period (1603-1857), famous for its high degree of seclusion from the world outside for good and bad.

凹 **Tsubi** – My favorite word for *cunt*, but rare in *senryû* except as the prefix for what we might call "pubic lice," *tsubijirami.* If it were more common, I might "quim" it.

▲ **Tsukuma matsuri** –> *Pot-wearing*

凸 **Turtle head** 亀頭 *kitô.* Glans penis in much of the Sino-sphere (not just senryu!)

凸 **Up-arch, Upbend, Up-curve** 上反 *uwazori* – The best penises, were supposed to arch up, like a mushroom growing on a slope.

凸 **Upper** 上付き *uwatsuki* or "up/above-attached." Same as *high-cunt*. Opp. a *downer*.

▲ **Vagina.** A clinical word seldom used in this book. => *Bobo, Octopussy*

▲ **Wakashu** => *young-crowd*

■ **Warring Era** Officially from 1489-1573, but, if you ask me, it really went on to 1603.

凹 **Wet-nurse** – The *uba* was probably more common in Japan and other countries without dairy products than in most parts of Europe. She is synonymous with the display of her large and open yet extremely hirsute vulva that spooked children, challenged men and dripped with desire.

凹 **Wide** 広い, ゆるい *hiroi* or *yurui*. Vaginal sex, sinful for bonzes. Opp. *Narrow* (anal sex)

▲ **Woman's Isle**. => Isle of Women.

▲ **Yome** => *Young wife*

凸 **Young-crowd** 若衆 *wakashu.* Usually translated "young men" or "young actors," I use the literal "young-crowd," but sometimes use the modern "gay" because they were proud of it whether out showing-off their finery or in their tea-shops. Some sold sex, but their always refreshing presence is what counts.

凹 **Young-wife** 娵・嫁 ***yome,*** literally "bride," but so called *for years* when she lives in the house of her mother-in-law/*shûto/old-wife*.

~~~~~~

If any reader wishes to have a fuller &/or better glossary, please make it & send it to me!
~~~~~~

目次 Index of 珍 Outrageous Ideas & Gross Things 物

目次 Index of 珍 Outrageous & Plain Names 名

一休大師盗む本書の最後の空白。

Zen Master One Rest, One *Break* if you prefer, Ikkyû steals the last free space in the book.

Because Microsoft Word is a radically wrong software that cannot efficiently handle mixed languages and columns, I could not do the book in a single file and each of the 30-odd files comprising this book had to be separately paginated (often a hellish task that makes me curse Bill Gates as I have never cursed anyone in my life). So, I cannot add pages to chapters already done and still sell the book before Xmas. But I came to realize that I needed a *man*-stink to balance the woman-stink and a *good* bonze to make up for the bad ones, so Ikkyû's here -

とんだ開眼一休はノロリ出し 77-29
tonda kaigan ikkyû wa norori dashi

a preposterous
eye-opening: ikkyû
hauls it out

一休の男根地蔵ハよくおぼへ 葉別 4
ikkyû no dankon jizô wa yoku oboe

ikkyû's member
the stone ksitigarbha well
remembers it

一休の褌・蛍のかざも混じたり 伊勢冠付
ikkyû no fundoshi · hotaru no kaza mo konjitari 文化一

ikkyû's loincloth
part of the bouquet is
fire-fly stink

Stone, wood or papier-mâché, bodhisattva of all types had an eye-opening ceremony. Painting in the pupil of the eye of the papier-mâché dharma when a task for which it was the charm is accomplished is the best known eye-opening. I have no idea how stone *jizô* were given the touch of preternatural life, but only Ikkyû *thus* baptized them. If you think such doings offset the boy-butt-buying, you might also enjoy Ikkyû's sea cucumber bm. in *Rise, Ye Sea Slugs!* Ikkyû was not only the prankster's prankster, but highly sexed and well-known for enjoying a relationship with Mori, a blind massager for whom he wrote a grateful poem about how her knowing hands restored his elderly manhood. Old semen was said to stink like fire-flies (inadvertently squash one, and you'll know). Ikkyû's Chinese poems on cock and cunt may be found in *A Dolphin in the Woods* (2007).

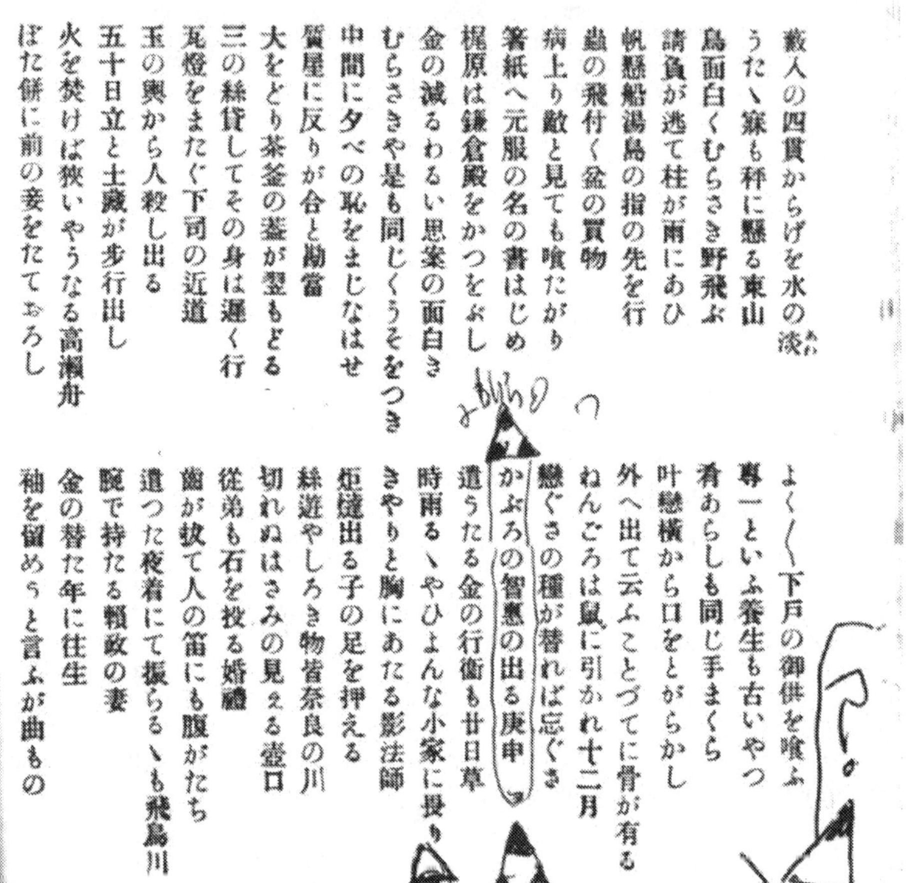

數人の四貫からげを水の淡
うたゝ寐も秤に懸る東山
鳥面白くむらさき野飛ぶ
請負が逃て柱が雨にあひ
帆懸船湯島の指の先を行
畠の飛付く盆の買物
病上り畝と見ても喰たがり
箸紙へ元服の名の書はじめ
梶原は鎌倉殿をかつをぶし
金の減るわるい思案の面白き
むらさきや是も同じくうそをつき
中間に夕べの恥をまじなはせ
質屋に反りが合と勘當
大をどり茶釜の釜が聟もどる
三の絲貸してその身は遅く行
瓦燈をまたぐ下司の近道
玉の輿から人殺し出る
五十日立と土藏が歩行出し
火を焚けば狹いやうなる高瀬舟
ぼた餅に前の妻をたておろし

よく／＼下戸の御供を喰ふ
專一といふ養生も古いやつ
肴あらしも同じ手まくら
叶戀横から口をとがらかし
外へ出て云ふことづてに骨が有る
ねんごろは鼠に引かれ十二月
戀ぐさの種が替れば忘ぐさ
かぶろの智惠の出る庚申
遣うたる金の行衛も廿日草
時雨るゝやひよんな小家に投り
きやりと胸にあたる影法師
炬燵出る子の足を押える
絲遊やしろき物皆奈良の川
切れぬはさみの見ゑる壺口
從弟も石を投る婚禮
齒が抜て人の笛にも腹がたち
遣つた夜着にて振らるゝも飛鳥川
腕で持たる賴政の妻
金の替た年に往生
袖を留めうと言ふが曲もの

いく通時雨て見てもをとこ山
細見を鶏呑にすると丸裸
立居に根太が鳴てはづかし
かまくらにいつ迄草の出來心
瘡は髪と指でをしへる
いまだ悋氣の付かぬ剛力
近いころ心から出て縫ならひ
たうがらし喰へば若衆も怖くなり
そのかみの人はたまかな峯の松
馬を見知て笑ふをどり子
石燈籠吉原からもなぶる也
春先は咄の高い飼鳥屋
庇の雪を喰て氣に入
云名付鼠舞して歸りけり
枇杷ばかり大きな顔で咲て居
つかみ合うても橘中の友
紫の足袋から懺悔はじまりて
乘物に和尚の袖も緋ぢりめん
御納戸茶女の智惠の廻り過
茶臺出す顔も近くて遠い物

120　武玉川　八篇

The above page with sixty *ku* is one of 936 such poem-packed pages in a tiny 1927 book 日本名著全集版行会の『川柳雑俳集』 which provides my access to the entire *Mutamagawa* (which only takes 290 pages). The *ku* I marked on the bottom row is the outrageous one about a young-crowd who eats chili peppers. I see another I could not read before (but now can) with a misleading note. The smudgy original is 25% smaller.

P ◆ O ◆ E ◆ M ◆ 初 ◆ 句 ◆ 索 ◆ 引 ◆ I ◆ N ◆ D ◆ E ◆ X

研究者諸君！ Please note that spaces do not count and most readers will have more fun with the other indexes. 敬愚

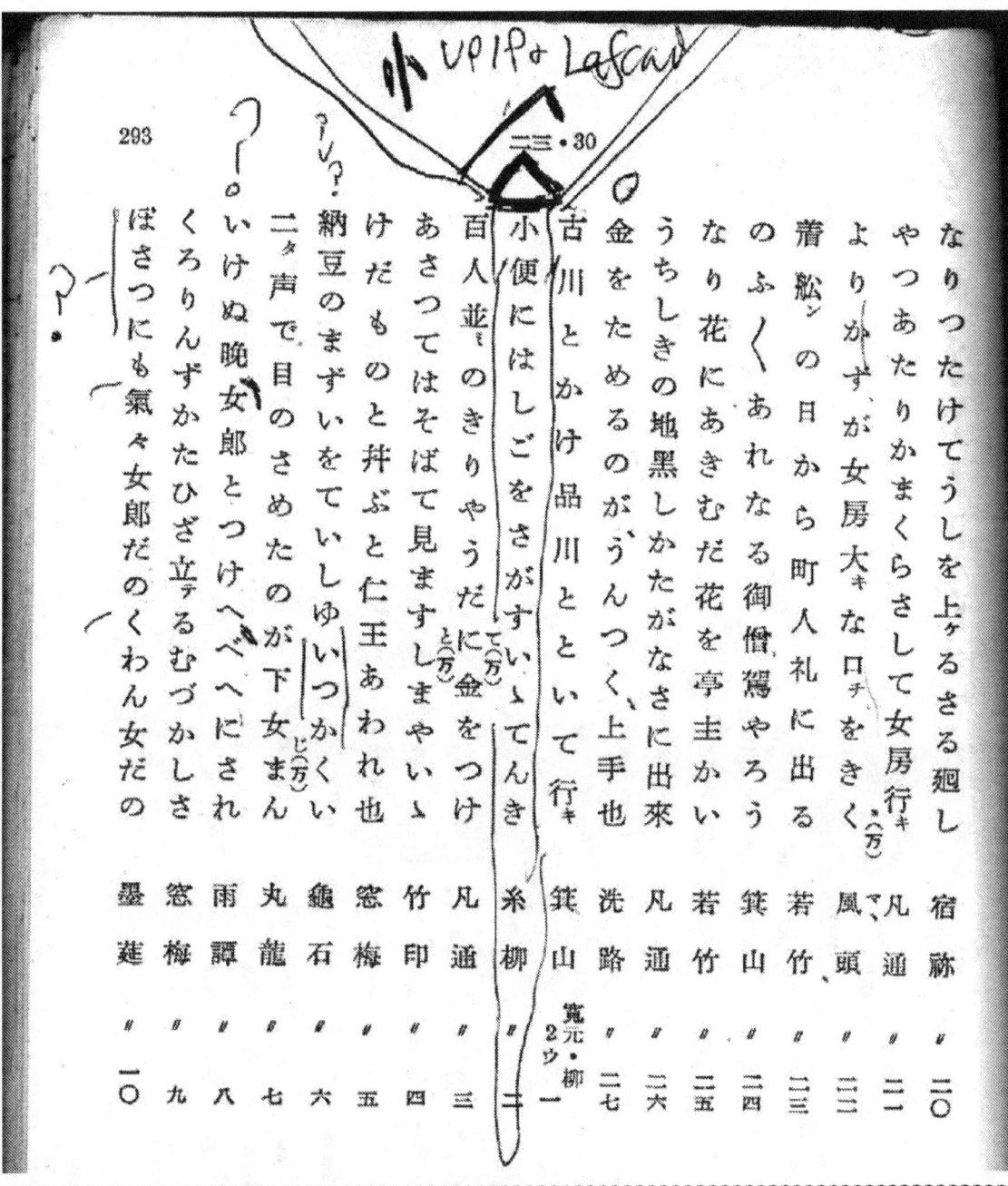

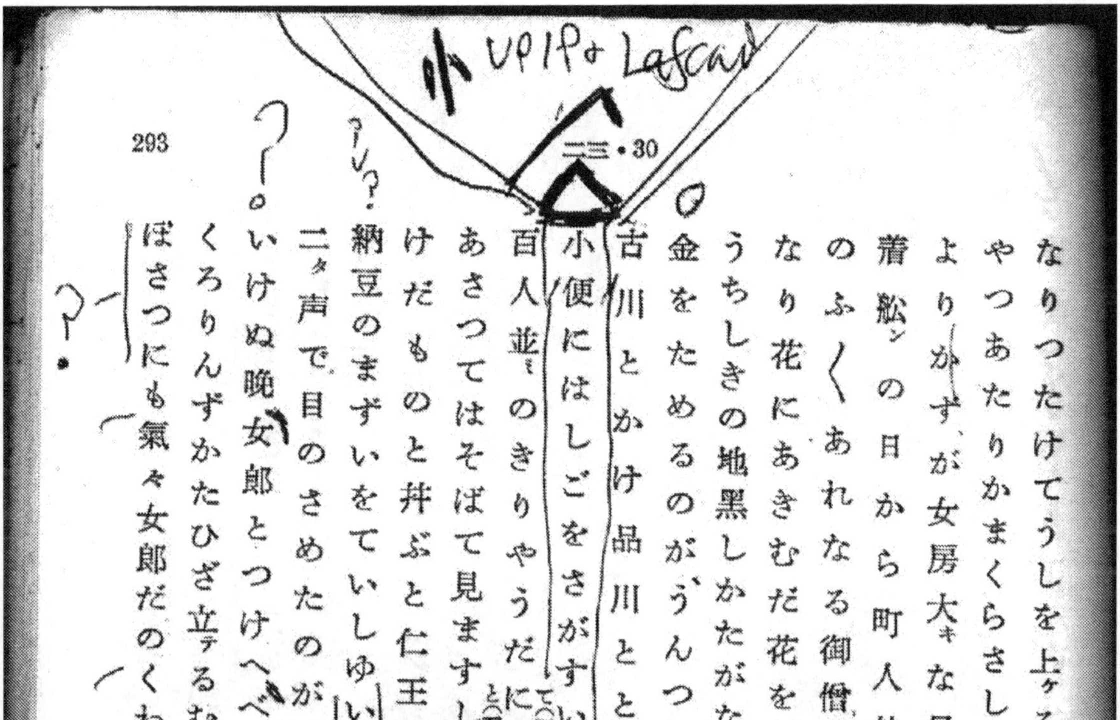

293　二三・30

なりつたけてうしを上ヶるさる廻し　宿跡 〃 二〇
やつあたりかまくらさして女房行キ　凡通 〃 二一
よりかずが女房大キな口チをきく　風頭 〃 二二
着松ンの日から町人礼に出る　若竹 〃 二三
のふくあれなる御僧鴛やろう　箕山 〃 二四
なり花にあきむだ花を亭主かい　若竹 〃 二五
うちしきの地黒しかたがなさに出來　凡通 〃 二六
金をためるのがうんつく上手也　洗路 〃 二七
古川とかけ品川といて行キ　箕山 寛元・柳2ウ 一
小便にはしごをさがすいゝてんき　糸柳 〃 二
百人並のきりやうだに金をつけ　凡通 〃 三
あさつてはそばて見ますしまやいゝ　竹印 〃 四
けだものと丼ぶと仁王あわれ也　窓梅 〃 五
納豆のまずいをていしゆいつかくい　亀石 〃 六
二タ声で目のさめたのが下女まん　丸龍 〃 七
いけぬ晩女郎とつけへべへにされ　雨譚 〃 八
くろりんずかたひざ立テるむづかしさ　窓梅 〃 九
ぼさつにも氣々女郎だのくわん女だの　墨蓮 〃 一〇

This is one of a small number of pages with pen-names attached in Iwanami's cheap pocket-book (24 vols.) *Willow*. I was looking for a different page with some cartoons I drew in the margin, but decided to introduce this instead because the *ku* (by thread-willow) that I circled whenever I read it should have been squeezed into *Micturition Mimesis*, next to Lafcadio Hearne's steeple piss! *Shôben ni hashigo o sagasu ii-tenki* (23-30) might be just

"Looking for a ladder while out to take a piss – a clear day,"

because he wants to clean the roof; then, again, it might be

"Looking for a ladder to take a piss – what fine weather!"

律義者・嗅今日は何日目じゃ　笠付類題集
お月見の豆に手を出しはじかれる　一六五
乗る処が赤いお船で寄せつけず　一一六
馬だからよしなと女房尻を向け　一一二
女武者馬に乗ってよせ付けず　八六
女房の馬で亭主の槍を寝せ　一一三
すっぽんも縮む女房のお月様　一〇五

女房が駄目なら、下女にでもと、手出しをしますが……

馬上だと断る相模見上げ果て　五八
お馬だよしなと下女ははねつける　三五

我慢するのは男根ばかりでなく、張形もお休みします。

お馬には牛は使わぬ長つぼね　新編六
（牛＝張形）

女が交合をしたくない時は、月経中でなくても、月経中と偽って、交合を断る手段に使います。男は女の生理をよく勉強して、日数を計算して騙されないようにしましょう。

今更に雲の下帯ひきしめて

月のさわりの空言ぞうき　（唐衣橘州）
—『万載狂歌集』十一（天明三）

さて、どうしても我慢できない夫にとって、夫婦喧嘩の生じない解決法は千摺で一時しのぎをすることです。

へ月に七日の不浄さえなくば
主にへんずりかゝしゃせぬ
—魔山人『赤湯文字』（昭和五四）

月七日十人組で弓削すまし　九一
（普通の男根なら五人組）

千摺じゃあまりにもわびしいと、もうひとつの穴を代用に考える夫もいますが、それをゆるしてくれる女房はとても感心な人です。

お馬なら屁の穴でもと馬鹿亭主　一〇五

七日間我慢すれば、解禁の日を迎えます。

七日ほど喰わず利生の居催促　新編二八
（利生＝男根の隠語）

女房が落馬をするとすぐに乗り　六五

This a page from *Cuntologia* – minus margins above and below – showing how senryu are used. There are no fewer than 13 senryu, most of which I used in the chapter on menstruation, and one song suggesting husbands should masturbate when their wives are *on the horse*. I recall reading and letting go *Willow* 九一 (91) *tsuki nanuka jûningumi de yuge sumashi* (month 7-days 10-man team-with, yuge takes-care[of it]): *Seven of thirty days Dôkyô makes do c̲ a ten-man team!* I let it go because I felt ten fingers were not much compared with the other hyperbole brought to bear on his massive endowment (ch.1). But *now* it hit me: He needs two hands to wrap *around* it! On this page, the author advises men to keep a note on their wife's period lest she use it for a headache.

*Re:*views of my books

In the course of writing/designing this book, I have finally come to notice something about the f-letter. When you italicize it, suddenly you have a tail, a slash where none existed before. All the other letters remain above the line if they are above it normally. Only "f" grows a tail "*f.*" I also can see that it has a hilt and a blade and one could pull it right up and out from a line and wield it as a scimitar. So far no one has attacked my books, at least not with anything sharp. One person tried *clubbing* my worst-seller (*Orientalism & Occidentalism*) at Amazon, but when I wrote him and said he forgot to mention what was in the book (he did mention it had notes with notes with notes – something I am rather proud of – but that was about it) before he insulted the book and me, and indirectly indicated that I was sharpening my tongue for battle, he kindly withdrew. Had his review contained a single valid complaint, I would put it here with the favorable ones, for I would much prefer another take me to task so I may defer from doing the same (I have been criticised in correspondence but not in public for trying too hard to destroy my authority – *Come on you guys* (no woman has so complained), I'm happy with the *author* and can do without the *ity*). Bull-shit enough. Here are snippets from reviews, with some additional comment. You may find more of the reviews on the review pages of www.paraverse.org or, at the sources. You may also find snippets of reviews of my first seven books, written & published in Japan/ese (反・日本人論＝工作者、誤訳天国＝白水社、英語はこんなにニッポン語＝筑摩文庫等). ★The reviewers are not responsible for what is in *this* book!

<u>*Rise, Ye Sea Slugs!* (1,000 *ku* re. sea cucumbers compiled & translated from Japanese). paraverse 2003. pp 480 $25.</u>

"I wondered, can one really devote 480 pages to haiku on sea slugs? The answer is emphatically 'yes.' Although difficult to read from beginning to end, this book contains great learning and insight, and deserves a wide reading among specialists and non-specialists alike."

"For many of the haiku, Gill gives multiple translations as a way of showing possible interpretations. I know of no other book of English translations of haiku that goes to such lengths to explain translations, which in Gill's hands are accurate, economical, and often elegant. In addition to being an accomplished translator and poet (over 100 of the poems are by the author, under the nom de plume keigu), Gill is an articulate defender of the art of translation."

"Gill is also a master of the discursive footnote, and at times I found myself reading along the bottoms of the pages, jumping among footnotes, and marveling at his often amusing and always reliable views of Japanese culture, both literary and everyday. For all the eccentricities one might expect (and does find) in a book devoted entirely to Japanese haiku on the sea slug, the author is an accomplished haiku writer, a very talented and engaging critic, capable of reading with an acute understanding of culture and cultural differences." –Thomas H. Rohlich, Professor of Japanese Language and Literature at Smith College, from *Metamorphoses:* the journal of the five college faculty seminar on literary translation (Spring 2005 (Vol. 13.1)).

~~~~~~

"Reading it, we see the deep affection of the Japanese for the phenomena of their own environment and culture. At the same time, we encounter one of the most original minds to take up the related subjects of haiku and cross-cultural communication. . . ."

"This single-topic tome may be our best English-language window yet into the labyrinth of Japanese haikai culture. If you have read Yasuda, Blyth, Henderson, Ueda, and Shirane, then read Gill. He will expand your mind. If you have not read those guys yet, then read Gill first. He's more fun." – William J. Higginson, author of *Haiku World*, in *Modern Haiku* (volume 35.1 winter-spring 2004).

~~~~~~

Author's note. Perhaps you have heard of Ponge and his object poems. The Japanese, or this ideal though natural ding en sich (sp?) demonstrate what is – and is not – possible, both directly and through metaphor.

~~~~~~
~~~~~~

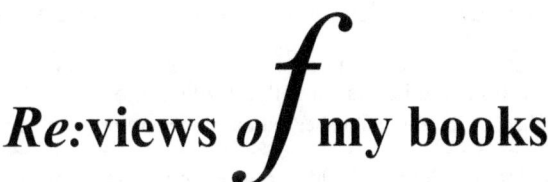

Re: ***Fly-ku!*** (Translations of fly & fly-swatting ku, + an in-depth study of Issa's famous fly-ku,"Don't swat!") 2005

"An American scholar and poet who writes in an extemporaneous style akin to that of Jack Kerouac; thinks like Herman Hesse, Koyabashi Issa, and Lewis Carroll, all rolled into one."

– Robert D. Wilson, publisher+editor of the on-line magazine *Simply Haiku* (2005-summer)

"For those with the patience, the unfolding of 600 variations on a theme, with elegant discourse, is a treat, and, at times, when the author delves into the lively back-and-forth on the internet, the past and present of haiku, or the root and uses of various Japanese words, it becomes quite jolly."

"Gill strikes us as no less than amazing. Why isn't he teaching at Yale, or the University of California, or Tokyo University? His references include no end of obscure Japanese lore, plus quotes and notes from such artists as Clare, Lovelace, Steinbeck, Dumont, Verdi, Satie, Blyth, Shakespeare, Emily Dickinson."

– Carlos Amantea, author of *The Blob That Ate Oaxaca* in R.A.L.P.H. (Review of Art, Literature, Philosophy & History)

Author's note. Not as much natural history in this wee bk. as in Rise, Ye Sea Slugs!, but a good discussion of the supposed anthropomorphic fallacy & a comparison of translations of "Don't swat/hit/kill" the fly.

Re: ***Cherry Blossom Epiphany*** (Three thousand *ku+ka* on blossom-viewing, including many by Sôgi) 2007, pp.740

"It was bad old Ezra Pound, acknowledging his heavy debt to haiku in translation, who affirmed that the first rule of poetry was "Make it new." This is something Gill has done more effectively, as far as remaking haiku in English goes, than anyone else around. . . .

"One of my favorites is on p. 375, where no less than seven translations are proposed, but four of them "sous rature," or _misekechi_ ['erasures shown,' literally]: in old Japanese, words crossed out in a manuscript but left legible enough that the reader can see what was discarded, and imagine why. (Publishers with accountants are not likely to tolerate this kind of haikaiesque mischief. Gill gets away with it only because he is his own publisher.) And (another reason, if needed) in his commentary Gill distances himself from the conventions of pedantry just as effectively as the haikai poets he translates departed from the venerable (and staid and eventually stuffy) traditions of classical linked verse to make something new." – Lewis Cook, professor of Japanese literature, CUNY (in a blog at one of Gaby Greves fine haiku *kigo* and Buddhism-related sites, in response to another's questions about my work.

"This book is exceedingly delightful – what word could be more accurate I cannot say! Here is a guide to allow every reader to play with their own translations of these poems – indeed all the important ingredients – are amply included: . . . nothing in this book is cut in stone – it is pure water, ever-flowing – and that is what is so inspiring about it, its generosity and delightful creativity!" – s.w. at mountainandrivers.org

Author's note. Professor Cook has a broader perspective and more discriminating vocabulary to bring to bear upon what I am doing than I have or ever will have. To my mind, the one thing that neither he nor anyone that I know of has attempted to evaluate is the success/failure of the ways in which I chapter, i.e. divide the poems into sub-themes, something different for sea slugs, flies, cherry blossoms and the New Year (The Fifth Season, below)

Re: ***The Fifth Season*** (2000 *ku* on 20 New Year themes & first book of ten in the IPOOH series 2007, pp.500

The New Year, once the Original, or First Season, of the *five* seasons of haiku, has been neglected in favor of the other four by Occidental translators. *The Fifth Season* finally gives this supernatural or cosmological season – one that combines aspects of the Solstice, Christmas, New Year's, Easter, July 4th and the Once Upon a Time of Fairy Tales – its due. The contents will delight lovers of literate non-fiction (*i.e.,* essay) and everyone interested in *celebration, cultural* and *folk ritual in Japan, haiku, light-verse, translation* and, because of the artful way the font is used, *book design*, as well. *This book brings the Moon back into the calendar and Humans back into haiku.* (As the reviews to date of this book have been mere introductions, I used my own words here.)

Re: ***Topsy-Turvy 1585*** (611 ways Europeans & Japanese are contrary according to Luis Frois): See *Bibliography.*

Re: ***Orientalism & Occidentalism*** (essays the relationship between the impossibility of perfectly translating between exotic tongues (English <=> Japanese) & antithetical stereotypes of culture, Japanese/Eastern *vs.* US/Western).

◎かの『反・日本人論』、『誤訳天国』のロビン・ギル、いまや◎

robin d. gill 著 paraverse press 出版の本の書評抜粋

~~~~~~

Rise, Ye Sea Slugs! （海鼠千句）について。五大学の文芸翻訳誌、Metamorphoses 2005 春号評者＝スミスカレッジ日本語学、日本文学教授トーマス・H・ローリックの書評より

ギルの手によるその翻訳は簡潔で的をえており、しばしば優雅な味わいがある。　これほど翻訳を詳細に説明してある俳句の英訳書は、私の知る限り他に類を見ない。すでに熟練した翻訳家であり、俳人でもある（本書中百句以上が敬愚というペンネームをもつ著者の作である）著者は、芸術としての翻訳の強力な擁護者でもある。どの句にも彼の翻訳のあとに続いて、それぞれ微妙に異なる解釈のあいだを日本文学、歴史、現代の文化についての余談、さまざまな色合いの逸話、ときには暴言までが自由に往来する。（中略）文学についても日常生活についても必ず信頼でき、しばしば愉快でもある彼の日本文化観に私は舌を巻くほかなかった。なにしろ徹頭徹尾ナマコが句題の俳句を集めた本と聞けば当然期待される（事実そのとおりの）風変わりな点はともかく、著者はくろうとの俳人であり、文化と文化間の違いを機敏に理解しながらものを読むことのできる優れた才能に恵まれた魅力ある評論家である。　興味津々の本書は、広く俳句愛好家、日本文学と海洋生物の研究者、プロ，アマをとわず翻訳家のすべてに喜ばれるにちがいない。

~~~~~~

同著について。*Modern Haiku* 現代俳句（2004 年冬春 35．1 号）*Haiku World:* 1996 の著者、ウィリアム J. ヒギンソン の５ページにわたる書評より

一人の翻訳者として、わたしはギルの俳句翻訳に対する姿勢は刺激的で挑戦的であると思う。彼は「翻訳者の原作に対する責任」（「対応する力」＝　ロバート ダンカン）という点で、果たすべき水準をきわめて高いところまで引き上げてきているのだ。（中略）この単一季語の大著は、日本の俳句文化の迷宮への、今までで一番優れた英語の窓口であろう。（中略）もし、ヤスダやブライスや、ヘンダーソンやウエダやシラネ＊［注：過去半世紀の俳句英訳名家］を読んだことがあるなら、ギルもお読みなさい。あなたの意識を深く広く拡大させてくれるから。そして、先の方々の著作を読んだことがないのなら、やっぱり先にギルをお読みなさい。彼のほうがずっとおもしろいから。

~~~~~~

科学者の評 ＝「凄い！惚れてしまった。小柄な我が友を何年も研究してきたが、悪態をつかれるか、さもなければ忘れられた存在でしかない、と思っていた。ナマコ文学をめぐる日欧の差！悲しいかな、互いに隔てられた科学と文学には、理論においてはむろんのこと、用語上ですら、とてつもないギャップが随所にみられる。両者を深いところで見事に融合した本で、科学者も納得させる。恐れ入りました。」Alexander Kerr 博士 = Web of Life プロジェクトの海鼠科担当、独語の海鼠研究（古典）の英訳、環境進化論の研究に従事する気鋭の生物学者。James Cook 大学属。

~~~~~~

F*ly*-ku*!*（蝿句）について。オンライン句誌『Simply Haiku』創立者かつ編集者ロバート・D・ウイルソンの書評より

書きぶりはジャック・ケルアック流即興を思わせ、ものの考え方はヘルマン・ヘッセ、小林一茶、ルイス・キャロル、このすべてを丸めて一つにしたような本なのだ。。。

~~~~~~

桜・花見三千古句の英訳ある 2007 年の新刊 ***Cherry Blossom Epiphany****:* The Poetry and Philosophy of a Flowering Tree、 又は、今までに、欧米で見逃れてきた新年部句、二千句ほど英訳ある ***The Fifth Season:*** *Poetry for the Re-creation of the World* のいずれの内容について、又上記書評の全文などは、http://www.paraverse.org で、ご覧になってください。英訳とはいえども、全句の日本語原文もその索引も全書に入っているから、英語が苦手の方も、一読を、おすすめできます。
~~~~~~

www.ingramcontent.com/pod-product-compliance
Lightning Source LLC
Chambersburg PA
CBHW081202240426
43669CB00039B/2738
9780974261850